COUNTRY AUSTRALIA

COUNTRY AUSTRALIA

THE LAND AND THE PEOPLE

Reader's Digest Sydney

Timber team, Myall Lakes, NSW. 1914

First edition
Published by Reader's Digest
Services Pty Ltd (inc. in NSW)
26–32 Waterloo Street, Surry
Hills, NSW 2010

Edited and designed by Capricorn
Press Pty Ltd (inc. in NSW)
3/9 Oaks Avenue,
Dee Why, NSW 2099

National Library of Australia
cataloguing-in-publication data:

Country Australia: the land and the people
Includes index
ISBN 0 86438 052 6

1. Australia – Dictionaries and
   encyclopedias
I. Reader's Digest Services   994′.003′21

Building Thornleigh Road, Kuring-Gai, NSW, 1934

Principal contributors
Peter Fray, BA (rural journalism), DipAg
Tony Rodd, BSc
Arthur Woods, MA(Oxon)

Design
Lawrence Hanley

Principal photographer
Kathie Atkinson

Principal artist
Alistair Barnard

Contributors
Paul Adam, MA, PhD
Alice Alston
Richard Beckett
Victor Cherikoff
Ian Close, BA(Hons)
Richard Fullagar, BA, PhD
Terry Gregory, BSc

J. Mark Howard, MA, DipEd
Neil Inall
Rod Metcalfe
Greg Mortimer, BSc
Alex Nicol
Melissa Sweet, BA (rural journalism)
Ian Watson, BA(Hons), PhD
Brian Woodward

Artists
Sue Cannon
Lawrence Hanley
Ian Marr
Jeanette Muirhead

Art assistant
Sue Cannon

Editorial assistance
Stuart Inder
Laraine Newberry
Jane Richardson
Phillip Rodwell

Research
Ursula Dubosarsky
Beverley Tunbridge

Production controller
Judith Clegg

Grubbing up a stump, Narara Viticultural Station, NSW, 1914

Contents

Budgee Budgee Public School, NSW, 1916

PART THREE: An A to Z of country Australia

Duncan Medhurst, one of the last
mounted mailmen in NSW, about 1950

SPECIAL FEATURES

Examining a Corriedale ram, Arrawatta Station, NSW, 1910

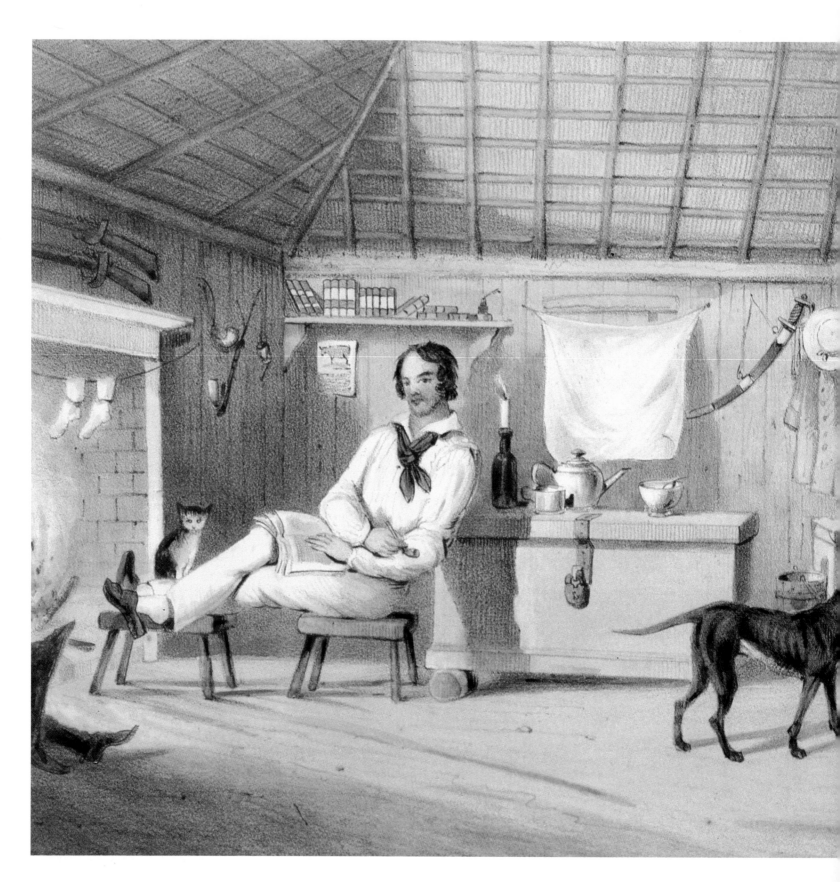

INTRODUCTION

The squatter's first home

Australia is one of the most urbanised nations on earth. Seven out of every ten people live in one of the country's 13 largest cities. In the late 1980s only 2.2 per cent of the population – a mere 363 622 men and women – earned their living from rural pursuits. Vast tracts of the outback support less than one person per square kilometre.

Despite these facts, most Australians like to think that they have a special relationship with the land and its workers. The characteristics traditionally ascribed to country people – generosity, resourcefulness, hard work and a laconic disregard for hardship – are greatly admired, and are still popularly thought by many to be peculiarly Australian traits.

The sad fact is, however, that few city Australians know much about their country at all. For many, the only glimpse they get of country Australia is from the windows of a speeding car on its way from one city or town to another. There is rarely anyone to ask about the sights that are seen in passing. It has been to satisfy this desperate need that **Country Australia** has been published. It takes readers beyond the boundary fence and into the homes and lives of country people. It shows what farmers do, how they live and how they earn their income. It looks at the folklore of the bush and the legendary figures – stockmen and shearers, squatters and selectors, bushrangers and goldminers – whose lives are Australian history. It identifies all the common wild plants, flowers, mammals, birds and reptiles that travellers might encounter, as well as showing what different crops, machines, stock and buildings look like, how they are used and what they do. But this is more than just a book of facts and figures. Our overriding aim in compiling this volume has been to promote a better understanding of the country in all its great beauty and diversity, in the hope that all Australians will wish to care for and preserve the unique heritage that has been placed in their care.

The book is divided into three parts. Part one – **The Making of Australia** – examines the forces, both natural and human, that created Australia as we find it today. Part two – **Living Landscapes** – examines the various habitats that are found around Australia – from tropical rainforests to farmland, and shows how communities of plants and animals live together within them. The heart of the book is in part three – **An A to Z of Country Australia** – where over 800 alphabetical entries cover topics from Aborigines to zircons.

For all its wide-ranging subject matter, however, this book is not intended to be a dry, conventional encyclopaedia. Obviously, almost any topic that has been covered could be greatly expanded – many, indeed, are the subjects of large books in their own right. The information we have included is highly selective, and attempts to give readers enough interesting and informative facts about each subject to satisfy any casual inquiry. We hope that it might also stimulate interested readers to seek additional information from other sources if they need it.

The arrangement of subjects in an A to Z format is straightforward, although there has been some minor juggling of a strictly alphabetical order to allow major topics a page or two of their own. Care has been taken to include information under the heading that we thought was most likely to be consulted, although the thorough index at the back of the book will direct readers to entries from other possible starting points. Cross references in SMALL CAPITALS are used sparingly in the text, only where it was thought that the reader would make better sense of the information presented by referring to another entry to obtain additional facts.

THE EDITORS

The farm house of W. Lawson, Esq., NSW

PART ONE

1

The Making of Australia

Origins of the continent

Two hundred million years ago, when the dinosaurs were supreme, the continents of the earth were united. Dinosaurs could walk from North America to Australia, given time. The united continents, which fitted together like a jigsaw puzzle, made up the ancient supercontinent of Pangaea. A huge V-shaped ocean, the Tethys Sea, lay between Australia and Asia, its point driving into Europe.

About 190 million years ago a rift severed Pangaea, separating North America from Africa. The future southern continents of Africa, Antarctica, Australia and South America and sundry pieces such as New Zealand, India and Madagascar, all made up the supercontinent of Gondwanaland, the rest forming the northern continent of Laurasia. Gradually the continents began to drift slowly apart.

The surface of the earth is divided into 'plates', most with lighter rafts of continents riding upon them. Australia is on the Indo-Australian plate, which is bordered by the Pacific, Antarctic, Eurasian and African plates. Well south of Australia, deep in the ocean, is the long Southern Ridge where material, often basalt, from below the surface is being deposited on the ocean floor, pushed up by convection currents in the fluid and semi-fluid interior of the planet. Here the plate is growing so that the surface, carrying Australia and New Guinea, is creeping forward, a few centimetres a year towards Asia.

There is another ridge in the mid-Atlantic where ocean floor growth is pushing the Americas and Eurasia-Africa apart. Elsewhere the oceanic edge of one plate is forced to dive beneath another, to melt again, as in the Java and Tonga Trenches. Sometimes colliding continents throw up mountain ranges, such as the Himalayas – born about 55 million years ago when India pushed against Asia. In these places the continental rocks are too light to dive beneath the adjacent plates and are scraped off to form mountains.

The edges of plates are areas of volcanic and earthquake activity, especially where the under-driving rock rubs against the rock of the upper plate. Sometimes the edges of two plates meet and grind past each other, as at the infamous San Andreas Fault in California where sooner or later there will be another earthquake rivalling the one that ruined San Francisco in 1906.

The mechanisms of plate tectonics, just outlined, led to the acceptance of the theory of continental drift by most geologists, although a number of biologists had long accepted it as almost the only satisfactory explanation for the distribution of many plants and animals such as marsupials and Antarctic beech trees.

The land masses did not separate quickly. For millions of years two separating continents may have remained in contact, like a banana skin being peeled slowly away, and even after separation there could remain an archipelago linking the two – as there is now between South America and Antarctica – so that some animals could still pass from one to another.

About 46 MYA, Australia was still connected to Antarctica through Tasmania, but the climate

Glossopteris *trees flourished during the Permian period. Fossilised leaves are found in the rocks of all southern lands and provide evidence that the continents were once joined together.*

The history of life on earth

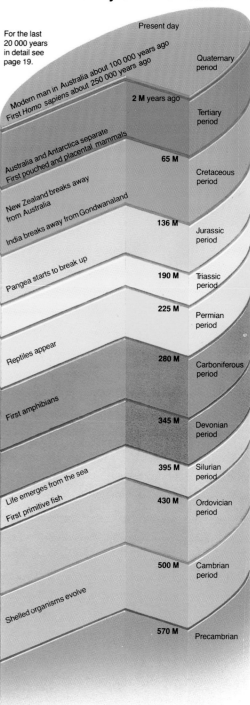

For the last 20 000 years in detail see page 19.

Modern man in Australia about 100 000 years ago
First *Homo sapiens* about 250 000 years ago

Australia and Antarctica separate
First pouched and placental mammals

New Zealand breaks away

India breaks away from Gondwanaland

Pangea starts to break up

Reptiles appear

First amphibians

Life emerges from the sea

First primitive fish

Shelled organisms evolve

Present day	
2 M years ago	Quaternary period
	Tertiary period
65 M	Cretaceous period
136 M	Jurassic period
190 M	Triassic period
225 M	Permian period
280 M	Carboniferous period
345 M	Devonian period
395 M	Silurian period
430 M	Ordovician period
500 M	Cambrian period
570 M	Precambrian

This time scale *covers the last 600 million years of the earth's history – from about the start of the Cambrian period, when the first creatures with hard skeletons evolved in the oceans.*

Australia's slow journey north

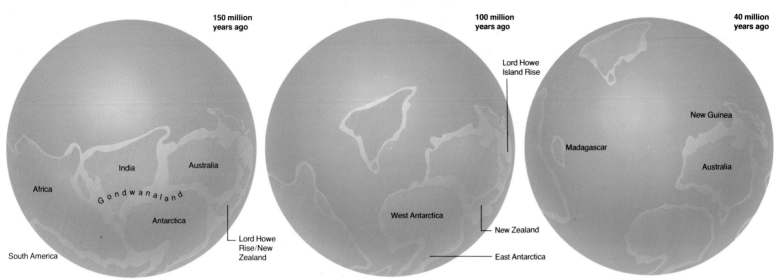

150 million years ago

India
Australia
Africa
Gondwanaland
Antarctica
South America
Lord Howe Rise/New Zealand

100 million years ago

Lord Howe Island Rise
West Antarctica
New Zealand
East Antarctica

40 million years ago

New Guinea
Madagascar
Australia

About 225 million years ago all the continents on earth were united in one great supercontinent called Pangea. This split into Gondwanaland and Laurasia about 180 million years ago.

India started to move northwards 130 million years ago, then South America broke away 30 million years later, followed by Lord Howe Rise/New Zealand 10 million years after that.

Antarctica and Australia separated about 53 million years ago and Australia reached its present shape about 28 million years later. It is now moving steadily north towards Asia at about 60 mm a year.

was merely cool, not glacial. The mass of Gondwanaland prevented the establishment of a circumpolar current. Much of the land was covered with temperate rainforest in which southern beeches were probably the most common trees. Marsupials and placental mammals had evolved during the Cretaceous period – the centre of evolution of marsupials was probably in Gondwanaland or the Americas, so they were widespread throughout Gondwanaland. Other animals shared by at least some of today's fragments of Gondwanaland are the parrots, and possibly the rattites – large, flightless birds such as emus and ostriches.

By 38 MYA, there was a seaway between Tasmania and Antarctica, and for the next 23 million years the continent drifted northwards at about 60 mm a year, with New Guinea at first still beneath the sea. About 15 MYA New Guinea approached Indonesia and the New Guinea Highlands were formed.

The changes in the shape of Gondwanaland and the drift northwards of Australia brought changes in climate. Drake's Passage, between South America and Antarctica, was opened by at least the early Miocene epoch, and the circumpolar current was established by the early Pliocene. The glaciation of Antarctica began about 25 MYA. Before that, when Australia was still in high latitudes, the weather was warm enough for rainforest to grow in much of the south. In the Eocene, at the time of separation, rainforest was spreading, and sea temperatures to the south of Australia were as high as 20°C.

During the Oligocene, however, sea temperatures fell to about 7°C and ice began forming in Antarctica.

By the early Miocene Australia had reached a low rainfall belt so that some parts of the north became arid, although parts of the south were still covered with rainforest, and grasslands began to appear. At the end of the Miocene, about 5.3 MYA, sea temperatures dropped to about 5°C and the climate became drier still. The arid regions reached their present extent during the late Pliocene.

During this vast period of time parts of Australia have been covered and uncovered by the sea. Much of the continent is made up of ancient rocks, up to 3600 million years old, which were planed down by erosion and are low-lying. For long periods sea covered the Nullarbor region, and isolated the east and west of the continent. This is why many plants in the southwest of Western Australia are found only in that area. The seaway between Tasmania and the mainland did not appear until the Oligocene or Miocene epochs but since then it has opened and closed at least eight times.

Much of Australia is now low and flat. The Great Dividing Range was created in the Cretaceous period by uplifting caused by movements of tectonic plates that opened the Coral and Tasman Seas. These movements produced steep slopes facing the sea, backed by plains.

The development of vegetation on the Australian segment of Gondwanaland has been traced partly by the study of fossil plant remains,

and also by the examination of fossil pollen. This is a recent field of research in Australia. So far studies have concentrated on the south-east part of the continent, which probably does not represent the whole of the country. Other factors also tend to give a false picture: pollen fossils are only found in areas with adequate rainfall; deposits contain a disproportionate amount of windborne pollen which is more likely to be dispersed than insect-borne pollen; and some important groups of plants do not have pollen which fossilises readily.

The oldest pollens that have been found belong to the conifers and come from the Cretaceous period. The first flowering plants to leave fossilised pollen were broad-leaved rainforest plants. The oldest of them belong to members of a group of plants which are today represented by holly. They lived in the Cretaceous period, and are older than some of the conifers. Many plant families appeared in the late Cretaceous and Tertiary periods, but the mistletoe family did not appear earlier than the middle Eocene. Sclerophyll plants – those with hard leaves which are adapted to dry conditions and poor nutrients, such as banksias and sheoaks – began to appear in the Palaeocene, but grass pollen is not found until the middle Eocene. Those plants which are dominant today – *Eucalyptus* and *Acacia* – are relative upstarts and their pollen is not found before the Oligocene.

Today Australia is a quiet continent where there have been few recent changes, apart from those brought about by the Ice Ages.

The last few million years

The last two million years are of particular interest to scientists, for it was in this period the modern plants and animals developed, and mankind evolved. It was also during this period that the Ice Ages occurred and sea levels rose and fell as glaciers and the Polar icecaps melted and froze again. After New Guinea and Australia had settled against the Sunda Arc – Indonesia and its associated islands – routes were open between Australia and Asia along which plants and animals could travel, although some sea barriers remained to stop many species. North-west of Australia, between the Indonesian islands of Bali and Lombok, and between Borneo and Celebes, runs Wallace's Line, which follows the continental shelf of South-East Asia. This has been a deep-water barrier since long before Australia and New Guinea reached the Sunda Arc. When Alfred Russel Wallace – Charles Darwin's colleague – first described it, it was thought to be a sharp line of demarcation between the Asian and the Australasian animals. It is true that no marsupials are found west of it until America, and few land-living placental mammals are found to the east, but it is no longer thought to be absolute. There is some mixing of animals on either side of the line.

The sea gaps were of little importance to flying birds and bats when sea levels made them narrow, but they did prevent the spread of larger land-living animals and any freshwater species which could not survive in salt water.

The earliest definite fossil bats found anywhere lived during the Eocene epoch in what are now Wyoming and France (see geological chart on p 21). The first Australian bats lived in the Miocene epoch – about 15 MYA. They probably began arriving in Australia in the mid-Tertiary, and have continued to come at times when sea levels have been low enough.

Rodents also made the passage to Australia, probably floating on rafts of vegetation carried out to sea by floods, but large mammals were unable to do so. All Australian rodents belong to the same family as the House Mouse, which is believed to have evolved about 25 MYA in Eurasia. They may first have reached Australia in the early Pliocene epoch, about 4.5 MYA. The Australian rodents fall into two groups – the so-called old endemics, and members of the genus *Rattus* – relatives of the cosmopolitan Brown and Ship Rats. The old endemics, which are varied, probably came in two waves, the first 4.5 MYA, the second within the last 2 million years. The ancestors of the native *Rattus* species arrived within the last one million years. The pests – the Brown and Ship Rats, and the House Mouse – may have first come with the earliest Dutch sailing ships.

Two million years ago, then, Australia contained all the major groups of plants and animals that are found here now, with the notable exception of humans. The mammals were represented by monotremes – which may well have evolved in this region – marsupials, rodents and bats. Many of the species were, however, different to those alive today.

The last Ice Ages, a series of glacial periods interspersed with warmer spells between about 120 000 and 15 000 years ago, affected the larger landmasses of the northern hemisphere far more severely than those in the south. But the effects on the sea were world-wide, for when much of the world's water was stored as ice, sea levels were low. When it melted, levels rose in every ocean. In the European Alps five glacial periods can be distinguished, but these are not so clear-cut in the southern hemisphere, and there is even doubt if the glacial periods in Australia coincided with those of the north.

In Australia during the last Ice Ages little of the country was covered with ice. Only the Australian Alps, much of the high country in Tasmania and possibly some very small parts of Western Australia had glaciers. The peaks of New Guinea, which was then connected to Australia by land, also had glaciers.

More is known about the last Ice Age than about earlier ones. It began about 120 000 years ago. The cold was at its most intense, and the ice covered its greatest extent, about 18 000 years ago. The sea level was also then at its lowest, and mainland Australia, Tasmania and New Guinea were joined in a single land mass, although still cut off by sea from South-East Asia. The climate was, of course, cold, but it was also very dry, so that there were sand dunes in the then interior of the continent, and, surprisingly, on Kangaroo Island and in eastern Tasmania. The areas of the south of the continent that are now covered by forest were more or less treeless, although some forest must have persisted as small patches in sheltered places. Rainforest species of plant and animals such as the Musky Rat Kangaroo, also hung on in small refuges, mainly in eastern Australia and New Guinea.

At some unknown – and greatly disputed – time during the last Ice Age, the first humans arrived in Australia. They were able to walk for most of the way from South-East Asia, but not all the way. Even when the sea was at its lowest level they would have had to make some sea crossings where the shore of arrival could not have been seen from the shore of departure and, for all the travellers knew, may not have existed. Their first occupation sites were on what is today the shallow continental shelf and are now covered by the sea.

During the Pliocene and Pleistocene epochs,

Fossils like these unearthed recently at Riversleigh Station in Queensland have added enormously to knowledge about the animals that lived in Australia from 15 million to 50 000 years ago.

Ice-eroded rocks, tarns, and other glacial features in south-west Tasmania were left behind after the last Ice Age. The ice melted around 15 000 years ago, and sea levels rose, cutting Tasmania off from the mainland.

the mammals and birds of Australia and other land masses included many more large animals than now exist. Perhaps the best known are the ox-sized diprotodon, and the mihirunag, which may have been the largest bird that has ever existed. Some of these animals belonged to groups which no longer exist, but many of them were closely related to living species. In the Pleistocene epoch, for example, there were kangaroos. They included many large species, among them the largest that has been found so far – *Procoptodon goliah* – which may have weighed as much as 300 kg. Twenty thousand years ago there were close relatives of the grey kangaroos which were twice as heavy as their living relatives. The appearance of gigantic forms may have been an evolutionary response to the country's aridity – the continent began to become arid about 15 MYA – because large animals are more efficient than small ones in their use of poor-quality food.

The reasons for the disappearance of large animals world-wide are unclear. They did, however, begin to vanish at about the same time that humans began to spread out into the world from their first home in Africa.

The emergence of modern Australia

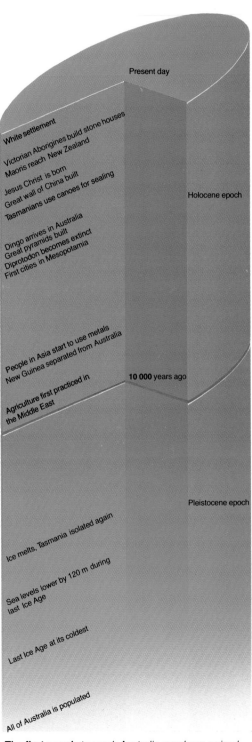

Present day

White settlement

Victorian Aborigines build stone houses
Maoris reach New Zealand
Jesus Christ is born
Great wall of China built
Tasmanians use canoes for sealing

Dingo arrives in Australia
Great pyramids built
Diprotodon becomes extinct
First cities in Mesopotamia

Holocene epoch

People in Asia start to use metals
New Guinea separated from Australia

10 000 years ago

Agriculture first practiced in the Middle East

Ice melts, Tasmania isolated again

Sea levels lower by 120 m during last Ice Age

Pleistocene epoch

Last Ice Age at its coldest

All of Australia is populated

The first people to reach Australia may have arrived 100 000 years ago. By 20 000 years ago the whole continent was populated, and 10 000 years ago it had a shape and climate like that of today.

Australia in the grip of an Ice Age

At the height of the last Ice Age, some 18 000 years ago, Australia was drier and colder than it is today, and might have looked roughly like this. Aboriginal travellers could have walked dry-shod from the far northern coast of New Guinea all the way to southern Tasmania. Much of the interior of the continent was covered by desert and sand dunes. Great dust storms swept across the continent taking clouds of material out to sea over both the western and eastern coasts. Permanent icecaps were to be found on the Tasmanian highlands, around Mt Kosciusko in the Snowy Mountains and on the highlands of New Guinea.

Kalimantan
Sulawesi
New Guinea
Icecap
Timor
Java
Port Moresby
• Darwin
• Alice Springs
Australia
Desert
• Brisbane
Perth •
• Sydney
Adelaide •
Canberra •
Icecap
• Melbourne
Icecap
Tasmania
• Hobart

The coming of humans

Twenty years ago it was believed that the Australian Aborigines had lived in Australia for about 8000 years before the arrival of the Europeans, and that during that time they had lived a virtually unchanged life. We now know that the first Australians came from Asia at some time during the last Ice Age, perhaps 120 000 years ago. The migrants would have had to make several sea crossings, perhaps as many as eight, to travel from South-East Asia, even when the sea was at its lowest. Later the seas rose, separating mainland Australia and Tasmania and New Guinea. Several Aboriginal traditions record the encroachment of the sea which, on low-lying, flat coasts, would have been as much as 5 km each year. When the sea was at its lowest, Australia was 2.5 million sq km larger than it is now. Doubtless the first occupation sites of the ancestral Aborigines were on this now sea-covered land, so the date of the arrival of the first Australians will probably never be known.

The belief that people lived on the present mainland about 120 000 years ago is based on indirect evidence from a soil core taken from Lake George in NSW. At a depth corresponding to this age there was a sudden increase in the amount of charcoal, indicating fires, and a decrease in fire-intolerant plants, coupled with an increase in eucalyptus pollen. This period had been no drier than earlier interglacial periods, so some anthropologists think that the increasing numbers of fires may have been due to the presence of people who used fire to keep the country open, as the Aborigines did thousands of years later. There is no evidence such as skeletal remains, or stone artifacts, of such antiquity.

Most ancient Aboriginal sites have been found in the more densely populated parts of the country because that is where most of the archaeologists live. There is therefore almost certainly a bias in the evidence of sites found. It would be expected that the first Australian sites still above water would be on Cape York, in the Northern Territory or in the north of Western Australia. However, the oldest site so far found in north Queensland – the Walkunder Arch Cave at Chillagoe – is only 18 000 years old, far younger than sites further south. However, there is some charcoal evidence, similar to that from Lake George, of human presence in the Atherton Tablelands 45 000 years ago. In Arnhem Land there are several rock shelters in the escarpment dating from 18 000 to 24 000 years ago, and in some of these the world's oldest ground-edge axes have been found. Even more remarkable is the waist on these stones which suggests that they were fitted into a cleft stick. In the north-west of Australia there are some sites about 20 000 years old, but the oldest known Australian Aboriginal site in Australia is much further south,

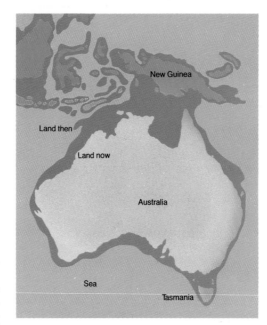

When sea levels were at their lowest, during the last Ice Age, only about 95 km separated Australia from islands to the north. A relatively short sea journey would have enabled settlers to reach the continent.

in a gravel pit on the banks of the Nepean River west of Sydney. It has yielded stone tools that have been dated to about 42 000 years ago, but this is near the limit for the radioactive carbon dating technique. There are sites of similar antiquity – 30 000 to 40 000 years – elsewhere in south-eastern Australia, and one of 38 000 years on the ancient flood plain of the Swan River, between Perth and Walyunga.

It is probable that the first Aborigines arrived somewhere on what are now the northern coasts, and spread over the following centuries along the coasts and large river valleys. It was only a few thousand years ago that some groups colonised the more arid regions of the continent. The oldest known site in central Australia is about 22 000 years old.

Nobody knows if all today's Aboriginal people are descended from one small group, or from several groups, arriving at different times. Thirty years ago Joseph Birdsell's three-wave theory ruled. He believed that the first people were small, oceanic Negritos who were later driven into Tasmania by a second wave, the Murrayans. Still later the Carpentarians settled the north. Today, after many genetic and morphological studies, Birdsell's theory has been abandoned. Even the prehistoric Tasmanians did not differ markedly from present-day mainlanders, although by the time they were virtually wiped out

by Europeans their small population had been isolated long enough for differences to have appeared. In the past, however, there may have been – to judge from fossil finds – at least two groups of people in the Pleistocene epoch, one showing characteristics close to modern Aborigines, and the other with more robust characteristics, and archaic features of the skull which had remarkably thick bone.

The most puzzling people are those buried at Kow Swamp in northern Victoria, in a Pleistocene graveyard that was used from about 15 000 to 9000 years ago. They had large, long skulls, the bone of which was up to 13 mm thick. Their eyebrow ridges were large, and their foreheads so flat and receding that some anthropologists wondered if they practised skull deformation on their children. This is, or was, common in some parts of the world, but very rare among historic Aborigines. Their jaws were massive and from above, the skulls were flask shaped. Despite their primitive appearance, it is clear from the presence of grave goods, including head bands of teeth, that these people had religious and aesthetic senses.

People with similar characteristics were found in other areas – for example, Cossack Man from Western Australia and Nitchie Man (buried with a necklace of 178 pierced Tasmanian Devil teeth) from NSW. These individuals may have lived only 6000 or 7000 years ago. An even more robust skeleton has since been found near Lake Garnpung in NSW, but its age is uncertain.

In stark contrast are the much more modern looking, although far older, ancient people of Lake Mungo who lived in the Willandra Lakes region of western NSW. When people first lived there, about 32 000 years ago, Lake Mungo was filled with water and fish. Mungo 'man', the first skeleton found, turned out to be Mungo girl: after her death she had been cremated – the world's first recorded case – and then her bones were smashed before burial. She was slender, small and round-skulled, and her eye brow ridges were small compared with those of robust skulls. Nearby there was another burial – that of an uncremated man who, on internment, had been coated with red ochre.

In recent years it has been recognised that the Aborigines' way of life was not unchanging for tens of thousands of years. There are, for example, two very different stone industries. In the earlier tradition during the Ice Age period, the people used choppers made from pebbles, cores of stone shaped like horse hoofs, and various kinds of robust scrapers. This so-called 'core tool and scraper tradition' gave way, at about the time of the arrival of the Dingo, to the small tool tradition in which flakes struck from a core were worked into a variety of forms, many of which were designed to be hafted on to spear shafts or other handles, with vegetable gum and twine. Later still stone was used less and less, its place being taken by bone and other organic materials. It may be, however, that bone was used just as much in earlier days: it does not survive as long as stone.

The idea that the Aborigines had only a small effect on the environment has also been abandoned. For thousands of years they used fire to keep the country open, and to encourage the growth of green feed for kangaroos. When Kangaroo Island was visited by Matthew Flinders in 1802, and by Nicolas Baudin later that year, both captains realised it was then uninhabited because there was no smoke. With the dispossession of the Aborigines of many Australian regions, once open, park-like country reverted to poor scrub within a few years. It is possible that the Aborigines' use of fire contributed to the disappearance of the large animals that once lived in Australia.

Yet another notion that has been revised is that before European settlement the Aborigines were always nomadic people, living in small groups, who made only the flimsiest, transitory shelters. But on various large rivers and swamps some groups built such ingenious fish traps that large groups could live there for months at a time. At Lake Condah in Victoria they lived in one place long enough to build at least 140 houses of stone, roofed with wood.

It was in this area, in a gravel pit on the banks of the Nepean River west of Sydney, that the oldest tools yet found in Australia were unearthed by researchers.

Evidence of Aboriginal occupation

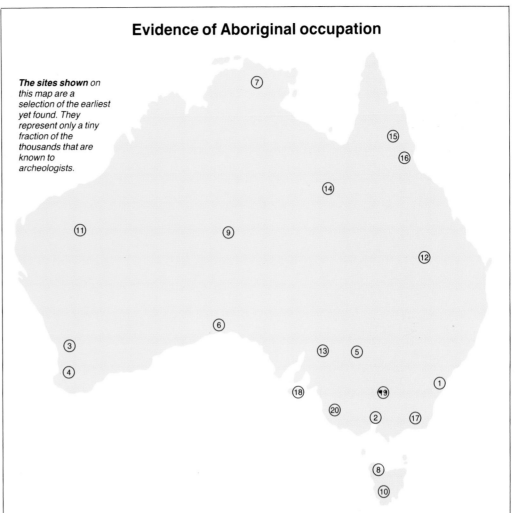

The sites shown on this map are a selection of the earliest yet found. They represent only a tiny fraction of the thousands that are known to archeologists.

The earliest dated Aboriginal site yet found – at Cranebrook – is about 42 000 years old. Clearly Aborigines reached northern Australia much earlier than this, but the first settlement sites are probably now under water – submerged when sea levels rose after the last Ice Age.

1 Cranebrook Terrace Tools found in a gravel pit here are 42 000 years old.

2 Keilor Tools and bones 40 000 years old have been found at this site.

3 Upper Swan River Tools from this site date back for at least 38 000 years.

4 Devil's Lair Discoveries at this site include 33 000-year-old tools, 29 500-year-old bone tools and a bone bead about 15 000 years old.

5 Lake Mungo This is the site of the world's earliest known cremation – 26 000 years ago. Tools and ochre 32 000 years old have also been found.

6 Koonalda Cave Aborigines decorated the walls of this cave 14 000 to 24 000 years ago – the oldest known example of Aboriginal art.

7 Oenpelli The world's oldest ground-edge hatchets have been found in rock shelters here and date back to at least 24 000 years ago.

8 Cave Bay Cave Bone points found here are 18 000 years old, but the cave was first occupied at least 22 500 years ago.

9 Puritjarra This 22 000-year-old site is the oldest yet found in central Australia.

10 Kutikina Cave The most southerly Ice Age site in the world. First occupied 20 000 years ago.

11 Mount Newman Rock shelter here occupied 20 000 years ago.

12 Keniff Cave Occupied 19 000 years ago.

13 Roonka Flat First visited 18 000 years ago.

14 Colless Creek This oasis in the arid region was used 18 000 years ago.

15 Early Man Shelter First traces of occupation date back for 13 000 years.

16 Walkunder Arch Cave Earliest dates of 18 000 years before present.

17 Clogg's Cave Remains are 17 000 years old.

18 Seton Cave The people who visited this cave 17 000 years ago probably died out when rising sea levels cut off Kangaroo Island.

19 Kow Swamp Skeletons between 15 000 and 9000 years old have been unearthed at this site.

20 Wyrie Swamp Australia's oldest wooden tools – including boomerangs – have been found here. They are around 10 000 years old.

White settlement

During the tens of thousands of years they lived alone in Australia, the Aborigines, with their fire-sticks, greatly changed the country's environments, but their impact was slight compared with that of the Europeans who have been here for just 200 years. One obvious change has been the covering of land with buildings – Australians are the most urbanised people in the world. Some of the effects of cities are obvious. Much of the soil is covered with brick or concrete, leaving only a patchwork of land in gardens and parks, little of which carries any native vegetation. Cities and towns also produce tonnes of waste – sewage, domestic rubbish, old building material and factory waste – all of which must be disposed of. As all the largest cities are coastal, and most of the largest inland towns are on rivers, the sea and the rivers have been used for getting rid of liquid wastes, including sewage.

Solid waste is either dumped on the surface, or used as landfill. Near the large cities suitable land for dumping has become scarce. A large city or town makes its own climate. Water falling on concrete obviously runs away into stormwater channels and drains and quickly wastes itself in the sea. Concrete absorbs heat, and releases it as the air cools, or reflects sunlight, while tall buildings cast shade over the ground for most of the day. The net result is that air temperatures in cities are usually a degree or two higher than those in the country. Another feature is the channelling of winds by canyon-like city streets which can make them very gusty.

In the past, before the introduction of burning restrictions and regulations on car emissions, cities such as Sydney suffered from smog which was trapped below long-lasting inversion layers.

Away from the cities, the Europeans have profoundly changed the landscape with forestry, grazing, farming and mining.

Many problems arose from the Europeans' complete ignorance, 100 or 200 years ago, of the functioning of ecosystems. They obviously had no experience of farming in Australian conditions, which differed greatly from those of temperate northern Europe. Attempting to use unmodified European farming methods led to erosion, and to the impoverishment of already nutrient-poor soils. Graziers tried to make their land carry the stock which it could support in the best years, with disastrous results to the stock and vegetation in drought years. They also denuded the land of growing trees by ringbarking and felling, thus opening it up to further erosion.

The sheep and cattle themselves changed the vegetation on which they grazed. They were the first mammals in Australia with hard, pointed hoofs, to which the plants were not adapted. Furthermore they eat a different selection of plants from those favoured by marsupials, and thus changed the composition of native pasture. Sheep in parts of NSW, for example, have grazed out saltbush and bluebush, which have been replaced by native grasses. The release of rabbits near Geelong in Victoria led to their spread over much of the continent within a few decades. They, like the sheep, are preferential feeders, and denuded large areas until they were partly checked by myxomatosis.

In the more arid parts of the country pasture plants are well adapted to periodic droughts, and although several hectares may be needed to sustain a sheep, the sheep grow good wool. In better-watered regions, however, exotic pasture plants, which respond better to fertilisers than native species that are adapted to impoverished soils, have been used with great success. A particularly successful combination has been subterranean clover and superphosphate. The clover provides the nitrogen which the soil lacks. In the south most of the introduced pasture plants – grasses and legumes – originally came from the Mediterranean region. In tropical Australia other species are used.

Arable farming has even more marked effects on the landscape than grazing, with a mixed vegetation cover being replaced by a single crop. Obviously grazing native mammals and crops are incompatible.

Most crops need fertilisers. Some areas also need trace elements for crops to be grown successfully. One problem with fertilisers has been the run-off of the excess into rivers and lakes which has caused the great multiplication of water plants, followed by serious oxygen depletion as plant material rots. Another problem sometimes caused by farming is the presence of pesticide residues in the environment. Some – particularly the chlorinated hydrocarbons – are very persistent, and can have effects as they pass through food networks, becoming more and more concentrated at each stage. In Europe and North America they have reduced the numbers of birds of prey, at least temporarily, but the problem does not seem to have been so severe in Australia.

Most rivers have been changed in some ways by Europeans. They have been polluted, and they have been dammed and had their courses changed. These processes have changed the water temperature and rate of flow, and often native fish species have declined.

Australia has never had a large proportion of forested land, although the early settlers at Sydney must have believed that the trees stretched as far as they did in Canada. Since

A fateful day for Australia, its Aboriginal inhabitants and its wildlife – the First Fleet, carrying the first permanent white settlers, sails into Port Jackson on 27 January 1788.

Within a few years of settlement, Europeans had changed the Australian landscape dramatically. Trees, like these being felled in 1917 (below), were cleared, and minerals, such as gold from Victorian mines (above), were extracted to bring prosperity to the growing colonies.

settlement, a large proportion of the eucalyptus forest has disappeared, and only remnants of the rainforests survive. It is true that foresters plant eucalypts to replace those that they crop, but the forester's ideal forest differs markedly from a natural one. To make growing and cropping easier the forester wants stands of regularly-spaced, even-aged trees, all healthy and sound, all maturing at the same time, with each block consisting of a single species. His object is the same as that of a wheat farmer, except that he is willing to wait much longer for his crop to 'ripen'. A natural forest, on the other hand, contains a variety of trees, some young, some mature and some dead or dying. Such a forest provides the resources – food and cover – needed by a wide variety of native animals which do not find them in abundance in an ideal forest.

Native trees provide mainly hardwoods. There have been extensive plantings of the soft wood species *Pinus radiata* which supports far fewer native species of animals.

The disappearance of native animals has more often been due to the destruction of their habitats, rather than as a result of human hunting. Thylacines may have been hunted to extinction, but the only kangaroo which has disappeared for this reason seems to be the Toolache Wallaby. It is possible that some of the species which have become extinct since European settlement were tottering on the brink at the time of first colonisation, and would have gone anyway. However, there is no doubt that many flourishing species have either disappeared or have had their ranges greatly curtailed by the

destruction of their habitats. Some species, on the other hand, have benefited from European settlement. Some possums, for example, have taken happily to city suburbs, eating fruit and flowers in gardens, and performing boisterous courtships in attics, while the great kangaroos have benefited from improved pastures and water supplied from artesian wells.

The part played by introduced animals and plants is often controversial. There is no doubt about the direct destruction wreaked by rabbits, but they may also have contributed to the decline of some burrowing animals, such as bilbies, by competing with them for sites. Feral cats, and possibly also foxes, destroy small native mammals and birds, and water buffalo in the north destroy billabongs and waterside vegetation. Here and there the Mallard is killing the Pacific Black Duck with love – by interbreeding. Other birds are probably less harmful because they tend to live in urban areas and to use introduced trees, and probably fill niches that would not be used by native birds. Introduced weeds such as the prickly pears in the past, and Bitou Bush today, drive out native vegetation.

Mining is the most destructive of all activities, although the area changed is very small. Much of it is carried out in remote areas, however, where it is intrusive, and the activity is not restricted to digging holes in the ground. Towns are built for workers, and railways and roads link the centres to the ports. When processing is carried on near the site, as with the copper smelting at Queenstown in Tasmania, the damage can extend for many kilometres.

Country homestead

PART TWO

2
Living Landscapes

Rocks and soil: food for plants

Geologically speaking, rocks are mixtures of minerals, of which there are about 30 different kinds. Usually they are hard, durable materials, although loose sand can technically also be counted as rock. The 12 commonest elements in the materials that form rocks – accounting for 99 per cent – are, in order, oxygen, silicon, aluminium, iron, calcium, sodium, potassium, magnesium, titanium, hydrogen, phosphorus and manganese. The commonest minerals are quartz (silicon dioxide or silica), orthoclase feldspar, plagioclase feldspar, augite, hornblende, biotite, olivine, calcite, magnesite, garnet and muscovite. All but calcite (calcium carbonate) and magnesite (magnesium carbonate) are silicates containing one or more of the elements listed above. Rocks therefore are mixtures composed mostly of the above minerals.

One of the first ways of classifying rocks is by their origin: igneous, sedimentary and metamorphic.

Igneous rocks are formed by the solidification of magma (molten material) on or close to the surface of the earth's crust. If the material flows over the surface the resulting rocks are called volcanic rocks. Plutonic rocks are those that have solidified below the surface in large masses; erosion of the overlying rocks may eventually expose them. When the magma pushes through fissures below the surface and solidifies there, forming comparatively thin sheets, the rocks are known as hypabyssal rocks.

The sheets formed between the bedding planes (usually horizontal) of already existing rocks are called sills, and those that cut across them (usually vertically) are dykes.

Magma that solidifies below the surface usually does so slowly enough for large crystals to form. When magma solidifies quickly on the surface the crystals are smaller. In extreme cases there is no crystallisation, and the resulting rock is a glass, such as obsidian. Some minerals crystallise at higher temperatures than others, and sometimes one kind of mineral crystal will change to another as the temperature falls.

There may also be differences in the composition of the magma at various places. Potash feldspar, muscovite and quartz are the last crystals to form. These processes lead to the formation of different kinds of igneous rocks: those with more than 66 per cent of silica are acid igneous rocks; those with less than 45 per cent are ultrabasic.

In between are the two commonest kinds of igneous rock: the acidic granite, high in silica, sodium and potassium but lower in iron, aluminium and manganese; and the basic basalt, which has relatively large contents of the metals. Basalt is a dark volcanic rock with very fine crystals and often much glass, which covers

Rocks can have three possible origins: they can be igneous – formed from molten material – like these basalt columns (right) in the Victorian Alps; sedimentary – deposited by wind and water – like this shale in Western Australia (below); or metamorphic – changed by heat or pressure – like this quartzite in Tasmania (above).

large areas on land and on the ocean floor. On cooling it often forms columnar shapes as at Kiama in NSW, and Cape Raoul in Tasmania. Granite is an acid plutonic rock, always crystalline, with the particles often of equal size although sometimes large crystals, often several centimetres across, are present.

Sometimes magma solidifies in the cores of volcanoes to form hard volcanic rocks. The surrounding, softer rocks erode away leaving the plugs standing. This was the origin of the Glasshouse Mountains in Queensland and the Warrumbungles in NSW.

Over millions of years rocks wear down, eroded by the weather. Expanding ice breaks off flakes, and cycles of heat and cold make the rocks contract and expand, cracking them. Glacial ice and debris scour the rocks below. Wind-blown sand grinds them, chemicals in rain soften them. Grain by grain the rocks break up, and if there is a slope, water carries the remains away. Sometimes the grains are blown away by the wind. All these processes are more severe in mountains, and consequently the mountains are gradually worn down, their bits deposited by water or wind on lower ground or in the sea. Eventually earth movements may raise mountains again, and the process is repeated.

The particles, when they are deposited, form sedimentary rocks. If the original rocks were igneous, chemical changes during the erosion remove some of the minerals leaving a much higher proportion of silica, so that many sedimentary rocks consist largely of quartz. As deposits build up, the layers below are subjected to pressure, compacting the rock. The grains then become cemented together by chemical processes. Uplifted sedimentary rocks are also eroded – as are metamorphic rocks – so the material of sedimentary rocks can result from any kind of rock.

Sedimentary rocks are deposited in layers and these can often be distinguished easily as strata or, on a much smaller scale, as thin layers. Sometimes evidence of water currents can be seen. Many sedimentary rocks bear fossils of plants and animals.

Limestones are sedimentary rocks formed by the precipitation of calcium and magnesium compounds in still water to form carbonates which settle and compact on the bottom. Some are organic in origin, formed by the remains of dead microorganisms, molluscs, coral and other animals. Coal is another kind of organic sedimentary rock. Other kinds include tuff, which is produced by material such as ash falling from a volcanic eruption.

The commonest sedimentary rocks, however, are sandstones in which the grains are 0.05 to 2 mm in diameter, siltstones (0.005 to 0.05 mm diameter, on average) and claystones, which have smaller particles. The last two are often grouped as mudstones. Shales are made up of clay particles, and will split into leaves, but unlike true clays, shales do not become plastic in water. There are also conglomerates which contain large pebbles or even boulders embedded in a finer rock.

Australia is an old continent which has seen little volcanic action, or mountain building, for millions of years. Consequently it is now a greatly eroded continent with vast areas of sedimentary rocks.

Metamorphic rocks are produced from igneous or sedimentary rocks by the action of heat or pressure, or both. Where molten magma touches an existing rock, for example, it can be changed, or metamorphosed. Folding of strata by earth movements will also produce metamorphic rocks. The best-known are probably slate and phyllite, which are comparatively little changed shales; schist, which is more profoundly changed shale and which often shows flakes of mica; marble, derived from limestone; and quartzite which is metamorphosised sandstone. The last differs little chemically from sandstone, but is harder and more compact.

Soil is obviously formed from minerals. The most fertile soils are derived from igneous rocks which contain the elements listed above. Sometimes, however, some igneous rocks such as serpentine also contain elements that are toxic to plants – chromium or nickel, for example.

In this greatly eroded continent there have been, over millions of years, few deposits of new igneous minerals on the surface, and most of what could be eroded has been eroded and deposited in the sea. In the soil that does remain, many of the useful elements have been leached out, leaving soils particularly poor in phosphorus, potassium and many trace elements. There are a few areas of good soils, mainly in alluvial flats in valleys or associated with basalt areas, but many are about as fertile as a sand dune. Native plants have evolved mechanisms and characteristics – such as sclerophylly – which help them to grow in these impoverished soils, but many introduced plants cannot be grown successfully for long without the application of nutrients.

Soil consists of far more than minerals and water. It contains, for example, the roots and other parts of plants, and other organic matter in various stages of decay. It also contains vast numbers of microorganisms, fungi, and animals, ranging from microscopically small nematode worms and single-celled amoeba and their relatives, through somewhat larger mites, insects and their larvae, to larger creatures such as earthworms. These are essential for plant growth because they recycle nutrients by breaking down organic materials, releasing nitrogen compounds. The earthworms and some of the other animals also make tiny tunnels which are essential for the passage of air and water.

A section through soil down to bedrock shows a series of layers or 'horizons' by which the particular soil can be classified. The horizons are the result of weathering and the movement of materials by water or by the action of the plants themselves. Usually an A horizon, the zone of accumulated organic matter, can be seen. It can be divided into an upper, darker A1 horizon, and a lower, lighter A2 or subsurface horizon. The B horizon below is the subsoil layer where the inorganic and mineral constituents gather. Below this is the C horizon which is the partially weathered bedrock. In its place there may be a D horizon if the soil material has been deposited from elsewhere. Different bedrocks and different climates – arid, where water evaporation exceeds rainfall for example – produce different soils, but it is difficult to compare Australian soils with those of other countries in this way. There are many different kinds of soils recognised in the Australian classification.

Many of the Blue Mountains' sandstone peaks west of Sydney are capped with a layer of basalt. There are striking differences between the plants that thrive in the rich basalt soils (right), and those that grow on the poorer sandstone beneath (above).

Water: the vital fluid

The Australian climate is determined by the continent's geographical position, size, shape, and topography. The term 'weather' should not be confused with 'climate'. The climate refers to the average or mean conditions of rainfall, wind and temperature over tens or hundreds of years. The weather at any time is merely a sample of these conditions, and a particular value, such as that of temperature, may be well above or below the mean for that time of the year.

The climate of Australia depends on its position in relation to the circulation patterns of the earth's atmosphere. These are driven by the sun which, because of the earth's tilt, is lowest in our sky in June, and highest in December when – on our midsummer's day – it is vertically above the Tropic of Capricorn which runs approximately through Alice Springs, Emerald and Rockhampton. It is impossible to detail here the global air movements, but their result for Australia is a tendency for weather systems to move from east to west in the north of the continent and from west to east further south. In between is the anticyclone belt, with the anticyclones moving west to east at about 800 km per day. In summer low-pressure areas are well to the south of Australia but they move north in winter so that many of the southernmost parts of Australia have winter rainfall – a Mediterranean climate – while north of about 20°S there is summer rainfall – a monsoonal climate. Between – in the arid region – there is no regular pattern for either winter or summer. Along the east of the country the mountains influence the weather so that rainfall is heavier between the mountains and the sea. Weather systems pick up moisture from the ocean so that around Cairns there are heavy rains throughout the year, and further south the winter-summer pattern outlined above is confused by the oceanic effects so that in most of NSW there is an even distribution throughout the year, although in places it can be erratic.

Maps showing the temperatures at various times by means of isotherms – lines joining places with equal temperatures – can be misleading for they usually show the corrected temperatures – those that would apply at sea level. Thus the temperature shown on a map for a spot in the Kenya Highlands could be several degrees higher than that shown by a thermometer at the place. Most of Australia is low-lying so the temperatures experienced are often close to those shown on the maps, but a comparison of Australian maps with those of, say, Africa, will give the impression that Australia is cooler.

Temperatures increase towards the tropics (more regularly in the winter) but with the seas and oceans modifying them in coastal regions. In general, the hottest region is around Marble Bar in Western Australia and the coldest is in the Alps. July is the coldest month, and January or February in the south and November or December in the north, are the hottest.

The general rainfall pattern has been outlined above. The driest area is east of Lake Eyre with an average (median) annual fall of about 100 mm. The wettest lies around Tully in Queensland (median 4203 mm), although parts of the high country of Tasmania, and the Snowy Mountains region approache this. The highest fall in a year was at Bellenden Ker in Queensland (11 251 mm). The proportion of the country with less than 200 mm on the average is 29.6 per cent: only 11.4 per cent has more than 800 mm.

Ecologically and agriculturally, the average annual rainfall is only one of the factors determining the effectiveness of rain. Obviously only the rain that does not evaporate can be used by plants, and the rate of evaporation depends upon the temperature. The annual evaporation from an open tank is greater than the rainfall everywhere on the mainland, except in the eastern highlands. The rain that does fall, however, rarely falls into a tank or a lake: most of it reaches the soil from which evaporation is slower. The nature of the soil and the topography are also important. In many places much rain runs away leaving relatively little soaked into the ground. Another factor is the intensity of the rainfall, often measured by dividing the total rainfall for the year by the number of rainy days in the year. Put simply, however, if 200 mm of rain falls in 24 hours, most of it would run away if there is an appreciable slope, probably causing erosion as well, but if that rain is spread over 20 days, more of it will stay in the area where it falls. The intensity ranges from about 3.8 mm per wet day in parts of the south to more than 15 mm per wet day in the north.

The average rainfall of a place gives no clue, however, to the variability there. It is obvious that in Australia many places suffer from droughts during which little rain falls for several years, and then when the drought breaks there may be a succession of very wet years. A simple method of measuring variability is to take the readings for a number of years, calculate how much each differs from the average value, then

An alarming storm bears down on a coastal NSW town. Australia's erratic and often extreme climate has made farming difficult over large areas of the continent.

Satellites reveal secrets of the world's weather

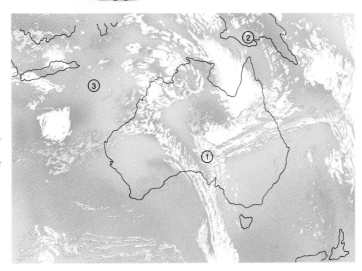

*The composite satellite view (above) of the southern hemisphere in early January (mid-summer) was obtained by a US weather satellite orbiting the earth at a height of 1450 km. It reveals: **1** Swirling clouds associated with mid-latitude low pressure areas (one of which is passing over southern Australia) as they are pushed along by strong westerly winds; **2** patchy clouds in the equatorial low-pressure band; **3** mostly clear skies in the sub-tropical high pressure zone, where the air is sinking.*

average these deviations and express the variability as a percentage. (100 times the average deviation divided by the mean). For example, if the mean was 200 mm, and for three years the rainfall was 100 mm, 50 mm and 310 mm, the deviations would be 100, 150, and 110, their average would be 120, and the deviation 40 per cent. In practice, of course, many more than three years are used in the calculation. Not surprisingly the lower the average annual rainfall, the greater the variability, and this applies world-wide, although not to the same extent in different regions. Australia comes out badly on this criterion. In areas with low average annual rainfall in Australia, the variability is much greater than in most other countries with a similar annual rainfall. This is another way of saying that many areas of Australia are more drought-prone and flood-prone than areas in other countries with a similar annual rainfall.

One simple measure of effectiveness of rain for the agriculturalist is to count all the rain over four-tenths of the evaporation from an open tank as effective. Thus, if a tank loses by evaporation 200 mm of water in a month, and the rainfall is 100 mm in that month, then the month's effective rainfall is 20 mm. On the average it needs five consecutive months to grow a crop – less in warmer regions. It follows that, therefore, if crops are to be grown in an area, they need five consecutive months with effective rainfall. This is, of course, an oversimplification. It does not take into account water that may be stored in the soil from one month to another, nor the nature of the crop. A water-greedy crop like sugarcane, for example, will need more water than wheat because it transpires more, and the losses may even approach those from a free surface of water. Furthermore most crops need a period with the soil more than merely moist which is the condition implied by an effective rain month: they often need at least one month with soaking rain. And finally the rainfall is variable: there may be years with five months effective rain and there may be years with drought.

Drought has been described as a period of months or years during which so little rain falls that the earth scorches, dams dry out, crops burn up and stock animals die. It is difficult to find a more 'scientific' definition than this list of the effects of drought. Droughts cannot yet be forecast with accuracy, but important droughts occur at intervals of, at the most, eight years, although few are as severe as that of 1979–81. The most disastrous since colonisation was that of 1895–1903. In the 1942–45 drought, sheep numbers fell from 120 to 90 million. The less devastating effects of later severe droughts have been attributed to the increase in sown pastures which, with their drought-evasive plants such as subterranean clover, maintain sheep longer in drought than do native pastures.

Communities of plants

The community of plants which grow in a given place depends on many factors such as the kinds of plants available, the rainfall and its pattern through the year and other features of the climate. Also important are the soil and its fertility, the topography and aspect of the site, and its history.

If some catastrophe such as a massive earthslide or volcanic action lays bare the soil or bedrock, or a fire completely destroys the vegetation, there is often a succession of plant communities, the composition of the final community depending to a large extent on the factors outlined above.

If the beginning is bare rock, the first colonisers are often lichens which over the years grow, erode the rock surface, and decay, releasing organic matter, and providing a habitat for soil microorganisms and later small soil animals. Eventually there is enough soil for small herbs and grasses to get a footing. They, in their turn, build up the soil and its organic matter, and provide some shelter, so that in time they are replaced by shrubs which shade out the herbs. Eventually, if the site is favourable, large trees will grow – the so-called climax vegetation. At each stage in the succession the communities tend to be more complex, with more and more interacting species of plants, animals and microorganisms, although eventually the numbers of kinds of large species may fall. In addition the biomass – the total amount of living material present – increases at each stage.

Similar successions occur with different starting points. At certain places along the NSW coast there are mangrove forests. Soil washed down from higher levels builds up around the roots, raising the soil level until it is too dry for the mangroves which are forced to extend seawards. They are replaced on the new, salt-laden, boggy land by meadows of salt-loving Beaded Glasswort *Salicornia quinqueflora*. Once again soil is washed down, the land is raised and becomes less salty, and is taken over by various shrubs and small trees such as sheoaks (*Casuarina*), paperbarks (*Melaleuca*) and *Banksias*. These eventually give way to eucalypts and *Angophoras* – if developers do not get there first. The whole process can be seen in a walk through the zones in an undisturbed area from the mangrove swamps to the higher ground inland.

Obviously the process does not always culminate in the climax vegetation of woodland and forest. Tall trees generally grow only where the soil is fertile, and where there is enough water. The process may be stopped by environmental limitations at some earlier stage, such as grassland, heathland or shrubland.

Plant communities vary greatly, but they have patterns in common. Usually one or a few species are the most important in the sense that they make up the majority of the plant matter in a particular place. In forests, of course, trees are the most common plants and generally in Australia they are various kinds of eucalypts. Their foliage shades the ground below and dictates what plants, if any, will be able to grow there, for all green plants need light. Their extensive roots also draw on a large volume of soil for water and nutrients, and thus help to determine which other plants can make a living. There is intense competition for resources within species and between species in a plant community for resources. These important species are the so-called dominants of the particular community.

Few forests are a tangled continuous mass of foliage from the floor of the forest to the tops of the trees. Generally one or more layers of foliage, or storeys, can be picked out. The uppermost one is, of course, that formed by the foliage of the dominant trees which in some dense forests may appear from the air as a continuous layer with here and there a particularly tall tree – an emergent – poking above the rest. Below this layer are the boles of the trees. If enough light gets through there will be one or more understoreys – perhaps one formed by shrubs and another, near the ground, by herbs or grasses.

The spacing of the dominant plants and their bulk are determined by the environment. In poor conditions, where competition for water is intense, they will be widely spaced, and the proportion of the land directly shaded by their canopies will be relatively small. Australian botanists have classified the varied types of Australian vegetation on the basis of the types of dominant plants, their height and the proportion of ground shaded by the foliage. The main groups have been subdivided on the basis of the kinds of understoreys, if these are present. The divisions are artificial, however, in that communities grade into each other, and many communities fall between two divisions, but they do characterise many widespread typical communities.

In early studies of plant communities which were mainly carried out in Europe and North America, the concept of particular groupings of interacting species developed – for example an ash-oak woodland. A community was considered almost as if it had a life of its own. Recently many plant ecologists have thought of a community at a particular site as being a collection of the plants of a region whose ecological ranges overlap. Thus two eucalyptus species may have overlapping ranges as far as soil acidity is concerned. If, for example, soil acidity varies from place to place at a site then, provided other requirements are met, the two species will occur together only in certain areas. As there are many such possible variables, such as temperature,

Plants that halt the sea's relentless advance

Four stages in the reclamation of a shallow estuary shore by mangroves are illustrated in the photographs (right). The estuary (below), on an inlet of Broken Bay, north of Sydney, is also a good illustration of the pressures placed on such areas by human activities.

Housing (5), land reclamation (6), and boating activities (7) are all conspiring to constrict the areas where mangroves can grow. Recognition of the importance of such forests for wildlife and fisheries may prevent them from being completely destroyed.

1 Mangrove seedlings take root when silt has built up on the sea bed, raising its level.

Vast numbers of tiny plants and animals live on the decaying carcase of a forest giant, gradually breaking it down and returning the nutrients it contains to the soil where they can be used again.

exposure, soil moisture and so on, the plant community at any particular place will be highly specific, and probably unique.

The plants of a community do not exist in isolation. There is a host of other kinds of living organisms on which plant communities are utterly dependent. If they were not there, a tree that died from old age would remain for years just that, an old dead tree, until it was perhaps destroyed by fire. All the nutrients that went into its growth would be locked up, and eventually the soil would be exhausted, and no more plants would grow. Only a limited amount of new mineral matter is brought in by rains, winds and ground water. In short the other organisms are essential to the community because they cycle the materials within the plants, ensuring that new plant growth will replace the old.

The plants are the primary producers. It is they which, by photosynthesis, capture the energy of sunlight and, from water and carbon dioxide use it to produce organic compounds. In doing so they release oxygen. Other organisms use the plants as a source of food. Plant-eating animals eat leaves, fruit, wood, bark and roots, releasing carbon dioxide, and producing faeces and nitrogen-rich excretions. Some animals attack dead plant and animal remains, and faeces, reducing them to smaller pieces which are more readily broken up by smaller animals, fungi and bacteria. Some fungi and bacteria also attack living plants. Earthworms and other animals bury dead plant material in the soil where it remains until it rots away, acting as a kind of sponge which helps to retain water in the system. The soil animals also keep the soil open by tunnelling so that there is enough air.

All these organisms produce carbon dioxide which is used by green plants, ensuring that carbon in the community is constantly cycled. One group of bacteria convert nitrogen-containing organic compounds into simple nitrates which can be taken up by the roots of plants. Others, however, produce nitrogen gas which cannot be used directly by the plants and may be lost to the atmosphere. There is, however, yet another group of bacteria which can capture nitrogen gas and change it into nitrogen compounds which can be used by plants. Some of these live freely in the soil, but others live in nodules on the roots of plants such as wattles.

Many fungi and other microorganisms form a felting on the roots of certain plants, and in return for nutrients from the plant they help with the intake of water, and also help to protect the roots from being attacked by harmful species. Many trees will fail to grow if planted in soil where there are no suitable fungi.

There are, of course, animals and other organisms in the community which prey on those that feed on the living plants or their remains. Energy and materials pass along many food webs. On the whole, however, material is cycled in such a way that the whole community, if it is the final stage of a succession, continues indefinitely until there is some drastic change caused by fire, deforestation, pollution, climatic change or some other catastrophe.

In some cases, however, it may be that the final stage of a succession cannot continue to exist for some reason. A forest may age so that the old trees are not replaced by new ones, and then a 'catastrophe' such as a fire may be needed to start the cycle again.

*2 **Roots and pneumatophores** in a mature mangrove forest trap mud and other debris.*

*3 **Mud flats** behind the mangrove forest are now beyond the reach of even the highest tides.*

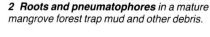

*4 **Mature sheoaks and eucalypts** grow on land that was once part of the sea floor.*

Life in the high country

Australia has relatively little mountainous country, and only about 11 700 sq. km is highland on which snow lies for more than one month in a year. This is only about 0.14 per cent of the country, but at the same time it is 28 per cent of the area of Switzerland and, it is said, for at least a short time in the winter there is more snow country in Australia than there is in Switzerland.

The snowline – above which there is continuous snow for at least one month – lies at about 900 m in Tasmania (6500 sq. km), at 1400 to 1500 m in Victoria (2250 sq. km), and at 1500 to 1700 m in the ACT and NSW (360 and 2600 sq. km respectively).

Areas in which the snow lies for one to four months is classed as subalpine. At these levels snow gums can grow. Above the tree line – usually at about 1800 m, although perhaps 150 m higher in sheltered places – is the alpine zone, the top of Mt Kosciusko (2228 m) being an example. Here the snow may lie for eight months, and in sheltered places, for all the year. Frosts can occur on any night of the year, and temperatures lie at or below freezing for weeks on end. Some 2540 mm of snow, rain and hail fall in a year, and much of the snow is blown into drifts by gales.

There are, however, no mountains on the mainland like the Matterhorn or Mount Cook, for most of the highland country in eastern Australia is relatively flat, although with deep, eroded gorges. Thus the topography, the relatively low altitudes and the nearness to tropical and subtropical zones combine to give a highland zone which is much less extreme than the European Alps or the Norwegian fjells. There is also a greater accumulation of soil on Australian hills than is to be found on the flanks of mountains of

Tasmania's highlands – *as here in the Cradle Mountain-Lake St Clair National Park – are more rugged than the alps on the mainland.*

other regions, and it rarely freezes beneath its snow cover. It is also rich in organic matter as decay is slower when it is cold.

Much of the Tasmanian highlands, on the other hand, is composed of dolerite so that the topography is rugged, although still nothing like the Matterhorn, and soil does not accumulate as it does in the Australian Alps. Furthermore, as Tasmania is a relatively small island, the climate is more oceanic, the winds are less severe and snow does not lie on the ground for long.

One feature that strikes a visiting European or American is the absence of conifers in the subalpine zone of the Great Dividing Range, and the presence instead of snow gums. Australia is the only place in the world where broad-leaved evergreen trees grow above the snow line. On the mainland the snow gums are *Eucalyptus pauciflora* and in Tasmania, *E. coccifera*. In Tasmania, however, some cold rainforest trees and shrubs, such as beeches and King William Pines, may reach subalpine levels, within the snow gums, or growing separately. Snow grass, belonging to a mainly northern hemisphere genus, *Poa*, grows among the gums and above the snowline.

In alpine and subalpine areas plants face the problems of a short growing period; the weight of snow above them in winter, or severe frosts when there is no protective snow; intense radiation from the sun on clear days; high winds; and in the summer, short periods of drought. The evolutionary response has produced small, rock-hugging plants with small spiny leaves, and often with a covering of down which acts as an air trap. Some species grow in tussocks or as cushions on the ground.

Many plants are found only in alpine regions, and often a species may be restricted to one or two peaks, having been isolated there for thousands of years. The Mt Kosciusko area alone has ten alpine plants that are unique. Among the buttercups, for example, Eichler's Buttercup grows on Mt Hotham and Dibbins Spur, the Western Tiers Buttercup on the Western Tiers in Tasmania, and the Kosciusko Buttercup on Mount Kosciusko.

The buttercup genus, *Ranunculus*, is one of several genera found in the Australian high country which are thought of as temperate plants in the northern hemisphere. They may have 'worked their way down' mountain chains to southern parts of the mainland and Tasmania during glacial periods in the past. Some of the other genera are *Gentianella*, mountain gentian, with one Australian species; *Euphrasia*, the eye-brights; *Veronica*, speedwells; and *Viola*, violets. Representatives of these genera can also be found in lowland areas, but all have alpine or subalpine species.

Alpine herbfields are common in the alpine

Snow gums *growing among granite boulders on the upper slopes of the main range near Mt Kosciusko.*

zone of the mainland, where they provide much of the colour and beauty of the high country. As the plants depend on having adequate soil, the herbfields are rarer in Tasmanian alpine regions. Plants of the daisy family are prominent, such as Billy Buttons, Pale Everlastings, Alpine Podolepis and Silver Daisies, but many other families are present. An unexpected plant is the creeping Fan Flower for this is usually associated with another extreme environment, the seashore. Grass Trigger plants are also found in lowland areas, but there is a more robust form which lives in alpine areas. In damp herbfields above 1300 m the grass-like leaves of the Sky Lily, which also occurs on the mountains of New Zealand, can form a sward.

The Twin-flower Knawel, of the speedwell family, is one of the commonest of plants in Australian and New Zealand alpine and subalpine areas. It is an example of the various plants which form compact cushions, only a few centimetres high, which hug the ground closely – an obvious adaptation for alpine conditions.

Cushion plants are prominent above the tree-line in Tasmania where the ground-hugging Creeping Pine, absent from the mainland, can also be found.

In subalpine swampy and peaty areas, in broad high valleys, closed or open heaths may develop with shrubs as the dominant plants.

The alpine bogs are also rich in sphagnum moss which retains great quantities of water.

Despite the apparent inhospitability of subalpine and alpine areas for animal life, many creatures do live there, even during the winter. In Australia the ground below the snow cover rarely freezes, and the snow protects any animals below it from freezing winds. In subalpine habitats some mammals are active above the snow. Ringtail Possums feed in the trees and wombats push down through the snow to eat the grass below. Some birds, such as magpies, may feed in the bushes and trees although, of course, most birds migrate to lower ground in the winter.

In the 1960s the CSIRO discovered remarkable activity in extensive burrows beneath loose snow in the Kosciusko National Park. They found two species of marsupial mice, two rodents and the Mountain Pygmy-possum foraging in the tunnels, or resting in grass nests in burrows.

One of the marsupial mice, the Dusky Antechinus, lives also in Tasmanian alpine heaths and woodland, but is also sometimes found in temperate rainforests. The marsupial mice are predators, living on small animals.

The Mountain Pygmy-possum was known as a fossil in 1895, long before it was discovered alive. It is the only mammal of Australia which always lives above the winter snowline. The first living specimen was found in a ski hut on Mt Hotham in 1966, and only a few have been captured since. As far as is known it is found only in an area of about 200 sq. km around Mt Hotham. There are about 300 individuals in the Park. It and the Dusky Antechinus are the only mammals which can be found at or near the summit of Mt Kosciusko in the winter.

Of the two rodents, the Bush Rat is widespread

Alpine herbfields on the slopes above Blue Lake, north-east of Mt Kosciusko. The lake is dammed by a moraine, a relic of the time during the last Ice Age when glaciers flowed down the slopes of these mountains.

Fierce winds have sculpted the snow on Mt Jagungal's summit marker. In the distance, some 36 km away, is the main range with Mt Kosciusko (2228 m), Australia's highest mountain, on the horizon.

in the east and south-west of the mainland. The Broad-toothed Rat, on the other hand, is rare. It is found in the mountains of Tasmania, and in the Alps, but also in wet sclerophyll forest in the Dandenong and Otway Ranges. All the mammals, apart from the marsupial mice, eat plants.

Most reptile and birds move down to lower ground in winter, but at least two frogs live above the snowline, and a third, the Sphagnum Frog of the New England district, often spends a week or two under snow. The striking Corroboree Frog (illustration p 183) of the Brindabella Ranges and Snowy Mountains, lives in sphagnum bogs at heights up to 1700 m. It was not discovered until 1952 and, the story goes, was so unusual that the Museum put it on one side thinking it was a hoax or an exotic species. The third species, also living in bogs, is the Baw Baw Frog which lives on Mt Baw Baw at altitudes over 1200 m.

The mountains have many remarkable insects. One scorpion fly, for example, has been collected a few times, but only on snow in Tasmania. The Kosciusko Grasshopper, a species which can change its colour with temperature can be common, and the two hairy cicadas – in which both sexes sing – are found only in high country, one on the mainland, the other in Tasmania. Possibly the most interesting insects however are the Bogong Moths (illustration pp. 94, 259) which breed in the lowlands, but AESTIVATE in caves and granite tors in the Snowy Mountains, covering the walls of their resting places.

Australia's unique grasslands

Large areas of Australia are covered with grasses, or plants that are so grass-like that most people would not distinguish between them. Many grasslands in the better watered areas are now improved pastures, carrying various introduced grasses and often clovers to increase the amount of nitrogen in the soil.

The pollen of true grasses first appear in the Australian fossil record only about 50 million years ago, relatively late compared with many other plant families. In eastern Australia grasses were uncommon until the Pliocene Period and became abundant only in the Pleistocene (see table p 19). In central Australia, however, they adapted to the increasing aridity and become more and more important from the middle of the Miocene Period onwards.

Hummock grasslands are typically, indeed,

uniquely, Australian. The hummocks are up to a metre in diameter and about 300 mm high, with flowering stems reaching 1.5 m. The foliage shades 10 to 30 per cent of the ground in the normal formation, and less than 10 per cent in open hummock grassland. The clumps grow outwards so that the centre is often dead and dry. The perennial, evergreen grasses which have sclerophyllous (hard-leaved) foliage are species of *Triodia* and *Plectrachne* (SPINIFEX). They are also often called, with good reason, porcupine grass. Between the hummocks there is little but red, bare soil, except perhaps for a few very scattered trees. After rains, however, short-lived flowering plants and grasses – also with sclerophyllous foliage – suddenly appear and produce their seeds.

This kind of grassland covers much of the

northern half of Australia – about 23 per cent of the continent – where the annual rainfall is about 125 to 350 mm, and the sandy soils are deep and lacking in nutrients. Nevertheless they are deep enough to hold any rain which does fall and this presumably compensates for their poor quality. Nitrogen levels are often about one-third, and phosphorus levels about one-half, of those in other arid soils, even ones that are normally thought to be impoverished. Hummock grasses often grow on the slopes of, and between the longitudinal dunes which are common in the arid interior.

The tussocks in tussock grasslands are smaller than hummocks. In northern Australia, from the Kimberleys to the Barkly Tableland in Queensland and around the eastern fringes of the Simpson and Great Stony Deserts, in areas with a rainfall of about 350 to 700 mm, there are large stretches of open tussock grassland on rolling plains with chalk-clay soils. The main grass is *Astrebla* or Mitchell Grass. The tussocks are from 600 to 1200 mm apart, have a diameter at their base of 150 to 230 mm, and reach a height of 450 to 900 mm. They shade 30 per cent or less of the ground. In good years there is a continuous cover of short grasses and flowering plants between the tussocks. Unlike spinifex country, this vegetation provides reasonable grazing for livestock at the time of the monsoonal rains. Trees, however, are very rare.

In parts of western Victoria, on heavy soils, there is a similar association, but with Kangaroo Grass *Themeda australis* and sometimes Wallaby Grass and other *Danthonia* species as the dominant plants. The tussocks are smaller than those of Mitchell Grass. Most of this land, however, has been cleared for farming.

A third example, also much reduced in area, is dominated not by a grass, but by iron 'grass', *Lomandra* species, of the GRASSTREE family, although *Danthonia* tussocks are also found. There are many herbs between the tussocks. The iron grass tussocks are about 300 mm tall and are found in the Mt Lofty Ranges, although many exotic plants now grow in that area as well.

Along flood plains in the north of Australia, on heavy black soils which crack in the dry season, there is closed grassland with a continuous cover of short or medium height grasses, with herbs scattered among them. Common species are *Oryza fatua*, a relative of cultivated rice, and *Eleocharis* species. The rice was one of the grasses used by the Aborigines who set fire to the grass and then winnowed the seeds from the ashes. The other plants, *Eleocharis* or spike-rushes, belong to the sedge family.

The Spinifex Hopping-mouse *Notomys alexis* is one mammal which has conquered the harsh environment of hummock grassland. During the

Most of the grasses growing on rolling, well-watered pasture land, and around cities and towns, are introduced species. Few native grasses are seen by city dwellers in their parks and gardens.

day it lives in a deep burrows, often a metre below the surface, and emerges at dusk to feed through the night on plants and insects, from which it obtains all the water that it needs. Among the marsupials which can be found sheltering in spinifex, in nearby soil cracks, or in the holes of hopping-mice or spiders are the insectivorous Kultarrs, which look like hopping-mice, but run on all four feet. Spinifex birds *Eremiornis carteri*, warblers, also live, not surprisingly, in spinifex country, but usually where run-off from watercourses makes the grasses grow thickly. Spinifex Pigeons, an emu-wren and six grasswrens may also be found among the spinifex. Common reptiles in the same area are Desert Skinks *Egernia inornata* which make shallow burrows at the base of spinifex plants or shrubs, Sand Monitors *Varanus gouldii* and Military Dragons *Ctenophorus isolepis*. Several members of the *Ctenotus* genus of skinks are also found in hummock grassland, and as many as seven species can be found living together. However, to avoid competition they divide up the habitat, and the day. Two hunt insects mainly between the hummocks, and the others hunt in the hummocks and around their edges, with three climbing above the ground. Two are active in the middle of the day, the others at cooler times. Furthermore they differ in size, and therefore catch different sizes of prey.

Desert Death Adders *Acanthophis pyrrhus* are one of the dangerous snakes which may be encountered in this country.

One advantage that reptiles have over mammals and the birds is their ability to starve for long periods if they cannot get food. Mammals and birds must move out, or starve to death,

Hummock grassland in the arid Pilbara area of Western Australia. These grasses are common throughout the dry north and centre of Australia. They are grazed in some areas, although most are untouched.

if they cannot eat frequently, although some mammals, such as dunnarts, can go into a torpid state for a time, or survive on stored fat.

The oddest inhabitants of spinifex grassland must be the burrowing frogs, such as the Desert Spadefoot Toad *Notedon nichollsi* and the Water-holding Frog *Cyclorana platycephala*, which come to the surface only after rain.

Some of these creatures live also in the tussock grasslands. Here the birds include various grass parrots *Neophema* spp., Singing Bushlarks *Mirafra javanica* – which are also found in less arid grasslands and cultivated pastures – Golden-headed Cisticolas *Cisticola exilis* and various finches such as Painted Firetails *Emblema picta*, which live in rocky gorges near arid grasslands. In all about 100 birds can be found in grasslands of various kinds, and about 18 of them are rarely found anywhere else. It is difficult, however, to define grassland birds as many species use trees in woodland, and visit grassy areas for food.

Mammals which can be found in less arid grassland without trees include the euros, mulgaras, Red and Pigmy Antechinuses, Long-tailed, Sandhill, Fat-tailed and Hairy-footed Dunnarts, Desert Mice, Sandy Inland Mice and, formerly, stick-nest rats. Long-haired Rats also live in dry grasslands, and in good years, when there is plenty to eat, they live up to their old name of Plague Rat. The name 'plague' referred to their numbers, not to any connection with Europe's 'Black Death'.

Different continents have developed different kinds of vegetation on their arid lands. Most of

Australia's arid land is relatively well covered by vegetation, compared with land in other continents where the climate and soil are similar, and where there are no true, shifting sand deserts of the Sahara type. Grassland is relatively uncommon in the more arid lands of other continents, but, on the other hand, Australia does not have the water-storing cactus and yucca communities found in American deserts or the succulent plant communities of Africa.

GRASSLAND

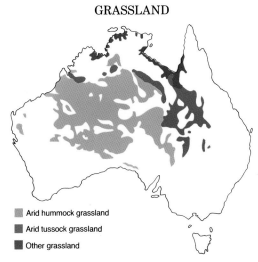

Arid hummock grassland

Arid tussock grassland

Other grassland

Areas where natural grasslands predominate. In regions that favour agriculture and grazing many of the native grasses have disappeared to be replaced by introduced species and clover for better stock feed.

Tussock grasses growing in the far north-west of Australia. Such areas are often extensively grazed by both sheep and beef cattle.

Scrubland and shrubland

Large areas of Australia are covered by vegetation where shrubs of various kinds are the most common plants. Shrubs are woody plants which are less than 5 m tall and they usually have either many stems growing from the ground or many branches arising from the stem close to the ground.

Shrubland grows in more arid areas than woodland with which it merges. Closed scrub – where plants cover more than 70 per cent of the ground – on the other hand, is usually found in fresh and brackish swampy areas where the dominant plants are paperbarks and tea trees, although coastal tea trees will also form closed shrubland on coastal sand dunes if sheltered from wind and salt. Such communities cover only small areas.

Mallee is a typical open scrub, with multi-stemmed eucalypts 2 to 8 m tall covering between 30 and 70 per cent of the ground. It grows on many calcareous and infertile sandy soils, in areas with an annual rainfall of 250 to 500 mm. The type of understorey depends on how dry and acid the soil is. Sometimes it is composed of grass with herbs. On deep sandy soils the grasses may be hummocks of porcupine grasses, and on calcareous soils, with heavier subsoils which retain water longer than the sand, tussock grasses grow. In the second case, scrubland often merges into open woodland with the mallee eucalypts looking more like trees. In other areas the understorey is composed of sclerophyllous (hard-leaved) shrubs. These are sometimes dense, particularly when the soil is calcareous and lies over limestones formed by old coastal dunes. When the soil is sand above heavy clays they may be less dense, with areas of bare ground and few grasses or herbs between. The eucalypt is often Yellow Mallee, an

SCRUBLAND AND SHRUBLAND

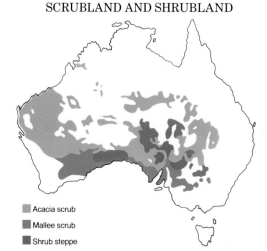

Acacia scrub
Mallee scrub
Shrub steppe

The areas covered by various communities of scrub and shrubs. Acacia scrubland, which occupies the largest area, is dominated by various hardy, long-lived species such as Mulga, myall and gidgee.

important honey species. Among the shrubs are Broom Heath-myrtle, Broom Honey-myrtle and Mallee Cypress-pine.

On its drier edges the community with its grassy understorey often shades into mallee combined with semi-succulent shrubs.

Where the dominant shrubs cover less than 30 per cent of the ground, and the plants are 2 to 8 m tall, the plant communities are called tall shrublands or tall open shrublands. These are found in semi-arid areas growing on a variety of soils where the rainfall is often less than 250 mm a year. Mulga is the most important example of the first type, and it grows on alluvial flatlands

and tablelands in the inland. In the south it meets the mallee, often with an abrupt change from one type of vegetation to the other.

Mulga shrubs are acacias, and very often Mulga itself, *Acacia aneura*. Once established this is a very drought-tolerant shrub which commonly lives for over 100 years and may reach 250 years of age. It cannot, however, live in areas with regular summer or winter droughts as it needs heavy summer rain to produce enough flowers, and heavy winter rain for the seeds to set. The seeds germinate in warm summer conditions, but the young plants need rain to become established. The fact that mulga is growing in an area means that there must be a suitable sequence of summer and winter rain about once every ten years for the community to continue. Unfortunately these conditions also encourage the build-up of rabbit populations which destroy many of the seedlings. Other acacias which take the place of *A. aneura* in some areas are myall, gidgee (or stinking wattle for its smell after rain), and lancewood.

There may also be an understorey of shrubs made up of sclerophyllous plants such as cassias or grasses and saltbushes. There is usually a layer of herbs as well, including members of the daisy, mallow, cabbage and amaranth families.

Other tall shrublands are found on rocky hillsides in parts of semi-arid southern Australia with acacias, cassias and other shrubs between 2 and 4 m tall.

Tall open shrubland – less than 10 per cent cover – may also be made up of *A. aneura*, but the pindan of northern Australia contains *A. holoserica* and Plectrachne hummocks. (Pindan country is the region of Broome-shrubland dominated by the Pindan Wattle *Acacia ancistrocarpa*.) In southern Australia, in the Big Desert and on the Ninety-Mile Plain there is the so-called mallee heath, composed of dense sclerophyllous shrubs and scattered dwarf mallee.

Heathlands are areas where the shrubs are up to 2 m tall and they can either be closed – with 70 to 100 per cent cover – or open – with 30 to 70 per cent cover. They are made up of sclerophyllous shrubs or chamaephytes – shrubs whose buds, which carry them over from year to year, are either at ground level or close to it. These areas are called heathlands because many of the shrubs resemble the heathers and lings found in Europe, although the Australian heaths belong to a separate family, the Epacridaceae. Australian heathlands are possibly the most colourful plant communities in the country since they contain many of the most attractive flowering plants such as native fuchsias. The coastal heaths of the south-west of Western Australia are particularly rich in species. The south-west corner in general is home to about 6000 species of flowering

Saltbush shrubland on the Nullarbor Plain. The bare spaces between the shrubs are sometimes clothed with grasses and other plants after heavy rain. Such areas usually receive only about 250 mm a year.

Dense mallee scrub on the coast near Port Lincoln on the Eyre Peninsula, South Australia.

Camels grazing on saltbush steppes, among mallee eucalypts. Surprisingly, areas like these can be grazed by stock, particularly sheep, which can extract a living from the sparse vegetation.

plants, and may well have the world's richest collection of plants outside the tropics. About 80 per cent of the species found there live nowhere else. In addition there is more diversity among some of the plant groups found there than anywhere else in the country. Around 37 of Australia's 50 or so banksias, and 106 out of 120 melaleucas all grow in the south-west.

Typical lowland heath plants grow on sandy, very infertile soils in higher rainfall areas. Among the many groups found in heaths are banksias, hakeas, acacias, kunzeas, grass trees, leptospermums and melaleucas.

Heathland is frequently burnt out, but the plants recover very quickly. Grasstrees in particular are well adapted to fire, and, indeed, are more or less dormant between burns.

The last type of shrubland is low shrubland where plants cover less than 30 per cent of the ground, and are less than 2 m in height. Best known are the vast areas of arid Australia, including much of the Nullarbor Plain, where saltbush and bluebush are most common. Bluebushes have deep roots and grow mainly on soils into which water penetrates quickly. Saltbush, which has shallow roots, grows best in areas where a hard sub-surface barrier prevents its roots from penetrating very deep. Bindyi may grow with the shrubs and, after rains, so do various ephemeral plants. This kind of country was once called shrub steppe, and will support sheep during droughts. Bluebushes, however, seem to be less able to withstand continuous grazing than saltbushes, because of the way in which they flower and reproduce.

Heathland is alive with birds because the cover and the flowers, and the insects which exploit them. However, compared with wood-land, the number of species is small – usually about 20 in a given area, and as little as 16 in the Sydney district. The birds include various pollinators, such as honeyeaters, as well as ground parrots, bristlebirds, thornbills, emu wrens, and some quails, nightjars and cuckoos. Similarly the number of mammals is usually small and few or none are found only in heath. Two tree-living species which regularly use the habitat are the Honey Possum and the Western Pygmy-possum.

About 50 species of birds can be found in shrub steppe, the most characteristic being Inland Dotterels, two quail-thrushes, Gibberbirds, the Orange Chats and a grasswren. Emus also live in shrub steppe, as well as in other areas. Various mammals spill over from arid woodland, among them various hopping mice, together with 'ordinary' mice.

Scrubland and shrubland – mulga and mallee – are home to about 29 species of mammals, including Western Grey Kangaroos, Red Kangaroos – which use mulga for shelter or feed after rain – scrub wallabies, nailtail wallabies and hare-wallabies. There are also small predatory marsupials such as phascogales, *Sminthopsis*, Western Pygmy-possums and various hopping-mice and other small rodents.

Roughly 160 species of birds live in mallee, the most famous, of course, being Mallee Fowl, although they are found not only in such areas. Seven species are found only in the mallee and they include Regent Parrots, Mallee Emu-wrens and Purple-gaped Honey-eaters.

The only birds found only in mulga scrubland are Bourke's Parrots, Chestnut-breasted Quail-thrushes, Slaty-backed Thornbills, and Grey Honeyeaters. In all about 80 or 90 species can be found in mulga.

Forest and woodland

In Australia forests are those communities of plants in which trees are dominant, and the tallest layer of foliage covers between 30 and 100 per cent of the ground. Dense forests (70 to 100 per cent) are RAINFORESTS. Open forests cover between 30 and 70 per cent. When the trees are sparse (10 to 30 per cent) or very sparse (less than 10 per cent), plant ecologists call such communities woodlands and open woodlands respectively. Trees, incidentally, are different from shrubs and bushes in having a single stem.

The differences between forests are more than a matter of mere geometry because the spacing of the trees is a result of factors such as the availability of water, the condition of the soil and the aspect of the site. Furthermore, in open forest the dominant trees are eucalypts which are not found in rainforest. Another common feature of many open forests and woodlands is the harshness, spikiness and toughness of the foliage of the plants of the lower storeys, a phenomenon called sclerophylly (literally 'hard-leafness'). This was at first thought to be an adaptation to dry conditions, but it is now known to be largely the result of the low levels of nitrogen, phosphorus and other nutrients in many Australian soils.

The foliage of the eucalypts themselves may cover the percentage areas mentioned above, but they do not shade it. The flat surfaces of the leaves of eucalypts are held vertically so that they do not receive the full heat of the sun and, consequently, they let light pass through.

Open forests are widespread in areas with an annual rainfall of 900 mm or more, in the tropical, subtropical and temperate parts of mainland Australia and Tasmania. Naturally, over such a wide range there are great differences in the complexity of forests and the plant species found in them. In general the trees have flat crowns so that the lengths of the trunks are much greater than the depths of the foliage.

In tall open forest the trees are 30 m or more in height, and sometimes even more than 60 m. There is one stand in Tasmania – the Andromeda Reserve in the Styx River Valley – which contains (or contained) the tallest hardwood tree in the world, a Mountain Ash *Eucalyptus regnans* which one authority in 1972 claimed to be 98.65 m tall. The reserve had a greater weight of timber to the hectare than any other forest in the world. Tall open forest is found in the wetter districts of Tasmania and Victoria, and in a few places in south-east Queensland (Flooded Gum *E. grandis* forest); eastern NSW (Blue-Gum *E. deanei*, *E. saligna* and Blackbutt *E. pilularis* forests), and south-west of Western Australia

Tropical woodland *clothes the slopes of the Hamersley Range in the north-west of Western Australia. Clumps of spinifex (*Trioda *and* Plectrachne *spp.) dot the bare red earth beneath the trees.*

(Karri *E. diversicolor* forest). The trees drop their branches, and also knock them off by rubbing against each other so that the cover may be not much more than 30 per cent. Consequently there is a dense understorey of tall shrubs and small trees, including species of pomaderris *Pomaderris*, daisy bushes *Olearia*, wax flowers *Eriostemon*, wattles *Acacia*, and, in damper places and gullies, tree ferns *Dicksonia*. Down on the ground there are grasses and smaller ferns and herbs of various kinds. This kind of forest is also known as wet sclerophyll forest. The foliage of the plants in the lower strata is not as harsh as that of dry sclerophyll forest plants.

In dry sclerophyll forests the dominant trees are some of Australia's 450 species of *Eucalyptus*. Typically there is an understorey of harsh-leaved shrubs, but in large areas of open forest in Victoria tussock grasses take the place of these sclerophyllous shrubs. Nevertheless the name 'dry sclerophyll' was extended to include them.

There are thus three types of open forest where the dominant trees are from 10 to 30 m tall, also loosely called dry sclerophyll forest. They are: grassy open forest with a well-developed layer of herbs and grasses, and only scattered bushes; shrubby open forest with many hard-leaved shrubs, but relatively poor development of herbs and grasses; layered open forest with well-developed layers of shrubs and herbs.

Low open forest (trees 5 to 10 m), which grow in poorer soils or in lower rainfall areas, can be divided up in a similar way.

At one time there were also large areas of brigalow forest in which the dominant trees were *Acacia harpophylla*, but most of it has been cleared for agriculture. The trees were usually 9 to 15 m tall, and there was a shrub layer containing other acacias, eucalypts and casuarinas, often with a layer of herbs as well.

Unlike rainforests, which survive in fire-proof pockets, open forests are often ravaged by fire, both natural and man-made. It seems almost as though eucalypts were made to burn. Their leaves contain volatile and extremely flammable oils so that the foliage burns easily. Many species readily shed branches and bark, as well as leaves, and in dry conditions these decay slowly and ignite easily. On the other hand most eucalypts can withstand severe fires. The bark protects the inner tissues for some time, and beneath the bark are specialised buds – epicormic buds – which shoot within a few days of the passing of a fire. The shoots may appear at first all over the tree, but eventually certain ones dominate and others decline. If the fire is so severe that the parts of the tree above the ground are killed, new shoots

WOODLAND

■ Humid woodland

■ Arid to semi-arid woodland

Woodland*, where trees cover less than 30 per cent of the ground, is widespread in Australia.*

often emerge from the LIGNOTUBERS below the soil. Many acacias also have lignotubers.

The shrubs in the understorey are more sensitive to fire, but usually there is a wealth of their seeds in the soil waiting for such an occurrence. Some of these seeds will not germinate until heat has cracked their hard outer coats, and some of the shrubs carry fruits which are also cracked by the heat, releasing their seeds. As a consequence, the shrub layer quickly regenerates, unless the fires are so frequent that they cannot set seed, and the supply of seeds in the soil is exhausted.

The eucalypts of tall forest, on the other hand, are usually sensitive to fire so that such a catastrophe can destroy the forest. The forest quickly begins to grow again from the seeds that have accumulated in the soil, producing, at first, dense stands of saplings. As time passes these thin out and after about 100 to 150 years the trees have matured once again. If a fire occurs before they can produce seed, however, the tall trees do not re-appear. Some stands of Mountain Ash in Tasmania are known to be more than 400 years

old and thus cannot have been subjected to a severe fire in all that time, but this is rare.

One characteristic of eucalypts, at least in Australia, is their susceptibility to disease and insect attack, particularly by termites, and their tendency to shed branches. These processes produce many hollow branches and trunks in a mature forest which provide a variety of mammals and birds with dens, roosts and nesting sites.

About 140 species of Australian birds can be found in eucalyptus forests, although most of them will also live in rainforest or woodland. A few birds, however, are restricted to the wet sclerophyll forest – they include Wonga Pigeons, Gang-gang Cockatoos, Powerful Owls, Bell Miners and Pilotbirds. The Superb Lyrebird is a species found in this habitat and in rainforest. Typical birds of the drier forests are some robins, quail-thrushes, warblers and thornbills. In general there is a smaller proportion of fruit-eating birds than in rainforest, but a greater proportion of nectar and blossom feeders.

There is also a wealth of forest marsupials such as Speckled Hare-Wallabies, Pademelons,

Red-necked Wallabies and other small kangaroos, possums and the Koala, as well as bats and rodents such as the New Holland Mouse. Many of these are also found in drier or wetter habitats. In recent years ecologists have discovered that some species are most numerous at some stage in the regeneration that follows a fire. The New Holland Mouse, for example, was 'lost' for more than a century until it was rediscovered in 1967 in Kuring-gai Chase National Park on the outskirts of Sydney. It apparently thrives best during the early and middle stages of regeneration, provided that a small number of animals have survived the fire in refuges. Leadbeater's Possum, another species once thought to be extinct, thrives at certain stages in the regeneration of wet, tall open-forest in Victoria. Fire, or at least fire occurring at natural intervals, is thus not the great calamity for forest wildlife that it seems to be. Indeed, it can be argued that many woodlands need a good natural fire every 50 years or so if the shrubs are to survive. In time they age and die, and often their seeds will not germinate until they have been subjected to heat.

FORESTS

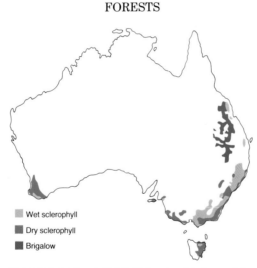

Wet sclerophyll

Dry sclerophyll

Brigalow

Forests have been divided into a bewildering variety of categories. Four basic types are illustrated here: dry sclerophyll (top left), wet sclerophyll (bottom left), open (below), and closed (right)

Subtropical and temperate rainforests

Tropical rainforests have many trees in common with Asian forests, and so do the subtropical rainforests and warm-temperate closed forests which are found in pockets from the Tropic of Capricorn to as far as Wilson's Promontory in Victoria. Among the features that can be seen are lianes and buttress roots, which become less prominent away from the tropics, although ferns and epiphytes are still common. Emergent Hoop Pines can be found as far south as the Queensland-NSW border. Other trees are usually not as tall as those in tropical rainforest, and there are rarely more than two layers of trees. Smaller varieties of trees with smaller leaves are found furthur south. The canopy is at about 10 to 30 m above the ground, with a layer of shade-tolerant trees below. In general, the further south, the less complex the plant community.

Often one species of tree will be the most common over a large area. Coachwood *Cerato-petalum apetalum*, which yields a valuable cabinet-maker's timber, and Hoop Pine are examples. The Hoop Pine is a close relative of the familiar Monkey Puzzle Tree *Araucaria araucana*, Norfolk Island Pine *A. heterophylla* and the Kauri *Agathis australis* of New Zealand.

In these rainforests the more important trees include Lillypilly *Acmena* sp., Red Cedar *Toona australis* – although many have been removed by timber-getters – Brush Box *Tristana conferta* and Yellow Sassafras *Doryphora sassafras*. which was once used medicinally as a tonic although,

like many other rainforest trees, it contains a toxic alkaloid.

There are also fewer species of birds and mammals to be found in these forests than in the tropical forests, although some species, such as Lewin's Honeyeater and the Topknot Pigeon, range from the tropical forests to those of Victoria. Some birds which are found only in the more southern forests include Regent Bower-birds, Rufous Scrub-birds, Albert Lyrebirds, Spine-tailed Logrunners and the Paradise Rifle-birds. Among the most common mammals are pademelons, Ringtail Possums, Mountain Brush-tail Possums, Long-nosed Bandicoots, various species of Antechinus and several rats. Parma Wallabies, until recently thought to be extinct in Australia, sometimes venture into rainforest. Fruit-bats are also common, and among the

reptiles is the jet-black 600-mm-long Land Mullet, one of the world's biggest skinks. It lives largely on snails and fungi, both of which are common in damp forest.

There is yet another kind of rainforest in Australia, strikingly different from those above. These are the forests found in cool temperate areas, or in high country in tropical and sub-tropical regions, and they contain plants that are mostly Antarctic in origin. Indeed, before the theory of continental drift was generally accepted, the Antarctic beeches – species of *Nothofagus* – were often cited as evidence for the drift theory by biologists.

Antarctic beeches, most of which are ever-greens, are often the dominant trees in these forests. They are found in high rainfall, tem-perate areas in Tasmania, parts of Victoria, and

Dense subtropical rainforest *in Cania Gorge, near Gladstone in Queensland (right). Staghorn ferns (above) are among the many epiphytes that can be seen growing on the trunks of rainforest trees.*

Only small pockets of warm temperate rainforest are left in southern NSW and northern Victoria. This stand is in Bulga National Park, east of Morwell in Victoria.

mountain country on the Queensland-NSW border, and also in New Guinea, New Zealand, New Caledonia and Chile. In Chile they form extensive stands in the southernmost parts of the forests which stretch down the Pacific coast, extending to within 50 km of Cape Horn. This long stretch of forest shows clearly, like rainforests in Australia, a gradual decrease in complexity and richness of plant and animal species with increasing latitude, from the complex tropical rainforests of the north to the simple cold, wet forests of the south.

There are about 40 species of *Nothofagus* in the world, of which three are found in Australia.

Of these, Tanglefoot *N. gunnii*, a small shrub, is found only in Tasmania where it grows in alpine areas. It is the only known native Australian tree which is deciduous in winter. It grows either alone, or in the understorey of forests dominated by Myrtle Beech. Myrtle or Tasmanian beech *N. cunninghamii* is a small leaved species with short, downy leaf-stalks which is found in Tasmania and Victoria. It reaches a height of 60 m with a girth of about 12 m. Its valuable wood, used in cabinet making, is called Red Myrtle. The Australian or Negrohead Beech *N. mooreii*, the species with the largest leaves (25–75 mm long), grows in NSW and Queensland; one of the best remaining areas of trees is in the McPherson Range above 1200 m. The trees, which grow to about 45 m, were once very common on the Great Dividing Range.

Antarctic beeches can spread only across land because their nut-like fruits cannot withstand long immersion in sea water, and are too big to be carried by birds or wind. Although they belong to the same family as European beeches and oaks which occur in the northern hemisphere, they themselves have apparently never grown there. They are thus truly plants of southern regions and provide further evidence to support the theory of continental drift. Some of the animals associated with *Nothofagus* also provide evidence to support the theory. For example, peloridiids: small, lacy-winged primitive BUGS which live in damp moss and liverworts in cold rainforests. They have almost the same distribution as *Nothofagus*, and are found only in southernmost South America, southeastern Australia (including Tasmania), Lord Howe Island and New Zealand. On Stewart and Lord Howe Islands, they live in moss, although there are no *Nothofagus* there. They were probably blown there by wind.

These rainforests may contain other trees such as the southern conifers including Huon Pines *Dacrydium* sp., *Athrotaxis* sp., a relative of the redwoods of California, and Southern Sassafras *Atherosperma moschatum*. The sassafras is in no way related to the American sassafras from which tea and root beer are made. It belongs to a small, southern hemisphere family of aromatic trees and smells like sarsparilla or nutmeg. It is a regularly shaped, conical tree about 10 to 20 m tall, with creamy flowers and a springy wood used for making clothes pegs. Sometimes these trees replace *Nothofagus* as the dominant species. Tree heights often range from 18 to 42 m, but although mosses, lichens and ferns grow abundantly on the trees, there are no strong lianes or buttress roots. Eucalypts and similar trees may sometimes grow within the forest communities in certainarias.

Temperate rainforests of this kind support fewer species of animals than do the subtropical and tropical forests. In 1963, in adjacent areas of subtropical and temperate rainforests on the mainland, two biologists recorded 254 individual birds, representing 32 species in the subtropical forest, but only 186 individuals and 22 species in the temperate forest. Two other scientists have recorded only 17 species of birds in the high rainforests of Tasmania, and some of these were not normally members of the community. The commonest birds in the Tasmanian forests are Yellow-Tailed Black Cockatoos, Pink Robins, Scrub-tits, Tasmanian Thornbills, Brown Scrub-wrens and White's Thrushes. The few mammals found in the forests include Tasmanian Pademelons, Tasmanian Devils, Spotted-tail Quolls, Red-necked Wallabies, Brushtail Possums and Swamp Rats. One native mouse – the Long-tailed Mouse *Pseudomys higginsi*, which lives in tunnels below the litter – is found only in cool rainforests in Tasmania.

There are few frogs in Tasmania, but the beech forests of the McPherson Ranges are the home of the Pouched Frog *Assa darlingtoni*, a 30-mm-long creature whose males have pouches along their sides in which their tadpoles develop. This species is found nowhere else except in adjacent subtropical rainforest. It lives beneath rocks, rotting logs and leaf litter. Another small frog of the MacPherson temperate and subtropical rainforests is Loveridge's Frog *Philoria loveridgei*. It too has unfrog-like breeding habits. Like all members of its genus it lives in a burrow in which it lays large eggs from which hatch, not tadpoles, but small froglets.

Cool temperate rainforest covers much of the rugged south-west of Tasmania. These Myrtle Beeches are in Mount Field National Park, west of Hobart.

Rainforests of the tropics

Rainforests are called closed forests by ecologists because the canopies of the trees form a continuous cover allowing very little light to filter through to the ground.

These forests need large quantities of water to flourish so they are found in Australia only in well-watered pockets along the eastern coast from Cape York to Tasmania, with small patches in the north-west of Western Australia. Thousands of years ago they covered much larger areas but were forced to contract as the Australian climate became much drier. Since the arrival of Europeans a large proportion of the little that was left has been destroyed. At present rainforests, such as the one on the Daintree River in Queensland, are battlefields for conservationists, developers and governments.

The trees which make up the forests seem to fall into two groups: ones that originated in the Indo-Malayan region and the other that came from the ancient supercontinent of Gondwanaland. The Indo-Malayan group was once believed to have entered Australia from South-East Asia in relatively recent times, after continental drift had brought Australia and New Guinea near to the Asian land mass (see p 18). Recently, however, some ecologists have suggested that these plants have been in Australia far longer. They point out that Australia's tropical rainforests are closer, in terms of general structure and contents, to rainforest in the Western Ghats of southern India than to those in South-East Asia or even New Guinea. Rainforest is a complete system, and must spread as a unit. They argue that it is unlikely that birds or other creatures could carry all the the components of the forest from India to Australia, if the areas were as far apart then as they are now. Since both continents were part of Gondwanaland, however, the two areas were once close together. They therefore suggest that the common plants probably came from Gondwanaland and that at least some of them originated in the parts of Gondwanaland that are now Australia. If this is the case, then some of the spread must have been from Australia, or other Gondwanaland continents, to Asia. They also argue that during periods when Australia was very dry, rainforest survived only in small wet areas, perhaps merely along rivers, and that during wetter times, they spread outwards from them. According to this theory the area of rainforests in Australia was expanding at the time of the arrival of Europeans, so that much of what is left is only a few thousand years old.

Tropical rainforests are found along the eastern edge of Cape York and are the most complex land-based ecosystems in Australia. In the Cairns-Tully rainforest, a 1.5-ha area was found to contain 160 different kinds of trees, which is probably more than can be found in any other Australasian or Asian forests. It is uncommon for two trees of the same species to grow near to each other. Many of the species are related to those found in Asia and there are no eucalypts, and few hardwoods, although there are relatives from the eucalypt and clove family, the Myrtaceae, and other families which are found in drier forests and woodlands. Such families, however, are represented by only one or two species. Members of these families which have become adapted to drier conditions probably evolved from species growing near the edges of the rainforest communities.

The trees in a rainforest can be roughly divided into three groups: those which will soon die and fall; mature trees which are healthy; and young, small, healthy trees which are growing in the gloom, but which will not have the opportunity to grow further until one of the old trees is destroyed. Then several of the young trees which grew near its base will compete for the space. There is a fourth group of tall trees – the emergents which push above the canopies of the others. In northern Australia these are usually Hoop Pines *Araucaria cunninghamii*, an undoubted Gondwanaland species. Other trees belong to such families as the laurels and Australian walnuts, citrus, though *Citrus* itself is absent, mahoganies, nutmegs, the waratah family – also of Gondwanaland origin – litchis and coffee. They reach a height of between 5 and 40 m, or more, and have evergreen leaves which are usually at least 45 sq. cm in area so that they can present as much chlorophyll as possible to the light which falls on them. Most leaves end in pointed extensions down which the water from the leaves drains to the ground. The trunks have extensive buttresses anchoring them to the soil.

Climbing plants – lianes – proliferate and, indeed, much of the foliage seen from above the forest belongs to them. Many of them are older than the trees themselves, and when their supports fall, merely tie themselves to the successors. In the Atherton Tablelands the main climbers and creepers include Matchbox Bean *Entada*, a member of the wattle family, snakewood *Lonchocarpus*, whose relatives in South-East Asia are a source of insecticides; and the prickly lawyer vines *Calamus*, which are palms. Most of the trees carry Staghorn and Elkhorn Ferns. They collect debris in their bowl-shaped holdfasts which matures into soil creating, in effect, tree gardens in which other plants grow. The other epiphytes – plants growing on other plants – include tree-orchids such as *Dendrobium*, *Sarcochilus* and *Cymbidium*. Strangler

A tropical rainforest creek at Cedar Bay, south of Cooktown in far northern Queensland. The forest here is noted for its prolific birdlife.

RAINFOREST

■ Rainforest

Small pockets of rainforest dot the east coast of Australia, western Tasmania and small areas of the extreme north-west of Western Australia. Exploitation is slowly reducing their area.

Fallen trees in Wallaman Falls National Park allow visitors a glimpse of the incredible profusion of growth in a tropical rainforest.

figs are common. Their seeds are dispersed by flying foxes and birds, and some lodge and germinate on branches of trees. A root drops from the young plant to the ground and it begins to grow. Eventually so many roots link the plant to the ground that the host tree is completely enveloped and dies. Then the fig takes its place.

Material that falls to the ground is quickly recycled for, in the damp soil with its even temperature, fungi and other rotting organisms, and huge numbers of different soil animals are very active. Most of the forest's minerals are in the trees so that when those are logged and removed there is a large loss in the resources.

The trees and other plants of the tropical rainforests contain hundreds of different kinds of chemicals which probably evolved as a defence against organisms that may attack the plants. Many of these chemicals, particularly the alkaloids, are found in a far greater variety than in any other area in Australia, and some of them have great potential in medicine. Unfortunately many of them will never be discovered if rainforests disappear at their present rate.

While some animals do live in the forest litter, or attack the trees, the great wealth of animal life – mammals, birds, insects and some reptiles – is to be found in the canopy, where the flowers are displayed. Some trees, however, have flowers growing on their stems and, it is thought, these attract shade-loving butterflies which pollinate them. In the rainforests of Cape York many of the animals are closely related to, or identical with,

species that live in New Guinea. Among the birds which are related to New Guinea species, and which are more or less confined to the northern forests, are Eclectus and Red-cheeked Parrots, Palm Cockatoos, White-tailed Kingfishers, Blue-breasted Pittas, Northern Scrub-Robins, Little Scrub-Wrens, Boat-billed and Black-faced Fly-catchers, Chestnut-breasted Cuckoos, and the Green-backed Honeyeaters. Among the more Australian rainforest birds are Trumpet Manu-codes of the bowerbird family, Golden and Tooth-billed Bowerbirds and several honey-eaters. Many of these birds keep to the canopy or fly above it, or live in dense vegetation, and are more easily heard than seen from the ground. Cassowaries – another bird with relatives in New Guinea – are restricted because of their weight to the forest floor, where they feed on fallen fruit. In mountain rainforest Golden Bowerbirds build their large bower on the ground, and display to any nearby females on a branch above it. On the edges of the forest, where it shades into wood-land, Yellow-billed Kingfishers may be seen.

The Queensland Blossom-Bat is one of the rainforest mammals which pollinate trees; they are found as far south as the Queensland-NSW border. Various flying-foxes are also important pollinators. The mammals in the rainforest which have New Guinea relationships include the two cuscuses, the two tree-kangaroos, the Striped, Long-tailed, Pygmy, Green Ringtail, Brush-tipped and Herbert River Possums. The Prehensile-tailed Rat, long known in New Guinea but

discovered in Australia only in 1974, lives in burrows but forages in trees, as does the White-tailed Rat. Two rainforest mammals which are Australian, rather than derived from New Guinea species, are the unique Musky Rat-kangaroo and Godman's Antechinus.

The rainforests are also the headquarters of Australia's small group of microhylid (narrow-mouthed) frogs, although New Guinea is the centre for the family. Many other frogs and reptiles are confined to or flourish in, these extremely rich areas.

Sinuous buttress roots anchor rainforest trees firmly to the ground. They may allow trees to stand with shallow roots in poorly aerated, swampy soils.

Wetlands, lakes and ponds

Australia may be the driest of the inhabited continents but there is still a small proportion of the country that can be classified as wetlands. Unfortunately, much of what was present when the Europeans arrived has disappeared. Some has been drained to produce grazing land or to modify the flow of rivers to prevent flooding, and some has been filled to provide building land. In 1970 a researcher estimated that in coastal NSW alone at least 60 per cent of wetlands used by water birds had already been drained. Millions of years ago, before the continent dried out, wetlands covered one-third of Australia, and, among other birds, supported flamingos.

In wetlands the water-table lies at the surface, or above it, for at least some of the time: Some wetlands may be wet for only one or two years at a stretch when rivers overflow; others may be wet for only part of each year. Technically, wetlands include land covered by salt water, such as mangroves and saltmarsh.

Bogs are wetlands in which the water is acid and where sphagnum moss is common. Often peat is formed in such conditions. Bogs are valued by archaeologists because the acidity prevents organic material from decaying so that animals, or animal products such as leather and clothing, are often wonderfully preserved, like the famous 'bog bodies' dug up in Ireland, England and Denmark, often the victims of ritual sacrifices. No such finds have been made so far in Australian bogs. Many Australian bogs are found in the high country in wet valleys, or in hollows where the growth of sphagnum moss is greatest in the centre so that it forms a raised bog. Alternatively the moss may grow like a blanket over a wide area and the result is called a blanket bog. These are, however, rare in Australia. Some bogs are found in hollows in sand dunes along the eastern coast where the water is acid and nutrients are in short supply.

Fens resemble bogs in that the vegetation decays to form peat, but the water is only slightly acid, if at all.

Swamp is wet, spongy land into which boots sink with a squelch. The term is used rather loosely for any such land and, in fact, includes many different communities of plants, ranging from cumbungi and reed swamps surrounding permanent waters to paperbark and sheoak swamps and even river plains that are frequently covered by water.

Apart from the examples in the mountains, most Australian wetlands are found near the coast, particularly between the Great Dividing Range and the sea, and in northern and north-eastern coastal regions. The only extensive wetlands in the inland are associated with the Murray-Darling River system. Among these are the billabongs and channels from the Paroo and the Macquarie Marshes to the river redgum swamps along the Murray and Murrumbidgee Rivers. In the north there are the famous wetlands of Kakadu National Park.

Lakes and ponds may be permanent or, like Lake Eyre, usually dry and filled only at infrequent intervals. Although ponds are often thought of as merely small lakes, the real difference between them is depth. A lake is so deep that there are parts of it where rooted plants cannot grow, whereas in a pond rooted water plants can grow in any part of it.

Lake basins are formed by earth movements, volcanic action, glacial action or by the damming of a valley by glacial debris. Billabongs are found beside meandering rivers.

Lakes differ greatly in their salinity. Some Australian lakes are seven times saltier than the sea. Australia's largest permanent lake, Lake Corangamite in Victoria, is saline while the water of some of the lakes in the Snowy Mountains is almost as pure as distilled water. There are naturally great differences between the plants and animals living in salt and freshwater lakes.

Some water plants – flowering plants and ferns, as opposed to algae – are found only in permanent ponds, lakes and rivers. These are the submerged species whose foliage does not reach above the surface. Some are rooted to the

Kakadu's wetlands *cover a vast area, particularly after the wet season. Areas like this paperbark swamp are home to a great variety of animals and plants, including one-quarter of all Australian freshwater fish.*

The waterlilies floating on this tranquil tropical swamp near Cooktown are a native species.

as single-celled protozoa, tiny rotifers or wheel animalcules – were identical with those found on other continents, but now more and more of them are being recognised as peculiarly Australian. Most of those found in salt lakes appear to have evolved from freshwater animals and not from sea-living ones, as might be expected. This is the case even in salt lakes that are not far from the sea. It seems likely that there are fewer species of animals to be found in Australian inland waters than there are in similar bodies of water in many other countries.

Wetlands lack many of the aquatic animals found in permanent waters, simply because they cannot survive the dry periods, but aquatic insect larvae are very common, as are some crustaceans. Wetlands are also home to many frogs, lizards and snakes.

Wetlands and permanent waters are also supremely important in the lives of Australian waterfowl – ducks and magpie geese – as well as birds such as herons, bitterns, brolgas and some waders. Unfortunately some of the richer and more extensive wetlands in the north have been irreparably damaged by introduced water buffalo, which destroy the vegetation at the edges, reducing the ground to muddy wallows. Another introduced animal, the pig, has also caused much damage. Unlike the buffalo, little can be said in favour of pigs which have made Macquarie Marshes their headquarters in eastern Australia. Pigs need wet places for wallowing, and marshes also provide good cover.

Wetlands do not get the publicity that threat-

Macquarie Marshes in NSW, recently in danger of drying out when the river feeding them was dammed, are once again home to vast numbers of water birds.

ened rainforests do. Neither are very plentiful in this dry continent, and both are being exploited. While the destruction of rainforest would have mainly local effects, the disappearance of wetlands would have a wide impact. They are essential for the survival of many nomadic species such as ducks, as well as for riverine fish which need them for spawning. They are also more easily invaded by alien plants than rainforests are. Rainforest plant communities resist the establishment of any foreign plants, but brambles, willows and exotic grasses and reeds grow profusely along river banks and in wetlands, and plants such as Salvinia, Water Hyacinth, Alligator Weed and Canadian Pondweed can change the character of a lake or pond.

bottom. The water milfoils – of which there are some native species as well as a number of exceedingly troublesome introduced weeds – are probably the best known examples. Some bladderworts are also submerged, except when flowering. They lack true roots but often have slender threads to give anchorage. They are named for the bladders on their leaves which catch small animals in the water.

There are other plants whose leaves float on the surface. Again some are rooted to the bottom and some are not. Two non-rooted examples are Salvinia Fern and Water Hyacinth, both of which are aggressive introduced weeds. Water lilies are well-known, rooted native floaters. Less noticeable are duckweeds *Wolffia*, which are the smallest of all flowering plants.

Finally there are the emergent plants which are rooted to the bottom, but which emerge above the water surface. The Common Reed, which can be 3 m tall, is the most familiar. This, and other emergent plants, may grow permanently on the fringes of a lake or pond, or periodically in wetlands, dying down when the water dries up.

Each kind of permanent water and wetland has its own distinctive population of animals – even rain puddles which last only a few weeks can be crammed with life. Until recently it was thought that many of the smallest animals – such

Pelicans feeding on the waters of Lake Alexandrina, at the mouth of the Murray River in South Australia. The lake, and the adjoining lagoons of the Coorong, are important wetland areas.

The fringe of the sea

It is difficult to work out how long Australia's coast is. Even if the distance along the highwater mark is accurately measured, decisions have to be made about how far up a river the coast extends. The calculation also depends on the amount of detail shown on the maps used. In 1980 Dr. Robert Galloway, a CSIRO researcher using 1:250 000 scale maps, concluded that the total length of the mainland and Tasmanian coasts was 30 270 km. Islands added an extra 16 800 km to give a total of 47 070 km.

About 39 per cent of the coast (excluding Tasmania) is tropical, with the remainder being subtropical. The difficulty in measuring the length of the coast is mirrored in the difficulty of counting Australia's islands. Official lists do not include many un-named small islands and island-reefs, despite the fact that a lot of these are important ecologically and, presumably, to ships' pilots. A Commonwealth list of 1912 allots 593 islands to Queensland, 321 to Western Australia, 115 to South Australia, 77 to the Northern Territory, 70 to Tasmania, 52 to Victoria, 39 to NSW and none to the ACT: a total of 1267 in all. Of these 866 are in the northern tropical region and 401 are in cooler southern waters.

Many islands are 'continental' – they are really parts of the adjacent mainland which have been separated by erosion or rising sea levels. Another common type, with many small, nameless examples, is the sandy cay which is formed by sand accumulating on coral reefs.

At various places along coasts material is either being eroded away by waves or water currents or deposited by the same agents. The erosion is also aided by the chemical effects of sea water. Sometimes the two processes may be going on simultaneously within a hundred metres of each other: waves erode a cliff in one part of a small bay, and shingle or sand is deposited in another. Wind also plays a part on sandy shores, piling the sand up into dunes which, if not stabilised by plants, gradually move inland. The gently-sloping face of the dune fronts into the prevailing winds which blow sand up and over the top to make a steeper slope on the lee side. Coasts are also subject to sudden changes – a beach may be almost eroded away overnight by a sudden storm.

The force of waves can be almost unbelievable. There is the famous case of Wick in Scotland where in 1872 an 800-tonne block of concrete, 'secured' by iron rods 90 mm in diameter, was dumped in the harbour by a storm. Later its 2600-tonne replacement was also torn away. The force of the waves was estimated to be 30 tonnes/m^2. Spray from waves often travels at more than 100 km/h, and the water itself also carries sand and rocks which pound at cliff faces. It is easy to see how the ocean can carve rocks into fantastic shapes.

The shape of cliffs is also determined by the relative hardness of the different layers. Often there is a notch at sea-level, with the rest of the cliff projecting above it. This is due to wave action, but in limestone cliffs, chemicals in the water also play a part. Another common feature is a platform at sea level which is formed by water washing across it. If the rock strata are horizontal, then the platform is flat, but if the strata are inclined, a serrated platform is the result. Sometimes part of the cliff is harder than the rest so that in time it becomes isolated from the land as a column or 'stack'. The best known Australian stacks are the Twelve Apostles at Port Campbell in Victoria.

Often an offshore island breaks the force of the waves coming in from the sea, and they are refracted towards the rear. Consequently rocky islands often have steep cliffs to the seaward, and a shallower slope on the land side.

When material is being deposited on a coast a number of different features can be formed, including mud flats, salt marshes, mangrove swamps, sandy shores and various formations around estuaries. Some of the material is carved from the land by erosion, and some travels with coastal currents either from rivers and estuaries, or from places where the coast is being eroded.

The plants found along all coasts can be divided into two groups: marine – for example, algae and some submerged flowering plants such as *Zostera* – or maritime. The second group are subjected to salty conditions and often to high winds. They can often be covered, or partly covered, for at least a few hours each day by salt water. They are, however, mostly flowering plants which are pollinated in ways similar to most other plants – by wind or insects. Further back from the sea, but still influenced by salt and wind, are the submaritime species.

Some plant species found growing on sandy foreshores in Australia are often found on shores in other parts of the world. Sheoaks *Casuarina*, for example, which are used for dune stabilisation in Australia, are common in coastal areas of Malaysia, Indonesia and many Pacific islands. Coconuts, although widespread on so many tropical shores are, however, a puzzle. Experiments carried out by members of the *Kon-tiki* expedition clearly showed that the nuts cannot withstand immersion in salt water long enough to achieve trans-oceanic migrations. However, many grow naturally on tropical Australian coasts and islands. Most of those found further south were planted deliberately either in the

Coastal dunes thrown up by the waters of the Southern Ocean, east of Albany in Western Australia.

Powerful, salt-laden winds and sandy soils have a profound effect on coastal vegetation.

hope of establishing a palm-oil industry, or to provide tourists with 'tropical' surroundings.

Plants that are to succeed in an unstable sand dune must be able to withstand being covered by sand from time to time, or to have their roots exposed. One of the most successful is Hairy Spinifex *Spinifex hirsutum* (see illustration p 200), which is quite distinct from the so-called spinifex of arid areas. It grows from stout underground stems which bind the sand, and produces porcupine-like clumps above the surface. The male and female flowers grow on separate plants. The introduced Marram Grass is also used to stabilise dunes. In England where churches, and even whole villages, have disappeared under encroaching coastal sand, it was a crime to disturb Marram Grass plantings, and penalties were severe under Queen Elizabeth I. A less happy introduction as a stabiliser of Australian dunes was Boneseed or Bitou Bush, a native of South Africa, which is now a major problem weed on the coasts of eastern Australia.

When the sand has been stabilised by Spinifex and other plants such as Sea-rocket and Coast Saltbush, other low-growing plants – such as fanflowers and the like – can become established. Once they have improved the soil small trees and shrubs such as Coast Wattles, banksias and tea trees can grow. Later the ground becomes suitable for larger trees such as angophoras and eucalypts. This sequence from bare sand to thickly-vegetated higher ground can be seen on many southern coasts.

Mangroves grow in silt washed down from the land, or that deposited on the seaward side by water currents. Their roots are buried in stagnant water and airless mud so knob-like projections – pneumatophores – poke above the surface to obtain oxygen. On southern coasts only one or

Lion Island in the entrance to Broken Bay, north of Sydney, is one of over 1200 islands that dot the waters surrounding the continent. Many are important breeding grounds for sea birds and are protected.

two species will be found, but on tropical shores there may be up to 29 species of mangroves. The still, organically-rich waters of mangrove swamps are extremely important as spawning grounds for fish, and as habitats for many other marine animals. Behind the mangroves there are often extensive saltmarshes with succulent plants such as samphire and various grasses and sedges.

Two major groups of birds use Australian shores – those which get their living from the open sea but come to the shore to rest and to build nests, and those which find their food on the shore itself. The last group contains many waders which nest in the northern hemisphere but migrate across the equator for the Australian summer. Among these are the curlews, sandpipers and many plovers. They are long-beaked and usually long-legged birds which probe beneath the sand or mud for worms and molluscs. Some waders such as the Sooty Oystercatcher and the Hooded Plover are residents.

Australia is unusual in that few sea birds nest on coastal cliffs as they do in other countries, although suitable sites seem to be common enough. Most large continental islands are also neglected. It seems as though the birds prefer islands from which they can see the sea in each direction. The islands of Bass Strait support gannets and millions of Short-tailed Shearwaters, probably Australia's commonest bird. Coral cays are also greatly favoured by nesting seabirds. In all about 26 species breed on Australia's coasts.

Mangroves are used by about 60 or 70 different species of birds, but only about a dozen are restricted to them. They include Striated Herons and Red-headed Honeyeaters which feed on insects and spiders as well as nectar.

Just as the coasts are the nesting places for some oceanic seabirds, the southern ones are also the home – during the pupping and mating season – to Australian and New Zealand Fur Seals, and from time to time to other species such as Leopard Seals.

Dense stands of mangroves fringe much of Australia's tropical coast – these are at Cape Tribulation, north of Cairns in Queensland. In some places the forest is so thick that progress on foot is impossible.

Deserts and arid lands

To most people outside Australia, this is a land of deserts and gum tree forests. It is certainly the driest continent, apart from Antarctica, and a country of low relief. A true desert has virtually no rain and no vegetation and, typically, is composed of shifting sands or bare rocks. The driest place in Australia is Mulka in South Australia where the annual mean rainfall over 57 years has been 119 mm, although over 41 years that of Troudaninna, also in South Australia, has been less – 104 mm. The world's driest place, the Atacama Desert in Chile, has had a complete drought for at least 400 years.

Australia has no true desert and climatologists class the centre of the continent as semi-arid. There are many areas with vegetation, even trees, unlike the Sahara and the deserts which border the Red Sea. However, using the term in its loosest sense, about one-third of the continent – between the 250 mm rainfall line in the south and the 380 mm line in the north (or 500 mm in some classifications) – could be called desert.

The arid zone is far from uniform, apart from its general flatness. Soils are sandy in the Great Victoria, Simpson, Tanami and Great Sandy Deserts, and in the Central Ranges, and clay, loam or stony elsewhere. The Pilbara and the Central Ranges contain some hills, but few are more than 1500 m high.

The arid lands are covered by a variety of types of vegetation, including shrublands of *Acacia* or *Eucalyptus*, low shrubland with saltbush, bluebush and similar plants, hummock grassland and tussock grassland. These associations of plants cover about 90 per cent of the arid

DESERTS AND ARID LANDS

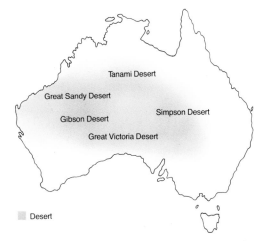

Arid and semi-arid country stretches over much of the inland of the continent.

Areas such as this around Ayers Rock may appear to be deceptively green and well-clothed with vegetation, but rain falls here on fewer than 20 days a year, and the median annual rainfall is below 400 mm.

zone, the rest being rock outcrops, creek channels and dried-out salt lakes.

Acacia shrubland is the most extensive, covering two million sq. km, about one-third of the total. Timber from the dominant tree, Mulga *A. aneura*, is familiar because it is widely used for making trinkets. It can grow on many kinds of soils, as long as they are not sandy or salty.

Hummock grassland probably comes nearer to the popular concept of a desert than any other formation in Australia. The plants are the infamous porcupine or spinifex grasses *Triodia* and *Plectrachne* which are little relished by domestic animals because of their harsh, spiky foliage. Tussock grasses, on the other hand, are grazed by sheep, as are saltbushes and bluebushes, despite the salt crystals on their foliage. Almost the only perennial plants found on the Nullarbor – 'no-tree' – Plain are a species of bluebush, *Maireana sedifolia*.

Eucalyptus shrublands are composed mainly of mallee species, which are eucalypts with multiple stems rising from a lignotuber – a swollen, underground stem. These and the *Acacias* can give the impression that the land is clothed with trees, yet the aridity is equal to that

of many treeless deserts found in other countries.

Here and there are patches of other groups of plants. In south-east Australia, for example, there are areas of low woodland, and to the surprise of visitors from the northern hemisphere, one of the dominant trees is often a conifer, Cypress Pine *Callitris columellaris*. The others are usually casuarinas and boonery *Heterodendrum*, which belongs to the hop-bush family. River beds, which are more often dry than wet, at least on the surface, can be lined by River Red Gums, a eucalypt. Even more remarkable is the grove of palm trees, *Livistonia mariae* (discovered by Ernest Giles in 1872) on a tributary of the Finke river, and the cycads, *Macrozamia*, which still live in the harsh Macdonnell Ranges. These, and certain fish, are all that is left from eons past when the centre was much better watered.

Such oases are rare, however, in the arid zones, and most animals and plants of the centre have had to evolve strategies to survive in such a dry environment. Furthermore, they have to cope not only with extreme heat in the day, but also with cold at night, for the relatively bare surfaces quickly radiate heat to cloudless skies.

Plants cannot move away when conditions are

The dead heart. Dunes march towards the shores of Lake Blanche, a dry salt lake in Western Australia's Great Sandy Desert. Marble Bar, to the west, holds Australia's heat-wave record – 160 days over 37.8°C.

severe, although some of them can, in a sense, hide. Deserts throughout the world are famous for their sudden blooming when the infrequent rains do fall, and the Australian deserts become among the most colourful. In the soil there are millions of seeds produced during the last rainfall. When the ground is wet they quickly sprout, and within a few days the ground is carpeted with ephemeral blooming plants, mostly members of the daisy family, which quickly set seed before withering away. There is, at the same time, a sudden increase in the numbers of insects, many of which are pollinators of the flowering plants. Some desert plants survive the dry periods not as seeds, but as rhizomes, tubers or similar underground structures. A few species have extremely long roots which can reach down to whatever water there is. None of these plants have their above-ground tissues greatly modified to conserve water – they are drought-evaders rather than drought-resisters.

Many desert plants survive by storing the water which they can get. The classic examples are the succulent cacti of the Americas, and some African plants which greatly resemble them. In such plants the stems are thick and fleshy, often spiny, and without conventional leaves. Cacti, other than introduced species, are not found in Australia, but there are some succulent species. These plants store water, and reduce water loss by restricting transpiration. They have thick skin and their water pores are set in grooves, or surrounded by hairs or spines. Many Australian desert plants which are not succulents reduce water loss in similar ways, and by rolling their leaves so that the lower surfaces, carrying their water pores, are protected. They can also wilt considerably before dying.

Animals, unlike plants, can move when conditions become bad, but it is only the birds and the large mammals, such as Red Kangaroos, which can move completely away from a drought-stricken area. Most mammals seek shelter from the sun during the day, and forage or graze at night. Small mammals such as Rabbit-eared Bandicoots, marsupial mice and rodents burrow, and in extremely hot periods may even AESTIVATE for a time. Within a burrow the temperature can be kept fairly constant and much lower than outside day-time temperatures, and the humidity is relatively high so that water losses are reduced. Nevertheless there are water losses, and often there is no surface water to drink for months at a time. Grazers, browsers, insect-eaters and meat-eaters will get fluid from their food, but seed-eaters have to get water by the oxidation of substances in seeds. This has been observed in some small desert rodents from north America, and presumably also occurs in Australian desert rodents.

The Pebble-mound Mouse *Pseudomys chapmani* has an interesting way of collecting water. It lives in the Pilbara, inside a mound of pebbles which it collects. Every morning it gathers small drops of dew which condense on the stones during the night. Another adaptation of small desert mammals is the production of a very concentrated urine as a means of conserving water.

Australian deserts have fewer species of seed-eating rodents than do north American deserts – 11 *versus* 33 – but many more grain-eating birds – 27 to 4 – and lizards – 150 to 57. The lizards eat a variety of food ranging from plants to insects and even small mammals. Goannas, dragon lizards and many skinks hunt during the day, but some skinks and the geckoes are active during the night or at dusk and dawn. Lizards shelter from the extreme heat in burrows, under tussocks of grass or stones, or beneath tree bark. They have one great advantage over the mammals and birds – as cold-blooded animals they need relatively little food and can go without for weeks.

The most unexpected desert animals are the frogs, which must keep their skins damp, or die. A few species avoid dying in droughts, which may last for years, by filling up with water after rain, burrowing deeply into the soil, and enclosing themselves in mucus. When heavy rain comes again they emerge and quickly lay their eggs which rapidly mature to young frogs before the surface pools dry out. Desert Aborigines often found them to be a life-saving source of water.

Palm Valley's unique trees are survivors from a time when the arid interior had a wetter climate.

Sahara-like dunes – like these on the fringe of the Nullarbor Plain – are rare in Australia.

Farmland: the never-ending struggle

Many people believe that as far as farming is concerned, 'Mother Nature' knows best. They support the use of farmyard manure rather than artificial fertilisers – which is good advice except that there is not enough to go around – and absolutely forbid the use of chemical pesticides.

Unfortunately for this belief, farming is one of the most unnatural activities that mankind has devised. Left to itself, and given enough time, a piece of land will become covered with a mixture of plants, the particular species depending upon factors such as the nature of the soil, the climate and the seeds available in the district. As time passes the vegetation becomes more and more complex and greater in total weight (biomass), until it reaches the climax vegetation for that particular site. The nature of the climax vegetation depends on many factors, including those listed above. In benign conditions in Australia it is often woodland or forest. Associated with the increasing complexity of the vegetation is an increase in the variety of animals and micro-organisms to be found. There are so many interactions between the organisms – so many pathways along which energy and matter (such as carbon and nitrogen) can flow – that few

species get completely out of hand and become harmful. However, there are some exceptions in natural conditions. In arid and semi-arid grass-lands, for example, a couple of seasons of good rains can lead to massive increases in rodents such as Long-haired Rats, once called, mis-leadingly, Plague Rats.

Farming – and crop-farming in particular – is an attempt to stop this process at some stage which suits the farmer. A wheat grower, for example, takes bare land which may once have supported mallee vegetation, and tries to hold it for a season at one stage in the succession. Furthermore he does his utmost to ensure that the land carries only a single plant, wheat. Furthermore that wheat is removed at harvest so that the land loses organic matter, phosphorus, potassium and other nutrients, and its cover. In natural vegetation, on the other hand, most of the materials, apart from some of the gases produced in decay and by respiration, stay within the plant community.

The growing of a single plant brings other difficulties. In a natural woodland, for example, plant-attacking organisms such as fungi and insects have to depend on scattered specimens

of their host plants, mixed with a variety of unsuitable plants. In a wheat crop such organisms do not have to worry about where their next meal is coming from, and if they can produce several generations in a single season, need have no concerns about the future of their offspring. Their food surrounds them.

There is yet another unnatural feature of annual crops. Generally there is some kind of rotation of crops. This is partly a pest-control measure in itself, and partly a means of re-plenishing the soil with nutrients. Legumes, for example, fix nitrogen, and replace some of the nutrients removed by earlier crops. In between, the land is bare for a time as a result of cultivation – unless the farmer uses another technique, such as a chemical herbicide to kill growth. Consequently there is little time for the natural enemies of crop pests to build up their numbers to such a level that they can keep the pests down. Also, unless they are able to eat a wide variety of food, few useful species survive from one year to the next. It is also usual for the pests of annual crops to spend most of their energy in reproduction. They multiply rapidly, take advantage of the food while it is there, and

Crops such as wheat *must be grown over vast acreages to be profitable. However, this type of farming involves a constant battle with pests and weeds.*

Farming has radically changed the face of much of Australia. Only a scattering of trees remain of the vegetation that once clothed this land.

then more or less disappear until the next season. Aphids are excellent examples – small, short-lived, prolific insects – they dispense with sex and wings when times are good because they are not necessary and simply waste energy which is more usefully, for the aphids, devoted to asexual reproduction (virgin births).

Some of the enemies of perennial crops, such as fruit trees, behave like aphids, but many of the pests in orchards adopt another strategy. They reproduce less quickly, put their energy into growing larger, living longer and often maintaining a territory. The Codling Moth of apples, for example, has some of these characteristics and few apples support more than one caterpillar each. Consequently a relatively small number of caterpillars can cause a great amount of damage. Perennial crops can build up a permanent population of natural enemies of pests which are also able to live off other resources such as pollen and nectar in the plants which often grow between the trees. Nevertheless they are rarely –

in Australian conditions – able to keep pests such as the Codling Moths under control.

Many crops suffer competition from weeds. These too are well suited to the unstable conditions of cropped land. They are colonising species which germinate quickly in bare soil when there is no competition from other plants. They grow rapidly and produce large numbers of seeds. There are also perennial weeds such as St Johns Wort and Skeleton Weed which can grow from small plant fragments left in the soil.

Many of these pests are introduced, and one reason for their success is that they have arrived without their natural enemies – parasites, predators and diseases – which keep their numbers down in their countries of origin. Biologists often try to redress the balance by importing some of these natural enemies, and sometimes this works, although there have been spectacular failures, such as the Cane Toad. In recent years other techniques have been tried, including the use of pheromones – chemical messengers released by organisms which influence the behaviour of their fellows, such as sex-attractants, for example – and by releasing genetically modified individuals to reduce the fertility of wild populations.

Unfortunately, however, these methods do not always work well enough, and farmers are often forced to use chemical pesticides as an alternative. After World War II the modern synthetic pesticides were developed, and they included the chlorinated hydrocarbons such as DDT. These were at first very effective – so effective, indeed, that many pest populations rapidly became highly resistant to them by evolutionary processes. They were also very persistent. One grave disadvantage was that they also killed many of the natural enemies of pests. As a consequence, the pests rapidly recovered when the effects of the insecticide had worn off, and they were no longer held in check by their natural enemies.

These problems have been greatest in cotton, a crop with a very long growing season which suffers from many different pests. The destruction of natural enemies, coupled with the development of resistance, brought new species of pests into prominence, the most important being the Bollworm caterpillars of *Heliothis* moths. In the Ord River region of Western Australia as in parts of Texas and Mexico, cotton was eventually abandoned by farmers because of the new pests.

Farmers still have to use pesticides, but they are now used in ways that are less environmentally harmful. Modern pesticides such as the organophosphates, carbamates and pyrethroids, are less persistent than DDT and they can be used with biological methods of control.

Farming and wildlife conservation have different objectives, but they are not entirely incompatible. Some farmers and graziers, for

FARM TYPES

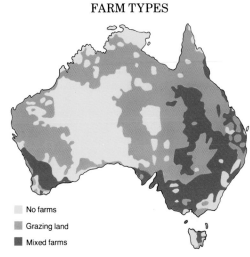

No farms

Grazing land

Mixed farms

Almost all the land that is capable of supporting livestock or crops is now in use.

example, either conserve or plant groups of trees to serve as wildlife refuges. They may also set out corridors of trees or bushes through their properties so that migratory species have routes along which they can travel, or by which non-migratory species can colonise new areas on the property. Yet others, troubled by those species of parrots which attack grain crops, yet not willing to destroy them, sometimes plant areas near the roosting sites with crops which they are willing to sacrifice to lessen the damage to their main crops. The building of farm dams has been of great benefit to many wildlife species, and some conservation-minded farmers even make artificial islands within them for birds.

Farm dams have benefited both farmers and native wildlife. Birds in particular use them as a source of food and water, especially when times are hard.

Wildlife in cities and towns

Europeans, and to a smaller extent, Aborigines, have changed most of the Australian countryside, but the changes have probably been greatest in the towns and cities where most of the natural vegetation has been destroyed, and the soil covered with bricks and concrete. With the disappearance of the native vegetation came a decline in the numbers of native animals.

Some municipal authorities have carefully preserved patches of native vegetation within their boundaries – King's Park (403 ha) in Perth is an outstanding example. Sydney seems exceptionally fortunate at first sight, for a survey in 1961 revealed that it had retained 23 300 ha of native vegetation – about one-quarter of the original area. Careful reading of the report showed, however, that the boundary chosen by its authors extended to the limits of the Metropolitan Water, Sewerage and Drainage Board's area, and thus included two large national parks – the Royal National Park (14 905 ha) to the south and Kurring-gai Chase National Park (14 656 ha) to the north. It is unfair to count these as urban areas when counting the numbers of different native species in Sydney, although there is no doubt that native animals stray from them into adjacent built-up areas.

There is no need to define urban habitats rigidly. They can be regarded simply as areas where the buildings are close together, interspersed with roads, railway tracks, gardens, recreation reserves, playing fields, factory sites and derelict land. In cities such as Sydney the seashore must also be included; it may encompass mangrove swamps and salt marshes. The 1961 survey estimated that there were 40 500 ha of 'man-made' vegetation – garden trees and shrubs, lawns and gardens – in Sydney.

In Britain suburban gardens are often richer in species of animals – particularly insects – than are nearby farmlands with their hedgerows and copses. No comparable surveys appear to have been made in Australia although one was suggested for the Bicentenary Year, but it is probable that the counts would be disappointing. In Britain the gardens contain mainly Eurasian and north American plants to which native animals readily adapt. Traditionally Australian gardeners have tried to grow, at least in the south, similar plants, and it is only recently that the movement for cultivating native plants has become strong. As a result most of the animals commonly found in city and suburban gardens are introduced species. This applies not only to the insects, but also to the birds. In Sydney, for example, the commonest birds in parks and gardens are House Sparrows, mynahs, starlings, Bulbuls, Feral Pigeons and Spotted Turtle-doves. Gulls are usually the only native birds to be seen, and they are there because, like most of the birds above, they are adept at scrounging from people.

Some native species have adapted well to the European-inspired gardens of south-eastern Australia. They include, among the insects, the day-flying Vine Moth which readily attacks Virginia Creeper, grape vines and fuchsias, several butterflies which feed on citrus, and the Queensland Fruit Fly. Among the birds there are Pied

Many species of birds, *such as these Sacred Ibises in a Sydney park, seem unconcerned about humans.*

Currawongs and New Holland Honeyeaters, which feed greedily on hibiscus flowers, and among the spiders the Redback, and in the Sydney region, the notorious Funnelweb flourish. Some suburbs suit possums which feed on garden fruits and flowers and which take over attics for breeding, if they can get into them. They may even be seen in Darlinghurst near Kings Cross in the heart of Sydney. All the backyard aphids and greenfly are introduced, however, as are virtually all the snails, slugs and woodlice, and the spade will reveal only northern hemisphere earthworms.

Many gardens and small parks (10 600 ha in 1961 in Sydney) contain trees and shrubs, and these are often natives such as eucalypts, figs and tea-trees. These should support native birds such as fairy wrens, but unfortunately they are more widely spaced than in native vegetation, and as they are separated by open space often consisting of well-manicured grass, there is no cover to protect the birds from predators such as cats and the currawongs. Silvereyes, on the other hand, often seem to do well in such conditions.

Some of the larger city parks, such as Centennial Park in Sydney, contain patches of native plants and often stretches of water. About 100 species of native birds have been recorded in the park, although the species vary from time to time. Cormorants are to be seen on most days and Musk Ducks, Dabchicks and herons are often to be found. Black duck, waterhens, gallinules, Black Swans and Coots are permanent residents, and are often very tame. Sacred Ibises have increased greatly in numbers there in recent years, descendants, it is said, of specimens which were released, or escaped from, Taronga Park Zoo. At times they can be seen flying in flocks over Sydney, or scavenging in Hyde Park in the centre of the city, although

Lakes in Sydney's Centennial Park *are home for many water birds – both native and introduced. Altogether, over 100 species of birds have been recorded as living within the park boundaries.*

they have long since disappeared from the lower Nile, their traditional home. Such municipal lakes are refuges for various waterfowl in dry periods. During a drought in the 1980s, for example, there were dozens of pelicans in Centennial Park, although only one or two remained in 1988. On the land are many birds such as parrots and cockatoos, Willie Wagtails and, of course, mynahs and Feral Pigeons.

Reptiles and amphibians are few in numbers in most cities although skinks are common in most suburban gardens of large cities, and Tiger Snakes persist on the outskirts.

All the larger cities of Australia are coastal, and wildlife can be abundant in places on the coast. Mangrove swamps, although unpleasant to visit, and the adjacent swamps and sands, are often particularly rich. Mangroves are important spawning grounds for many marine fishes, but they often also support many birds. Towra Point, which projects into Botany Bay, 15 km from the Sydney GPO, is a staging point for migratory waders which breed in the Arctic. More than 20 species have been recorded, including Mongolian Dotterels, whimbrels, curlews, Sharp-tailed Sand-pipers and Bar-tailed Godwits. The point is also used by other waterbirds including terns, spoon-bills and ibises. Much of the area is now a nature reserve but, unfortunately, recent engineering work in the bay has shifted the currents so that Towra Point is threatened with erosion. In addition sea urchins is destroying the seagrass.

Towns, surprisingly, can sometimes protect a native species by isolating them from dangers to which rural populations are subjected. The Native Cat or Quoll, for example, lived around Nielsen Park in Vaucluse, Sydney, until 1964, although it had become uncommon outside the city. It has been suggested that the population was isolated from a disease which spread through rural animals years ago.

There are, of course, many introduced mam-mals in urban areas, to the detriment of the few natives that remain. Feral cats abound, and even well-fed pet cats will take birds when they can. Black and Brown Rats and the House Mouse are abundant and some years ago there were free-living white rats in the grounds of a Sydney university. Feral pigs have been reported in the outskirts of some larger cities, even, sometimes, living under houses and emerging at night without the householders being aware of them.

Finally there are the animals which most naturalists disdain – those that live in houses. In 1960 the agricultural economist George Ordish wrote *The Living House*, a fascinating history of an English Elizabethan manor house, not in terms of its human inhabitants, but of the other animals, invited and uninvited, which lived there. Many of the creatures mentioned would be found in some Australian homes today, including such unwelcome guests as fleas, bedbugs and cock-roaches. Most countries have two groups of cockroaches – those which are more or less cosmopolitan and live as human 'guests', and those that live in the bush or its local equivalent. The domestic species are becoming more common world-wide. Many domestic spiders are also introduced – the most familiar in Australia is the harmless *Pholcus phalangoides* or daddy-long-legs spider, which makes untidy webs in corners. Even some Redback spiders, inhabitants of outside lavatories, could be Black Widows descended from spiders brought to Australia with American equipment during the war.

The fashion for native gardens (above) should attract more native animals and birds to cities than did the formal parks and gardens of introduced plants (left), which were once favoured by many Australians.

The wide, brown land

The Australian continent has a land area of 7 682 300 sq. km and is the lowest, driest (except for Antarctica) and flattest of all the earth's continents. Its highest point is Mount Kosciusko, NSW, which rises to 2228 m and its lowest point is on the dry bed of Lake Eyre at 15 m below sea level. Nearly 90 per cent of the continent is below 500 m, and the average height is only about 300 m. Half of Australia has a median rainfall of less that 300 mm a year and over three-quarters receives less than 600 mm a year.

The continent is divided into six states and two federal territories which are (with their areas and populations in 1984): New South Wales 801 600 sq. km, 5 412 000; Victoria 227 600 sq. km, 4 078 500; Queensland 1 727 200 sq. km, 2 507 000; South Australia 984 000 sq. km, 1 353 900; Western Australia 2 525 500 sq. km, 1 383 700; Tasmania 67 800 sq. km, 437 400; Northern Territory 1 346 200 sq. km, 138 800; Australian Capital Territory 2400 sq. km, 244 600. The total population of the Commonwealth was 15 555 900 people of which 12 271 400 were born in Australia, 2 363 100 were born in Europe and 481 400 were born in Asia. At the time of the 1981 census there were 159 897 Aborigines and Torres Strait Islanders living in Australia. Australia is also one of the most urbanised nations on earth with over 70 per cent of the population living in cities or towns.

Little detail is visible on this view of the earth taken by US astronauts from about 160 000 km in space. What is striking, however, is how brown Australia appears, and how isolated it is from its neighbours.

New Guinea

ARU SEA

Torres Strait

C Wessel

Prince of Wales I **Thursday I** C York

Gove Peninsula

Groote Eylandt

Gulf of Carpentaria

Cape York Peninsula C Melville

Princess Charlotte Bay

Mitchell R

• Cooktown

CORAL SEA

Mornington I

• Normanton

Great

• Cairns

Tableland

Rockingham Bay

Hinchinbrook I
Great Palm I **Barrier**
• Townsville

• Mount Isa

• Cloncurry

Charters Towers •

Whitsunday I

QUEENSLAND **Reef**

• Mackay

Georgina R

Diamantina R

Thompson R

Barcoo R

• Longreach

Great

• Rockhampton

Gladstone •

Hervey Bay

TROPIC OF CAPRICORN

Simpson Desert

Dividing

Sandy C

• Charleville

Fraser I

Warburton R

Cooper Creek

Strzelecki Creek

• Roma

Range

Moreton Bay

Toowoomba •

Moreton I
Brisbane

Goondiwindi •

• Gold Coast

Warrego R

Culgoa R

• Lismore

Paroo R

Macintyre R

• Moree

• Grafton

• Bourke

Range

• Armidale

NEW SOUTH WALES

Tamworth •

Smoky C

• Broken Hill

Darling R

• Kempsey

Dividing

Port Macquarie

Menindee L

• Dubbo

Taree

Port Stephens

Lord Howe I

Main Barrier Ra.

Mudgee •

Orange •

Newcastle

• Mildura

Bathurst •

Port Jackson

Murray R

Lachlan R

Great

• Sydney

Murrumbidgee R

• Wollongong

Adelaide

• Murray Bridge

Wagga Wagga •

Goulburn

ACT • **Canberra**

Kangaroo I

Albury-Wodonga •

Jervis Bay

• Cooma

Batemans Bay

• Bendigo

VICTORIA

▲ **Mt Kosciusko**

Twofold Bay

Mount Gambier •

Grampians

Ballarat •

TASMAN SEA

L Corangamite

Geelong •

Melbourne

Pt Hicks

C Otway

Port Phillip Bay

Westernport

Wilsons Promontory

King I

Flinders I

Hunter I

Bass Strait

Cape Barren I

Eddystone Point

Devonport •

• Launceston

TASMANIA

Port Davey

SW Cape

Hobart

Tasman Peninsula

SE Cape

Storm Bay

SOUTH PACIFIC OCEAN

CLIMATE ZONES

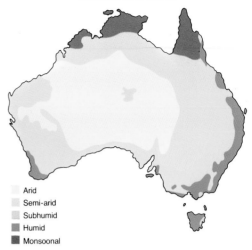

Arid
Semi-arid
Subhumid
Humid
Monsoonal

HUMAN DISTURBANCE

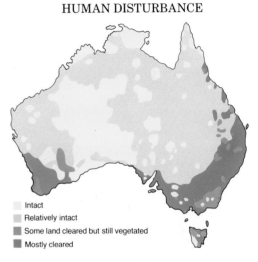

Intact
Relatively intact
Some land cleared but still vegetated
Mostly cleared

NATIVE PASTURE

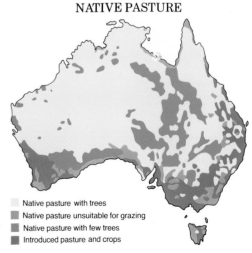

Native pasture with trees
Native pasture unsuitable for grazing
Native pasture with few trees
Introduced pasture and crops

The impact of European settlement has been felt over virtually all of Australia to some extent. Only the arid interior has escaped unscathed.

Dipping sheep

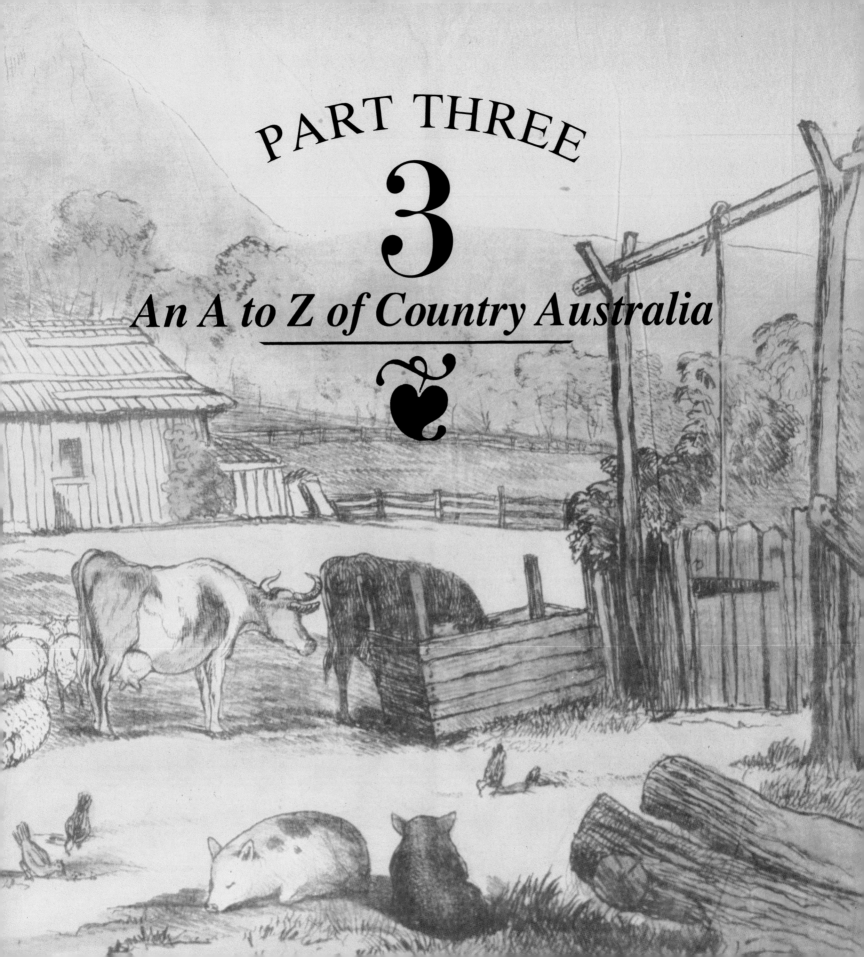

PART THREE

3

An A to Z of Country Australia

ABORIGINES

There is an increasing willingness on the part of European Australians to understand more about the indigenous inhabitants of this continent – the Aboriginal people whose culture is so different from that of the colonising British. In some respects it is misleading to regard Aborigines as a people with a single distinctive culture, because within this racial group there are hundreds of distinct languages – as different as English and French. Some groups lived a rather nomadic life-style and others had established villages with stone buildings when Europeans arrived. Although it is difficult to estimate how many Aborigines lived in Australia before this invasion, researchers suggest that the figure was probably less than one million. Many Aborigines were killed by diseases and wars, but the current Aboriginal population is probably about the same as it was in 1788. Despite mixed marriages, Aboriginal people are proud of their rich culture.

Aborigines have lived in Australia for at least 40 000 years, as reckoned by archaeologists. Their ancestors probably originally crossed from islands to the north of Australia in small groups, possibly by canoe. Their original settlements are now 150 m or more under the sea because at the time of their arrival much more of the world's water was locked up in the polar icecaps. Various studies confirm that Aborigines are most closely related to their nearest neighbours to the north, such as people from New Guinea and islands of south-east Asia.

But traditional Aboriginal mythology – in contrast to that of native Pacific Islanders, for example – enshrines the belief that they have always lived on this continent, since the Dreaming. The Dreaming is a continuing tradition which embodies concepts, stories and events about Aboriginal kinship, religion and cosmology. The Dreaming constitutes for Aborigines a plan of life which not only provides the context for everyday existence and relationships, but also explains creation and allows contact with the spirit world, not unlike Christianity or any of the other great world religions. In different parts of Australia the power of either a great Father or great Mother was held responsible for the creation of the world and Aboriginal culture.

Aborigines are born into specific kinship relationships, like all people, but relationships such as father, mother, brother and sister are sometimes used differently from the way Europeans use these forms. Aborigines use the kin terms when speaking to each other, and the terms specify various responsibilities, such as who can marry whom, as laid down by the Dreaming. Aborigines are also assigned status within a class system which groups together people of the same class. The nature of these classes varies for different groups, but each Aboriginal community is divided into two, four or eight groups – sometimes into a combination of such divisions, which makes their social life and responsibilities perhaps the most complex of any human groups anywhere in the world. These

Few Aborigines now choose to live in the traditional way, as hunters and gatherers. However many people, such as these from the far north of Australia, possess all the skills needed to survive happily in the bush.

When Europeans arrived in Australia they found the continent occupied by a proud and independent people. This group was photographed in Victoria in 1858.

divisions are associated with particular spirit beings, places, animals and plants. It is these which specify very precise responsibilities about land management, the performance of rituals and social responsibilities. These divisions also influence marriage rules and the routines of everyday life. Aborigines assert that white people have lost their dreaming because, compared with the very ordered Aboriginal view of life and the landscape, white people seem to live in a chaotic social world, with little respect for the land on which they depend.

In contrast to the extremely rich spiritual life of Aborigines, their traditional material culture was relatively simple, at least in the eyes of most Europeans. However, although Aborigines used spears and spear-throwers rather than bows and arrows, and did not make pottery or metal machines, there can be no doubt that their traditional toolkit of stone, wood, bone and skin was exactly right for their way of life. Few white people could survive as comfortably as Aborigines did in the dry interior of the continent, or in the subantarctic conditions of south-west Tasmania during the last ice-age, 18 000 years ago.

Aboriginal culture is alive and thriving today in all parts of Australia, from Tasmania to the Kimberleys in the far north-west of the continent. By far the best way for non-Aboriginal people to understand this highly spiritual culture is to listen to Aborigines themselves, to read their published poems and stories and to visit their own museums or keeping places.

Some Aboriginal people have accepted part of the European culture and have produced remarkable inventions and outstanding works of art. But Aborigines, like other racial groups are proud and jealous of their heritage. Despite the great losses suffered at the hands of a colonising culture, an increasingly united Aboriginal movement throughout Australia is reasserting the traditional values and rights, both within and apart from European culture.

One of the most obvious material remains of

Aboriginal occupation is art, which is found on rock surfaces over the entire continent. Aboriginal people have considerable knowledge of the natural environment which still provides a wide variety of materials for their arts and crafts. The artists employ a variety of styles, techniques and media, and Aboriginal art still retains its own distinctive quality.

Throughout most of Australia, Aborigines used to paint on bark, but it is in the Northern Territory that these paintings are most spectacular. They portray stories which are special to the Dreaming of the artist. Creatures such as the Rainbow Serpent have special significance because of their role in creating features of the landscape. A variety of symbols are used to represent individuals, groups of people, camping places and natural features. Thus each painting incorporates different levels of meaning: it tells a story; it provides a map; and it explains how the landscape was formed and why it is significant to people who are initiated into that particular Dreaming. Only the artist has the knowledge to reveal the whole story behind each painting, and certain levels of meaning may be restricted to those appropriately initiated.

Four main colours are used in bark paintings: red and yellow from ochres, white clay and black charcoal. Originally, natural plant juices were used to mix the colours, but now a water-based glue is used. The bark itself is cut from a eucalypt tree and flattened to produce a rectangular slab, the largest of which may be to 2 m long. A background colour may then be applied, followed by the intricate designs and figures, often painted with fine, human-hair brushes. Kangaroos and other animals are sometimes shown in x-ray style, revealing their skeleton and internal organs.

Aborigines have been painting the walls of caves and rock shelters for over 10 000 years. Engravings, made by pecking the rock with a stone, were first made nearly 20 000 years ago. The paintings and engravings depict similar kinds of stories about events, places and religious subjects as do bark paintings. This rock art is found on the walls of caves and shelters where Aboriginal people lived, as well as on special, sacred sites where religious and other ceremonies were performed.

Several distinctive styles can be identified for different places and different periods of time over the last 20 000 years. In the western desert, for example, circle and line designs dominate, whereas in parts of northern Australia there are spectacular galleries with fish, animals and spirit figures – with strange heads and elongated bodies. Animal tracks are a common subject and some rock walls are covered with emu and kangaroo prints. Another common subject is the hand stencil, where a human hand had been placed on a wall with fingers outspread. Ochre is then mixed and sprayed through the artist's

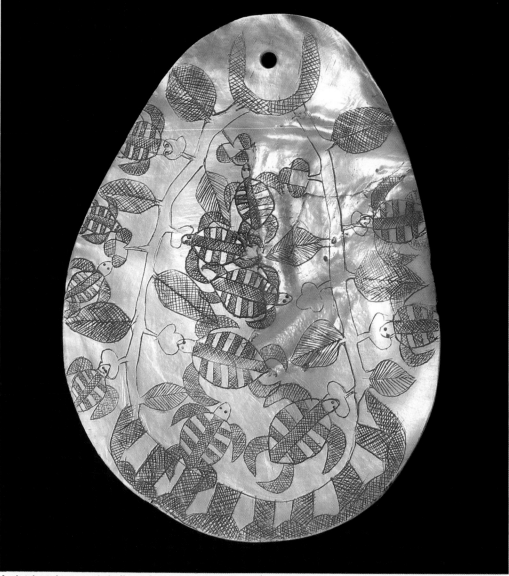

An intricately-carved shell pendant made by people from the Kimberley region of Western Australia. Such ornaments were hung either from the neck or the waist, and were often traded with people from the inland.

mouth over the hand, leaving a colourful stencil. Some of the rock paintings portray animals which are now extinct in Australia and these must have been painted thousands of years ago.

Aborigines paint and decorate many objects apart from bark and rock walls. Body painting is particularly intricate, and the preparation of these paintings for ceremonial dances takes many hours, following special religious rites. The earth itself is sometimes sculpted and painted in ceremonial designs. Body painting and earth sculpture do not last for very long, but the intricate details have a similar intimate relationship with the land and Aboriginal religion. Some modern Aboriginal artists also paint in oil and water colour.

Bags, mats and baskets are made from vegetable fibres and reeds. The vegetable fibres are dyed with natural plant juices and twisted together to form a strong string. The strings are then woven together forming colourful patterns, with a series of complicated knots. Aboriginal women make many kinds of bags including small carrying bags, called 'dilly bags'. The bags, mats and baskets also illustrate, with their colourful patterns, stories related to the Dreaming, and particular patterns are the copyright of particular clans and groups of women.

The carefully carved wooden boomerang is probably the most famous hunting and fighting weapon of Australian Aborigines. In fact there are several kinds of boomerang and in some places in northern Australia, boomerangs are not used as weapons at all, but as musical instruments. In concert with didgeridoos and other instruments, two boomerangs are clapped together to beat out rhythms during corroborees and other ceremonial dances.

Only a few Aboriginal boomerangs are designed to return. The carved upper curve and the longitudinal curve and twist create an aerodynamic wing which, when correctly thrown, returns to its starting point in the hands of the thrower. These boomerangs are used to capture birds which respond as if the boomerang were an attacking hawk. The frightened birds, such as ducks, are thus forced to fly into huge nets, strung out across rivers. These returning boomerangs sometimes have elaborate grooves which are thought to assist in their flight.

Other kinds of boomerangs, much larger and heavier than the returning type, are designed to strike and stun large animals such as kangaroos. The spinning arms of the boomerang hits the animal with great force, sometimes cutting and killing it. These heavy-duty boomerangs can also be used as clubs and butchering knives. Hunting and fighting boomerangs also have elaborate decorations and carry the special markings of a particular hunter.

Archaeological evidence has shown that Aborigines have been using boomerangs for thousands of years. Ancient specimens have been found in Wyrie Swamp in South Australia which are at least 10 000 years old. Stencils of boomerangs have also been found on painted walls of caves and rock shelters.

Music is also important to Aborigines, and didgeridoos are a unique Australian invention. These strange musical instruments are made by cutting down a small hollow branch or tree. The hollow centre is scraped smooth and the outside

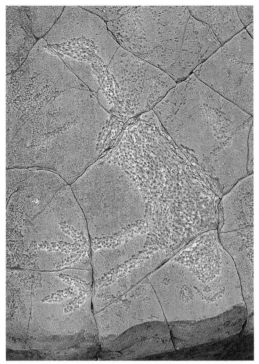

Complex rock paintings and carvings can be seen in many parts of Australia. The bird (above) has been pecked into rock at Mootwingee, in the far north-west of NSW, and the elaborate gallery (below) is at Kakadu in the Northern Territory.

Aborigines in north Queensland used baskets like this to prepare food. They were loaded with crushed cycad seeds and placed in water to leach out poisons.

is carved and painted with elaborate designs, symbolising religious places and mythical events. Didgeridoos are made in all sizes and can be up to several metres long. With practice it is possible for an amateur to learn some of the skills required to play them. The lips are closed in and around one end of the hollow instrument, somewhat like blowing a trumpet. From then on all breath comes in through the nose and out through the mouth – both at the same time. As air is sucked in through the nose, air is also forced out through the lips by inflating the cheeks. This causes a continuous drone, a little like that of bagpipes. However, with skill it is possible to create a wide range of notes, and even to talk through the instrument. Traditional didgeridoo music is played at ceremonial dances in accompaniment with other instruments.

Aborigines are skilled in using natural objects for making necklaces, ornaments and toys for children. Necklaces and rattles are made by stringing together different kinds of seashells and the fruits and nuts of certain plants. Beautiful echidna-spine necklaces are particularly elegant, with their natural brown and white colouring. Emu eggs and nuts from the Boab tree are also carved with natural landscapes and animals.

All these items can be found in Aboriginal craftshops and local museums, which usually supply details of each carving and painting. The particular artist or craftsman often describes what the designs mean, and the particular stories which relate to their traditional land. Some items are not for legal sale because of their religious importance, which restricts those who can see the objects.

ACACIA

Acacias, commonly known as wattles, are one of the larger groups of woody plants. There are around 1000 species world-wide, and about 750 of them are found only in Australia.

Representatives grow in nearly all habitats and regions of the continent – from the edges of rainforest to the arid centre, from coastal fore-dunes to subalpine heaths. They range in size from dwarf shrubs to tall trees, some of them yielding valuable timber.

The term wattle is very old and refers to flexible twigs or branches which can be woven together to make portable fencing (hurdles), or to provide a support for plaster work in buildings (WATTLE AND DAUB). In Britain, the main source of wattle was hazel. The first settlers in Australia found a small tree around Sydney Cove which had flexible branches that were ideal for plaster work. They called this tree wattle or blackwattle (hence Blackwattle Bay). In fact, although this plant has globular heads of cream flowers, it is not an *Acacia* at all. Its botanical name is *Callicoma serratifolia*, and it is related to the coachwood found in rainforests. However, the similarity of its flowers to those of *Acacia*, and the fact that some *Acacia* species were later used as a source of wattle sticks, led to the term wattle being applied to all *Acacias*. A number of species are, however, also widely known by Aboriginal names, or names given by the early pioneers, for example, Myall, Boree, Mulga, Brigalow, Gidgee, Dead-finish, Hickory and Raspberry Jam (from its smell).

The fluffy cream to deep golden yellow flowers of *Acacia* are one of the most familiar sights in the Australian bush, and one *Acacia* – the Golden Wattle *Acacia pycnantha* – is the floral emblem of the Commonwealth. *Acacias* can be divided into two great groups based on the structure of their flowers – those species with flowers in globular heads and those in which the flowers are in the form of spikes.

The fruit of the *Acacia* is a pod, similar to that of the pea family, and its seeds have a very hard, impervious coat. Many species do not germinate until after a bushfire has heated the coat sufficiently to allow moisture to penetrate it. In order to get wattle seeds to grow in a garden it may be necessary to scratch the hard outer coating first, or alternatively to treat them with boiling water for a short time.

Acacias were once very important as a source of tannin, which was extracted from the bark. The first known shipment of wattle bark extract left Australia in 1823, and by the end of the nineteenth century thousands of tonnes of wattle bark were being exported each year. However, the industry in Australia was soon overtaken by that in South Africa – ironically based on plantations of Australian *Acacia* species.

Acacias have many other uses. Some species produce GUMS which have a wide variety of applications, and in the late nineteenth and early twentieth centuries Australian *Acacia* gums fetched high prices abroad. The larger species also yield valuable timber, such as that of the Tasmanian Blackwood *Acacia melanoxylon*. Many varieties were also once used by Aborigines, both for food and because they had medicinal properties.

Acacias may one day prove to be valuable for rehabilitating degraded land. Nitrogen-fixing bacteria live in the roots of most, if not all, species, which means that they are important for soil fertility in regions where they grow.

Bright yellow sprays of wattle flowers are a familiar sight in the bush. Many common names have been given to Acacia species by bushmen, such as Mulga, Brigalow, Boree and Gidgee.

ACRE

The acre is a measure of land which has been used for hundreds of years. Originally it was the area that could be ploughed by a yoke of oxen in one day. Not surprisingly, one acre tended to vary from the next so, in the 13th century, the English monarchy ruled that an acre should be a standard size – an area 40 poles long and 4 poles wide, or 43 560 sq. ft (4047 sq.m). This acre has been used over the years by Australian farmers. Apart from describing the size of a farm, acres are also used in calculations such as stocking rates (so many sheep or cattle per acre) and fertiliser rates (so many pounds per acre). Often, paddocks are named according to their acreage – 'ten-acre' and 'hundred-acre' paddocks abound. The advent of the metric system and the hectare, equalling 2.471 acres, has done little to reduce the importance of the acre in the day-to-day conversations of most Australian farmers.

AGATE

Australia is renowned for its beautiful agates. These are a spectacularly coloured, very fine-grained type of quartz with thin concentric layers, like an onion. The layers are usually black, white, brown, red and grey, but they can sometimes be yellow, green and blue. Natural colouring is due to small amounts of iron, but sometimes artificial pigments are introduced to produce specimens with exotic colours. Agate is a semi-precious stone that is cut and polished for jewellery and ornaments.

Agates usually occur in rocks formed from molten lava. When lava flows from a volcano it has holes in it produced by steam and gas – like bubbling porridge. As the larva solidifies fluid fills these cavities and eventually hardens to form agate. Individual layers in an agate can be so fine that 15 000 measure only 25 mm. Agates are found throughout Australia in areas where volcanoes once existed.

AGISTMENT

In feudal times peasants were charged agistment for grazing their cattle in royal forests. Nowadays, Australian farmers charge agistment for stock – usually cattle, sheep or horses – which graze on their properties. Farmers may agist stock out when their area is in drought. Stock-owners, particularly in inland Queensland and NSW, will send stock long distances to agist them where there is some feed. Depending on the agistment agreement, the owners may have to regularly check and maintain their stock's water supplies and fencing. Sometimes farmers will also agist stock out to fatten them before sale – for example put them on a neighbour's crop or post-harvest stubble before sending them to market. Others who invest in stock without owning land will agist their stock out from the time of purchase to the time of sale. Rather than pay cash for agistment, some small owners prefer to swap grazing for labour on a casual basis. On a smaller scale, many horse-owners, particularly those living in or near towns, also have their stock on permanent agistment.

AGRICULTURAL CHEMICALS

The use of agricultural chemicals has increased dramatically over the last 40 years as farming and livestock management have become more technical. Almost all plant and livestock producers now use a wide range of chemicals to control pests, weeds and diseases. Indeed, it has been estimated that without chemicals, one-third of Australia's rural production would be lost.

Awareness about the safety of chemicals has increased in recent years. A number, most notably DDT, have been banned, and strict regulations now govern the use of all chemicals. Farmers generally have become more safety conscious in applying chemicals.

Herbicides are used to control weeds in crops, pastures, orchards and horticulture. They can be applied before or after weeds emerge, and kill on contact or remain in the soil for later action. There has been a trend toward using herbicides instead of cultivation to control weeds as part of minumum or no-tillage operations. These methods are widely believed to be better for soil structure and cheaper than conventional cultivation practices. Pesticides and fungicides are not as widely used as herbicides. Farmers will not generally use them unless there is evidence the damage posed by the pest or disease outweighs the cost of spraying. Herbicides, pesticides and fungicides can be applied over a wide area – by aircraft or a boom spray pulled behind a tractor – or they can be spot applied.

A wide range of chemicals are also used in livestock production. Horses, cattle and sheep are drenched for internal parasites and dipped or sprayed for external parasites, such as lice or ticks. There are also vaccines for a wide range of diseases. Hormones are used to promote fertility and growth in sheep and cattle. Young pigs are often given antibiotics in their food and water to control infections that cause scours.

Scientists are continually refining agricultural chemicals because pests, weeds and diseases tend to build up resistance to them. Sheep worm's resistance to drenching, for example, has become a major problem for the industry. Many scientists have therefore turned their attention to biological and alternative forms of control. The Oriental Fruit Moth, for example, a pest of peach and nectarine orchards, can now be controlled by release of a synthetic version of the smell put out by females to attract mates. The chemicals drive the male moths into confusion – and save the fruit from attack.

AGRICULTURAL MACHINERY

In the early days, the inventiveness of Australian farmers was severely tested by the necessity of having to adapt farm implements to new conditions, and by the need for equipment to clear and prepare virgin land for farming.

The Bull-Ridley stripper, developed in South Australia in the early 1840s, H.V. McKay's stripper-harvester of 1884, and mechanical shears – invented in the late 1800s – were among the most notable Australian inventions. Perhaps the greatest contributions to Australian farming was made by the STUMP JUMP PLOUGH and spring-loaded cultivator – developed in the late 1800s – and so named because of their ability to ride over obstacles, thus avoiding breakages. Both allowed much new land to be used for cropping. Indeeed, they are still used on newly-cleared land today where stumps are a problem.

Sugarcane harvesters were also a notable Australian invention. About two-thirds of the machines sold around the world today are supplied by Australian manufacturers.

These days, farmers must invest more and more money in equipment in order to remain efficient and competitive. The value of machinery on an average, broadacre grain farm is probably close to $1 million.

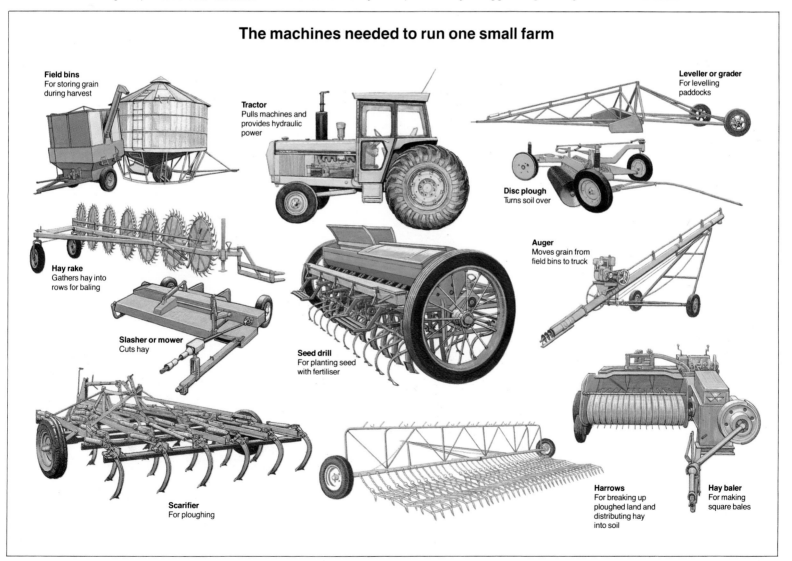

The machines needed to run one small farm

Field bins
For storing grain during harvest

Tractor
Pulls machines and provides hydraulic power

Leveller or grader
For levelling paddocks

Disc plough
Turns soil over

Hay rake
Gathers hay into rows for baling

Auger
Moves grain from field bins to truck

Slasher or mower
Cuts hay

Seed drill
For planting seed with fertiliser

Scarifier
For ploughing

Harrows
For breaking up ploughed land and distributing hay into soil

Hay baler
For making square bales

ALDERFLY

Alderflies are usually seen gliding or flying slowly and awkwardly near cold, clear streams and ponds in late afternoon or early evening, but they can fly quickly when disturbed. They are often large insects with a wing span of up to 160 mm. The adults have long antennae, bulging eyes, two pairs of well-veined similar wings, and a flexible, soft abdomen. They have chewing mouthparts, but are believed not to feed during their short adult life which is devoted to mating and egg laying. Their water-dwelling larvae, which also have chewing mouthparts, and prominent gills along their sides, hunt near the bottoms of streams, and pupate on the banks just below the surface, emerging when the water level falls. They are an important food for fish. They take their name from the alder, a common European tree found near streams and ponds. There are about 16 Australian species.

ALGAE

The term algae takes in a great range of plant forms, from tiny single-celled organisms to massive kelps. Given their diversity, it is easiest to define algae by the features they do not have – roots, stems, leaves and flowers. Superficially many of the larger algae appear to be arranged into stems and leaves, but closer examination shows that they do not possess the characteristic features of these organs from flowering plants.

Algae are usually thought of as living in water, as indeed most species do. Nevertheless, there are species found on wet rocks and tree trunks, or on soil. One of the most familiar of these land living algae is *Trentopohlia*, which produces the brilliant orange, felt-like growth on rocks, tree trunks and fence posts in the eastern highlands of Australia.

In most water bodies algae provide the major source of food on which the whole ecosystem depends. In the open ocean, and in most areas of freshwater, the most important algae are the phytoplankton – floating, normally single-celled plants. Viewed under the microscope, phytoplankton have many different shapes, but they are normally invisible to the naked eye. However, under certain circumstances there can be so many phytoplankton in the water that they can colour it. During occasional 'red tides' million of tiny plants multiply and stain the sea red – there can be over a million cells to every litre of water. The phosphorescence which can sometimes be seen in a boat's bow-wave and wake is also produced by phytoplankton.

Although phytoplankton are usually beneficial to humans, a small number of species may produce toxins, which if absorbed by shellfish, for example, may subsequently cause health problems. In freshwater, large numbers of phytoplankton may taint drinking water and make it unsuitable for human consumption.

ALP

True alpine ranges consist of recently folded mountains, whereas the so-called Australian Alps are a high, dissected plateau. The highest parts range from about 1800 m to 2230 m – at the summit of Mt Kosciusko. They form a long curve, part of the Great Dividing Range, roughly 120 km long, from Mt Kosciusko in the north, through Mt Feathertop, Victoria, (1922 m) to Mt Bogong, also in Victoria (1983 m). The mountain tops are flat with outcrops of resistant rocks. The summits are above the tree-line (about 1700 m) but, except where rocks outcrop, are well covered with grasses and flowers. The highest parts of Mt Bogong are made up of outcrops of granite which were pushed up through soft slates and schists. Its sides are steep. Mt Feathertop is composed of basalt-capped slates with gentler slopes. Kosciusko is built of hard granite, and has many steep cliffs and deep gorges, with evidence of glaciation. The Alps are the source of the Murray, Murrumbidgee, Snowy and Mitchell Rivers, and the site of the gigantic Snowy River Scheme.

Virtually the whole of the Snowy Mountains *appear in this photograph taken from an American spacecraft. To the right are Lake Eucumbene (top) and Lake Jindabyne. From Lake Jindabyne the deep valley of the Thredbo River cuts almost through the range to the far side. The valley above is that of the Snowy River, which finishes below Mt Kosciusko. The long arm of Lake Eucumbene almost touches the Kiandra-Adaminaby road.*

ALPINE PLANTS

In Australia alpine plants are found only in the higher mountains of the south-east – the Snowy Mountains in NSW, the mountains of the Australian Capital Territory, the Victorian Alps and the mountain areas of Tasmania. On the mainland this means altitudes above about 1200 m, but in southern Tasmania alpine plants descend much lower. At lower levels there is localised alpine vegetation in 'frost hollows' – flat valley bottoms where cold air collects at night.

The term alpine plant is usually applied to colourful plants, such as snow daisies and eyebrights, which carpet high areas in summer, but in Australia there are also many shrubs and a few trees which can be found near the tops of the highest mountains. The commonest, and often the only tree in the alpine region is the SNOW GUM *Eucalyptus niphophila*. In many areas there is also a dense layer of shrubs, especially on steeper slopes. In the Kosciusko region alone there are 200 species or sub-species of alpine plants, of which 21 are endemic.

Because of the short growing season, most alpine plants do not start flowering until November or December, and most are finished by about February. January is the best month to see alpine flowers.

AMBER

Amber is a resin that once oozed from pine trees that grew about 10 million years ago. Today it is found as a fossil in some coal deposits, such as those at Morwell and Lal Lal in Victoria. Amber is hard, smooth and waxy and varies in colour from perfectly transparent pale-yellow through deep-orange to an opaque ivory. It burns at a high temperature and gives off a pleasant aroma of pine trees. It is easy to carve and has been valued since prehistoric times as a gemstone. Sometimes insects, pine needles and plant remains are found preserved in amber and such specimens are highly prized.

AMETHYST

Amethyst is a semi-precious stone that was once said to bring peace of mind to those who wore it. It is a variety of quartz which ranges in colour from pale-purple to deep-violet. Small amounts of iron are responsible for the beautiful colouring. Clusters of crystals are often found, as well as perfect single crystals. These form in cavities in volcanic rock, or in veins that cut across granite. Sometimes the rock surrounding amethyst crystals is weathered away and then they are washed into streams, where they can sometimes be found as waterworn pebbles.

Amethyst is found around Beechworth in Victoria; Stanthorpe and Haberton in Queensland; Emu River in Tasmania; the Flinders Ranges and Kangaroo Island in South Australia; and Hardey River in Western Australia.

ANABRANCH

This word (pronounced anabrank) is used only in Australia, for part of a river that branches off and links up with the main stream later on. Several of Australia's inland rivers have anabranches, such as the Condamine west of Toowoomba, the Barwon near Mungindi, and the Lachlan near Lake Cargelligo. The Great Anabranch of the Murray is about 480 km long, leaving it south of Menindee and re-entering it below Wentworth and the junction with the Darling River.

A multitude of anabranches of the Diamantina River flow into Goyder Lagoon, near the far north-eastern border between South Australia and Queensland.

ANGOPHORA

There are seven species of angophoras, and all are confined to the eastern states, chiefly Queensland and NSW, from the coast inland to around Bourke and Cunnamulla, and in the south just crossing the Victorian border into east Gippsland. All except one species have rough, scaly bark, but it is this species with smooth, orange-cream to red-brown bark and often twisted limbs which is the angophora known to most people, at least in NSW. This is the Smooth-barked Apple *Angophora costata*, and it is a common tree on sandstone ledges near Sydney, extending north into central Queensland. The rough-barked species are also commonly known as 'apple', because their twisted limbs reminded early settlers of apple trees. A common place-name in some regions is Apple Tree Flat, referring to the widespread *Angophora floribunda*, which often grows along valleys.

Angophoras belong to the EUCALYPTS in the broad sense, although they are traditionally grouped into a genus of their own. Their separate petals and sepals are what distinguishes them from the eucalypts.

ANIMAL

The word is sometimes loosely applied to fur-bearing or hairy creatures which suckle their young. But these form only a small group – properly called mammals – within the animal kingdom which includes birds, fish and insects – in fact everything from the amoebas to humans.

All life on earth is divided between the animal and plant kingdoms. Plants are basically those life forms which can manufacture their own food. Animals must get their nourishment from plants or from other animals. Consequently they need to move, either to search for things to eat or to avoid being eaten. They also need a mouth to take in their food and a digestive system to break it down so that it can be used.

More than a million different types, or species, of animals are known to exist in the world, and new ones are still being discovered. Animals can be classified according to the way they are built. There are 26 major groups called phyla. Of these groups, 25 are made up of invertebrates – animals without backbones. Insects are by far the most numerous invertebrates: there are about 800 000 species. Many of the more familiar animals belong to a sub-division of the remaining phylum and are known as vertebrates – animals with backbones. These are further subdivided into five groups: fish, amphibians, reptiles, birds and mammals.

Strict international rules govern the scientific naming of organisms so that the names may be used throughout the world, even by scientists who cannot speak each other's language. Common names cause confusion: the Australian Magpie, for example, is not related at all to the European Magpie, despite their superficially similar appearance.

For the purpose of classification, phyla are subdivided, step by step, into classes, orders, families, genera (singular: genus) and species (singular: species). In large groups there may be other levels for convenience, such as subfamilies. The Housefly *Musca domestica*, for example, is a species in the genus *Musca*, family Muscidae, Order Diptera (two-winged flies), Class Insecta, Phylum Arthropoda. Fossilised remains of prehistoric creatures have helped to establish the evolutionary chain from which the present rich variety of animal life has developed over millions of years. Many fossil animals bear a strong resemblance to living species in the same area, demonstrating the continuity of life on earth over millions of years.

Australia has a diverse and unusual collection of native animals because it has been isolated from the rest of the world by vast oceans for many millions of years.

ANIMAL BEHAVIOUR

Every animal is born with a set of instincts that fit it for survival, help it to find and attract a mate or, in the case of social animals, equip it to live among others. What may appear to the casual observer as aimless behaviour – the gliding of a bird, the fluttering of a butterfly, the gambolling of a rabbit, has a specific purpose. Behaviourists – scientists who study animal bahaviour – know that all animal activity is meaningful, and most of it is instinctive.

However, instincts can sometimes be a trap, especially if there is a change in environment. A garden spider taken to a place where there is nothing to catch will expend its energy uselessly in spinning its intricate web, because web-spinning is something it does instinctively. The animals which, as individuals and as a species, have the best chance of surviving a drastic change of environment are those which, as well as acting instinctively, are able to learn from experience.

These findings are only relatively recent. For many years the study of animal behaviour was little more than the collection of anecdotes and the attribution to animals of human emotions and desires. Ethology – the specialised study of all the kinds of innate and learned behaviour which animals use to keep alive and reproduce came of age as a science in 1973. In that year the Nobel Prize was awarded to three animal ethologists – Karl von Frisch, Konrad Lorenz and Nikko Tinbergen.

When studying particular behaviour, ethologists look for the stimulus which triggers it, but they also look for an evolutionary basis – the particular processes of natural selection that have led to its development. They try to study their subjects in their natural habitat or if not, in conditions as close to natural as possible. Their work demands many hours of patient observation, recording and measuring, although the task has now been made much easier with the introduction of slow-motion photography and electronic recording equipment such as video cameras. Some other workers in animal behaviour carry out experiments with their animals in very unnatural conditions. They may, for example, study the learning and memory retention of animals by running them in mazes, rewarding successes with food and punishing failures with mildly unpleasant electric shocks, and finding how well performance improves with constant repetition.

Some kinds of behaviour are stereotyped. Tinbergen and his colleagues worked largely with birds, particularly geese and gulls. A nesting female Greylag Goose *Anser anser* will retrieve an egg which rolls out of the nest by drawing it inwards with her beak. If the egg is gently taken away during this action the movement is completed without the egg. This stereotype action is invariable – once it starts, it has to go on to the very end. It is as though an internal program had been switched on and must be completed. It is innate or instinctive.

Ethologists call this a 'fixed action pattern'. These patterns can, however, be modified or, rather, have other actions superimposed on them. In the case of the goose, she adjusts for the egg's wobbling as it rolls by moving her beak from side to side, but if there is no egg, and therefore no wobbling, she moves her head in a straight line. But she must have some stimulus to start the egg-rolling action. Some part of the vast amount of information that is pouring into her sense organs must be the sign stimulus, as it is called. This has to be filtered out from all the other stimuli and acted upon.

The stimulus is the egg outside the nest. To be more accurate, it is the egg-like thing outside the nest because the goose will retrieve almost any smooth, rounded object – from a real egg to a large yellow balloon. Interestingly only females in a nest display this fixed action pattern.

Other kinds of behaviour are inborn. They appear fully fledged in an animal when it reaches a particular stage in its development, and often do not change with practice or age. These are the instinctive behaviours. Sometimes, however, behaviour patterns are learned, either by practice or, in higher animals such as birds and mammals, by learning from the parents or other members of the species. Instinctive behaviour appears stereotyped – programmed, as it were – although it is difficult for observers to be certain they are making an objective judgment. One clue that a piece of behaviour is instinctive is its performance in response to an inappropriate stimulus.

One example is the Greylag Goose and the experiment with the yellow balloon. Another is the response of male sticklebacks (small, spiny European freshwater fish) in the reproductive state, when they have developed a red belly. Such males will attack each other. One year, however, Tinbergen noticed a red-bellied male in his Dutch laboratory going into the attack although it was alone in its aquarium. After a few days he realised that this happened just as a red post-office van was passing the window. Subsequent experiments showed that the males would attack even crude models (such as a half-red, half-white disc with an eye painted on it) but ignore an accurate model of a male fish which lacked the red markings.

One simple form of learning is habituation. Young gulls instinctively freeze when anything flies overhead, but as they grow older they respond only to hawk-shaped birds. Even then the stimulus is relatively simple and researchers needed only to use cut-outs with the bird's shape. In one ingenious experiment the model, when 'flown' from left to right, displayed the short neck and long tail of a hawk, but when it was sent in the other direction the model had a long neck and short tail – it was goose-like. The habituated gulls froze for the first and ignored the second.

It is easy to see how these developments evolved. Birds which never froze would be picked off by hawks, thus would never reproduce, and those which continued to freeze when there was no need to would probably get less to eat and would be less likely to reproduce than those which learned not to be scared of their own shadow.

Another simple form of learning, imprinting, was made famous by Lorenz and his geese, although it was half-recognised much earlier by Pliny the Elder. The first living creature a gosling sees on hatching, provided that it is big enough but not too tall, is treated by the bird as its mother. After a female had been removed just before hatching, a clutch of goslings saw Lorenz crouching nearby, learned that he was their mother, and followed him accordingly. Here again is an example of instinctive behaviour modified by learning.

Then there is social behaviour, which involves the interaction of two or more animals of the same species, and must almost always occur at least during mating, except in animals which reproduce without mating. It should be distinguished from mere aggregation which may involve no interactions. Thousands of butterflies, for example, may settle in one sunny spot but take no notice of each other.

Social behaviour is most highly developed in the higher vertebrates and in social insects; it brings many advantages such as mutual defence from predators, division of labour (in bees), and improvement in the care of the young. The individuals of a group are, however, competing for at least some resources (such as territories, mates or food). Hence aggressive behaviour has evolved. Two males will compete for a mate, for example, or for territory. These battles rarely result in serious injury, except in humans. One will retreat or show some submissive behaviour which signals to the other that he concedes defeat – the kind of behaviour seen often in dogs. The victor does not go in for the kill because if he did the desperate loser could injure him.

In many social animals, bouts of aggressive and submissive behaviour establish a hierarchy or pecking order in which, for the time being at least, each individual recognises its place. Once established, the pecking order makes further battling over food – which would waste energy and bring the risk of injury – unnecessary. Those at the bottom, however, are at a disadvantage as they get less food and a smaller chance of mating. Consequently, as a juvenile grows stronger it will try to rise in the order.

All social behaviour depends largely, of course, on communication. This can take various forms. The posture of a submissive dog – head and rump up, forequarters on the ground, tail drooping – says quite clearly 'I submit'.

Sound is another means of communication, although it does draw the attention of potential predators, so it is often used only at certain times: during the reproductive period, as an alarm signal, or for group co-ordination among animals such as birds and monkeys which live in cover. Insects such as grasshoppers and cicadas use sound in courtship.

Movements and other visual signals are very important, and range from a deer flashing a white tail to signal danger, to the complex dance of honey bees which tells hive mates how far away a food source is, and in which direction.

Chemical communication is also very important, although since we have such a relatively poor sense of smell we have only realised recently how important the chemical senses are to other animals. The dog lives in a world of odours which tells it which other dogs have been around, whether or not they are on heat, and whether they regard a certain area as their territory. Many mammals use their faeces or secretions of various glands as boundary markers. Social insects such as ants and termites communicate largely by chemicals, and the reproductive behaviour of many animals – particularly insects – is facilitated by chemical signals. Many male moths, for example, are brought to a potential mate by her release of incredibly small quantities of complex chemicals called pheromones.

In Australia there is an active band of animal behaviourists, particularly among the bird biologists (see, for example, KOOKABURRAS). Mammalogists have been making intensive studies of marsupials, particularly the hierarchies in KAN-GAROOS and the birth behaviour of pregnant females. This research involves long hours – often during the night – making careful observations, and the subsequent analysis of the results by sophisticated statistical techniques. Animal behaviour has come a long way from those earlier collections of anecdotes.

ANT

Ants are among the most obvious of all insects, and Australia has about 1000 of the world's 10 000 species. They are found everywhere, from the lowlands to the mountains, living in their nests which are below ground, in old logs or even in living plants. Colonies may vary in size from only a few individuals to tens of thousands. They are closely related to BEES and WASPS and like them have queens (winged, later wingless), males (winged) and workers (wingless sterile females). Some species have more than one kind of worker: for example soldiers – which are large – and ordinary workers of different sizes. All female eggs have the same potential – whether they develop into queens or workers depends on the food they are given and other factors.

Most species have nuptial flights, usually on warm, humid days, which are synchronised for all the nests in a district, increasing the probability of breeding between different colonies. Too much inbreeding can reduce the vigour of a colony of ants. After mating, the males die, and surviving fertilised queens found new colonies. Some species, such as ARGENTINE ANTS rarely have nuptial flights.

Ant eggs hatch into legless grubs, totally dependent on workers for care and nourishment. They, and the pupae (misnamed 'ant eggs' by aquarium keepers), can be seen being carried to safety when a nest is disturbed.

Some species have become parasitic on other ants. A queen and her workers invade a nest, kill the host queen, and live at the expense of the host workers. Eventually a colony made up only of invaders remains. Other parasitic species – one BULL ANT *Myrmecia inquilina*, for example – have no workers and are totally dependent on their hosts. In some countries certain slave-making species go 'blackbirding' for workers from other nests.

Some ants are predators and some are vegetarians. Many collect seeds. Some species 'farm' various BUGS on foliage or roots, tending, sheltering and protecting them. In return they collect honeydew – a sweet secretion – and in the process encourage their spread. In arid areas several species store up honeydew and nectar in special swollen workers called honey-pot ants, which were prized by Aborigines.

Ants communicate largely by chemicals called pheromones. Some, for example, lay trails to and from food supplies, and others signal danger by releasing an alarm pheromone.

Among the most commonly encountered species are the large (13–14 mm) non-stinging Meat Ants *Iridomyrmex detectus*, which make the familiar gravel-capped mounds, and the small (2.5–3-mm) White-footed House Ant *Technomyrmex albipes*, which nests indoors and out.

A nest of Green Tree Ants Oecophylla smaragdina *is constructed from leaves. Adults draw the leaves together and cement them in place with silk they squeeze from their own larvae, which they carry in their jaws.*

The Yellow-footed Antechinus, common on the east coast of the mainland, is one of few small native marsupials to be commonly seen around suburban houses and gardens.

ANTECHINUS

Antechinuses – once called broad-footed marsupial mice – are small, meat-eating marsupials related to the native cats (Dasyuridae). There are nine species in the genus *Antechinus*, and one each in two separate sub-families – *Parantechinus* and *Pseudantechinus*.

Best known of the nine species is the Yellow-footed Antechinus *Antechinus flavipes* which grows to an average body length of 120 mm, with a 100-mm tail. Females are a little smaller than males. Their head is greyish, lighter around the eyes, and the rest of the body is brown with a black tip to the tail. They live in many parts of east, south-east, north-east and south-west Australia, and are sometimes seen in suburban gardens. They feed at night, mainly on insects, but also on small animals such as mice, leaving the skin behind, inside-out. They have quick, darting movements, and can run upside down beneath branches. Copulation may last 12 hours, and soon after mating the males (perhaps not surprisingly) all die. This leaves the mother and young free from his competition.

The Fat-tailed Antechinus *Pseudantechinus macdonnellensis* (body 95–105 mm, tail 75–85 mm) is found throughout the arid areas of inland Australia, where they sometimes live in termite mounds. In a good season, when insects are plentiful, the tail grows fat.

ANT-HOUSE PLANT

Ants and plants interact in many ways. Ants use plant material – seed-harvesting and leaf-cutting ants, for example – and they also benefit many plants by dispersing their seed. In some Australian plant communities a high proportion of species have seeds distributed in this way. In other cases plants rely on ants to protect them from harmful insects. One particularly interesting relationship has developed between ants and the so-called ant-house plants.

Ant-house plants are EPIPHYTES – they do not grow on the ground, but on trees or shrubs. As these epiphytes do not have roots in soil – nor do they draw nourishment from their hosts – they face particular difficulties in obtaining sufficient nutrients to survive.

To overcome this problem the plants have chambers which contain ant nests. The ants deposit organic matter in some of the chambers, and it seems that as this material breaks down any nitrogen and phosphorus released is absorbed by the plant.

There are over 150 species of ant-house plants found in the tropics, but relatively few live in Australia. Those that do are restricted to northeast Queensland – north of Townsville – but they do not live in rainforests. Most are found in *Melaleuca* (paperbark) woodlands and in mangrove forests.

A labyrinth of passages and chambers within the fleshy tuber of an ant-house plant makes an ideal ant's nest and it is quickly colonised.

Ant house
Cut away

Passages

ANTHRAX

Anthrax is a potentially dangerous blood disease which can be caught through the skin from infected livestock, or from their products (one name is wool-sorter's disease). There are occasional human cases in Victoria and NSW. Dead farm animals found in a paddock should be treated with caution. The causal organism is *Bacillus anthracis*.

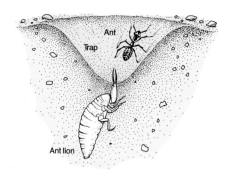

Foraging ants that venture too close to an ant lion's trap can do little to save themselves from the formidable jaws that await them at the bottom of the pit.

ANT-LION

Ant-lions are the larvae of large dragonfly-like insects – closely related to LACEWINGS – with clubbed antennae and which are often attracted to lights in summer. The larvae have sickle-shaped jaws for capturing prey. They lie almost covered with sand at the bottom of a small conical depression which they have dug, waiting for ants or other crawling insects to stumble down into their jaws. They may hasten the prey's descent by flicking sand at it. Some species have a narrow 'neck' which is almost as long as the rest of its body. In dry areas the traps may be out in the open, but in rainy districts they are often under a rock ledge or other cover. One of the commonest species is the blotch-winged *Glenoleon pulchellus* which has a wingspan of about 60 mm, and whose larvae make a pit about 30 mm in diameter.

APHID

Most of Australia's 100 or so aphids (commonly called greenflies or blackflies by gardeners) originated overseas – only a few are native. New species are still arriving.

These notorious BUGS suck sap from the leaves, stems and roots of plants. Aphid populations survive by building up numbers as quickly as possible. To do so they dispense with sex for most of the year, and produce living, young wingless females rather than eggs. While the host plant remains soft enough there are many wingless generations – producing unneeded wings wastes resources – but as the plant begins to harden some nymphs develop wings and fly away to colonise fresh plants.

In mild weather it takes a week or less for a newly born aphid to become mature and to begin reproducing herself. A typical female can produce about 120 young. Consequently a single female could have almost three million million great-great-great-grand-daughters after six weeks, weighing perhaps 800 000 tonnes if all survived. Obviously this does not happen – there would not be enough food and, in any case, many of the developing aphids are killed before they can reproduce by parasitic wasps, predatory ladybirds, haverflies, birds and diseases.

In colder parts of the world many species pass the winter as eggs, often on a different kind of plant from that used in the summer. As the days shorten and grow colder some of the females produce winged males as well as winged females. These mate, and the females lay eggs on the winter host, usually a tree. In the spring there are a few generations on the tree, then winged females begin to colonise summer hosts. In most of Australia where the weather is warm enough for aphids to reproduce throughout the year, this part of the cycle is dropped, and males may never occur.

Aphids spread many virus diseases, damage plants by sap-sucking, and excrete honeydew – a sugary liquid which encourages the growth of black sooty mould on foliage.

Popular apple varieties

Granny Smith

Delicious

Red Delicious

Golden Delicious

Jonathan

Bonza

APPLE

Apples are grown in all Australian states, with the 'Apple Isle' – Tasmania – named in their honour. Australia's main apple growing regions are in the temperate areas of Tasmania's Huon Valley, Western Australia's south-west, the areas around Orange, Bathurst and Batlow in NSW, Queensland's Granite Belt in the state's south-east, the Adelaide Hills in South Australia and in Victoria's north and south.

Around 17 million boxes (weighing 18 kg) of apples are produced annually. The harvest varies considerably each year as the crop in at least one region is usually hit by frost, drought, hail or wind damage.

Most apples are sold fresh on the domestic market, although the demand for juicing apples is growing. They are also sold for canning and cider making. South Australia and Western Australia usually sell most of their fruit for the domestic market within the state, as quarantine restrictions impede easy movement to other states. Apples have traditionally been exported to Britain and Europe but, with these markets constricting, exporters are looking to develop markets in south-east Asia, particularly Malaysia.

The apple industry has undergone major rationalisation over the last decade with many small growers being replaced by large operations. This has helped offset the high capital costs of more sophisticated technology.

Apples are still mainly harvested manually by seasonal labour, although mechanical harvesters and aids have been developed and are becoming more common. Apple trees last for between 10 and 15 years and new stock is propagated by grafting or budding. This allows varieties to be bred to suit market requirements and particular climatic conditions.

Granny Smith is perhaps the most famous Australian variety, being first cultivated by Maria Ann Smith at Earlwood, NSW, in the 1880s. The sweeter varieties, such as the Red and Golden Delicious, are becoming more popular than the tart varieties of Granny Smith and Jonathans.

ARCHER FISH

The archer fish are famous for lurking just below the water surface and shooting down insects and other animals above them with spurts of water. The fish forms a tube in its mouth, through which it squirts water droplets by pushing its tongue up against a groove in its palate. Its most remarkable feat, however, is to aim the spurt, since its eyes are below the surface, and the light rays from the prey are refracted. It has, in reverse, the same problem that humans have when trying to poke something in a pond with a stick.

There are six species, three of which occur regularly in fresh water in northern Australia. The widespread Common Archer Fish *Toxotes chatareus* (see illustration p 177), which can

grow to 400 mm in length, can aim accurately at prey 1.5 m away. The Western Archer Fish *Toxotes oligolepis* (to 150 mm) is found only in the Kimberley region. The so-called Primitive Archer Fish *Toxotes lorentzi* (to 230 mm) of the South Alligator and Daly River systems is uncommon.

ARGENTINE ANT

The Argentine Ant *Iridomyrmex humilis* is a notorious pest because it forms huge, diffuse colonies from which the workers pour out to swarm throughout a building to search for food and water. Fats, proteins and sweetstuffs are all greedily gathered. The ants bite, but fortunately they do not sting.

The ant was first discovered in Buenos Aires in 1866, and reached North America – where it is now a major pest – probably in coffee cargoes. It was first reported in Australia in 1939 at Balwyn, Melbourne. It has since been found in Western Australia, NSW and Tasmania, but determined efforts are being made to prevent its permanent establishment. The ants are small (2.5 to 3 mm) light-to dark-brown with only one knob on the waist. They lay food trails in lines. When crushed they do not smell of formic acid, but have a musty odour. They can form colonies which fuse in winter, each having many queens, and they expel all other ants from the area.

If their presence is suspected it must be reported to the state Department of Agriculture, or the local council. Pharaoh's Ant *Monomorium pharaonis* is another troublesome introduced ant which often colonises hotels, flats and hospitals, particularly in the south.

ARTIFICIAL INSEMINATION

Artificial insemination, or AI, has been known of since the Middle Ages, but has only been used to improve livestock over the last 30 years. It is mainly used in Australia on dairy cattle, but also on beef cattle and, to a lesser extent, sheep and pigs. AI involves collecting semen from the male and inserting it in the female's vagina when she is in oestrous – also known as in-season or on-heat – when fertilisation is possible.

Ram semen must be used soon after its collection, although methods for preserving it longer are being developed. Bull semen, however, can be frozen. AI allows the qualities of a superior sire to be spread over a large number of females. A bull might service 100 cows a year, although it theoretically produces enough semen to service 7500 cows. Through AI a bull can service up to 2000 cows a year. AI has given cattle breeders much greater access to a small pool of superior sires. Semen is stored in straws which can be sold for as much as $20 000 if the donor is a top stud animal. AI has also enabled breeders to cross their stock with exotic overseas breeds without breaking quarantine laws.

Australia through artist's eyes

Early colonial paintings were studies of flowers, animals and places intended as scientific records. When landscapes came to be painted for art's sake, they were interpreted by men whose academic training had conditioned them to work in a certain way. They were unable to express the light, colours and lines of their new surroundings. Their attempts to portray the country often divulged their longings for the softer views of Europe, and even distaste for the untamed or what they saw as monotonous. They forced their works into borrowed moulds. Only in the 1830s was Australia depicted realistically. Conrad Martens, the first free-settler professional artist, arriving in 1835, produced numerous watercolours that were largely free of imported ideas. However, he preferred to paint scenes that were naturally and grandly romantic, such as Sydney Harbour. John Glover, on the other hand, an Englishman who emigrated to Tasmania in 1831 at the age of 64, was romantic but a realist too. He put on canvas what he saw and loved. Both he and Eugene von Guerard were affected by the quality of the Australian light. Von Guerard, an Austrian, lived in Victoria between 1853 and 1881. He felt duty-bound to be exact, without imposing ideas or ideals, or emphasising the exotic as others did at the time.

In the 1880s, as more and more inhabitants were

Many early European artists, like the convict Joseph Lycett who painted this view of the Nepean River west of Sydney in the early 1820s, had trouble coming to terms with the Australian landscape. Vegetation in particular retained distinctly European shapes and colours.

Charles Condor's painting Under a Southern Sun, *executed in 1890, brilliantly captures the light and colour of the bush.*

Australian-born, the search for a national identity gained momentum. The Heidelberg painters, led by Tom Roberts, were influenced by French Impressionism and its preoccupation with the atmosphere that surrounded a subject. Australian Impressionists, still feeling the urge to record the country, took a more factual approach, but they gloried in the light and colour of the landscapes. In the ardently patriotic hands of Roberts, Frederick McCubbin, Arthur Streeton and Charles Conder, the gum tree became a national symbol. Their paintings were suffused with their delight in the Australian landscape with all the glare, the grey-greens of the bush, the vast shimmering expanses and the colours – not bleached by the sun, but there to be discovered.

The 1930s saw Russell Drysdale interpret the country with a new, unsentimental vigour. Since then, Australia's subtle colours and vagaries of light have been celebrated in ways impressionistic, figurative and abstract – the abstract represented notably by Fred Williams. No longer are the visions clouded with remnants of inappropriate cultures.

ASBESTOS

The word asbestos comes from the Greek meaning unquenchable. It is a fibrous mineral which has the remarkable property of being able to be woven into a cloth which will not burn. It is therefore used for fireproofing, and as an insulation against heat and electricity.

There are two common types of asbestos – white and blue. Blue asbestos (crocidolite) is found in veins in long grey-blue fibres with a silky sheen. White asbestos (chrysotile) is the main source of the mineral and it occurs in veins and seams. Good asbestos fibre is fine and pliable with a greasy feel.

Asbestos has been mined in Australia at a number of places, notably at Barraba, NSW; Marble Bar and the Hamersley Range in Western Australia and at Rockhampton in Queensland.

ATOMIC BOMB TESTS

On 3 October 1952 Britain exploded an atom bomb over the sea near the Monte Bello Islands, some 90 km from the north-west coast of Western Australia. It was followed 12 days later by an explosion at Emu in the Great Victorian Desert, about 250 km west of Coober Pedy. After another 12 days, another bomb was exploded at Emu. Two more were exploded on land in the Monte Bello Islands in May and June 1956. Between September 1956 and October 1957, seven more bomb tests took place at different spots all roughly 35 km north of Maralinga, a village created on the edge of the Nullarbor Plain for the hundreds of scientists and servicemen.

In 1984, the South Australian government returned 75 400 sq. km of tribal lands near Maralinga to the traditional Aboriginal owners. A large section had to be excluded because of contamination. Near Maralinga itself, within the 3817 sq. km Prohibited Area, is a fenced-off area of about 225 ha. Here more than 800 tonnes of radioactive materials are interred in 21 pits, and scattered in and on the ground are an estimated 100 000 metal particles contaminated with plutonium. The debris is not from the atom bomb tests but from a series of 700 experiments held secretly between 1959–1963. Plutonium was used on 30 of them. In 1967 Britian did some cleaning up. Larger pieces of soil glazed by heat were picked up; one crater was filled in; ground around the explosion points was ploughed and covered with fresh soil. In 1979, Britian removed 11.4 tonnes of radioactive matter and about 900 g of plutonium. Concrete plinths were put up to mark the sited of all bomb explosions and some of the experiments. Material was buried in pits which were capped with concrete and fenced.

In 1985 a Royal Commission found that there was little radioactivity left on the Monte Bello Islands, the Emu site and some of the Maralinga sites. But it recommended Britian should decontaminate the area.

Taranaki atomic bomb test site near Maralinga, SA. A bomb was exploded here some time in 1956 or 1957.

AURORA AUSTRALIS

Occasionally in southern Australia streamers, curtains, flashes and beams of coloured lights are seen shimmering and dancing across the night sky. The aurora australis – or southern lights – originates in the sun. Because of its very high temperature, the sun's atmosphere constantly expands outwards, emitting vast quantities of electrically charged particles. When they reach the vicinity of the earth, most of the particles are deflected by the earth's magnetic field towards the poles. Cascading to about 100 to 10 km above the surface the particles bombard atmospheric gases such as oxygen and nitrogen. Energy is given off as light. Auroras are connected with the occurance of sunspots.

AVOCADO

The avocado is a pear-shaped, green-skinned fruit grown in tropical and sub-tropical regions from northern NSW to northern Queensland. There are also plantings in Western Australia and in the Northern Territory.

Avocados have been grown on Australia for more than 30 years, but their popularity did not become widespread until the late 1970s, when several farmers and city investors 'rediscovered' the fruit. In the past ten years production has increased eight fold to around 15 000 tonnes a year. By the early 1990s, Australia is expected to produce more than 30 000 tonnes a year.

Avocado trees take around five years to produce their first commercial crop. They are harvested during July and May, depending on the area's climate. Most of Australia's crop is consumed locally.

Most of the 11 common varieties of avocados were developed in California, although they originated in Guatemala, Mexico or the West Indies.

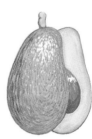

AXEMEN

Axemen are a special breed, a brotherhood linked by more than deftness at placing the axe so precisely that it can be almost impossible to tell where individual strokes have been put; or skill at sharpening a Kelly to razor keenness (Kelly is slang for the standard axe, once made by a company bearing that name but now mostly made by Hytest, a Melbourne firm); or the ability to judge in a split second how to deal with a knot suddenly revealed in the log that can gap (nick) the axe edge and make it useless. Richard Beckett in his book *Axemen, stand by your logs!* captured the special quality of the fraternity, the mateship that originated with the axemen of the cedar forests of NSW. Tough, hard-living men as they were, they knew that working alone in the gloom of the forests could cloud men's minds, so they worked in pairs.

One of the earliest recorded competitions took place in Ulverstone, Tasmania, in 1874: two men had a race to fell trees of 1.2 m in diameter. Competitions increased at local shows or sports meetings in NSW, Victoria and Tasmania, spurred by the development of the 'Tasmanian' axe made especially for Australian hardwoods. Matches were rather chaotic affairs, with dozens of competitors starting together. Once in Tasmania, 67 started but as they were scattered all over the field the judges could not decide the winner. At a competition in Latrobe, Tasmania, in 1891, the United Australasian Axemen's Association was formed. It organised the sport along today's lines, with handicapping and divisions, and an elimination system of heats, semi-finals and finals.

Competitions always include underhand and standing block events. In the underhand event, the axeman stands on his block and cuts through it with downward blows. In the standing block event, he stands beside his block and cuts a scarf (a V-shaped cut) on one side, then turns and cuts a back scarf to topple the block. In treefelling or jiggerboarding, the axeman climbs a pole by means of three steel-tipped boards which he places in notches he cuts, to reach the block nailed to the top of the pole; having cut a scarf, he descends and repeats the process on the other side, and severs the block. In butcher's block competitions, two axemen compete in pairs, cutting through a block either from opposite sides or from the same side after the initial scarf has been opened up on each side.

The hardwood used in competitions varies from state to state. It can include messmate, stringybark, jarrah, karri, white gum, turpentine. Before competitions, logs are kept in special sheds, hosed or blanketed with wet hay to prevent drying and splitting. For championships, with eight axemen competing, all logs are taken from one tree trunk. Trees tend to be denser or tougher at the base, and competitors draw lots for their logs.

Axemen buy their standard axes direct from the factory and prepare them themselves. Weight varies, but an average would be around 3 kg. Original handles are almost always replaced with one of a preferred weight and length. The secret of a good axe is in the grinding, and each man has his own secret technique. Laborious hours with a rubstone give the final razor finish to a racing axe.

Accidents are now rare but in days of harder living, competitions could be dangerous after 'lunch', with competitors teetering off their logs in underhand events. In 1923, an axemen's trousers got snagged on the chocks holding a block; he turned, swung, and cut his leg right off. He recovered. Spectators probably took longer to get over it.

This form of the sport is peculiarly Australian and New Zealand. The loggers and lumberjacks of the United States and Canada hold competitions involving softwood with lighter, shorter-handled, double-bladed axes. Axemen in Basque Spain and Finland hold endurance contests with competitors racing to cut through several sizeable logs. A world championship is held at Sydney's Royal Easter Show, but other world championship events take place in every state and in several towns in New Zealand.

Competitive woodchopping contests, like this at the Royal Easter Show in Sydney (above) originated in Tasmania among men who spent their lives cutting timber by hand (left). The record time for cutting through a standing block (as shown above) 12 in (305 mm) in diameter is 13.7 seconds. In the hard hitting contest, where a competitor must cut through the wood with the fewest number of strokes, a 12-in block has been toppled by just 19 blows.

B

BAMBOO

Bamboos are a group within the grass family, distinguished by tall, rather woody stems which, unlike the stems of other grasses, keep their green foliage for years. Australia has only three bamboo species, confined to the Northern Territory 'Top End' and the rainforests of north Queensland. In coastal Queensland and NSW a common giant bamboo up to about 20 m tall, believed to be an Indian *Bambusa* species, is often seen in dense clumps. The native *Bambusa arnhemica* grows to about 6 m high, with thin stems, and can be seen beside the Arnhem Highway on the way into Kakadu National Park.

BANANA

Bananas are grown in the sub-tropical districts of NSW, Queensland, Western Australia and the Northern Territory, although more than 90 per cent of the annual, 140 000-tonne, harvest comes from far north Queensland near Innisfail and Cairns, and the north coast of NSW. Queenslanders may be nick-named 'banana benders' but NSW is home to the 'Big Banana' – a huge artificial, banana monument at Coffs Harbour. Each plant produces one bunch of bananas a year. This is called a hand and can weigh several kilograms. The hands are often covered with dark plastic bags to speed ripening. Most of the crop is harvested between November and January. The main varieties are William's hybrid, Lady Finger and Cavendish.

Two popular varieties of bananas – Lady Fingers (top) and William's hybrid – and a typical tree in fruit. *Australian growers produce around 140 000 tonnes of fruit each year from around 8000 ha of trees. Most of the fruit comes from Queensland and northern NSW.*

BANDICOOT

There are two families of bandicoots – the true bandicoots and the BILBIES.

The name bandicoot is borrowed from a large Indian rat. Bandicoots forage for food such as earthworms and insects they dig from the ground leaving little conical holes. Their fur is harsh and pulls out easily. Although bandicoots have long snouts, some species are called short-nosed, and others long-nosed. One of the most common of the four short-nosed species is the Southern Brown Bandicoot *Isoodon obesulus* (male, body length 330 mm, tail 120 mm) which is found in scrubby areas of south-west and south-east Australia, Tasmania and Cape York. It is nocturnal and aggressively territorial.

There are five long-nosed bandicoots: four *Perameles* species and the Rufous Spiny Bandicoot *Echymipera rufescens* (300–400 mm, 75–100 mm), common in north-east Cape York, although mainly found in New Guinea.

The Long-nosed Bandicoot *P. nasuta* (310–425 mm, 120–155 mm), which ranges along the east coast, is the usual culprit when holes are found in suburban gardens. Of the others, one is confined to islands in Shark Bay, WA, one occurs in parts of Victoria, although more commonly in Tasmania, and one is believed extinct.

The last specimen of the Pig-footed Bandicoot *Chaeropus ecaudatus* (230–260 mm, 100–150 mm) was taken in 1907 near Lake Eyre.

BANKSIA

Banksias are some of the best known native plants, because of their easily recognised flowers, and from their role as the villains – the Big Bad Banksia Men – in May Gibbs' stories. The name commemorates Sir Joseph Banks, who, along with the Swedish botanist Daniel Solander, collected the first specimens when Captain Cook landed at Botany Bay in 1770. The species collected by Banks still survive today in the woodland and heath at Kurnell. Banks himself did not publish the botanical results of the *Endeavour* voyage and the plants collected were described by others.

The genus *Banksia* is restricted to the southern hemisphere and many varieties are found in both Australia and South Africa. All Banksias are woody plants, ranging from small shrubs to tall trees which can grow up to 20 m high. Most species have hard, leathery leaves and are usually found in woodland and heath, normally in well drained soils, although a few species grow in swampy, wet conditions. A feature of those habitats is the regular occurrence of fire. Many species have a fire-tolerant trunk – often with a thick gnarled, corky bark or a subterranean woody stock or LIGNOTUBER from which they re-sprout. Other species are killed by fire but regenerate from seed.

More than 70 species have now been identified, with two centres of distribution – the south-west of Australia, where nearly 60 species are found, and the east coast. In both regions some species are widely distributed while others are restricted to small areas. Only one species, *Banksia dentata*, occurs in both eastern and western Australia and it is found in open sclerophyll forest on the northern monsoonal fringe of the continent. It is also the only species found outside Australia, extending to New Guinea and the Aru Islands.

Banksias are pollinated by birds, small marsupials and some insects. Some species produce large quantities of nectar, which is why early settlers often called them honeysuckle. Only a few of the many flowers in each spike produce

Common in eastern Australia, ranging from the tip of Cape York to north of the Hawkesbury River, the Northern Brown Bandicoot Isoodon macrourus *is frequently seen at night in suburban gardens.*

The spectacular banksia blossom – this species, Banksia coccinea, *is from Western Australia – is made up of hundreds of individual flowers. Early settlers called the plants honeysuckle because of their abundant nectar.*

seed – those that do develop into woody, two-valved follicles. Every fruit contains two seeds, each of which bear a papery wing. The follicles take at least a year – and in some species two years – to mature. Follicles may open spontaneously, but in many cases they remain closed until exposed to the intense heat of a bushfire.

Several Western Australian species are exploited commercially, with large numbers of flowering stems being picked every year. A number of species are cultivated but horticultural development is in its early stages. The full commercial potential of the Banksia is yet to be realised. Most Banksias in the wild grow in soils that are low in nutrients. Fertiliser should therefore only be applied to cultivated species cautiously, otherwise it may reduce flowering and shorten the life of the plant. If fertiliser is used, it should be in a slow-release type, preferably low in phosphorus, as increased phosphorus has been shown to be toxic to a number of types. In general, Banksias are fairly free of diseases and pests.

BAOBAB

The Australian Baobab, or 'Boab' *Adansonia gregorii*, is the only member of this unique group of plants outside Africa and Madagascar. It is restricted to the Kimberley region of north-western Australia and should not be confused with the Bottle Tree of Queensland, which is only a distant relative. The Baobab can become a large, widely spreading tree of up to about 20 m high, leafless in the dry season, and its swollen trunk can reach a diameter of up to 5 m. The wood is soft and spongy and the Aborigines are said to have squeezed drinking water out of chunks cut from the trunk. The large whitish flowers appear in the wet season and are

pollinated by bats. They are followed by hard, globular brown fruits about 100 mm in diameter, within which the seeds are packed in a floury white substance which provided an Aboriginal foodstuff. One of the best known Baobabs is the Prison Tree at Derby, WA. The hollow interior of this old tree was once used as a prison.

BARBED WIRE

Before the invention of barbed wire, fences were made of stone, or were of the wooden post-and-rail type. Wire fences existed, but the cable was made of a single wire which was either round, or flat with a serrated edge, and not very strong.

The first barbed wire patents were taken out in the United States in the 1860s, but there are claims that it was developed in New Zealand at the same time. The invention did not become widespread until an Illinois farmer, Joseph Glidden, saw some barbed wire at a fair, improved on it, and in 1874 invented a practical machine for its manufacture. The advantage of barbed wire over other fencing wire is that it has two wire strands twisted together which provided extra strength and permits expansion and contraction in heat and cold without breaking. The barbs, which stop stock leaning on and breaking the fence, are about 25 mm long and are twisted around the wires at about 100-mm intervals. The tips are usually cut diagonally for greater sharpness.

Barbed wire was first produced in Australia in the 1870s by a company called Australian Wire Industries (now a part of BHP)

SPIKY BARRIERS

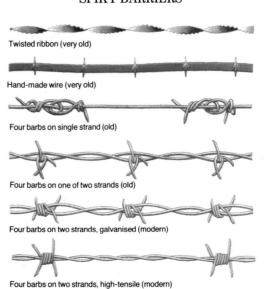

Twisted ribbon (very old)

Hand-made wire (very old)

Four barbs on single strand (old)

Four barbs on one of two strands (old)

Four barbs on two strands, galvanised (modern)

Four barbs on two strands, high-tensile (modern)

Five varieties of barbed wire, from the thousands that have been developed since the first patents were taken out in the 1860s. Barbed wire collectors in the USA even have a magazine that caters to their hobby.

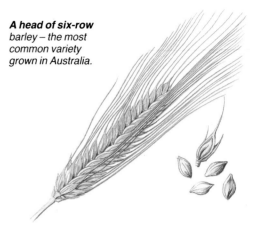

A head of six-row barley – the most common variety grown in Australia.

BARLEY

Barley is Australia's second most important grain crop after wheat. The main growing districts are in the grain areas in western, southern and eastern South Australia. The area planted with barley is steadily increasing and now exceeds 3.5 million hectares. There are two basic types – six-row and two-row – although many varieties have been bred to suit different regions and markets. The number of grain sites across the width of a full head determines whether it is a six- or two-row barley.

Six-row barley, the most common type, is used as protein in stock feeds. A small amount is also milled to provide pearled barley for human consumption, mainly used in soups and casseroles. Two-row barley is usually processed into malt for making beer and spirits. Barley is suited to lighter sandier soils than wheat. It needs a long, cool ripening period.

BARRAMUNDI

The name barramundi is Aboriginal and has been applied by Europeans to more than one kind of fish. The commercially important barramundi, however, is *Lates calcarifer* (illustration p 177), one of the giant perches. The family it belongs to contains about 20 species, ranging from Africa to Australasia. The Australian species is found from the Persian Gulf to northern Australia. This large carnivore can reach a length of 1.8 m and weigh 60 kg. It has a pointed head with a protruding lower jaw and small teeth, red eyes, a humped back and two dorsal fins – the first with seven or eight spines, and the other with one spine and several soft rays. Barramundi prefer to live in slow, permanent streams where the temperature is over 20°C. They mature in fresh water, and spawn in estuaries and shallow coastal waters. After spawning the adults return to fresh water, and older males may then change sex. They are a popular sporting fish, greatly valued on the table, and are considered a good candidate for commercial fish-farming.

BASALT

Basalt is a fine-grained, dark-grey to black rock that cooled from lava which spilled from volcanoes onto the earth's surface. It is made up mainly of the minerals plagioclase feldspar and pyroxene but, because the molten lava cooled very quickly, its crystals are generally microscopic in size.

There are large areas of basalt throughout Australia, and in western Victoria there are fresh basalts that were probaly formed at about the time when the first Aborigines came to Australia. Most basalt in Australia is found in vast, solidified flows, some over 900 m thick. Some basalt lavas develop vertical joints as they cool. In places regular hexagonal columns are formed, and at Spring Bluff in Queensland the columns are so perfectly formed that they can collapse during mining. Basalt weathers to form very rich soil. The rock is used for road metal, concrete aggregate and as a building STONE.

Hexagonal basalt columns in Victoria's Organ Pipes National Park were formed from a lava flow that filled this valley about one million years ago.

BAT

Bats are the only flying mammals, although some others can glide. They are a very successful group of animals and their order – the Chiroptera or 'finger-wings' – is second in numbers only to the rodents. There are about 1000 species of bats in the world, which means that one in seven mammal species is a bat. No one is sure of the exact number in Australia, but there are probably more than 55. Unlike the marsupials, they entered the continent from the north when it had moved near to Asia after drifting away from the ancient super-continent of Gondwanaland.

A bat's wing is a thin membrane extending from its shoulder to the base of its thumb, then to the tips of its fingers, its ankle and, finally, its tail. Bat knees, and consequently their feet, point backwards. Many bats have apparently grotesque growths on their noses called noseleafs, and on their ears called traguses. These flaps help them to direct their ultrasonic squeaks accurately, and to judge with equal accuracy the direction from which the echoes come, for many bats navigate and find prey by means of echolocation (see diagram). None is blind, however, as is sometimes commonly believed.

The FLYING FOXES or fruit bats do not use echolocation, and consequently have normal faces – often dog-like – and most have claws on their thumbs and second fingers. Their tails, if they have any, are short.

The remaining bats only have claws on their thumbs, and they eat mainly insects and other small animals. In winter, when insects are scarce, many of these small bats become torpid. Their body temperature falls to that of the surrounding air so that their metabolism – and their need for food – is reduced as much as possible. There are five families of bats in Australia: the false vampires, the horseshoe bats, sheathtail bats, mastiff bats and 'ordinary' bats.

False vampires are found in Africa, Asia and Australia, but only one species is unique to this country. The Ghost Bat *Macroderma gigas* (mean body length 115 mm, forewing 105 mm) is the largest bat, apart from the flying foxes, in the world. It has large eyes, long ears which are joined above its head, and a prominent noseleaf and tragus. Its fur is grey, lighter below. During the day it lives in caves and mineshafts in the northern half of Australia and emerges at night to capture insects and small animals, including other bats. Some are caught on the ground. It is the only Australian flesh-eating – as opposed to insect-eating – bat. Ghost bats are rare, although there are still some very large colonies.

Horseshoe bats are a group which range from Europe to Australia. They have a complex noseleaf which is horseshoe-shaped, hence their name. There are eight species in Australia. Most widespread is the Eastern Horseshoe-bat *Rhinolophus megaphyllus* (body 44 mm, tail 40 mm,

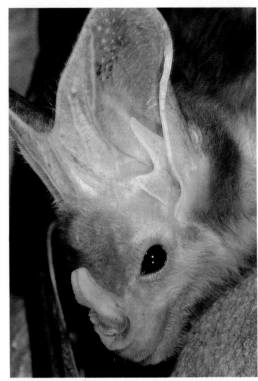

Bizarre structures on the Ghost Bat's nose and ears (above) help it to direct and receive the ultrasonic sounds it uses to navigate. Australia's only carnivorous species, Ghost Bats can take quite large prey (right) which they carry to a regular feeding site.

forearm 47 mm). This greyish-brown or orange animal roosts in warm, very humid caves from Cape York to north-eastern Victoria. It is common from place to place in the tropics. The other horseshoe-bats live in northern, tropical, parts of the continent.

The tail of a sheathtail seems to poke up through its flying membrane from below, although it is, in fact, covered by a thin extension of the membrane. The tail can be pushed backwards and forwards which may help to make the limbs more mobile, and provide some kind of flight control. The bat's face is pointed and lacks a noseleaf, although there is a tragus. Sheathtail bats have narrow wings and many fly quickly. Of the seven Australian species, the most widespread is the Common Sheathtail-bat *Taphozous georgianus* (mean body length 73 mm, tail 18 mm, forearm 64–71 mm) which is found all across Australia in tropical and subtropical areas. The animals hunt above vegetation and water, flying slowly and catching various insects, but particularly beetles. They roost in deep caves, rock fissures and the mouths of mines. In some parts of Western Australia and Queensland they are said to be found in every cave, and it has also been suggested that Europeans have

increased their distribution by providing them with abandoned mines to roost in.

Mastiff bats are so called because of their faces. They lack a noseleaf, although their ears have a tragus. They are also called free-tailed bats because their tail pokes out behind their flight membrane. They have long, narrow wings and can scuttle quickly across the ground where they sometimes capture insects. Some, however, cannot take off from the ground. Mastiff bats are found in every continent except Antarctica. There are six Australian species and four are common, at least in some parts of their range. Eastern Little Mastiff-bats *Mormopterus norfolkensis* (body 45–55 mm, tail 31–40 mm, forewing 36–38 mm) are sometimes called Norfolk Island Mastiff-bats, although they have never lived there, except in the imagination of a former curator of the British Museum. They do occur, although uncommonly, in coastal areas from southern Queensland to south of Sydney. They are woodland bats, roosting in hollow trees and under bark. White-striped Mastiff-bats *Tadarida australis* (mean body length 92 mm, tail 43 mm, forearm 61 mm), the largest Australian species, live over most of the southern two-thirds of the mainland and are common in some places. They hunt above the tree canopy and on the ground,

and roost in small colonies or alone in hollow trees, under bark or in buildings. Their upturned noses and wrinkled snouts give them an appearance which some people find ferocious.

'Ordinary' Bats are presumably called ordinary because they belong to the largest family. They are very well represented in Europe and north America, where the world's first bat experts worked. They live on all continents, except

HUNTING IN THE DARK

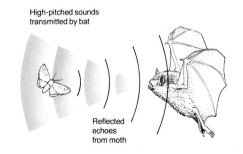

High-pitched sounds
transmitted by bat

Reflected
echoes
from moth

To find food and avoid obstacles at night a bat emits high-pitched sounds. Echoes of the sound reflects from objects, such as moths, and are picked up by the bat which locates and captures its prey in flight.

Antarctica, and extend further into cold regions than other bats because they are efficient hibernators. The family is very variable. Most do not have a noseleaf, but some long-eared bats have a small one. Their tails are relatively long with the membrane reaching, or almost reaching their tips. There are about 28 Australian species.

One of the rarest is the Golden-tipped Bat *Phoniscus papuensis* (body 50–60 mm, tail 40–50 mm, forewing 35–39) which has dark-brown fur tipped with gold. They were thought to be very probably extinct in Australia until 1981 when one was trapped at Cairns. Since then they have been found in several eastern coastal forests, even as far south as southern NSW, near the Victorian border. They probably capture insects from trees in rainforest, and can apparently hover if they need to.

There is no doubt that bent-wing bats are abundant. They are called bent-wings because the last joint of the third digit on each hand is so long that it has to be bent when the wing is folded. Tails and bodies are about the same length. The Common Bent-wing Bat *Miniopterus schreibersii* (body 52–58 mm, tail 52–58 mm, forearm 45–49 mm) is found in coastal regions of north-western Australia and the east coast from Cape York to South Australia. The animals spend much of their year at widely scattered roosts in caves, storm-water channels and buildings, but in spring the females move to warm, humid nursery caves which may be hundreds of kilometres away. There, after birth in December, there can be 3000 young bats to each square metre of ceiling, waiting for their mothers to suckle them. The colonies break up in February and March, and the young may disperse for long distances. The bats usually feed above the tree canopy in wooded valleys. The Little Bent-wing Bat *M. australis* (43–48 mm, 43–48 mm, 36–40 mm), which ranges from Cape York to northern NSW, has similar habits and often shares roosts with the common species. It catches insects below the tree canopy.

Gould's Wattled Bat *Chalinolobus gouldii* (mean lengths, 70 mm, 45 mm, 44 mm) is a common dark-coloured species found throughout Australia, except for part of the Northern Territory and Cape York. They are one of comparatively few species to be seen in Tasmania. They live in forest, mallee and urban areas, roosting in buildings, birds nests, and tractor exhaust pipes, among other places. They gather in colonies of about 30 individuals, although sometimes there may be up to 100.

The smallest Australian bat is the Timor Pipistrelle *Pipistrellus tenuis* (38–49 mm, 22–34 mm, 27–34 mm) of northern Australia. Another small species is the widespread and common Little Cave Eptesicus or Little Brown Bat *Eptesicus pumilus* (mean 46 mm, 36 mm, 33 mm) which roosts in caves and similar places.

BAUXITE

Bauxite is the chief ore of aluminium, one of the world's most useful metals because of its unique combination of lightness, strength, electrical conductivity and resistance to corrosion. Bauxite is a soft earthy rock with the colours of the Australian landscape – white, grey, yellow and red.

Bauxite is formed in tropical or subtropical areas when water dissolves some of the constituents of the surface rocks, leaving behind the aluminium. The immense bauxite deposits around Weipa and Gove on the Gulf of Carpentaria, in north-west Western Australia and in the Darling Range near Perth make Australia a major source of aluminium.

BEECH

The true beeches *Fagus* spp. are strictly northern hemisphere trees, although they are sometimes planted in Australian gardens. Their counterparts here are the Antarctic beeches *Nothofagus* spp., which are of great evolutionary interest because they are also found in New Zealand and South America, and their fossil pollen is common in Antarctica. Researchers claim that this is further evidence that all of the continents were once joined together.

BEE-EATER, RAINBOW

Rainbow Bee-eaters *Merops ornatus* (210–240 mm with long tail) are beautiful, long-billed birds with short legs. They are usually seen in groups hawking and swooping gracefully, wings vibra-

HOME FOR BEES

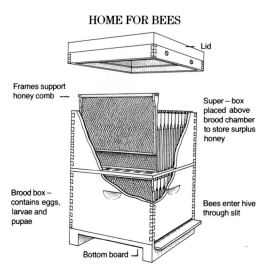

Lid

Frames support honey comb

Super – box placed above brood chamber to store surplus honey

Brood box – contains eggs, larvae and pupae

Bees enter hive through slit

Bottom board

A traditionally-designed commercial beehive provides the insects with a convenient home. The 80 000 or so workers in a large hive might accumulate as much as 200 kg of honey in a good season – only one-third of which is used for their own consumption.

ting rapidly then held rigidly out to glide as they hunt flying insects, a large proportion of which are bees and related species. The birds remove the stings by rubbing the abdomens against bark. Sometimes they roost together in hundreds.

Bee-eaters are found in most parts of mainland Australia, wherever there are flying insects. The female lays four to seven white eggs in a long tunnel in a sandy bank or slope. At other times the birds live entirely in trees. The young stay in the tunnel until they are ready to fly, their early feathers wrapped in waxy sheaths to protect them from dust.

Most Australian Bee-eaters migrate to New Guinea and further north for the winter, although some in northern Australia overwinter there. Hundreds pass across the Torres Strait, and many migrate over Western Australia.

BEEKEEPING

There are an estimated 12 000 beekeepers in Australia, of whom about 2000 are commercial. An average hive produces around 70 kg of honey and beeswax annually. Mechanical honey extractors are used to spin the honey out of the combs. Plastic hives are slowly replacing the traditional timber hives because of their durability. Many beekeepers find it necessary to move their hives around large areas to 'follow the blossom' and to keep their bees producing year-round. Roughly 40 per cent of Australian's honey is exported, mainly to West Germany, the United States, the United Kingdom and some Asian countries. The world market is dominated by China and Mexico. The domestic market is quite stable, each person on average consuming almost one kilogram of honey each year.

Australian honeybees have a worldwide reputation for quality and for being relatively disease free, and are exported to Canada and Middle-Eastern countries.

BEES

There are more than 1600 known species of bees, and many more have yet to be described by scientists. They resemble WASPS, but feed their grubs on pollen and nectar rather than on animal food. Few form the large colonies associated with the introduced honeybee *Apis mellifera*. Australian bees vary in length from a few millimetres to 20 or 30 mm, but all have hairs which are branched, visible only with a powerful microscope. Bees are supremely important pollinators of plants.

Most bees carry pollen in a patch or basket of hairs on their hind legs. They have biting mouthparts and a long tongue for probing flowers. Most bees are solitary. A female makes a nest – usually in a burrow in the soil, in a plant stem or in rotten wood – which contains sealed cells, each with an egg and a supply of pollen and honey. After laying she dies and the larvae fend for themselves. Often, however, there will be thousands of these burrows close together, made by separate females. In some species females share a small nest and a few are reproductive – there are no workers. In yet other species adult females remain in the nest for a time, caring for the developing young.

The most complex behaviour is found in the honeybee's family which contains 14 species, namely the honeybee and the small, stingless native bees *Trigona* of the northern part of the continent. These bees have queens, drones (males) and workers. The last do all the work – the foraging, tending and feeding the larvae in the cells, ventilation of the nest by wing-fanning, guard duties, and so on. Honeybee workers graduate from indoor to outdoor jobs as they age. Honeybees form new colonies when the original nest is overcrowded. The queen leaves the nest, followed by many of the colony's workers in a swarm, but first she has placed eggs in special royal cells, well supplied with royal jelly by the workers, to produce new queens. Some of these mate, and leave with their swarms. Finally an emerging queen kills all the other queens, mates, and becomes the new queen of the old colony. After mating the helpless drones are neglected and die. Meanwhile scouts from the swarm have found a new site in a hollow trunk, chimney or similar place, and the swarm

THE BEE'S STING

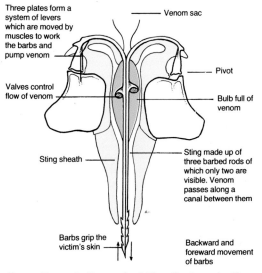

Three plates form a system of levers which are moved by muscles to work the barbs and pump venom

Venom sac

Valves control flow of venom

Pivot

Bulb full of venom

Sting sheath

Sting made up of three barbed rods of which only two are visible. Venom passes along a canal between them

Barbs grip the victim's skin

Backward and foreward movement of barbs

Bees sting only if provoked. The sting is worked by a series of articulated plates which dig the barbs into the victim and pump in venom.

How bees talk to each other

A group of worker bees are shown the direction in which they must fly in order to find a new source of food more than 100 m from the hive.

If a honeybee finds a fresh source of food, she tells her fellow workers where it is by dancing inside or outside the hive. The round dance – quick, circular movements flown first in one direction, then the other – means food is within 100 m or so. The waggle dance – a figure-of-eight with loops separated by a straight run – means the food is further away. The bee wags her body on the straight run only. If she dances upward on the comb the food is in the direction of the sun. Upward wagging runs 30° to the right means food is 30° to the right of the sun.

A honeybee arrives to feed from a flower. Many female bees gather nectar, both to feed themselves and to carry back to the nest where it is converted into honey. Workers also gather pollen – which is brushed up and carried on hairs on their back legs – and this is also used to feed growing grubs.

and the queen have moved in. The workers use their wax to begin a new comb, and the new colony is established. This account applies to 'wild domestic' bees. Beekeepers try to control their hives and to prevent swarming.

Indeed, one of the goals of bee-breeding is the reduction of swarming. If a swarm is found a local beekeeper will gladly deal with it. To contact one, consult your local Department of Agriculture, or an apiarists' association.

The native bee *Trigona* nests in hollow trees. A new colony is formed by workers finding a new site, transporting building material there and establishing the nest in readiness for a new young queen to come across later. The old and the new colony keep in contact for some time. Unlike honeybees which store honey in cells, the native species make wax honeypots.

Among many interesting bees in Australia are the large-headed, solitary bees called megachilids which cut semicircles of leaf – often from roses – to line their cells; the colletids which line their cells with a cellophane-like material; and several parasitic or cuckoo bees which lay their eggs in the nests of other species.

Some common Australian bees

There are over 20 000 species of bees world-wide with probably as many as 3000 species in Australia alone, although many of them are yet to be scientifically described. The great majority are solitary and only very few species live in large, organised nests. Most notable are the introduced honeybee and the stingless native bee *Trigona*. The honeybee is the most commonly seen, and many native species are usually overlooked by casual observers either because they are solitary, or because they are small and inconspicuous – some are only four to five millimetres in length.

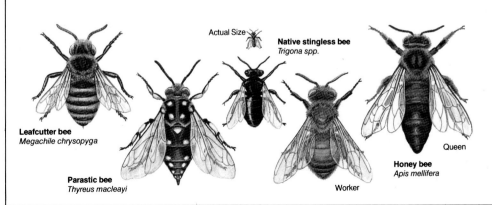

Leafcutter bee
Megachile chrysopyga

Parastic bee
Thyreus macleayi

Actual Size

Native stingless bee
Trigona spp.

Queen

Honey bee
Apis mellifera

Worker

BEETLE

Beetles are INSECTS with hard 'skins' and hard forewings – called elytra – which meet in a straight line and cover the flying wings which are folded beneath. There are about 280 000 known species of beetles in the world, far more than in any other order of animals. There are almost 20 000 known Australian species. Many lead hidden lives and rarely fly, so are consequently overlooked by casual observers. Nevertheless they are often attractively coloured, and are popular with collectors.

Beetles have biting and chewing mouthparts. In most beetles the elytra cover all – or nearly all – of the abdomen although in the coach beetles or 'staphs' they are short and most of the abdomen can be seen. The only kinds of insects which they could be confused with are the SHIELD BUGS, but these have sucking, beaked mouthparts. Almost anything edible is eaten by one kind of beetle or another, although few are parasites, either of other beetle species or of vertebrates, and then only externally. Larvae vary from legless grubs – sometimes called weevils – to active, long-legged hunters, or fat, C-shaped, short-legged grubs such as those of CHRISTMAS BEETLES. All have well-developed heads, often brown, and no false legs on the abdomen. Beetles and their larvae are found in all parts of the country, from the tidal fringe to mountain tops. Apart from two small groups, all Australian beetles fall into one of the following two major groups.

The first group contains almost all of the water and ground beetles, most of which are long-legged, active hunters of other insects, both as adults and larvae. Many have metallic colouring. They include the Bombardier Beetle *Pheropsophus verticalis* which is 10–15 mm long with a black elytra and four yellow spots. It lives under stones in damp places and squirts out a cloud of hot vapour when disturbed.

The second group contains the other beetles. The scarabs and their relatives are easily recognised by their antennae, which have plates that spread like the fingers of a hand. CHRISTMAS BEETLES and DUNG BEETLES are typical examples, as are the stag beetles which range from 10 to 50 mm in length. The jaws of male stag beetles are often very large.

The coach beetles have long bodies and very short elytra, so they look like earwigs without pincers. They are from 1 mm to about 20 mm in length. The pupae of some are parasites of certain FLIES, and others are guests in the nests of birds and social insects, where they feed on scraps and are tolerated by their hosts. Some can cause a blistering of the skin.

The tenebrionid beetles make up one of the largest families. Its members are very varied in size and shape and usually dull brown or black. They include the widely-spread flour beetles which are a few millimetres long, and the 10–15-mm-long *Tenebrio molitor* whose larvae are the meal worms fed to pet lizards.

Beetles are economically important. Some are pests, but many recycle organic matter in the soil, and others are pollinators.

ANATOMY OF A BEETLE

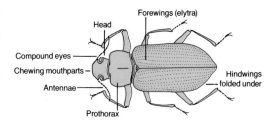

A typical beetle showing the important parts of its anatomy. Despite the extraordinary variety of shapes, colours and sizes of beetles, all have certain common features which distinguish them from other insects.

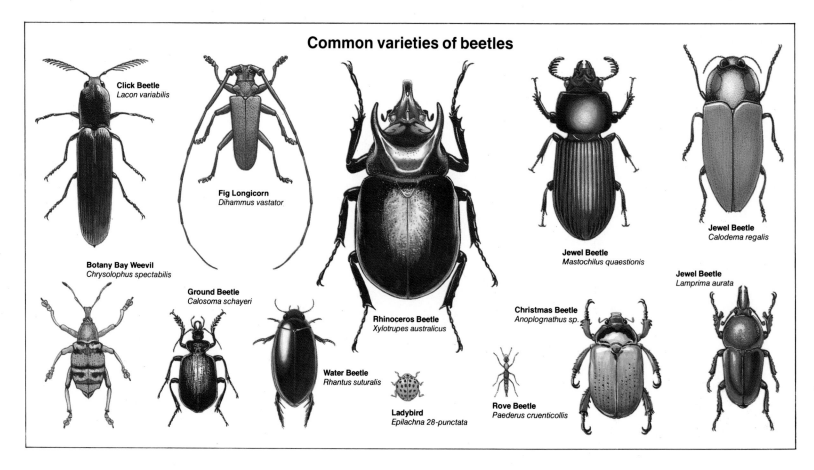

Common varieties of beetles

Click Beetle
Lacon variabilis

Fig Longicorn
Dihammus vastator

Botany Bay Weevil
Chrysolophus spectabilis

Ground Beetle
Calosoma schayeri

Rhinoceros Beetle
Xylotrupes australicus

Water Beetle
Rhantus suturalis

Ladybird
Epilachna 28-punctata

Rove Beetle
Paederus cruenticollis

Christmas Beetle
Anoplognathus sp.

Jewel Beetle
Mastochilus quaestionis

Jewel Beetle
Calodema regalis

Jewel Beetle
Lamprima aurata

BELLBIRD

The name bellbird is used for two unrelated Australian birds – the BELL MINER, a HONEYEATER, and the Crested Bellbird, *Oreoica gutturalis* (200–220 mm) one of the Australian robin or thickhead family. This bird ranges over most of mainland Australia, reaching coastal districts in the west and south, and lives in arid country and eucalyptus scrub. The male has a crest which it can raise. The birds feed on insects – especially caterpillars – and seeds. They often place injured hairy caterpillars around the rims of their nests – although the nestlings do not eat them, and nobody seems to know why they do it.

BELL MINER

The Bell Miner *Manorina melanophrys* (180–190 mm) is a yellow-beaked, olive-brown HONEY-EATER which lives in densely forested south-east Australian gullies, where it feeds in flocks on foliage insects, particularly scales and lerps (see BUGS). As they flit about the trees the birds communicate with each other by their bell-like call, each bird uttering a single note at a time. The birds apparently breed at any time of the year, and may breed more than once, but only the females brood the eggs. Bell Miner individuals will, however, feed the nestlings of their neighbours. The Noisy Miner, *M. melanocephala* (250–290 mm), also lives in colonies, but in more open woodland, in eastern Australia and Tasmania. It feeds mainly on insects.

BERRY FRUITS

Strawberries are Australia's main berry crop, followed by raspberries. Blueberries and kiwifruit – also known as Chinese gooseberries – are the newest and most rapidly expanding berry industries. Because berry growing is labour-intensive, some farmers allow customers to pick fruit themselves for lower prices.

Victoria is the country's largest strawberry producer, followed by Queensland, Tasmania, South Australia and Western Australia. Victorian strawberries are sold fresh, while some of those from other states are processed. A strawberry winery on Queensland's Sunshine Coast, turns about 60 000 kg of fresh fruit into 30 000 bottles of strawberry wine a year.

Tasmania and Victoria are the significant raspberry producers, while blueberries grow mainly in Victoria, Tasmania, south-east Queensland and along the NSW coast. Like other berry fruits they are a good export because they are out of season in northern hemisphere markets when they are being picked here.

Kiwifruit are another popular crop. Originally from China, they were renamed by aggressive New Zealand marketers who pushed the green-fleshed fruit to new popularity. A vine crop, kiwifruit are mainly grown in NSW and Victoria. There are smaller plantings in other states.

BETTONG

Bettongs are miniature nocturnal kangaroos which are as small as cats, or even smaller. They live in dry country where one, the Boodie or Burrowing Bettong *Bettongia lesueur* makes burrows, or 'renovates' those made by rabbits. It can grow to a length of 400 mm (body) plus a 300-mm tail. A hundred years ago it ranged from Western Australia to NSW, but now survives only on some islands off the Pilbara coast of Western Australia. It eats fruit, seeds, fungi and termites.

The Tasmanian Bettong *B. gaimardi* has been extinct on the mainland since about 1900, but is common on the island. It spends the day in a dense, concealed nest of grass and bark, and emerges at night to feed. The Brush-tailed Bettong or Woylie survives in a few areas of eastern and south-west Australia.

BILBY

The Bilbies form one of the two families of BANDICOOTS. They differ from true bandicoots in having long silky fur, hairy tails, long rabbit-like ears and by living in burrows. One, the Lesser Bilby or Yallara *Macrotis leucura* (male: body length 240–270 mm, tail 125–170 mm) lived in the Centre, but is probably now extinct, the last clue to its existence being a skull found in an eagle's nest in 1967. When it went into its burrow it sealed the entrance behind it, leaving only a small depression on the surface. The Greater Bilby or Dalgyte *M. lagotis* (300–350 mm, 200–290 mm), a delicate animal with a black and white crested tail, is endangered. One reason is probably the competition of rabbits for burrows, although predators, livestock and fire are all threats to it. The Dalgyte feeds at night on insects, seeds, bulbs, fruit and fungi.

The Tasmanian Bettong Bettongia gaimardi *is the only member of its family that is not endangered. These small, rarely seen, nocturnal animals feed mainly on seeds, roots, fungi and bulbs.*

Once widespread in arid areas *throughout the continent, the Greater Bilby* Macrotis lagotis *is now found only in the deserts of central Australia, although a few also live in the Kimberley region of WA.*

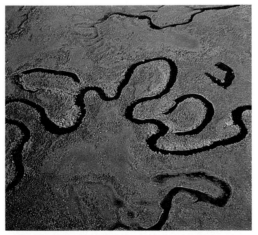

Several billabongs *flank the main course of the Serpentine River in Tasmania. Some exaggerated loops will clearly be cut off from the river at some time in the near future. The scars of many dried-up billabongs can also be seen.*

BILLABONG

Billabongs were made famous in Australia – and elsewhere – by the song *Waltzing Matilda*, in which the swagman drowns himself in a billabong rather than be captured by troopers. The name is used to describe a loop in a river that has become cut off from the main stream, and is left as a curved lagoon. Sometimes billabongs may rejoin a stream when the river floods, but often they dry up as the river moves further away. Viewed from the air, the land on either side of many Australian rivers, especially those such as the Murray which meander across flat country, is dotted with the scars of thousands of dried up billabongs. In other countries the same feature is called a mort lake or an oxbow lake.

The name is derived from two Aboriginal words: *billa* meaning 'a pool or stretch of water' and *bong* meaning 'dead'.

Billabongs are one of the traditional homes of BUNYIPS – a fact that has given rise to one theory about their origin.

BIRD

Birds evolved from reptiles, probably around 150 million years ago. Scales were replaced by feathers, except on the legs. Feathers are excellent insulators, helping to maintain a high, constant body temperature. Birds can thus be active when the cold leaves reptiles lethargic. Most birds can fly, and those that cannot, such as penguins, are descended from birds which once could. Many of their bones contain air spaces – extensions from the lungs – to lighten them. The lungs themselves and the heart, four-chambered, like that of a mammal, have evolved to assist flight which is powered by huge muscles anchored to the highly modified breast bone. The skull has been lightened, and the heavy jaws and teeth of the reptilian ancestors have been replaced by a light horny beak. At the other end the long tail with its bones has been replaced by a short stub.

A bird's digestive system consists of a gullet, a stomach and an intestine, and finishes in the cloaca – a combined digestive, excretory and sexual opening. The first, muscular, part of the stomach is the gizzard, used for grinding food. It may contain swallowed stones or grit to help with the process. Many birds have a large crop for storing food.

Feathers are the hallmark of the birds. There are six types, the most important being the contour feathers, which cover the body surface, and the flight feathers. When fully formed, feathers are dead structures. Each consists of a central shaft, the bare part of which, the hollow quill, is inserted in the skin. Further along is the solid rachis, carrying the flat webs of the vane on each side. Each web consists of hundreds of parallel barbs which, in their turn, carry barbules which criss-cross with those of other barbs. Finally some of the barbules carry microscopic hooks which engage with tiny grooves on the adjacent barbules, giving the vane its stiffness. Sometimes the hooks and grooves 'unzip' but a bird can fasten them together with its beak while preening. Down feathers, found beneath the contour feathers in many birds such as ducks, lack the hooks. They are insulating feathers. A single flight feather of a large bird can carry more than a million barbules.

The beaks of birds show how they get their living. The long curving bills of curlews are used for probing mud and sand; the stout bill of the House Sparrow makes short work of seeds, and the hooked bills of eagles and hawks deal swiftly with their prey. The wide-gaping bristly bill of the frogmouth scoops up insects, the broad long bill of the spoonbill is well suited to catching prey floating in water and the pointed bill of a honey-eater is ideal for probing flowers.

Wings also vary. Albatrosses, for example, have long, narrow glider-type wings which are ideal for soaring with scarcely a wing beat;

A pair of European Greenfinches Carduelis chloris *perform an aerial ballet.*

herons have relatively short, wide wings which makes their flight seem lazy and slow.

The 8000 to 9000 birds of the world form a Class, Aves, of the vertebrates and around 750 are found in Australia or in nearby waters. About 368 are peculiar to this continent.

A few families of birds are restricted to Australia, for example emus, lyrebirds and scrub-birds, while others, such as the honeyeaters, magpies, currawongs and the bower-birds, are almost confined to this country. Notable absentees include the woodpeckers and, apart from introduced species, the finches.

Many species of birds are territorial. Most birds defend a small space around themselves, although many will submit to the presence of their mates, or other birds during activities such as mutual grooming. Territories are extensions of this space, and there are four main types: a large breeding area where nesting, other reproductive activities and foraging take place; a large feeding area, but with most of the food found elsewhere; a small nesting area, as with colonial sea birds, ibises and galahs – in colonial birds all members of the colony help to defend the area from attacks by predators such as skuas; a generally small mating area – not used for nesting – such as the arenas and bowers of bowerbirds. The occupant of a territory defends it vigorously, usually by song and aggressive displays, against any intruders, but however aggressive it may be within its own territory, it becomes submissive if it strays into another and is challenged. This change in behaviour as a bird leaves its territory and enters another ensures that blood-letting is rare. It is obviously of no advantage to a bird, especially one with young to look after, to become damaged unnecessarily.

Some birds, particularly resident species, maintain their territories throughout the year. Many birds which doggedly defend territories during breeding leave them and may flock with others for the rest of the year. Various reasons have been put forward to explain territorial behaviour in animals, including restricting the population size to a suitable level, making pair-bonding easier, ensuring that there is enough food for the young, checking the spread of disease, and making the defence of the nest or den easier.

Mating is preceded by courtship in which one bird, almost always the male, displays by song, dance, feather-flaunting or some other means, before the other. Display stimulates the partner to receptiveness but also strengthens pair-bonding, and, because the display is usually highly specific, makes attempted mating between different species unlikely.

Birds reproduce by laying eggs – hard-shelled structures containing the embryo and enough food for development up to hatching – after which the chicks are fed by the parents. Egg

HOW A BIRD FLIES

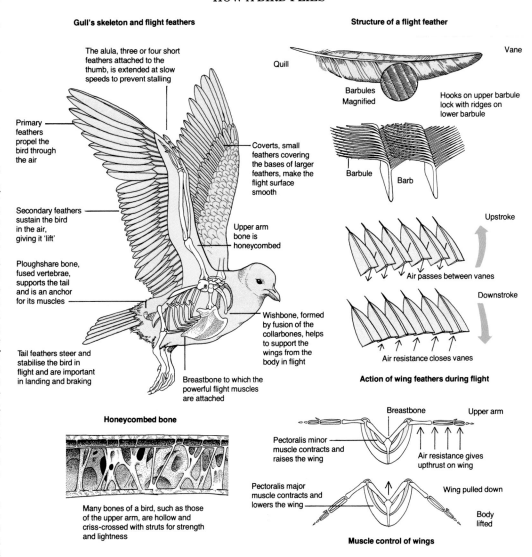

Gull's skeleton and flight feathers

The alula, three or four short feathers attached to the thumb, is extended at slow speeds to prevent stalling

Primary feathers propel the bird through the air

Secondary feathers sustain the bird in the air, giving it 'lift'

Ploughshare bone, fused vertebrae, supports the tail and is an anchor for its muscles

Tail feathers steer and stabilise the bird in flight and are important in landing and braking

Coverts, small feathers covering the bases of larger feathers, make the flight surface smooth

Upper arm bone is honeycombed

Wishbone, formed by fusion of the collarbones, helps to support the wings from the body in flight

Breastbone to which the powerful flight muscles are attached

Structure of a flight feather

Quill
Vane

Barbules Magnified

Hooks on upper barbule lock with ridges on lower barbule

Barbule
Barb

Upstroke
Air passes between vanes

Downstroke
Air resistance closes vanes

Action of wing feathers during flight

Honeycombed bone

Many bones of a bird, such as those of the upper arm, are hollow and criss-crossed with struts for strength and lightness

Breastbone
Upper arm

Pectoralis minor muscle contracts and raises the wing

Air resistance gives upthrust on wing

Pectoralis major muscle contracts and lowers the wing

Wing pulled down

Body lifted

Muscle control of wings

Birds can fly in two ways, either by gliding or soaring when the wings are outspread and used as aerofoils, or by flapping. In the downstroke of flapping flight, the power stroke, the feathers are closed flat to meet maximum air resistance and lift the bird. The wings move downwards and forwards and the primaries are bent up at their ends. In the upstroke, a rapid recovery stroke, the wings are raised in an arc and the primaries twist open, allowing air to pass through them with as little resistance as possible.

shape and colour is characteristic of the species, but birds which nest in holes usually lay white eggs which are visible in the gloom, and eggs laid on the ground, on a few wisps of grass, are well-camouflaged. Nests vary greatly in form and materials. Many are open cups but some are hollow balls, sometimes with a funnel-like entrance. Building materials include grass, twigs, cobwebs, lichens, leaves, mud and saliva.

With most birds, incubation, care of nestlings and training is carried out by both parents, but one may perform all tasks – male only with emu

and cassowaries, and female only with bower-birds. On hatching some birds are well-feathered, have open eyes and are able to run, but most are born blind and naked. Mound-builders have unusual nests: they bury their eggs in large mounds of decaying – and therefore warm – vegetable matter. The hatchlings leave the mound and are then self-sufficient. Cuckoos, and some other, non-Australian birds including a duck, lay their eggs in the nests of other birds and are thus parasites.

Many animals make noises but bird calls are

justly famous because of their beauty and, to human ears, musicality, or because, like the curlew's or the Kookaburra's, they are evocative. Birds call or sing to communicate with members of their own species, or to threaten others, but in doing so they reveal their presence to predators. Small animals, such as birds, usually have calls with high frequencies. The sounds are produced in an organ in the throat called the syrinx, situated where the windpipe branches. It consists of muscles and membranes which vibrate as air rushes past them, producing the noise. In the perching birds the syrinx is complex, particularly in the true song birds, and can produce the patterns of pulsed sounds we call bird song. In the other orders, and in the primitive perching birds such as the lyrebirds, the syrinx is less complex, yet the lyrebird can mimic the songs of dozens of other species, while the song of the crows, advanced perching birds, is far from musical to human ears.

Birds can detect a range of frequencies similar to those heard by human beings. Ultrasound to us is, therefore, ultrasound to them – although owls, which hunt partly by sound, can hear high-pitched squeaks. Many birds can detect song

THE TOOL FOR THE JOB

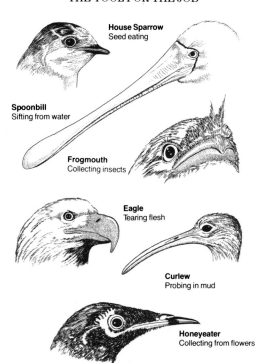

A bird's bill is a feeding tool. The extraordinary variety of shapes and sizes that can be seen attests to the great range of foods on which birds can live. Species that do not live on one type of food throughout the year have an all-purpose bill, which may be adapted perhaps to seed- eating in in summer and insect-eating at other times.

pulses separated by only one or two milliseconds (thousandths of a second). We can distinguish these as separate sounds only with the aid of complex electronic equipment. Presumably, then, a bird can pack a large amount of information into a very short song.

Songs and calls have many functions. In reproduction the male uses it to attract and court a female, to advertise what kind of bird he is and thus avoid mating with a similar but different species. He also uses it to mark the limits of, and to defend, his territory. Song may also be used to encourage the young to eat. Other functions include the coordination of flock behaviour, and the passing on of information about enemies, alarm calls, and assembly calls (for food). Birds also sing to perfect their songs, and, some people suggest, for pleasure. The last reason is doubtful because a noisy bird reveals its presence to potential enemies and, presumably, needless noisiness would be eliminated by natural selection.

The development of song is controlled by sex hormones. It has been found that female canaries can be made to sing like males by injecting them with male hormones – therefore making them more marketable – but they lose their powers quickly. The learning of a song is complex, and varies from species to species. Many experiments have been carried out in which birds were isolated when young so that they could not learn by imitation. Some species produced more or less perfect songs, while others developed a primitive version which could be improved by exposing them to normal birds, as long as they were not too old. Many species have been found to have dialects – the song in one district is more or less uniform, but quite different from songs elsewhere. In the Kosciusko National Park, for example, three populations of the Olive Whistler *Pachycephala olivacea* live in three river basins, isolated from each other by high mountains and each has a distinct dialect.

In the strict sense bird migration means the shift in the mass of the population from a breeding area to an overwintering area, followed by a return. It differs from nomadism in which birds move from one area to another more irregularly, in an opportunistic fashion – moving to places where rain has recently fallen, for example, or where gum trees have come into bloom. Many of Australia's birds are nomadic because of the continent's dry and erratic climate. Migration also differs from dispersion in which birds, generally the new generation, leave the area of the parents' territory in which they were raised, to find territories of their own. The best known examples of migration are those in which the birds leave the hemisphere in which they breed to avoid the winter, with its lack of food, to go to the other hemisphere. It is most common in insect- and invertebrate-eating birds

This tiny bird's feather from Koonawarra, Vic. is one of the oldest yet found. The rocks in which it was discovered are between 125 and 110 million years old.

which nest in temperate or cold areas. The nearer the poles the species nests, the more likely, and more marked, is its migration. In the Australian summer, for example, many species of the sandpiper family arrive from northern Asia or even Europe where they have nested. The reverse – breeding in Australia and spending the Australian winter in the northern hemisphere – is relatively uncommon. The best example is the Short-tailed Shearwater which migrates in a huge figure-of-eight to the northern Pacific. Migrations of local interest are those which take place within Australia – often a northwards movement during winter – from Australia to the islands to the north, across the Tasman Sea, and from Antarctic and subantarctic islands to Australia in the winter. Some birds may also move from highlands to the lowland during the winter. In some Australian species it seems that some individuals stay put while their fellows migrate.

The means by which birds find their way – and particularly young birds flying separately from their parents – is still the subject of intense research. Navigation by the sun and stars plays a part without doubt, and there is evidence that some birds have a magnetic sense of direction. In other countries many species follow well-defined flightways, but these are not so clear-cut in Australia. Young birds flying alone must have some inherent genetic map, but this is not yet properly understood.

BIRDS, COMMON

There are about 750 species of birds in Australia: about 125 do not breed here, 20 or so are introduced, and 368 are peculiar to this continent. There are roughly 8600 in the world. The following pages contain drawings and brief descriptions of 164 'common' species. Any list of common birds will be inconsistent for several reasons. Obviously, in a country as large as Australia a bird common in one region may be unknown in another. The most numerous bird in Australia is probably the Short-tailed Shearwater or Muttonbird, but it can be seen only along southern coasts, and spends most of the year far away at sea. Many common birds are difficult to see and may be silent, and are thus often not detected. This list includes those birds which were observed 1000 times or more in the survey carried out by the Royal Australasian Ornithologists Union and published in their *Atlas of Australian Birds*. It also includes some species which were not so frequently seen, but which could not be left out – such as the Cassowary, for example. These might be called familiar birds, although uncommon. In addition, at least one example is given from all except four of the families represented in Australia, even if none of the members of the family can be classed as common or familiar. The Paradise Riflebird is an example. The missing families are the Tropic Birds, Frigate Birds, Pittas and Bulbul.

For the record, the ten most commonly reported birds in the RAOU's survey were: the Australian Magpie (52 945 sightings); the Willie Wagtail; the Australian Magpie-lark; the Welcome Swallow; the Black-faced Cuckoo-shrike; the Galah; the White-faced Heron; the Laughing Kookaburra; the Australian Kestrel and the Common Starling (31 764).

Birds of Australia

EMUS AND CASSOWARIES
These birds are flightless. Emus are common over most of the continent, whereas Cassowaries are restricted to rainforest on Cape York Peninsula. In the same order are Ostriches, introduced to SA

Southern Cassowary
Casuarius casuarius

Emu
Dromaius novaehollandiae

GREBES
Small to medium diving birds that build floating nests in fresh to brackish water

Australasian Grebe
Tachybaptus novaehollandiae

Great-crested Grebe
Podiceps cristatus

PENGUINS
All 18 penguins are restricted to southern seas Only one, the smallest, breeds in Australia

Little Penguin
Eudyptula minor

PELICAN FAMILY
Fish-eaters with webbed feet

PELICAN Familiar large fishing birds seen throughout Australia

Australian Pelican
Pelecanus conspicillatus

CORMORANTS These fresh and saltwater birds are often seen with outstretched wings, drying their plumage

Great Cormorant
Phalacrocorax carbo

Little Pied Cormorant
Phalacrocorax melanoleucos

Little Black Cormorant
Phalacrocorax sulcirostris

DARTERS Called Snakebirds because of their long flexible necks. They frequent inland waters

Darter
Anhinga melanogaster

PETRELS Small to large migratory sea birds that usually nest in large island colonies

Short-tailed Shearwater
Puffinus tenuirostris

GANNETS AND BOOBIES Often seen at the coast diving from great heights

Australasian Gannet
Morus serrator

ALBATROSSES Large, stocky oceanic birds with long wings and gliding flight

Shy Albatross
Diomedia cauta

QUAILS, PHEASANTS AND TURKEYS

Fowl-like, scratching, ground-feeding birds with short round wings

MOUND BUILDERS Turkey-like birds which incubate their eggs in huge mounds of sand and decaying vegetable matter

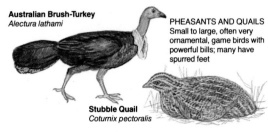

Australian Brush-Turkey
Alectura lathami

PHEASANTS AND QUAILS Small to large, often very ornamental, game birds with powerful bills; many have spurred feet

Stubble Quail
Coturnix pectoralis

BUTTON-QUAILS, RAILS, CRANES AND BUSTARDS

Ground-feeding birds with long necks and often long legs for wading

BUTTON-QUAILS Small; females larger and more colourful.

Painted Button-quail
Turnix varia

RAILS AND CRAKES Secretive; poor fliers; wetland birds, often with long toes for walking on floating vegetation

Dusky Moorhen
Gallinula tenebrosa

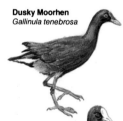

BUSTARDS Bulky, long-legged running birds of open plains

Australian Bustard
Ardeotis kori

Eurasian Coot
Fulica atra

CRANES Very large and stork-like with long legs, necks and bills. Fond of dancing

Brolga
Grus rubicundus

Purple Swamphen
Porphyrio porphyrio

JACANAS Small, tropical birds with four very long toes

Comb-crested Jacana
Irediparra gallinacea

DUCKS, GEESE AND SWANS

Aquatic fowl with long necks; excellent swimmers.

DUCKS, GEESE AND SWANS Water birds with fully webbed feet, the males usually more colourful than females

Plumed Whistling-duck
Dendrocygna eytoni

Black Swan
Cygnus atratus

Maned Duck
Chenonetta jubata

Australian Shelduck
Tadorna tadornoides

Cape Barren Goose
Cereopsis novaehollandiae

Musk Duck
Biziura lobata

MAGPIE GEESE Large, with partly webbed feet, grazers of tropical wetlands

Pacific Black Duck
Anas superciliosa

Grey Teal
Anas gibberifrons

Magpie Goose
Anseranas semipalmata

HERONS, STORKS, IBISES, SPOONBILLS

HERONS, EGRETS AND BITTERNS Long-legged wading birds with long necks and dagger-like bills; often plumed in breeding season

IBISES AND SPOONBILLS Wading birds with down-curved or spoon-like bills for probing mud

White-faced Heron
Ardea novaehollandiae

Australasian Bittern
Botaurus poiciloptilus

Sacred Ibis
Threskiornis aethiopicus

STORKS Very large birds with long necks and legs, heavy bills and partly webbed feet

Black-necked Stork
Ephippiorhynchus asiaticus

Great Egret
Ardea alba

Yellow-billed Spoonbill
Platalea flavipes

DAY-TIME BIRDS OF PREY Strongly-built with short necks, hooked bills and powerful talons

OSPREY Large fishing hawk seen around most of the coastline except in Victoria

Osprey
Pandion haliaetus

HARRIERS Large, with owl-like faces, small heads. Low, sailing flight over open country with upswept wings

Swamp Harrier
Circus approximans

EAGLES Large to very large with soaring flight and powerful legs and talons

Wedge-tailed Eagle
Aquila audax

White-bellied Sea-Eagle
Haliaeetus leucogaster

HOVERING KITES Small, usually grey and white, hovering with dangling legs. Found over most of mainland Australia

Black-shouldered Kite
Elanus notatus

SOARING KITES Medium size, hunting in pairs for rabbits and small mammals

Whistling Kite
Milvus sphenurus

FALCONS AND KESTRELS Small to medium size with pointed wings. Falcons soar then fall at great speed on flying prey, whereas kestrels hover then drop on ground prey

Peregrine Falcon
Falco peregrinus

Australian Kestrel
Falco cenchroides

Brown Falcon
Falco berigora

GOSHAWKS AND SPARROWHAWKS Medium size, powerful, agile; swift fliers

Brown Goshawk
Accipiter fasciatus

Collared Sparrowhawk
Accipiter cirrhocephalus

PLOVERS, WADERS AND GULLS Many of these birds are summer vistors which nest in the northern hemisphere and thus are seen only in their non-breeding plumage

PLAINS-WANDERER Resemble button-quails but with longer legs

Plains-wanderer
Pedionomus torquatus

OYSTERCATCHERS Conspicuous black and pied waders, common around all Australia

Pied Oystercatcher
Haematopus longirostris

PLOVERS, LAPWINGS AND DOTTERELS Small to medium-sized, with short necks and bills, common throughout Australia

Black-fronted Dotterel
Elseyornis melanops

Red-capped Plover
Charadrius ruficapillus

Masked Lapwing
Vanellus miles

THICK-KNEES AND STONE CURLERS Medium-sized running land birds, short-billed with camouflaged plumage. Active nocturnally

Bush Thick-knee
Esacus magnirostris

Painted Snipe
Rostratula benghalensis

STILTS AND AVOCETS Slim waders with long bills, upturned in avocets.

Black-winged Stilt
Himantopus himantopus

Red-necked Avocet
Recurvirostra novaehollandiae

SKUAS, GULLS, TERNS, NODDIES Mostly white or grey seabirds with long pointed wings.

Silver Gull
Larus novaehollandiae

Crested Tern
Sterna bergii

SANDPIPERS Waders of coastal mudflats.

Greenshank
Tringa nebularia

PRATINCOLES Small, dry-plain waders with forked tails and very long wings

Australian Pratincole
Stiltia isabella

Eastern Curlew
Numenius madagascariensis

DOVES AND PIGEONS
Stocky fruit- or seed-eaters with soft bills, among the fastest flying birds

CUCKOOS AND COUCALS
Insect- or fruit-eating birds with long tails. Cuckoos are tree-dwellers and are nest parasites. Coucals are ground-nesting, poor fliers, and care for their own young

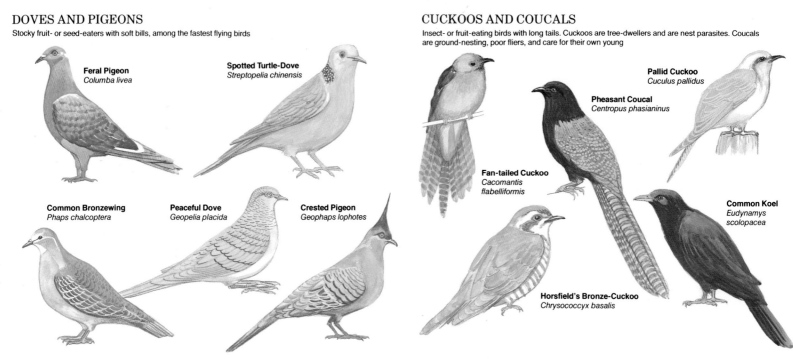

Feral Pigeon
Columba livea

Spotted Turtle-Dove
Streptopelia chinensis

Common Bronzewing
Phaps chalcoptera

Peaceful Dove
Geopelia placida

Crested Pigeon
Geophaps lophotes

Pallid Cuckoo
Cuculus pallidus

Pheasant Coucal
Centropus phasianinus

Fan-tailed Cuckoo
Cacomantis flabelliformis

Common Koel
Eudynamys scolopacea

Horsfield's Bronze-Cuckoo
Chrysococcyx basalis

PARROTS AND COCKATOOS
Noted for their brilliant colouring, they have strong hooked bills and feed mostly on fruit, seeds and nectar. Australia has the most diverse collection.

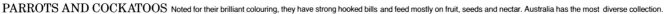

COCKATOOS Large parrots usually of one or two colours, with mobile crests

LORIKEETS Usually green, swift-flying parrots with brushy tips to their tongues for feeding on blossoms and nectar

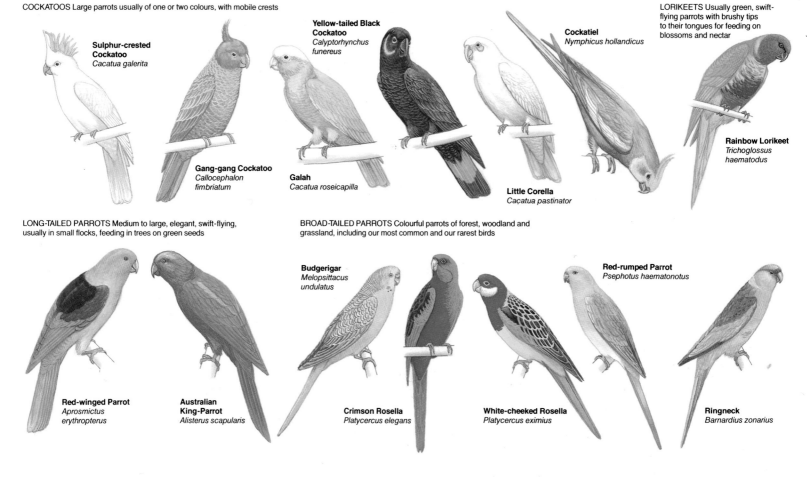

Sulphur-crested Cockatoo
Cacatua galerita

Yellow-tailed Black Cockatoo
Calyptorhynchus funereus

Cockatiel
Nymphicus hollandicus

Gang-gang Cockatoo
Callocephalon fimbriatum

Galah
Cacatua roseicapilla

Little Corella
Cacatua pastinator

Rainbow Lorikeet
Trichoglossus haematodus

LONG-TAILED PARROTS Medium to large, elegant, swift-flying, usually in small flocks, feeding in trees on green seeds

BROAD-TAILED PARROTS Colourful parrots of forest, woodland and grassland, including our most common and our rarest birds

Budgerigar
Melopsittacus undulatus

Red-rumped Parrot
Psephotus haematonotus

Red-winged Parrot
Aprosmictus erythropterus

Australian King-Parrot
Alisterus scapularis

Crimson Rosella
Platycercus elegans

White-cheeked Rosella
Platycercus eximius

Ringneck
Barnardius zonarius

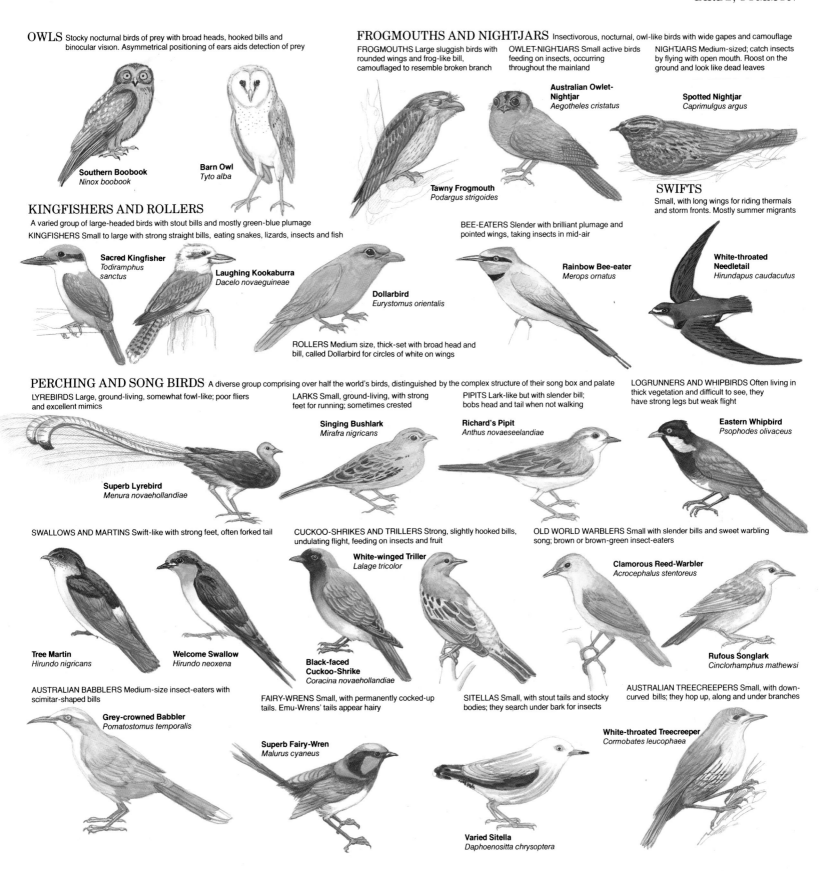

OWLS Stocky nocturnal birds of prey with broad heads, hooked bills and binocular vision. Asymmetrical positioning of ears aids detection of prey

Southern Boobook
Ninox boobook

Barn Owl
Tyto alba

KINGFISHERS AND ROLLERS

A varied group of large-headed birds with stout bills and mostly green-blue plumage
KINGFISHERS Small to large with strong straight bills, eating snakes, lizards, insects and fish

Sacred Kingfisher
Todiramphus sanctus

Laughing Kookaburra
Dacelo novaeguineae

Dollarbird
Eurystomus orientalis

ROLLERS Medium size, thick-set with broad head and bill, called Dollarbird for circles of white on wings

FROGMOUTHS AND NIGHTJARS Insectivorous, nocturnal, owl-like birds with wide gapes and camouflage

FROGMOUTHS Large sluggish birds with rounded wings and frog-like bill, camouflaged to resemble broken branch

OWLET-NIGHTJARS Small active birds feeding on insects, occurring throughout the mainland

NIGHTJARS Medium-sized; catch insects by flying with open mouth. Roost on the ground and look like dead leaves

Australian Owlet-Nightjar
Aegotheles cristatus

Spotted Nightjar
Caprimulgus argus

Tawny Frogmouth
Podargus strigoides

BEE-EATERS Slender with brilliant plumage and pointed wings, taking insects in mid-air

Rainbow Bee-eater
Merops ornatus

SWIFTS

Small, with long wings for riding thermals and storm fronts. Mostly summer migrants

White-throated Needletail
Hirundapus caudacutus

PERCHING AND SONG BIRDS

A diverse group comprising over half the world's birds, distinguished by the complex structure of their song box and palate

LYREBIRDS Large, ground-living, somewhat fowl-like; poor fliers and excellent mimics

Superb Lyrebird
Menura novaehollandiae

LARKS Small, ground-living, with strong feet for running; sometimes crested

Singing Bushlark
Mirafra nigricans

PIPITS Lark-like but with slender bill; bobs head and tail when not walking

Richard's Pipit
Anthus novaeseelandiae

LOGRUNNERS AND WHIPBIRDS Often living in thick vegetation and difficult to see, they have strong legs but weak flight

Eastern Whipbird
Psophodes olivaceus

SWALLOWS AND MARTINS Swift-like with strong feet, often forked tail

Tree Martin
Hirundo nigricans

Welcome Swallow
Hirundo neoxena

CUCKOO-SHRIKES AND TRILLERS Strong, slightly hooked bills, undulating flight, feeding on insects and fruit

White-winged Triller
Lalage tricolor

Black-faced Cuckoo-Shrike
Coracina novaehollandiae

OLD WORLD WARBLERS Small with slender bills and sweet warbling song; brown or brown-green insect-eaters

Clamorous Reed-Warbler
Acrocephalus stentoreus

Rufous Songlark
Cinclorhamphus mathewsi

AUSTRALIAN BABBLERS Medium-size insect-eaters with scimitar-shaped bills

Grey-crowned Babbler
Pomatostomus temporalis

FAIRY-WRENS Small, with permanently cocked-up tails. Emu-Wrens' tails appear hairy

Superb Fairy-Wren
Malurus cyaneus

SITELLAS Small, with stout tails and stocky bodies; they search under bark for insects

Varied Sitella
Daphoenositta chrysoptera

AUSTRALIAN TREECREEPERS Small, with down-curved bills; they hop up, along and under branches

White-throated Treecreeper
Cormobates leucophaea

OLD WORLD FLYCATCHERS Small to medium birds that now include Old World thrushes and robins; feed on small invertebrates in leaf litter

White's Thrush
Zoothera dauma

Blackbird
Turdus merulus

'THICKHEADS' This varied family includes the Australian robins, whistlers and shrike-thrushes, the monarch flycatchers and the fantails

AUSTRALIAN ROBINS Look like European robins, but the breast is not always red

Eastern Yellow Robin
Eopsaltria australis

Jacky Winter
Microeca leucophaea

FANTAILS Flycatchers which fan and close their tail feathers, and include the Willie Wagtail, one of Australia's best-known birds

Grey Fantail
Rhipidura fuliginosa

Willie Wagtail
Rhipidura leucophrys

MONARCH FLYCATCHERS Large-headed with broad bills, and bristles around the mouth; strong colour patterns; have crests which they raise if agitated

SUNBIRDS Tiny, brilliant birds which feed on insects and nectar

Yellow-bellied Sunbird
Nectarina jugularis

Restless Flycatcher
Myiagra inquieta

WHISTLERS AND SHRIKE-THRUSHES Large round heads with robust, sometimes hooked bills, and attractive songs

Crested Bellbird
Oreica gutturalis

Grey Shrike-Thrush
Colluricincla harmonica

Rufous Whistler
Pachycephala rufiventris

FLOWERPECKERS Small, fruit-eating birds, often with iridescent plumage

Mistletoebird
Dicaeum hirundinaceum

AUSTRALIAN CHATS Small, with bills and tongues like honeyeaters' but shorter

Crimson Chat
Epthianura tricolor

HONEYEATERS A large and varied family, from tiny to large, usually dull-coloured. Most have long, down-turned bills, and channelled or grooved tongues, with brush-tipped segments on the end

Eastern Spinebill
Acanthorhynchus tenuirostris

Spiny-cheeked Honeyeater
Acanthagenys rufogularis

Red Wattlebird
Anthochaera carunculata

SCRUBWRENS AND THORNBILLS Small, stout-billed eaters of insects and seeds

White-browed Scrubwren
Sericornis frontalis

Weebill
Smicronis brevirostris

Noisy Friarbird
Philemon corniculatus

New Holland Honeyeater
Phylidonyris novaehollandiae

Yellow-faced Honeyeater
Lichenostomus chrysops

Yellow-rumped Thornbill
Acanthiza chrysorrhoa

Noisy Miner
Manorina melanocephala

BUTCHERBIRDS AND CURRAWONGS Medium to large, usually pied with long hooked bills. They have attractive songs, live in small family groups, and may become tame

Australian Magpie
Gymnorhina tibicen

Pied Currawong
Strepera graculina

Pied Butcherbird
Cracticus nigrogularis

Grey Butcherbird
Cracticus torquatus

WEAVERS Stocky, brightly coloured, with stout conical bills, eating seeds and some insects

Zebra Finch
Taeniopygia guttata

Red-browed Finch
Neochmia temporalis

House Sparrow
Passer domesticus

STARLINGS Gregarious well-built birds of medium size; strong fliers eating seeds, insects and refuse

Common Starling
Sturnus vulgaris

Common Mynah
Acridotheres tristis

AUSTRALIAN MUDNESTERS Gregarious and noisy. The Chough is crow-like but with red eyes and white patches on wings in flight. Build cup-shaped nests

White-winged Chough
Corcorax melanorhamphus

Apostlebird
Struthidea cinerea

PARDALOTES Small, big headed birds which search the outer leaves of eucalypts for insects

Striated Pardalote
Pardalotus striatus

FINCHES Small introduced seed-eaters, with strong conical bills

European Goldfinch
Carduelis carduelis

DRONGOS Glossy black, tree-dwellers with forked tails and stout bills; catch insects in flight

Spangled Drongo
Dicrurus bracteatus

BIRDS OF PARADISE Rainforest tree-dwellers, rather crow-like, but the males often have metallic, iridescent plumage. They eat insects dug from rotting wood, and fruit

Paradise Riflebird
Ptiloris paradiseus

MAGPIE-LARKS Common throughout the mainland, they eat insects and snails, and are often gregarious, building nests of mud

Australian Magpie-Lark
Grallina cryanoleuca

WHITE-EYES Small greenish birds with brush-tipped tongues, feeding on nectar, insects and fruit

Silvereye
Zosterops lateralis

ORIOLES Tree-dwellers of medium size with strong bills curving slightly downwards, and stout feet for hopping

Olive-backed Oriole
Oriolus sagittatus

BOWERBIRDS Medium-sized, eating mainly fruit. The males make bowers for courtship display on the forest floor, and are more brightly coloured than the females

Satin Bowerbird
Ptilonorhynchus violaceus

WOODSWALLOWS Small and plump, with broad pointed wings; they can only hop on the ground. The flight is a mixture of flutter and glide

Dusky Woodswallow
Artamus gyanopterus

RAVENS AND CROWS Medium to large with strong bills. All being black with white eyes, they are difficult to distinguish from one another

Australian Raven
Corvus coronoides

91

BITOU BUSH

This South African shrub *Chrysanthemoides monilifera*, sometimes called Boneseed, was originally introduced into Australia as an ornamental garden plant, and later planted by some soil conservation authorities for stabilisation of coastal sand dunes. It has now become thoroughly established along large stretches of Australia's temperate coast and is a greater threat to the native vegetation than any other introduced plant. Bitou Bush is a spreading shrub which grows to a height of about 2.5 m and is easily recognised by its broad, shallowly-toothed leaves with cobwebby hairs when young, bright yellow daisy flowers and a black berry containing a hard bony seed.

BLACKBERRY

Although often regarded as one of Australia's worst weeds, blackberries are only a problem in a restricted area in the south-east of the continent, in wetter mountain and foothill areas east of Adelaide and south of Brisbane, and also in Tasmania. In Western Australia they have a very limited foothold in the far south-west. The blackberries found there belong to a group which also includes a few native Australian species known as native raspberries. The weedy blackberries are scrambling shrubs which grow to about two metres high and spread by suckering into dense masses of long, prickly canes. They bear sprays of white or pale pink flowers between November and December and the fruit ripens in about February, which is the best month for blackberry-picking.

Blackberry is now a noxious weed in most states.

BLACKSMITH

Every large station's cluster of buildings included a smithy. There horses were shod; carts and drays were made and mended; ploughshares and innumerable other pieces of equipment were fashioned and repaired; branding irons, bolts and links for harness were shaped; water tanks,

The employees at Mr Percy's blacksmith shop take time off during a busy day to pose for a photograph. In 1914, when this group assembled outside their ramshackle works in North Sydney, their skills were in enormous demand. Four years later the horse population of Australia reached its peak: one horse to every two people.

troughs and pumps were welded and riveted; even the tools used were made there. The blacksmith was often the highest paid worker below the manager.

Every town had its blacksmith's shop, a sociable place where on wet days especially there would be a knot of men swapping yarns. Teamsters would boil their billies on the forge and eat their dinners in the shop. Sometimes bullocks too were shod, or cued, with two-part shoes on their cloven hoofs. Small boys watched as the striker swung his sledgehammer to shape the glowing piece of iron on the anvil. The apprentice worked the great bellows, which were often two metres long.

Until ready-made shoes became available, blacksmiths made them from bar steel. Sid Tiedeman – a blacksmith in the Manning area in the 1910s – said a skilled worker could make four shoes in a quarter of an hour. Shoes varied in form and weight according to the horse, its work and the roads it travelled. A shoe for a carriage horse might weigh 500 g, one for a draught horse as much as 2 kg. They had to be shaped precisely to avoid straining tendons. Fitting them was also highly skilled work. Nails too close to the outside of a hoof could split it; nails too near to the sensitive part of the foot could hurt or bring on lameness. Shoeing a newly broken horse might need a wary eye and some hasty footwork.

Cars and lorries began to appear around 1910. By about 1925 many blacksmiths had had to become service station operators and smithies were turned into welding shops.

BLACK SOIL PLAINS

The black soil plains are found in sub-humid areas where the annual rainfall is between 500 mm and one metre. Black earths made up of organic matter have accumulated to a depth of about 600 mm or more and the subsoil can trap and hold considerable amounts of water. The soils are black when damp to depths below that reached by the plough and, unlike most others, can sustain their fertility, thus making them popular with wheat farmers. When dry they are brownish in colour.

There are valuable farming areas on the black soil plains, especially on the north-west slopes of

Roads that crossed the black soil plains were notorious in the days before sealed surfaces made motoring safe. Even light rain turned the surface into a greasy quagmire that ensnared many cars and horse-drawn vehicles.

the Great Dividing Range, the Liverpool Plains of NSW, and on the Darling Downs and central highlands of Queensland. Smaller areas are found in other states.

BLACK STUMP

Near Coolah, in north-western NSW, is an area the local Aborigines called 'the place where the fire went out'. By 1826 land nearby had already been named the Black Stump Run. In that year Governor Darling proclaimed the limits of the area of the colony in which land might be let or sold and in which settlement might be allowed. The Black Stump Run was named as a boundary. The run gave its name to an inn and staging post which stood 10 km north of Coolah on the Gunnedah road – a well-known landmark from 1850 until it burnt down in 1908. Thus Coolah claims to have the original Black Stump – the proverbial last outpost of civilisation. But Munduberra, west of Gayndah, also has a black stump landmark, and Johnsonville, east of Bairnsdale, and Merriwagga, between Hillston and Griffith also claim to have had the stump which was the origin of the saying.

BLOWFLY

There are about 135 FLIES in the blowfly family in Australia, but *the* blowfly is the widespread *Lucilia cuprina* (illustration p 179), a nineteenth-century introduction from South Africa or India. This metallic green fly – a little larger than a housefly – is the species which is mostly responsible for striking sheep. The female is attracted to sheep fouled with faeces or urine, or suffering from fleece rot, and lays her eggs on or near the skin in batches. The maggots scrape at the skin with their hook-like mouthparts, and enter the flesh which they soften with an enzyme that they excrete. When fully grown the larvae pupate in the soil. Severe attacks may kill the sheep. Less severe attacks reduce its condition and cause a break in the wool. Merinos, which have many folds in the skin, are particularly susceptible. Control is by the controversial MULESING – cutting the skin round the vulva so that when it heals it is stretched taut – tail-docking, and insecticidal jetting. The CSIRO is carrying out promising field trials using genetically-engineered flies with reduced fertility to control the population.

BLUE GUM

The name blue gum is one of the most notorious examples of ambiguity among the common names of native trees. In different parts of Australia it is used for at least four well known eucalypt species, none of them closely related. However, they are all medium to large, mostly smooth-barked trees, with greyish streaks in their bark. The Queensland Blue Gum *Eucalyptus tereticornis* is the eucalypt with the widest north-south distribution, occurring from east Victoria to north Queensland and also in southern New Guinea. A member of the red gum group, it is known in NSW and Victoria as Forest Red Gum. The Sydney Blue Gum *Eucalyptus saligna* is a rapid-growing tall straight tree of the wet forests of coastal NSW and southern Queensland. Its bark is a smooth bluey-grey. Tasmanian Blue Gum *Eucalyptus globulus* is the Tasmanian floral emblem. In the very wet forests of Tasmania, this is one of the largest trees, almost as tall as the giant Mountain Ash. Striking features are its semi-fibrous bark, broad, bluish juvenile leaves, and sickle-shaped adult leaves which are up to 500 mm long. The South Australian Blue Gum *Eucalyptus leucoxylon* is a common tree of south-eastern South Australia and western Victoria.

BLUE HILLS

This famous Australian radio serial by Gwen Meredith was a sequel to her earlier success – *The Lawsons* – and traced the fortunes of a number of country families. It was broadcast by the ABC four times a week from February 1949 to September 1976, for a total of 5795 episodes, and was so popular that for years it was estimated that nearly half the listening audience throughout Australia tuned in to it regularly. The success of *Blue Hills* has been attributed to the author's thorough knowledge of the details of life on the land; her invention of credible characters; an interesting, well-constructed plot based on unfolding family relationships and her use of natural dialogue. Her skills were complemented by good casting, production and acting.

Blue Hills began with the Tanimbla family of Dr Neil Gordon and his wife Lee, played by Queenie Ashton, who remained with the series throughout, later also playing Granny. It widened to include the Howards, Roberts and Mac-Arthurs. Nellie Lampart played the long-running character Hilda.

Other serials popular in the early days of radio were *Dad and Dave* which began in 1936 and ran for 15 years; *Dr Paul*, which was probably the most listened to radio serial in the world, and ran from 1949 to 1971; *When a Girl Marries* (1946–65); and *Portia Faces Life* which was broadcast in 3444 episodes from 1952 to 1970.

BLUEBUSH

Australia has around 60 species of bluebush – small perennial shrubs with blue-green fleshy leaves – which grow to about one metre high. Fruits range from showy red to drab straw-coloured. Most species are very drought resistant and may be heavily grazed by stock in bad seasons, although they are generally avoided in favour of more palatable grasses and herbs when conditions are good. Very few species have been brought into general cultivation.

BLUE-RINGED OCTOPUS

Blue-ringed octopuses are found all around the mainland and Tasmanian coasts. The more tropical species is the somewhat larger *Hapalochloena lunulata*. The southern one, *H. maculosa*, is rarely more than 200 mm from arm-tip to arm-tip, yet an adult contains enough venom to kill ten men. The venom is the saliva, injected by the animal's sharp, parrot-like beak. The octopus is reluctant to bite, but will if handled. The brilliant blue rings which flash on the darkening body when the normally brownish animals are disturbed induce some people to pick them up. More sensible animals regard the display as a warning. The octopus normally hunts by night in shallow water, but can be stranded in seashore pools.

The bite is relatively painless, but the venom causes progressive paralysis, preceded by tingling of the lips, vomiting and collapse. Victims need mouth-to-mouth resuscitation.

Vivid blue rings warn potential aggressors that this inconspicuous-looking creature can kill. Either one of two species can be found almost anywhere around the coasts of mainland Australia and Tasmania.

BLUE-TONGUED SKINK

There are ten species of blue-tongued lizards or skinks. All but one are confined to Australia, and one or more are found in all parts of the country. They are between 150 and 500 mm long with relatively short limbs, each with five fingers or toes. Many are heavily built. The tongue is usually vividly coloured and shown – with an angry hiss – in aggressive or defensive displays. However the lizards are sluggish and their bite is only superficial.

Best known is the Eastern Blue-tongued Lizard *Tiliqua scincoides* which grows to a length of about 500 mm (illustration p 236). It eats invertebrates, mice and fruit.

Bogong moths appear in the height of summer and seek cooler conditions in the Snowy Mountains, living together in vast numbers until later in the season.

BOGONG MOTH

Bogong moths are famous for aestivating – the summer-time version of hibernation – in huge numbers in caves in the Australian Alps. The MOTHS are drab, grey-brown insects with a wingspan of about 40 mm. Their caterpillars are cutworms in the plains of south-east Australia, living in the soil, and emerging at night to feed on fleshy plants, including crops. At the start of summer adults migrate to the Alps where they mass, like tiles on a roof, at densities of 14 000 or more per square metre in caves and crevices in granite tors (and nowadays in some buildings). Aborigines used to gather from many kilometres around to feast on the moths, sweeping them into nets, and roasting them quickly on hot stones. The reliability and quantity of this food made large ceremonial gatherings possible. Now the only creatures which benefit from the moths' behaviour are parasitic worms which attack them only in the caves. Bogongs are among the commonest moths that flutter around lights in Sydney on summer nights.

BORONIA

This group of about 70 decorative flowering shrubs is found right around Australia, but not in the centre. The plants seldom grow more than two metres tall and they have oily, aromatic or rank-smelling leaves and four-petalled flowers which are mostly pink, less commonly white, yellow, bluish or brownish. In some species the flowers are flattened and starlike, or they may have cupped petals. Perhaps the best known is the beautifully scented Brown Boronia *Boronia megastigma*, a native in Western Australia, but long grown in Victoria as a cut flower and for perfumery. Near Sydney *B. ledifolia* and *B. pinnata* make displays of pink blossom on the sandstone in winter and spring respectively. The rarer Native Rose *B. serrulata* has deep pink globular flowers. In the Victorian MALLEE the Blue Boronia *B. caerulescens* is common, with starry lilac-blue flowers.

BOTTLEBRUSH

Many Australian plants have flower spikes which are brush-like, including *Banksia*, *Melaleuca*, *Calothamnus*, *Beaufortia* and, at a smaller scale, many species of *Acacia*. The common name bottlebrush is, however, applied specifically to plants of the genus *Callistemon*, with its typical 'bottlebrush' flowers.

Most Callistemons are very hardy and grow easily in many different types of soils and conditions. They enjoy full sun and are amongst the most popular species of native plants for use in gardens, parks and streets.

There are about 25 species which are found in areas that range from swampy wet heath to dry rocky slopes. Callistemons are found all over Australia, although there are more species in the east, and only a few in the west.

The flowers come in a range of colours – scarlet, pink, violet, yellow, white and green, often highlighted by a dusting of pollen. The most widely grown species – and many hybrids have been developed by nurserymen in recent years – are those with scarlet flowers. The flowers of some species produce large quantities of nectar which attract honeyeaters. The crushed foliage is often fragrant.

Most species are shrubs, but a few will grow into small to medium sized trees.

BOTTLE TREE

The name is usually used to refer to the Queensland Bottle Tree *Brachychiton rupestris*, but the name is less commonly applied to some other *Brachychiton* species, or to the BAOBAB of north-western Australia. The Queensland Bottle Tree is found only in the south-east quarter of Queensland, from near Toowoomba on the south-east, north to around Mackay and inland to Roma. In natural bottle-tree scrubs, the tree's thick trunk is usually elongated – like a beer-bottle in shape – but planted trees often have a more flask-shaped trunk like a chianti bottle. Large areas of bottle-tree scrub have been cleared for cattle-grazing. Although Bottle Trees are often left standing, their seedlings do not survive in cleared paddocks.

BOULDER

Boulders are pieces of rock varying in size from about that of a tennis ball to larger than a house. They are formed by the natural processes of wind and water wearing down rocks. Some of the more spectacular boulders seen in Australia, like the Devils Marbles in the Northern Territory, are rounded tors of granite. These are formed by water which penetrates fractures in the granite until the rock starts to break up. The outer part of the granite block also gets both hotter and colder during a day than the inner part, causing layers to peel off, thus forming a rounded tor.

BOWERBIRD

The Bowerbird family is found only in Australia, New Guinea and adjacent islands. Bowerbirds are probably closely related to BIRDS OF PARADISE. Males have a special place – called an arena – in which they display to attract females, and where they often mate. The arena is usually on the ground, although some bowerbirds build an elaborate structure from plants – the bower – which they often decorate with small, brightly coloured objects.

The Satin Bowerbird *Ptilonorhynchus violaceus* (270–330 mm), for example, builds a bower consisting of an avenue of interwoven thin sticks, with a north-south alignment, and decorates them by painting them with a mixture of charcoal and saliva, which it rubs on with its beak. He further decorates the display platforms at both ends with natural and artificial brightly-coloured objects – usually blue to match his eyes. If a female approaches he flies down and displays – with a stiff gait – before her. After mating she nests some distance away. The male's song is a mixture of croaks, rattles, loud whistles and mimicry of other birds. Outside the breeding season Satin Bowerbirds gather in flocks and may raid orchards.

Male black and yellow Regent Bowerbirds

A collection of painstakingly gathered blue objects surround the bower of a Satin Bowerbird – both natural and man-made objects are collected. The rows of sticks are woven together and painted with charcoal and saliva. Bowers are always aligned north-south.

Sericulus chrysocephalus (240–280 mm) are much showier and perhaps in compensation build a less elaborate bower – an avenue of twigs, painted yellow with saliva and leaf juices, on a platform of sticks, usually hidden in a bush. They live in rainforest ranging from the Hawkesbury River, near Sydney, to south Queensland. The dull Fawn-breasted Bowerbird *Chlamydera cerviniventris* (260–290 mm) of Cape York builds an extremely elaborate bower, painted green, on a raised platform.

BRACKEN

Bracken *Pteridium esculentum* is one of the most widespread species of fern in Australia. It is very similar in appearance to the northern hemisphere old world bracken *P. aquilinum* and some botanical researchers think that there is only one widespread species. Its stems are up to 1.5 m long, brown and stiff, and carry large, deeply-divided fronds with narrow yellow-green to dark-green leathery segments.

There is good evidence that bracken has spread considerably since European colonisation. Dense growths now smother large areas of former pasture. The large accumulation of dead fronds are highly inflammable and fire, when it occurs, helps other ferns to gain a foothold, making the problem worse.

The extensive underground creeping stems of bracken are covered with rusty red hairs. They also contain starch and may have been used by Aborigines for food. However, the young fronds are poisonous and can cause cancer.

BRANDING

Farmers and graziers throughout the world have been branding livestock, mainly cattle and horses, for many centuries.

Australian graziers brand calves and young horses with a registered brand which is specific to a property or company. The mark allows identification of stock and discourages would-be thieves. On most properties, branding is carried out at the same time as castration and vaccination of calves. The branding irons are heated in a flame until red hot and are then pressed into the animal's rear upper flank or rump. It must be pressed firmly enough to prevent hair from growing again, without causing unnecessary damage or injury. The mark will then be visible on the coat or hide for the beast's lifetime. Most cattle properties have one or two well known brands. Stock are given another brand, or are cross-branded, when brought in from another property or owner. Sheep are branded with fluid, but ear tags are used for more permanent identification.

A newer method – freeze branding – is becoming popular, especially among horse owners. This involves freezing out the hairs and skin pigment with very cold brands.

Prince Alfred Bridge, which crosses the Murrumbidgee River and its river flats between Gundagai and South Gundagai, was built between 1863 and 1865, and became one of the longest bridges in NSW. The centre section is made from iron with piers that were cast at Mittagong. The bridge is no longer in use.

BRIDGE

Creeks, gullies and rivers caused early travellers in vehicles acute discomfort and delays. The smallest gully became rutted or boggy; running creeks had rough beds; rivers fordable one day raged in flood the next. Australia's abundant, straight, tall hardwood trees proved ideal for bridges and were the chief material for several decades, but the oldest surviving bridge (1825) was built of stone, at Richmond, Tas. The oldest remaining mainland bridge, over Lapstone Creek near Penrith, was finished in 1833.

Bridges fall into four groups: beam or girder, arch, suspension and cantilever. Arch bridges like the one at Richmond, and Sydney Harbour Bridge, bear their own weight and need solid foundations at each end. Truss bridges are a development of the beam and their strength derives from the combination of top and bottom members and various forms of bracing. They enabled wider spaces to be spanned after their introduction in the 1850s. One of the oldest crosses the Karuah River at Monkerai, NSW. Suspension bridges – expensive to construct – are only built where the terrain is unsuitable for piles. Of the few in Australia, a multiple-span example crosses the Fitzroy River at Rockhampton. Cantilever bridges cross wider spaces again.

In the 1860s and 1870s, the railways needed great numbers of bridges, of iron and steel, at first in combination with timber, to take the great weights. Roads across navigable waterways, particularly the Murray and Darling Rivers, required movable bridges. Several, like the first, at Bourke (1883), lifted vertically. Bascule bridges (drawbridge-like) can be seen at Menindee and Carrathool. Australia's oldest swing bridge (1883) – still operated by hand winch – crosses the Latrobe River near Sale, Vic. Iron and steel eventually gave way to reinforced, prestressed concrete.

BRIGALOW

Brigalow is the common name both for the tree *Acacia harpophylla*, and for the region west of the Great Dividing Range, stretching from northern NSW for over 1000 km northwards into central Queensland.

The tree generally averages about 15 m in height, although it can grow to 24 m in areas where the rainfall is higher. Woodland dominated by Brigalow is often very dense, and can be almost impenetrable. The densest areas were called 'scrub'.

Little of the original Brigalow scrub now stands. Techniques developed in the 1880s – using huge rollers – enabled settlers to clear vast areas for agriculture.

Around the turn of the century, PRICKLY PEAR, introduced into Australia in the late 1830s, reached plague proportions in the Brigalow. It was not until the introduction of the Cactoblastis Moth in 1925 that the scourge was finally brought under control.

BRISTLEBIRD
The three species of bristlebirds are so named because of the clumps of stout bristles at the bases of their bills, which may protect their eyes as they run through heathland, foraging for insects and berries. Habitat destruction has meant that the Western Bristlebird *Dazyornis longirostris* (180–200 mm) is now restricted to a small area near Albany, WA, although it once ranged as far as Perth. The Rufous Bristlebird *D. broadbenti* (230–270 mm) has not been seen in Western Australia since 1906, but it is still found from the Otway Ranges in Vicoria to the mouth of the Murray. The Eastern Bristlebird *D. brachypterus* is found in patches from southern Queensland to Marlo, Vic.

BROLGA
The Brolga *Grus rubicundus* is one of two cranes found in Australia. It ranges from Victoria to north Queensland, the Northern Territory and northern Western Australia, favouring open swamplands, although birds are sometimes found in the Simpson Desert. Brolgas feed on animals, seeds, tubers of sedges and sometimes on grain. In the dry season they form large, wide-ranging flocks, but they move to their swampland breeding grounds in the wet season. The Sarus Crane *G. antigone* of Cape York is very similar to the Brolga, but the red extends further down its neck. Cranes are noted for their stately dancing – solo, in pairs or in groups. Bowing and bobbing, with outstretched wings, trumpeting now and then, they advance and retreat.

BROMELIAD
The best known member of this American family is the PINEAPPLE, grown in plantations in tropical and subtropical eastern Australia, from about Coffs Harbour northward. Its fruit is really a compound fruit, formed from a spike of fruitlets which are fused together. Apart from the pineapple, many bromeliads are grown in Australia as ornamental plants. In the south enthusiasts grow them indoors or in glasshouses, but in warmer coastal climates many are used in outdoor landscaping. Most bromeliads have a rosette type of growth, and many of the EPIPHYTES have their leaf bases so tightly overlapping that they hold a reservoir of rainwater at their centres. They commonly have brilliantly coloured flowers.

BROWN SNAKE
There are six species in this group of slender-bodied, small-headed snakes, although there is great variation among them. The Eastern Brown Snake *Pseudonaja textilis* which grows to 1.5 m is the second most common cause of serious bites in Australia. It ranges from South Australia to north Queensland. Adults are uniform in colour, and range from light tan to almost black. They are active by day, and very fast if threatened, striking several times. They are found in areas ranging from arid scrub to wet forest, and eat small mammals and reptiles. All brown snakes are egg-layers. The Western Brown Snake or Gwardar *P. nuchalis* 1500 mm is not as aggressive.

The dugite *P. affinis* 1500 mm is an aggressive snake of south-western Australia and southern South Australia.

BRUCELLOSIS
Brucellosis is a disease of livestock, particularly cattle and sheep, which causes abortion. The variety in cattle – caused by the bacterium *Brucellosis abortus* – can infect people, usually through contact with the animals. It produces a debilitating, recurring illness. Acquiring the disease from milk is uncommon with cows, but more common with the types that affect sheep and goats. The disease was notorious among servicemen in Malta when it was a naval base. It has been suggested that brucellosis caused Beethoven's deafness.

BUDGERIGAR
Wild Budgerigars *Melopsittacus undulatus* (175–185 mm) are small highly-nomadic PARROTS which follow flushes of grass seeds in the interior of Australia. Their range reaches the coast in the far west. Specimens seen in non-arid areas are almost certain to have escaped from aviaries and may often be distinguished by their non-wild plumage. Flocks usually consist of less than 100 birds which roost in trees at night. They usually breed from August to January in the south, and from June to September in the north. In experimental conditions they can survive without water for months, but in the wild they drink every day if they can, immersing their heads in water. When conditions are good Budgerygahs can multiply rapidly and in some years may be the country's most abundant parrot. During courtship the male feeds the female by regurgitation. However, the female prepares the nest unaided and broods her four to six round, white eggs alone.

BUFFALO FLY
The Buffalo Fly *Haematobia irritans exigua* is a small (3.5–4-mm) blood-sucking relative of the house-FLIES which was introduced to the mainland at Port Essington in the Northern Territory in 1838. It is now widespread in most of northern Australia, attacking cattle and WATER BUFFALO. The flies push their way through the hair to the animal's skin. One bull can carry several thousand, more or less permanently. Infested cattle lose condition, and often rub sores on their hides. The larvae breed in fresh dung, and the introduction of DUNG BEETLES was directed partly against this pest. If cattle are unavailable the flies will attack people.

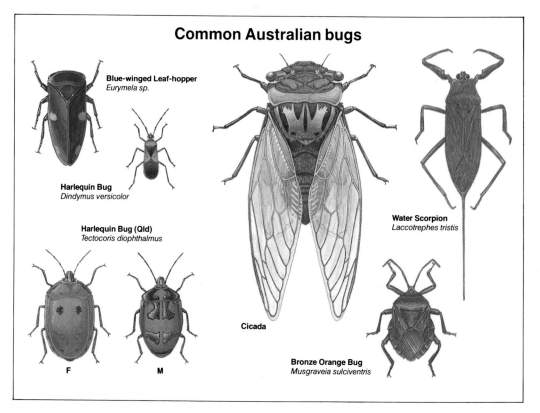

Common Australian bugs

Blue-winged Leaf-hopper
Eurymela sp.

Harlequin Bug
Dindymus versicolor

Harlequin Bug (Qld)
Tectocoris diophthalmus

F

M

Cicada

Water Scorpion
Laccotrephes tristis

Bronze Orange Bug
Musgraveia sulciventris

Setting off for town in the buggy from Yandilla station on the Darling Downs, Queensland in 1886. Buggies were the most common of all family vehicles.

BUG

Bugs are quite different to BEETLES and other insects and are distinguished by their sucking mouthparts which are drawn out into a beak. They also almost always have two pairs of wings. Among the bugs are some of the smallest and some of the largest insects and they are found in all types of country. There are two groups of bugs. The first – the Homoptera – contains many families, including such familiar ones as CICADAS, APHIDS and SCALE INSECTS. All are plant-sap suckers, and none live in water. Other examples are the mainly tropical lantern flies, which have a wingspan of 25–40 mm. These are brightly coloured insects which often have a big 'snout'. The froghoppers or spittle bugs are usually small, although one kind can grow to a length of 9 mm.

The second group – the Heteroptera – contains many families of carnivorous, plant-feeding and water-dwelling insects. Among them are the nirid or capsid bugs, a very large group of rather delicate green or brown, mostly sap-sucking insects. Some suck the blood of other insects. The lace-wing bugs are aptly named. The assassin bugs, with their strong, curved beaks, are fierce hunters of other insects. The wingless, introduced Bedbug *Cimex lectularius* belongs to this group, as do the SHIELD BUGS.

The water-living bugs include the long-legged water striders which skate and hunt on water surfaces, the predatory backswimmers which swim – to us – upside-down under water, the water boatmen and the giant 70-mm-long water-bugs or 'toe-biters'.

BUGGY AND SULKY

Horse-drawn vehicles once came in great variety. Coaches, omnibuses, open drags and hansom cabs were essentially public vehicles, to be hired or for use by fare-paying passengers. Types for family use included fairly large vehicles such as the brougham, victoria, buckboard and station wagon. More numerous, however, were the lighter one-horse vehicles known as gigs, dog-carts, sulkies and buggies. The name trap was also sometimes used for light one-horse family vehicles in general.

There were variations between the use of the names in Britain, the USA and Australia. In general, however, in Australia the gig was a very light two-wheeler, widely used by people such as doctors, who had to travel frequently on their own. The dog-cart, also a two-wheeler, had seats back and front. The sulky was a two-wheeler with a single bench seat, but it normally had a fairly large space behind for luggage, and this might have another, narrower, seat for children. Finally, there was the buggy which in Australia was a medium-sized vehicle, usually a four-wheeler, and usually also with a folding hood. Buggies and sulkies were the most common of all family vehicles.

BULBUL

The noisy Red-whiskered Bulbul *Pycnonotus jocusus* (200–220 mm) was introduced into Australia from the Orient in 1880, and is commonly seen in parks and gardens. It is firmly established around Sydney, but less securely in Melbourne. Bulbuls are rarely found deep in the bush – apart from in privet-infested gullies – preferring, like the House Sparrow, human company and some of the fruit that people grow. It also eats some insects and flower buds. Its distinctive song is likened to a staccato 'kinkajou'. The Red-vented Bulbul *P. cafer* was established in Melbourne in 1917, but has not been seen since 1942.

BULL

The beast in the mob of cattle which is the largest, heaviest, bellows the loudest and moves in the most stately, authoritative manner is generally the bull. Bulls – mature uncastrated male cattle – are used for breeding and to produce semen for ARTIFICIAL INSEMINATION. They are rarely slaughtered for meat. Bulls are capable of reproduction from about nine months of age, but are not usually used to service cows before they are 18 months old. Sometimes bulls run with a mob of cows year-round, but in more intensive operations they are usually only put with cows which are ready to mate. 'Teaser' bulls are used to find out which cows are ready to mate.

BULL ANT

Carnivorous bull (dog) and jumper ants are the most primitive of the ants. They are found only in Australia and New Caledonia, although 22-million-year-old fossils have been found in the Baltic. Bulldogs – usually red or brown and black – are about 25 mm long, and the slenderer black and yellow jumpers about 12 mm. Bulldogs make underground bushland nests which they defend aggressively, holding on with their huge mandibles while they sting painfully. Their venom is closer to that of wasps than to that of higher ants. Jumper ants make small mound nests, and attack with little leaps. The ants are widely spread in the southern half of the mainland and Tasmania. Some people suffer shock when stung, and need medical help.

Defensive bulldog ants, confronted on a bush track, will rear up as if to attack a human intruder. They can inflict a painful sting, which can be serious for some.

BULLOCK

Bullocks are mature male cattle which have been castrated. They are normally three years of age or older. They are not to be confused with steers, which are castrated when younger.

Castration – the removal of an animal's testicles – ensures that bullocks are less aggressive than bulls, and are able to mix freely with other males. Bullocks are raised for beef, mainly on extensive properties where cattle are often marketed at a later age. They are also used by intensive beef and dairy producers to identify cows which are ready to mate. A marker, known as a straddle, is attached firmly to the bullock's underside and when the bullock mounts a female, a dash of colour from the marker is left on her back.

Bullocks played a major role in the early settlement of Australia – harnessed in teams and pulling laden wagons of produce.

BULLOCK TEAM

Bullock teams played a major part in opening up the Australian continent for white settlement. The bullock driver was known as a bullocky and together with the drover and the squatter was one of those legendary, larger-than-life outback figures of early Australian devolopment, immortalised by writers such as Joseph Furphy, Henry Lawson, C.J. Dennis and Katherine Susannah Pritchard. The bullocky was depicted with long-handled whip, wearing a red shirt and moleskin trousers recounting long yarns in colourful language around a campfire, while his bullocks stole the squatter's grass.

Bullock teams were seen around Sydney within a few years of first settlement. The bullocks were originally gelded domestic cattle, but cattle were later crossed with Asian Water Buffalo and breeds were developed that had greater strength and willingness to work. They were yoked in pairs and assembled in teams of about 18, each team pulling a wagon or dray.

Bullocks provided the first means of heavy transport and carried supplies to inland towns, outback stations and the mining fields, returning to the cities with timber, minerals, wool and harvested crops. The siting of many of today's towns was determined by the needs of nineteenth-century bullock teams. Often a store or hut was placed at daily intervals along bullock tracks. Preferably it was by a creek. The track eventually grew into a road – some highways still follow the winding routes of old bullock tracks – and the store or hut into a settlement.

During the second half of the nineteenth century bullock-teams in some areas were replaced by horses and camels on longer journeys, and with the development of motorised transport in this century they have been superseded by tractors and trucks. They are still useful in particularly hilly areas.

BULRUSH

The name bulrush (also bullrush) was originally applied to a tall sedge *Schoenoplectus lacustris*, but it is now more commonly used for species of *Typha*, the reed maces. These have characteristic dense, chocolate-brown fruiting heads, which eventually break up to release numerous fluffy individual fruits.

There are three species of *Typha* in Australia which are difficult to tell apart. The Aboriginal name is cumbungi. The underground stems were used as a source of both starch and fibre to make twine. Bulrushes are usually found around swamps and shallow, slow moving water courses. They tend to occur in dense patches and sometimes need to be controlled.

Two teams of bullocks haul huge logs along a dusty country road in the late 1920s, urged on by the whips – and no doubt a few well-chosen phrases – of their drivers, the 'bullockies'. In the early days bullockies were often ex-convicts. Their stockwhips had handles 2.5 m long and plaited hide thongs that stretched for four metres or more.

This fanciful bunyip decorated a page from C. Moynihan's nineteenth century poem The Feast of the Bunya. '*From the dense scrub at midnight / Is heard a fearful noise, / The gins draw closer round the fire, / And tremble for the boys. / For well they know the bunyip, / From out the clear lagoons, / Hath come to swallow up the youths, / Now absent two full moons.*'

BUNYIP

The bunyip was an aquatic animal, greatly feared by the Aborigines as a devourer of women and children. It was said to be large and furry, but there was no agreement about its exact shape, although all agreed that it roared. Some Europeans reported sighting strange water creatures – the explorer Hamilton Hume, for example, saw an animal like a 'manatee or hippopotamus' in Lake Bathurst, NSW, in 1821, and E.S. Hall reported that it had a bulldog's head and made a noise like a porpoise. Some reports were hoaxes: a Hunter River, NSW, newspaper in 1847 recorded one which it claimed had a human face and feet turned backwards (see YOWIE).

There are several possible bases for bunyip reports. They could be seals, animals which would be rarely seen by Aborigines who lived away from the coast. Seals do sometimes stray long distances inland. The Aboriginal bunyip may be based on folk memories of some of the large marsupials which were still present when they colonised Australia, or on their bones found by later Aborigines. The roar has been attributed to booming bitterns, but one explanation accounts simultaneously for the roar, the bulky animal and the aquatic association. This claims that Aboriginal bunyip traditions are relatively modern, and may be based on the first encounters with cows, bogged and bellowing. It is also said that some bunyips proved to be musk ducks when they were shot.

BURNING OFF

Many farmers 'burn off' once a year – or use controlled fires to destroy the many tonnes of straw and weeds left over in paddocks after the harvest of cereal crops like barley, wheat and oats. Burning off is usually conducted in late summer or early autumn when the straw, or stubble, is dry. Before farmers light the stubble, they plough around the perimeter of the paddock to form a firebreak and prevent flames from jumping into other paddocks or burning fence lines. Many farmers believe a 'good burn' is the best way to destroy unwanted straw which could hamper the next season's sowing, or carry over plant diseases into another crop. However, machines are now available that allow farmers to plant directly into the stubble. On many farms, stubble can reduce soil erosion and provide stock with shelter during the winter.

BURR

This term is used for any small, non-fleshy fruit of a plant bearing hooked or barbed spines or bristles, adapted to cling to animals' fur or birds' feathers, thus spreading the seeds. Humans are generally only aware of burrs for their nuisance value – when they stick to socks, trouser-bottoms or shoelaces – or more importantly when they lower the value of the wool shorn from sheep. Burrs are found on a wide range of plants, but are more common on fleshy plants than on trees and shrubs, and in the cooler or more arid areas than in wet coastal forests. In the inland many of the plants that carry burrs tend to grow on hard, stony soils.

BUSH

The early white settlers of Australia were mainly towns people. To describe landscapes different to those of the Old Country they used country words, but with different meanings. Some words they discarded altogether: Australia has no woods, no coppices and no thickets. Bush – in England another word for shrub – first appeared in 1801 as an adjective, and in 1803 as a noun meaning out of town, unsettled or sparsely settled regions. This is its meaning today in southern Africa, Canada and in cities of Australia. To a New Zealander bush is dense forest – what the Australian colonists called brush. To country people in Australia bush is open forest, or somewhere vague.

By the end of the 19th century – with about half the population in Sydney, Melbourne and Adelaide – Australia's writers and artists, searching for a unique national identity, began to romanticise the bush and its heroic pioneers, its rural bandits, its laconic, stoic male inhabitants. The romantic myth lingers on in a country where over two-thirds of the population live in cities of 100 000 people or more.

BUSHFLY

Bushflies *Musca vetustissima* are close relatives of houseflies, and probably entered Australia with the Aborigines. The rather silvery bushflies can be recognised by two longitudinal dark marks on the tops of their bodies. There are four on the larger houseflies (illustration p 179). Bushflies become more active as the day warms up, but they become lethargic as it gets cooler again. The flies avoid deep shade, rarely coming indoors. Females need protein from sweat, tears and saliva and carbohydrates from flowers for their eggs to mature. Eggs are laid in the faeces of large animals, and the recent introductions of exotic DUNG BEETLES were directed against this pest. In colder areas bushflies die in winter.

COMMON BURRS

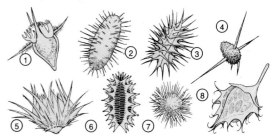

Eight of Australia's more troublesome and widespread burrs: *1 Bogan Flea* Calotis *sp.; 2 Bathurst Burr* Xanthium spinosum; *3 Burr Medic* Medicago polymorpha; *4 Galvanised Burr* Sclerolaena *sp.; 5 Spiny Burr-grass* Cenchrus *sp.; 6 Australian Carrot* Daucus glochidiatus; *7 Biddy-biddy* Acaena *sp.; 8 Native Dock* Rumex brownii.

BUSH HUMOUR

Australian bush humour might have its origins among the large numbers of Irish settlers in this country, and the supposed propensity of the Irish to delight in exaggeration. It may have developed from the loneliness of the outback, and the bushman's need to talk at length to any fellow human being that he chanced across. It might even have its roots in the strength of Australian beer, and the traveller's tendency to linger as long as possible in the shade of a bar. Whatever its background, bush humour depends for its success on the ability to tell the most improbable lie while keeping a straight face. It also depends on the co-operation of the listener who is expected to accept the story at face value, and to immediately counter it with – if possible – an even more outrageous lie.

Yarn spinning contests are still a part of many bush festivals and a true champion can go for many hours without acknowledging that there is anything in the least unusual in the stories he has just told.

Particularly successful yarns are picked up by story tellers all over the country, cherished like national treasures, polished, added to and repeated at the first opportunity. It is not unusual to find a yarn spinner in a small bush pub who has three or four carefully prepared and very funny stories which he will delight in parading at the drop of a hat for the amusement of a stranger. Sometimes he will even have an accomplice, an equally polished straight man, to feed him the necessary lines on cue.

A typical story, that is often repeated all over

'With th' fences an' other improvements, I'd say th' property's about doubled its original value.'

Eric Jolliffe, *Pix*, 1947

Australia, concerns the prodigious strength of a wharf labourer who could carry three bags of wheat – 480 awkward pounds – at a time up the gangplank of a ship.

The story relates how he would balance one bag across his massive shoulders then reach down and tuck another under each of his arms before running up the plank that separated the ship from the shore. On one occasion the plank broke under the strain, pitching the strong man into the harbour. His mates on the wharf saw him surface twice, splutter each time as if he was trying to say something and then sink again. They watched in horror as he struggled back to the surface, giving every indication that he would

sink back for the third and fatal time before he finally shouted to his watchers: 'If one of you bastards doesn't throw me a rope soon I'll have to let go of these bags!'

The funny side of bush life

Bert Bailey (left) played Dad, and Fred MacDonald, Dave, in all the Dad and Dave films of the 1930s.

The Rudd family were presented to Australia in a short story in 1895. It became the first chapter of *On Our Selection*, published in 1899. Dad, the bewhiskered, battling cocky; patient Mother; gangling, shrewd Dave; his brother and sister Joe and Sarah, and the dairymaid Fanny, starred in eight more *Selection* novels, a play, four films, and a radio series of 2276 episodes over 15 years. The Rudds' comic misadventures on their poor selection in the southern Queensland outback were chronicled with harsh vitality by Steele Rudd. His real name was Arthur Hoey Davis, himself a selector's son, eighth in a Darling Downs family of 13. *On Our Selection* had sold a quarter of a million copies by 1940. All the *Dad and Dave* films, made in the 1930s, starred Bert Bailey as Dad, and Fred MacDonald as Dave. When the radio series ended in 1951, Dad and Dave were firmly ensconced in Australian folklore.

Ken Maynard, *Australasian Post*, 1966

'By cripes, Clarrie, it looks as if this crop is goin' ter have a short life.'

A primitive bush shack at Gembrook, east of Melbourne, in 1905. Poles hold the bark roof in place and prevent the slabs from curling. The walls seem to be made from saplings, possibly with mud to fill gaps between them.

BUSH HUT

Homes in timbered country that was being cleared were made of planks 50 mm thick and up to 450 mm wide. Many ironbark slabs, almost indestructible, survive in their original buildings, or removed and recycled. Lengths of about 2.5 m were slid horizontally between battens nailed to large corner posts sunk a metre into the ground, or stood vertically on foundation blocks. Sophisticated slab huts had 20-mm wide strips of galvanised iron nailed over the cracks on the outside. The slabs shrank as the timber seasoned,

and newspaper was stuffed into the gaps to stop the worst of the wind from whistling in. Newspaper also served as lining for the walls. Before corrugated iron, bark for the roofs came from the trees that provided the slabs, or a tree still standing could be peeled – no matter that it killed the tree. The bark was flattened by being dried with the inside positioned towards a fire, then pressed under some timber. The bark strips were lashed to rafters with greenhide, and poles were laid across to stop them curling. Inside the ceiling was calico or hessian. A tattered length

of canvas, slung from a frame, formed the door.

Many early huts and houses were built in the shape of a cross. The sitting area was at the centre, protected from the heat outside, and with doors on all four sides that could be opened up to form a breezeway.

Few early dwellings incorporated kitchens because of the risk of fire. Kitchens were separate rooms, or lean-tos.

BUSHMAN
See entry p 106.

BUSH TUCKER

Damper dampened hunger, but often lay like lead in the stomach. It was the staple bush food, needing only flour and water, and baking powder if available. It could be kneaded on a piece of bark. The swaggy's mixing bowl was a (fairly) clean old flour bag that lined a hole scooped in the ground. Johnny cakes used the basic damper recipe – perhaps refined with a pinch of Eno's fruit salts – divided into palm-sized scones and cooked on the embers for a couple of minutes each side. Damper also formed the topping for bush pie – meat stew fancied up with a crust in the last minutes. Puftaloons were damper patties fried, and sinkers were balls of damper dough dropped in a stew, or boiled in sweetened water and eaten with syrup. Damper and golden syrup – cockies' joy – kept many country people alive in the Great Depression of the 1930s.

Bush food needed to satisfy tired men instantly. It was mostly heavy, monotonous and nutritionally unbalanced. Almost anything that walked, crawled or flew was tried for variation, giving rise to the legendary bush dish which had many versions: take one galah (cockatoo), pluck and cook with an ironbark slab (or boot stuffed with rocks) until slab is soft, then throw bird away and eat slab.

Meat featured large in the bush diet, often salted, using saltpetre and brine. If a pot for the curing was not available, meat could be rubbed with salt, or salt mixed with saltpetre, sugar and vinegar; then left covered from flies by day and out at night for two or three weeks. The choice was usually mutton, mutton or mutton. Cold meat could be enlivened with bush chutney – one tin dark plum jam, half a bottle Worcestershire sauce; mix well.

Drover's plum pudding was boiled rice and sweetened water, with a handful of raisins thrown in at the end. A step up the culinary ladder were brownies, needing butter, brown sugar, mixed fruit and baking powder. It was a poor shearing shed that did not serve these biscuits at smoko.

Billy tea – black because there was no milk – was usually so strong that one nickname for it was 'Jack the Painter' because of the stain it left around the drinker's mouth.

TRADITIONAL BUILDING METHODS

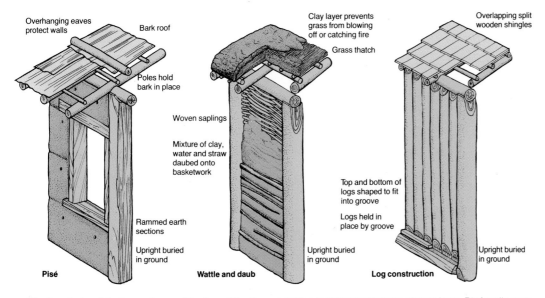

Most early bush huts used a combination of the three primitive building techniques shown here. Pisé walls were built of rammed earth; wattle and daub of woven twigs plastered with a mixture of mud and straw; and slab walls of saplings or shaped planks inserted into grooves. With slabs walls the slabs could be either vertical, as here, or horizontal. Thatched roofs were not much used, perhaps because of the risk of fire.

Common Australian bushes and shrubs

Bushes, sometimes also known as shrubs, are any woody plants that are not as tall as trees, and which do not die back to the ground each year. Australia has many thousands of native species. In some areas most of the plants are shrubs, as they are on coastal heaths, for example, or on saltbush steppes. It is only possible here to show a few examples from the major groups, some of which contain hundreds of species. The plants are listed under their botanical names, and are grouped according to their families. Common names are given where they exist.

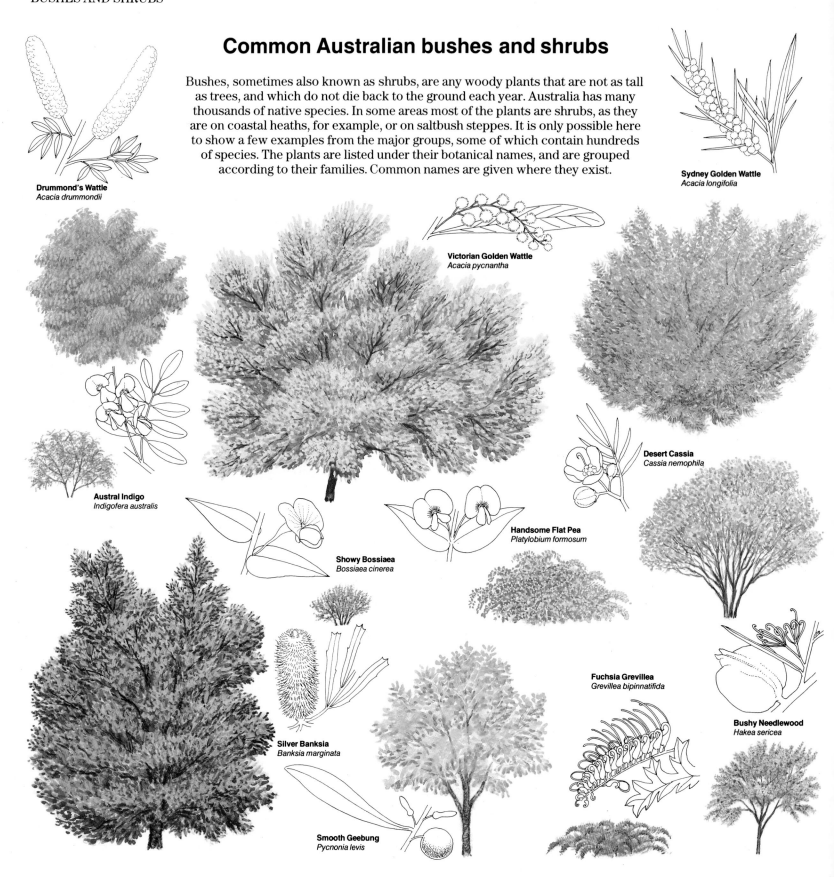

Drummond's Wattle
Acacia drummondii

Sydney Golden Wattle
Acacia longifolia

Victorian Golden Wattle
Acacia pycnantha

Austral Indigo
Indigofera australis

Desert Cassia
Cassia nemophila

Showy Bossiaea
Bossiaea cinerea

Handsome Flat Pea
Platylobium formosum

Silver Banksia
Banksia marginata

Fuchsia Grevillea
Grevillea bipinnatifida

Bushy Needlewood
Hakea sericea

Smooth Geebung
Pycnonia levis

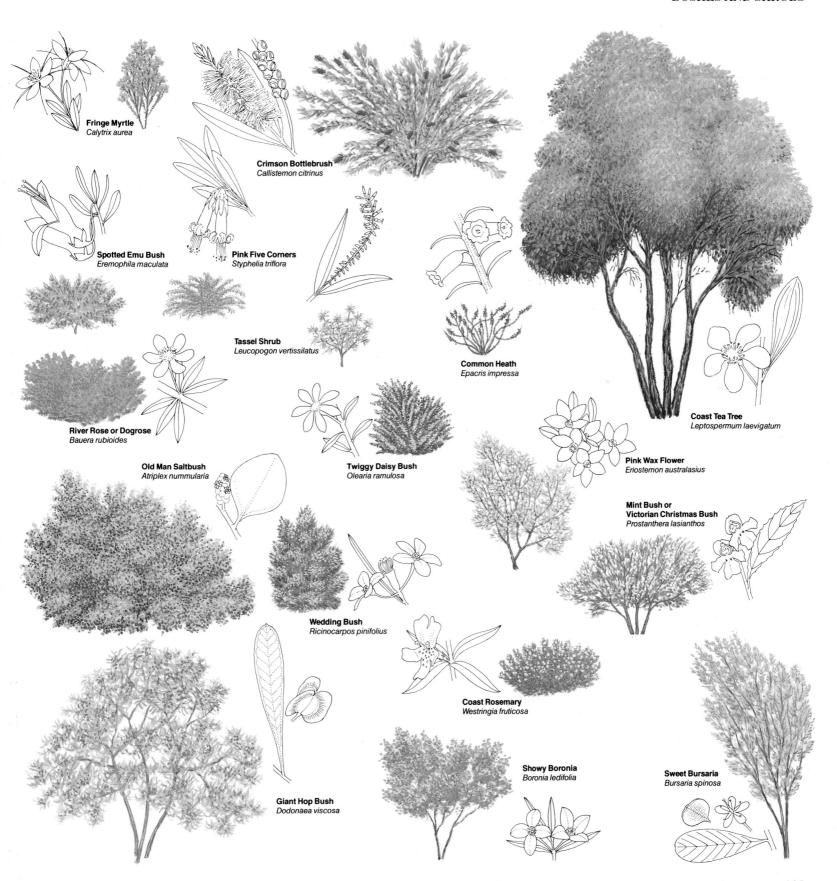

Fringe Myrtle
Calytrix aurea

Crimson Bottlebrush
Callistemon citrinus

Spotted Emu Bush
Eremophila maculata

Pink Five Corners
Styphelia triflora

Tassel Shrub
Leucopogon vertissilatus

Common Heath
Epacris impressa

Coast Tea Tree
Leptospermum laevigatum

River Rose or Dogrose
Bauera rubioides

Old Man Saltbush
Atriplex nummularia

Twiggy Daisy Bush
Olearia ramulosa

Pink Wax Flower
Eriostemon australasius

**Mint Bush or
Victorian Christmas Bush**
Prostanthera lasianthos

Wedding Bush
Ricinocarpos pinifolius

Coast Rosemary
Westringia fruticosa

Giant Hop Bush
Dodonaea viscosa

Showy Boronia
Boronia ledifolia

Sweet Bursaria
Bursaria spinosa

103

BUSHFIRE

Fires frequently sweep though many areas of Australia, but the south-eastern corner must be among the world's most fire-prone areas. There has hardly been a decade since white settlement when there has not been a major fire or series of fires in this area. There have been many human deaths, and communities are regularly threatened or even wiped out.

The reasons for this situation are not hard to find. The topography of much of the country is very rugged, so that once a fire starts it is difficult to control. Gullies between hills also make perfect chimneys for fires which can race up hillsides, burning all in their path. Long hot summers with low rainfall also provide plenty of ideal fuel, of a type that is among the most combustible in the world.

Native Australian eucalypts – or gum trees – contain high concentrations of oils which are extremely inflammable. In very hot fires a lot of the oil in a tree can be vaporised before the fire reaches it, causing it to explode into flames. Such fires can move at terrifying speed – leaping from tree-top to tree-top – and have trapped and killed many firefighters.

Fire has always been a part of the Australian environment. Some native plants have seeds that will only germinate after they have been exposed to intense heat, and many trees have special adaptations for recovering after a fire, such as epicormic shoots and LIGNOTUBERS. Aboriginal hunters often deliberately lit fires, both to flush out game and to provide fresh grazing and therefore better hunting. Some researchers at the CSIRO have suggested that there have not been enough fires since white settlement, and that some areas might be improved by more burning.

Despite the fact that fire costs the country dearly – both in financial terms and in loss of life – bushfire fighting is poorly funded and largely voluntary. But many thousands of public spirited people, apart from those keen to protect their own property, give up considerable spare time to maintain equipment and take preventative measures, apart from going readily into dangerous situations when a fire occurs. Country-wide, there are about 300 000 members of around 7000 bushfire brigades.

Every small community in Australia has its own brigade. Depending on the size of the community, it will have one or two four-wheel drive trucks fitted with water tanks and power pumps, two-way radio sets, and manual knapsack sprays. Often the trucks – tanker units – are by no means new, in fact some still in use are mounted on World War II Blitz Wagons. Members of the brigade often store equipment at home, and often supply some of their own as well, such as chainsaws, or tanker-trailer units that they take out to the paddocks when harvesting.

Each brigade has a captain, and he controls

Bushfires, particularly large ones, present a terrifying spectacle at close range. In major blazes temperatures of nearly 1400°C have been estimated inside fires, and they may reach almost 2000°C.

the fighting of a fire in his area, unless it is very large. He is responsible to a regional officer, sometimes employed by the local government, sometimes by the state fire authority. The regional fire control officer's responsibility lasts 24 hours a day, seven days a week, all year.

State governments can declare certain days 'days of extreme fire danger'. On these days no fire whatsoever can be lit in the open, and strictly speaking it is an offence even to strike a match for a cigarette out of doors.

Burning off of scrub and stubble to reduce potential fuel for a fire is essential. Each state except Queensland declares a fire season in which no burning off can be done without a permit; neighbours have to be informed. In Queensland, permits are needed year-round, and neighbours must actually give permission. In some areas local councils can make landholders create firebreaks, or contribute towards the cost of making them.

Community help is vital in fighting fires. Local radio stations broadcast information throughout the season, and a fire captain may ring the station and ask them to put out an appeal for help from neighbouring brigades if a situation becomes serious. For that reason radio sets are always on, even in many country town offices, during the fire season.

In some states of Australia the state emergency services controller has the power to declare a fire an emergency. He will do this when he believes the situation to be beyond his control. When this happens the state government will make heavy machinery available from organisations such as the National Parks and Wildlife Service. The armed forces may also be called in to help.

Although for most people who watch television news programs, firefighters seem to spend their time beating back flames at the fire front, this is not really what large-scale firefighting is all about, especially in rugged or difficult terrain.

The fire captain will know well the area where the fire is burning. He will watch the wind direction and calculate how the local topography will push a fire towards firebreaks like rivers and roads. One method of stopping a fire is to deprive it of fuel by burning ahead of it. Quite often fires are fought without using water at all, but by making firebreaks, cutting back vegetation, and raking the ground back to the soil. Graders are often used to widen firebreaks.

In recent years experiments have been carried out in Australia using aircraft to water bomb particular 'hot spots' in fires, using either plain water or water with a fire-retardant chemical added to it. The aim is to allow heavy machinery to get as near to the fire as possible so that firebreaks can be created to contain the blaze and allow it to burn itself out.

Many native Australian plants – like these grasstrees – produce new green shoots quickly after a fire. On some eucalypts trees, epicormic shoots grow from concealed buds under the bark, and these produce new leaves which allow the tree to survive until the crown regrows.

Fire sweeps through grassland on South Australia's Yorke Peninsula. When hot weather follows good falls of rain, thousands of square kilometres of grassland can be burnt out in one single fire.

Weapons in the war against fire

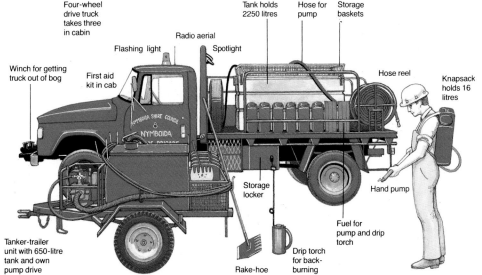

Four-wheel drive truck takes three in cabin

Radio aerial

Flashing light

Spotlight

Tank holds 2250 litres

Hose for pump

Storage baskets

Winch for getting truck out of bog

First aid kit in cab

Hose reel

Knapsack holds 16 litres

Storage locker

Hand pump

Fuel for pump and drip torch

Tanker-trailer unit with 650-litre tank and own pump drive

Rake-hoe

Drip torch for back-burning

Bushfire fighters use a relatively small collection of simple tool when fighting fires. Beaters – either a spade or a wet bag on the end of a pole – are still popular in an emergency, although they can be very tiring to use for any length of time. Care must also be taken to ensure that sparks are not spread onto unburnt fuel nearby. Hoe-rakes – also called McLeod tools for their inventor – help to clear debris quickly from the ground, and are useful in constructing firebreaks. Drip torches, using either kerosine or diesel fuel, enable firefighters to burn firebreaks in front of an oncoming blaze. A knapsack spray – with a hand-operated pump that can send a jet of water for six metres and a spray for rather less – is useful for mopping up around the edges of a fire.

The Modern Bushman

The bushman's traditional skills – those that enable a man to live and earn an income in the Australian bush – are still practised today. A few new tools, such as four-wheel drive vehicles and chainsaws, may have made some tasks easier, but they are not a substitute for hard-won knowledge about the land and its inhabitants, knowledge that is still passed on from generation to generation.

There is never any shortage of work to be done on a property, and even the most efficient owner needs help from time to time. Often he can call on a neighbour to lend a hand. Perhaps he is owed a favour, or it will be understood that he will be available to help at some time in the future. Neighbours might cooperate in putting up a boundary fence, or in making a team to speed the task of getting ripe crops in on time.

Casual labour is also available to hire, although not always at short notice. The son of a neighbour might not be fully employed, and will be glad of the money, so too may a nearby smallholder who is struggling to make a living. Even the owners of quite large properties sometimes go and work during slack periods – the extra cash is always welcome.

Specialists are rare in the country. Any competent man will be expected to be both ingenious and master of an extraordinary range of skills. He will not need to be told what to do or how to do it, and he will not need to be supervised. If asked to put up a fence, for example, he could be expected to choose the best line, fell the most appropriate trees, make the posts, dig the holes and strain the wire.

And what does one pay for skilled labour of this calibre – for a man who will turn up at seven in the morning with all his own equipment, work hard all day, with perhaps half an hour off for lunch (on the job), and leave at dusk? In 1988 the going rate was just $55 a day – around $7 an hour.

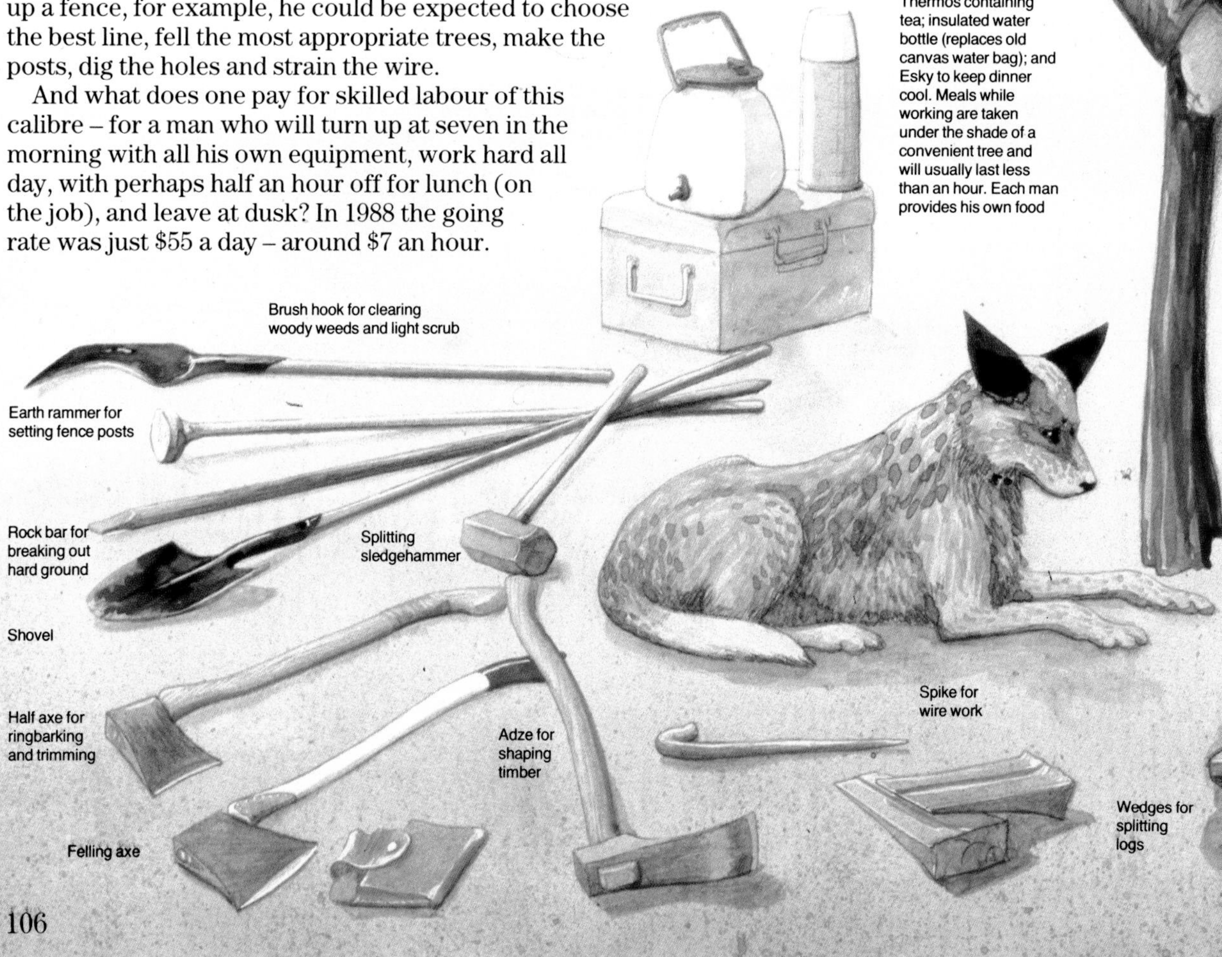

Ready for a day's work. The tools, animals and equipment that might be needed by a worker in cattle country in northern NSW. Obviously all of this equipment would rarely be needed on any one single day, but a lot of it is carried in the back of his four-wheel drive truck anyway. Workers in other parts of the country – in wheat or sheep-growing areas, for example – would need a different range of tools. There is, however, increasing pressure on farmers to diversify, which means that many more new skills have to be mastered.

Most bush workers dress neatly, despite the fact that they are usually doing dirty work. The typical uniform is a King Gee shirt, jeans or moleskins, elastic-sided working boots, a Drizabone coat for wet weather, and a hat (always)

Thermos containing tea; insulated water bottle (replaces old canvas water bag); and Esky to keep dinner cool. Meals while working are taken under the shade of a convenient tree and will usually last less than an hour. Each man provides his own food

Brush hook for clearing woody weeds and light scrub

Earth rammer for setting fence posts

Rock bar for breaking out hard ground

Shovel

Splitting sledgehammer

Half axe for ringbarking and trimming

Adze for shaping timber

Spike for wire work

Greenhide stockwhip

Felling axe

Wedges for splitting logs

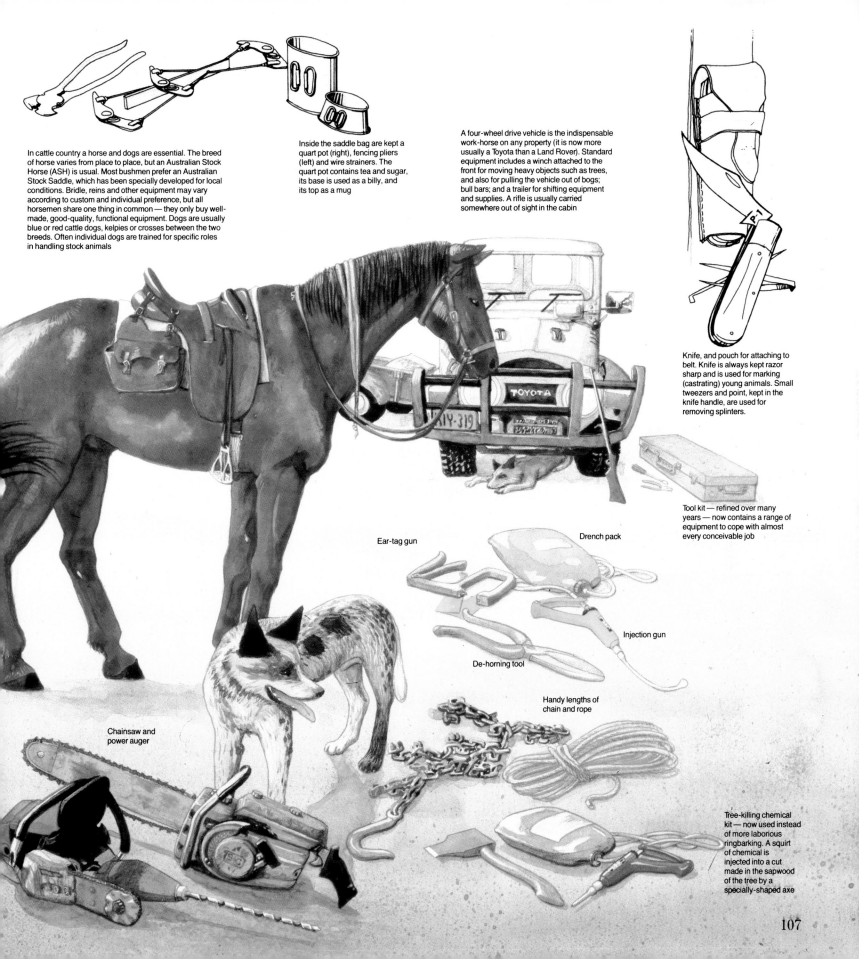

In cattle country a horse and dogs are essential. The breed of horse varies from place to place, but an Australian Stock Horse (ASH) is usual. Most bushmen prefer an Australian Stock Saddle, which has been specially developed for local conditions. Bridle, reins and other equipment may vary according to custom and individual preference, but all horsemen share one thing in common — they only buy well-made, good-quality, functional equipment. Dogs are usually blue or red cattle dogs, kelpies or crosses between the two breeds. Often individual dogs are trained for specific roles in handling stock animals

Inside the saddle bag are kept a quart pot (right), fencing pliers (left) and wire strainers. The quart pot contains tea and sugar, its base is used as a billy, and its top as a mug

A four-wheel drive vehicle is the indispensable work-horse on any property (it is now more usually a Toyota than a Land Rover). Standard equipment includes a winch attached to the front for moving heavy objects such as trees, and also for pulling the vehicle out of bogs; bull bars; and a trailer for shifting equipment and supplies. A rifle is usually carried somewhere out of sight in the cabin

Knife, and pouch for attaching to belt. Knife is always kept razor sharp and is used for marking (castrating) young animals. Small tweezers and point, kept in the knife handle, are used for removing splinters.

Tool kit — refined over many years — now contains a range of equipment to cope with almost every conceivable job

Ear-tag gun

Drench pack

Injection gun

De-horning tool

Handy lengths of chain and rope

Chainsaw and power auger

Tree-killing chemical kit — now used instead of more laborious ringbarking. A squirt of chemical is injected into a cut made in the sapwood of the tree by a specially-shaped axe

107

BUSHRANGER

The name bushranger is of Australian origin, and was first applied mainly to escaped convicts who had taken to the bush and lived by robbery. Conditions in the colonies encouraged bushranging, for escaped convicts had practically no chance of leaving the country, and there were no cities where they could stay unrecognised among the crowds. On the other hand, there was plenty of wild bushland, in which it was difficult for police to find them.

Tasmania, where the convicts included a high proportion of hardened criminals, was the first area to be seriously troubled by bushrangers. In 1809 Governor Bligh, who had been released by the rebels in Sydney, and had gone to the Derwent in the ship *Porpoise*, wrote about 'a set of Free Booters (Bushrangers they are called)', and claimed that 'about sixty, and some of them well armed, are now in the Woods'. One notorious Tasmanian bushranger was Michael Howe, who led a gang reported at one time to number about 30, but was ambushed and killed by a policeman and a stock-keeper in 1818. Another was Matthew Brady, who was captured and hanged in 1826. During the next few years, vigorous measures taken by Governor Arthur practically eliminated bushranging in the island colony. The only notable Tasmanian bushranger after that was Martin Cash, who operated very successfully for a while in the 1840s, but was finally captured after a chase in which he mortally wounded a policeman. Although he was condemned to death for this offence, such was his reputation for chivalry and avoidance of violence that the sentence was commuted to life imprisonment. He then proved such a model prisoner that after several years he was given a ticket of leave and settled down as a farmer and highly respected member of the community at what is now the Hobart suburb of Glenorchy, where he spent the rest of his life.

On the mainland the first bushranger was Black Caesar, an escaped negro convict, whose haunts were in an area now comprising Sydney's south-western suburbs, and who was shot dead in 1796 near what is now the suburb of Strathfield. However, bushranging did not reach proportions comparable to those in Tasmania until the great increase in population from about 1814, and the spreading of settlement over the Blue Mountains. In 1814 it was reported that a gang of 17 bushrangers was operating around the Cowpastures (now Camden), and by 1830 the position was so serious that police were given the power to arrest suspects without a warrant. Particularly notorious were Bold Jack Donahoe, who operated mainly from Windsor to Bringelly and was shot dead in 1836 near Campbelltown, and the crazed ex-convict John Lynch, who terrorised the Berrima district in NSW. Before hanging in 1841, Lynch confessed to killing nine

Cash, Jones and Kavenagh *escaped together from Port Arthur by swimming naked from Eaglehawk Neck to the mainland. Their gang, 'Cash and Co', became notorious throughout Tasmania.*

people with an axe – but claimed that he did it by divine guidance.

After the abolition of transportation to eastern Australia in 1852, bushranging by escaped convicts ended. At the same time the gold discoveries provided a new motive and new opportunities for highway robbery. At the height of the rushes many robberies occurred on the roads between the Victorian fields and Melbourne, but those responsible do not appear to have worked from hideouts in the bush, and can hardly be called bushrangers.

The second great period of bushranging came in the 1860s and 1870s, mainly in NSW. Most of those involved in it were free-born, but often of ex-convict parentage, and from the poorer classes. In many cases they farmed small properties, from which it was hard to make a living, and they were therefore under constant temptation to indulge in petty theft, or to go further and steal horses, cattle or sheep. Other small farmers tended to sympathise with them, and to help them when they were on the run. This caused frustration among the police, who therefore often tended to use arbitrary methods, which in turn caused increased opposition.

In NSW the most famous bushrangers of this period were Frank Gardiner and Ben Hall. The former was twice convicted of horse-stealing before taking to the bush in 1861, and organising a gang with hideouts in the Weddin Mountains south of Forbes. In the following year, in a deed now commemorated by a plaque a little out of Eugowra on the road to Orange, the gang robbed a coach, escorted by police, taking £3277 in cash and 2718 ounces (over 85 kg) of gold. Gardiner was captured in 1864 and sentenced to 32 years' jail but the harshness of the sentence aroused great sympathy for him. In 1874, following the presentation of a widely-supported public petition, he was freed on condition that he leave NSW, and he finally migrated to California.

Ben Hall was of ex-convict parentage, and was widely believed to have been driven to a life of crime by police harassment. After being tried for highway robbery in 1862, but acquitted, he returned to the small pastoral property which he had leased near Forbes, to find that his wife had left him. On another occasion, while he was in police custody on suspicion, his home was burned down and most of his stock killed. Shortly after this he took to the bush, became leader of the remnants of Gardiner's gang, and carried out a series of daring robberies before

Law and order in the colonies

The system of courts and police forces by which law and order are maintained today evolved slowly. Phillip had only one court, consisting of a Judge Advocate and six military or naval officers. Later Governors also appointed Justices of the Peace (unpaid and usually untrained) to act as magistrates In 1814 a Supreme Court under a judge was set up, and in the 1820s the first full-time paid magistrate was appointed. During the next few decades, the colonies all acquired court systems basically the same as they are today.

As for the police, Phillip had none, and had to appoint a 12-man team of convict constables to keep order at night. The development of a regular police force did not begin until the time of Governor Macquarie (1810–22). Even then, the ordinary foot police soon proved unable to cope with well-mounted bushrangers, and so in 1825 a number of soldiers were formed into a mounted police unit, with special uniforms similar to those of British dragoons. This practice was extended and taken up by other colonies, so that most of the police encountered by bushrangers on the run were in fact mounted troopers.

Mounted police – *such as these in Victoria – were formed to combat the threat of bushrangers, and also to keep order on the goldfields and to help catch runaway convicts, often with the help of Aboriginal trackers.*

The body of 'Mad' Dan Morgan propped up at Peechelba Station where he was shot in the back by a station hand in April 1865. His head was later severed from his body, shaved and sent to Melbourne University to be studied by curious scientists.

Henry Johnson, alias Harry Power, in irons shortly after his capture in the King River Ranges near Beechworth, Vic., in 1870. Ironically, Ned Kelly's grandfather, James Quinn, received a reward of £500 for the part he played in Power's eventual capture.

Martin Cash – 'the Gentleman Bushranger' – was sentenced to death for the murder of a constable, but strong public opinion resulted in his being sent to Norfolk Island for life instead. He eventually got his ticket of leave and emigrated to New Zealand.

Ben Hall, whose body is buried in the cemetery at Forbes, NSW, was only 27 when police caught up with him in May 1865. Official reports later claimed that there were 15 bullets in his body, but widespread rumours claimed the real number was more than 30.

Frank Gardiner, who rode with Ben Hall and Johnnie Gilbert, was sentenced to 32 years in jail after his capture. Released in 1874, he sailed for San Francisco where he ran The Twilight Saloon until he was reputedly shot dead in a poker game in 1903.

Frederick Ward – Captain Thunderbolt – had a seven-year career as a bushranger before being fatally wounded by police at Rocky River in May 1870. His grave in the town of Uralla, south of Armidale, NSW, was a popular tourist attraction for many years.

being shot dead by police in 1865. He was perhaps the best organiser among all bushrangers, taking care in particular to equip his men with horses of top quality – often stolen racehorses so that they could outdistance the police. He also had a reputation for a strong sense of humour.

Others in the 1860s were Frederick Ward CAPTAIN THUNDERBOLT, in New England, Thomas and John Clarke of Araluen, who were hanged in 1867, and the aptly nicknamed Daniel Mad Dog MORGAN. The 1870s produced Andrew George Scott *Captain Moonlight*, who took to the bush with five others in 1879 after serving a gaol term for bank robbery. A brilliant confidence man, who posed as a lay preacher, he nevertheless had only a brief career, being captured in 1880.

The Kelly gang was the most famous of all. In 1877, after repeated clashes with the police since boyhood, Ned KELLY and his brother Dan, who was wanted for horse stealing, went into hiding in the Wombat Ranges, south of Wangaratta in Victoria. They were soon joined by their friends Joe Byrne and Steve Hart, and when they came on the camp of a police party at Stringybark Creek, Ned shot three of them dead in cold blood. All four were then declared outlaws. They carried out two particularly daring bank robberies, at Euroa in Victoria and Jerilderie in NSW. At the latter they locked up two policemen, herded most of the population into the hotel, and then dressed as police to rob the bank. Finally they were trapped by police in the inn at Glenrowan, Vic. Ned, with the top half of his body clad in armour made for him by a blacksmith, was shot in the legs, captured, tried for murder, and hanged in Melbourne on 11 November 1880. The other three had died in the battle at Glenrowan.

Famous bushrangers and their haunts

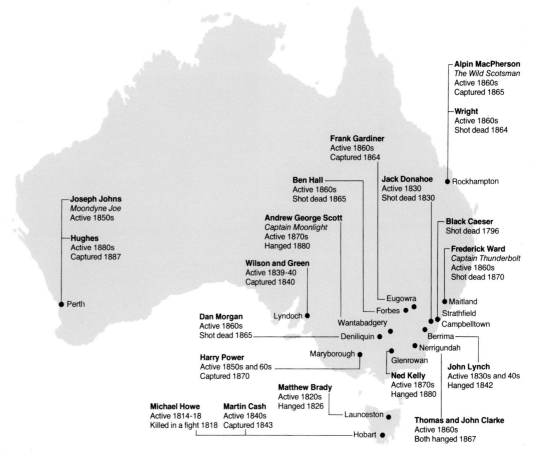

The haunts of 20 of Australia's better-known bushrangers. In most cases they have been linked to the places where they eventually met up with justice. Obviously most operated in south-eastern NSW because that was where most people lived during the heyday of bushranging, in the 1860s and 1870s.

BUSHWALKING

In 1982 a NSW Government survey distinguished between bushwalking – 'an activity which attracts enthusiasts as well as recreationists' – and 'walking to scenic points or for pleasure'. Bushwalking must be pleasurable because membership of the 170 or so clubs in Australia increases every year, despite the fact that, as the survey showed, most bushwalkers prefer walking alone or in small informal groups. Clubs can shortcut hard experience regarding clothes and gear, and introduce walkers to such arts as lighting a fire in difficult conditions, and safely crossing a raging creek. But for unorganised walkers the very many well-marked and often sketch-mapped trails in national parks and state forests mean that advanced skills in navigation and bushcraft are not needed – only a modicum of common sense. Knowing trails well, park rangers can warn of arduous or eroded stretches, and a number of books describe popular parks' tracks, grading them easy, medium and hard. To manage 30 km in a day is possible, but walkers over rough terrain and carrying gear for camping go about 10 or 15. 'Scrub bashing' – which is generally uncomfortable and undesirably disturbs vegetation – can be as slow as one or two kilometres a day. Several very long tracks have been cleared and marked, such as the 400-km Bibbulmun Track between Kalamunda and the south coast of Western Australia; the 450-km Hume and Hovell Track between Gunning and Albury; and the Heysen Trail, eventually to be 2000 km long between Cape Borda on Kangaroo Island and Mt Babbage in the Flinders Ranges.

BUSTARD

The only Australian bustard, the Kori Bustard *Ardeotis kori* is 1.1 to 1.2 m long with a wing span of 2.3 m (the female is smaller). It ranges to India, Africa and New Guinea. Unfortunately this large, palatable bird – like its 20 or so relatives in other countries – has drastically declined in numbers because of hunting and the destruction of its habitat. The same species occurs in Africa, where 18-kg cock birds have been reliably recorded. If these measurements are accurate, this is the world's heaviest flying bird. Australian specimens are not known to reach this weight, although one cock weighed 14.5 kg. Unfortunately, although they can fly well, they are reluctant to do so and prefer to walk away from danger or freeze, thus making themselves easy targets for hunters.

BUTCHERBIRD

The four butcherbirds of Australia *Cracticus* spp. are strong, highly territorial, black, grey-black or pied predators. They can be confused with the Australian Magpie or the Currawongs, but their large bills are hooked, their legs short and weak, and their eyes dark. The northern Black Butcherbird *C. quoyi* (420–440 mm), lives in rainforests and mangroves where pairs establish permanent territories of about 10 ha in extent. The Grey Butcherbird *C. torquatus* (260–300 mm), and the Pied Butcherbird *C. nigrogularis* (320–360 mm), are found over most of Australia. The Black-backed Butcherbird *C. mentalis* (250–270 mm), lives on Cape York. Butcherbirds generally swoop on any small prey and often wedge it in a branch to dismember it.

BUTTERFLY

See entry opposite.

BUTTON GRASS

Button grass *Gymnoschoenus sphaerocephalus* is in fact not a grass but a sedge. It is very widespread in south-eastern Australia, but is most commonly associated with south-west Tasmania. Indeed, for many bushwalkers south-west Tasmania and button grass plains are virtually synonymous.

In south-west Tasmania, button grass occurs in two different situations. On poorly drained sites it forms large, tall tussocks, producing a community avoided, where possible, by walkers. However, it is also found as smaller, lower tussocks on the button grass plains – a healthy community on better drained sites which covers vast areas of the south-west. Most, probably all, of the button grass plains once supported forest – frequently temperate rainforest. However, as a result of repeated burning, the forest has retreated and been replaced by button grass. The original increase in burning which lead to this dramatic vegetation change was probably caused by Aborigines, but in recent times Europeans have been responsible for many fires. Button grass is extremely inflammable and, despite the generally wet climate, the button grass plains will carry fire only a few hours after rain.

BUTTRESS ROOT

These are a striking feature of some rainforest trees. They take the form of projections from the trunk base, broadening as they near the ground. Some, known as plank buttresses, are very thin and flat. They probably allow trees to stand with only a very shallow system of surface roots in poorly aerated soils.

Button grass plains *cover large areas of south-west Tasmania. The clumps can grow very quickly in good conditions, and will rapidly cover the ground once seeds become established.*

BUTTERFLY

There is no sharp distinction between butterflies and MOTHS, which together form the INSECT order Lepidoptera. However, in general butterflies are brightly coloured, and moths are drab; butterflies fly in the day and moths at night; butterflies hold their wings vertically at rest, moths do not; butterflies have clubs on the tips of their antennae, moths do not. The last rule works best, the only exception being one group of butterflies, the Skippers, which have antennae that gradually thicken towards the ends and are hooked at the tips. There are six butterfly families represented in Australia, but one, that of the beaks, has only one species. Families and their species numbers are: skippers (Hesperiidae, 106); swallowtails (Papilionidae, 18); whites (Pieridae, 31); danaids, browns, admirals, painted ladies etc. (Nymphalidae, 79); beaks (Libytheidae, 1); blues and coppers (Lycaenidae, 124). Many butterfly collectors, like stamp collectors, find any slight difference between two specimens an excuse to invent a new name. Thus many of the species are divided into numerous subspecies on the basis of often unimportant differences.

The skippers are small to medium-sized butterflies with thick bodies, short wings and hooked antennae. They fly spasmodically and in a jerky fashion during the day or at dusk. Their colours are rather dull browns with yellow, white or clear spots. Wings are sometimes folded flat.

The swallowtails are so named because most European species have tailed hind-wings, as do some Australian ones. Their pupae, which are often iridescent, are fastened by their tails to plant stems, and are supported by a girdle of silk round their upper parts. Adults are large, often brightly coloured, and the sexes are frequently markedly different. The most spectacular examples are the strictly protected Cape York

LIFE CYCLE OF A BUTTERFLY

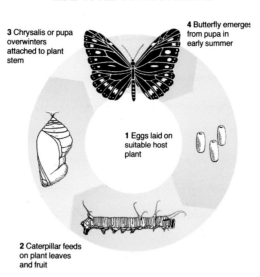

3 Chrysalis or pupa overwinters attached to plant stem

4 Butterfly emerges from pupa in early summer

1 Eggs laid on suitable host plant

2 Caterpillar feeds on plant leaves and fruit

The life cycle of the Common Australian Crow is typical of many butterflies. Little is known about the life expectancy of adult insects in the wild.

ANATOMY OF A BUTTERFLY

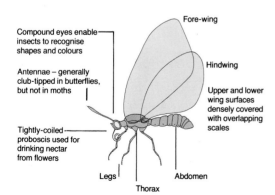

Compound eyes enable insects to recognise shapes and colours

Antennae – generally club-tipped in butterflies, but not in moths

Tightly-coiled proboscis used for drinking nectar from flowers

Fore-wing

Hindwing

Upper and lower wing surfaces densely covered with overlapping scales

Legs

Thorax

Abdomen

The best way to distinguish between butterflies and moths is to examine their antennae – those of butterflies are club-tipped or have thickened ends, while those of moths are feathery or finely pointed.

Birdwing *Ornithoptera priamus*, and the Richmond Birdwing *O. richmondia* from northern NSW and southern Queensland.

The whites are butterflies which commonly have white or yellowish upper-surfaces to their wings, although often with black spots and margins. Under-surfaces are white or splashed with yellow, black or red. Most familiar is the Cabbage White *Pieris rapae* which came from New Zealand in 1937.

The nymphs include a wide variety of small to large butterflies, all with undeveloped forelegs. Many fly and bask in the sunshine. *Danaus plexippus*, the Monarch or Wanderer Butterfly, is a remarkable, large chestnut brown insect with prominent black lines on its wings, which have a span of 110 mm. It is a North American species that has colonised eastern Australia, having crossed the Pacific Ocean by its own efforts. Wanderers feed on poisonous milkweed and related plants which makes them distasteful to birds. Blues and coppers are usually small butterflies whose wings have dull, camouflaged under-surfaces, but blue or coppery upper-surfaces. As they fly they are easily seen, but when they land they close their wings and are almost invisible. The wood-louse-like caterpillars of many blues shelter in ant nests, where they are prized by their hosts for the attractive substances they produce. They emerge at night, with an ant escort, to feed.

A Wanderer butterfly is born (right). The insect must sit on the pupa case for several minutes while its wings dry and tiny capillaries fill with blood.

Common butterflies of Australia

There are 382 species of butterflies so far recorded in Australia, of which 174 are restricted to this country alone. Of the rest, 112 are found throughout the Australian region and 96 are also found elsewhere in the world.

Most of Australia's butterflies prefer to live in tropical or subtropical areas. A total of 320 species have been found in the wet north of the continent, 195 have been recorded in the wetter coastal areas of the south-west and south-east (including Tasmania) and 92 in the dry interior. A total of 175 species are found *only* in the north, while just three are found *only* in the Centre.

The 42 butterflies illustrated on these pages are some of the more widely distributed and interesting species. Representatives of five of the six families found in Australia are shown. Missing are the beaks, which have just one local representative.

DANAIDS, BROWNS AND NYMPHS

Common Eggfly
Hypolimnas bolina nerina

Common Brown Ringlet
Hypocysta metirius

Red Lacewing
Cethosia cydippe chrysippe

Meadow Argus
Junonia villida calybe

Tailed Emperor
Polyura pyrrhus sempronius

Australian Painted Lady
Vanessa kershawi

Common Brown
Heteronympha merope merope

Glasswing
Acraea andromacha andromacha

Common Australian Crow
Euploea core corinna

Evening Brown
Melanitis leda bankia

Australian Admiral
Vanessa itea

Wanderer
Danaus plexippus plexippus

Lesser Wanderer
Danaus chrysippus petilia

Blue Tiger
Daneus hamatus hamatus

WHITES AND YELLOWS

Lemon Migrant
Catopsilia pomona pomona

Common Pearl White
Elodina augulipennis

Australian Gull
Cepora perimale scyllara

Wood White
Delias aganippe

Cabbage White
Pieris rapae rapae

Common Grass Yellow
Eurema hecabe phoebus

Imperial White
Delias harpalyce

Caper White
Anaphaeis java teutonia

SWALLOWTAILS

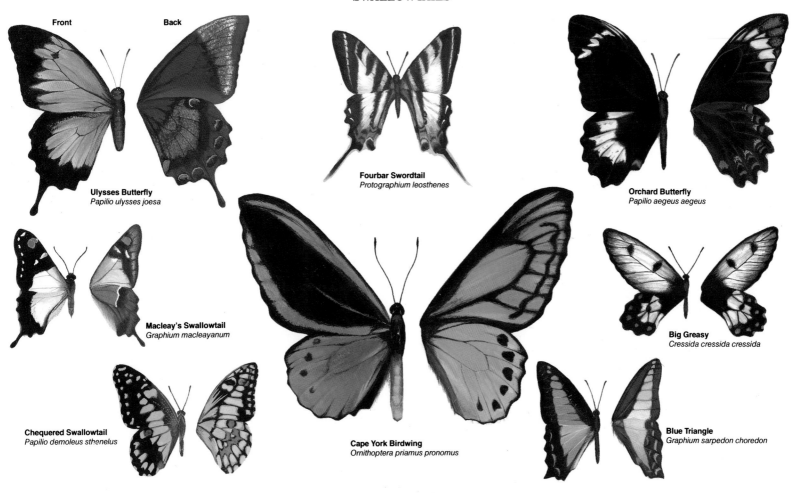

Front **Back**

Ulysses Butterfly
Papilio ulysses joesa

Fourbar Swordtail
Protographium leosthenes

Orchard Butterfly
Papilio aegeus aegeus

Macleay's Swallowtail
Graphium macleayanum

Big Greasy
Cressida cressida cressida

Chequered Swallowtail
Papilio demoleus sthenelus

Cape York Birdwing
Ornithoptera priamus pronomus

Blue Triangle
Graphium sarpedon choredon

SKIPPERS

Brown Awl
Badamia exclamationis

Regent Skipper
Euschemon rafflesia

Eastern Flat
Netrocoryne repanda repanda

Orange Palmdart
Cephrenes augiades sperthias

Eliena Skipper
Trapezites eliena

Flame Skipper
Hesperilla idothea idothea

BLUES AND COPPERS

Amaryllis Azure
Ogyris amaryllis

Fiery Jewel
Hypochrysops ignitus ignitus

Copper Jewel
Hypochrysops apelles apelles

Small Copper
Lucia limbaria

Common Grass Blue
Zizina labradus labradus

Western Jewel
Hypochrysops halyaetus

113

CABBAGE TREE PALM

The name 'cabbage tree' was used by early sailors and explorers for any palm or palm-like plant with a terminal leaf-bud that could be used as a fresh vegetable. This group of about 16 species of palms with fan-shaped fronds extends around the north and east coasts of Australia, from the Hamersley region in Western Australia to the far east of Victoria. There is also an isolated stand of these palms along one short stretch of the Finke River valley in central Australia. Along the south-east coast, from about Noosa in Queensland through NSW and just into Victoria, is found the common Cabbage Tree Palm *Livistona australis*, mainly on coastal swamps, dunes and headlands.

CACTUS

Cactus is popularly used for a wide range of succulent or spiky plants. However, the true Cacti all belong to one family, the Cactaceae, and are mostly leafless plants in which the succulent green stem performs the task of photosynthesis. Many cacti are fiercely spiny. The very sharp, needle-like spines are in clusters at regular intervals on the stems, with a tuft of woolly hairs at the base of each cluster. This hair tuft is the characteristic feature by which cacti can by recognised. Cacti are native to the Americas but many have been introduced into Australia. The most significant are the PRICKLY PEARS, which became major weeds in some regions. Many other cacti are grown by enthusiasts, who often have large collections of the smaller kinds in glasshouses. In the tropics and subtropics some of the night-blooming cacti with large white flowers are commonly seen in gardens.

CADDIS FLIES

Caddis flies can be seen in cooler areas flying at dusk, dawn or during the night, near the water in which their larvae develop. They resemble small brown moths to which they are related, but their wings and bodies are covered with hairs, and scales are rare. Wing-spans usually range from about 10 to 30 mm. Mouth parts are reduced, but can take water or nectar. One species lives in lakes three times saltier than the sea. Caddis fly eggs are laid in gelatinous strings, in or above the water on foliage, and are sometimes camouflaged with hairs from the female's body. Most larvae – some of which have gills on their abdomens – live in cases made of sand grains or fragments of plants, each characteristic of a particular species. Members of one group construct nets at the mouths of their cases. Most eat both plants and animals. There are about 260 Australian species.

CAMEL

The only wild camels *Camelus dromedarius* (mean head and body length 3 m, height at highest point, the hump, 2.1 m), anywhere in the world are in Australia. Camels have been domesticated for so long it is impossible to be sure of their natural range, but it almost certainly included parts of Arabia and possibly the fringes of the Sahara. They were not known in Egypt before 500 BC at the earliest, but both kinds of camels (these and the Bactrian) were known and distinguished in Mesopotamia by about 2000 BC.

Once it began to dawn upon Europeans in Australia that the Centre might be desert, camels became desirable imports. The NSW and South Australian governments contemplated bringing them from India, but the first to arrive came in 1840, as a private venture.

Some were imported for stage shows and circuses, but in 1860 the Royal Society of Victoria brought in 24 from India, with an ex-Indian Army soldier and three 'Afghan' handlers. These camels, and two others, joined the ill-fated Burke and Wills expedition. Two survived, and were released. The merchant-pastoralist Thomas Elder was the most important early importer: in 1866 he landed 121, of various kinds, from Karachi in Pakistan. Elder walked them inland and established a stud farm.

Camels and their Afghan handlers – mostly Moslems from what was then northern India – carried out many transport tasks in inland Australia besides exploration. In the peak year, 1919, the official count of domestic camels was 12 649 but there were probably at least 20 000. In 1941 – at the last census – there were 2267. As the car and the truck replaced them they were released, and became the ancestors of the modern feral mobs.

The estimated feral population is about 25 000, mainly in the Centre, but with one or two isolated populations. They prefer sandy ridge-dune country. They can eat a wide range of plants, including extremely bitter or thorny ones shunned by other animals, and also plants that are rich in salts.

Sometimes camels move away from the arid regions and cause damage to fences, watering

Camels played a vital role in opening up much of inland Australia. These animals were part of an expedition led by Alfred Canning leaving for the Kimberley area of Western Australia in 1906. Camel trips in central Australia are now popular with tourists as the only way of seeing some areas.

points and even crops in settled areas. Australian camels are remarkably free from disease, and consequently a number have been exported back to the Middle East.

CAMOUFLAGE AND MIMICRY

Almost every animal, whether hunter or hunted, makes use of camouflage to escape its enemies or to deceive its prey. For the majority of animals concealment depends on body colour and patterning. Colour has another function too – one which sometimes conflicts directly with the need for camouflage. For as well as concealing, it can also reveal. These contradictory roles of colour are well illustrated in birds, where the males are often boldly coloured to attract mates, while the females, which usually look after the eggs and chicks, are drab.

The simplest way for one animal to elude another is to be indistinguishable from its surroundings. Thus a green grasshopper disappears among grass and leaves and the Australasian Bittern among waterside reeds and rushes. Some animals are even capable of changing colour to suit their surroundings.

However well an animal merges with its surroundings, the 'solidness' of its body may still betray it. As light shines from above its back is highlighted and its belly put in shadow. To counteract this effect many animals have a dark-coloured back and a light-coloured belly.

Some animals put on a terrifying act to frighten a predator away. If a bird penetrates the camouflage of some species of moths, the moths suddenly lift their forewings to reveal two large eye spots on their hind wings. The startling effect on the predator gives the moth time to escape. The moth is playing on the bird's fear of its own enemies, such as cats and owls, which it recognises by their eyes.

Using colour not to camouflage, but to advertise, is another way of scaring off enemies. Vivid patterns of black, white, red and yellow are displayed as 'warning colours' announcing the unpleasant taste or sting of the animal wearing them. The black-and-yellow body of a wasp says 'sting' to members of the entire animal kingdom, not just to humans.

Some harmless and edible animals have bright colours which mimic those of poisonous or distasteful creatures. In this way the mimic shares the protection of the animal with warning colours, and deceives its enemies. Many flies resemble wasps in shape and colour. To get full benefit from these disguises the mimics must live in the same area as their models.

CANE TOAD

Cane toads *Bufo marinus* are the only true toads in Australia, where they are an exotic species. They originally came from Latin America where they range from Mexico to Brazil, breeding in fresh and sometimes brackish water, but about the end of last century they were taken to many West Indian and Pacific countries for pest control, especially in sugar cane. They were brought from Hawaii and released in Australia in 1935 to control, it was hoped, *Lepidoderma albohirtum*, a native chafer beetle whose larvae attack cane. They have failed to do this, although there are claims that they have been of value in some other countries. Now the toads have become pests by sheer force of numbers. They have the distinction of being the only organism introduced for biological control which may have to be controlled biologically itself. Populations are also very large in Papua New Guinea. One unpleasant feature is the mess made when cars run over them. Another is the poison in their skins, and particularly in the parotid glands which are conspicuous just behind the toad's eyes. Many household pets which tried to eat toads, have been poisoned. Cane toads commonly reach a length of 150 mm. They breed in any stretch of permanent or temporary water, still or slow-moving. At present they occur in coastal and sub-coastal north-eastern Australia from northern NSW to Cape York, but the range is expanding.

CAPE BARREN GOOSE

Biologists argue whether or not the Cape Barren Goose *Cereopsis novaehollandiae* is a goose at all. It is not a goose anatomically, but it behaves like one, grazing on land and rarely taking to water. The birds have earned the dislike of

Potent poison oozes from a parotid gland on the side of a cane toad Bufo marinus. *The toads are capable of squirting the poison for distances of up to one metre into the eyes of an attacking animal. Snakes, cats and dogs will die within an hour of eating a toad, and there have been cases of children being poisoned by them, although as yet there have been no recorded deaths.*

farmers in the southern coastal regions where they occur, because of the damage they do to pasture through eating and fouling. They are uncommon birds and were once near to extinction. Like real geese they make good eating and were much hunted, especially in the days of the early sealers.

Males establish small territories. Pairs probably mate for life. Nests may be on the ground, or up to six metres above ground, in bushes or trees, but wherever they are, the birds like to have a clear view. When the young are about six weeks old they are left by the adults and gather in small flocks. The geese were introduced into New Zealand in 1915, but not very successfully, since they have only been reported occasionally since that time.

CAPTAIN THUNDERBOLT

This noted bushranger was born in Windsor, NSW, in 1835, his real name being Frederick Ward. In 1863, while serving his second prison sentence for horse-stealing, he escaped from Cockatoo Island prison in Sydney Harbour. During the next several years he carried out many robberies, at first in the Bourke district, but later in New England and the Hunter Valley. He concentrated on holding up mail coaches, and in avoiding violence he gained a reputation as 'the Gentleman Bushranger'. He was shot dead by a policeman in 1870, and was buried at Uralla. Thunderbolt Rock, close to the New England Highway not far from that town, was supposed to have been one of his lookouts.

Brilliant camouflage conceals a wood moth from all but the sharpest-eyed predator. The moth must position itself vertically on the tree trunk to get the maxiumum advantage from its remarkable protective colouring and patterning.

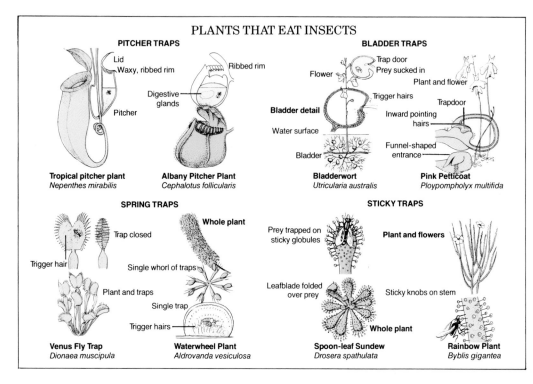

PLANTS THAT EAT INSECTS

PITCHER TRAPS

Lid
Waxy, ribbed rim
Digestive glands
Pitcher

Tropical pitcher plant
Nepenthes mirabilis

Ribbed rim

Albany Pitcher Plant
Cephalotus follicularis

BLADDER TRAPS

Trap door
Prey sucked in
Flower
Plant and flower
Trigger hairs
Trapdoor
Inward pointing hairs

Bladder detail
Water surface
Bladder
Funnel-shaped entrance

Bladderwort
Utricularia australis

Pink Petticoat
Ploypompholyx multifida

SPRING TRAPS

Trigger hair
Trap closed
Whole plant
Single whorl of traps
Plant and traps
Single trap
Trigger hairs

Venus Fly Trap
Dionaea muscipula

Waterwheel Plant
Aldrovanda vesiculosa

STICKY TRAPS

Prey trapped on sticky globules
Plant and flowers
Leafblade folded over prey
Sticky knobs on stem
Whole plant

Spoon-leaf Sundew
Drosera spathulata

Rainbow Plant
Byblis gigantea

CARNIVOROUS PLANT

Carnivorous plants have a curious fascination for many people, and their cultivation is now a popular hobby. Australia has one of the largest and most diverse collections of carnivorous plants found in any continent. The species in Australia can be divided into four groups on the basis of the method they use for capturing prey – flypaper traps in SUNDEWS, pitfall traps in PITCHER PLANTS and suction traps and spring traps in the species that live in water.

For most species, insects provide the major prey, although other small invertebrates may become victims. Tales of plants capturing small

An insect-eye view *from the inside of a pitcher plant. Downward-sloping hairs compel visitors to a well of fluid at the bottom of the pitcher, where they drown and are dissolved by enzymes in the water.*

mammals and birds, while feasible, if unlikely, in the case of some tropical pitcher plants, do not apply to any Australian species.

All species of carnivorous plants have green leaves and carry out photosynthesis. The carnivorous habit is thus not essential for growth, but capture of insects may provide important nutrients that are otherwise in short supply. The great diversity of carnivorous plants in Australia, particularly in the south-west, may reflect the low amount of nutrients, especially of phosphorus, in many soils.

CARP

The carp family is one of the largest among the bony fishes. Its members have no teeth in their jaws, although there are some in their throats, no adipose fins (see TROUT) and usually have barbels (sensory whiskers) near their mouths. The European or Common Carp *Cyprinus carpio* (illustration p 177) which grows to 1.2 m and a weight of more than 60 kg, probably originated in Asia, but is now one of the most widespread of all fishes. It was brought to Australia in 1872. It is a hump-backed, thick-bodied fish with a small mouth that has a pair of barbels at each corner. It is believed that there are three stocks in Australia: one in the Sydney region (since 1908), one in the Riverina, and one in Victoria.

Carp will eat both plants and animals. They have a habit of sucking in and straining mud, which makes the water turbid and is detrimental to other fish. The Mirror Carp is a variety with a row of large, mirror-like scales.

CART

Three carts soon supplemented the wheelbarrows that were the colony's sole means of transport in 1788. They were pulled by 24 convicts chained to the shaft. Bullocks were first used in 1796, six or eight hauling up to two tonnes, yoked in pairs to the single pole, plodding about 14 km a day. Until the 1850s four-wheeled vehicles were rare outside major towns. Two-wheeled carts were more easily extricated from bogs and were better able to avoid rocks, ruts and stumps. As roads gradually improved, four-wheeled drays became standard. Broadly speaking, a cart has two wheels and two shafts, a dray four wheels and a single pole, but the terms are loose. Low-sided box wagons came in from

Two-wheeled carts *were more popular than four-wheeled drays on primitive roads because they could be hauled out of bogs more readily, and they were easier to steer around obstacles such as stumps and rocks in the way.*

America in the 1850s; drawn by 16 or 18 bullocks or 14 horses, they took loads of up to eight tonnes. Covered wagons with outward-leaning sides were introduced by German immigrants to South Australia, and at the turn of the century many families used them for the laborious journey to the Mallee. Around 1900, table-top wagons, without sides but with platforms sloped to make loads settle inward, carried 14 tonnes and more. Twenty years later, all were obsolete.

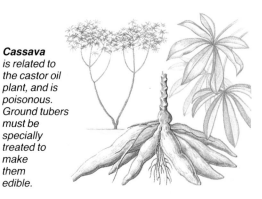

Cassava *is related to the castor oil plant, and is poisonous. Ground tubers must be specially treated to make them edible.*

CASSAVA

Around 400 million people, most of them in Africa and Latin America, eat around 120 million tonnes of cassava a year. It is one of the most important sources of food starch in countries like Zaire, Togo and Nigeria. In Brazil, the largest Latin American user, cassava is used in bread making. In Australia, the crop is still in the early stages of development, and is not grown on a large scale. There is a small commercial crop in Queensland.

Cassava is grown for its large tuberous root, which is several times larger than the part of the plant above the ground. The tubers store starch and moisture, enabling the crop to survive long periods of low rainfall or drought.

CASSIA

Australia has around 20 native cassias, of which three are trees confined to Queensland's east coast. The remaining shrubby species are spread over most of the continent, but are most conspicuous and colourful in the dry inland. Cassias are legumes, with seeds in flattened bean-like pods, but without a pea type of flower. The flowers are more open and cup-like, nearly always golden-yellow in colour. They show a remarkable adaptation to pollination by beetles, with five small stamens shedding pollen and five larger, sterile stamens, called 'fodder stamens', on which the beetles munch, and in so doing brush off pollen and carry it away.

CASSOWARY

The three cassowary species are restricted to Australia and New Guinea. The Southern Cassowary *Casuarius casuarius* (1.2–1.5 m) occurs in rainforest in north-east Queensland and New Guinea. It has a large bony casque or helmet on its head which protects the bird as it barges through the undergrowth. The hairy body feathers and spine-like flight feathers – if a flightless bird can be said to have flight feathers – are adaptations to thick undergrowth. Cassowaries eat fallen fruit, seeds, fungi, dead small animals and snails. Normally they are solitary and apparently territorial but come together for courtship – a circular dance by the male – and breeding when the female lays about four eggs on the ground. These are incubated by the male who looks after the chicks until they are about nine months old. The female is thus able to mate with more than one male. The long claw on the inside toe is a formidable weapon, useful in the defence of chicks. Cassowaries roar, rumble, boom and hiss.

CASTOR OIL PLANT

This is a giant herb *Ricinus communis* that generally appears on waste ground in urban areas where it seeds itself profusely. Originally native to India, it was introduced to Australia as

The castor oil plant is the source of a once popular laxative. All parts of the plant have been used in medicines, although the seeds are very poisonous.

a commercial oilseed, but it was never a success. The seeds contain a highly poisonous protein-like substance – ricin – a few milligrams of which can kill a person if it is injected into their bloodstream. The poison is destroyed by heat in the process by which castor oil is extracted and refined from the seeds.

CASTRATION

Castration turns young rams into wethers, colts into geldings and young bulls into steers. Farmers usually castrate male animals by removing their testes with a sharp knife or scalpel. Sometimes tight rubber rings are placed around calves' and lambs' testes, which then drop off after a few days. Chemical castration, involving hormonal injections, is also being developed. Castration, also known as gelding or cutting, stops male animals reproducing and inhibits the release of male hormones. Gelded animals are usually easier to handle and more stocky than their sexed counterparts. But they also have a slower growth rate and therefore tend to put down fat more quickly.

CATERPILLAR

A caterpillar – the name probably comes from the Old French for 'hairy cat' – is the larva of a MOTH or BUTTERFLY, but the word is sometimes used for larvae that resemble them. Butterfly and moth caterpillars have biting and chewing mouthparts which also carry silk-spinnerets. Their antennae are short and have three segments. Behind each is usually a group of six eyes, but some caterpillars are blind. Each of the three segments of the thorax usually carries a pair of five-segmented legs, ending in a claw. There are also false legs on the abdomen. These are unsegmented swellings with rings of minute hooks for traction.

Because caterpillars lose their colour when preserved in spirit, identification is based on the arrangement of the hairs, the number and position of the false legs and their hooks. Caterpillars have several means of defence (see MOTHS and BUTTERFLIES). Some have stinging hairs and spines, some live in cases, and some have excellant camouflage colouring. The larvae of many geometrids (the inchworms or loopers) are shaped and coloured like twigs. Several caterpillars are brightly coloured, often in black and red, or black and yellow. This is a warning to birds that the caterpillar is distasteful or poisonous, although sometimes a caterpillar may be merely mimicking an unpleasant one. Many swallow-tail caterpillars push out a brightly-coloured, evil-smelling horn when disturbed, and others vomit their last meal. Caterpillars grow by n oulting their skin periodically.

The brilliantly coloured larva of the moth Neola semiaurata *eats mainly acacias. Caterpillars are found in a bewildering variety of shapes and colours, and they often have elaborate defences against predators.*

CATFISH

There are two closely related families of catfishes in Australia. Both have the sensory whiskers (barbels) around their mouths – which gives them their common name. They are slimy, have scaleless skins and venomous spines. The fish of one family – the fork-tailed catfishes – have a crescent or forked tail, and those of the other have an eel-like tail. There are at least 11 eel-tailed catfishes in Australia, as well as some undescribed species. Several are called tandans. The Silver Tandan or Central Australian Catfish *N. argenteus* (up to 200 mm) is found in inland river systems and the Gulf of Carpentaria. The Dewfish or *the* Catfish *Tandanus tandanus* (illustration p 177), which grows to a length of 900 mm, is the largest of the group and is found in south-east Australia, South Australia and in the Murray-Darling river system. It is a carnivorous bottom feeder.

CATTLE

The Australian cattle industry is considered one of the most efficient in the world. Along with wheat and wool, it forms part of the backbone of both the rural and national economies. It is also one of the most geographically diverse rural pursuits, being found in all states and territories. At present about 23 million head of cattle are run throughout Australia.

Different breeds of cattle are well adapted to almost all of the climates and conditions found in Australia, from the temperate southern states to Queensland's tropics and the arid interior. The key to the industry's success has been the availability of large tracts of land, allowing cattle grazing at low stocking rates, and native and introduced parture grasses and legumes. Most cattle are run on such grasses and not, as in the United States, Japan and some parts of Australia, on high-cost, grain-based feedlots. Australian grass-fed beef is recognised as one of the leanest, low-cost forms of high quality red meat that can be found in the world.

However, like all other rural sectors, the cattle industry has suffered its share of disasters, usually the result of market disruption, climate or over-production. In some cases, all three have been to blame. The most noted 'cattle crashes' occurred in 1843, 1897, 1914, the late 1930s and the mid 1970s. In 1976, for instance, the temporary closure of Australia's single most important market, the USA, caused a dramatic drop in beef prices and massive reductions in the size of the national herd. In more recent times, the discovery of pesticide residues in beef shipments to the USA almost cost the industry more than $1 billion worth of markets in North America and Asia. Fortunately, the industry narrowly escaped that fate with no great loss of money or reputa-

Popular breeds of cattle from around Australia

Northern and southern cattle producers tend to run different breeds, although there is some overlap. Northern graziers favour the larger, hardier breeds such as Brahman, Santa Gertrudis and Droughtmaster. Northern cattle must be resistant to the blood-sucking cattle tick, and be tolerant of hot, dry periods. In the south traditional British breeds such as Hereford, Shorthorn, Angus and Devon, as well as European breeds such as Simmental and Charolais, are more common. Other breeds – such as Murray Grey, Braford and Belmont Red – are adapted to particular areas of Australia.

Hereford
A beef breed from Herefordshire, England, and first introduced into Australia in 1826. Now found throughout the continent

Poll Hereford
First imported from the USA in 1920, this breed of beef cattle is now one of the most popular and numerous in Australia

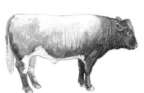

Poll Shorthorn
Developed from early Australian shorthorn cattle last century, this beef breed is now found throughout Australia.

Holstein-Friesian
This breed was imported into Australia in the 1850s from the Netherlands. It is now the most numerous dairy cow in Australia

Illawarra
A dairy breed developed on the south coast of New South Wales. Cows produce large quantities of milk from poor pasture

Angus
This breed originated in Scotland, and produces excellent meat. Herds are mostly found in south-eastern and southern areas of Australia

Brahman
Developed in northern Queensland, this beef breed has now spread to all states. Brahmans are particularly resistant to cattle tick

Santa Gertrudis
First introduced into Australia from the USA in 1952, this breed of beef cattle has now spread to all states

Jersey
This classic dairy breed was first imported into Australia in the 18th century. More than 40 per cent of all dairy cows are Jerseys

Ayrshire
This diary breed has diminished in popularity in recent years. The first animals were imported into Australia in the 1850s

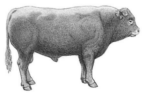

Limousin
The harsh conditions in central France, where this beef breed originated, have made it ideally suited to parts of Australia

Devon
One of the oldest English breeds, Devons first came to Australia in the early 1800s. Cattle are renowned for their excellent meat

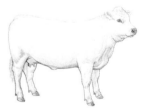

Charolais
This breed of beef cattle was only introduced into Australia in 1969. The cattle were originally developed in central France

Guernsey
Only small numbers of this English dairy breed are found in Australia — most of them in south-eastern coastal areas

Red Poll
A very old British breed that arrived in Australia in the 1850s. Red Polls yield both good-quality beef and milk

Murray Grey
The first Murray Grey cattle were bred in the upper Murray River valley in 1905. They can now be found throughout Australia

Simmental
Originating in Switzerland, and one of the oldest (dairy) breeds in the world, Simmental cattle first arrived in Australia in 1972

South Devon
Originally dual purpose — beef and milk — nearly all South Devons are now bred for meat. This is the largest of the British breeds

tion. The international standing of the Australian cattle industry is very important because around 50 per cent of its production is exported. The main markets are the USA, Japan, Canada and Taiwan. Small amounts are also sent to south-east Asian countries such as Malaysia. The lower-priced offal cuts like liver are exported to the European Economic Community.

Cattle were introduced to Australia with the First Fleet in 1788. However, the early settlers made little distinction between beef and dairy cattle during the first few decades of European settlement, and the industry's development was erratic. But by 1843 cattle were being permanently grazed by Edward Henty at Portland Bay in Victoria. The development of the Victorian industry was well under way when, four years later, Joseph Hawdon drove the first mob of cattle into South Australia. The first real moves to develop the northern beef industry were made during the mid 1800s when explorers, like Allan Cunningham, F.T. Gregory and Alexander Forrest, began exploring the arid interior of the continent.

From around 1870, the northern half of the country, with its large areas of native grassland, proved ideal for the establishment of sprawling cattle stations. Some covered thousands of square kilometres. Pastoralists like Sir Sidney KIDMAN, the Durack family and then the English Vestey family developed large holdings in northern Queensland, the Northern Territory and the north of Western Australia. Often these great 'empires' ran many thousands of cattle, which were mustered annually. Today, families like the Coutts brothers from Ayr, south of Townsville, still play an important role in the industry, along with large companies and individual graziers.

The Australian cattle industry can be divided

A scene of rural peace. For city Australian, few sights are more typically 'country' than cattle grazing in green fields. In fact, most of Australia's cattle have to extract a living from rather harsher surroundings.

EATING 15 KG A DAY

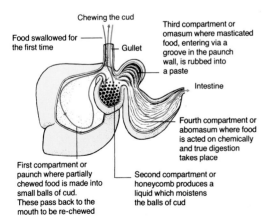

Chewing the cud

Food swallowed for the first time

Gullet

Third compartment or omasum where masticated food, entering via a groove in the paunch wall, is rubbed into a paste

Intestine

Fourth compartment or abomasum where food is acted on chemically and true digestion takes place

First compartment or paunch where partially chewed food is made into small balls of cud. These pass back to the mouth to be re-chewed

Second compartment or honeycomb produces a liquid which moistens the balls of cud

A Friesian cow weighing 570 kg needs about 15 kg of food a day. To accomodate this vast quantity of matter, and to process it thoroughly, the cow's stomach is separated into four compartments.

into roughly two sections: the north and south.

In the southern temperate states of NSW, Victoria and Tasmania, around 40 per cent of the national herd is grazed on introduced clover, medic and grass pastures at high stocking rates. The vast majority of the 450 to 660 kg 'finished' cattle end up on the domestic market, either in a butcher or supermarket display, or a restaurateur's plate. In the Northern Territory, north Western Australia and central and northern Queensland, the cattle are more extensively reared, mostly on native grasses.

Like their forebears and other members of the rural community, modern cattle producers face many hazards, such as pests, disease, drought and fire. But one of the most enduring and costly hazards is perhaps the cattle thief or duffer. Some of the early settlers turned to duffing due to the shortage of meat in the developing colony. Usually the thieves drove the mobs of stolen cattle to safe places in the hills, where the stocks' brands were changed or disguised in readiness for sale. Small landholders and ex-convicts, who were not favourably disposed towards the pastoralists and squatters, often helped the duffers or were less than helpful to authorities. Although these sympathies have largely disappeared, cattle duffing is still a problem on the vast properties in

northern NSW, and Western Australia. A fast truck and well-trained cattle dogs can help to foil the best efforts by police and landowners to catch thieves.

WHERE AUSTRALIA'S CATTLE LIVE

Beef cattle areas

Intensity of colour represents the general distribution of beef cattle. Dairy cattle tend to be concentrated in lusher coastal areas, and close to major rivers.

CAVE

A cave is a hole in the ground large enough to contain humans; a cavern is simply a large cave. There are three kinds of natural caves: those formed by wind or wave erosion, those formed by volcanic action and, on the grandest scale, those formed by the chemical action of water in limestone regions.

Erosion caves can be found in any rocks which are soft enough to be eroded by wind-borne particles or waves, but they are not very deep unless some line of weakness is exploited by the action. They are not common over much of the interior of Australia because of the very low relief, but wave-eroded caves above or below present sea levels are frequent enough in coastal cliffs. Many erosion caves are little more than overhangs which have been exploited in the past by Aborigines as shelters or art galley sites.

Caves resulting from volcanic action are rare in Australia. They are formed when lava solidifies on the surface but flows away beneath, leaving tunnels and cavities. Eventually the roof falls in places, revealing the space below. Some examples have been found in parts of Queensland, in basalt country west of the Burdekin River and north of Charters Towers.

The most extensive caves are found, however, in limestone country, and some have passages many kilometres long. Water charged with carbon dioxide is acidic and eats away the limestone, enlarging cracks and crevices into passageways and caverns. Sometimes the water disappears, leaving air-filled caves; sometimes the cavities remain filled with water.

Limestone caves are of two kinds: those found in formations where the limestone is relatively young and the beds of stone unfolded, and those formed where the limestone has been thrown up by rock movements to form barriers to surface streams. The limestones of the Nullarbor Plain were laid down over many millions of years in a series of beds. The top layer, the Nullarbor Limestone, varies in depth from about 15 to about 60 m, and is almost perfectly level on the surface. Such country is called karst, after an area of Yugoslavia which the Venetians denuded for ship timbers.

There are no surface streams on the Nullarbor; any rain that falls is quickly lost down crevices. Eventually much of it finds its way underground to the sea along the Great Australian Bight. Most of the limestone is solid and more or less impervious to the water, so cave formation depends upon there being joints. Presumably the caves were carved out at some time during the last two million years when the climate was, occasionally, wetter. Surface features include sinkholes where the water has, over long periods, widened small fissures in the rock, and karst windows where the roof of part of a cave has collapsed (see photograph p 235).

Some of the shallower Nullarbor caves reach depths of up to 21 m, and are thus restricted to the top two levels of limestone (the Nullarbor and the 'unnamed' limestones). Few of their larger tunnels extend horizontally more than about 60 m. At the lower levels the walls are often perforated with numerous small tubes a few centimetres in diameter. The deep caves are in the third layer of limestones (Wilson Bluff), and are reached through narrow sinkholes through the upper layers. These lead down to reach large, simple caverns up to a kilometre or more long. They are usually 12 to 16 m high and 24 to 36 m wide, but can reach heights of 48 m and widths of 60 m. In places the floors of the caverns are below the levels to which the rocks are water-saturated so that underground lakes have formed. The different levels of the two kinds of caves probably correspond to different sea levels in the past.

One of the largest of the deep caves is Cocklebiddy in Western Australia, discovered in 1930, which was penetrated to a length of 6240 m from the entrance in 1983. Most of the tunnel is flooded, apart from two large air spaces (Rockpile Chamber and Toad Hall) and a couple of smaller ones. At the entrance the water level is about 100 m below the plain's surface, and the deepest known part of the tunnel is about 30 m below this.

There are other deep, water-filled caves in limestone country in the Mt Gambier region of South Australia, including the notorious Shaft where diving is forbidden since four explorers died from nitrogen narcosis (unconsciousness induced by the presence of the gas) in 1973. The sinkholes of the district should not be confused

A curtain of stalactites – in what is often called an organ pipe formation – form a solid wall across Cave Jewel at Augusta in Western Australia.

Spectacular mushroom-shaped pillars of flowstone, also at Cave Jewel in Western Australia. Deposits of calcium carbonate take hundreds of years to build up.

Tiered stalagmites grow steadily towards the roof of Mammoth Cave at Margaret River in Western Australia. The world's largest stalagmite is in Australia.

Thousands of delicate stalagmites hang suspended from the roof of Lake Cave near Margaret River, Western Australia. Amazingly, a few blind, white creatures eke out a precarious living in this silent underground world.

counterparts and form columns. When the water oozes out along a long fissure a shawl may be formed. Sometimes curly formations – helictites or 'mysteries' – are common but there is doubt about their origin. Calcite may form in water that has collected in hollows on the floor to produce basins of gem-like crystals.

While Australia cannot claim the largest or deepest caves in the world, it does claim the largest stalagmite – 15 m tall with a basal circumference of 30 m, although there is a taller one (29 m) in France. Cave guides often claim that stalagmites take millions of years to form, but in one Australian cave a group of visitors broke some stalagmites. Sixteen years later they had added about 50 mm of new growth. The deepest cave so far discovered in Australia is in the remote south-west of Tasmania near Mt Anne. There, in Anne-A-Kananda cave, a complex tangle of passages plunge to 373 m. Speleologists are still exploring the area, and it is quite likely that deeper passages will be discovered.

Living in the dark

Australia has few creatures – like this pale, spindly cave spider – which spend their entire lives in the dark. Many more venture into caves to find food.

Many animals live in caves, or use them, but only a few in Australia live in total darkness. Such creatures are called troglobites, and they are often blind and without pigmentation. If they are arthropods, such as insects and centipedes, they often have long limbs and many erect sensory hairs. Two fishes – an eel and a gudgeon – are found in the caves at North West Cape in Western Australia. In an exploration of 47 caves on the Nullarbor, Dr Aola Richards found 97 kinds of arthropods, but only 11 – six centipedes, three spiders, a cockroach and an isopod crustacean – were troglobites. The cockroach ranged from the twilight zone to, in one cave, a site 4.5 km from the entrance. In Tasmania two species of troglobite carabid beetles have been discovered.

All these creatures depend directly or indirectly on energy sources from outside the cave, as plants cannot grow in the dark. They live on a diet of bird and bat droppings, organic debris, dead animals, fungi, and each other.

with the flooded volcanic craters. By 1984 more than 12 divers had lost their lives cave-diving in this region.

Other examples of this type of cave in South Australia are found at Naracoorte, where the overlying terrain is swampy. They are also found in Western Australia on North West Cape, and between Cape Naturaliste and Cape Leeuwin, where Mammoth Cave is the most spectacular.

The limestone caves of eastern Australia are of the second type. Hard strata of resistant limestone, up to 400 million years old, rear up through beds of softer rocks through which rivers and creeks can carve their courses. When these are blocked by the limestone, they can – by chemical action – eat passages through them. In time the courses in the softer rocks are deepened so that a new system of passages, at a lower

level, may be formed. Sometimes the rivers have left archways, as at Jenolan Caves, NSW. Alternatively the river may disappear into the limestone and reappear on the other side. Other examples are Bungonia, Wombeyan, Wellington and Yarrangobilly Caves in NSW, Buchan Caves in Victoria, and those at Chillagoe and Mungana in Queensland.

Many limestone caves, with the notable exception of most of those on the Nullarbor, are well furnished with stalactites and stalagmites. These are formed by the slow dripping of the calcium bicarbonate water from the roof. A long-suspended drop partially evaporates and leaves a ring of calcium carbonate. A long series of drops eventually produces a stalactite. Droplets evaporating below on the floor build up stalagmites which may eventually grow up to meet their

CATTLE DUFFING

The Americans call it rustling, but in any language it is just plain theft. Often stock disappear from saleyards where they are being held overnight. Sometimes a truck backs up to a gate on a lonely road and loads a few head for quick slaughter. Occasionally a few vanish from a travelling mob on the road.

Skins – from both cattle and sheep – that are sold in Australia must have the ears with them so that marks can be checked, and the owner identified if necessary. Cattle offered for sale must have a tail tag for the same reason. Auctioneers will often refuse to sell animals to the vendor's neighbours – the legitimate presence of another brand on a property could be used to disguise the theft of more stock.

CATTLE GRID

Long outback journeys are sometimes made tedious by constantly having to slow down to cross seemingly endless eroded cattle grids or ramps. Impatient motorists should bear in mind that the alternative is a series of gates, which would take even longer to open and close.

Grids interrupt a fence line with a trench about one metre deep and two metres wide dug across the road. Parallel bars – usually made from light railway line or galvanised water pipe – are laid across the trench 150 mm apart.

Sometimes, where a grid does not have elaborate side guards to prevent stock from stepping around it, bushmen will deter cattle with a simple device – a cut-out metal dog which swings threateningly from a fence post close to the road and the grid.

CEDAR

This name was originally applied to the Cedar of Lebanon and other conifers with aromatic timber. It is now used for a number of broad-leaved trees with similar reddish, durable, easily-worked timber, including Australian Red Cedar *Toona australis*. This rainforest tree was once common in valleys of the east-coastal ranges, from around Milton in NSW northward to the Atherton Tableland in north Queensland. From the earliest period of European settlement it was the most highly valued native timber, and by the middle of the last century had been almost eliminated by timbergetters in accessible areas near towns or major rivers in NSW. In recent times it was popularly believed to be almost extinct, but in fact this is an exaggeration, there being many trees in rainforest regrowth, even quite close to Sydney, and large trees survive in inaccessible gullies in rugged range country, including the Blue Mountains. Red Cedar is one of the very few deciduous trees of temperate forests, and can be detected from a distance by its leafless branches in winter, and its flush of reddish new leaves in spring.

CENTIPEDE

Centipedes, which rarely, if ever, have exactly 100 legs, are carnivorous and have venomous jaws, although none of the Australian species is dangerous to human beings. Their bodies are long and flattened, and have from 15 to 177 body segments, depending on the species. Each trunk segment carries a pair of legs. The head has long antennae, and usually groups of small eyes, although some are blind. Members of the largest Australian species are about 100 mm long

Most centipedes live in soil and litter, and some are active tunnellers. The swift, very long-legged, 35-mm long House Centipede or 'Hairy Nanny' *Allothereua maculata* sometimes enters damp houses. When attacked it sheds quivering legs. It may cause panic, but it is quite harmless, and even useful. Otherwise the most familiar species is the large yellowish *Scolopendra morsitans*, found under stones, logs and litter.

Centipedes have a bad reputation, but only one confirmed fatality has been recorded anywhere in the world. Some large Australian species can inflict a painful bite if provoked.

CHAT

Members of the Australian chat family, with its five species, are found only in Australia. Chats are closely related to the honeyeaters. Three – Crimson Chats *Epthianura tricolor* (110–120 mm), Orange Chats *E. aurifrons* (105–120 mm) and Yellow Chats *E. crocea* – are gregarious, nomadic birds which live in the dry interior, feeding on insects found on the ground. White-fronted Chats *E. albifrons* (120–130 mm) are also gregarious, but they live in southern regions in heathland and samphire swamps near water. Gibberbirds *Ashbyia lovensis* (125–130 mm), in contrast, live on gibber plains in the Lake Eyre Basin where they eat spiders and insects. They are not, apparently, highly nomadic, although they are the Australian bird most adapted to living in a desert. During courtship males rise stepwise to about 30 m, tweeting as they do so, then drop vertically to the ground.

CHEESE

The world's only cheese factory in the tropics – at Millaa Millaa on the Atherton Tableland – produces Cheddar. Australia's first white settlers made Cheddar, and Cheddar makes up about two-thirds of the 170 000 or so tonnes of cheese made in Australia every year. But about 50 of the world's other 1000-odd types of cheese are increasingly being made locally: non-Cheddar cheese production doubled between 1980 and 1986. Almost all are drawn from European countries, although Australia can claim as its own the semi-hard table and cooking cheese Pastorello, and the world's first poly-unsaturated Cheddar, made in 1976 at Wauchope. Most of Australia's several dozen cheese factories are found in high-rainfall coastal areas in each state, but there are factories at Wagga Wagga and in the Murray River Valley, and an establishment in Leeton produces true Pecorino from sheep's milk. The sheep are milked twice daily on a rotary milker; the product is called Merino.

Cows' milk for cheese must be pasteurised to

kill bacteria – heated fast to 72°C, then brought rapidly back to 4°C. Cheese-making involves coagulating milk into curds which are cut and heated to release the whey; salted; pressed; and left to mature. The type of cheese is determined by the strain of bacteria and the amount of rennet – both promote the formation of the curds; the degree of acidity allowed to develop; the creaminess of the milk; the moisture left; and the length of maturing time. Hard cheeses such as Parmesan and Emmental can be matured for as long as two years. Some large factories are highly mechanised – one of the eight Kraft establishments, at Allansford near Warrnambool, was among the world's first almost totally mechanised cheese factories.

CHICKPEA

Chickpeas are one of a number of grain legume crops that have attracted considerable interest in the past five years as an alternative to cereal crops. Others in this group include PIGEON PEAS, LUPINS, faba beans and cowpeas.

Grain legumes, or pulse crops, contain a higher amount of protein than other field crops, and also add nitrogen to the soil. At present there are

Everyone on a farm is expected to help when there is work to be done. There are plenty of tasks that call for nimble fingers rather than strong backs.

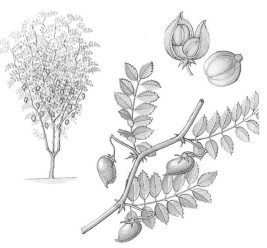

Kabuli chickpeas – with large, white seeds – were originally grown in the Mediterranean region where they are still widely used in cooking.

around 50 000 ha of chick peas planted in Queensland, NSW, Victoria and, to a lesser extent, Western Australia.

Chickpeas are a whitish or brown round grain grown during winter, primarily for export to Asia, India, Middle Eastern countries, the United Kingdom and the United States. They are usually eaten by vegetarians as a source of protein. In India, the world's largest consumer of chickpeas, they are milled to form a thick soup called dahl. In the Middle East, chickpeas are ground to make a thick paste known as hommous.

Farmers also use chickpeas as a 'disease break' to cleanse the soil of plant diseases found in cereal crops. The two main types of chickpeas are the desi and the kabuli. The desi type, which account for about 85 per cent of the world's production, are used for both stock and human consumption, and suit low rainfall areas. Kabuli are large, plump, white seeds which are more difficult to grow, but generally bring higher prices. They suit irrigation.

In other parts of the world, chickpeas are known as Bengal gram or Garbanzo bean.

CHILDHOOD

For many country children last century, childhood ended not long after they could walk and talk. Tots of three and four would feed fowls and collect eggs, gather kindling and bring in calves to pens, shepherd sheep and scare birds from crops. Five- and six-year-olds would join the circle husking corn until midnight, shivering as June and July winds blew into the barn. They would winnow grain, tossing it in the air so the breeze blew the husks aside. They would sift the grain again, and again and again, removing more husks in a year-round chore.

Without the labour of wives and children,

many settlers would have had to give up their battle for independence and return to the cities. The labour-intensive dairy farms relied particularly on children. Large families – ten or twelve children were quite usual – made the struggle more difficult.

Much of Australia's farm land was cleared with the aid of children. Sons of ten or eleven would chop down small trees at waist height, strip off the bark and arrange them around stumps to dry off so that they could later be burned. Smaller boys would pick up dropped pieces from the larger trees being burned, heaping them around stumps and ensuring they smouldered until the stumps were gone. When at last the land was ploughed, children would pick up roots ripped up by the plough, piling them to be carted to the house for firewood. At harvest time – whether it was hops, hay, corn or grapes – girls and boys worked from daybreak to dusk, longing to hear their mother's cooee calling them to breakfast, or to see her peg a shirt on the clothes line as a signal that tea time had come. Boys, already men at eight or nine, would pitch sheaves of hay up on the cart and, once in the yard, pitch them down again for stacking. Children would sew the tops of bags of wheat, although it was as much as a lad of ten or twelve could do to shift a bag weighing 100 kg.

In *A Fortunate Life*, Bert Facey wrote about childhood near Narrogin, WA. To reach his uncle's selection, Bert aged seven and his small cousins walked 225 km in three weeks behind a cart. While his uncle began the clearing, Bert's task was to set snares for possums, skin them and peg out the skins, worth a shilling each. At eight, he was sent to work on a nearby farm for five shillings a week and his keep. This was in 1902, when earnest efforts to end child labour in city sweatshops and factories had been going on for some 20 years. Primary school education had become compulsory from the 1870s, but little could be done to enforce regulations when girls were needed to look after little ones while their mother was ill, or producing yet another child. At shearing or harvest time schools emptied to a welter of imaginative excuses.

Book learning may have been intermittent, but these children acquired self-reliance and courage. They learned to ride almost as soon as they could walk, mounting from a log or stump and cantering away bareback through landscapes whose features, animals and plants formed their world. Sundays were for swimming in waterholes, scaling trees to great heights after possums and birds' eggs, fishing, yabbying, or for simply roaming around the land.

Modern children on farms are still expected to help in any way that they can and to be self-reliant and responsible. However, they are no longer expected to work at adult tasks to the limit of their endurance.

THE CHINESE

The presence of Chinese in Australia is today accepted, even publicised. People flock to shops and restaurants of the Chinatowns of Sydney's Haymarket and Melbourne's Little Bourke Street. In Ballarat and Bendigo 19th-century Chinese joss houses have been reconstructed. All of this is in sharp contrast to the intense hostility shown towards Chinese immigrants throughout most of Australia's history.

This hostility was largely due to racist prejudice, but there were other reasons. Chinese came to the goldfields – especially to Victoria in the 1850s and to Queensland's Palmer River in the 1870s – in such numbers that it seemed possible that they might outnumber Australia's European population. Moreover it was feared that they might undermine Australian wage standards and cause undesirable divisions in colonial society.

Opposition to Chinese immigration was the main motive for the adoption of a Federal 'White Australia' policy in 1901. However from 1958 the policy was gradually relaxed and finally dismantled. Chinese from Hong Kong, Malaysia and Singapore have become numerous among immigrants. A high proportion of Vietnamese refugees admitted to Australia have also been of Chinese ethnic background.

CHRISTMAS BEETLE

Christmas BEETLES are typical chafers with fingered antennae and claws that cling to little boys' skin. They are large, often golden, beetles that usually emerge in December – just as their Northern Hemisphere relatives, the maybugs, emerge in May. Their heads are easily seen from above, and the tips of their abdomens protrude. Adults feed on eucalypt leaves and can defoliate a tree. Their larvae – white, fleshy, C-shaped curl-grubs – feed on roots and humus and are often turned up by keen gardeners.

CHRISTMAS BELLS

Christmas bells belong to a small group of Australian plants, *Blandfordia*, which are members of the lily family. The name was given in honour of the Marquis of Blandford – subsequently the 5th Duke of Marlborough – a keen British amateur botanist and gardener who lived in the 19th century.

The large waxy bell-shaped flowers, varying in colour between species from red through orange to yellow, often figure in decorative design as well as being very popular as cut flowers. Flowering is mainly concentrated in the high summer season.

The most popular species as a cut flower in NSW is *B. grandiflora*, which grows in swampy wet heath in sand dunes from Gosford northwards. For many years, the main source of flowers has been from the wild, but they are

Not only did Chinese immigrants come to labour on the goldfields, but some enterprising individuals also opened restaurants. John Alloo's Chinese Restaurant was in the main street in Ballaarat, Vic. in 1855. European diggers also apparently ate there, because the signs above the door are in both English and Chinese.

easily grown in cultivation, although flowers are not produced until plants are three years old. In the wild, flowering is most prolific in the first few years after bushfires, and in the past, flower collectors have been responsible for the frequent firing of coastal wet heath in order to promote flowering in subsequent seasons.

CHRISTMAS BUSH

Over most of Australia, high summer is not the major flowering season for native plants, but there are nevertheless a number of species whose spectacular flowering displays in the period from November to January have earned them the title of Christmas Bush (or Tree). In Western Australia, the Christmas Tree is the brilliantly orange-flowered *Nuytsia floribunda*, the world's largest parasitic flowering plant (see MISTLETOE). In the same state *Hakea preissii*, with masses of orangy-red flowers is referred to as Christmas Hakea. The Tasmanian Christmas Bush is *Bursaria spinosa*, known in other eastern states as blackthorn. A small thorny shrub with sprays of creamy sweet-scented flowers, it is superficially similar to the European Blackthorn *Prunus spinosa*.

The Victorian Christmas Bush is *Prostanthera lasianthos*. It is the largest of the mint bushes, with a wide distribution from southern Queensland to Tasmania. It is found along creeks and as part of the shrub layer in wet sclerophyll forest, but it is now also widely grown in gardens. The foliage has a menthol (minty) smell. Flowers are normally white, although some strains have very pale mauve or pink flowers.

The NSW Christmas Bush *Ceratopetalum*

gummiferum has compound leaves which are bright yellowy green when young, becoming darker when older. The flowers have white petals and open in November or early December. After the true petals die, the calyx (sepals) enlarges and turns pinky red – the papery calyx lobes look like petals. In a good flowering year, the whole bush can be clothed with red.

THE CHURCH

In the early years of British settlement churches played little part in the colonists' social life. Very few of the convicts had been churchgoers, and it was August 1793 before the colony's chaplain, Rev. Richard Johnson, finished building the first church. When free settlers became more numerous, the position began to change. Governor Macquarie built several imposing churches, including St James in central Sydney, St Luke's at Liverpool and St Matthew's at Windsor, which became not only centres of worship but important social gathering places. As settlement spread further, the great difficulty of each denomination was to contact its scattered adherents. Many small congregations were formed, and the country clergyman became a familiar sight in the bush as he travelled on horseback or in a sulky from one to another.

The second half of the 19th century was an age of church-going, and many imposing churches were built then. However the problem of small congregations outside the main population centres remained. In more recent times, because of the increased mobility brought about by the motor car, the tendency has been for congregations to be consolidated, some church

Patrons at the Roxy Gardens Theatre *in Leeton, NSW in 1935 had to take careful note of the weather forecast before setting out for a night at the pictures. Cinemas in many outback towns once looked like this, with chairs made simply from strips of canvas suspended between two poles.*

Tiny churches, *like this one near Tumbarumba, NSW, are a common sight in the bush. Many are now deserted, their interiors in ruins. The cemetery may still be used by local families, but the faithful usually only have to make a short car trip to join a larger community in the nearest town.*

This is also true of many middle-sized provincial cities. Bathurst, for example, had four cinemas as early as 1910, but now, with a population of over 22 000, has none.

CITRUS FRUIT

Australia produces around $200 million worth of oranges, grapefruit, lemons, mandarins and limes each year. Fresh citrus fruit are available throughout the country in most months apart from winter and are grown in all states except Tasmania and the Northern Territory.

The citrus industry is centred along the banks of the River Murray in South Australia, NSW and Victoria. The Victorian town of Mildura is known as the orange capital of Australia. Other important growing centres include NSW's Murrumbidgee Irrigation Area, the central coast and central west, and in Queensland around Mundubbera and Gayndah. In Western Australia, a smaller producer compared to other states, oranges are grown just north of Perth.

Around eight million citrus trees are grown by 4500 producers. Oranges, with around six million navel or valencia trees, are by far the most important crop, followed by lemons, mandarins and grapefruit. A small quantity of limes, either Tahitian or West Indian, is grown in Queensland, Western Australia and the Murray River region.

Around 60 per cent of the citrus crop is used by the processing industry, mainly in the manufacture of juice and other drinks. Around one-third of the crop is sold on the domestic fresh market, while the remainder is exported.

Including fresh and processed products, the average Australian consumes an estimated 45.5 kg of citrus fruit a year.

Australia imports several thousand tonnes of South American and European citrus during the winter months. These imports have been criticised by Australian growers, who have to compete with cheap, subsidised orange juice concentrates from countries such as Brazil.

CLANCY OF THE OVERFLOW

A personality of this name is featured in two of the best-known of 'Banjo' Paterson's poems, namely *Clancy of the Overflow* and *The Man from Snowy River*. There has been much conjecture about Clancy's possible identity, strong claims being made on behalf of a noted horseman named Thomas Michael Macnamara. Paterson himself, in a letter to the *Sydney Mail* on 28 December 1938, said that 'This ballad had its being from a lawyer's letter which I had to write to a gentleman in the bush who had not paid his debts.' However he made no reference to any particular person providing a model for Clancy. As for 'the Overflow', it may have referred to a station of that name, or to country onto which a river such as the Macquarie or the Lachlan sometimes overflowed.

buildings being abandoned. However there are still quite a few small congregations which may be visited by a clergyman once every few weeks, as in the pioneering days.

THE CINEMA

Motion pictures began their popularity in the early 1900s. By 1920 there were about 700 cinemas in Australia, and by 1955 1700, including many massive city theatres where an extra element of fantasy was added by elaborate decorations and special visual effects, such as a blue artificial sky with twinkling stars lit from above and moving clouds projected from below.

'Going to the pictures' was throughout the 30s and 40s the most popular form of entertainment, total attendance reaching 138 million in 1955. But the coming of television, and the video recorder, forced most suburban and country picture theatres to close.

The social impact of this change has been considerable, especially in country towns. In the cities people might go to the cinema without seeing anyone they knew; but in a typical country town going to see a film usually involved meeting friends and acquaintances, and was a major social activity for both children and adults. Today, however, many small towns have either no picture theatre, or have infrequent screenings.

Sirens of summer

The shrill singing of cicadas on a hot, breathless summer's afternoon is one of the most evocative of Australian sounds. These extraordinary insects have fascinated generations of children because of their size and beauty, and the more common varieties have been given names such as Black Prince, Greengrocer and Double Drummer. Their lives are hardly less surprising than their strange appearances.

Cicadas are often wrongly called LOCUSTS in Australia, for they are unrelated to the grasshoppers and are, in fact, large BUGS. As bugs they have sucking mouthparts which they use for extracting fluids from plants. They have glassy forewings and their main eyes are large so that their head appears triangular from the front, with a strong beak below. The insects also have three simple eyes which shine like jewels.

Three lifesize cicadas – (above and right), and (below) the empty case of a nymph. No one is sure how long Australian cicadas spend underground, but some researchers have suggested that it may be from four to six years.

Voices from the distant past

Most people recognise cicadas not by their appearance, but by their sound. In a year when there are large numbers about the noise can be deafening. In almost all species only the males have voices. The exceptions are the two species of hairy cicadas which are found only in south-eastern Australia and Tasmania, although there are fossils, 60 to 200 million years old, from other parts of the world. They differ from true cicadas in various ways. The ancient Greek poet Xenarchus knew nothing of Australia, and thus of the hairy cicadas, so he may be excused for his observation 'Happy the cicadas' lives, for they have voiceless wives'.

The noise is produced by a pair of thin membranes – the tymbals – which lie high on the flanks of the abdomen, near the front. Each has several ridges. In most cases a plate lies over the tymbal. Inside the animal a strut connects the tymbal with the large muscle which is attached to the floor of its abdominal cavity. Below the tymbals, surrounding the muscles, are air-filled chambers. When the muscle is contracted, the tymbal pulls inwards until suddenly it clicks over.

When the muscle relaxes, the tymbal clicks back to its original form. Apparently a series of clicks is started by an impulse from the nervous system, but after the first click the impulses arise from within the muscle itself. This allows a much faster rate of clicking than can be achieved by a series of nervous impulses. Many insects with very fast wing beats use a similar system. The ridges on the tymbal are important in regulating the nature of the sound, and, indeed, each cicada species has its own specific song, which can be recognised even by observant humans. Ears, found in both sexes, are tightly stretched membranes, called tympana or mirrors, which are close to the tymbals. It could be thought that they are too close – considering the volume of sound produced by a male – but it is believed that the tympana are slackened by the male when he begins to trill. He is therefore virtually deaf to his own music. Hairy cicadas do not have tympana so females must hear their serenaders in some other way.

Cicadas usually sing together when the temperature and time of day are right for a particular species. In south-eastern Australia they are supposed to begin the week after the Melbourne Cup – in early November. Some people find the noise deafening, even unbearable. According to Richard Sharell in his book *New Zealand Insects* the Maoris describe a noisy party as *Me kihi kei te waru* – 'like the cicadas in the eighth month' and English as He reo kihikihi – 'the cicada language'.

The female has a stout egg-laying apparatus with which she cuts slits in twigs before partly inserting a bean-shaped egg. The damage may cause the twig to die, especially on peach and other fruit trees. The damage is most likely at the end of a dry summer on trees near bushland, and may be severe enough to distort growth. After a few weeks the nymphs emerge, fall to the ground, and burrow to feed on the fine roots of trees.

The structure of a nymph is easily seen from the cast skin which is usually found clinging by its claws to a tree after the emergence of the adult insect. This usually takes place early in the morning. The beak can clearly be seen, as can the strong burrowing forelegs. Sometimes a nymph makes a hill or tube of mud as it emerges from the soil in which it may stay for days.

Years spent under the ground

Despite the fact that cicadas are familiar to most people, remarkably few studies of their life histories have been made. It is believed that the insects live as nymphs for several years. In the southern USA it is known that certain species – the periodic cicadas – spend 13 years as nymphs (17 years in the north of the country), and that there are 'flushes' of cicadas at those intervals. One biologist has pointed out that as 13 and 17 are prime numbers they are divisible by only 1 and 13 or 17 respectively – and argued that this would make life difficult for any predator or parasite specialising in them. They too would have to have 13- or 17-year life spans to synchronise. A 2-, 4- or 14-year cycle, for example, would not fit. Australian species are not believed to have such long nymphal lives.

Cicadas have many natural enemies besides small boys. The introduced House Sparrow is adept at catching adults, some moth caterpillars are external parasites upon them, and two solitary wasps, *Sphecius pectoralis* and *Exeirus lateritius* stock their underground nests with cicadas as food for their developing grubs. The native Cicadabird *Coracina tenuirostris* has a call like a cicada, and it eats them. Some researchers have suggested that the call is a lure.

Black Princes and Yellow Mondays

Cicadas have a special fascination for children who have given many of the common special names. Some decades ago the rather uncommon Black Prince *Psaltoda argentata* was eagerly hunted as there was a rumour that specimens brought high prices because of an allegedly high iodine content!

Common species are the Green Monday or

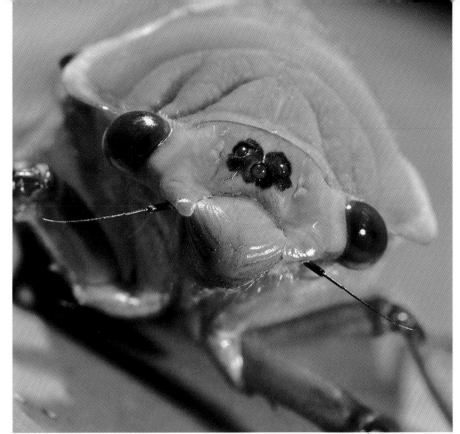

Five eyes stare from the head of a Greengrocer cicada, one of the largest varieties. The largest cicada in Australia is probably the Double Drummer, which can have a wingspan of 130 mm or more.

Greengrocer *Cyclochila australasiae* (with a yellower form called the Yellow Monday), the Floury Miller or Baker *Abricta curvicosta*, and the black and red Double Drummer *Thopha saccata* which has an enormous, 130-mm wingspan.

Bladder cicadas have swollen abdomens and leaf-like wings: the largest, which grows to 35 mm long is *Cystosoma saundersi* of southern Queensland and northern NSW.

Singing in unison

Anyone who has lived near cicadas will know that dozens – perhaps hundreds, it's hard to tell – begin singing at once. This coordination is easily explained. It is probable that the insects sense the time of day – for many organisms have a built-in clock – and if the temperature is high enough they are primed for singing at a certain time or light intensity. It then takes only one male to burst into song for all the others within hearing to start. The process resembles that of a dog disturbed at night. It begins to bark and within seconds it starts a chain reaction that can spread over an entire town.

The sudden cutting off of cicada song is harder to explain. It is doubtful that all the insects are influenced to stop simultaneously by the same environmental change – although they might be primed to do so – and it is improbable that the fact that one has stopped would be noticed by all the others amidst the general noise. Perhaps, however, one pauses, and his nearby rivals stop. Then, maybe, silence spreads like a chain reaction, but incredibly quickly.

AN EXTRAORDINARY LIFE CYCLE

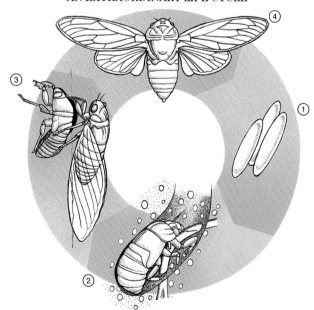

Cicada eggs (1) are deposited in slits cut at the ends of branches by a female. Within weeks the tiny larvae – looking like large fleas – hatch and drop to the ground below. There they dig into the soil until they reach a tree root where they construct a clay cell in which they remain for perhaps four to six years (2). Fully-grown nymphs tunnel up through the soil to wait just below the surface for the right conditions. When these occur the nymph emerges, climbs a tree and attaches itself with its front claws. The insects then splits open its outer skin (3) and emerges ready – after its wings have dried – to fly away (4) and mate.

CLEAR FELLING

Clear felling is the name given to an operation that removes all the trees from a forested area. The usual technique is to go through a forest and remove any millable timber, and when that has been done, to take everything else that is left for wood chipping.

Sometimes no attempt is made to remove millable timber and everything is chipped. Forests considered to be low-grade by the timber industry may simply be clear-felled and the timber burned before the land is replanted with fast-growing softwood species.

Clear-felling is now out of favour in Australia and battles are still being fought between conservationists and the timber industry with claims and counter-claims being made by both sides. However, it is now generally accepted that clear-felling exposes the soil to erosion and destroys a wide variety of plants and animals.

A scene of devastation west of Eden, on the NSW south coast, as land is clear-felled ready for pine planting. Timber industry policy is now not to recommend clear-felling on land not already cleared for agriculture.

CLEARING

Every phase of agricultural expansion in Australia has been accompanied by its own particular style of land clearing, and in most cases the results have been disastrous.

At the end of the gold rush, pastoralists saw an opportunity to make use of the sudden glut of cheap labour that became available, and thousands of hectares of trees were ringbarked. The job was usually carried out by gangs of Chinese who could get no other form of work.

After World War I returning troops were given blocks of land in the Soldier Settlement Scheme. Much of it was extremely difficult to work – either useless crown land or uncleared portions of large stations. It was during this time that the

Mallee country in southern NSW and Victoria was opened up.

Mallee is a eucalypt with a LIGNOTUBER from which new shoots sprout after a bushfire. The trees are particularly difficult to clear because the roots have to be laboriously removed to prevent the trees from growing again. The work was hard on the men and horse-teams who had to do it. Many men were still suffering from war wounds and horses were frequently 'staked' on the spindly trunks of broken trees. Ironically, vast amounts of sandy soil were blown away from the Mallee as soon as the cleared land experienced its first drought and strong winds, creating huge dust storms.

CLICK BEETLE

Householders are sometimes disturbed on quiet nights by a clicking sound: a search often reveals an elongated beetle on its back on the linoleum, jumping up as it tries to right itself. This is a click BEETLE which leaps by forcing a peg on the thorax into a cavity behind it, thus flexing the body suddenly. There are over 600 species in Australia. The LARVAE of some are the wireworms – so-called because of their toughness – which feed on roots and which caused havoc in Britain during World War II when old grassland was ploughed to grow potatoes. *Lacon variabilis* is a pest of sugar cane in Queensland. Other larvae are hunters of animals in soil and dead wood.

The larvae of some other species are carnivorous, and prey on the larger wood-boring beetles, such as the longicorns.

The great labour involved in clearing virgin forest in order to establish a farm is brought home in this photograph from the turn of the century.

THE SOMERSAULTING BEETLE

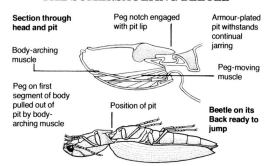

When a click beetle falls on its back it rights itself by somersaulting. It arches its back so that a notch on the peg locks with a lip on the edge of the pit. Under the tension of the peg-moving muscle the peg slams into the pit, throwing the beetle into the air.

Australian climate records

Carefully recorded observations of the daily weather conditions over a long period can be used to construct the climatic record of a place. In Australia, a climatic record can be traced back to the arrival of the First Fleet in 1788 when Lieutenant William Bradley took routine temperature and humidity measurements on board HMS *Sirius* in Sydney Harbour. Later, in 1859, the Government Observatory started to take regular weather measurements at Observatory Hill in Sydney. Nowadays, the Commonwealth Bureau of Meteorology organises the collection of weather observations at hundreds of locations all over Australia so that, at least in recent times, a comprehensive climatic record of most of the country is available. The record allows researchers to identify extreme weather conditions and to see if there are long term patterns to events such as droughts.

State or territory	Highest annual rainfall	Highest day's rainfall	Highest temperature	Lowest temperature
New South Wales	4540 mm Tallowwood Point, 1950	809 mm Dorrigo, 21.2.1954	52.8°C Bourke, 17.1.1877	−22.2°C Charlotte Pass, 14.7.1945
Victoria	3738 mm Falls Creek, 1956	375 mm Tanybryn, 22.3.1983	50.8°C Mildura, 6.1.1906	−12.8°C Mt Hotham, 13.8.1947
Queensland	11 251 mm Bellenden Ker, 1979	1140 mm Bellenden Ker, 4.1.1979	53.1°C Cloncurry, 16.1.1889	−11.0°C Stanthorpe, 4.7.1895
South Australia	1851 mm Aldgate, 1917	222 mm Stansbury, 18.2.1946	50.7°C Oodnadatta, 2.1.1960	−8.2°C Yongala, 20.7.1976
Western Australia	2601 mm Karnet, 1964	747 mm Whim Creek, 3.4.1898	50.7°C Eucla, 22.1.1906	−6.7°C Booylgoo, 12.7.1969
Tasmania	4504 mm L. Margaret, 1948	352 mm Cullenswood, 22.3.1974	40.8°C Bushy Pk, 26.12.1945	−13.0°C Shannon, 30.6.1983
Northern Territory	2966 mm Eliz. Downs, 1973	545 mm Roper Valley. 15.4.1963	48.3°C Finke, 2.1.1960	−7.5°C Alice Springs, 12.7.1976

CLOUD

Water vapour is a dry, invisible gas which takes on the appearance of a cloud as it condenses on to airborne particles, such as dust or vegetable matter, to form liquid droplets. Most cloud droplets are very small (about 20 micrometers in diameter) and remain aloft because updraughts in the cloud are strong enough to overcome the tendency of water droplets to fall.

Most clouds form because of updraughts in the atmosphere. As moistened air rises it expands, because the weight of air above it is less, and cools to the point where it becomes saturated. A cloud then forms and any subsequent upward movement gives the cloud a characteristic shape. Vertical movement of air may occur as air rises over a mountain, producing orographic clouds; as it is pushed upwards by the passage of a cold front, giving frontal clouds, or because the air becomes buoyant when it lies over a hot surface, hence convective clouds. Each process produces clouds of a different shape.

The shape of clouds has occupied poets and romantics from time immemorial, but the best-known scheme by which clouds are identified was proposed by an Englishman, Luke Howard, in 1803. Howard proposed that clouds be grouped according to genera, species and varieties, and given a Latin name, in a botanical fashion. Thus, a cumulus (Latin – heap) congestus (Latin – swollen) pileus (Latin – cap or hat) is a low white cloud, of fluffy cauliflower appearance and which has capping clouds aloft.

The best way to identify basic cloud forms is to divide them according to altitude: high clouds (8–20 km above sea level), middle clouds (2–8 km) and low clouds (0–2 km). Each level produces distinctive clouds. High clouds are composed entirely of ice crystals because the air is very cold at high altitudes; middle clouds contain a mixture of ice and water; whereas low clouds are composed mostly of liquid water because temperatures near the ground are often not low enough for freezing to occur. Therefore, low clouds (cumulus, stratocumulus and stratus) appear to be more solid because of a concentration of water droplets (and also because they are closer to the observer). Middle clouds (altocumulus and altostratus) have a white and/or grey appearance – but often allow sunlight through. High clouds (cirrus, cirrocumulus and cirrostratus), being mostly ice crystals, are more transparent and usually have a detached and fibrous appearance because they are blown about by strong winds at high altitudes. Another group, including nimbostratus and cumulonimbus clouds, may extend from low to high levels in the atmosphere and consequently have a dark, foreboding appearance because they obscure the sunlight, sometimes turning day into night, and often bring torrential rain.

Some commonly seen clouds

Cirrus or mare's tail clouds are the highest. They are made up of ice crystals and are usually between 8 and 20 km above sea level.

Altostratus are middle-level clouds which may be between two and eight km above the earth. Sunlight can often filter through them.

Nimbostratus are middle-level clouds which form a dark grey layer, generally covering the whole sky, and thick enough to hide the sun or moon.

Cumulus is low cloud which forms itself into domes or towers – the upper part often resembling a cauliflower. Rain or snow often falls from large cumulus.

Cumulonimbus is low, heavy and dense. It billows up forming huge towers and sometimes develops an anvil shape on top. Lightning is often seen playing inside.

The base of a large cumulonimbus cloud at dusk. The strange rounded shapes are called mammatus and are caused by downdrafts within the cloud.

CLOVER

Many different types of clover – including those found in garden lawns – are grown in Australia's southern regions for grazing and for seed and hay production. These include strawberry, cupped, woolly, rose, red, purple, white, shrubby and crimson clover.

However, the annual subterranean clover family – so named because its seed is buried beneath the ground – is by far the most important. Together with superphosphate, it has been responsible for allowing the development of hundreds of thousands of hectares of land in the wheat and sheep areas. The value of subterranean clover was first noticed by Adelaide Hills farmer Amos Howard late last century, but it has only been widely used in the last 50 years. Previously, species originating from Great Britian – such as red and white clovers – were most common, although they did not suit a wide range of climates. However, introduction from the Mediterranean of annual legumes, including subterranean clover, which suited winter growing seasons and dry summers greatly expanded the areas where pastures could be grown. Subterranean clover seeds are sought out and grazed by sheep, providing fodder over dry seasons. By fixing nitrogen into the soil, the clover also increases the yields of cereal crops with which it is grown in rotation. Trials have shown that subterranean clover pasture can increase soil nitrogen levels by more than 60 kg per hectare in a year. This is equivalent to the effect of applying about 300 kg of fertiliser to each hectare of land.

Subterranean clover is the largest pasture seed crop in Australia. Most of the seed crop is grown in South Australia and Western Australia, often under irrigation.

COACHWOOD

A relative of the NSW Christmas Bush, Coachwood grows into a much taller tree, and was formerly exploited for its timber. This is tough, close-grained and of medium density, and before the days of motor cars it was regarded as the best native timber for the bodywork of coaches, hence its common name. Coachwood is found almost only in NSW, from the Queensland border ranges south to Batemans Bay. Some temperate rainforests at medium altitudes in the coastal ranges consist almost entirely of Coachwood trees. It is particularly common in the sheltered valleys of the Blue Mountains. Its trunk is recognisable by the near-smooth grey bark with large paler patches of a minute lichen. The toothed, simple leaves give off an aromatic smell when crushed which resembles new-mown hay. Sprays of white flowers are followed by starry dull-red fruit which, like those of the Christmas Bush, are usually seen around the end of the year in December or January.

In a scene reminiscent of America's Wild West a Cobb and Co. coach rattles across a rough dirt road on its way from Broken Hill to Tibooburra in the far north-western corner of NSW in 1910.

COAL

Coal is an unusual rock as it is composed almost entirely of once living material. It is the remains of the lush forests that grew over huge areas of swampy land in Australia millions of years ago. When the trees and plants died they did not rot in the normal way because of the swampy conditions. The plant debris piled up and was eventually covered by sand and mud. As it was compressed by the overlying material the water was gradually squeezed out until what remained was almost pure carbon, or coal.

Peat is an early stage in this process. It still contains a lot of water and is little more than a loose mass of plant material in which individual leaves and stems can still easily be recognised. Small deposits of peat form in Tasmania and the highest parts of the Snowy Mountains.

Brown coal or lignite is similar to peat, but it has been buried longer – about 40 million years – and deeper. There are large brown coal deposits in East Gippsland, Victoria, and the Riverina district of NSW. Bituminous coal has been compressed even more, until it is black, with well developed bright and dull layers.

Most of the coal in Australia is bituminous and is between 150 and 200 million years old. The highest quality coal is anthracite. It is hard and compact with a brilliant black colour, but it is not common in Australia.

Australia is one of the world's leading coal producers. It is mined mainly along the east coast. Most of is used as an energy source, especially in the generation of electricity, but also as a source of gas and oil.

COBB AND CO.

This, the most famous of Australian coaching companies, was immortalised by Henry Lawson in his poem *The Lights of Cobb and Co.* The last of its coaches to run is now in the Queensland Museum, Brisbane; and others are preserved at the Power House Museum and Vaucluse House in Sydney; the National Museum in Melbourne, and the Gaol Museum and Cultural Centre at Hay in the south-west of NSW.

The company was founded in Melbourne in 1853 by Freeman Cobb and three other Americans, in response to the need for better transport between that city and the goldfields. The first route was from the city to Sandridge (Port Melbourne), but services were soon added to the goldfields and elsewhere in Victoria. The coaches used were of the American Concord type, which were much more suitable for Australian conditions than English coaches. Their bodies were swung on leather straps, made of up to eight thicknesses of buffalo hide, which helped to soften bumps, but caused a rocking motion which sometimes gave passengers motion sickness on long journeys.

After changing hands four times, the company was bought in 1859 by a company headed by James Rutherford. By this time railways were offering strong competition on some of the Victorian routes, but new services were opened in NSW, and in 1862 the company's headquarters were moved to Bathurst. Once again railway competition soon caused it to look further afield, and in 1865 a Brisbane to Ipswich run was opened. During the next several years the Queensland operations were extended greatly, and by the 1870s the company was harnessing over 6000 horses a day in the three colonies combined. At the same time, however, it was being forced to concentrate on thinly inhabited areas, since the railways were spreading ever further outwards from the capital cities. This trend was accompanied by diversification into pastoral activities, shipping, railway construction, and iron-making at the Estbank works in Lithgow. In 1881 the Queensland operations were formed into a separate company, whose last route, between Yeulba and Seurat, did not close until 1924.

COCKATOO

The cockatoos are a group of crested parrots which usually live in groups and are almost restricted to Australia and New Guinea. The largest of Australia's 13 species is the Palm Cockatoo *Probosciger aterrimus* (550–580 mm) of northernmost Cape York – a red-cheeked, black bird. There are five smaller, seed-eating black cockatoos, and all but one – the glossy Black-Cockatoo of eastern Australia – collect in large noisy flocks. The Cockatiel *Leptolophus hollandicus* (320 mm, including long tail) has recently been accepted as a cockatoo but its habits are a mixture of those of cockatoos and of other parrots. It is a flocking nomadic bird which eats seeds from the ground.

The five *Cacatua* cockatoos are the Pink or Major Mitchell Cockatoo of the interior, the Sulphur-crested Cockatoo of eastern and northern Australia and Tasmania – which is a familiar and very noisy pet – the two CORELLAS, and the GALAH.

The final species, the Gang-gang Cockatoo *Callocephalon fimbriatum*, is a remarkably tame, red and grey species of south-eastern Australia. It spends summer in the high country, and winter in the lowlands, even in the suburbs of Melbourne and Canberra.

COCKROACH

Most countries have two kinds of cockroaches: native species which live out-of-doors and are often attractively coloured – bush cockroaches in Australia – and a selection from a suite of cockroaches which are now so widespread that no one is sure where they originated. These are the notorious pest cockroaches and include the so-called German Cockroach *Blatella germanica*, which is brown with two dark stripes on the front of its body and about 15 mm long; the American Cockroach *Periplaneta americana*, 35 mm long with yellow edges on its thorax; the Australian Cockroach *P. australasiae* which is very similar to the American Cockroach, but a darker brown with brighter yellow patches,

Some native and imported cockroaches

Bush cockroach
Polyzosteria aenea

Bush cockroach
Panesthia sp.

Smoky Brown Cockroach
Periplaneta fuliginosa

Bush cockroach
Platyzosteria sp.

Australian Cockroach
Periplaneta australasiae

Oriental Cockroach
Blatta orientalis

and the Smoky Brown Cockroach, which is a uniform dark brown.

Cockroach eggs are laid in groups in purses which are dropped or glued to a surface. The nymphs resemble the adults, but are wingless. Domestic species foul food with faeces and evil-smelling exudations, and probably carry diseases. There are about 450 Australian species.

Cockroaches have changed little since they lived on dark forest floors in Carboniferous times, more than 280 million years ago, and many pessimists believe they will outlive the human race if there is a catastrophe.

COCONUT PALM

There has been much debate about whether the Coconut *Cocos nucifera* is native in Australia. Its presence was recorded on some tropical Australian beaches as early as the beginning of last century, but it could have been brought there by Malay traders. Whatever the case, most Coconut Palms now found in Australia have been deliberately planted, often with the idea of attracting tourists by 'swaying palms' reminiscent of the Pacific islands. The palms are essentially a tropical species, hardly surviving south of the Queensland-NSW border, and not producing good coconuts much south of the Tropic of Capricorn in the Rockhampton-Gladstone area. In Australia the trees are mainly found within a kilometre or two of the seashore, most commonly right on the beach. Fallen coconuts are usually plentiful since Australians lack expertise both in climbing the palms and in dehusking the nuts.

COFFEE

Coffee is no newcomer to Australia's wet, tropical districts. In the early twentieth century, farmers on the Atherton Tableland in north Queensland established a few small coffee plantations. Unfortunately, the crops were destroyed by pests, disease and finally, in 1918, a cyclone. In the late 1970s, a few pioneers started growing coffee, the world's most popular non-alcoholic drink.

Again, the Atherton Tableland was chosen, but nowadays the hard coffee 'cherries' are harvested by machines, not pickers. New varieties have allowed coffee to be grown as far north as the Cape York Peninsular and south to Murwillumbah in northern NSW.

There are also small plantations near Townsville, Bundaberg, Maryborough, and on the Sunshine Coast, north of Brisbane. There are 57 coffee species, but only four are grown commercially. Most of the world's harvest is arabica coffee, mainly from Brazil, Kenya and New Guinea. The robusta variety is used for instant coffee. Australia is a small producer by world standards and the lack of suitable land is likely to stop it ever becoming self-sufficient.

COLONY

On 22 August 1770, to a volley of muskets on Possession Island off Cape York, James Cook in the name of King George III laid claim to New Wales. Perhaps reminded on the way home that the name already existed for territory near Hudson's Bay in Canada, he changed it. The colony of New South Wales, created in 1786, included all of mainland eastern Australia. Van Diemen's Land, named by Abel Tasman in 1642, was added to the colony in 1788. Its name became closely linked to penal settlements, and by the time it became a separate colony in 1825 free settlers preferred Tasmania, the name that was formally adopted in 1855.

For the third colony, in 1829, the name Hesperia – land of the west – was suggested, but the establishing act of British Parliament referred to 'settlements in Western Australia'. This was the first time Matthew Flinders' preferred name for the continent appeared officially, New Holland having been used before. The Swan River colony (Perth) of 1829 was the first settlement in Western Australia: the King George's Sound township (Albany) had been founded in 1826, but was not transferred to Western Australia from New South Wales until 1831.

In 1834, Liberia, Williamsland – for the reigning King – Felicitania and Central State were turned down as names for the next colony in favour of the sober South Australia.

The settlers of the Port Phillip district of New South Wales finally achieved separation in 1851. To their anger their northern boundary was moved from the Murrumbidgee south to the Murray River, so denying them the rich Riverina. They spurned Phillipsland, because of its association with penal settlements, and added yet another Victoria to the world's atlases. It was the Queen herself who, rejecting Cookland, proposed Queensland when at last the Moreton Bay and other northern squatting districts of New South Wales became a colony in 1859.

The colonies became states upon federation on 1 January 1901. In 1911, the Commonwealth gained jurisdiction over the new Australian Capital Territory, and over the Northern Territory, which had been part of New South Wales until 1863, and then part of South Australia. The often-changed boundaries of New South Wales even embraced the islands of New Zealand between 1839 and 1841.

CONIFER

Australia has relatively few native conifers – cone-bearing trees – although they are believed to have been much more numerous in the vegetation of the ancient super-continent Gondwanaland, 50–150 million years ago. The existing conifers fall into three main groups.

The cypress-pines, which contain about 10 species, are scattered through most of Australia, but are particularly common in the semi-arid interior. The White Cypress-pine *Callitris glauciphylla* forms dense forests on some flat areas of northern inland NSW – for example in the PILLIGA SCRUB – and in south-central Queensland.

The Araucarias, Kauris and Podocarps of the eastern Australian rainforests include the widespread Hoop Pine *Araucaria cunninghamii*, which grows from Dorrigo in NSW to Cape York. This tall tree is often seen in silhouette on coastal ranges in Queensland, and has been grown in plantations for its valuable soft, whitish timber. Bunya Pines *A. bidwillii* are found only in a small area of south Queensland and are noted for their huge cones containing large seeds, once roasted and eaten by Aborigines. Queensland Kauris *Agathis robusta* grow into huge trees on and near Fraser Island, also in the Cairns-Atherton area, but are now too rare to be cut for timber.

The Tasmanian conifers include the famous HUON PINE which is found only in river valleys of the south-west corner of Tasmania. King Billy Pine *Athrotaxis selaginoides* and Pencil Pine *A. cpressoides* are found in the central mountains, and several shrub conifers are also found only in the mountains.

Apart from these native species, there are many exotic conifers which have been planted in Australia, for timber or for ornament. Foremost among timber species is Radiata (Monterey) Pine *Pinus radiata*, of which there are extensive forests in south-eastern NSW, Victoria and the far south-east of South Australia. Other *Pinus* species are planted in more subtropical east coast areas. The cypresses are widely planted for ornament or as windbreaks, and in cooler mountain areas species of Spruce, Fir, Larch and Douglas-fir are also planted as ornamentals.

CONVICT BUILDING

During a period of 80 years over 163 000 convicts came to Australia. In the early years especially they formed the great majority of the work force, and therefore nearly all the buildings left from those times were constructed by them. Such buildings are to be found mainly in NSW and Tasmania, with a fairly large number also in Western Australia, which received fewer convicts, but at a later period. The areas which now form Victoria and Queensland received convicts in relatively small numbers, at times when the history was still part of NSW. South Australia received none.

The most accessible convict buildings in Sydney are in or close to Queen's Square, including the Hyde Park Barracks, the Mint Building – both of which have been renovated and are used as museums – St James Church and the central edifice of Parliament House. Residences include Experimental Farm Cottage and John Macarthur's Elizabeth Farm House

Convict buildings at Port Arthur (above) in Tasmania – some of which are still intact – are a grim reminder of a brutal era in Australian history. Also in Tasmania are the convict-built warehouses at Salamanca Place in Hobart (below). Ruined remains of the Great North Road, north-west of Sydney (right), are little known.

(both at Parramatta) and Cadman's Cottage (near Circular Quay). Notable buildings in outer Sydney or nearby towns include St Matthew's Church and the Court House in Windsor, St Luke's at Liverpool, Government House at Parramatta and the Great North Road at Wiseman's Ferry.

In Tasmania the most impressive buildings are the ruins of Port Arthur. Intact buildings include many in Hobart's Battery Point district, and a number of warehouses in Salamanca Place. Accommodation for tourists is also available throughout Tasmania in various convict-built colonial cottages.

In Western Australia the convict establishment was centred on Fremantle, where surviving buildings include the gaol, three blocks of terrace houses for warders in Henderson Street and the former mental asylum which is now the Fremantle Museum and Arts Centre.

In other states perhaps the most conspicuous convict building is the former windmill in Brisbane's Wickham Terrace.

CO-OPERATIVE

Australia has several thousand co-operatives, the great majority of them building societies and credit unions, which are buyers' co-operatives. The 400-plus agricultural co-operatives are mostly sellers' co-operatives. Foremost among the principles underlying all co-operatives are that they should be voluntary and democratic. They are owned and controlled by their members. Membership is open to anyone who wants to trade with that co-operative. Interest on shares, if any, is strictly limited because share capital put in by members is used to service the business, and not as investment for capital gain. The first aim of co-operatives is to provide services to members. Profits or savings are distributed in proportion to the members' uses of the co-operative. For example, a potato farmer who sells 300 tonnes in a year through a co-operative will receive a smaller proportion of any trading surplus than one who sells 2000 tonnes. All co-operatives should co-operate actively – not compete with others.

The first co-operative was formed in Rochdale in England in 1844, to counteract hardship to workers caused by competition. Australia's first was formed in Brisbane in 1859, and the movement quickly took hold across the country. Co-operatives sometimes met vigorous opposition from speculators who took advantage of the farmers' need for ready money to buy produce at low prices, and held back the reselling until they could take large profits.

Some agricultural co-operatives are formed to buy, for example, fertiliser or seed. Some are for sharing machinery. But most are for marketing, which includes packing, storing and sometimes processing. All of Australia's rice is produced, processed and marketed co-operatively. Dairy co-operatives operate most of Australia's butter factories and handle about half its liquid milk. Most fruit is canned in co-operative plants. Many a rural co-operative is its town's major employer. Australia's largest co-operative in number of members (19 000) is Westralian Farmers Co-operative Ltd, which is both a buyers' and sellers' organisation.

COPPER

Copper was the first metal to be mined in Australia. There are copper mines in every state, but most production comes from four large underground mines at Mt Isa in Queensland, Cobar in NSW, Mt Lyell in Tasmania and Mt Gunson in South Australia. Copper can occur as pure metal – native copper – or in combination with sulphur as in the common ores bornite, chalcopyrite, chalcocite and covellite. Copper pyrites, which is brassy yellow, is sometimes mistaken by amateur prospectors for gold (see FOOL'S GOLD). The brightly coloured green malachite and blue azurite are sources of copper metal as well as being beautiful gemstones.

Most copper is used in electrical wiring and as an alloy with other metals such as zinc to make brass, and tin and zinc to make bronze. These, and many other minor uses, make copper second only to iron as a metal that is essential to modern industrial civilisation.

CORELLA

There are two species of these white cockatoos, the Long-billed Corella *Cacatua tenuirostris* (370 mm), which have some red on their necks, and the shorter-billed Little Corella *C. pastinator* (350–420 mm). To confuse matters, some Little Corellas of south-west Australia have long bills for digging out corms and bulbs and were until recently thought to be *C. tenuirostris*, but may prove to be a third species.

Long-billed Corellas have declined since European settlement, and are now found only in an area between Melbourne, south-east South Australia and the Riverina in NSW, but Little Corellas are widespread and possibly expanding. They nest in tree hollows, and chew the inside each morning to provide fresh litter, which may eventually kill the tree. They form flocks, sometimes up to 70 000 in the Kimberley Region, which feed on the ground, mainly on seeds. Sometimes they damage small grains, such as sorghum in the Northern Territory.

Long-billed Corellas prefer to live along wooded watercourses among farmland, and Little Corellas in a variety of woodland, scrub and pasture, with water nearby. Both species will flock with other cockatoos such as the Sulphur-crested and the GALAH, and, like the other cockatoos, they are ground-feeders. They are also particularly noisy.

CORMORANT

Although the name is from French *patois* for sea-crow, cormorants are not found only near the sea. The four Australian species can often be seen on inland fresh waters. The Black-faced Shag *Leucocarbo fuscescens* (600–700 mm) of southern coasts, is, however, completely marine. The other four species are found in many parts of Australia, and one, the Great Cormorant *P. carbo* (700–900 mm), is found virtually everywhere. Yeast and little Black Cormorants have black plumage: other species have white chests.

Cormorants swim with their bodies low in the water, and dive for fish, returning to the surface to feed. Beneath the water they swim with their webbed feet, using their wings for steering. In proverbs they are reputed to be gluttons, but the belief that a cormorant with its wings out-stretched is easing fish down its gullet is false. It is drying its wings because its plumage is not waterproof. If it were, the bird would be far too buoyant to dive very deep or stay under for any length of time. Cormorants have a strong, direct flight, usually low over the water, sometimes in skeins. They do not fly far out to sea. They generally breed in colonies, nesting in trees or bushes, or on the ground. Guano – excreta – deposited by dense colonies of Pied Cormorants *Phalacrocorax varius* was mined during both World Wars and in colonial times at Shark Bay in Western Australia as a source of fertiliser.

CORRUGATED IRON

In 1850 the imported roofing material of a new building in Melbourne made an article in the *Argus*: 'It forms, we understand, the cheapest and lightest covering for roofs...pleasing in appearance, very durable...' Fifteen years later, corrugated iron had replaced shingles of sheoak or hardwood as the standard roofing material in country towns. Its corrugations gave it strength beyond its thickness by making it rigid in one direction, and provided drainage channels for rainwater. It was cheap, owing to a process for corrugating with shaped rollers patented in England in 1844. Being light it needed only a light frame to support it. It was easily transported without risk of damage. Galvanising – or coating with molten zinc – made it corrosion-resistant. In the 1870s, a new machine produced curved sheets, and shop awnings, verandah and band-stand roofs became convex or concave, relieving the hard lines of a material that did not age with any grace. Inland, where timber was in short supply, corrugated iron walls became common. The corrugated iron water tank meant that isolated houses no longer had to be close to a creek or have a well. In 1895, its use was described as 'the most abominable abuse that has crept into Colonial Architecture', but 90 years on it has gained affection and is occa-sionally used in prestigious constructions.

COTTON

Between April and July, roadsides in some parts of Queensland and NSW are littered with a white fibre which looks like wool. It is, in fact, cotton. The cotton harvest – which earns Australia more than $700 million a year – is under way.

Around 200 000 ha of cotton are grown under irrigation in north-west and central NSW and central and southern Queensland. The main cotton centres are Moree, Narrabri, Wee Waa, Trangie and Bourke in NSW and St George, Emerald and some parts of the Darling Downs in Queensland. Some farmers in the more marginal cotton areas grow the crop without irrigation, despite lower and less predictable yields.

After harvest, the pure cotton is removed from the rest of the hard shell or boll, within which it grows on 1 to 1.5-metre-high stalks. This process is called ginning and occurs at one of several multi-million dollar gins spread around NSW and Queensland. Cotton was first introduced into Australia with the arrival of the First Fleet in 1788. The industry developed, aided by world shortages, to reach a production peak in 1871. However, a series of natural and market disasters reduced the size of the industry until it recovered in the 1920s.

The modern industry which has a worldwide reputation for quality, was developed by several former United States cotton growers in northern NSW in the late 1960s and early 1970s. In the past five years, the industry has developed rapidly to become the world's fourth largest cotton exporter after the USA, Mexico and India. The industry regularly produces more than one million bales of cotton a year.

Only four out of thirty known species of cotton are grown commercially. Cultivated species – from Asia and America – have long hairs on their seeds which can be spun into yarn.

A fine expanse of corrugated iron covers the roof of a homestead on the banks of the Swan River in Western Australia. This ubiquitous building material has become a feature of country architecture in Australia.

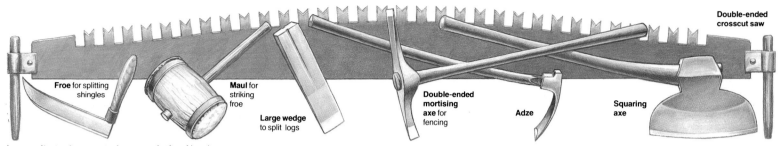

Froe for splitting shingles

Maul for striking froe

Large wedge to split logs

Double-ended mortising axe for fencing

Adze

Squaring axe

Double-ended crosscut saw

Ingenuity is the great characteristic of bush carpentry, as demonstrated in the examples illustrated here. Before the recent introduction of portable power tools, such as chain saws, all work had to be carried out using hand tools. Rural carpenters had a small range of simple tools adapted to their needs (above), with which they could fell trees, cut them up, and convert them into gates, fences, stockyards and even buildings. A lot of work carried out by skilled men 100 years ago still stands today.

An old axe head doubles as a washer on this post.

Two small trees and an old plough make an effective and eye-catching property sign west of Bourke in NSW.

A dilapidated slab hut, perhaps 100 years old, still in use on a Hunter River property, NSW.

Old hand-cut rails form part of a stockyard fence.

The Country Kitchen

Nowadays, country kitchens differ little from those in the city, but for a long time they lagged behind in convenience and cheeriness. By the 1940s, most city homes had gas or electric stoves, but the fuel range or stove was still standard in the country – adding hugely to the work and discomfort of women such as the farmer's wife whose typical day is described here.

5.00 am Enter the kitchen with a candle, bleary eyed. Remove ashes from stove. Get newspaper and kindling from the box outside the back door. Fill kettle and fit it into the matching ring directly over the flames – by the time the range is properly going, the kettle is boiling, ready for the day's first pot of tea. While waiting, put out milk by the back door for the cats. Take saucepan of chook food from the top of the stove to the back verandah to cool so older daughter can mix it with bran and feed fowls before school. **6.30 am** Feed the two pigs with yesterday's slops boiled up last thing at night. Cook breakfast – two eggs and chops for everyone, fried bread and more tea. **7.30 am** Wash up in hot water drawn off from the stove, swishing soap ends around in it in the little wire cage. Get out preserved eggs from the box in the larder and wipe off Vaseline and sawdust. Last week's 20-lb (9-kg) bag of flour is almost gone – add to list for the next weekly trip to the town: '1 bag of flour, 5 lbs sultanas and two tins of treacle'. Put some wood in the stove. **8.30 am** Bake a pound cake, and a dozen rock buns for husband and two contract fencers for morning tea. Set milk to set on top of the stove, and skim off the cream when it clots. Scald the pan thoroughly so tomorrow's milk won't be turned sour. **9.30 am** Mince yesterday's mutton for a shepherd's pie. Fetch in potatoes from the clamp in the barn, rubbing off bits of straw and some of the earth that was heaped over them. Keep potato peelings for the pigs and after boiling, add the water to the fowls' pail. Put some wood in the stove. **10.30 am** Fetch the mugs in from the verandah where husband and men have come for their tea – they're working near the house. One has brought a sheep's head as he's slaughtered today – put it on with some carrots and onions for a broth. **11.30 am** Mix and knead bread and leave it near the stove to prove. Since for once husband will be in for dinner (the fencers bring their own), cut a few good thick slices of yesterday's bread, with some of the mutton left out from the mincing. Some curds are being strained in a flour bag in the larder – mash them up with a fork, add salt and some chives for cottage cheese. Add the whey that drained off to the bucket of pig's swill. Husband will round off his dinner with two slices of cake and three cups of strong tea. **12.30 pm** Mop down lino and polish with own mixture of beeswax and turpentine. Scrub the kitchen table.

Sit down and write letter. Put wood in the stove. **1.30 pm** Refill kerosene lamp and wash its chimney. Refill refrigerator with kerosene. **2.30 pm** Put wood in the stove. Test its heat with some white paper in the oven – it goes black so the oven needs cooling with a basin of cold water set inside. Next time the paper goes honey-colour so in goes the bread. **3.30 pm** Take tea to the men. They get warm bread and quince jam, and the rest of the cake. Set cottage pie and tapioca pudding in the oven for tea. Open jar of bottled plums done in the Fowlers' last summer. **4.30 pm** Put some wood in the stove. **5.30 pm** Set cabbage and runner beans on to boil, long and slow. Send children to feed pigs, fowls, cats and the dog. **6.30 pm** Put wood in the stove. After tea, do the ironing. **7.30 pm** Sit down with some knitting and a newspaper by the kitchen stove, listening to its gentle roar.

31 Wood box got a piece dropped in every time someone went to the dunny and passed the wood heap on the way back. The hottest and slowest-burning woods were gidgee in Queensland, red gum or yellow box in Victoria, ironbark in NSW

32 Hearth stone was sometimes of shaped river stone or slate, but often of cement painted green with paving paint once a year, when the stove front was painted with silver-frost and the top with blacking

33 Dresser, stained and varnished, held Willow Pattern crockery

34 Box of money traditionally lived on top of the dresser

35 Pantry with flyscreen door housed some of the average 200 jars of preserved fruit and vegetables bottled each year; sugar and flour in sloping bins on the floor; dried fruit, brown sugar and rice in large old biscuit tins; preserved eggs in the glass jars that batteries came in; bottles of lemon essence, and coffee essence with chicory; stoneware bottles with ginger beer brewing

36 Kerosene lamp wick dipped in vinegar made the lamp burn brighter. The glass had to be washed, and the wick trimmed, every day

37 Candle was for going to bed. A hurricane lamp was taken to the dunny

38 Silent Knight kerosene refrigerator, an extravagant item in this house, had to be filled about twice a week. A few ice chests were still around in the 1940s; they did not hold much; had to be emptied of meltwater daily; and few icemen were around

39 Meat safe with wire sides for ventilation either hung from the ceiling or had feet in kero-filled cups to stop ants invading

40 Recipe books' most-thumbed pages dealt with baking and sweets such as passionfruit flummery and bachelor pudding, and one ways to vary the interminable diet of mutton like: "Sauce: two dessertspoons of plum jam, half teaspoon mustard and three tablespoons of Worcester". White sauce covered everything from boiled mutton to beans

41 Enamel bread bin

42 Cupboard with screen wire for jams sat in dish of water against ants

43 Kerosene tins came in boxes which were much in demand for storing a variety of things such as kindling by the stove. Old kero tins themselves found a multitude of uses

23 Hearth tools were used every couple of hours when stove was stoked

24 Toasting fork made from fencing wire

25 Oven mitt was sometimes needed just to open the oven door, the stove got so hot

26 Fuel stove needed constant attention. It often brought the kitchen temperature above 35°C in summer. Its damper regulated heat, but it had to be finely controlled with more fuel or by leaving the oven door open to get the right heat for cooking particular dishes. Its flue had to be cleaned three or four times a year

27 Flatirons of different sizes made ironing a more or less continuous process

28 Kettle fitted into the ring housing the top lid to the stove so that in the morning it could sit directly over the flames from the kindling. By the time the stove got properly going, the kettle was boiling

29 Oil-cloth, carefully zigzagged along one edge, covered the mantelpiece

30 Pendulum clock with loud tick often sat in the middle of a row of descending-size canisters marked for sugar, sago, tea, salt and spice, or beside a raffia-decorated biscuit tin

12 Floor cloth often began life as part of a flour bag

13 Mouse trap was often baited with raw meat sprinkled with sugar

14 Lead waste pipe

15 Lino, invented in America in the 1860s, was cheap, easily cleaned and resilient. It needed polishing every week, with a mixture of beeswax and turpentine

16 Newspaper lined the lino

17 Pine table top was scrubbed every day, with powdered bath brick then soap, or a mixture of sand, soft soap and lime

18 Beaded jug covers and muslin-covered wire meat covers were essential armaments in the war with flies

19 Teapot, used about seven times a day, often had a knitted cosy with a pompom

20 Pastry slab of marble or timber

21 Rolling pin of hoop pine

22 Kitchen chairs were sometimes washed with water in which onions had boiled, for a bright finish

6 Pig's bucket took every scrap of food waste not already used for fowls, dogs or cats

7 Sugar soap and ammonia were invariably found under the sink. Ammonia was used for soaking collars and frying pans, washing windows, tweed dresses, blankets, brushes and combs

8 Sunlight soap did the work of half a dozen special cleaners today. Odds and ends were put in a little wire basket and swished around in washing-up water

9 Tin opener and washing-up mop hung on the wall

10 Tongue-and-groove timber lining, smoke stained from the stove, had to be washed down every year

11 Window was not considered important and was often small

2 Corner shelves held enamel saucepans. If used for eggs, milk saucepans had to be washed up cold.

3 Exposed pipe ran water from the tank, which took the run-off from the roof

4 Porcelain sink was liable to get blocked if a teapot was emptied down it

5 Draining board, pine or terrazzo, often had a wooden plate rack above

1 Flypaper combatted flies feebly. It was left for months and became thoroughly unattractive

COUNTRY PUB

The precise number of country pubs in Australia is not known, but it exceeds 5500. Each town has at least one pub, while some country towns consist of nothing other than a pub. Conargo, in the south-west of NSW, comprises a pub and no more than 12 houses. The pub was established to service a major road junction; the town followed. At Newnes, west of Sydney, only the pub is left in an old mining town that has now disappeared. Although there are still many pubs left, there is no doubt that their numbers are declining. Sydney used to have 'a pub on every corner', but there are few major corner hotels these days. Country towns have fared little better, although the decline in numbers is slower there. Reasons for the decline are difficult to pinpoint, but they are linked to changes in lifestyle and stricter drink-driving regulations, among other factors. Despite smaller populations, there are over twice as many pubs in country areas as there are in the city centres. In NSW there are 600 metropolitan pubs servicing 3 million people, and 1300 country pubs for a further 2.5 million people.

Much debate centres around Australia's oldest pub. The *Surveyor General Hotel* at Berrima, 160 km south-west of Sydney, claims the title of 'oldest continuous licensed pub', having originally been established as a coach house in the early 1830s. The *Macquarie Arms* at Windsor, 50 km to the west of Sydney, and the *Lord Nelson* in the heart of the city's rocks area also lay claim to the same title. Pubs elsewhere claim to be the oldest on an original site, while still others claim to be in the oldest building. However, records are obscure and such disputes will never be satisfactorily settled, especially when local pride is at stake.

Equally in dispute is the location of the largest and smallest pub and the longest and shortest bar. The title for the longest bar is not held by a pub at all. It belongs to the Working Man's Club at Mildura on the Murray River which has a bar 87 m long served by 33 pumps. However, many would argue that it is a false title because the whole bar is very rarely opened.

Country pubs are distinguished by their names and positions. Each town generally has a pub that bears its name. Additional pubs in the same town are commonly called the Royal, Criterion,

Queensland still has some of the best traditional country pubs, like the Shamrock Hotel in Townsville (above). Interiors (below) are designed for drinking, with few of the frivolous amenities popular in city bars.

Railway, Grand and Exchange. In recognition of the fact that many country pubs were also home to the local bookmaker, they were called the Tattersalls (after a London horse market founded in the 18th century).

In closely settled areas country pubs are rarely more than 100 km apart, representing an hour's motoring. The distance used to be that which could be covered in a day's ride or coach journey. In less densely settled regions, pubs were established at major points along stock routes or highways. Road junctions, watering sites and river crossings all became sites for pubs. They were established to meet the needs of the drovers and bullock drivers who were always on the road. Those that are picturesque have now become tourist attractions in their own right. Pubs in the remote outback – along the Birdsville Track and throughout the Centre – are distinguished by their rough exteriors, often little more than corrugated iron. Queensland probably still has some of the most architecturally distinguished country pubs, with their elaborate woodwork, verandahs and high ceilings. However, the timber structures are very expensive to maintain and may not last much longer. Increasingly, throughout country Australia, the old style pubs are giving way to air-conditioned brick buildings which may be more comfortable, but lack the atmosphere of the traditional pubs.

Regional brews

Very few regional beers are still sold in Australia. Perhaps the best known, and one of the oldest, is Boag's brewed in Tasmania. Other regional beers still available include Southwark and Coopers in South Australia, Cascade in Tasmania and West End from Western Australia. But they are all now available nationally. Regional beers have been disappearing since the 1930s when refrigeration and road and rail transport allowed the big companies to expand their distribution. Most of the major distribution centres such as Grafton and Wagga had their own breweries until recent years. Until 1980 most beers were sold on a state basis. A gentlemen's agreement between the major brewing companies stopped interstate trading. That broke down in the early 1980s, and now nearly all beers are marketed on a national basis, particularly those of the big two brewing giants: Carlton and United, and Bond Brewing.

COUNTRY ROAD

Of Australia's 800 000 or so kilometres of roads, roughly two-thirds are unsealed, with earth or gravel surfaces. Roughly can be all too right, but the cost of sealing can be $100 000 a kilometre. Even resealing – needed every six or seven years – costs about $2.50 a sq.m. Most earth roads are useable only in dry weather. Some earths pro-

duce little dust, and if traffic is light do not need much maintenance. Sand and clay usually have to be surfaced with another material.

Most rural roads in Australia are covered with a layer of gravel about 100 mm thick. How often they have to be graded varies according to the amount of traffic and local rainfall. Inland, gravel roads such as the Cobb Highway in NSW, between Wilcannia and Booligal, is graded (at a cost of about $125 a kilometre) only two or three times a year, but the Monaro Highway south of Bombala, NSW, with a good deal of truck and tourist traffic and a higher rainfall, needs grading every four or six weeks. A grader can do light maintenance work over some 15 to 25 km a day, usually passing six times over the same stretch to bring material in from the side, cut down high ruts, fill low spots and remove corrugations. It is believed that corrugations form when the surface material lacks clay binder, or when gravel breaks down quickly into small particles. Tyres bounce off raised spots, pick up speed and come down hard, compacting the material into small ridges. Grading corrugations evens them out for only a short time, sometimes merely days. Before new gravel is added all over a road, corrugations are tyned – ripped up with prongs on a grader. Reshaping and building up the road shoulder takes at least eight passes of the grader and sometimes only two or three kilometres roadwork can be completed in a day.

COUNTRY TOWN
See entry p 143.

COUNTRY WOMEN'S ASSOCIATION

In the pioneering stage of Australian history the loneliness of rural life in the outback must have been felt particularly by women. However, it was only when means of transport and communication improved that country women succeeded in founding organisations aimed at improving social amenities for themselves and their children.

The most notable of such organisations has been the Country Women's Association, which consists of a separate association in each state and in the Northern Territory, with the Country Women's Association of Australia acting as a national co-ordinating body. The first state association was that of NSW, founded in 1922 under the presidency of Grace Emily Munro.

The CWA aims at bringing women together in order to provide them with a more pleasant social and cultural life, and at obtaining better recreational, educational and health facilities for country areas. Activities have included the provision of rest rooms, meeting rooms, baby health centres and libraries in country towns; the promotion of better educational opportunities for country children; the founding of holiday homes at the seaside and in mountain resorts, and of residential clubs for country visitors in the

Corrugations are a feature of gravel road familiar to all Australian motorists. Exactly what causes them is still not fully understood, but in some areas they can develop very quickly, often within a few days, on freshly graded roads.

cities; the organising of music and drama groups; provision of instruction in handicrafts, first aid and physical culture; and co-operation in the provision of hostels for country children who are attending schools away from their homes. Currently, national membership of the CWA totals about 56 000 women.

COW

Mature female elephants, whales and seals are all known as cows. So, too, are the bovine animals upon which Australia's rich milk and beef industries are based.

Cows are female cattle over the age of about two and a half years, that have borne two or more calves. Their pregnancy usually lasts about nine and a half months. Cows are selected for their fertility, ability to rear one healthy calf a year, and for their milking, mothering and physical characteristics. A cow's protectiveness of its young varies between breeds, with Brahman mothers being noted for their fierce maternal instincts.

Selection of good breeders is essential, as the size of a calf at birth, and its later development, is largely determined by the dam. On average, a cow rears seven calves in its lifetime, although high performance breeders can produce up to 12. During their last two months of pregnancy, dairy cows are not milked and are known as 'dry' cows. After the new calf is born the cow produces large quantities of milk for about 300 days; during this lactation period she is reimpregnated and the cycle starts again.

CREEK

A creek in Australia differs from a river only in size. In Britain and elsewhere many different names are used for what are called creeks in Australia, such as beck, bourn, brook, burn, rill, runnel and stream. The choice depending upon local dialect and geography. Undoubtedly early settlers from the British Isles and elsewhere used many of these names, but virtually all have been replaced by creek which has been used in Australia since the 1790s.

Originally the word had the meaning of sea-inlet, and was used in this sense by Chaucer: 'He knew . . . euery cryke in Britaigne and in Spayne', particularly one that was unexplored. Inlet is the meaning in Britain, there being many examples near the mouth of the Thames. The features of Australian creeks are similar to those of Australian rivers, although on a smaller scale. They are often tributaries of rivers, although some may reach the sea while still known as creeks. Like rivers, some are permanent and some flow only seasonally or intermittently.

Lush tropical rainforest growth lines the banks of a tiny creek in Eungella National Park, west of Mackay, on the central Queensland coast.

CRICKET

Crickets are related to grasshoppers. Their antennae are at least as long as their bodies and females have a large egg-laying apparatus. When they have ears they are on the 'knees' of their front legs.

Some male crickets sing by rubbing their forewings together. The 'cricket by the hearth', belongs to the gryllid family – a typical example being the 20 mm-long black Field Cricket *Teleo-*

gryllus commodus, a crop pest which often comes indoors. In 1936 crickets – probably of this species – thrice short-circuited the power supply of a Melbourne radio station in one day, silencing it each time. King crickets are large, usually pale, insects which emerge at night and sometimes find their way into houses. Their huge powerful jaws can draw blood from the unwary while they are being ejected.

Most crickets lead hidden lives, but tree crickets live on foliage. There are about 300 species in Australia.

CROCODILE

Apart from mosquitoes, fleas and their like, Estuarine or Saltwater Crocodiles *Crocodylus porosus* (to 7 m, rarely more than 5 m) are the only animals in Australia which would consider an adult human being as a meal. They live in coastal rivers and swamps in north and north-eastern Australia, but are sometimes seen far out to sea. They range from east India and Sri Lanka to Fiji, and once lived in south China.

Freshwater Crocodiles *C. johnstoni* (3 m) are found in the far north of Australia, in permanent

A large and dangerous Estuarine Crocodile Crocodylus porosus *basking on a mud bank. Estuarine Crocodiles grow much larger than the Freshwater species, and they also have a much broader snout.*

A partly submerged Freshwater Crocodile Crocodylus johnstoni *could easily be mistaken for a floating log at first glance. The narrow, pointed snout is the best means of identifying this species.*

fresh water. Unlike Estuarine Crocodile they are harmless to humans except, possibly, when cornered and wounded. They have narrow, smooth snouts compared with those of Estuarine Crocodiles. An Estuarine Crocodile lays her eggs – about 60 – during the wet season, high on a bank beneath a mound of leaves, whereas Freshwater females lay about 20 eggs at the end of the dry season in a sandbank, covering them with sand. Both species feed at night on suitably sized animals. During the day they bask in the sun.

Crocodile stomachs contain stones and gravel, used in grinding food or – some people suggest – as ballast. They have four-chambered hearts, like birds and mammals and they have a bony false palate so that they can breath with their nostrils protruding from the surface while their mouth is open below. Their hind feet – but not their front feet – are webbed.

During the 1980s several people have been killed by Estuarine Crocodiles. Until a few years ago many of the larger ones were shot for the sake of their valuable skins. It is possible that with the relaxing of hunting pressure, since they became protected, the proportion of large, potential man-eaters has increased. Large specimens are certainly common, even near cities like Darwin. It is difficult to say how long they can live in the wild: certainly not the 500 to 1000 years claimed by some writers, but an age of 50 or 100 years is possible.

Despite various Alligator Rivers, there are no alligators in Australia.

CROP SPRAYING
The use of aircraft in agriculture has developed since World War II. Light aircraft are now used in some areas to seed crops and spray them with fertilisers, herbicides and insecticides. Crop spraying is most common in extensive grain growing areas, such as northern NSW, Queensland's Darling Downs and Western Australia's wheat belt.

Crop spraying is usually carried out by contractors and is more costly than land-based methods. It is favoured when action is crucial for pest or weed control, but tractor use is prevented by, for example, wet conditions. It is also used on crops such as cotton and sun-flowers which cannot be easily sprayed from the ground once the crop reaches a certain stage of maturity. Spraying has attracted controversy over the years because of aircraft accidents and the dangers of chemical drift. The Aerial Agricultural Association of Australia has aimed at improving both pilots' and farmers' safety consciousness.

Light aircraft are also widely used for seeding pastures, particularly in rough, inaccessible areas, and rice. Aerial top dressing of pastures with fertiliser is also common. Some NSW farmers have found ultralight planes effective in scaring away birds from crops.

CROPS
Australian agriculture can be roughly divided into two major sections – the livestock and cropping sectors. Each makes roughly the same financial contribution to the economy.

The cropping sector is made up of several broad groupings – WHEAT, coarse grains, oilseeds, SUGAR, COTTON, grain legumes, RICE, seeds and fruit and vegetables.

Wheat is by far Australia's single most important crop. It is grown in all states, particularly in the temperate regions of Western Australia, South Australia, Victoria and NSW. Most of the crop – which is used either to feed stock or in the manufacture of flour – is grown during the winter months and harvested between October and January.

BARLEY, OATS, MAIZE and SORGHUM are members of the coarse grain group of crops. They are mostly used to feed stock, although barley is the basis of brewing malt. Coarse grains are grown all over Australia in a range of climates. Barley, the most common crop after wheat, is grown in temperate areas.

Over recent years, grain legumes have become very popular with many farmers. This group includes LUPINS, lentils, faba beans, SOYBEANS, mungbeans, CHICKPEAS, field peas, cow peas and PIGEON PEAS. The microscopic organisms which grow around the roots of grain legumes attract the important nutrient, nitrogen, in the soil.

Cotton, rice and sugar are all crops specific to a certain area or climate. Rice is grown only in the Murrumbidgee and Murray River areas of NSW and, to a lesser extent, the Burdekin scheme, south of Townsville. Sugar requires high summer rainfall and temperature. Therefore it is grown only in the coastal belt between Grafton, NSW, and Cairns in Queensland.

Like rice, cotton is best grown under irrigation and, like sugar, it requires relatively high temperatures to grow successfully. For these reasons, it is mainly confined to inland areas of NSW and Queensland.

CROW
There are five Australian crows – members of the family Corvidae – and all are black with white eyes. Two are called crows, and the others are called ravens. It is notoriously difficult to identify Australian crows in the field because the differences between them are often very minor.

The Little Crow *Corvus bennetti* (450–480 mm) is a gregarious, nomadic bird of the inland, which may also be found on the west coast. There birds breed in loose colonies in trees and on telegraph poles. Their nests are made with sticks and mud, and sometimes cause short-circuits. Like most crows they feed wherever they can, and will often scavenge on refuse tips. They warble and creak rather than crow. The Torresian Crow *C. orru* (480–540 mm) lives in the northern two-thirds of the continent, competing with the Australian Raven where their ranges overlap. Flocks form in autumn and winter, but established pairs maintain permanent territories of about 100–200 ha. Their call is a staccato caw.

CROWN LAND
In 1770 on Possession Island at the top of Cape York, James Cook claimed the eastern half of Australia, which he called New South Wales, for the British crown, and thus began the English system of crown tenure in this country. Under English common law all land is vested absolutely in the crown or the state. Even freehold land which we tend to think of as 'private' ultimately derives from the crown and governments can place restrictions on an owner's use and rights to dispose of it.

The early governors began the process of the gradual alienation of crown land firstly by free grants to settlers and officers to encourage development, then by land sales and pastoral leases. After the crossing of the Blue Mountains much land was occupied illegally by squatters, and legal title only conferred later. Many lands have been removed from the crown estate for public purposes such as water catchment areas, forestry and national parks.

Crown land today represents the remaining parts of the continent which have not been sold, leased, dedicated or permanently committed for some purpose. Although there is a tendency to think of crown land as 'unused' or 'waste' land, much if it is used for particular purposes. The lands are under the ultimate control of lands departments in each state and territory, but are often administered locally by local councils or other public authorities.

Most council reserves are crown land which are held in trust by local councils and shires, but the lands departments have veto over the way the reserves are used. Travelling stock reserves, beachfronts, much river frontage, council caravan parks and many school sites are crown land, as are village commons, showgrounds and racecourses.

There are also day-to-day tenancies of crown land called permissive occupancies which allow for temporary private occupation of the land. Jetties, boatsheds and ocean swimming pools are examples of these.

CUCKOO
There are 11 parasitic cuckoos in Australia, and one non-parasitic – the Pheasant Coucal *Centropus phasianinus* (600 mm). The Oriental Cuckoo *Cuculus saturatus* (280–340 mm) breeds in Eurasia and spends the period from November to April in Australia. The rest breed here.

Parasitic cuckoos lay single eggs in the nests of the species they prefer, choosing a moment

4 Banks were built to withstand the ravages of eternity. The old building still stands, but nowadays the manager is usually merely passing through on his way to a city posting, where all the important decisions are made.

5 Local newspaper office. Many country papers are still owned by a local family firm that also does small printing jobs. Local feuds, incomprehensible to outsiders, are carried in the paper's weekly pages.

6 There will be at least two stock and station agents in a town of this size. The position is one of real power in any small community. A local man will know everybody's business. He will sell building blocks, advise of subdivisions, organise the sale of major properties and advertise clearing sales and auctions. He will also extend credit to regular customers and can therefore exercise considerable influence over decisions that property owners may make.

7 Police station with old police lock-up behind.

8 Court house.

9 Country Women's Association rest rooms.

10 Accountant's offices.

11 The respectable hotel is frequented (in the back bar) by the local doctors, lawyers, dentists and, of course, the squatters when they are in town. It is the nearest thing there is to a meeting place for professionals. There is a room where meetings can be held and evening meals are available. The accommodation is good, although most travellers these days have deserted pubs for motels. Patrons here do not get drunk.

12 There are always at least two pubs in any town — one used by the professionals and one by the workers — council roadmenders, shearers, and visiting teams of railway fettlers. This pub is also home to the local rugby league, fishing, darts and bike clubs. The patrons may organise a cricket team and arrange Melbourne Cup trips.

13 The Returned Services League (RSL) Club, complete with World War II artillery piece. The club's Chinese restaurant is one of the few places where it is possible to get a cheap meal after 8 pm on Saturday nights. In any town the RSL and the Rowing (or Tennis) Club are at opposite ends of the social scale. However, because the RSL has a larger meeting hall it is usually used for important social functions. Both clubs occupy prime pieces of real estate.

14 The old inn, now converted into a historical museum. The exhibits are maintained by a dedicated band of amateur historians, and the building is painted by members of either Apex or Rotary. The enterprise suffers from lack of funds and usually opens on Thursday and Sunday afternoons only.

15 The Roman Catholic church, school and general religious property of the faith are always at or near the top of a hill in any country town in Australia. If the town does not run to a hill then they occupy the biggest bump on the land.

16 Presbytery.

17 Catholic Community Centre.

18 Anglican church with rectory on the left, and youth and Sunday School hall behind.

19 Uniting church.

20 Masonic temple.

21 Towns of any size usually have at least two public schools, and there are endless arguments over which is academically superior. If the town is large enough to support a private school it will be down the hill from the Catholic church, and its children, of both sexes, will wear uniforms, including blazers.

22 Hospital.

23 A well-built chambers building is the solid, professional heart of any country town. It houses the backbone of the local establishment — doctors, lawyers, solicitors and surveyors.

24 Pastures Protection Board.

25 The Post Office, built about the same time as the first bank, normally reflects the twin Victorian virtues of dignity and solidity. The fact that it was one of the first buildings in the district reflects the importance of the service to country people. The postman still knows all the local property owners, and probably a lot of their private business as well.

26 The movies have long gone and the cinema has become two shops where potted palms and Swedish fabrics sit uneasily next door to 'R-rated' video tapes in what is the most obvious manifestation of city lifestyles in the town. The shops tolerate each other, but members of several local churches are not happy.

27 The hardware chains are spreading their tentacles into the country in the same way that they are in the city suburbs. Racks of expensively packed nails and screws have replaced the traditional bags and boxes — although many items can still be bought individually or in bulk at the produce store.

28 The town's second cinema — also killed by television and video recorders — has been converted into squash courts.

29 The old mill, now converted into an antique shop and restaurant by a local community nurse who lives on a nearby farm. She and her banker husband plan to establish a 'boutique brewery' to serve the tourist trade.

Anatomy of a country town

Country towns were once isolated and self-contained. Their inhabitants cared little for the 'big city', which they read about in newspapers and visited only reluctantly. Town life and gossip were far more interesting. A few remote outback towns have changed little today, but much of the isolation and character of towns has been swept away with the introduction of modern transport, and particularly television. Here Hal Porter remembers an evening in Bairnsdale, where he grew up in the 1920s.

1 The main street remains the real heart of any country town, despite the many changes that have taken place over the years. Much more than just a collection of shops, especially for people from surrounding properties, it is a place where you can find the bustle of urban life and have a chat about the weather.

2 So far council members have resisted moves to have the old Town Hall and council chambers building demolished, and a 'modern' block put up in its place. This was done in many towns in the 1960s, and the results are almost invariably regarded as monstrosities.

3 Council administrative offices and library.

He [the driver] stopped at Cook's Corner, Main Street, the town's centre for lolling, gossiping, watching the world pass by. We descended . . . at the crossroads of a deserted and mostly locked-up world. It was after sunset, sevenish, silent as a stopped watch, not a creature in sight. The shop veranda posts with their horseless hitching rings, perspectively vanishing westward, petered out, I knew, opposite the State School, at grocer Scott's but, in that shadowless, subtler twilight between twilight and sunset, seemed to run on endlessly, to world's end. Here and there, far far apart, three or four greengrocer / fruiterer / confectioners' were still open – Neely's, Russo's, Alice Dean's, perhaps old Mrs King's. So was Chic Saunder's billiard saloon . . . Nothing else. The bars of the town's eight hotels had been an hour or more closed, and no lights glowed behind their polychrome windows of creased and warty glass. The fashion of putting up shutters on shop-windows was nearly extinct, but a few of the old small shops had their up as though it were sixty years earlier and brick-chuckers expected from Bulltown, Hogtown, Cowtown, Ramtown, and Stonewall, nefarious gold-rush shanty settlements on Good Luck Creek . . . All other shops were merely shut, and their window displays would remain unlit when darkness fell . . .

'So there we were, darkness still an hour off, in a street to be sealed and little-frequented until next morning – grain store, saddlery, smithy, dressmaking salon, hairdresser's, pharmacy, newsagency, ham-and-beef store, fancy good shop, auctioneer's office, and cash butcher's, family grocer's, and O. Gilpin's chain store, and jeweller's and hardware merchant's, and – a matter of some interest to us – every tea-room and three-course-luncheon restaurant in Bairnsdale, and conceivably the length and breadth of Gippsland.'

Late afternoon in Peel Street, Tamworth, NSW in 1906. A scene that captures all the charm of another, unhurried age.

when the nest is unattended. They usually throw one of the host's eggs out at the same time. Many cuckoos have a hawk-like appearance which may prevent the host from interfering. Often the cuckoo's egg looks like that of the host, at least in shape and colour. After hatching, the fledgling cuckoo ejects host eggs and fledglings, eventually gaining all the attention of the adults, which may be smaller than the cuckoo. A female may lay several eggs in a season. Almost all cuckoos are insects eaters.

The Coucal is a long-tailed bird which lives on, and nests on, or close to, the ground. It is a poor flyer and will climb trees and then glide to the ground or another tree.

CUNJEVOI

This Aboriginal word is used by Europeans for both a plant of the arum group, and for the Sea Squirt *Pyura praeputalis*. Adult Sea Squirts are fleshy creatures, about 150 mm long, surrounded by a tough coat or tunic. They live firmly attached to rocks at the water's edge, up to a level which is exposed at extreme low tides, usually in large colonies. At the top they have two openings – or siphons – through which water passes in and out of the animal. When disturbed, or trodden on, the creatures squirt out any water inside them as a jet – hence their popular name.

CURRAWONG

Australia's three Currawongs are closely related to BUTCHERBIRDS and the Australian MAGPIE, but they differ in having bright yellow eyes. Their bills are pick-like and stronger than the magpie's, and their legs are stronger than those of the smaller butcherbirds. Currawongs eat a wide variety of foods – including carrion – and can be seen using their beaks to lever off pieces of bark to get at grubs underneath. They breed in solitary pairs, defending a territory, in highland forests. Currawongs have swooping, undulating flight.

Pied Currawongs *Strepera graculina* (440–480 mm) whose call gave the group its name, are found up to 400 km inland along the eastern side of Australia, from Cape York to Victoria, but not in Tasmania. There may be more than one million of the birds in south-eastern Australia. Some stay in the high country, forming flocks. These birds and the slightly larger Black Currawongs *S. fuliginosa* of Tasmania and the Bass Strait Islands, are sooty black with white on their wings and the tips of their tails. Grey Currawongs *S. versicolor* (450–510 mm) are found in southern Australia from Western Australia to NSW, and in Tasmania in woodland and forest.

CUSCUS

Cuscuses – there are two species – are closely related to the familiar Brushtail Possums found in many Australian city suburbs. In Australia they live in northern Cape York where they are reasonably secure, although not common. They move deliberately in trees, gripping the branches tightly with their feet and largely naked tail. They eat both plants and animals, and in captivity will eat tinned dog food.

Spotted Cuscuses *Phalanger maculatus* (body 348–442 mm, tail 315–430 mm) are blotchy grey and white, with males being more spotty than females. Their faces are round and furry, with small ears and red-rimmed eyes. Their appearance and behaviour may have been responsible for early reports of monkeys in Queensland. They mainly come out at night.

Grey Cuscuses *P. orientalis* (350–400 mm, 280–350 mm) are darker coloured animals with a shape closer to that of a typical possum. They only come out at night and are believed to spend the day in a den. They have long canine teeth – a cuscus characteristic – but are thought to be mainly vegetarian.

Travellers on Cape York *stand a good chance of seeing a Spotted Cuscus* Phalanger maculatus, *particularly at night with a spotlight. The attractive creatures are widespread, and were once hunted by local Aborigines.*

CYCAD

A good proportion of the world's cycads – palm-like plants – can be found in Australia. Popularly regarded as 'living fossils', because they reached their greatest diversity and geographical spread around 100 million years ago, cycads are still actively evolving in some regions, and the living species are not closely related to the early fossils. The only parts of the world richer in cycads than Australia are Central America, the West Indies and southern Africa. In Australia most are found close to the east coast, in Queensland and NSW, with a few scattered across the tropical north. A few isolated examples are also found in central and south-west Australia.

At first glance cycads look like palms, but in fact are cone-bearing plants with pollen-cones and seed-cones on separate plants. The pollen-cones are long – mostly measuring between 200 and 600 mm – and release their pollen all at once in great clouds into the wind. The seed-cones are fatter, being made up of broad fleshy scales to each of which are attached two or more large seeds, up to the size of hen's eggs. The starchy, nutlike seeds are poisonous – Captain Cook's crew suffered illness after trying them as food when stranded at Cooktown – but they were eaten by Aborigines after long treatment in running water, followed by roasting. The foliage causes slow poisoning of livestock, resulting in a paralysis of the legs known as 'staggers'. Landowners in some regions have therefore gone to considerable trouble to eradicate cycads by poisoning and other means.

Australian cycads are also known by a number of other popular names such as 'Burrawang' for *Macrozamia communis*; 'Zamia palm' for *M. moorei* and 'Byfield fern' for a species of *Bowenia* growing in coastal Queensland.

LIVING FOSSIL

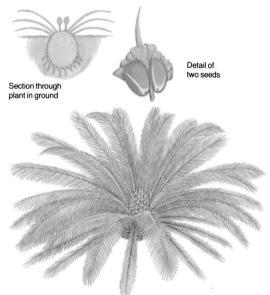

Section through plant in ground

Detail of two seeds

A female cycad *and cone, with a detail of the bright red seeds. The seeds are poisonous unless specially treated to remove the toxins. Aborigines used to eat them, and also made use of the stalks of male plants as a medicine.*

D

DAIRY FARMING

The Australian dairy industry supports around 18 000 farmers in all states. Only the Northern Territory does not have an efficient dairy farming and manufacturing sector. The residents of Darwin, Katherine, Batchelor and Tennant Creek receive milk from the Atherton Tableland in far north Queensland. In fact, the transportation of milk in large refrigerated tankers from Millaa Millaa, near Cairns, may be the world's longest milk run.

The largest milk producing state is Victoria. Around 950 000 cows, mostly Friesians, graze in the dairy centres of northern, western and eastern Victoria. Victoria provides more than 60 per cent of the nation's annual fresh milk production of 6.1 million litres. It also provides more than 80 per cent of manufactured dairy products, such as butter, skim milk powder and whole milk powder together with 60 per cent of cheese. NSW and Queensland also have large dairy industries, dedicated mainly to supplying fresh milk to the cities of Brisbane, Townsville, Rockhampton, Sydney, Wollongong and New-castle. The south coast of NSW and north and south-east coastal areas of Queensland also produces cheese.

The Australian dairy industry has expanded enormously since the early to mid 19th century, when milk was supplied by odd collections of mixed breed cows.

Mechanisation first came to dairy farming in 1875 when T.S. Mort invented the first practical method of refrigerating milk. This allowed the industry to expand away from cities and towns to cheaper, more suitable agricultural areas. Despite such developments, Australia was not self-sufficient in dairy products until 1897. Today, modern dairy farms are heavily mechanised. Cows can be automatically fed, washed, milked and recorded.

The Australian dairy industry has always concentrated on supplying fresh milk to the large capital cities – a policy that has had both benefits and drawbacks. For more than 120 years most city-dwellers have been able to purchase fresh milk on a daily basis. However, the development of state-based industries, designed to supply the fresh milk market, has encouraged over-production and occasional 'milk wars' between states. These arise when one state tries to sell fresh milk across the border. Some people argue that each state industry should be allowed to enjoy the highest priced market in return for guaranteeing year-round supply. Others say milk should be like any other product and be traded freely between states.

The dairy farmer's life is one of the most demanding in the country. Cows have to be milked twice, and sometimes three times a day, every day of the year. This means that the working day starts before dawn and finishes long after dark. Even when milking is over, there are always paddocks to fertilise, stock to move or treat and yards to clean.

The average dairy farmer has around 120 cows, usually Friesians, or the Channel Island breeds of Jersey and Guernsey, and occasionally Illawarra cattle.

DAM

Whether they be small and muddy, or large enough to go waterskiing on, dams are a focus of country life. They attract livestock, birds and wild animals from kilometres around, especially in dry seasons. They also often become a farmer's fishing hole, as many contain YABBIES, eels and fish – including barramundi, perch and catfish. With increasing interest in aquaculture, some dams are now being stocked for commercial farming. The house dam is also often used as the local swimming hole.

Most importantly, however, dams store water, whether for livestock, irrigation or household use. They are usually excavated in a gully or on a slope so that they can be filled by run-off. The water may then be pumped to where it is needed by motor or windmill. Stock sometimes water direct from the dam.

Dams are usually installed by contractors

Milking time in a dairy near Bega on the NSW south coast. Australia's first large dairy farm was established not far to the north of here in 1820. Modern milking machines (above) have taken at least some of the drudgery out of one of the country's most demanding types of farming.

54 Together with the railroad, the abattoir, timber mill and stockyards once brought prosperity to a district. Today the abattoir, if open, probably deals with feral goats for the Asian trade. In some districts, however, there is hope yet with the formation of co-op abattoirs. If there is a timber mill it is almost certain to be running down its operations.

55 Modern shopping complexes are welcomed by country people — regardless of their architectural merit (or lack of it). They bring with them lower prices and provide a hint of the excitement of city living.

56 The small local river floods low-lying parts of town after heavy rain. Locals used to catch cod and golden perch in it, but these days only European carp and trout are caught.

57 The town's first rural mansion, in its own grounds. It was built either by the local timber mill owner or a produce merchant, and is now owned by a lawyer who dabbles in Murray Grey cattle.

58 An old homestead, built in the 1840s, has always belonged to one family. They are fairly private and take only a minor part in town affairs.

59 Cellars and vineyards established by a local solicitor growing Shiraz and Hermitage grapes without irrigation.

60 The house and adjoining junkyard — filled with the rusting bodies of pre-World War II American cars — is owned by a local eccentric. He is popularly believed to be a millionaire.

First the river and then the railway. *The river gave hope in the driest of all continents; the railway brought a temporary end to the grey isolation of the bush. The conjunction of the two formed the nucleus of the town. Now they are almost relics of a bygone age, made redundant by the growth of rapid road and air transport and the introduction of large concrete water pipelines. As members of one of the most urban nations on earth, each Australian has his or her own personal image of a country town. Most are derived from images conjured up by the words of Henry Lawson and 'Banjo' Paterson. The reality is often different. A country townscape changes as much as that of a city, albeit more slowly. This amalgam is derived from many towns and many histories, but the flavour is very much that of Australia.*

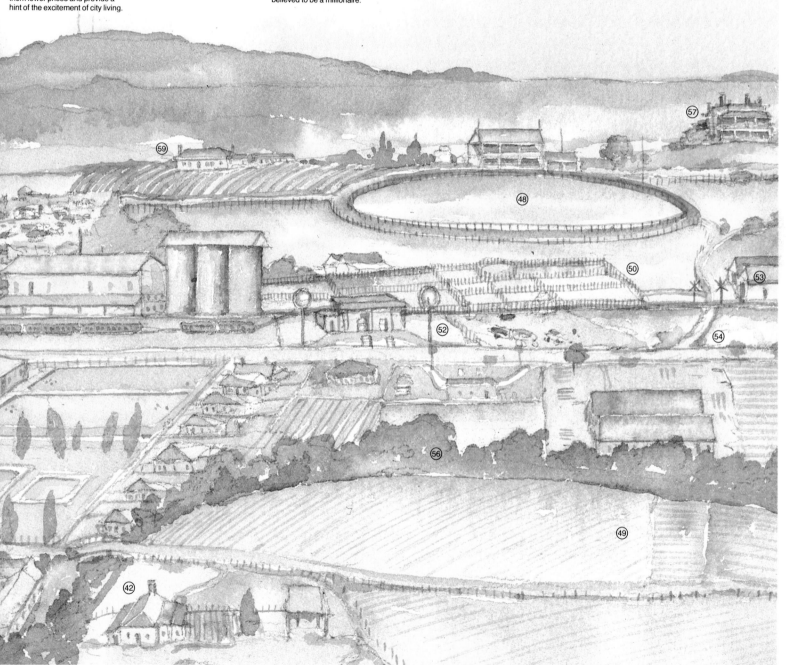

30 'Peggy's Coffee Shop' is downstairs while upstairs are flats rented to teachers and 'bank johnnies' by the owner, a local electrician.

31 The Craft Cottage was founded by a committee which formed itself into a limited company. Regular exhibitions are held of work by talented local painters and craftspeople.

32 Paragon Cafés dot the Australian heartland. They are invariably run by Greek families, but no longer serve steak and eggs, salmon sandwiches and pots of tea. Steak sandwiches, fishburgers and instant coffee have replaced them. On Fridays the wives of local graziers drop in for lunch while their husbands meet friends at the pub.

33 The large old general store 'established in 1908' closed in the 1960s. A supermarket chain has taken over the building.

34 This is probably one of the oldest stores to have survived without change. The proprietor still sells conservative, good quality clothes and accessories, such as Akubra hats, English-made jackets, brogues, braces, collar studs, cuff links and badger's-hair shaving brushes.

35 It was the 1920s before Australians reluctantly built memorials to the dead of World War I. These days they provide a focus to town festivities and a finishing place to the annual Anzac Day march.

36 Palm trees planted to celebrate the Relief of Mafeking (1900) during the Boer War.

37 Town and district information board.

38 The Bicentennial Park, newly landscaped, and equipped with modern lavatories.

39 Bowling club.

40 The motel was established in the grounds of the old mill. The mill manager's residence, built in the 1860s, is now the reception office and restaurant.

41 The council or community hall is invariably freezing on winter nights and stifling hot in summer. For lack of an alternative it is used for amateur theatricals, slide lectures, scout meetings and gatherings of local committees.

42 The first area of any town to be settled was usually a convenient stopover used by drovers and shepherds. The buildings of this original settlement are now rather down-at-heel, if they have not disappeared altogether.

43 The fast-food chains thrive in many a country town, particularly if a main highway channels hungry travellers through its centre. Fast-food outlets are always popular because they do away with the unpredictability of small cafés. At least patrons always know what they are going to get when they order a meal.

44 As in America, the railway was supposed to bring with it prosperity for all. But in Australia the railway was only slightly ahead of the road trailer. Infrequent services and run-down rolling stock mean that few people now catch the night mail to get to the 'Big Smoke'. Those that can afford it fly, or drive their own cars.

45 The average country railway station can be a sad place these days, with empty and neglected waiting rooms and closed buffets. But the façades are still generally well-maintained. The main traffic is now coal and wheat, not people.

46 The local produce store is still one of the most vital shops in town, stocking everything from star posts to canvas water bags, horseshoes, irrigation pipe, galvanised nails and cast iron pots. Sadly, few are now run as family concerns but have become franchise operations with links country-wide.

47 The small light-engineering works specialises in making grain and feed bins, water troughs, gates, general galvanised pipework and even barbecue equipment. They will also undertake specialised tasks like making branding irons, repairing truck chassis and forging special equipment and tools. This is the modern-day version of the village blacksmith, but traditional hand-forging skills have been replaced by those of the electric welder.

48 Racecourse and grandstand.

49 'Chinaman's gardens.'

50 The stockyards in a regional centre are vital to the local economy. Auctions, organised by local stock and station agents, are held frequently, and when prices are good, one million dollars' worth of animals might be processed in an average month. Most graziers prefer to sell their animals at auction and few private deals are made between neighbours.

51 Council garbage tip, cleverly located so that prevailing winter winds blow acrid smoke through the centre of town.

52 Service stations.

53 Abattoir.

A new day dawns over mist shrouded valleys and hills near Dungog in NSW. First light signals the start of another working day for most country people.

using bulldozers, other heavy machinery and, sometimes, explosives. They are built on clay or silt, as under-lying sand or gravel can allow water to seep away, emptying the dam. Construction is based on scientific principles to stop banks from collapsing and to minimise evaporation. Dams also have spillways, to cope with flooding during heavy rain and to prevent dam walls from bursting when the pressure is too great.

STORING PRECIOUS WATER

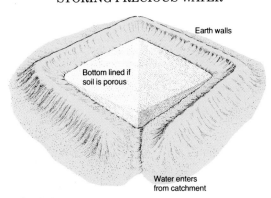

Earth walls

Bottom lined if soil is porous

Water enters from catchment

Earth dams must be expertly constructed and sited if they are to catch and hold water. Sometimes the base must be lined in areas where soil is not impervious.

DAMPER

This was the first bush bread, which can be traced back to soda bread eaten by the Irish. Originally it was unleavened, consisting of a dough made with plain flour and water, which was baked in the ashes of a hearth. Early instructions were quite specific in stating that the 'cake', sometimes known as a Johnny cake, should be no more than 50 mm thick, although it could be of any diameter. Modern damper is now made either with self-raising flour or plain flour, and bicarbonate and soda or baking powder. Until it became fashionable in 'colonial' restaurants, damper was always regarded as a poor substitute for yeast bread.

DAMSEL FLY

Damsel flies are attractive, small, slim DRAGON-FLIES, about 50 mm long, which normally hold their wings together and perpendicular to their bodies when at rest. The fore and hind-wings have a similar shape and are narrow at their base. Nymphs differ from those of typical dragonflies in having two or three gills on their tails, which can also be used as paddles for swimming. There are about 92 Australian species, and they are found in most areas that are close to water.

DANCES

Country dances have undergone a revival in Australia in recent years. They are of two types – the formal and the informal. Formal country dances are the Bachelor and Spinster's Ball, the Matron's Ball and the Picnic Race Ball. Informal dances are the traditional woolshed dance and general 'get-togethers'.

There is no specific Australian dance step. Young people dance to modern pop songs while the Barn Dance, Pride or Erin and other traditional steps are still popular with those over 40. American-style 'square dancing' has a large following in some areas.

Most dances are held at the local town or school hall, or sometimes at a hotel or club if they have a room large enough. Woolshed dances are very rarely held in the proper venue any more. The old woolsheds were often separate from the shearing sheds, and lanolin grease from the wool gave their timber floors a good polish. Woolsheds now are too small and smelly for a proper dance, since they generally double as shearing sheds.

Music is sometimes provided by travelling bands, which still tour the country playing at traditional dances. Regional pop bands or discos cater for the young.

DAWN

Dawn is a vague word. Even scientists take it as either the time of first light or the twilight interval between first light and sunrise. It can mean sunrise itself – surprisingly, twilight means pre-sunrise light as well as after-sunset light. Sunrise is the time when the first segment of the sun becomes visible. In fact, because of the bending of light rays by the earth's atmosphere, observers see the sun before it has really risen above the horizon. When the sun is close to the horizon, both at sunrise and sunset, it appears higher by about half of one degree. At the moment observers first see the sun, its centre is actually nearly one degree below the horizon. The diameter of the sun is about half a degree. The sun appears to move – of course in reality it is the earth that moves – through one degree every four minutes.

Dawn is the coolest time of day. During the day the sun heats the earth by short-wave radiation, and the earth emits this heat into space by long-wave radiation. When the sun goes down, the earth continues to emit radiation, cooling down until the sun begins to heat it once more the following day.

DAWN CHORUS

A bird sings to advertise its possession of a territory. One suitable time for this is at the beginning of the day, as the sun rises. If several neighbouring birds of a species sing at the same time, they learn of each other's presence and whether or not a property has fallen vacant during the night because of a visit by a cat or some other predator. When migrants are arriving – which often occurs at night – a bird which has established a territory soon learns if a rival has arrived, and a new arrival quickly discovers whether or not it has found a vacant plot. A bird sings most often during its breeding season, although some sing or call at dawn from time to time throughout the year.

Many birds sing territorially at other times of the day as well, but the dawn chorus is particularly striking because, with luck, the world is otherwise quiet, and because the sunrise acts as a trigger so that there is a concerted outburst of songs. To the Aborigines the Kookaburra's early song was a signal for the sky people to light the great fire.

DEER

There are no less than six species of deer living wild in Australia. Fortunately they are scattered, and restricted to small areas so that they do little harm, in contrast to those of New Zealand which are responsible for severe erosion in mountain districts. One species, the Rusa Deer *Cervus timorensis* has even enjoyed official protection in the Royal National Park south of Sydney.

The established species with their countries of origin, the date of their first importation, and their distribution, follow. The measurements are mean head and body lengths, shoulder height and tail lengths of (larger) males.

Fallow Deer *Dama dama* (1520 mm, 880 mm, 230 mm); Britain; before 1850, probably 1834; all states except Western Australia and the Northern Territory. These are the common park deer of Britain, usually brown with white speckles on their backs, but variable. Antlers on adult males are partly flattened. They were probably not originally from Britain, and folk tradition says that the Romans introduced them. There are about 7000 to 8000 in Tasmania on 40 000 ha of grazing country.

Chital Deer *Axis axis* (1640 mm, 930 mm, 250 mm); India (and probably Sri Lanka), about 1812, but not established. They came on many boats calling at India and Sri Lanka. The only established herd is near Charters Towers, Queensland, and it is descended from four animals released in 1866. Chitals are brown with lighter dappling and a distinctive dark muzzle band. They are seen in herds of up to 100.

Red Deer *Cervus elaphus* (2000 mm, 114–122 mm, 120–150 mm); Britain, some from parks, and some from the Highlands; said to have been kept successfully in Tasmania in 1830, but certainly brought from Windsor Great Park in 1860. Their Australian distribution includes the watersheds of the the Brisbane and Mary rivers in Queensland, the Grampians in Victoria, and the headwaters of the Snowy River in NSW. Red deer are red in summer, greyish brown in winter and may be seen in groups either of stags, or of females and immatures.

Hog Deer *A. porcinus* (115–1350 mm, 580–720 mm, 140 mm); India, Burma and Sri Lanka (extinct), 1858. These sheep-sized deer live in coastal scrublands and swamps in small, isolated groups along parts of the south-east coast of Victoria, and on some islands in Corner Inlet to which they are believed to have swum. There is an annual hunting season.

Rusa Deer *C. timorensis* (1570 mm, 940 mm, 200 mm); Indonesia, and various islands to which they have been introduced. They were the last of the deer to be introduced, from about 1868. They have greyish-brown, sometimes rough fur. They are found near Sydney, and on some Torres Strait Islands.

Sambar *C. unicolor* (2160 mm, 1270 mm, 300 mm); India and Ceylon, ranging to the Philippines – a forest deer; several introductions in the 1860s. Sambar are large, dark animals with large ears. They have a build sufficiently like that of a cow for the latter to have been shot in error on dark nights. They are the most successful introduction, flourishing mainly in south-west NSW, the ACT, and south-eastern Victoria, especially in the forests of Gippsland. Very shy animals, they are seen in pairs or family groups.

Red deer *are thought to the easiest variety to handle on a farm, and some herds are now kept to supply the small market for venison. These are in the Hunter Valley, north of Sydney.*

DENGUE FEVER

Dengue or break-bone fever is a virus-caused disease transmitted by the yellow fever mosquito *Aedes aegypti*, a species introduced into Australia. The classical form of the disease is rarely fatal although it can be be extremely uncomfortable with fever, severe joint pains and headaches. It is this form that sometimes occurs in warmer parts of Australia. Recently, however, a severe form with drastic effects on the blood – haemorrhagic dengue – has appeared in some Pacific Islands, especially among children.

DESERT

A true desert has virtually no rain and no plants, and its surface consists of bare rock or shifting sand. Australia has little true desert of the type found in the Sahara or on the shores of the Red Sea. Much of what is called desert in Australia is better called semi-arid country, for it has some vegetation, such as tussock grasses and some small shrubs.

Desert, in this looser sense, is that large area of Australia – about one-third – bounded by the 250-mm rainfall line in the south and the 380-mm line to the north.

The surface of a desert is subjected to extremes of temperature – very hot in the daytime, and cold at night, since there is no cloud cover to prevent radiation loss. Consequently stones expand, contract, and fracture. Rain, although rare, falls from time to time, and there is more erosion than in well-watered areas, since the desert surface is broken up and not protected by plants. Rivers sometimes run, and there may be floods, which deposit silt and debris in low-lying areas producing playas – claypans or dry salt lakes. After rain, however, the desert blooms as plants clothe the land until the heat withers them again.

The wind also shapes the landscape, eroding cliffs which characteristically rise steeply from the desert floor, or forming DUNES. In many areas the wind removes loose sand and dust, leaving the larger burnished stones which form the surface of gibber plains.

The Gibson Desert is a vast area of dunes and gibber plains, whereas most of the Great Victoria Desert is covered by dunes. The Great Sandy Desert is composed of sand hills, with its centre a stony desert. Sturt's Stony Desert, is largely gibber plain, sand dunes and claypans. The Simpson Desert also has sand dunes and claypans, which are usually dry.

DEW

Dew occurs when air containing water vapour comes into contact with surfaces sufficiently cool to cause the air to reach its dewpoint temperature. At this temperature, the air can no longer maintain its moisture in vapour form, and water condenses out. Dew mostly occurs between sunset and sunrise when nighttime cooling takes place. The depth of dew depends on the availability of moisture, the overnight temperature drop, and prevailing wind – calm conditions are naturally best. A heavy dewfall in Australia can deposit as much as 0.5 mm a day. Most dew evaporates quickly once the sun comes up.

Because Australia is such an arid country, many of its plants and animals take advantage of dewfall as an important natural supply of moisture. Even sailors once collected dew for drinking water – they would hang fleeces over the sides of their ships at night, and wring the dew into containers in the morning.

DIAMOND

Diamond is the hardest of all naturally occurring substances. It is 1000 times harder than quartz. Because of its hardness and brilliant lustre, or 'fire', it is one of the most valued gemstones. It is usually colourless and composed of pure carbon which has been baked and compressed at extreme temperatures in the earth's crust. Artificial diamonds have been produced by using pressures up to 4.3 million kg/sq.cm and temperatures of 750°C.

Small fragments of diamond and clouded diamonds are used in industry for cutting and abrasion, while larger stones are used for jewellery. Diamonds are found in Australia, notably in the Kimberleys in Western Australia.

Some of Australia's first diamonds were discovered among gravel on the alluvial tin fields near Copeton, NSW, late last century. Children kept them in jars – naming them 'shineys' – until they were identified. The first stones sent to Holland for cutting were returned as 'too hard'.

DIBBLER

Dibblers *Parantechinus apicalis* (body 145 mm, tail about 110 mm) are one of the rarest of the carnivorous marsupial mice. They formerly lived in part of south-west Australia, but had not been seen for 83 years when, in 1967 a pair was trapped accidentally by the photographer Michael Morcombe at Cheyne Beach. Morcombe, who was trying to capture honey possums, kept the unrecognised marsupials for some time to observe their behaviour, before having them identified by experts. Later two dead specimens were found on farms about 225 km north-east. Less than ten have been captured since, and no other evidence has been found of their survival.

They are white-freckled greyish animals with white rings round their eyes. Those found lived in heathland with *Banksia*, and a reserve has been established around the site. The Dibbler's range was probably getting smaller before European settlement, but habitat destruction has made the animal still rarer.

DIE-BACK

Australia does not have very much forest cover, and during the past 200 years the area of forest has been considerably reduced. With increasing awareness of the importance of trees has come concern over the widespread occurrence of die-back in many parts of the continent.

Die-back is a term that encompasses several, often poorly understood, phenomena. It does not simply refer to the death of trees, but rather to a decline in vigour which often, but not inevitably, leads to death.

The first stage in die-back is a thinning in the tree crown, starting with the death of foliage at the ends of twigs which progresses in towards the trunk. After a large proportion of the crown has died, eucalypts may produce numerous clusters of new shoots from branches and the trunk. This new growth is of so-called epicormic shoots, and in many eucalypts is also produced after fire. These epicormic shoots may develop into a restored healthy canopy but if die-back continues there may be several cycles in which new shoots are produced, followed by their death. Eventually the tree's reserves are exhausted and death follows. There are two broad categories of die-back: forest die-back which affects trees in native forests, and rural die-back which affects trees in farmland.

Although there are many causes of forest die-back, in most cases the immediate cause is infection by fungi. Rural die-back is a much more complex phenomenon which varies from place to place and from year to year, with no single cause. This makes it difficult to suggest immediate remedies. However, recent research may provide a better understanding of the problem and lead to solutions.

The elusive Dibbler Parantechinus apicalis *has only recently been rediscovered at Cheyne Beach, WA. Despite intensive efforts by researchers, only a handful of individuals have so far come to light. Dibblers were much more widespread in south-west Australia in the early days of European settlement.*

Severe die-back *near Armidale, in northern NSW. Hundreds of square kilometres of farmland are affected by the phenomenon in this area.*

DINGO

There is always controversy about the Dingo: not only about its impact on livestock, but also about its origins, and even whether it still exists in the pure form. There is no doubt that it is a dog *Canis familiaris* although it is placed in the subspecies *dingo*. However, the origin of the dog itself is controversial. Are all dogs the descendants of one kind of wolf, or are there different lines, each descended from different kinds of wolves; or are some of them descended, at least in part, from jackals? Or did the dog exist in the wild as a dog before it was domesticated?

Recently some biologists have taken to calling the domestic dog a wolf, *Canis lupus familiaris*, because some dogs will interbreed successfully with wolves. On the other hand there are differences between the genes of wolves and domestic dogs. In that respect the Dingo falls in with the domestic dogs. The oldest known domesticated dogs came from central Asia and are dated at about 12 000 BP (Before Present), whereas the Dingo is believed to have arrived in Australia no more than 4000 years ago, after the seas rose, cutting off Tasmania and flooding much of the continental shelf. This fits in with the modern notion that it was introduced over the sea by humans, and must have been domesticated to have travelled in canoes or on rafts. Later it became feral.

Some breeds of dogs, for example greyhounds, can be traced back at least 5000 years, so the Dingo may not even have been a particularly old breed of dog. One puzzling fact is that apart from some remains in Timor, no similar wild dog – fossil or still living – is found in adjacent islands or countries, though some living dogs in the Indus Valley region do resemble it. This led one researcher to suggest that it was brought to Australia by seafaring people, and that it could be descended from working dogs of south Asia.

Aboriginal people in European times would often bring Dingo pups into camp and raise them, but some pre-European Aboriginal sites – less than 1000 years old – have revealed graves in which dogs had been carefully buried, and the skeletons of some of these show redomestication – taming and breeding under human control. Otherwise all Dingo remains are similar to modern wild Dingoes.

Dingoes have a narrower snout than similarly-sized dogs such as kelpies; larger bony swellings over the ears; larger although more slender canines and bigger shearing teeth. Males range in size from about 860 to 980 mm (head and body) with a 290- to 3800-mm bushy tail. Bitches are smaller. Colour varies, but a Dingo is typically ginger with white points, although some are black and tan, or even completely white. There is disagreement about how pure Dingoes now are. CSIRO studies claim that there has been much interbreeding with domestic animals in populated areas, and even some in the Centre. The consequences are that the cross-breeds breed more often than pure dingoes – domestic bitches come on heat twice a year, Dingo bitches only once a year – and possibly that cross-breeds form bigger packs. Normally mating occurs from autumn to early winter, and a litter usually consists of three to four pups.

Dingoes are distributed throughout the Australian mainland, and feed on whatever is available. Mammals make up about 60 per cent of their diet and birds and reptiles the rest. Rabbits provide a large proportion when plentiful. When hunting small game Dingoes are usually solitary. When hunting larger animals such as wallabies or Eastern Grey Kangaroos several will co-operate. They will also take sheep – hence the existence of a fence, longer than China's Great Wall, which is supposed to exclude them from southern and eastern Australia.

Newcomers to the bush *are often startled to hear Dingoes howling at night. Although they belong to the same species as domestic dogs, Dingoes do not bark. Few pure-bred Dingoes now exist – most having interbred with feral dogs. Probably the last pure-bred population lives in forests between the Great Divide and the sea.*

DIRECTION

It is probably easier to get lost in Australia than in almost any other country in the world. The dense forest and bush that covers most of the continent – except for the arid interior – and often rugged terrain make direction finding difficult, even for those with bush skills. No one should venture into the bush without a map and compass, and a thorough knowledge of how to use them. Nevertheless, even an expert, properly equipped, will get lost from time to time. Usually, however, this will only be a temporary state of affairs, provided there is a map and compass to hand.

If you should get lost without a map or compass there are a number of simple techniques that may help you to find your way to safety, if you remember some basic facts.

The sun rises in the east and sets in the west – as do the stars and the moon. At its highest point in the sky – at noon – the sun will be due north. When you stand and face north, east is 90° to your right and west is 90° to your left. South is directly behind you.

There are a number of simple ways of finding north and south – at least approximately. Perhaps the most common involves using the sun and a watch (not digital). Point the number 12 at the sun and then north is about half way between 12 and the hour hand. A more accurate way is to remember that the sun moves 15° every hour.

Moss usually grows on the southern side of a tree, fallen log or rock, because there it receives less direct sunlight. Check on several trees in the neighbourhood before making any decisions – a single example may be shaded by other objects in the vicinity.

FINDING SOUTH

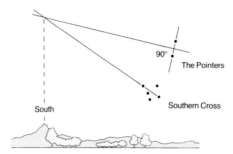

On a clear night it is a simple matter to find south. In your imagination draw a line in the sky linking the two stars on the main axis of the Southern Cross, and another at right angles to the Pointers. The point where they intersect is directly above due south.

Provided that you know the time before or after noon you can estimate where north is from the sun's present position by measuring off the correct number of degrees along the horizon. The distance across four knuckles on a clenched fist is about 8°, and across four outstretched fingers 15°.

If the sky is cloudy, and it is hard to work out exactly where the sun is, place a match upright on the 12 of your watch. Move the watch until the shadow of the match runs through the centre of the watch, then bisect the angles as before.

You can also find north by placing a stick in the ground. Make sure the stick is vertical then draw a circle on the ground around it. The shadow of the stick will slowly move. Mark the shadow on the ground every 10 or 15 minutes. If you join up these marks you will get a curved line. The points where the line cuts the circle will be due east and west.

At night, provided the sky is clear, it is a simple matter to find due south by using the Southern Cross constellation and two stars called the Pointers, which are nearly always visible from anywhere in Australia. Remember, however, that the stars change their position during the night, but that the pattern remains the same.

Draw an imaginary line through the long axis of the cross – the two stars furthest apart. Draw a second line between the Pointers. Bisect this line at right angles. Continue this bisecting line until it crosses the line through the Southern Cross. Drop a vertical line from this point to the horizon. Note where it falls in relation to some landmark that you will be able to recognise in daylight.

Two final natural direction indicators that may be useful to confirm your orientation are: that moss always grows on the shaded, southern side of a log or tree, and that in northern Australia termites build their giant mounds on an accurate north-south axis.

FINDING NORTH

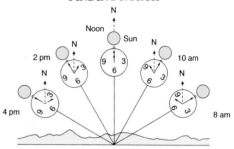

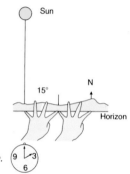

To find north, point the 12 o'clock digits of a watch at the sun – north is then about half way between the number 12 and the hour hand. Or you can calculate the number of minutes before or after noon and divide by four to get the number of degrees the sun is east or west of north. Use your hand to estimate the angle.

DISEASES OF STOCK

Australia is free of many stock diseases – including rabies and foot-and-mouth – partly due to strict quarantine rules and also to the protection given by being an island. Nevertheless, many diseases cause substantial losses. Some, like goitre, are related to nutritional deficiencies, while diseases like LEPTOSPIROSIS and BRUCELLOSIS are caused by viruses or bacteria. Others, like footrot and abscesses, are due to environmental factors. Most can by prevented or treated through vaccination or other techniques.

Brucellosis and tuberculosis are highly contagious cattle diseases, which can also affect humans. A national eradication program has reduced their incidence to northern Australia, and they are expected to be virtually eliminated within the next decade. Leptospirosis is another infectious cattle disease which affects humans, and can be vaccinated against or treated Tetanus, an acute infectious disease in sheep and cattle, can also be vaccinated against. Blue tongue is a serious insect-borne viral disease, found only in northern Australia. Originating in Africa, the strain present in Australia has not been found elsewhere.

Anthrax, a fatal disease of stock and man, occurs mainly in central NSW and occasionally in Victoria. It is sometimes known as 'the silent death' because it strikes so suddenly. Affected properties are quarantined. Blackleg can also cause sudden death in stock, but can be vaccinated against.

Many stock diseases can also be related to

nutritional factors – selenium deficiency, for example, can cause infertility in ewes and wasted muscles. A major sheep disease in Western Australia, lupinosis, occurs when sheep eat fungus-infected lupin stubble. Annual rye-grass toxicity is also a serious problem in Western Australia, and in South Australia to a lesser extent. It has killed over 12 000 sheep and 1000 cattle.

Stock also suffer parasites such as ticks, buffalo fly, lice, round worm and tapeworm. Most can be treated with some form of chemical application. The worst parasite affecting sheep is probably liver FLUKE, which occurs in high rainfall tableland regions and irrigation areas in all states except Western Australia.

DOCKING

Long tails may look attractive on young lambs, but in practice they are often a target for deadly blowflies. Lambs are therefore docked – have their tails cut – at an early stage. The length of the animal's tail is very important as one which is too long or too short can make sheep susceptible to flystrike.

Docking is usually done at marking, when the lambs are castrated, vaccinated and have identifying tags inserted in their ears.

DOG FENCE

The world's longest fence runs 5500 km from South Australia to Queensland, and is designed mainly to protect the principal sheep grazing areas of eastern Australia from attacks by Dingoes. The wire fence, between 1.5 and 2 m high – depending on the animals it is designed to

LONGEST FENCE IN THE WORLD

Dog fences protect sheep grazing areas in south-east and south-west Australia from attacks by Dingoes. Some stretches also keep kangaroos and rabbits out of major wheat growing regions.

A stretch of the dog fence in South Australia. Some parts of the fence in that state are to be electrified using solar panels so that any break will automatically set off an alarm to warn maintenance crews.

exclude – is usually buried 300 mm underground. In Western Australia another long stretch of fence encloses roughly the south-west corner of the continent. Altogether, Australia has a total of around 10 000 km of vermin-proof fences of various types.

Maintenance of the fences is a major problem for all of the state governments involved. Some parts of fences are up to 100 years old and will quickly corrode, particularly when exposed to salt. Sand often drifts over stretches of fencing, and the wire may be breached by kangaroos and emus. In Queensland 23 men work full time maintaining the fence, patrolling it in pairs. These days plastic wire is replacing the traditional variety, and it is hoped that this will double the fence's 20-year life expectancy.

At various times other fences have been built to control the spread of rabbits, kangaroos and other farming pests. In the 1880s and 1890s thousands of kilometres of fencing were erected in a desperate attempt to prevent rabbits from taking over the whole of Australia, but with little success. Despite the fact that the bottom of the wire was buried deep underground, the rabbits still managed to dig under it. Corners were also particularly weak points because rabbits would simply gather there in large numbers, jumping on each others' backs until they scaled the wire.

THE DOG ON THE TUCKER BOX

In 1932 Prime Minister Joseph Lyons unveiled a monument, featuring the statue of a dog sitting on a box, beside the Hume Highway near Gundagai. The location, known as Five-Mile Creek, had been a favourite stopping place for bullock drivers in early colonial days, and now attracts great numbers of passing motorists – even though the main highway no longer passes the monument.

The story on which this monument is based has its origin in a bush song of the 1890s, which tells of the trials of 'Bill the Bullocky':

His team got bogged on the Five Mile Creek,
Bill lashed and swore and cried,
'If Nobby don't get me out of this,
I'll tattoo his bloody hide';

But Nobby strained and broke his yoke,
Poked out the leader's eye,
And the dog sat in the tucker box,
Five miles from Gundagai.

The word 'sat' is actually a polite variation of the word used in the oldest version of the song. Later songs on the same theme have perpetuated it, and have substituted 'on' for 'in' the tuckerbox.

Why, however, should the story have become so well-known? One reason was the popularity of *The Road To Gundagai*, written by Jack O'Hagan in 1922, and used as the theme song of the *Dad and Dave* radio serial. It did not mention the dog, but the popularity of the characters Dave and Mabel led O'Hagan to back it up with another song:

My Mabel waits for me,
underneath the bright blue sky,
Where the dog sits on the tucker box,
five miles from Gundagai.

And so the anonymous, misbehaving dog became part of Australian folklore.

Bill the Bullocky's dog – immortalised in rhyme by Jack Moses in his song Nine Miles from Gundagai – was celebrated in this monument unveiled by the Prime Minister, just outside Gundagai, in 1932.

Working Dogs

It is a paradox that the working dog is at the one time the most prized and despised animal in rural Australia. It is a rare stockman who does not boast about his dog – of its intelligence and his devotion to his four-legged helper. For all that, most of the working dogs in Australia are poorly fed, poorly trained and the fact that they work so well is usually more of a tribute to their breeding than to their trainers.

Kelpies are the best known of Australian sheep dogs. Several colour combinations are possible – black, black and tan, red, red and tan, fawn, chocolate and smoke blue.

Border Collies were bred in Scotland as sheep dogs and are still popular in many parts of Australia.

Red Cattle Dogs are the same breed as Blue Heelers, but with different colouring. Almost every litter of Blue Cattle Dogs contains at least one red pup. The dog's part-Dingo ancestry is quite obvious.

A number of pure breeds are recognised by bushmen as working dogs. The Border Collie, the Kelpie and the Blue Heeler – also known as the Queensland Blue – had their origins overseas, in Britain, but the last is the odd one out, having some Dingo in its make-up.

The Blue Heeler is a smooth-coated, stocky dog with a great broad head. It comes in metallic blue or red roan colours and, unlike its sheep dog cousins, is most often used to 'hunt away' or drive stock ahead of it. It is allowed to bite – something that sheep dogs are not allowed to do – and will naturally 'heel' or nip at the hooves of large stock to get them moving. The Blue Heeler is thought to be descended from the Smithfield Blue, an English working cattle dog. Imported to this country to work stock it was soon found that the dog's usual weapon – its bark – was all that was needed to send half-wild cattle into the bush, never to be seen again. Clearly what was needed was a cattle dog without a bark. The native dog, the Dingo, has no bark. It is a silent hunter, and the marriage of the Smithfield Blue and the non-barking Dingo produced just the combination needed to get wild cattle moving, but not before the dog was within working distance and able to control them effectively.

Border Collies are handsome black and white dogs, either smooth-coated or long-coated. Some say they do not work as well as Kelpies in hot, open country, while others say they work closer and are more aggressive than Kelpies. Each dog has its own traits.

The Kelpie is known as Australia's own working dog and there is an old story that all Kelpies are descended from a particularly good Scottish bitch called 'Kelpie' – Gaelic for a water spirit. All of her offspring were known as 'Kelpie's pups' or just Kelpies.

The crucial first test

From the day a stockman picks up his new puppy he waits anxiously to see if it has an 'eye'. In other words, is it interested in working stock. The farm chickens are usually the first target. A pup that will stalk a couple of chickens until they start to run, and then dash to the front of them to frustrate their escape will bring a smile of delight to the face of its new owner.

The dash to the head of the stock to cut off their escape is the secret of a working dog. A pup that sees the chasing of chickens as a game, and is content to run along behind, is useless. A working dog has the instinct to kill bred into it. The rush to the head of the group of stock is the action of a hunter that preys on a herd. Its aim is to turn a fleeing mob back onto itself, to get the animals to mill about in confusion, and to use that confusion to go in for a kill.

The first thing that a good handler will teach his pup

Blue heelers – also known as Blue Cattle Dogs or Queensland Blues – are originally descended from English cattle dogs, although their origin is difficult to establish accurately.

Kangaroo Hounds were the first dogs to be developed in Australia. Used as fast hunting dogs, they were a cross between a Greyhound and a Deerhound.

Dingoes – the first Australian dogs – came to Australia with Aborigines about 4000 years ago. They are too independent to be used for work.

is to sit. A pup that has learned that lesson can be stopped in an act of mischief, corrected in a false move or, if necessary, kept out of harm's way. Once a pup has learned its name and how to sit it is taught to 'cast' – to leave its handler on command and run to the head of a group of sheep. Patient trainers teach this trick with a small group in a large yard. The pup can see all of the sheep and they cannot get away from it. It therefore learns quickly, and that builds confidence. Lazy trainers tie the pup to the collar of an older dog and send them both to work in a paddock. The older dog finds the towing hard work so it cuts in closer to the group than it would normally do, or the group goes so fast that they get away from the frustrated older dog and its ward and bad habits are learned.

A good cast is a wide cast. The dog should go away from his handler in a wide semi-circle to the front of the group of animals. In that way they do not see it coming and run or scatter in a panic. Also any single sheep, or small groups separated from the main mob will be turned back into it. The handler will usually signal the dog with his hand (to go left or right) and tell it to 'get away back'. Sometimes the dog may respond to a whistled command. Once the dog has gone to the front of the mob and turned it, the sheep are under control, and with a wave of his hand the handler can send the dog either to the left or the right, hold the

animals together, and lead them in any direction he wants to. In this case the handler rides in front, and the dog brings the animals along behind.

Dogs with other skills

Not all the work on a station, however, is mustering sheep and cattle in open paddocks. There is also work to be done in stockyards and in loading animals on to trucks. Usually these jobs call for a different type of dog – one that will work very close to the animals. The weapons of a good yard dog are its ability to bark – to 'speak up' on command – and its ability to 'back'.

The fastest way to get sheep into a pen, up a race or into a truck is to send a dog to the front of the group, and to bring it back through them. The sheep run to get away from the marauder and end up by going exactly where the handler wanted them to. When sheep are jammed into a loading race or stuck in a gateway, the only way to get a dog to the front may be over their backs. A good backing dog will run across the backs of a group and drop in front of them.

Likely pups are taught to 'back' by pushing them about in a wheelbarrow. The next step is to put a bale of hay in the barrow to make the balancing act a bit more difficult. Finally, the handler places the pup on the backs of some sheep held in a confined space so that it cannot fall between them.

Good yard dogs must be able to 'back' – to run over the backs of stock to get into position to force them up a ramp or into a yard where necessary.

DONKEY

Descended from wild asses of arid parts of northeast Africa, donkeys have adapted all too well to inland Australia. Some were brought to Australia in the 1860s, and for decades donkeys did useful work as pack animals and in large teams. Made redundant by motor vehicles, many were released to roam the country. Feral donkeys are now a major problem in the Northern Territory and Western Australia. They cause erosion, compete with cattle for feed, and hinder mustering.

In dry conditions the donkeys form aggressive mobs of up to 500 around water, preventing cattle from drinking. They also harm the habitats of small surface mammals and burrowing species. Little use can be made of them. There is no market for live animals or for donkey meat for human consumption. Even the skin does not make good leather with its many large pores. Every year in Western Australia alone about 30 000 are shot from helicopters, but at least a million more thrive.

Asses, strictly speaking, are the wild Asiatic and African members of the horse family, but the word is used loosely for donkeys. Donkeys *Equus asinus* can breed with horses. The progeny are always infertile. A male donkey and female horse produce a mule; a female donkey and a male horse produce a hinny.

DOWSING

Dowsing defies explanation. An American physicist has found that many dowsers are sensitive to tiny disturbances in the earth's magnetic field, so it is the dowser who unknowingly causes the rod to move. But there are documented cases of dowsing at a distance – a rod passing over a map and indicating water or minerals. Sceptics scoff at it as being scientifically impossible, but US marines in Vietnam divined enemy mines and

TYPES OF DOWSING RODS

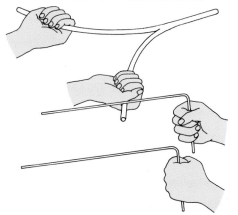

Two types of dowsing rods: the traditional forked stick and a pair of bent wires. Most experts agree that it is the person and not the tool that counts in dowsing – those who possess the ability can use anything.

tunnels, and in the USSR, geologists use the method for geological mapping. Dowsing has been and still is a valuable art in dry Australia, some practitioners combining it with their well-drilling businesses.

Dowsers – also called diviners – claim that they can gauge not only the direction of flow of water but the depth of a stream or metal. Ross Henderson, a diviner in Tasmania, claims to analyse soil, his rod rising over deficiencies, and dipping over excesses, of trace elements and fertilisers. The rod may be a wire bent into an L, whalebone, blades of grass, or the classic tool – a forked stick with branches about 500 mm long. Some diviners use a pendulum instead. In the case of a positive reaction, the pendulum swings clockwise on its string, or the rod tips up, and for negative reactions, vice versa. Dowsers say that when there is a reaction, the rod seems to exert a fierce power. Some need to wear leather-soled shoes; for others it does not matter. The practise goes back for millenia: in North Africa a cave painting 8000 years old shows a dowser holding his divining rod.

DRAGONFLY

Dragonflies are long, strongly-flying insects which hawk for other flying insects, or pounce on them from a perch. Their legs are arranged so that they can scoop up their prey while in flight. They differ from the closely related DAMSEL FLIES in having huge, bulbous eyes which meet – they are well separated in damsel flies – and in stretching out their wings in a straight line when they are resting. Both groups mate in flight.

Dragonflies have been called 'birdwatchers insects' because of their bright colours, swift flight, and complex behaviour which includes guarding a territory. They often stray far from water, and some species migrate long distances. There are about 190 species in Australia, and they can be found in most areas, provided that breeding sites are near enough.

DRIED FRUIT

About one-third of Australia's grapes become currants, raisins or, mostly, sultanas. This important industry – which exports roughly half the 100 000 tonnes or so produced every year – began in 1887. The Canadian brothers George and William Benjamin Chaffey – who had set up irrigation colonies in California – were granted 120 000 ha of land in the Murray Valley for experiments in irrigation here.

The settlements of Mildura and Renmark faltered in the 1890s in the rural slump, and with transport and irrigation problems, but after World War I the industry expanded, aided by soldier settlement schemes at Barmera and Chaffey. The Sunraysia region around Mildura, particularly on the Victorian side, produces most of Australia's dried vine fruits, thanks to Depres-

sion labourers who dug its drainage ditches. Smaller quantities come from the Swan Valley near Perth, around Kerang and Swan Hill in Victoria, and around McLaren Vale, Angaston and Renmark in South Australia. The white grapes used for raisins (Muscat gordo blanco and Waltham Cross) and for sultanas (mostly Sultana) are also sold fresh and used for wine. The small red grapes Zante currant and Carina are used only for currants.

Currants and early sultanas can simply be dried, but raisins and later-harvested sultanas are dipped in or sprayed with a solution of potash, oil and water to aid drying by sun and breezes on many-tiered racks 50 m long. Many growers now dehydrate the fruit in tunnels created by plastic sheeting around the racks, with fans distributing heated air. A labour-saving method of drying fruit on a trellis was developed by CSIRO in the 1960s. It involves pruning away about half the leaves to expose the grapes and start the drying process, then spraying with the drying emulsion. Mechanical harvesters that can strip a hectare of vines in an hour shake the fruit from the plants after two or three weeks.

Three to four thousand tonnes of prunes, nearly all from d'Agen plums, come from the Griffith and Young areas of NSW every year. Most other dried tree fruits come from the Riverland region of South Australia, around Berri and Renmark. Apricots are the most important. Kamaradin or fruit leather is made from a variety of fruits – combined or alone – minced then dried in slabs, to be eaten straight or reconstituted and made into pies. Consumption of dried fruit is nearly three kilograms per person a year.

DRONGO

There seems to be no good reason for using the names of the drongo or the GALAH as an insult. Spangled Drongos *Dicrurus bracteatus* (about 300 mm) are handsome, glossy black, slightly iridescent, red-eyed birds with fish-forked tails. They are found in north-west Australia and along the east coast from Cape York to Victoria.

Drongos eat large insects which they catch by pouncing from a perch or gleaning from foliage. They are aggressive to larger birds which they consider a threat to their nests – the common Indian species is called the King Crow because of its bravery towards crows which are bigger – but well disposed to smaller birds which, it is said, will nest for protection in a tree where a Drongo builds its seemingly fragile nest. The Spangled Drongo has a large repertoire of metallic notes and a creaking whistle.

DROUGHT

'For months at a time the sun shines remorselessly from a sky like beaten copper; sometimes the clouds come sweeping up at nightfall, flattering only to deceive – for no rain seems to fall from them. The grass grows brown and dry, shrivels in the furnace breath of the hot winds, and disappears; the grim, red, tortured earth burns like fired iron through the leather-shod foot of man and the horn-protected hoof of the horse, crumbles into a dusty powder, and is blown aside by every breeze.

'The rivers run slower and slower, becoming a mere chain of stagnant waterholes, and finally dry away altogether, leaving a ghastly fence of poisoned corpses set in the hardened slime. Even

Boom and bust is a characteristic of the Australian bush that Europeans farmers have found hard to come to terms with. The indigenous life of Australia has adapted to alternating good and bad seasons.

the deep pools and artificial tanks give but small resistance to the strangling foe, and their banks resound with the pitiful clamour of the bleating flocks and lowing herds that come to them in vain.

'The air is full of the stench of decaying carcases, and vibrates with waves of impending calamity. Wild things of the woods become tame in this common adversity; gaunt emus stalk fearlessly up to the very verandahs of the houses; kangaroos, mere shadows of their former selves, stand like tawny ghosts on the bank of the fast-drying waterhole...

'Day after day the flocks grow pitifully less as the grim enemy closes with them, leaving his victims dead on every side.

'The settler, powerless to render assistance, rides every grim morning through the rotting ranks, counting his losses and waiting, waiting for the raising of the siege.'

Such was the harsh reality of drought in 1908 for Will Oglivie in his book *My Life in the Open*. Generations of Australian farmers and graziers since have faced the same enemy.

A drought is said to occur when there has been a substantial shortfall, over a period of months or years, in the amount of rain which usually occurs

at a place. A map of the incidence of drought in Australia between 1965 and 1980 shows that drought conditions occurred for up to 40 per cent of those fifteen years in the southern half of the continent.

Australia is particularly susceptible to drought because of its generally low and variable rainfall, and also because of high evaporation rates over most of the continent. Major droughts to have occurred in Australia since systematic records were kept took place during: 1864–68; 1880–86; 1888; 1895–1903; 1911–16; 1918–20; 1944–45; 1963–65; 1972; 1977–78; and 1982–83. Of these, the 1982–83 drought is the worst on record because most parts of Australia were affected. The lack of rain was most marked in northern Australia because of the extreme lateness of the monsoon, but large parts of south-eastern Australia also experienced the lowest rainfalls on record. Agricultural production dropped by 25 per cent, many towns had water rationing, the dryness of the countryside gave rise to dust-storms and the devastating Ash Wednesday bushfires raged through Victoria and South Australia.

It is difficult to predict droughts because they occur irregularly, and are the end-product of complex global atmospheric patterns. It is thought that droughts in Australia may be linked to atmospheric pressure differences between the eastern and western Pacific Ocean, but meteorologists have been unable to establish the exact nature of the link.

Strategies for survival

There are few parts of Australia – however dry – that have no plants at all. Those that do survive in the arid inland must either evade or resist the effects of prolonged drought.

Evaders do not experience drought when they are growing. They survive dry periods as seeds, but take advantage of breaks in the drought to grow quickly, flower and produce new seeds. The seeds of such species often contain substances that prevent germination. Heavy rain is needed to remove these substances, so that plants do not start to grow after a light shower.

Plants that resist the effects of drought do so by adopting a number of strategies. Where water is available at some depth under the surface, deep roots may enable a plant to continue growing, even when the surface is dry. River Red Gums *Eucalyptus camaldulensis*, frequently seen along dry river beds in the outback, survive by this means. Other species minimise water use by having small, hairy or tough leaves.

However, even these resistant species will eventually die if the drought is exceptionally long. Only the so-called resurrection plants – which become very dry and shrivelled, but can absorb water when it rains – will survive under extreme circumstances for any length of time.

A sea of yellow everlasting flowers Helichrysum bracteatum carpet sandy, semi-desert in the far west of NSW (above). In a few weeks' time the bare red soil will be baking under the glare of a summer sun. River Red Gums (left) can only survive long, dry periods by drawing water from deep underground. Their presence often indicates the course of a subterranean stream.

DROVER

The stockman who moves mobs of cattle or sheep on foot, rather than by truck, is a drover. Sometimes the trip is aimed at getting the stock to market, but very often these days it is an attempt to keep animals alive in times of drought. The sheep or cattle are put out on the LONG PADDOCK, and just moved to wherever there is feed available.

Facilities, such as the land set aside on which stock can be driven, camping spots and watering points, are controlled by Pastures Protection Boards. These are committees of local land-owners who control a lot more than just the movement of stock, and a drover must apply to them to get a permit to move animals. This allows him access to food and water along the way, and to travelling stock reserves where he can camp. In return, the drover must keep the animals moving – he is not permitted to camp in one place until all the feed is eaten out.

Droving is a skilled job. The stockman must know the country ahead of his animals; he must know where he can get water at the end of a day's travelling and, most importantly, where the feed is growing. He moves stock at their own pace – they cannot be driven too quickly or they will want to 'camp' after only an hour or two on the road. It is best to let them move off in the morning at their own speed, and to travel at 'feeding pace'. Animals treated like that will travel much further in a day, with less stress, than those that are constantly pushed.

With large mobs, two or more drovers will be employed. One will travel ahead, checking on open gates or side roads where stock might stray. He will also act as a brake on the mob, keeping them within reasonable limits, although a big mob will spread out for many kilometres along the road. Smaller groups can be handled by one drover with the help of a very experienced dog, which travels in front, holding the group together. Drovers are required by law to place signs both behind and in front of travelling animals to warn motorists of the hazard ahead.

A drover is paid according to the percentage of the mob that he delivers to the destination. The contract will allow him a few animals for rations, but the value of any stock lost comes out of his final payment.

Drovers are usually accompanied by a tribe of dogs. In the days when there were more drovers working, they were always a good source of experienced working dogs, and often pups were given to them to 'break in'. The role of travelling dogs – a lot of work and not much food – gave rise to the expression 'poor as a drover's dog'.

A drover will often talk about his 'plant' – the tools of his trade. At one time this would have included a horse-drawn wagon in which the drover and his crew could sleep if necessary. It also acted as a store for provisions and feed for

Traditionally supposed to be overworked and underfed, drover's dogs were nevertheless treated by most stockmen with the care that they deserved. They were essential when large mobs or cattle or sheep were being moved.

the horses. These days the wagon has given way to a truck capable of carting the horses from place to place. A well set-up plant will also have portable fencing to contain the animals at night, together with all the equipment necessary to keep the drover on the road for a couple of months. In recent years, it has been not unusual to see the owners of a property – husband, wife and children – take all their stock on the road during a drought to keep them alive.

DUCKS AND GEESE

Australia has a strange selection of ducks and geese, besides a swan that is black. None of the four so-called geese are geese, and one duck – the extremely rare Freckled Duck *Strictonetta naevosa* (480–590 mm) – is closer to the swan than it is to the duck. They have a mixture of anatomical features which link them to the waterbirds which were the common ancestors of all ducks, geese and swans.

The 'geese' are the CAPE BARREN GOOSE, the Magpie Goose, and the two Pygmy-geese. The two whistling ducks – which whistle with wing-beats – have anatomical and behavioural features in common with swans and geese. The more widespread is the Plumed Whistling Duck (415–560 mm) found throughout northern and much of eastern Australia.

The Australian Shelduck *Tadorna tadornoides* (550–680 mm) was once called the Mountain Duck, although it prefers large brackish lakes near the coast. It is found in western and south-eastern Australia and in Tasmania, where it feeds in flocks on land and water plants, including some pasture species.

The black and white Magpie Goose *Anseranas semipalmata* (710–920 mm, males larger than females) has a slightly hooked bill, long legs and partly webbed feet. Magpie Geese are now more or less restricted to northern Australia, where they feed on plants in the open in marshes during 'the wet', or on plains during 'the dry'.

The familiar dabbling ducks belong to the

genus *Anas*. Males and females have different plumage, except when the males moult to their post-nuptial plumage. There are five species, not counting vagrants, the best known of which are the Pacific Black Duck *Anas superciliosa* (470–580 mm) and the somewhat larger European Mallard *A. platyrhynchos* which, unfortunately, interbreeds with native species. Both are common in public parks.

The Blue-billed Duck *Oxyura australis* (350–440 mm) and the Musk Duck *Biziura lobata* (470–630 mm), which both occur in south-east and south-west Australia and Tasmania, are also skilled divers. The former is largely vegetarian and the latter carnivorous. Both have spectacular courtship displays with the males splashing clouds of water behind as they rush forward. A male Blue-billed Duck may pursue a female under water. The male Musk Duck has a bag beneath its bill which smells of musk. It enlarges and smells even more in the breeding season.

The common breeds of domestic ducks – such as the Khaki Campbell and Aylesbury – are descended from the Mallard or Wild Duck of Europe and North America. This is an introduced species in Australia, where it interbreeds freely with native Pacific and Black Ducks. An interesting change in the species since its domestication – which is very recent – is that the drake now mates with several females, whereas in the wild it is monogamous. The domestic goose is descended from the Greylag Goose *Anser anser* of the northern hemisphere. Despite the long domestication, it has changed very little from the wild bird, apart from its colour. The only other common ducks that have been domesticated, and then only for ornamental purposes, are the Mandarin *Aix galericulata* and the Muscovy Duck *Carina moschata*.

DUNE

Sand dunes are familiar features of sea shores and deserts, and are formed by the action of wind on loose sand. Dunes cover many thousands of square kilometres in the deserts of the world yet, surprisingly, they differ greatly from one region to another.

Dunes may be either fixed or mobile. The first are usually formed when the sand drifts against some obstacle.

There are three main types of mobile dunes. Barchans, which are formed when the wind blows constantly from one direction, are crescent shaped, with the points forming downwind. Sand blows up over the shallower windward slope and falls down the steeper lee one, and the dune moved forward. They are common in the Sahara Desert and in American deserts, but not in Australia where longitudinal dunes – seifs – are usually found. These form when there are two common directions for the wind: one arm of a crescent dune is elongated by the side wind.

Domestic breeds of ducks and geese

Chinese White Goose — Chinese Brown Goose — Emden Goose — Indian Runner Duck — Buff Orpington Duck

Muscovy Duck — Mallard — Pekin Duck — Rouen Duck — Khaki Campbell Duck

Some seifs have been traced for hundreds of kilometres. Transverse dunes occur where there is plenty of sand, and they have a profile similar to that of a barchan.

The Simpson and the Great Victoria Deserts are two areas where dunes are found. They are often 6 to 30 m high, and about 400 m apart.

DUNG BEETLE

Australia's cattle drop an estimated 350–450 million pats of dung each day, most of which lies around for months because there are no native dung beetles which can consume such large masses. The native species are adapted to the small pellets dropped by marsupials. Each beast makes 400 sq. m of pasture a year temporarily useless by covering it with dung. Furthermore, BUFFALO FLIES, BUSH FLIES, biting MIDGES and parasitic worms develop in the dung. This problem of dung persistence seems to be confined to Australia, and since 1968 the CSIRO has been releasing large numbers of introduced dung beetles – most of them from Africa – mainly in the north of the continent.

Many dung beetles roll the dung up into balls in which they lay their eggs. The balls are buried in tunnels, beneath, within or near the dung. One species is the Sacred Scarab of Egypt, where the dung ball was looked upon as a sun symbol by the ancient Egyptians.

Many beetles collected abroad were found to have mites living on them. As some are potentially harmful, the beetles were surface-sterilised before being allowed into the country. However,

it has now been realised that some of these mites may be important as destroyers of worms and fly larvae, which may compete with the newly hatched beetle grubs for dung.

CANE TOADS have been seen assembling around fresh pats and swallowing dung beetles as they arrived. This was considered a threat to the campaign – each toad can eat 80 beetles a night – so the chief scientist contemplated introducing giant *Heliocropis* beetles, which might be able to eat their way out of a toad, and if not, at least give it fatal stomach ache. In India these beetles make dung balls coated with clay that are so large they were once thought to be ancient cannon balls.

Fifty or more species have been released in Australia, the plan being to establish a collection of beetles to suit the various climatic regions where they are needed. One of the most successful was the first, *Onthophagus gazella* (from Africa, *via* Hawaii).

Some dung beetles *cut pieces of dung and fashion it into balls which they roll away and bury, either for their own consumption, or for larvae to feed on.*

DUNNART

Dunnarts, of which there are 12 known species, were formerly called narrow-footed marsupial mice. They are divided into narrow-tailed dunnarts, and fat-tailed dunnarts although this description is of little help in identification because fat-tails have fat tails only when conditions are good and the living is easy. Most are the size of a House Mouse *Mus musculus*.

The Common Dunnart *Sminthopsis murina* (64–104 mm body, 68–99 mm tail) is a mouse-grey, narrow-tailed carnivore which rests during the day in nests of grass and leaves, emerging at night to feed on insects and similar animals. It is found in the south-west and south-east of the continent, and in north-east Queensland. The greatest numbers of animals are seen a year or two after fires. The tail of the Long-tailed Dunnart *S. longicaudata* is more than twice as long as its body. Very few specimens have been found, and all are from arid regions of the western half of Australia. Several other dunnarts are known from very few specimens.

The nocturnal Fat-tailed Dunnart *S. crassicaudata* (body 60–90 mm, tail 40–70 mm) in contrast is widespread in some open parts of southern Australia, although not on the east coast. Numbers may have increased following the clearance of land for farming.

DUNNY

A dunny is an Australian outback lavatory – especially the outdoor variety. They can be made from anything that comes to hand, ranging from a few corrugated iron sheets bent around some convenient bush poles with a bag door, to elegant structures complete with fitted weatherboards and elaborate fretwork eaves.

Sometimes they stand naked, leaning in the direction of the prevailing wind, 30 m behind the house. Often they nestle under the shade of a convenient tree for shelter, wreathed in choko vines. Pepper trees are favoured as protection, never gum trees which have a disturbing habit of dropping branches without warning on hot summer days. Often a pair stand as lonely sentinels at the back of a church or bush hall. Even today, many houses on the outskirts of cities and in quite large country towns still have outdoor lavatories.

Inside there may be anything from a simple box seat astride a septic tank, to a couple of strategic poles suspended over a long drop – a deep pit that requires no more than an occasional sprinkle of earth or lime. There are reputed to be two- and even four-holers still in use around some shearers' quarters.

Seasonally-used dunnies are traditional refuges for snakes, spiders (particularly red-backs) and possums. Country folklore abounds with tales of strange encounters in dunnies particularly on dark, stormy nights.

A lonely dunny – badly in need of a coat of paint – stands neglected at the back of a small country church. Infrequent use makes such shelters a welcome refuge for a great variety of local wildlife – particularly snakes and spiders. Many country tales tell of unexpected encounters in such places, particularly on dark nights.

DUSK

Sunset colours are due to dust and smoke. At the end of the day, the sun's rays travel further through the atmosphere than when the sun is directly overhead. Particles of dust and smoke scatter the light: first the blue rays, then the green are reduced in intensity, leaving the yellow and finally the longest, the red rays to reach the viewer directly.

The sun sometimes appears larger at dusk because particles of varying density in the atmosphere act like a magnifying lens.

Dusk in the tropics is much shorter because the earth's surface is moving faster there than it is at higher latitudes. Viewers therefore see the sun disappear over the horizon more rapidly. The last vestiges of daylight have gone by the time the centre of the sun is 18° below the horizon – the end of 'astronomical twilight'. On the shortest day of the year, 22 June, astronomical twilight at the equator lasts an hour and a quarter. At the latitude of Perth or Sydney it lasts about half an hour more, and in Hobart about one-quarter of an hour longer still. 'Civil twilight' – during which it is light enough for daytime activities to continue – lasts until the centre of the sun is 6° below the horizon. Near the equator this means about 25 minutes; in Melbourne about 40 minutes.

The ruddy glow of an outback sunset is usually due to dust in the air. Over much of Australia dusk, or twilight – the period from sunset to darkness – is very brief.

DUST

Dust is so much a part of Australian outback life that an Australian country singer – Slim Dusty – named himself after it. The dust – more commonly called bulldust in the country – lies thickly along outback unsealed roads and tracks, or collects in depressions in arid country.

The particles are fine – less than 0.002 mm in diameter – and once lifted into the air by a passing car settle only very slowly, unlike sand particles (0.02 mm diameter or more) which fall almost immediately to the ground. Bulldust comes from rocks that have been weathered away and also from deposits left behind by rivers. Much of the dust in inland Australia is blown from claypans.

Sydney Baker – a pioneering writer on the Australian language – stresses that bulldust must not be confused with bull dust, another outback product which is heard rather than seen.

DUST STORM

Dust storms – sometimes misnamed sand storms – are common in many arid countries, including inland Australia. Dust is lifted from the ground and reaches heights of thousands of metres, but sand rarely rises more than one metre.

Unfortunately, dust storms can also originate in cropping and pastoral districts during drought, when most of the vegetation cover had been dried or eaten out. On one afternoon in February 1983 the skies of Melbourne were so full of dust

Clouds of dense dust billow from the back of a car travelling fast along a freshly-graded outback road in Queensland. Particles as fine as talcum powder remain suspended in the air behind cars – cutting visibility down drastically – for many minutes after they pass, particularly if there is no wind.

A vast pall of dust about to engulf the tiny wheat farming town of Narrandera, on the Murrumbidgee River in south-western NSW, in 1903. Millions of tonnes of soil have been lost from freshly-cleared land in such storms.

blown from west of the city that car headlights had to be switched on hours before their usual time. Over 200 000 tonnes of topsoil were swept from the land in western Victoria in that one storm, much of it being lost out to sea. Dust may be blown even greater distances – from the Gobi Desert of Central Asia, for example, to the plains of northern China where there are vast stretches of wind-deposited soil, or loess, up to 300 m deep. In southern Australia there are many 'parna' areas which are covered with a thin layer of wind-blown silt deposited long ago. Loess deposits do not always tell of a hot dry climate in the past; they may also form during cold dry periods. In Europe there are many loess deposits laid down near the edges of the great ice sheets which once covered the continent.

DYKE

Magma is molten rock – the thick blood of a volcano. As it rises towards the surface from deep within the earth it buckles and cracks overlying rocks, and then fills the cracks. In time it cools and solidifies. These sheets of volcanic rock filling cracks are known as dykes. They range from a few centimetres to hundreds of metres in thickness. They are generally much longer than they are wide, and many have been traced for miles. Most dykes have straight, parallel walls. The dykes are usually harder than the surrounding rocks so they form prominent ridges when exposed by erosion, such as the famous 'breadknife' in Warrumbungle National Park, NSW. Dykes have even been recognised on the moon. In satellite photographs they are seen as long thin lines.

HOW DYKES ARE FORMED

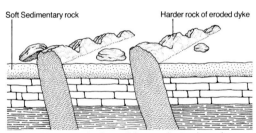

Soft Sedimentary rock   Harder rock of eroded dyke

The resistant rock of two dykes projects above layers of softer strata. Depressions occur when the situation is reversed, and the strata are harder than the dykes.

The most famous dyke in Australia – the 'breadknife' in Warrumbungle National Park, NSW. This 90 m-high slab of trachyte, formed 13 million years ago, has been revealed as surrounding rocks have weathered away.

161

EAGLES, HAWKS AND FALCONS

Australia has 24 daytime birds of prey, six of which are falcons, hobbies or kestrels (genus *Falco*) and 18 eagles and their allies. In both cases the females are larger than the males.

All the *Falco* species are widespread in Australia. The most famous is the magnificent Peregrine Falcon *F. peregrinus* (male 380 mm female 480 mm) which occurs in all continents except Antarctica. Peregrines, the Australian Hobby *F. longipennis* (male 300 mm) and the Brown Falcon *F. berigora* (male 450 mm) catch most of their prey in flight, but the Australian Kestrel *F. cenchriodes* (male 310 mm) hovers and drops onto prey on the ground.

Eagles are generally large birds, although the female Little Eagle *Hieraetus morphnoides*, a widespread mainland species, is only 550 mm long. The Wedge-tailed Eagle *Aquila audax* (female 1.0 m, wing span to at least 2.5 m) is the fourth largest eagle in the world.

The Little Eagle hunts by flying lazily over woodland, or by waiting on a perch, whereas the Wedge-tail soars at a great height, riding thermal currents, and swoops down on prey ranging from rabbits to small kangaroos. It is also a carrion eater. The Wedge-tail is found throughout Australia, including Tasmania, and is sometimes even seen over cities.

The White-bellied Sea-Eagle *Haliaetus leucogaster* (female 840 mm) eats carrion but also catches fish, tortoises, and rabbits. It is found all around the coast and along major river systems.

EARTHQUAKE

Earthquakes are literally ground-shaking events. They result from the build up of strain in rocks due to earth movements. The strain mounts until the rocks break and there is a huge release of energy, rather like bending a piece of wood until it breaks. This release of energy can occur at any depth in the earth's crust. Fortunately, Australia is not in a major earthquake zone.

There are several methods used for indicating the strength of an earthquake. The best known is the Richter scale. On this scale a magnitude one earthquake is equivalent to the energy released from 0.5 kg of TNT, while a magnitude eight earthquake is equivalent to the power of 60 000 one-megaton bombs.

In Australia there is one earthquake bigger than magnitude six about every five years, compared to the world average of about 140 per year. Fortunately there is no record of anybody being killed by an earthquake in Australia. The Simpson Desert is probably the most active earthquake area on the continent. The largest known earthquakes in Australia, however, were centred near Perth – at Meerberrie in 1941, and at Meckering in 1968. Both measured 6.9 on the Richter scale.

EARTHWORM

There are about 3000 species of worms in the world, but one group – the lumbricids – are famous as world travellers. They are found almost everywhere, and owe their dispersal to humans who carried them in soil on plants and possibly even on feet. These wandering earthworms often displace native species. They have done this in most Australian gardens, where three introduced species are the ones most commonly seen.

Earthworms have segmented bodies and no legs or distinct head. The common earthworm lives in deep, permanent burrows which are about one metre deep, but others have shallow temporary ones. All earthworms move through

Giant Gippsland earthworms *Megascolides australis can reach great lengths. The largest accurately measured specimen was 2.18 m long, unextended, and 3.96 m when naturally extended. The worms live only in wet river slopes of southern Gippsland, Vic.*

Railway officials survey damage *(right) caused by the Meckering earthquake of October 1968. The lines in the foreground were raised three metres above their original level. Despite considerable damage, this earthquake was mild, only measuring 6.9 on the Richter scale.*

the soil in the same way. They anchor the rear of their body with hooked hairs that grow on each segment, force the pointed front of their body through soil crevices, then anchor it and draw the rear after it. When soil is compact they eat their way through, swallowing the soil as they go.

Australia is home to one of the world's largest earthworms – the giant Gippsland Earthworm *Megascolides australis* – which lives only in an area of about 100 000 ha in the Gippsland district of south-eastern Victoria.

EARWIG

Earwigs got their name because of a common belief in Europe that they crawl into ears. This arose from the observation that they creep into crevices and lie with as much of their bodies as possible touching the surface – hence the use of plant-pots stuffed with straw as traps. They have long antennae, a long parallel-sided body, and short, hard forewings covering large, ear-shaped hind wings. They are rarely seen to fly, and some are wingless. They have a pair of pincers on their tails, used for mating and defence.

Nymphs resemble adults, and in some species the mother guards the young. Most will eat plant or animal food. The introduced European Earwig *Forficula auricularia* is common in cool regions.

ECHIDNA

There are only two species of echidnas – one of which is found only in New Guinea. The other, the Short-beaked Echidna *Tachyglossus aculeatus* (length 300–450 mm) lives in both New Guinea and Australia, including Tasmania. Echidnas belong to a group of animals called MONOTREMES, the only other member being the PLATYPUS. Echidnas have one abiding interest – termites and ants – and can be found virtually wherever these occur. In hot, dry areas they shelter in crevices during the day, feeding mainly at night. In other regions they can be active in the daytime during winter.

Spines, which are sometimes hidden by the ordinary hairs in the Tasmanian variety, defend the animal superbly. When disturbed they roll into a tight ball with the spines pointing outwards, but if the ground is soft they may burrow vertically downwards at great speed, leaving the spines sticking up like thousands of periscopes. Males have a spur on their hind legs like that of the platypus, but it does not inject venom, despite statements made to the contrary in some popular books.

The claws or the long snout are used to make a hole in an ant or termite nest, and insects are quickly collected by the extremely long sticky tongue. They are crushed between horny pads on the back of the tongue and the roof of the mouth.

Echidnas mate in July and August, and lay a single egg about two weeks later, probably

Eastern Australia has the world's largest earwig, *Titanolobis colossa* which grows to 55 mm in length and is found in rainforest and bush. Some earwigs are fur parasites of bats.

EEL

The best-known Australian eels are the freshwater eels which have long, cylindrical bodies. They mature in freshwater but when adult they return to the sea to spawn, often crawling across damp ground, or tumbling over dams to make the journey. They travel into deep oceans, spawn and then, presumably, die. The leaf-like larval eels migrate to the river mouths, a journey which may take years. There they transform into 'glass eels' and then elvers – which are miniature eels – and begin, in reverse, the migration their parents made, often climbing dams and barriers blocking the way in doing so.

There are four species in Australia. The Short-finned Eel *Anguilla australis* (to 1.1 m) lives in south-eastern Australia, Tasmania, New Zealand and Norfolk Island. It probably spawns in the Coral Sea near New Caledonia as does, it is thought, the Long-finned Eel *A. reinhardtii* (to 2.0 m). The Northern Eel *A. bicolor* (to 1.2 m) spawns near Sumatra. The first two species are being fished commercially in Victoria.

directly into a temporary pouch. The egg is incubated for about ten days and the young is suckled for about three months, after which it has a covering of short spines, and it is time to leave the pouch. Its behaviour for the next few weeks is unknown, but juveniles are not usually seen about until they are about one year old.

Powerful front claws allow Echidnas Tachyglossus aculeatus *to tear apart ant and termite nests in search of their favourite food. When threatened, they either roll themselves into a ball, protected by their sharp spines, or rapidly bury themselves in the ground.*

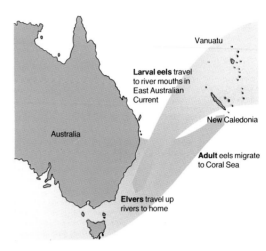

Vanuatu

Larval eels travel to river mouths in East Australian Current

New Caledonia

Australia

Adult eels migrate to Coral Sea

Elvers travel up rivers to home

Freshwater eels *from the east coast of Australia spawn near New Caledonia, a journey which involves a swim of over 1200 km from the mainland.*

ELECTRICITY

The existence of electricity has been known for centuries, but only in the second half of last century was it harnessed effectively.

Before 1879 the first electric lights in Australia helped workers complete the International Exhibition in Sydney. But it was country towns that were the first to introduce electric street lighting – Sydney and Melbourne were slow off the mark because they already had well developed gas lighting. Tamworth was the first town in Australia in 1888, followed closely by Young, Penrith, Moss Vale and Broken Hill by 1890. Thargomindah in far south-west of Queensland became the first town in that state to electrify its streets in 1893, when it set up a generator powered by water from a local artesian bore.

From 1920 the belief grew that electricity was the agent of a brighter, cleaner, more modern future. The electricity systems in each state, which until then had been in municiple and private hands, came under increasingly centralised and public control. Victoria and Tasmania were the first to develop state grids.

But in other states, even by 1945, country people only had access to mains electricity if they lived near a large town. In the 20 years after World War II, however, the electricity authorities in the larger states developed and integrated their respective grids. Subsidies were given to meet the costs of providing electricity to isolated areas. In the 13 years to 1959 the number of NSW farms served by electricity rose from 20 per cent to 65 per cent. Today mains electricity has replaced diesel generators, wood-fuel boilers and wind generators for all but the most isolated farms and communities.

EMERALD

Emerald is the grass-green variety of the more common mineral beryl, but it is perhaps the most valuable of all gems. Perfect specimens have a greater value than DIAMOND or RUBY, but they are extremely rare. Emerald is composed of the rare metal beryllium plus aluminium, silicon and oxygen. The gems are usually found in veins cutting across granite rocks. The richest deposits in the world are those at Muzo, Columbia. Small numbers of good quality stones have been recovered from Emmaville, NSW. There was a short-lived industry there and many small, attractive stones were cut. Some gems have also been discovered at Poona Hill, WA.

EMU

Emus *Dromaius novaehollandiae*, which can reach a height of 2 m, are the world's second largest living bird. Adult females weigh about 41 kg, and males about 36 kg, whereas a male ostrich has been weighed at 156 kg. They are nomadic, wandering birds, although in parts of Western Australia at least they make regular seasonal migrations, to the north-east in autumn, and to the south-east in spring. In a year an emu can cover several hundred kilometres, part of it in short bursts of 48 km/h, longer stretches at a steady 40 km/h.

Wings are short and have no quill feathers. The feathers are unusual in having two plumes, and no vanes, so that they appear hairy.

Emus mate in summer and autumn, but after the female lays her green eggs on the ground she departs, leaving the male to sit on the eggs and to tend up to 20 striped chicks for as long as 18 months.

Emus eat many foods, including plants and insects. They have been accused of spreading LANTANA seeds. They occur throughout Australia.

EPIPHYTE

Any plant that grows on another plant, but without actually invading its living tissues is an epiphyte. They are most abundant and conspicuous in rainforests. In fact their presence is one of the ways in which rainforest is defined. Orchids, ferns, mosses and lichens account for the great majority of epiphytes. A typical epiphyte clings to the trunk of its host tree by aerial roots. Its water supply comes entirely from rain, mist and dew. Many epiphytes are adapted to surviving dry conditions in a very dried-out state, or have very succulent tissues, although others depend on the humidity of their environment remaining at almost 100 per cent. The plants get their nutrition from decaying bark and

Epiphytes cling tenaciously to the trunks of these rainforest trees, which are among the most southerly in Australia. They are growing in the gorge of the Minnamurra River, not far south of Sydney.

leaves, and also from air-borne dust. Epiphytes frequently have ways of trapping such falling debris and concentrating them around their roots. The funnel of fronds of the Bird's-nest Fern, often found in Australian rainforests, is a good example.

In Australia epiphytes are common only in the high-rainfall areas of the east coast and ranges, including Tasmania. Apart from some of the hardier mosses and lichens, South Australia and southern Western Australia have virtually no epiphytes. In the monsoonal rainforests of the far north there are also very few epiphytes, owing to the length and severity of the dry season.

In eastern rainforests epiphytes range from (in tropical lowlands) large ferns and orchids – often in great variety and abundance on the upper branches of large trees – to mosses and lichens only, with perhaps a few smaller ferns lower on the trunks, in the cool-temperate areas of Tasmania and the mountains of the south-east. Wetter eucalypt forests are notably lacking in epiphytes, even though adjacent rainforest may have plenty. The most likely explanation is that the bark of rainforest trees provides a better hold for their roots than eucalypt bark, which either sheds its outer layer every year, or is full of tannins that are toxic to the plants.

EROSION

The erosion of rocks and soil on a grand scale over millions of years by wind and water has produced today's landscape. Erosion by wind and water on a small scale over 200 years has produced disaster. Bad farming methods have led to the loss of topsoil and the impoverishment of much good agricultural land in Australia. The country's first farmers came from Europe, where wind and rain are rarely intense enough to remove great quantities of unprotected soil, but the use of cultivation methods which worked well in Europe was often disastrous in Australia. Once the layer of natural vegetation had gone, rain and wind began to wash away the soil, often

Water has carved the banks of this deep erosion gully in the north-east of NSW into fantastic shapes. It is possible to visualise the enormous volume of soil that has been lost, just in this one small area alone.

forming gullies or miniature gorges. Repeated cultivation and cropping can also lead to the oxidation and removal of organic matter from the soil, which helps to preserve its structure and its resistance to erosion. The felling or ringbarking of trees also opens up the land to erosion by wind.

Cultivation, such as ploughing, is necessary from time to time to remove weeds, expose soil pests to dehydration or predators and to produce a suitable tilth for sowing. However, on slopes or in hilly country the plough should follow contours so that water flowing downhill is impeded by the ridges. After heavy rain the field should resemble a miniature terraced paddy, not a collection of tiny Grand Canyons. A relatively recent technique is chemical ploughing. Crop residues are not burnt or ploughed in, but treated with a herbicide such as paraquat which kills the plants, but is inactivated by the soil. The sod remains as a protection against erosion, and at sowing time it is either scarified, or has holes punched through it.

ESTUARY

An estuary is the meeting place of a river and the sea, where fresh water, laden with sediment, meets salt water. There the river drops much of its burden of silt and clay to form mudbanks, which may line the shores, or fan out to form a delta through which the river flows.

Twice a day the tides rise and fall, covering and uncovering the mudbanks and saltmarshes, and pushing salt water up the river. Where the river and sea waters meet they do not simply mix to form brackish water. Freshwater is lighter than seawater, and tends to flow over the top of it in a layer.

Estuaries are difficult places for plants and animals to live, but despite the problems they, and the nearby sea, are rich in animal and plant life, largely because the river brings down large quantities of food and minerals.

EUCALYPT

To most city-bred Australians eucalypt is just another word for 'gum tree', but to bush people 'gum' has the narrower meaning of a eucalypt with smooth bark – for example Blue Gum – in contrast with the rough-barked groups of eucalypts which are called ironbarks, stringbarks and boxes. To a botanist eucalypt is the collective common name for all members of the genus *Eucalyptus*, consisting of up to 800 species – depending on how broadly species are defined. All except a few of which are peculiar to Australia. The term eucalypt can also be extended to include the smaller genus *Angophora*.

It is often thought that eucalypts are found everywhere in Australia, but this is not the case. Over large areas of the far inland, even in places where trees and shrubs are abundant, only wattles and other small trees can be seen. There may be one or two eucalypt species – such as River Red Gums – scattered along stream beds. In the east and north, rainforests are a major habitat with few or no eucalypts; in fact their absence had been proposed as part of the definition of Australian rainforest.

Identification of eucalypts poses great problems for the inexperienced. Near any of Australia's capital cities it is possible to recognise the major groups and species with a little study and guidance. Because of the large number of species and the limited geographical range of each, there are very few species shared by any two state capitals. Brisbane and Sydney (including nearby ranges such as the Blue Mountains), for example, share about 20 species out of a total of around 115; Sydney and Adelaide about six out of 110; Adelaide and Perth two out of 61; Darwin and Sydney share none out of 107. There is also a great change in the species encountered between the coast and the dry inland, or during a climb into the mountains from the coast.

The simplest classification of eucalypts is by bark types, although, unfortunately, it often results in closely related species being placed in different groups. However, it is a first step in the recognition of eucalypts in the bush. Some of the main groups based on bark types are detailed below. This classification is most useful in eastern Australia – in the west and far north it is not so applicable.

Gums: a large number of species with smooth bark, or rough only at the very base, often streaked or blotched in various shades of dull cream, pink, grey, orange or yellow. The smooth surface is due entirely to the annual shedding of an outer layer of bark, usually in early summer, often persisting as long curled strips hanging from the branches. The Gums include many unrelated groups of species, and are common in most parts of Australia.

Boxes: a name applied to many species with smooth-barked upper limbs, but with rough bark on the trunk, and often on bases of limbs. However, some species with bark like this are called peppermints, blackbutts and ashes, so it is not a consistently-used name. Many of the boxes do form a natural group, related to the ironbarks. In south-eastern Australia one of the best known is the Yellow Box *E. melliodora*, famous for the pale, viscous honey it yields. The Coolabah is also a Box.

Ironbarks: a natural group of species with hard, grey deeply-furrowed bark.

Stringybarks: another natural group, confined virtually to the temperate east and south-east, with thick, bristly, fibrous bark.

Bloodwoods: also a natural group, chiefly tropical but extending down the east coast and into the Centre. They have a loose flaky or scaly bark, often exuding a dark red gum. The famous Red-flowering Gum, and its close relative Marri, are isolated representatives in the far south-west.

Ashes: also a group of mainly tall, slender trees that grow in almost pure stands in the mountains of the south-east. They have varying lengths of rough, fibrous bark on the lower trunk, with smooth bark higher up. The most famous is the Victorian and Tasmanian Mountain Ash *E. regnans*, the tallest known flowering plant (exeeded in height only by the Californian Redwood, a conifer). Alpine Ash *E. delegatensis* is a valuable timber species of the Snowy Mountains and Victorian Alps.

EURO

Strictly speaking the name Euro is applied to the one subspecies of the Common WALLAROO, *Macropus robustus* (male body length 1.1 – 2.0 m, tail 550–900 mm; females are much smaller and lighter in colour). The other subspecies is the WALLAROO or Eastern Wallaroo. The latter, which has long grey fur, is found on the eastern and western slopes of the Great Dividing Range, while the Euro, shorter-haired and more reddish,

Euros Macropus robustus erubescens *are closely related to the shaggy, dark grey Common Wallaroo. They are common, and are found over most of the continent, west from the slopes of the Great Divide.*

lives to the west, ranging to the coast. The animal's snout is bare and black. Euros vary so much that they were once thought to be three separate species.

Euros are also sometimes called Hill Kangaroos because they spend the day in small groups in shelter provided by the rocks of escarpments and stony hills. In the evening they leave the shelter to begin grazing, mainly on grasses, spinifex and herbs.

Although Euros are wide-ranging, their distribution is patchy, depending on the presence of suitable day-time shelter. They are, however, an abundant species which has to be culled from time to time, and since Europeans provided water, they have spread in some places. In good conditions they can breed throughout the year.

EVOLUTION

No zoologist or botanist, except possibly a few who had contrary religious beliefs before they began their studies, doubts the reality of evolution. Evolution is the development, over millions of years, of all the varied organisms now alive, from one – or at the most – a few much simpler ancestors. There is an immense amount of consistent evidence for this. It includes the fossil record, but goes far beyond it to many branches of anatomy, physiology, biogeography and genetics.

Darwin's contribution was not the *discovery* of evolution, but the amassing of a great amount of evidence that it had occurred. He also provided a mechanism, still accepted in its essentials by most evolutionists. The arguments are now about the rate of evolution – whether it was constantly slow and steady or at times rapid on a geological time scale.

Darwin noted that organisms produce offspring very like themselves, but with some differences from their parents, and from each other. He also noted that organisms produce far more offspring than will survive to reproduce themselves. He therefore concluded that any individuals better fitted to the environment would have a better chance of reproducing and passing on their favourable characteristics to their offspring, while those less suited would often fail to do so.

This is the process of natural selection, and can be seen at work on a minor scale in the spread of resistance to pesticides in insects, or the spread of darker forms of moths in polluted districts, where the normally well camouflaged original forms would show up on blackened trees. This can happen within a few generations but larger changes – such as the development of wings or hair – takes far longer. There has, however, been plenty of time – about 3000 million years. Since Darwin, the theory has been greatly refined by its integration with modern knowledge of genetics.

The intrepid explorers

European settlers first landed in Australia in 1788, but it took them 25 years just to cross the Blue Mountains, and even after 50 years they had explored less than one-third of the vast island continent.

Close on the heels of the explorers came the squatters, intent on claiming and settling the new discoveries. This small party was searching for a sheep run some time in the middle of last century.

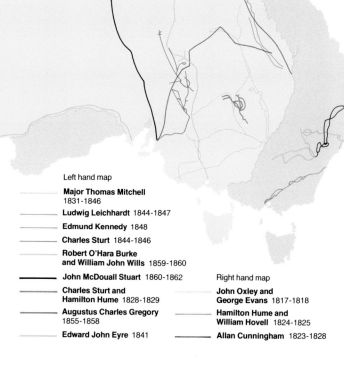

Left hand map

	Major Thomas Mitchell 1831-1846
	Ludwig Leichhardt 1844-1847
	Edmund Kennedy 1848
	Charles Sturt 1844-1846
	Robert O'Hara Burke and William John Wills 1859-1860
	John McDouall Stuart 1860-1862

Charles Sturt and Hamilton Hume 1828-1829	
Augustus Charles Gregory 1855-1858	
Edward John Eyre 1841	

Right hand map

John Oxley and George Evans 1817-1818	
Hamilton Hume and William Hovell 1824-1825	
Allan Cunningham 1823-1828	

P art of the reason for the slow progress of exploration was the fact that for many years the European population was very small. Moreover, the government did not want settlement to spread far and wide, because this would have increased the cost and difficulty of maintaining law and order in the convict colony.

The natural environment, too, presented many challenges. First, the Blue Mountains, west of Sydney, were suprisingly difficult to cross because of their peculiar formation. They consist of a plateau, cut into deep valleys. Explorers followed the valleys, only to find that each one ended in cliffs, and if these were climbed, more valleys and cliffs were met. One explorer, George Caley, likened it to travelling over the roofs of houses in a town.

Robert O'Hara Burke. His ill-fated expedition left Melbourne amid fanfares in 1860 and ended tragically on the shores of the Gulf of Carpentaria a year later, with the deaths of all except one member of the exploring party.

Across the mountain barrier
In 1813 Gregory Blaxland, William Lawson and William Charles Wentworth solved the puzzle. By following a ridge they were able to advance far enough to see that the remainder of the way would be easy. Several months later the colony's chief surveyor, George William Evans, continued to a point beyond the site of modern Bathurst, and discovered two inland-flowing rivers, the Macquarie and the Lachlan.

Before long, more inland-flowing rivers were discovered. In 1824 Hamilton Hume and William Hovell, travelling south to Corio Bay, on which Geelong now stands, crossed the Murrumbidgee, Murray (which they called the Hume), Mitta Mitta, Ovens and Goulburn Rivers. Alan Cunningham who travelled north to the Darling Downs in 1827, crossed the Namoi,

Dumaresq, Gwydir, Barwon and Condamine Rivers. In following these streams, explorers were hampered by the dryness of most of inland Australia. Few of the rivers were large enough to be followed by boat. Moreover the rainfall varied greatly from year to year. During droughts, many rivers dried up, and in wet seasons they sometimes spread over the countryside, forming swamps where there was no clear channel to follow. John Oxley met this latter problem when he tried to follow the Macquarie River in 1817 and the Lachlan River in 1818.

Sturt's epic journey
Captain Charles Sturt avoided Oxley's difficulty by setting off along the Macquarie River by boat in a drought year, 1828. He succeeded in passing the marsh, but was then caught by the opposite extreme, when the river dried up completely.

Proceeding on foot across the parched landscape, the explorers came to the Darling and Castlereagh Rivers. Sturt then concluded, correctly, that all the

Camels played a major part in opening up the dry interior of the continent. These belonged to the Elder Scientific Exploring Expedition, shown here setting out from the Everard Ranges in South Australia in June 1891 to fill gaps between the tracks of the heroic explorers of the 1870s.

northern inland rivers flowed into the Darling.

In 1829 he set out to trace the Murrumbidgee, and after launching a whaleboat and a skiff, proceeded by water to the Murray and down it to Lake Alexandrina. There he saw the narrow channel where the Murray makes its way across sandbanks to the sea. He concluded that all the southern rivers flowed into the Murray, and that a stream entering the Murray from the north was the Darling. He had, in fact, worked out the general shape of the whole, extensive Murray-Darling river system.

Sturt's discoveries were followed up by Major Thomas Mitchell, who travelled along unexplored portions of the Darling and Murray and through the western district of Victoria. By 1840 practically the whole of south-eastern Australia had been explored.

Penetrating the far north

Further north, in what is now Queensland and the Northern Territory, resistance by Aborigines was more determined than in the south-east. Edmund Kennedy, leader of an expedition on Cape York Peninsula in 1848, was fatally speared. Of the 11 Europeans with him six died of starvation, while three others disappeared and are thought to have been killed by hostile Aborigines.

By this time the remaining unexplored areas were mainly in the centre and west of the continent, where the great obstacles were the enormous distances to be covered, the searing heat of summer, and the extreme lack of water. Edward John Eyre came close to dying of thirst as he pushed along the shore of the Great Australian Bight from South Australia to Western Australia in 1841. Sturt, trying to reach the centre of the continent in 1844, was trapped in a gorge with a water hole for six months, during which the temperature reached 58°C.

Into the dry heart

Ludwig Leichhardt made an epic journey from the Darling Downs to Port Essington (north-east of Darwin) in 1844. Then in 1848 he and six others set out in the hope of crossing the continent from east to west,

The heroic efforts of explorers meant little without the patient work of the surveyors who mapped their discoveries. Men, like these painted by S.T. Gill in central Australia, spent months painstakingly measuring and recording the country through which they passed.

but were never seen by Europeans again. During the following decade A.C.Gregory travelled from the coast of Arnhem Land to central Queensland, and from southern Queensland to Adelaide.

Then in 1860 Robert O'Hara Burke left Melbourne in an attempt to cross the continent from south to north. He reached Cooper's Creek, left some men there, and pushed on with only his second-in-command, W.J. Wills, and two men named Gray and King. They reached the Gulf of Carpentaria, but Gray died on the return journey, and they came back to Cooper's Creek just seven hours after the men there had given up hope and left. Food had been buried at the foot of a tree with DIG carved on its trunk, but in spite of this, Burke and Wills died soon after. King was helped by Aborigines, and was rescued by a search party three months later.

Meanwhile John McDouall Stuart had also set off to cross the continent, starting from Adelaide, and in 1862, on his third attempt, reached the north coast. Ten years later the Overland Telegraph was constructed along his route, and this made it easier for explorers such as P.E. Warburton, John Forrest and Ernest Giles to penetrate unknown parts of Western Australia. By 1880 Australia's main geographical features were known, and the exploration of the remaining patches of territory was comparatively easy.

Jacky Jacky, the hero of Edmund Kennedy's tragic expedition along the Queensland coast between 1848 and 1849. His single-handed dash for help saved the lives of the three who survived out of the party of 13.

EXTINCT ANIMALS

There are many kinds of fossil animals to be found in Australia. Most of these prehistoric creatures lived in environments which were often quite different from those found in the same areas today. This goes without saying when the animals concerned lived in the sea, and their remains are to be found in, for example, central Queensland. Land-dwelling animals also lived in quite different habitats millions of years ago. Many of today's arid areas were then covered by lush rainforest.

The main evidence of past animal life comes from fossils which, by the nature of things, are often fragmentary. Nevertheless a skilled palaeontologist can learn much from one or two bones, particularly if they are similar to corresponding bones in an existing identified fossil, often one from another country. Other evidence comes from the cave art and legends of the Aborigines who arrived in Australia when many extinct animals were still in existence. Aboriginal folk memories may be responsible for stories of creatures such as the BUNYIP.

Many fossil bony fish have been found, as well as several very primitive forms, if the term 'fish' is used in a very wide sense. The Southern Four-eyed Fish *Arandaspis prionotelepis* from the Northern Territory, for example, is one of the world's oldest vertebrates. It was an ostracoderm – a fish without paired fins, that had the front of its body and its head heavily armoured. Like modern lampreys, it had no jaws. Most intriguing were paired openings – the pineal 'eyes' – on the top of its head. The marine Gogo Fish *Harry-*

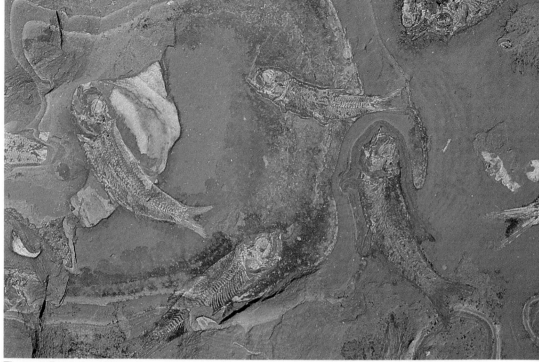

These well-preserved fish once swam in lakes that covered land around Dubbo, in central NSW, about 200 million years ago. At that time all of the southern continents were joined together in one vast supercontinent.

toombsia elegans was an arthrodire – a jawed fish with armour on its head and trunk, the two sections being articulated. It was discovered in the Kimberleys, which have also yielded the widespread armoured fish *Bothriolepis* which lived in fresh water elsewhere in the world. Clearly Australian animals started being different very early on.

Lungfish, related to the modern species, were once widespread in Australia, and are known from rocks formed up to 100 million years ago.

Early amphibians have also been found, among them labyrinthodonts, which were superficially more like salamanders than frogs. *Siderops kehli* is an unusual example because of the size of its head – which was twice as wide as its shoulders – and because it was relatively modern. The animals lived in south-eastern Queensland as recently as 212 million years ago. They were about 2.5 m long, and had jaws filled with almost 200 dagger-like teeth.

Australia had many ancient reptiles. Some of the best preserved bones of flying reptiles known as pterosaurs – often depicted in Hollywood films – have been found in central Queensland. The Queensland species was probably a moderately large, marine fish-eater.

Also from Queensland, and South Australia, come the remains of Ichthyosaurs *Platypterygius australis*, dolphin-shaped reptiles with four paddles, which hunted in the shallow seas that once covered parts of Australia. They were 6 to 7 m long, and were thus much smaller than the famous *Kronosaurus queenslandicus* – a 14-m monster, with a 3.5-m head, well supplied with teeth. It was a pliosaur, a short-necked creature which resembled the popular image of the elusive Loch Ness monster.

Among several known Australian dinosaurs were the Minmi *Minmi paravertebra*, an armoured creature, probably 3 m long, with unique vertebrae; the Sauropod *Rhoetosaurus brownei*, a four-legged, plant-eater about 15 m long; and some carnivorous dinosaurs, although none as awe-inspiring as *Tyrannosaurus*. Most

The fossilised bones of a Diprotodon are unearthed by scientists at Tambar Springs in northern NSW. Diprotodons, *the largest known masupials, stood two metres at the shoulder and were three metres long.*

Australian dinosaur fossils have also been unearthed in Queensland.

Other interesting extinct reptiles include giant pythons such as *Wonambi* (5 m) and *Montypythonoides* (7 m); a giant goanna, *Megalania prisca* (possibly 7 m long and eight times the weight of a Komodo dragon); and a recently discovered mammal-like reptile, the Dicynodont, which has yet to receive a scientific label.

Although the remains of giant penguins, coucals, mound birds, and flamingoes are among bird fossils found in Australia, the most interesting species were the Mihirungs – giants birds with hoof-like toes, which were still around when the Aborigines arrived (the name is Aboriginal). Although emu-like, they were not closely related to any modern birds.

Birds belonging to the genus *Dromornis*, which lived five million years ago, are believed to be the largest that have ever lived. Tracks of an unknown species, about 20 million years old, have been found in some parts of Australia. There is, however, much older evidence of Australian birds. Five well preserved feathers from Koonawarra in Victoria see p 84), are estimated to be 143 million years old.

The earliest mammal fossils from other parts of the world are about 200 million years old, and until recently Australia's oldest mammal fossil was *Wynyardia bassiana* from Tasmania, which was similar in shape and size to a Brush-tailed Possum. Then, in 1984, Alex Ritchie of the Australian Museum found a 28-mm-long jaw fragment with teeth among a collection of opalised fossils from Lightning Ridge in NSW. This was found to be more than 100 million years old. It is believed to be the remains of a MONOTREME ancestor of both platypuses and echidnas. Other fossil anteater ancestors are recent, and similar to modern forms, although they are often much larger.

So far no complete marsupial remains earlier than *Wynyardia* are known, so what the original Australian marsupials looked like is not clear at this stage, although they probably resembled American opossums.

Among the most famous of Australia's extinct animals is the *Diprotodon*, which survived until after the arrival of the Aborigines. It was a rhinoceros-sized, plant-eating animal, somewhat like a huge wombat in appearance. It was the first Australian fossil mammal to be described – by Sir Richard Owen in 1838. In later fossils the brain was relatively small compared with the older species, much of the skull being taken up by air spaces so that the actual thickness of the

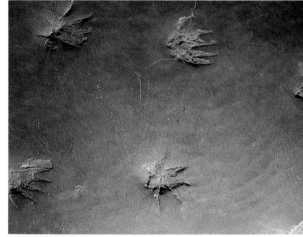

About 230 million years ago an ancient amphibian called a labyrinthodont waddled across mud flats near Sydney, leaving tracks that are still sharp today.

bone was about 1 mm. The animal's nose may have been extended forward as a short trunk.

Also well known are the marsupial lions, although for many years there was much argument over their role. One group believed they lived on melons. Now there is no doubt they were efficient carnivores. The most striking feature of their skull is the enlargement of the premolar teeth which act as huge shears. In recent years many remains have been found, and it is known that the animals had a very large, mobile, clawed thumb with which they may have held their prey until it suffocated. The panther-sized *Thylacoleo carnifex* lived about two million years ago, but there were smaller forms at various other times in the recent past.

The most famous of the extinct kangaroos were *Sthenurus* and *Procoptodon* which, unlike modern kangaroos, had hindfeet with a single toe. They had short, deep faces with eyes set in front, and could raise their arms above the head to drag down branches from a considerable height. Some were about 3 m tall.

Other outstanding Australian fossil finds include remarkably preserved bat fossils, closely related to fossils found in France, and freshwater dolphins from Victoria. The most interesting discovery, however, has been the large number of giant species – such as *Diprotodon*, palorchestids, rat kangaroos and wombats – which survived until well after the arrival of the Aborigines, perhaps 100 000 years ago.

There are two theories about their disappearance: the first is that they were wiped out by humans (a theory applied to similar animals on other continents), and the second is that they could not survive a period when Australia became very much drier. Many Australian scientists now seem to favour the second theory.

The treasure of Riversleigh

Fossil discoveries at Riversleigh station, about 20 km north-west of Mt Isa in Queensland, are immensely exciting to scientists wanting to unravel the evolution of animals from 10 to 15 million years ago. They are also important to the rest of the world because the fossils of Australia, isolated from Asia for 45 million years, can be used to test theories of evolution. The Riversleigh site was known to scientists from 1901, but it was only in 1983 that its richness became apparent. While investigating a promising region revealed by aerial photographs, Dr Michael Archer of the University of NSW looked down at his feet and saw some 'petrified spaghetti'. Hearts pounding, he and his colleagues crawled among the razor-edged rocks and spinifex. In ten minutes they uncovered the remains of more than 30 animals new to science. Since then another 70 have been discovered. Intensive work on the site by palaeontologists and an army of volunteers has barely touched the region.

Perhaps the most important discoveries have been the fossils of some bats that can be linked by the structure of their teeth to bats from France dated to 18 million years ago. This means it is now possible to date the fossils, and relate them to the rest of the world.

Riversleigh has also yielded remains of a 7-m snake now scientifically known as *Montypythonoides*; huge freshwater crocodiles; a partly tree-living, Dingo-sized marsupial lion; a carnivorous kangaroo; a tiny koala; and giant birds, numerous frogs and even insects.

The rocks of Riversleigh station (above) have yielded fossils of enormous importance to both Australian and world science. Among many remarkable finds is the perfectly-preserved skull of a 25-million-year old platypus, shown here with that of the smaller modern animal (right).

FARMING

When James Ruse became Australia's first farmer in November 1788, it is unlikely that even he, a forward-thinking and inspired convict, would have dreamt about the eventual size and importance of the industry he pioneered.

In the space of 200 years, Ruse's 30-acre (12-ha) 'Experimental Farm' at the present site of the city of Parramatta, west of Sydney, has spawned a primary industry which regularly contributes around $18 billion to the economy, and roughly one-third of all export income.

However, such achievements have not come without hardship, tears and fatalities. Ruse – and nearly every farmer to follow in his plough's wake – experienced drought, flood, plague and all manner of natural and man-made disasters.

Despite the many advances which allow farmers to survive and beat the disasters and economic downturns, life on the land can still be a hard slog, with long back-breaking hours and little or no pay. Around 170 000 farms in Australia directly support 393 000 workers, including 250 000 farmers, 120 000 wage earners and several thousand unpaid family helpers. These people are engaged in a range of agricultural pursuits from intensive piggeries, poultry units and fruit production to the extensive cropping and grazing properties of the inland. Australia's farm population, as in other developed nations, is experiencing a rapid decline in numbers. In the 1920s, the Australian government could boast of having a million farmers on a million farms. Many of these property owners were SOLDIER SETTLERS, who had been granted land following World War I. However, many of these soldier farmers, and several hundred thousand more experienced farmers, have left the land in the past 60 years due to the development of labour-saving machinery, increases in the economic size of properties and, in many other cases, financial hardship. The banker – calling to collect overdue debts, or to tell the farmer to sell the property or face eviction – is still a constant threat for many. According to the Australian Bureau of Agricultural Resource Economics (ABARE), about 12.5 per cent of wheat farmers still have debts exceeding $250 000. Further, around 17 000 farmers on all types of farms are in danger of bancruptcy in the next few seasons. But of course this is not the case for all farmers and graziers. Those who have remained debt-free and who have spread the risks by diversifying earn a living way well above that of the average weekly wage. According to the ABARE, the average farm income is around $30 000 a year, while 20 per cent of farmers (34 000) earn at least $80 000 a year. Most primary producers also enjoy many tax advantages over their city counterparts and, in the final analysis, always have their land's asset value to fall back upon. In short, most farmers are asset rich and, in comparison to the city wage-earner, income poor. This statement becomes even more pertinent given the hours worked by most farmers. The average 'cocky' physically works more than 60 hours each week, including many weekends.

Australian farms, which take up about 485 million hectares, can be roughly categorised by the type of activity they are used for. Extensive grazing – whether for sheep or cattle – uses the largest area of land. About 27.5 million hectares of sown and improved pastures, coupled with at least three times that amount of unimproved paddocks, support the nation's 164 million sheep and 20 million beef cattle. The dairy industry, which is largely based on the coastal regions within easy distance of most cities, also accounts for a further 2.5 million cattle, mostly of the distinctive black and white Friesian breed. The number of farmers engaged in the varying rural enterprises is constantly changing as producers respond to market and other economic forces. Over the past few years, there has been a marked shift away from wheat to sheep due to the high value of wool. The national wheat crop has fallen to around nine million hectares from 13 million hectares in 1983–84. Other crops, such as barley, oats, oilseeds and grain legumes, account for a further nine million hectares of land. The climatic variations within each state also dictate what farmers produce. Western Australia, for instance, is well suited to wheat production and often contributes one-third of the nation's output. Products like red meat and wool, however, are grown in every state.

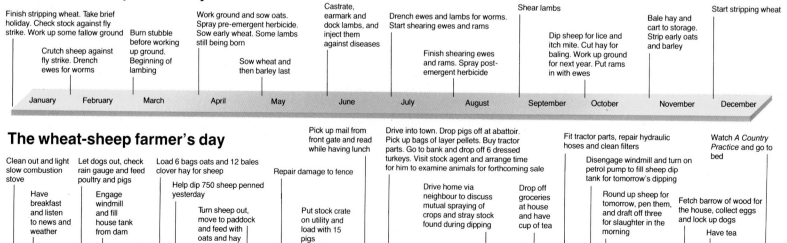

The wheat-sheep farmer's year

January	Finish stripping wheat. Take brief holiday. Check stock against fly strike. Work up some fallow ground
	Crutch sheep against fly strike. Drench ewes for worms
February	Burn stubble before working up ground. Beginning of lambing
March	Work ground and sow oats. Spray pre-emergent herbicide. Sow early wheat. Some lambs still being born
April	Sow wheat and then barley last
May	
June	Castrate, earmark and dock lambs, and inject them against diseases
July	Drench ewes and lambs for worms. Start shearing ewes and rams
	Finish shearing ewes and rams. Spray post-emergent herbicide
August	
September	Shear lambs
	Dip sheep for lice and itch mite. Cut hay for baling. Work up ground for next year. Put rams in with ewes
October	
November	Bale hay and cart to storage. Strip early oats and barley
December	Start stripping wheat

The wheat-sheep farmer's day

5 am	Clean out and light slow combustion stove
	Have breakfast and listen to news and weather
6	Let dogs out, check rain gauge and feed poultry and pigs
7	Engage windmill and fill house tank from dam
8	Load 6 bags oats and 12 bales clover hay for sheep
	Help dip 750 sheep penned yesterday
9	Turn sheep out, move to paddock and feed with oats and hay
10	
11	Pick up mail from front gate and read while having lunch
	Repair damage to fence
	Put stock crate on utility and load with 15 pigs
12 noon	
1 pm	Drive into town. Drop pigs off at abattoir. Pick up bags of layer pellets. Buy tractor parts. Go to bank and drop off 6 dressed turkeys. Visit stock agent and arrange time for him to examine animals for forthcoming sale
2	Drive home via neighbour to discuss mutual spraying of crops and stray stock found during dipping
3	
4	Drop off groceries at house and have cup of tea
5	Fit tractor parts, repair hydraulic hoses and clean filters
	Disengage windmill and turn on petrol pump to fill sheep dip tank for tomorrow's dipping
6	Round up sheep for tomorrow, pen them, and draft off three for slaughter in the morning
7	Fetch barrow of wood for the house, collect eggs and lock up dogs
	Have tea
8	Watch A Country Practice and go to bed

170

A wheat-sheep farm

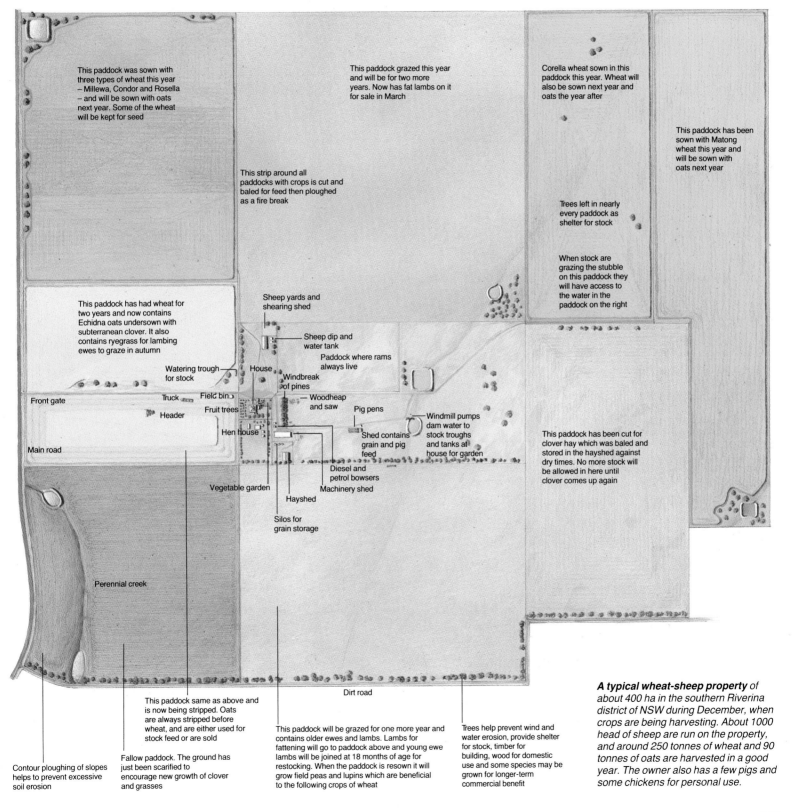

This paddock was sown with three types of wheat this year – Millewa, Condor and Rosella – and will be sown with oats next year. Some of the wheat will be kept for seed

This paddock grazed this year and will be for two more years. Now has fat lambs on it for sale in March

Corella wheat sown in this paddock this year. Wheat will also be sown next year and oats the year after

This paddock has been sown with Matong wheat this year and will be sown with oats next year

This strip around all paddocks with crops is cut and baled for feed then ploughed as a fire break

Trees left in nearly every paddock as shelter for stock

When stock are grazing the stubble on this paddock they will have access to the water in the paddock on the right

This paddock has had wheat for two years and now contains Echidna oats undersown with subterranean clover. It also contains ryegrass for lambing ewes to graze in autumn

Sheep yards and shearing shed

Sheep dip and water tank

Paddock where rams always live

Watering trough for stock

House

Windbreak of pines

Front gate

Truck

Field bins

Woodheap and saw

Pig pens

Windmill pumps dam water to stock troughs and tanks at house for garden

Header

Fruit trees

Shed contains grain and pig feed

Main road

Hen house

This paddock has been cut for clover hay which was baled and stored in the hayshed against dry times. No more stock will be allowed in here until clover comes up again

Vegetable garden

Diesel and petrol bowsers

Machinery shed

Hayshed

Silos for grain storage

Perennial creek

Dirt road

This paddock same as above and is now being stripped. Oats are always stripped before wheat, and are either used for stock feed or are sold

Contour ploughing of slopes helps to prevent excessive soil erosion

Fallow paddock. The ground has just been scarified to encourage new growth of clover and grasses

This paddock will be grazed for one more year and contains older ewes and lambs. Lambs for fattening will go to paddock above and young ewe lambs will be joined at 18 months of age for restocking. When the paddock is resown it will grow field peas and lupins which are beneficial to the following crops of wheat

Trees help prevent wind and water erosion, provide shelter for stock, timber for building, wood for domestic use and some species may be grown for longer-term commercial benefit

A typical wheat-sheep property of about 400 ha in the southern Riverina district of NSW during December, when crops are being harvesting. About 1000 head of sheep are run on the property, and around 250 tonnes of wheat and 90 tonnes of oats are harvested in a good year. The owner also has a few pigs and some chickens for personal use.

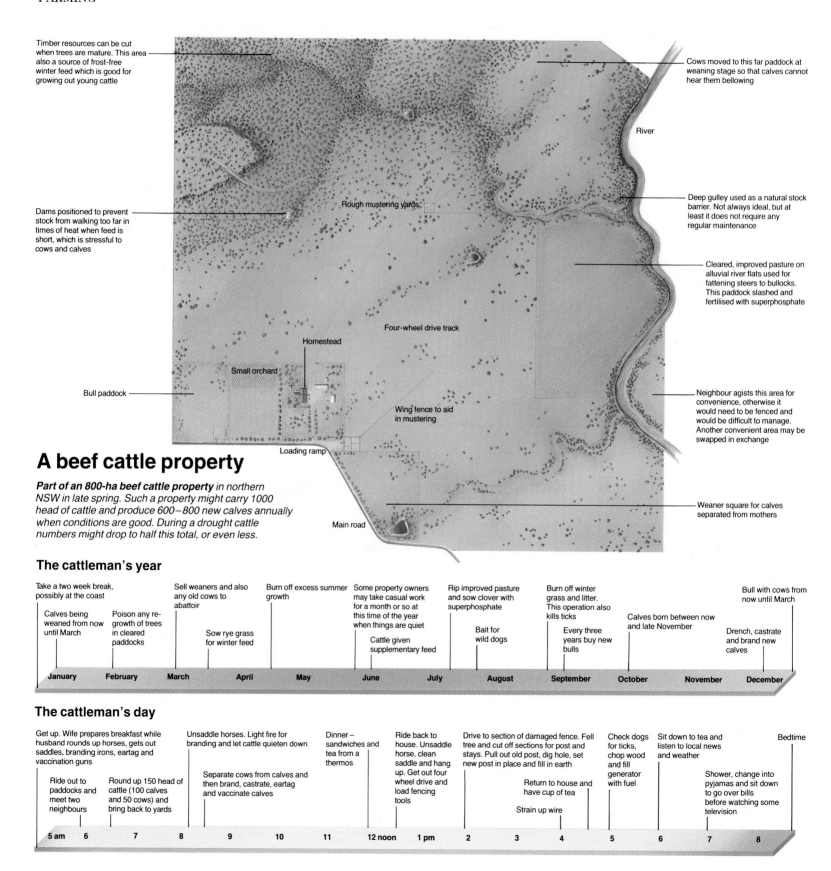

Timber resources can be cut when trees are mature. This area also a source of frost-free winter feed which is good for growing out young cattle

Cows moved to this far paddock at weaning stage so that calves cannot hear them bellowing

River

Dams positioned to prevent stock from walking too far in times of heat when feed is short, which is stressful to cows and calves

Rough mustering yards

Deep gulley used as a natural stock barrier. Not always ideal, but at least it does not require any regular maintenance

Cleared, improved pasture on alluvial river flats used for fattening steers to bullocks. This paddock slashed and fertilised with superphosphate

Four-wheel drive track

Homestead

Small orchard

Bull paddock

Wing fence to aid in mustering

Neighbour agists this area for convenience, otherwise it would need to be fenced and would be difficult to manage. Another convenient area may be swapped in exchange

Loading ramp

A beef cattle property

Part of an 800-ha beef cattle property in northern NSW in late spring. Such a property might carry 1000 head of cattle and produce 600–800 new calves annually when conditions are good. During a drought cattle numbers might drop to half this total, or even less.

Main road

Weaner square for calves separated from mothers

The cattleman's year

Take a two week break, possibly at the coast

Calves being weaned from now until March

Poison any re-growth of trees in cleared paddocks

Sell weaners and also any old cows to abattoir

Sow rye grass for winter feed

Burn off excess summer growth

Some property owners may take casual work for a month or so at this time of the year when things are quiet

Cattle given supplementary feed

Rip improved pasture and sow clover with superphosphate

Bait for wild dogs

Burn off winter grass and litter. This operation also kills ticks

Every three years buy new bulls

Calves born between now and late November

Bull with cows from now until March

Drench, castrate and brand new calves

| January | February | March | April | May | June | July | August | September | October | November | December |

The cattleman's day

Get up. Wife prepares breakfast while husband rounds up horses, gets out saddles, branding irons, eartag and vaccination guns

Ride out to paddocks and meet two neighbours

Round up 150 head of cattle (100 calves and 50 cows) and bring back to yards

Unsaddle horses. Light fire for branding and let cattle quieten down

Separate cows from calves and then brand, castrate, eartag and vaccinate calves

Dinner – sandwiches and tea from a thermos

Ride back to house. Unsaddle horse, clean saddle and hang up. Get out four wheel drive and load fencing tools

Drive to section of damaged fence. Fell tree and cut off sections for post and stays. Pull out old post, dig hole, set new post in place and fill in earth

Strain up wire

Return to house and have cup of tea

Check dogs for ticks, chop wood and fill generator with fuel

Sit down to tea and listen to local news and weather

Shower, change into pyjamas and sit down to go over bills before watching some television

Bedtime

| 5 am | 6 | 7 | 8 | 9 | 10 | 11 | 12 noon | 1 pm | 2 | 3 | 4 | 5 | 6 | 7 | 8 |

A horticultural farm

A 40-ha horticultural property on the banks of the Hawkesbury River, west of Sydney, growing fruit and vegetables on rich alluvial river flats.

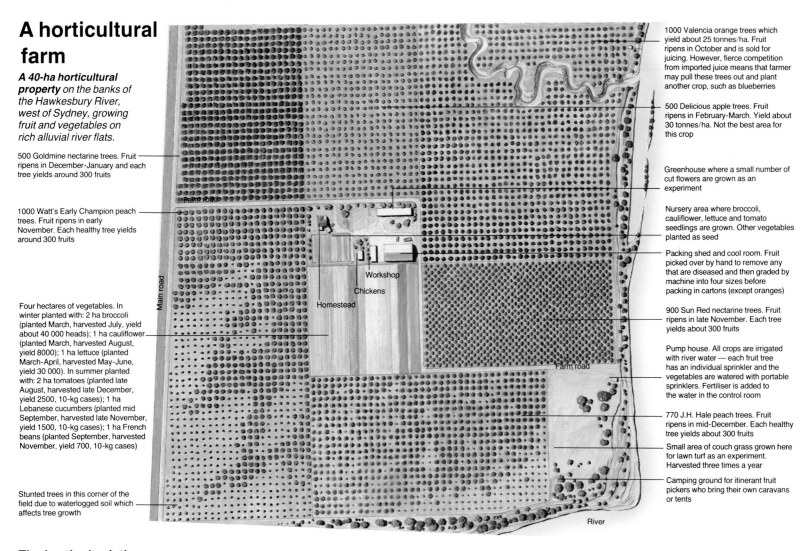

500 Goldmine nectarine trees. Fruit ripens in December-January and each tree yields around 300 fruits

1000 Watt's Early Champion peach trees. Fruit ripens in early November. Each healthy tree yields around 300 fruits

Four hectares of vegetables. In winter planted with: 2 ha broccoli (planted March, harvested July, yield about 40 000 heads); 1 ha cauliflower (planted March, harvested August, yield 8000); 1 ha lettuce (planted March-April, harvested May-June, yield 30 000). In summer planted with: 2 ha tomatoes (planted late August, harvested late December, yield 2500, 10-kg cases); 1 ha Lebanese cucumbers (planted mid September, harvested late November, yield 1500, 10-kg cases); 1 ha French beans (planted September, harvested November, yield 700, 10-kg cases)

Stunted trees in this corner of the field due to waterlogged soil which affects tree growth

Plant road

Main road

Workshop

Chickens

Homestead

Farm road

River

1000 Valencia orange trees which yield about 25 tonnes/ha. Fruit ripens in October and is sold for juicing. However, fierce competition from imported juice means that farmer may pull these trees out and plant another crop, such as blueberries

500 Delicious apple trees. Fruit ripens in February-March. Yield about 30 tonnes/ha. Not the best area for this crop

Greenhouse where a small number of cut flowers are grown as an experiment

Nursery area where broccoli, cauliflower, lettuce and tomato seedlings are grown. Other vegetables planted as seed

Packing shed and cool room. Fruit picked over by hand to remove any that are diseased and then graded by machine into four sizes before packing in cartons (except oranges)

900 Sun Red nectarine trees. Fruit ripens in late November. Each tree yields about 300 fruits

Pump house. All crops are irrigated with river water — each fruit tree has an individual sprinkler and the vegetables are watered with portable sprinklers. Fertiliser is added to the water in the control room

770 J.H. Hale peach trees. Fruit ripens in mid-December. Each healthy tree yields about 300 fruits

Small area of couch grass grown here for lawn turf as an experiment. Harvested three times a year

Camping ground for itinerant fruit pickers who bring their own caravans or tents

The horticulturist's year

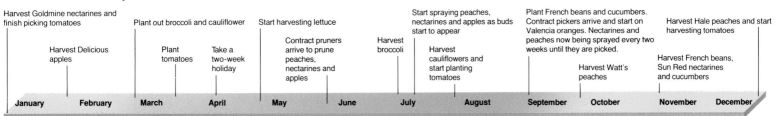

Harvest Goldmine nectarines and finish picking tomatoes

Harvest Delicious apples

Plant out broccoli and cauliflower

Plant tomatoes

Take a two-week holiday

Start harvesting lettuce

Contract pruners arrive to prune peaches, nectarines and apples

Harvest broccoli

Start spraying peaches, nectarines and apples as buds start to appear

Harvest cauliflowers and start planting tomatoes

Plant French beans and cucumbers. Contract pickers arrive and start on Valencia oranges. Nectarines and peaches now being sprayed every two weeks until they are picked

Harvest Watt's peaches

Harvest Hale peaches and start harvesting tomatoes

Harvest French beans, Sun Red nectarines and cucumbers

January	February	March	April	May	June	July	August	September	October	November	December

The horticulturist's day

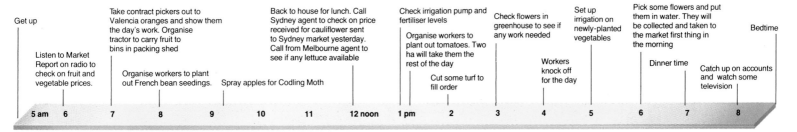

Get up

Listen to Market Report on radio to check on fruit and vegetable prices.

Take contract pickers out to Valencia oranges and show them the day's work. Organise tractor to carry fruit to bins in packing shed

Organise workers to plant out French bean seedlings.

Spray apples for Codling Moth

Back to house for lunch. Call Sydney agent to check on price received for cauliflower sent to Sydney market yesterday. Call from Melbourne agent to see if any lettuce available

Check irrigation pump and fertiliser levels

Organise workers to plant out tomatoes. Two ha will take them the rest of the day

Cut some turf to fill order

Check flowers in greenhouse to see if any work needed

Set up irrigation on newly-planted vegetables

Workers knock off for the day

Pick some flowers and put them in water. They will be collected and taken to the market first thing in the morning

Dinner time

Catch up on accounts and watch some television

Bedtime

5 am	6	7	8	9	10	11	12 noon	1 pm	2	3	4	5	6	7	8

A striking fault revealed in a road cutting below Parliament House in Canberra. The displacement of rocks on either side of the two fractures can easily be traced. The entire section of rock is about five metres high from the top to the bottom.

FAULT

Faults are breaks in rocks where one section of rock slides past another. They are caused by rocks being compressed, stretched or twisted until they tear. They were first recognised in the coalfields of northern Europe in the 18th century when miners found that some coal seams suddenly disappeared, then reappeared elsewhere. Movement on faults can occur on any scale from a few millimetres to hundreds of kilometres. The Alpine Fault in New Zealand is a good example of a large-scale fault where the western side of the country has slid several hundred kilometres to the north of the eastern side. Other faults cause sections of rock to be raised or depressed. Uplifted blocks – or horsts – expose a fresh face called a scarp. Perhaps the best known example of a scarp in Australia is the eastern edge of the Grampians in Victoria. Whatever the scale, the faults are a clear display of the huge forces at work within the earth.

HOW FAULTS ARE FORMED

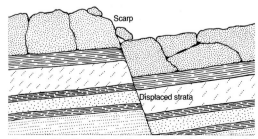

Scarp

Displaced strata

A normal fault, similar to the example photographed above. Major movements at fault lines often result in earthquakes – some of them devastating.

FERAL ANIMAL

Many animals introduced by Europeans have escaped from control and have adapted to life in the bush – often very successfully. Many have become major problems because they destroy delicate environments and compete against native animals, often driving them from an area. Cats, dogs, rats, rabbits, pigs, goats, camels, cattle and water buffalo are all problems in various areas.

Cats may have reached Australia before Europeans because there are reports that some Aborigines considered them to be native. They could have arrived with Indonesian or other visitors to the north. Even so, many of the feral cats today are descended from ones which escaped from European control, or were deliberately dumped.

Toms range in size from 450–600 mm, with tails from 240–340 mm, and weigh between four and six kg. Females are smaller. Colour varies in the ways it does in domestic animals. It is possible and widely believed that after some generations in the wild, feral cats are larger than domesticated ones. Ion Idriess, the writer, saw one 'as high as a hefty, medium sized dog' on Cape York Peninsula.

Feral (and stray) cats are found throughout the mainland and Tasmania, from rainforests to deserts, where they can survive without drinking water. One CSIRO expedition killed 70 in a few weeks near a camp in the Kimberleys.

Cats hunt mainly at night, resting during the day in rabbit burrows and similar retreats. They feed on various animals up to the size of a possum. Their main item of food seems to be, however, rabbits. The stomachs of 33 feral and stray cats in agricultural districts of western Victoria contained mainly carrion, rabbits and mice, and no native animals. But in timbered country in the eastern highlands, most of the diet of 95 killed cats had been native rats, mice and possums, with some birds.

Cattle were among the first feral domestic animals in Australia. There were two bulls and five cows remaining from the First Fleet on 1 May 1788, but by 9 July both bulls and four cows were missing, presumed killed. In 1795, however, their descendants – a herd of about 60 – were found more than 60 km from Sydney at Cowpastures (now Camden).

When beef cattle are allowed to roam free it is difficult to decide whether they are feral or not. They may all be owned by someone, but any that escape mustering and dipping for years can hardly be said to be under control. Some certainly became feral in the Northern Territory when the settlements at Port Essington and Raffles Bay were abandoned and their livestock released. In 1976 it was estimated that there were about 95 000 feral cattle in Australia.

The First Fleet's 74 pigs probably belonged to a variety like the Tamworth – a long-legged, long-faced animal – similar in many ways to the wild boar of Europe. They may have been given the freedom of the settlement to forage in the surrounding bush, so that some may have escaped within months of Sydney's establishment.

Pigs need damp places to live, such as swamps and river courses, but with this restriction they are found from Victoria and NSW through Queensland to the north. There are also populations in the Northern Territory, northern Western Australia and on Flinders and Kangaroo Islands. They must wallow frequently in mud or water, and need cover from the sun in hot areas. They will eat both plants and animals and have a digestive system similar to that of humans.

Pigs often come close to domestic stock and may transmit diseases to them. Feral pigs are reservoirs for brucellosis, leptospirosis and Murray Valley encephalitis, and could harbour exotic diseases such as foot and mouth, and swine fever, if they were ever introduced.

The numbers fluctuate, being lowest after prolonged drought, but in 1976 the Australian population was estimated – probably underestimated – as 975 000. In 1977, 91 per cent of the NSW Pasture Protection Boards reported pigs in their areas.

Packs of feral dogs – formed from runaway farm animals or pets – often wreak havoc on domestic livestock, especially sheep.

FERN

In fossil form, ferns date back more than 300 million years; today's ferns are among the most primitive plants on earth. Prehistoric ferns were generally much larger than those of today; tree ferns reaching 30 m high formed the world's first forests and the wood of those trees is the basis of present-day coal deposits. There are now about 10 000 species of ferns worldwide, and about 400 live in Australia.

Ferns are flowerless plants, reproducing by means of spores, not seeds. They are perennial and the leaves first appear as coils which unroll. On the undersides of the leaves, spores are formed in minute, club-shaped sacs, called sporangia, which are usually covered with a flap. The spores are dispersed by wind or animals. Each grows into a green, scale-like disc, called a prothallus, often less than 12 mm long, which has male and female organs. Sperms are produced and travel in a film of rainwater to the female organ to fertilise egg cells from which new plants develop.

Most ferns are found in moist, shady places because they need water for reproduction and because the delicate fronds dry out easily. However, some are found in dry rocky areas and are called 'resurrection plants'. The sporophytes of these species can dry out completely and resume functioning as soon as water is available.

A maze of stone walls once spanned the Darling River creating small ponds in which fish were trapped and caught by Aboriginal hunters. Many of Australia's shallow rivers must once have had traps like this.

FIELD

To city dwellers, 'field' conjures up romantic visions of golden wheat rippling in the sun. This is probably a reflection of the European and North American use of the term to describe an area of cleared ground used for cropping or pasture. However, most Australian farmers use paddock in this context. To them a field is something to play football on. In contrast, British farmers know the paddock as a small area, usually near the homestead, where a few horses and house cows are run.

Nevertheless, field does have some relevance for Australian farmers and graziers. Annual field days are an important event on most calendars. Farmers and graziers gather to attend field days where they can see the latest equipment and technology. Field days are far more commercial than country shows, attracting most major rural suppliers and often leading to purchases worth many millions of dollars. Like country shows, they also provide an excellent opportunity to catch up on local gossip.

FIG

Historically this is the common name of the edible fig *Ficus carica*, but the meaning is often broadened to include any member of the largely tropical rainforest genus Ficus, of which there are about 2000 species worldwide. The most remarkable feature of figs, by which they are instantly recognised, is their flower-bearing structure, popularly called the 'fruit'. This is a fleshy container, on the surface of which are crowded hundreds or thousands of tiny white, pink or purplish flowers. This corresponds to the short, crowded flower-spike of their relatives the mulberries, but with a very important difference – in the figs the spike is turned inside-out, with the flowers on the inside. The opening at the top is very small and partly blocked by scales. This amazing structure is closely connected with the fig's method of pollination, which depends on tiny wasps. These hatch and grow inside the closed fig and the adult wasp eventually eats its way out and may enter another fig through the temporarily opened pore at the top. The full story is very complex, involving different wasps for each different species of fig.

There about 50 species of fig that are native to Australia. The greatest numbers are found in the rainforests of north Queensland, with a few extending down the east coast as far as Victoria. Others are found west across north Australia and one species lives in central Australia, where it grows over rocks. Some of the rainforest figs are giant trees, but start life as EPIPHYTES high in other trees, quickly sending roots to the ground. After some years these make a sheath of interlocking roots around the host's trunk and ultimately fuse together and kill it – such figs are known as 'strangler figs'.

Around Sydney, and on the NSW coast and ranges, the most common species is the Port Jackson Fig *F. rubiginosa* which grows to a large spreading tree. They are often a sign of calcium in the soil because they grow on shores of estuaries, on the sites of Aboriginal MIDDENS.

FINCH

The term 'finch' is used loosely for several kinds of stout-billed, largely seed-eating birds. The true finches have only two introduced species in Australia. One, the Goldfinch *Carduelis carduelis* (125–135 mm) is one of the happier introductions because of its beauty and its liking for thistle seeds.

The grass finches of Australia are weaver birds. Although most of them weave large dome, flask or bottle nests, often with side entrances, few of them nest in colonies, or build the spectacular nests of the village weavers and social weavers of other countries. There are 19 Australian grass finches, although four are called mannikins. One of the latter is the Nutmeg Mannikin *Lonchura punctulata* (110–120 mm) an introduced colonial-nester.

Australian grass finches are popular cage birds. One of the most beautiful and widespread is the flocking Zebra Finch *Taeniopygia guttata* (100 mm), a bird that is usually found throughout the arid inland grasslands.

FIREFLY

The name firefly is usually used for phosphorescent beetles of the family Lampyridae. The adult females are often wingless, and are sometimes called GLOW-WORMS, although in Australia and New Zealand this name is usually used for the larvae of tiny fungus gnats.

The glow of phosphorescent animals is produced in specialised tissue or organs, and involves reactions with an enzyme luciferase which can be extracted and used to make cold light in a test-tube.

There are about 16 of the beetles in Australia, mostly in the north, although one is found in the Blue Mountains west of Sydney. The lights are presumably used in courtship. In some tropical countries many beetles flash in unison but this does not seem to occur in Australia.

The larvae inject corrosive saliva into snails and suck out the resulting fluid. One British species was introduced into New Zealand in an attempt to control pest snails.

FISH TRAP

Aborigines ate many kinds of fish from the sea, estuaries and freshwater lakes and streams. Sometimes a hook and line was used, but larger numbers could be obtained by trapping them in stone dams. Once the fish were trapped they could easily be speared, netted or taken with special conical-shaped baskets placed at outlets. Sometimes the fish left in traps were poisoned.

In rivers, large stones were piled up to form a dam or channel through which fish had to pass. Fish – including eels which migrate inland from the sea – were caught in large channels made from earth, and in stone weirs on the edges of seasonal lakes in western Victoria. As the water-level rose and fell in the lakes, different fish traps would come into operation. Some fish traps may be thousands of years old, but most of them are probably younger.

On coastal reefs and in shallow sandy bays, walls and dams were also built with large stones. The pools would fill up as the tide came in and, as it dropped, the fish would be left behind to be gathered easily by hand.

Fish traps are quite rare and if they are discovered they should be reported to the local museum or National Parks officer. The stones should not be disturbed.

Common freshwater fish of Australia

Australia has been very dry for much of its recent geological past, and as a result few species of freshwater fish are found in its rivers and lakes. Even those that are found have evolved relatively recently from sea fish, and are often just as much at home in estuaries, or even the open ocean.

More interesting are those species which live in the rivers and creeks that flow into the inland. There they must live and breed in water that is sometimes becomes extremely stagnant and low in oxygen. Some wait until floods bring fresh water before breeding, while others carry their eggs in the mouths, or drape them over their bodies, so that they can be moved to better areas. There are only four true freshwater fish – those that did not evolve in the sea – the most interesting of which is the QUEENSLAND LUNG FISH.

About 230 species of freshwater fish have been recorded in Australia, of which 49 are really sea fish that sometimes enter rivers, 20 enter estuaries or the sea at some time in their lives and 16 (at least) were introduced. Some introduced species, particularly the European Carp have been very successful in Australia rivers.

Some of the more widely-distributed, common and interesting species are illustrated here.

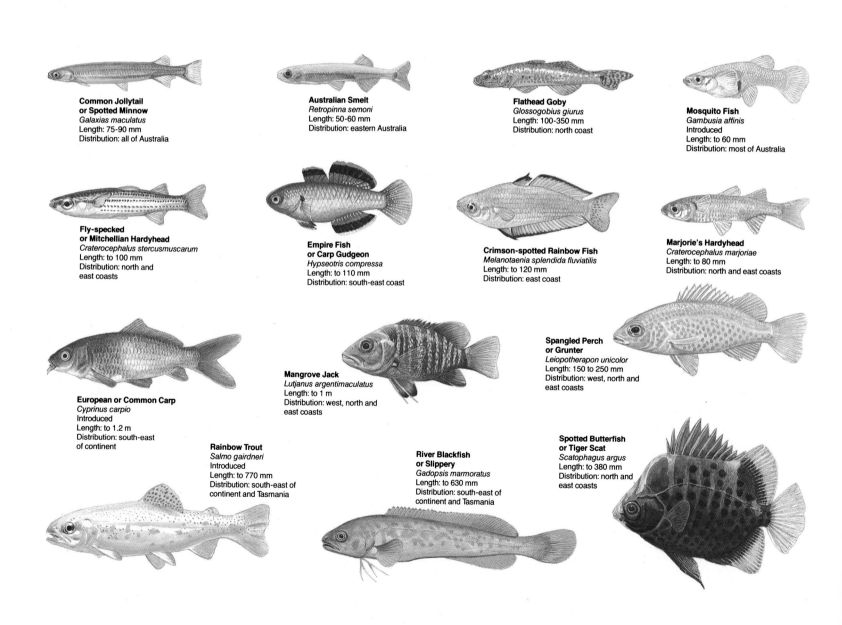

Common Jollytail or Spotted Minnow
Galaxias maculatus
Length: 75-90 mm
Distribution: all of Australia

Australian Smelt
Retropinna semoni
Length: 50-60 mm
Distribution: eastern Australia

Flathead Goby
Glossogobius giurus
Length: 100-350 mm
Distribution: north coast

Mosquito Fish
Gambusia affinis
Introduced
Length: to 60 mm
Distribution: most of Australia

Fly-specked or Mitchellian Hardyhead
Craterocephalus stercusmuscarum
Length: to 100 mm
Distribution: north and east coasts

Empire Fish or Carp Gudgeon
Hypseotris compressa
Length: to 110 mm
Distribution: south-east coast

Crimson-spotted Rainbow Fish
Melanotaenia splendida fluviatilis
Length: to 120 mm
Distribution: east coast

Marjorie's Hardyhead
Craterocephalus marjoriae
Length: to 80 mm
Distribution: north and east coasts

European or Common Carp
Cyprinus carpio
Introduced
Length: to 1.2 m
Distribution: south-east of continent

Mangrove Jack
Lutjanus argentimaculatus
Length: to 1 m
Distribution: west, north and east coasts

Spangled Perch or Grunter
Leiopotherapon unicolor
Length: 150 to 250 mm
Distribution: west, north and east coasts

Rainbow Trout
Salmo gairdneri
Introduced
Length: to 770 mm
Distribution: south-east of continent and Tasmania

River Blackfish or Slippery
Gadopsis marmoratus
Length: to 630 mm
Distribution: south-east of continent and Tasmania

Spotted Butterfish or Tiger Scat
Scatophagus argus
Length: to 380 mm
Distribution: north and east coasts

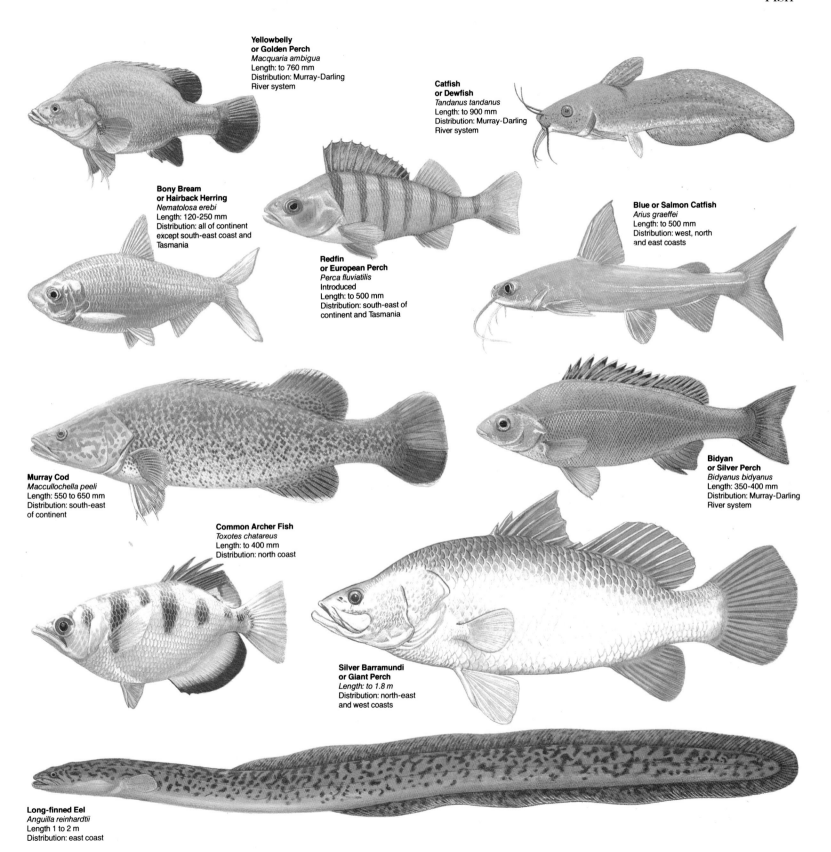

**Yellowbelly
or Golden Perch**
Macquaria ambigua
Length: to 760 mm
Distribution: Murray-Darling
River system

**Catfish
or Dewfish**
Tandanus tandanus
Length: to 900 mm
Distribution: Murray-Darling
River system

**Bony Bream
or Hairback Herring**
Nematolosa erebi
Length: 120-250 mm
Distribution: all of continent
except south-east coast and
Tasmania

Blue or Salmon Catfish
Arius graeffei
Length: to 500 mm
Distribution: west, north
and east coasts

**Redfin
or European Perch**
Perca fluviatilis
Introduced
Length: to 500 mm
Distribution: south-east of
continent and Tasmania

Murray Cod
Maccullochella peeli
Length: 550 to 650 mm
Distribution: south-east
of continent

**Bidyan
or Silver Perch**
Bidyanus bidyanus
Length: 350-400 mm
Distribution: Murray-Darling
River system

Common Archer Fish
Toxotes chatareus
Length: to 400 mm
Distribution: north coast

**Silver Barramundi
or Giant Perch**
Length: to 1.8 m
Distribution: north-east
and west coasts

Long-finned Eel
Anguilla reinhardtii
Length 1 to 2 m
Distribution: east coast

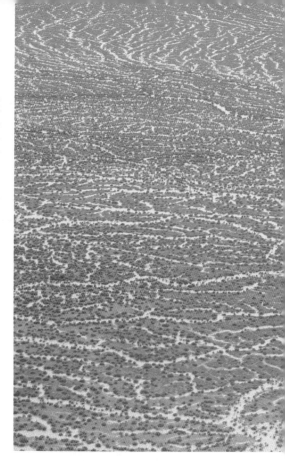

FLAME TREE

The fiery red flowers of the Flame Tree *Brachychiton populneus* make it stand out among the dark green foliage of other rainforest species. This medium-sized tree of east-coast rainforests is found from the Illawarra region south of Sydney to far north Queensland, and is also found in New Guinea. In the south it is one of the few deciduous native trees, and produces spectacular masses of small, coral-red flowers on bare branches in late spring. The trees are sometimes called Flame Kurrajong, because they belong to the same group as the KURRAJONG, and Illawarra Flame because they were once common in the Illawarra region, which has now mostly been cleared of rainforest. For many years Flame Trees have been planted widely in streets, parks and gardens and they can make a wonderful ornamental tree, but sometimes they flower erratically.

FLANNEL FLOWER

There are 17 species of flannel flowers. One species is found in both Australia and New Zealand, and the rest are found only in Australia.

The 'petals' of flannel flowers are really modified leaves that surround the flowers. The flowers get their name from the hairy 'petals' which look as if they are made from flannel. The best known flannel flower *Actinotus helianthi*, widespread around Sydney, looks very like the European alpine plant edelweiss, but the resemblance is only superficial. There is a diminutive relative, *A. minor*, which also flourishes only in Sydney's sandstone areas.

FLEA

Fleas are blood-sucking insects which can spread diseases. In 1984, in Sydney, they held up the mail because sorters refused to work in a flea-infested building.

All adult fleas – there are about 70 species in Australia – attack mammals or birds, but they are not very specific. The dog's flea is often a Cat Flea *Ctenocephalides felis*, and the cat's a Dog Flea *Ct. canis*. Most of the introduced species will bite human beings, at least when they are very hungry.

Adult fleas are small, bristly insects protected by a thick outer layer and with bodies that are flattened so they can slip through fur or feathers. They jump well to escape or to transfer to a new host. Most adult fleas spend only part of their time on their victims, but Sticktight Fleas embed their mouthparts in the host and cling on.

The long, thin, blind, white legless LARVAE develop in debris, feeding on organic scraps and, if possible, the faeces of adults which contain undigested blood.

The Human Flea *Pulex irritans* is thought to have become less common in most of the world this century.

FLOOD

While much of the Australian continent is arid, its highly variable rainfall – especially on the east coast – means that floods are fairly common. Major floods have occurred this century in 1910–11, 1929–31, 1949–50, 1954–55, 1971, 1974, 1976 and 1982.

Tropical cyclones are perhaps the major cause of flooding in the north of the continent. In January 1974 Cyclone Wanda caused severe flooding in Brisbane as one metre of rain fell in a few days. Over 10000 houses were destroyed or damaged, and 14 people lost their lives as floodwaters swept though the city. At one point the Brisbane River reached 6.6 m above its normal level. The greatest amount of rain ever to fall in one day in Australia, since records were kept, deluged Bellenden Ker in northern Queensland with 1140 mm during Cyclone Peter on 4 January 1979.

Other floods may be caused by prolonged winter rains from mid-latitude cyclones, such as caused flooding in Perth in August 1963, or from rain-bearing low pressure systems which remain stationary for a number of days and cause persistent heavy rain.

Like droughts, floods are only a hazard when they affect human settlements. If a flood is considered to be dangerous when it reaches a depth of one metre, and has a speed of more than one metre per second, then most of northern Australia experiences substantial flooding each year during the wet season. However, when human and animal life have adapted appropriately, flooding is not a problem. For example, it has been estimated that only one community of 200 or more people, and 200 buildings, would be at risk if the Gulf of Carpentaria had a flood of a severity likely to occur only once every 100 years. If similarly severe flooding occurred in the less well-prepared Murray-Darling drainage system, nearly 90 communities and 12000 buildings would be at risk.

FLUKE

Flukes are parasites and are members of a group which also contains tapeworms. Adult flukes usually live in the internal organs of animals – for example in the lungs, intestine or bile-ducts of the liver – although some, such as those that cause bilharzia, thankfully absent from Australia – are parasites of the blood system.

The Sheep Liver Fluke *Fasciola hepatica* is the most important species in Australia. It infests sheep and cattle, and sometimes people. It is one of the largest flukes in the world and can grow to a length of 30 mm.

Another fluke, *Austrobilharzia terrigalensis*, has the most direct effect on humans. The eggs are carried by seabirds, excreted and hatched in water, and when larvae come in contact with people, the result is the common 'bather's itch'.

LIFE CYCLE OF THE LIVER FLUKE
(*Fasciola hepatica*)

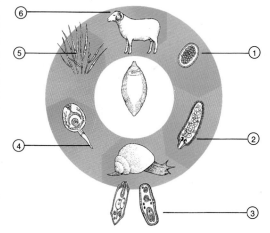

Sheep Liver Flukes are a major problem in Australia. Each fluke lays at least 45 000 eggs (*1*), which pass out of the animals with faeces. They must reach water to develop, but once there the tiny larvae hatch (*2*) and swim to a freshwater snail and enter it. Once inside the snail the larvae change into two new forms (*3*) – cercariae – which leave the snails after a few months (*4*). The cercariae attach themselves to grass or water plants (*5*) and wait to be eaten or drunk by grazing animals. Once inside a sheep (*6*) the tiny flukes find their way to the liver, and from there to the bile ducts where they may stay for up to two years.

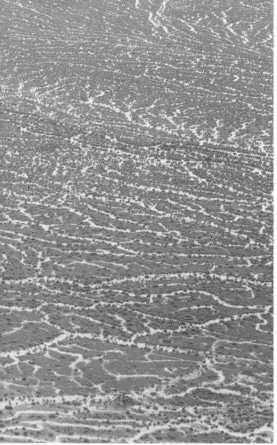

Vast quantities of floodwater overflow tributaries of Coopers Creek, which runs from central Queensland to the Channel Country. Much of this valuable water will end up in Lake Eyre, where both plants and animals will flourish for a time.

FLY

The true flies form an immense group of insects of great importance. More than 85 000 are known in the world, and there are more than 6700 species in Australia.

The forewings of flies are used for flying, but the hind wings have been reduced to small knobs on stalks which function like a gyroscope to control stability in flight – essential in an insect that can fly very fast. Mouthparts are basically used for sucking, and are like a sponge at the end of a tube. In many – such as MOSQUITOES – they have become adapted to piercing and sucking. The legless larvae vary from the maggots of houseflies – which are virtually headless – with hook-like appendages for dealing with food, to the wrigglers of mosquitoes.

Most larvae probably originally scavenged in organic matter, but some have turned from this to attacking plants or to living as parasites in the eggs of locusts, or caterpillars and other animals. Many live in water and feed on organic debris and micro-organisms. Adults also live on a variety of foods such as nectar, honeydew, fluids from decaying animals, fruit, beer (vinegar flies) and almost anything edible that can be softened with saliva (houseflies).

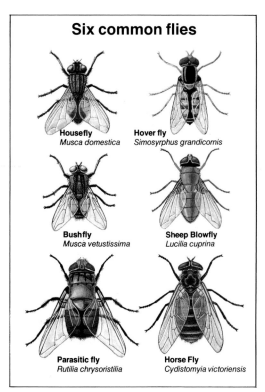

Six common flies

Housefly
Musca domestica

Hover fly
Simosyrphus grandicornis

Bushfly
Musca vetustissima

Sheep Blowfly
Lucilia cuprina

Parasitic fly
Rutilia chrysoristilia

Horse Fly
Cydistomyia victoriensis

FLYCATCHER

These birds catch insects in flight – often dashing from their perch to do so – but the name is given to many different kinds of birds which all have this habit in common.

Most Australian flycatchers can be grouped as monarch flycatchers. These are large-headed, broad-billed birds, and a typical member of the group is the well-named Restless Flycatcher *Myiagra inquieta* (160–210 mm), a black and white bird which often hovers around foliage picking insects and other creatures off leaves and bark. It resembles the Willie Wagtail *Rhipidura leucophrys* (190–210 mm) which is a fantailed flycatcher in the same family.

FLYSTRIKE

Flystrike is one of the major problems facing the Australian sheep industry. It occurs when blowflies lay their eggs on moist or damaged patches of a sheep's skin. The eggs hatch into maggots which attack the sheep, causing death in extreme cases as well as a loss in wool quality. Crutch strike is the most common form, although pizzle (on rams and wethers), tail and belly strike are also common. Flystrike has become more difficult to control because blowflies have developed resistance to insecticides. Preventive measures include crutching and the controversial practice of MULESING. Research is being undertaken into alternative controls, including breeding sterile blowflies.

THE FLYING DOCTOR

Because vast areas of Australia are sparsely inhabited, aerial medical services have been of great importance. A move to establish them was begun in 1917 by Rev. John Flynn, director of the Presbyterian Church's Australian Inland Mission. However the idea had to wait until an Adelaide electrical engineer, Alf Traeger, had developed a two-way radio set, powered by foot pedals, by which people living in isolated stations could communicate with a flying doctor base.

The first service was established in 1928 and others soon followed. However the expense of running such a large organisation became too great for the Australian Inland Mission, and the Flying Doctor Service of Australia – a voluntary organisation – was formed, financed by contributions, subscriptions and government grants. The use of the prefix 'Royal' was authorised in 1955. Today the RFDS operates from bases in Cairns, Mt Isa and Charleville in Queensland; Broken Hill in NSW; Launceston in Tasmania; Port Augusta in South Australia; and Kalgoorlie, Jandakot, Geraldton, Carnarvon, Meekatharra, Port Hedland, Derby and Wyndham in Western Australia. Aerial medical services are also operated by the Northern Territory Department of Health, from bases in Darwin, Gove and Alice Springs. In some cases a doctor flies to a patient, in others the patient is brought by air to a base hospital, and in minor or non-urgent cases advice may be given by radio. The radio networks of most of the bases are also used for the education of outback children as SCHOOLS OF THE AIR.

An injured stockman receives on-the-spot treatment from the Flying Doctor. The service began in 1928 with a De Haviland DH50 operating from Cloncurry in Queensland. In the first year Dr Vincent Welch and his pilot flew over 32 000 km and attended 255 patients. Until the introduction of the service there was no medical help available to people on isolated stations.

A Grey-headed Flying-fox (left) *feeding on the blossoms of a Turpentine tree. The colony (above), of several thousand, is in a northern Sydney suburb.*

FLYING-FOXES AND FRUIT-BATS

Flying-foxes, fruit-bats and their relatives are vegetarians. They differ from ordinary insect-eating bats in having two claws on each wing, and in not using echolocation for navigation and locating prey. Consequently their faces do not have the grotesque nose outgrowths and ear flaps of some other bats. Their eyes are also relatively large and they are, indeed, often fox like. All the Australian species belong to the same family, which ranges from Africa, through southern Asia, to Australia.

The four species of flying-foxes assemble in 'camps' to hang, roosting, in trees during the day, and move off to their feeding grounds at night, often flying as far as 50 km. Normally they feed on blossoms and fruit of native trees, but when these fail – as was the case in 1986–87 – they can do great damage in commercial orchards.

Grey-headed Flying-foxes *Pteropus poliocephalus* (mean body length 253 mm, forearm 161 mm) are dark-brown, but with a yellow mantle and grey head. They range from mid-Queensland to Victoria, mainly in coastal regions, and form large camps when blossom is plentiful, usually in forests or on islands, but sometimes in urban areas. Breeding has been recorded as far south as Nowra. After mating in March or April the camps break up. The partly-naked single young are born in October, and are carried for some weeks by their mothers until their fur has grown. Then the young are left at the camp while the mothers forage. The species has at least 20 different communication calls.

Little Red Flying-foxes *P. scapulatus* (211 mm, 132 mm) are a nomadic species and are found along the north and east coasts, from mid-Western Australia to Victoria. They feed on blossom and nectar, and orchard fruit when these fail. Black Flying-foxes *P. alecto* (240–260 mm, 150–182 mm) are the largest species, with a similar distribution to the Little Red. Spectacled Flying-foxes *P. conspicillatus* (220–240 mm, 155–175 mm) are found only in north-east Queensland.

Bare-backed Fruit-bats *Dobsonia moluccense* (300 mm, 135–155 mm) are found on north-eastern Cape York, and are the only member of their group in Australia which camps in caves or under boulders, forming roosts of up to 100 individuals. They are fond of flowering bananas. Queensland Tube-nosed Bats *Nyctimene robinsoni* (100–110 mm, 60–70 mm) have nostrils which extend forwards 5 or 6 mm, and yellow or light green spots on their wings and ears. The tubes may be an adaptation for breathing, and the spots make excellent camouflage when the bats roost in sun-flecked foliage. They are found along the east Queensland coast, as are Queensland Blossom-bats *Syconycteris australis* (50 mm, 38–43 mm) which feed on nectar and pollen. The Northern Blossom-bats *Macroglossus Cogochilus* (61 mm, 40 mm) are found across the extreme top of Australia.

FOOL'S GOLD

Amateur prospectors are often disappointed when flecks of golden-coloured minerals in their pans turn out to be fool's gold. Weathered flakes of mica have a deceptively gold-like appearance, but strictly speaking fool's gold refers to the mineral pyrite, also known as iron pyrites, newchum gold or mundic. Pyrite is made up of iron and sulphur. It has a brass yellow colour and is often found as perfect cubic crystals. It is easily distinguished from gold, because gold can be cut with a knife, but pyrite can not.

Pyrite is found associated with gold, notably at Mt Lyell in Tasmania. It is sometimes mined by itself as a source of sulphur, from which sulphuric acid is made.

FOREST

Australia has a great variety of forests, and how much is described as forest depends on how a forest is defined. In the sense of stands of trees yielding useful timber, forests occupy only a small fraction of Australia's total area, but in the sense of any land with a cover of trees, they occupy a major part.

The richness of a forest depends on the resources the area can provide. The tallest and densest forests are found in places with high and reliable rainfall, where the soil is rich in mineral nutrients, and where there is some protection from strong winds and very low temperatures. This richness can be measured in terms of biomass – the total mass of vegetation per hectare. One of the most basic ways of classifying forests, therefore, is to divide them into classes according to the height of the canopy and the spacing of the tree crowns. This classification gives two main classes of forest – closed and open – in which open forests are further divided into tall open, open and low open.

Closed forests are the same as RAINFORESTS in Australia. They are forests in which the tree crowns prevent between 70 and 100 per cent of sunlight from reaching the ground beneath.

Open forests are a broad category that takes in most of the eucalypt forests of Australia. They are forests in which the tree crowns prevent between 30 and 70 per cent of the sunlight from reaching the ground beneath. Open forests are divided into three major groups according to the height of the dominant trees.

The first group is tall open forest – also known as wet sclerophyll forest – where the tallest trees are over 30 m high. These forests are found only in the higher rainfall parts of Australia, on deeper, although not necessarily very fertile soils. In many of the areas in which they occur it is likely that, in the absence of bushfires, they would ultimately change into rainforests, as there are usually several rainforest species growing in their lower layers.

In eastern Australia they are found on the coastal strip, and on the Great Dividing Range, with the dominant eucalypts changing from north to south, and from sea level to the mountains. In subtropical Queensland and NSW, also in mountain areas of tropical north Queensland such as the Atherton Tableland, the eucalypts include such species as Blue Gum, Flooded Gum, Tallowwood and Blackbutt. In the slightly cooler tablelands of NSW they include members of the ash group such as Brown-barrel, New England Blackbutt and Messmate. Further south, in the hills of eastern Victoria and adjacent NSW, the very large Shining Gum and Eurabbie appear. In southern Victoria and Tasmania is found Australia's tallest tree – the Mountain Ash – reaching almost 100 m, while in the subalpine zone of the Snowy Mountains and Victoria's Bogong High Plains are stands of the similar Alpine Ash.

In western Victoria, South Australia and most of Western Australia there is virtually no tall open forest, except in a few moist, sheltered areas such as valleys in the Grampian Ranges and in South Australia's far south-east. In the far south-west of Western Australia are found that state's only tall forests. The tallest is the Karri forest, although there is very little of it, and Jarrah forests on better sites commonly exceed 30 m in height. In the far north of Australia the only tall open forest is found over very limited areas of Cape York Peninsula and in Arnhem Land, where stands of Darwin Stringybark and Darwin Woollybutt may reach a height of 30 m.

All types of tall open forest in Australia are exploited for timber, mostly with intensive forest management, although stands are also preserved in some national parks.

The second class of open forest – called simply open forest – has trees between 10 and 30 m high. This class, together with low open forest, are often called dry sclerophyll forest. They differ from wet sclerophyll forest because their understories contain heathy shrubs or grasses, and not rainforest-type plants and ferns. Open forest covers quite large areas of Australia, and all the state capitals are situated in open forest areas. Many different eucalypts are the dominant trees, and in a few types of open forest, such as brigalow for example, acacias dominate. Large areas of open forest have been cleared for agriculture and grazing, and some also for plantations of exotic pines, so that on the better soils and flatter country there is not much of it that remains undisturbed. Over large areas, in fact, it is found only in road reserves between property fences. There is some timber-getting in open forest areas, but generally not for large-scale sawmilling because the trees are too crooked and are mostly hollow. In parts of NSW and Western Australia some areas of open forest are harvested for wood chips.

The last class of open forest is low open forest, where the trees are under 10 m tall. This stunted, scrubby type of forest grows in areas that are dry, cold or windy, or where the soil is too infertile or poorly drained to support taller forest. Much of inland Australia is covered with low open forest, dominated by eucalypts or acacias. When the trees become more widely spaced such areas may be called woodland. A large proportion of this type of forest remains relatively undisturbed, as the soils are unsuitable for agriculture or grazing, and the trees are too small to yield useful timber. An exception is in the Western Australian wheat belt, where, with the aid of a lot of fertiliser, it has been found that wheat crops can be obtained from low open forest country. As a result large areas of this previously idle land have been cleared.

Types of open forest

Tall open forest is very similar to rainforest, except that the tree crowns are not as densely packed.

Patches of open forest are found around most major cities, but much has been cleared for agriculture.

The stunted growth in low open forest is due to poor soil and bad climate. Most of it remains undisturbed.

FORESTRY

Forestry is practised in only a small part of Australia but it is nonetheless an important industry. Australians use more timber than they produce. Apart from cutting back consumption, the only way to redress this imbalance is to increase production. The most likely way to achieve this seems to be to increase the area of tree plantations.

Over the past 50 years the area of pine plantation has grown from a few hectares to something over 100 000. The largest areas are in Victoria, south-eastern NSW, and the far south-east of South Australia, and with few exceptions the species planted is Monterey Pine *Pinus radiata*. Large areas of this pine have already reached their final felling age of 40 to 45 years and have been replaced by seedlings. Forestry is also widely practised in native forests, in particular the taller eucalypt forests of the high-rainfall east coast and ranges, and the giant Karri forests of the far south of Western Australia and their less spectacular but no less valuable neighbours, the Jarrah forests.

The main elements of management are balancing the timber gained by tree growth against the amount cut annually, so as to sustain the yield indefinitely. More controversial is forestry in rainforests, and in poorer eucalypt forests for production of woodchips for export.

FOSSIL

Fossils are the remains of extinct organisms left in rocks. Often, however, scientists use the word more widely, and include any organic trace that is buried and preserved. Thus tracks, tunnels and faeces can all be fossilised.

Fossils are usually formed when the remains or traces of organisms are covered by water or wind-borne sediments before they are completely destroyed. In the following years – or millions of years – further deposits build up above, covering the fossils with sedimentary rocks, often to a great depth. Eventually, earth movements or erosion may bring the deposits to the surface where they are found.

It is rare for soft parts of plants and animals to be preserved, although in exceptionally dry places an animal may be mummified. Sometimes fossil bones or shells may be virtually unchanged chemically, but more often the original chemicals are replaced by minerals. At times, as at Riversleigh in Queensland, this process is so precise that electron microscopic studies can be made of the material. Often the original remains disappear entirely, but their place is taken by rock material which seeps in to form a cast.

Fossilised tracks are fairly common. Usually they are left in a muddy surface which dries and is then covered with sediment. At Winton, Queensland, there is a remarkable collection of trackways, the result of a stampede 100 million years ago, of a flock of small dinosaurs fleeing away from a larger carnivorous one, and also a much trampled watering hole where they drank. Such fossils can reveal almost as much about dinosaurs as the massive skeletons in museums.

FOX

Foxes *Vulpes vulpes* were introduced from Europe so that the unspeakable could go in hot pursuit of the uneatable. Author Eric Rolls wrote that many native animals such as Dingoes and wallabies were chased in the traditional fox-hunting fashion before the fox was introduced, but that the quarry was more often than not referred to as 'Reynard' in the gossip columns of the day. Consequently he had some difficulty in deciding whether some of the early reports discussed foxes or pretend-foxes. One early hunt composed of officers and other sportsmen, obtained a fox from England (one of eight sent in 1855), released it at Randwick in Sydney, chased it along Maroubra Bay and killed it inland from there. This may have been the first real fox and fox-hunt in the country. Most of today's foxes,

Introduced foxes have adapted very successfully to life in Australia – the only places where they are not found are the tropics and Tasmania. They are the largest predators, after Dingoes and feral dogs.

however, are probably descended from some released near Melbourne in the 1860s. These, and possibly others, populated Australia from the deserts to the coasts, but did not colonise tropical Australia or Tasmania.

Foxes are predators and scavengers. They will

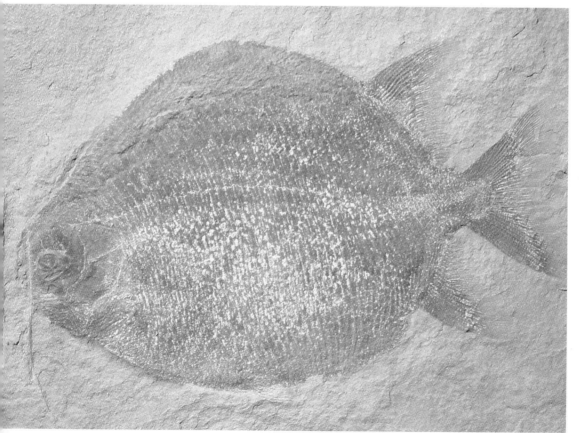

Fossils, such as this 200-million-year-old fish from Somersby, north of Sydney, can tell scientists a lot about the way in which plants and animals have evolved over the past 570 million years.

eat insects, earthworms, fruit, small mammals – particularly rabbits – and carrion. In densely vegetated country they may rely on native animals, and have been blamed for the decline of animals such as lyrebirds. Sick lambs are taken, but healthy ones are apparently usually left alone. Foxes hunt at night and stay under cover during the day, often in burrows. Recently skins have become valuable and there has been much hunting – not by packs, but by people with guns.

FRILLED LIZARD

Frilled Lizards *Clamydosaurus kingii* (to 900 mm) are the dragon lizards which appear on the backs of Australian 2c coins, and which – for some inexplicable reason – became, with koalas, of great interest to the Japanese in the 1980s. They are widespread in the northern half of Australia, from south-east Queensland to north-east Western Australia, and are also found in New Guinea, in dry sclerophyll forest and woodland. They are tree-climbers and eat small vertebrates and insects which they hunt during the day, mainly on the ground, and particularly after rain. Their most conspicuous feature is their frill which lies in a fold around their necks when at rest, but which can be opened to threaten foes. The lizards vary in colour according to where they live, ranging from grey to red and yellow.

When frightened the lizards can run quickly on their hind legs, seeking the safety of a tree (illustration p 236).

FROGMOUTH

Frogmouths – a family of 12 species ranging from Sri Lanka to Australia – make superb broken branches as they pass the day sitting bolt-upright in a tree. The wide-billed frogmouths are night-time insect, spider and centipede hunters which sit in a tree, or fly from perch to perch, till they see prey below on the ground. They fly down, killing the prey with their large bill at the moment that they land. The largest of the three Australian species is the Papuan Frogmouth *Podargus papuensis* (500–600 mm) which will tackle small rodents. In Australia they are found only on Cape York, where the Marbled Frogmouth *P. ocellatus* (370–410 mm) also lives. Most widespread is the Tawny Frogmouth *P. strigoides* (350–530 mm).

FROGS AND TOADS

According to most textbooks, amphibia – frogs and toads in Australia – are animals that have not completely divorced themselves from water. Eggs are laid in water, young (tadpoles) develop in water, and they change into adult frogs, which often live partly on land – hence the name 'amphibia' – meaning 'in both ways life'.

Australian frogs, however, do not always follow the textbooks – as might be expected in a land where surface water is often scarce. Despite

Common frogs and toads

Giant Barred Frog
Mixophyes iteratus

Garden Tree Frog
Litora Caerulea

Desert Tree Frog
Litoria rubella

Turtle Frog
Myobatrachus gouldii

Corroboree Frog
Pseudophryne corroboree

Water-holding Frog
Cyclorana platycephala

Cane Toad
Bufo marinus

the fact that much of the continent is dry, there are about 174 known species of frogs in Australia, and many more probably await discovery. There is also one introduced species, the only true toad – the CANE TOAD *Bufo marinus*. Some frogs live even in sand-plain deserts, but all are subject to drying out and their behaviour must be modified to prevent this. In Europe, a better watered continent, there are, in contrast, only about 14 species.

There are four families of native Australian frogs, but the relationships of some of them to frog families in other parts of the world is not certain. Among the more interesting species is one that is found only in a small area of south-east Queensland, *Rheobatrachus silus*. This frog has unique reproductive habits: the female swallows the young tadpoles and they develop into small froglets in her stomach. When the time comes for them to be 'born', the mother rises to the surface and out they pop. Later research has shown that the young release a chemical substance which turns off the mother's secretion of hydrochloric acid while they are in residence. It is possible that this discovery will lead to a treatment for gastric ulcers.

The Pouched or Marsupial Frog *Assa darlingtoni*, which is found only in the McPherson Ranges and adjacent mountains on the border between Queensland and NSW, also has peculiar breeding habits. The male has pouches on the sides in which the tadpoles develop, and which become longer as the tadpoles grow.

FRUIT

In botany this word has the very general meaning of any seed-containing structure produced by fertilisation of a flower – in contrast to the plain English meaning of an edible, sweet object that comes off a tree. Australian native plants produce an astonishing range of shapes and sizes of fruits, although only a small number are fleshy and edible (see FRUITS, NATIVE).

Eucalypt fruits are the familiar 'gumnuts', varying in size from about 2 mm across in some Coolibahs, to the massive woody fruit of the West Australian Mottlecah – up to 100 mm in diameter. In most eucalypts the fruit remains on the tree for years, growing more woody, sometimes only releasing its seed after the tree is scorched by a bushfire. The shapes of these woody fruits vary enormously.

Hakea is a widespread genus with mostly woody fruits which split open into two halves when dried, releasing two seeds. Some are quite large, often with interesting surface patterns.

Banksias have fruiting 'cones' which consist of the old flower-spike with the true fruits – in structure rather like those of Hakeas – scattered randomly among the dead flowers. These were the 'Big Bad Banksia Men' of May Gibbs' children's books.

Rainforest trees produce some of the most interesting and attractive dry fruits. One is Crow's Ash or Native Teak *Flindersia australis* with large prickly pods which split open into a starlike structure with five segments.

FRUIT FLY

This name is used both for the tiny flies that are attracted to ripe fruit, vinegar, beer and wine, and the true fruit flies, whose maggots infest fruit. The latter are usually brightly coloured and the most important species in Australia are the widespread Mediterranean Fruit Fly *Ceratitis capitata* (5.5 mm) of Western Australia, and the yellow and brown Queensland Fruit Fly *Dacus tryoni* (9 mm). The Mediterranean fly was once found in eastern Australia but it was forced out in the 1940s by the Queensland fly as it spread south. Both attack a wide variety of native and introduced fruits to lay their eggs beneath the skin. The larvae usually pupate in the soil. There are about 130 native species.

The presence of fruit flies in a district interferes with fruit exports, so quarantine stations on state borders are essential.

FRUIT, NATIVE

Travellers in the Australian bush are not greatly struck by the number of wild edible fruits they see. All the same, in most areas of the country there are at least one or two plants yielding edible fruit, even though they are often small or rather acid. As with many other groups of Australian plants, it is in the rich rainforests of the east coast, particularly in the tropics, that the greatest wealth of fruit-bearing plants is found.

People without local knowledge of edible plants are often afraid that eating an attractive-looking wild fruit might result in their being poisoned. With one notable exception in Australia, it is a reasonable rule to follow that, if a fruit is palatable, then it is harmless, at least in moderate quantities. This does not hold so true for the seeds, or for wild nuts. Fruits with an obvious bitter – rather than sour or acid – flavour, or with milky sap, should be treated with greater suspicion. The exception among palatable native fruits – fortunately confined to far North Queensland rainforests – is the notorious Finger Cherry *Rhodomyrtus macrocarpa*. Although sometimes eaten with no ill effects, this has on several occasions caused permanent blindness by damaging optic nerves.

In the far north, for example on Cape York and in Northern Territory's 'Top End', many wild fruits are still eaten by Aborigines, and much has been written about their food plants. Only a few are noted here. Pandanus or Screw-palm is common on seashores and beside swamps and streams. The orange to red fruit in large globular heads, are edible, but the soft pulp from the inner end must first be boiled or baked. Also on seashores is found the Morinda *Morinda citrifolia*, which has an elongated compound fruit which smells bad, but is edible fresh. The red Wild Apple *Syzygium suborbiculare*, a small tree of sand dunes and dry scrub thickets, has large crisp fruit which can be eaten fresh, roasted or boiled. Cocky Apple *Planchonia careya*, a very common shrub or small tree with red leaves in the dry season and floppy white 'shaving brush' flowers, has a fruit like guava which is soft and tasty when fully ripe. It is found as far south as Rockhampton, usually in open eucalypt forest. Around Cape York and in the Gulf Country the Nonda Plum *Parinari nonda* is widespread. It is a small tree with hard, cylindrical yellowish or brownish fruit with floury flesh.

In the taller, dense rainforests of the coast and ranges, extending from North Queensland well into NSW, many different wild fruits are found. The most conspicuous are probably the various species of Lilly Pilly and Native Cherry *Syzygium* and *Acmena* which are white to pink, purple or red, often rather crisp and aromatic. They are mostly rather flavourless fresh, but can be boiled with sugar to produce a good jelly. A north Queensland fruit with a good flavour is the Herbert River Cherry *Antidesma dallachyana*. These are small but profuse, red-brown and acid. The Bolwarra *Eupomatia laurina* is a shrub with a larger pale yellow fruit like a guava, quite edible fresh. The plants are found along the whole length of the east coast. Davidson's Plum or Ooray *Davidsonia pruriens* is a small Queensland tree with profuse plum-sized bluish fruits hanging on long stalks, These are acid to eat fresh, but are excellent stewed.

The more temperate eucalypt forests and woodlands of eastern and southern Australia yield fewer and mostly smaller edible fruits. Native Currants *Leptomeria* are leafless, broom-like shrubs with small translucent green to red berries which are quite tasty, although acid. The related Ballarts or Native cherries *Exocarpos* are similar shrubs or small trees with small hard fruits carried on a swollen, juicy stalk which is the edible part. They are widely distributed in

Some edible native fruit

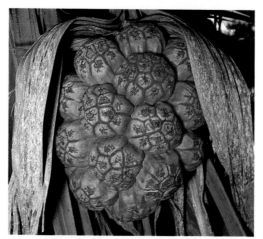

The orange or red fruit of the Pandanus or Screw-palm of northern Australia can be eaten fresh.

The fruit of a Cocky Apple, common in northern Australia, resembles a guava, and is soft and tasty.

The small, citrus-like fruit of Desert Limes are too acid to be eaten fresh, but they can be cooked.

Boobiallas – this is Myoporum montanum *from Dalby in Queensland* – are edible, although bitter.

eastern Australia. A group of small twining plants with soft, edible fruit are the Apple-berries or 'Dumplings' *Billardiera*, which are reasonably common in southern Australia. Related to the introduced BLACKBERRIES are the Native Raspberries *Rubus*, found in wet eastern forests and in the southern mountains. Their berries are perfectly edible fresh, but some are quite tasteless.

In the plains and wooded low hills of the dry inland there are a surprising number of edible native fruits. The Native Pomegranate or Wild Orange *Capparis mitchellii* is a small tree with a dense spreading crown which bears a spherical, hard-skinned fruit with many seeds embedded in pulp. When fully ripe the pulp is quite pleasant to eat. The Desert Lime *Eremocitrus* is a prickly, suckering shrub with masses of miniature, pale greenish citrus-like, fruit, rather too acid to eat fresh. These are both plants of the heavier soils of inland Queensland and northern NSW. Further south and west, in the saltbush country and in Central Australia, Nitre Bush *Nitraria billardieri*, a spreading, tangled shrub, has soft brownish berries with a pleasant, slightly salty flavour. A few of the saltbushes have edible fruit, in particular Ruby Saltbush *Enchylaena tomentosa*, a low shrub with narrow succulent leaves and small brilliant red berries. A group of widely distributed shrubs with edible although bitter fruits are the Boobiallas *Myoporum*. Their small white, pink or yellow fruits have juicy flesh around a hard stone. Mention should also be made of the QUANDONG *Santalum acumintum*, the largest and tastiest of the inland fruits. It is bright red and spherical with a round, pitted stone. The fruit can be eaten fresh, although it is fairly acid, but it is prized for making jams and jellies. Quondongs, although widespread, are not common in most areas.

FUNGUS

This important group of organisms has traditionally been included with the plants, but in modern classifications of living things it is regarded as a Kingdom on its own, distinct from both the Plant and Animal Kingdoms. To most people fungi are mushrooms and toadstools, but these are the fruiting-bodies of just one of several major groups. The various moulds and mildews, as well as yeasts, a large range of 'rots', 'rusts', 'blights' and other plant diseases, together with human and animal diseases such as tinea and ringworm, are all types of fungi. The toadstools and other fruiting-bodies always arise from masses of threadlike, mostly colourless *mycelia* which riddle the soil or rotting logs, and make up the more permanent part of the fungus.

Fungi are present everywhere, and their minute spores are always floating in air-currents around us, waiting to grow on, or in, some suitable material. For food they only need water and organic matter, which they can absorb directly.

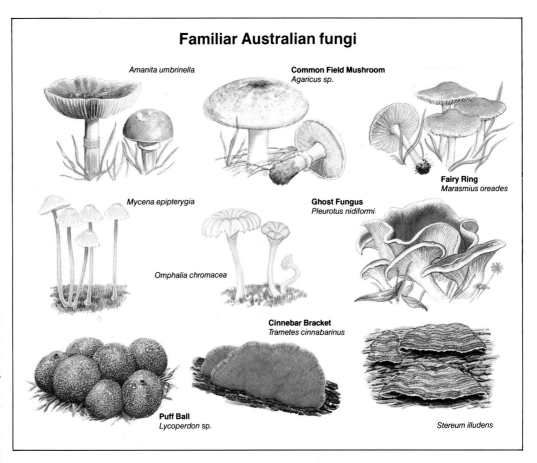

Familiar Australian fungi

Amanita umbrinella

Common Field Mushroom
Agaricus sp.

Fairy Ring
Marasmius oreades

Mycena epipterygia

Ghost Fungus
Pleurotus nidiformi

Omphalia chromacea

Cinnebar Bracket
Trametes cinnabarinus

Puff Ball
Lycoperdon sp.

Stereum illudens

They do not need light-energy, as green plants do.

Fungi grow best where it is warm and humid, as it is in a rainforest. There, together with insects and other small animals, they are responsible for the rapid decay of dead wood and fallen leaves. There are two major groups: those that attack living plant or animal tissues, and those that live on dead materials.

In moist forests the fruiting-bodies of many fungi are commonly seen. These include toadstools, which, like edible mushrooms, are gilled fungi; polypores, which have pores rather than gills on the undersides of their cap – these include bracket fungi which are hard to the touch; as well as many odd groups, such as the basket fungi, earth-stars and puff-balls.

FUNNELWEB SPIDER

Funnelweb spiders, found only in south-east Australia and Tasmania, are primitive spiders with parallel, downward pointed fangs, which must rear up on their back legs to strike effectively. All are probably potentially lethal, but human deaths – about 25 this century – have only been caused by the Sydney Funnelweb *Atrax robustus* (female body length about 30 mm) and, as far as is known, only by males. His venom is about five times more toxic than hers.

Until the release in 1980 of an antivenene, many bites were fatal, although often the spider does not inject enough venom to cause serious illness.

A typical funnelweb is a large black or brownish-black, relatively hairless spider with a shiny head-thorax, and with conspicuously long spinnerets on its abdomen. The male, which is slenderer than the female, often has a spur on its second leg, used in mating. It clamps the female's legs and reduces the risk of the male's attending a funeral rather than a mating. Most species live at the end of a funnel of silk in a tunnel or crevice under a rock, log or house, or in a tree trunk. In the mating season males may wander far from their burrows. Despite widespread beliefs to the contrary, funnelwebs can jump no more that about 20 or so millimetres.

The Sydney species is found from Newcastle to Nowra and inland to Lithgow. Other funnelwebs are found further north, and in Victoria. There is an isolated population around Mt Lofty in the southern Flinders Ranges, and on the southern end of Eyre Peninsula. Recent studies indicate there are probably at least 34 species.

Move the victim of an attack as little as possible as this spreads the venom. If the bite is on a limb apply a firm bandage to the full length of the limb and splint it (see p 338).

GALAH

Galahs *Cacatua roseicapilla* (350–360 mm) are among the most beautiful of Australia's cockatoos. During the non-breeding season they group in flocks of 30 to 1000 birds which fly and forage together on fallen seeds. In the breeding season they separate into pairs, and nest in tree holes that may be used by the same pair for several years in succession. They defend a small territory around the hole, but forage and drink elsewhere, usually within a radius of about 10 km. They can fly at 50 km/h.

When the fledglings are old enough to leave the nest, after six–eight weeks, they are taken to a crèche of up to 100 other young and are left there while the parents forage. The fledglings can fly almost as well as adults, except for one aspect: they tend to crashland. After about two months in the crèche, the young birds are left to fend for themselves.

Galahs are usually found in savanna woodland and open grassland over almost all of Australia, but they can be seen in city suburbs occasionally.

GALAXIA

There are 20 species of these small, scaleless, minnow-like fishes in Australia, most of them living in the southern half. They are long, more or less tubular, and have a single dorsal fin set well back above their anal fin. Some spawn in fresh water and spend time at sea as juveniles before returning. As they are small fishes they are preyed upon by introduced trout, and some populations may have declined as a result. The climbing galaxias can scale steep waterfalls and rocks, using their paired fins to cling and move.

The best-known galaxia is the widespread Common Jollytail (illustration p 176).

GALL

A great variety of swellings can be seen on the leaves and twigs of many native trees and shrubs, sometimes looking like fruits or misshapen flowers. It is usually their sizes and odd positions that give them away as galls, which are formed as a result of attacks by insects or microorganisms. The attackers introduce minute quantities of growth-altering chemicals into the plant tissues, causing a tremendous multiplication and expansion of cells into predetermined shapes. In the case of insects, galls provide food and protection for the insect's grub, the eggs being inserted at the same time as the substance is injected. Most of the large shiny galls on eucalypts are insect galls, produced mainly by various wasps.

GARDEN

In 1862, on the way to her brother's station near modern Bowen, Queensland, Rachel Henning visited a homestead built only two years before, 'with a veranda covered with passion-vine and a garden full of petunias in most brilliant flower. We begged a whole bundle of cuttings...' She and her sister within a year created a flower garden around their house and a separate kitchen garden with an orchard. The eagerness to establish a garden stemmed as much from a longing to bring familiarity to new surroundings as from the need for vegetables and herbs. It was often the women who found comfort in gardening, although it was hard labour as well. Without hoses, water was carried in heavy wooden pails with a yoke over the shoulders. The need to water was not understood by the early settlers, who were used to a damp climate, and many of their fruit trees died.

The first gardens had been planted for survival's sake, but by 1793, when the spectre of starvation had retreated, a visiting Spanish botanist reported geraniums at Government House at Parramatta. Many cottage flowers were shipped from England on the advice of Sir Joseph Banks. Besides the hollyhocks, roses, phlox and lupins, unfortunate imports were thistles, and prickly pear and lantana from South America. Market gardens became familiar as former Chinese miners saw the chance offered by a swift rise in population. Front gardens in the towns were generally given to flowers, with vegetables at the rear of the house. Away from settlements, cottages often stood at the far end of a block, with vegetables, herbs and fruit trees nearest to the house, flowers by the road. Gardens were stiffly formal with gravel paths between geometric beds – a development which was a deliberate contrast to the unruliness of the Australian bush.

GARNET

Garnets are fairly inexpensive gem stones, widely distributed throughout Australia. They are noted for their elegant crystal shape, rich colours in all shades except blue, and hardness – about the same as quartz. Garnets have different chemical compositions, and as the amounts of calcium, iron, magnesium, manganese, titanium and chromium change, so does the colour. White or colourless garnets are rare. Garnets are often found in stream beds or occasionally beach sands, but few are of good quality. Most are just waterworn fragments sieved from gravel areas.

Colourful flower beds and square, bright-green lawns in a country garden are a sharp contrast to the dry, grey-green chaos of Australian bushland.

GAS

Natural gas is one of nature's ready-made products, which today has become an important energy source for commercial and industrial uses. It should not be confused with the gas produced by artifically heating coal. Natural gas has about double the heating capability of coal gas, as well as being cleaner burning.

Natural gas is a fossil fuel produced when microscopic plants and animals are buried for millions of years. The process is the same as for the formation of coal and oil, but at a high enough temperature gas will escape from the rotting remains and pass up through the rocks like water through a sponge. The gas is stored in the spaces between the grains of the rocks, notably in sandstone and limestone.

FORMATION OF NATURAL GAS

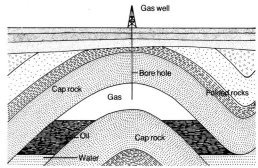

Reservoirs of oil and gas trapped in folded rocks deep underground. Weathering has removed all traces of the structure from the surface of the earth.

GATES AND FENCES

Australia's first fences were post and rail, made of bush timber, the uprights morticed top and bottom and the rails tapered either end to fit snugly. The work was done with an adze. The gate was a slip rail – saplings that would slide easily in and out of morticed holes.

Early gates were hand-made, and the pattern of the gate, the number of cross-bars and the style of bracing often gave a clue to the origins of the land owner. Each county in England had its own pattern and these were faithfully duplicated in the new country.

Post and rail gave way to post and wire. Usually six or eight strands of wire were threaded through holes bored in split bush timber. Barbed wire on top of the fence was introduced to control cattle. However, the barb gives way to plain wire in the corners, or near a fence post. Cattle are most likely to force a mounted stockman into the fence there.

Steel posts or star pickets that can be hammered into the ground are now the usual intermediate posts in fencing panels, and wire netting – either rabbit-proof or ringlock, a wider mesh – has been introduced to control rabbits, lambs or pigs. Wooden gates have given way to either commercially or home-made pipe and netting gates.

The bushman's inventiveness has seen the perfection of flood-proof fences across creeks and waterways. These are designed to fall flat under the pressure of water and debris. Electric fencing, either temporary or as a single strand on a permanent fence, is popular.

Erecting a fence is usually a contractor's job, with the payment being so much per kilometre. The effectiveness of a fence will depend entirely on getting the right tension, or 'strain', on the wire. It takes experience to tie the wire tightly after straining it.

Contrasts in fencing – a modern wood, steel and wire fence (above) and an old post and rail fence (below). Country people judge a property owner by his fences – a badly made or poorly maintained boundary fence indicates a careless worker.

Metal gates have replaced wooden ones almost everywhere. Tradition has it that wooden posts must be made of timber that grows on the property – imported posts will rot more quickly in the ground.

'Cockies gates' – easy-to-remove panels in the fencing – are used where it is necessary to get large machinery in or out of paddocks.

GECKO

Members of this family of lizards are found in all warmer parts of the world, and there are about 86 species in Australia. All are small with soft bodies and well-developed, five-toed limbs. They come out at night and are excellent climbers, with pads on their feet for that purpose. Some can even cling to a sheet of glass. Their eyes resemble those of snakes in having no moveable lids, and in being covered with transparent 'spectacles' which are shed with their skin. Geckoes clean their eyes with their long, fleshy tongues.

All Australian geckoes lay eggs and feed on insects and similar prey, and sometimes other lizards. A few in the north have become house-geckoes, being drawn by the insects attracted to lights. One of the most widespread species, from Western Australia to NSW, is the Spiny-tailed Gecko *Diplodactylus ciliaris* (85 mm) which varies in colour, but is often reddish. The two rows of spines on its tail make it easy to distinguish from other species.

GEEBUNG

This NSW Aboriginal name was originally used for some species of the shrub *Persoonia*, but it is now commonly applied to all of the 50 or so species of this group. A feature that unites them is the small edible yellowish fruit, with a hard stone and sweet, juicy flesh. The sticky flesh has caused children in Western Australia to christen the fruits 'snotty-gobbles', a name which has stuck for some species. Another feature is the four-petalled small yellow or orange flowers.

The great majority of geebung species are found in the higher-rainfall areas of eastern Australia, including Tasmania. One species is found right across northern Australia in monsoonal eucalypt forest. Its fruits are a popular food of the Aborigines.

GEMSTONES

Five thousand years ago tomb paintings from the Nile Valley depicted traders busily dealing in precious gemstones like EMERALD and lapis lazuli. The large DIAMONDS of history like the Kohinoor came from India, and were so valuable that the despotic rulers of India and ancient Persia were once at war to win them. Gemstones are minerals possessing a combination of desirable qualities of great beauty, durability and rareness. Apart from diamonds, gemstones have no technical utility and their only use is for body adornment because of their clarity, colour and sparkling internal fire.

Precious gemstones are minerals capable of being cut and faceted to display their inner beauty. AMETHYST, GARNET and BERYL are more common examples while RUBY, emerald, diamond and SAPPHIRE are rare. In the earth's crust diamond is as rare as one drop of water in 30 000 olympic swimming pools full of water.

Ornamental gemstones on the other hand are mostly translucent or opaque stones which can be quite plentiful in nature, but are valued because of their attractive colours and patterns. AGATE, JADE, TIGER'S EYE, turquoise and OPAL are examples. The best quality opal is not as durable as precious gemstones, but can be as valuable because it is so rare.

Of the several thousand known minerals only about 100 are designated as gemstones, and even though all of these occur in Australia, only diamond, opal and sapphires are of economic importance.

Most gemstones originate from granite and basalt, but are found in river sands and gravels, particularly throughout eastern Australia, where the rainfall is higher and there are more suitable types of rocks than there are in the west.

Some parts of Australia are rich in gem and ornamental minerals – particularly the opal fields and the sapphire fields of northern NSW and Queensland. The big opal producers are the South Australian fields of Coober Pedy and Andamooka. Lightning Ridge, NSW – source of the unique black opal – gives professional prospectors little return for a lot of hard work. TOPAZ is found in the gravels of the Tate River and amethyst at Mt Barunda in northern Queensland. Central Queensland boasts sapphire from Rubyvale and chrysoprase from Marlborough. New England and the north-west slopes of the Great Divide in NSW is a treasurehouse of gem minerals, with jade, ZIRCON, petrified wood, cairngorm, diamond and many others being found in creeks and rivers. Australia's main diamond fields lie in the Kimberley region of Western Australia, in stream gravels and the original host rock. These deposits are being developed commercially on a large scale.

Cut and uncut examples of many precious and semi-precious stones are shown here.

Garnet
Harts Range, NT

Garnet
Bingara, NSW

Boulder opal
Yowah, Qld

Opal
Lightning Ridge, NSW

Opal
Lightning Ridge, NSW

Diamonds (uncut)
Copeton, NSW

Ruby

Ruby
Alice Springs, NT

Beryl
Emmaville, NSW

Beryl crystal
Torrington, NSW

Sapphire
Rubyvale, Qld

Sapphire
Inverell, NSW

Chrysoprase
Marlborough, Qld

Agates
Mt Agate, NSW

Chrysoprase
Marlborough, Qld

Gemstones found in Australia

Quartz crystal
Kingsgate, NSW

Amethyst crystals

Amethyst

Quartz
Tingha, NSW

Topaz
Mt Surprise, Qld

Zircon
Uralla, NSW

Topaz
Tingha, NSW

Aquamarine beryl
Torrington, NSW

Zircon
Harts Range, NT

Tiger's Eye
Pilbara, WA

Topaz crystals
Mt Surprise, Qld

Tiger's Eye
Pilbara, WA

Emerald
Kiandra, NSW

Jasper
Lord Howe Island

Emerald
Emmaville, NSW

Tourmaline crystal
Harts Range, NT

Jade ring
Cowell, SA

Jasper
Tamworth, NSW

Sardonyx
Bellata, NSW

Jade
Nundle, NSW

Green Tourmaline
Harts Range, NT

Pink Tourmaline
Harts Range, NT

Locations in brackets
show where specimens
illustrated were found.

189

GHOST TOWN

Settlements which were once populous but are now either completely deserted or are only a small fraction of their former size are often called ghost towns. Most of Australia's ghost towns fit the second description, which is only to be expected since the towns have all been built since 1788, and there has not been time for the vast climatic changes which have depopulated many settlements in other continents.

Among the most impressive ruins are those at Port Arthur in Tasmania, which was a convict settlement from 1830 to 1877. Since 1972, when the whole district was declared a historic reserve, the old buildings have been well maintained and some renovation work carried out.

Nearly all other Australian ghost towns are either former mining settlements or ones which provided services for the mining industry. Thus Cooktown – at the mouth of the Endeavour River in far north Queensland, where Captain Cook repaired the *Endeavour* – was founded in 1873 to service the nearby Palmer River goldfield. Before long it had 64 hotels, a main street three kilometres long, and a population officially estimated at about 25 000 Europeans and 30 000 Chinese. Today it contains about 1000 people.

Port Douglas, further south in the Cairns district, boomed in the 1880s because of gold, silver and tin mining, and at one time had a population of 8000. This declined to about 100 in the early 1960s. Since then, however, tourism has provided a new lease of life.

In NSW, the former gold-mining town of Gulgong has not shrunk as sharply as the two Queensland examples. Nevertheless its population of nearly 2000 is small compared to that of its boom years in the 1870s. Several buildings from that time, including the post office, police station and the former opera house, are still standing. Australia's $10 banknote carries a drawing of Gulgong in its prime, and a portrait of Henry Lawson, who lived there as a boy. A number of Lawson's stories and poems are based on his memories of Gulgong, so that the ghost of the old town is preserved in his words, as well as in its remaining buildings and the relics in its historical museum.

Clunes, where Victoria's first payable gold was discovered in 1851, is similar to Gulgong in that it has shrunk to a small fraction of its population of the gold-rush days. However, few historic buildings have survived. On the other hand, Hill End in NSW, which once had a population of about 30 000 but is now almost deserted, still has many of its old buildings. Since it was proclaimed a historic site in 1967 a number of them have been restored, and the township has enjoyed a tourist boom. Memories of gold-rush days are preserved in the remarkable collection of photographs taken by Bernard Holtermann.

Other former gold-mining towns now deserted or almost deserted, include Halls Creek in the north-west of Western Australia, and Waukaringa, 40 km north of Yunta in South Australia. Halls Creek was the site of Western Australia's first notable gold discovery, in 1885, and within a year it had a population of about 3000. Today's population of less than 1000 live in a new township, 14 km away from the old site. Waukaringa was the scene of a minor rush in the 1880s and 1890s, but is now completely deserted.

Gold-mining has been the main activity that has caused Australian settlements to boom and fade, but other forms of mining have played a part. Newnes and Glen Davis, near Lithgow, NSW, were both established to work the district's shale oil deposits. The former's works operated for a mere four months in 1911 and then from 1914 to 1923, when it finally became uneconomic. Glen Davis produced crude oil from 1940 to 1952.

Silverton, in the Barrier Ranges of western NSW, was founded in 1880 when silver ore was discovered, and flourished briefly. In 1883, when mineral discoveries were made at a 'broken hill' on Mt Gipps station, 24 km away, residents of

GHOST TOWNS

Some of Australia's better-known ghost towns. Most of them declined when nearby mineral deposits were worked out.

Lucknow, NSW, was founded on gold and prospered in the 1860s when the general store (right) was built. Gradually returns declined, although some mines (seen above in 1900) were still working in the 1940s. Today (below), little remains of the town.

Silverton referred to the new find as a 'hill of mullock' and dismissed it as insignificant. But Silverton's fall was soon as rapid as Broken Hill's rise. In 1889 Silverton's last mine closed, and the town now exists mainly as a recreation centre for Broken Hill residents. There is a strong feeling of being in a ghost town because Silverton's few surviving buildings from the 1880s – including a hotel, a fine stone church and the gaol (preserved as a historical museum) – stand out starkly in a landscape from which the lightly built miners' houses have disappeared.

It is rare for a town to become completely deserted and then to come back to life. A minor example is provided by Innamincka, in South Australia, situated on Coopers Creek at the point where Sturt crossed it on his unsuccessful attempt to reach the centre of the continent in 1844, and not very far from where Burke and Wills died. The settlement began as a customs post, since it was not far from the border between South Australia and Queensland. A police post was established in 1882, and a hotel and general store in 1886. In 1928 the Australian Inland Mission opened a nursing hostel there, and it became a regular landing place for the

Flying Doctor Service from Broken Hill. By 1952, however, the police station, hostel and nursing home had all closed, and the township deserted. In the 1970s the development of Gidgealpa gas field and an increase in tourism led to the opening of a hotel-motel, although Innamincka's rebirth cannot be said to be vigorous. The main relic of old Innamincka is the world's largest bottle heap – once nearly 200 m long, but now depleted by the ravages of time. As the author George Farwell wrote: 'According to prejudice, you could find that heap the text for a sermon, or the touchstone of the traditional Australia.'

Australia contains a few towns of which the original buildings are now deep under water. The residents of Tallangatta, in north-eastern Victoria, were moved to a new township in 1955–56 as their old homes were gradually submerged because of an enlargement of the Hume Reservoir. In NSW, Jindabyne residents were moved when the waters of Lake Jindabyne, formed by the damming of the Snowy River, engulfed their old homes, and the people of Adaminaby were re-located when the old township was covered by water in another part of the Snowy Mountains Scheme.

The Victorian town of Walhalla boomed during the 1850s gold rush, and was still thriving in the 1870s (above). Now (below) only a handful of houses remain.

GHOST GUM

The chalky white or pale salmon-pink bark gives the distinctive *Eucalyptus papuana* its common name. It is found in a broad belt right across the tropical north of Australia. One of the small group of 'paper-fruited bloodwood' species, which flower, ripen and shed their fruit entirely within the wet season, Ghost Gums extend from the coast far into the arid interior. They are perhaps the best known trees of the 'Red Centre' where they grow on cliffs and rocky slopes of the central Australian ranges. Albert Namatjira's striking watercolour paintings of the 1940s and 50s drew attention to the Ghost Gums of this region. Tourists sometimes confuse them with River Red Gums, also common, but mainly found in the bottoms of gorges and distinguishable by greyish streaks in their bark.

GIBBER

Australians call them gibber plains, the Americans call it 'desert armour' and explorers Burke and Wills complained that the ground was 'covered with sharp, dark brown stones that were terrible to walk on'. The legendary stony deserts of Australia extend in patches from near Port Augusta to beyond the Northern Territory border. The gibbers are small pebbles which cover the desert floor in a thin, almost impenetrable layer. In places they are so tightly packed that water cannot soak into the soil. Gibbers are formed when strong desert winds erode the surface rocks into smooth, highly polished stones, often with a veneer of iron and silica called desert varnish. Any fine sand is blown away to form dunes elsewhere.

Camels crossing gibber plains in South Australia. Early explorers, such as Charles Sturt who has a stony desert named after him in far north-western NSW, had great difficulty in crossing these hard, barren stretches of country. The stones cut and bruised the feet of both horses and camels, as well as those of the men.

GIDGEE

This name – sometimes spelt Gidyea or Gidgea – is used for the species of wattle *Acacia Cambagei*. It is a small to medium sized tree with a dense, bushy head of grey-green foliage and dark grey, flaky bark. It is an inland, east Australian species, occurring through a wide belt of Queensland from around Mt Isa south-east to near Roma and well into north-western NSW. It also extends into the Northern Territory, west of Camooweal. In the Georgina Basin, on the border between Queensland and the Northern Territory, it is replaced by Georgina Gidgee *A. georginae*, a smaller, more gnarled tree, the leaves of which contain fluoroacetic acid, making them extremely poisonous to grazing animals. To the east and south-east, Gidgee is replaced by BRIGALOW. Both are trees of low, flattish country and both grow in dense stands. A memorable feature of Gidgee is the stink produced by a stand of it in wet or humid weather – rather like the smell of a tannery. Bush people go to some lengths to avoid camping near it.

GINGER

This ancient spice is grown around Caboolture, Nambour and Gympie, and particularly around the processing factory at Buderim, Qld. Although a perennial, it is usually grown as annual. Plants left in the ground produce a smaller, more fibrous root, the part which is used. Because the flowers are usually sterile, propagation is from pieces of the root, planted in September. The high quality ginger – to be crystallised, put in syrup, made into marmalade, toppings or spreads – is harvested in February and March when the roots have almost no fibre, and taste mild. The remaining crop is harvested between May and August, mostly for dehydrating and grinding into spice. Roughly one-sixth of the annual crop of between 6000 and 7000 tonnes is sold fresh.

Ginger, a native of the East Indies, has been cultivated in Queensland since the 1920s. The leafy stems grow up to one metre high and leaves are 150 to 300 mm long.

A Sugar Glider feeding from gum blossoms. The flap of skin which enables these tiny possums to cover such great distances in the air – at least 50 m – is difficult to see here, but it extends from wrist to ankle. When stretched taut it turns the glider into a parachute.

GLIDER

Three species of POSSUMS have evolved as gliders. Gliding is made possible by a membrane – an extension of the body skin – which stretches from the forelegs to the hindlegs. In the Greater Glider *Petauroides volans* (body 350–450 mm, tail 450–600 mm) it extends from elbow to ankle; in the Feathertail Glider *Acrobates pygmaeus* (65–80 mm, 70–80 mm), really a PYGMY-POSSUM, from elbow to knee; and in the rest, from wrist to ankle. The animals have long tails which help them to steer and balance. The largest, the Greater Glider, can plane about 55 m from a high tree, with an angle of descent of about 40°. The next largest, the Yellow-bellied Glider *Petaurus australis* (280 mm, 433 mm) has a shallower angle of descent, and can thus glide further, about 100 m, crying noisily as it does.

Gliders are found along the eastern side of the continent, but the best known species, the Sugar Glider *B. breviceps* (170 mm, 170 mm) extends to northern Western Australia and Tasmania. It feeds on insects, honeydew (*see* APHIDS) and the sap of eucalypts. In cold weather half a dozen or more will huddle in a nest. The Feathertail feeds on manna, nectar, sap and insects at night. Like other pygmy-possums it can become torpid in cold weather.

GLOW WORM

Several insects produce a cold light called phosphorescence or luminescence by a complex chemical reaction in specialised tissues and organs. Among them are glow worms, the larvae of tiny fungus gnats *Arachnocampa*, which hang in groups from sticky webs which they build in caves and under rock ledges. The light attracts prey. In NSW they are found at Bundanoon and in some old railway tunnels. The name is also sometimes used for FIREFLIES.

GOANNA

The name goanna is a corruption of iguana, a kind of lizard which does not occur in Australia. This country has about 20 out of the world's 30 or so species of goannas, which are called monitor lizards elsewhere. None are found in Tasmania. The Perentie *Varanus giganteus* (illustration p 236) is Australia's largest, and probably the world's third largest, lizard, and can reach 2.4 m in length. They live in arid regions from western Queensland to Western Australia, and are distinctively coloured with a rich brown background embellished with cream or yellow spots, edged with black and brown, and with lighter underparts. They live on the ground in rock crevices and feed on small vertebrates, insects and carrion.

Gould's Goanna or Sand Monitor *V. gouldii* (to 1.5 m or more) is the most widespread species, living on the ground throughout mainland Australia, apart from the extreme south-east. Colour varies enormously, inland species tending to have brighter patterns than the dark eastern coastal varieties. They can flee with surprising speed, and a large specimen will sometimes rear up spectacularly, supporting its body on its hind legs and tail as it runs. Their diet is similar to that of the Perentie.

The Lace Monitor *V. varius* (to 2.0 m) is the second largest monitor (illustration p 236). Its other name, Tree Monitor, refers to its habit of escaping up trees. It ranges from Cape York through NSW to eastern South Australia and generally lives in forests. Colour varies, but many are dark bluish-black on their upper parts, with scattered light-coloured scales. This species often lays its eggs in a burrow in a termite nest. A smaller species is the Short-tailed Monitor *V. brevicauda* (to 2.5 m) which lives in spinifex and ground litter in sandy areas from eastern Queensland to Western Australia. Another tiny species, the Pygmy Mulga Monitor *V. gilleni* (300 mm), also lives in desert areas, but in crevices and under the bark of trees. In contrast the Mangrove Monitor *V. indicus* (1.0 m) lives in rainforest and mangroves along northern coasts, and includes fish in its diet.

In the past goannas were used as a source of medicinal oil. Although Goanna Salve (a registered trade name) is still sold it presumably no longer contains goanna oil, because all Australian reptiles are protected. Nevertheless today's product is enjoying a boom with current exports worth $100 000 and with potential sales to the USA – where the salve has been approved by the Food and Drug Administration – of millions of dollars a year.

Originally the fat from around the kidney was used, but old goannas build up layers of fat beneath their skins and this did not go to waste.

A dead goanna was split lengthways and placed, belly down, in the full sun on a sheet of iron until all the fats oozed out. The oil, or the salve made from it, was reputed to have wonderful penetrating power – so great that it was supposed to seep through glass bottles. It was mixed with a snake bite antidote based on bracken. No longer did victims have to cut a cross over the bite and rub in Condy's crystals. All that was necessary – optimistic manufacturers claimed – was to rub the patent mixture over the intact skin and let the goanna oil do the rest.

GOAT

Captain Phillip brought 19 goats with the First Fleet to provide milk *en route* and to found a herd. Later, Angora and Cashmere herds were established, but the projects failed and some of these animals ran wild. Hardy goats were also a convenient source of milk and meat in mining and railway construction camps. When these broke up the goats would be released.

Feral goats can now be found over most of Australia, with the greatest concentrations in Western Australia, western NSW and nearby parts of South Australia. They avoid rainforests, wetlands and deserts. The total population is estimated to be 200 000–350 000. Goats are agile, browsing animals notorious for causing erosion and destroying vegetation. But they also have a role as weed controllers.

Goat farming for mohair and cashmere is one of Australia's newest and most rapidly expanding rural industries. Farmers began keeping Angora goats for mohair in the 1860s. Most have built their herds by crossing purebred bucks with feral does. Goats are also kept for meat and milk. The milk from dairy breeds Saanen, British Alpine and Anglo-Nubian is prized by consumers allergic to cows' milk.

GOBY

The goby family is the largest among the fishes with about 1800 species, most of them living at sea or in estuaries. It contains the smallest fishes and also the smallest vertebrates – the Pygmy Goby *Pandaka pygmaea* of the Philippines only reaches a length of 7.5 mm.

The pelvic fins of gobies are joined to form a sucker. Some have scales and some are scaleless. Males are usually larger and more brightly coloured than females. There are seven known Australian freshwater species, the smallest of which is the Bug-eyed Goby *Redigobius bikolanus* (to 30 mm), a fish with an elongated body and large eyes on its back. It is found in northeast Australia and also in other countries. The Flathead Goby *Glossogobius giurus* (to 350 mm) is a large-mouthed, sluggish, carnivorous bottom-feeding fish, with a protruding lower jaw, and olive to brown and white colouring (illustration p 176). It is found in northern Australia.

Common goat breeds

Angora
Mohair – a fine, strong, lustrous fibre – is produced from Angora goats

Toggenburg
Originating in Switzerland, Toggenburg goats are kept for milking

Anglo-Nubian
This breed of dairy goat is the second most popular in Australia

Cashmere
This is a generic term applying to goats which grow cashmere – a fine textile fibre

British Alpine
A high-producing dairy breed that was developed in the late 19th century

Saanen
The most popular breed in Australia, and the highest-producing dairy goat

GOLD

Gold mining brought a great increase in Australia's population and prosperity during the 1850s and 1860s, and continued to be an important industry until the early 20th century. It declined sharply after World War I, but recent rises in the price of gold have brought a revival in output and profitability, with Western Australia the main producer, followed by the Northern Territory and Queensland.

One day early in 1851 Edward Hargraves, accompanied by a youth named John Lister, was picking his way along Summer Hill Creek, in the Bathurst district of NSW. Hargraves was concerned because the creek was dry, but Lister, who was acting as guide, assured him that there would be water further on. Coming at last to a pool, the older man – according to his own colourful account – told Lister that they were standing on top of a goldfield. He proceeded to wash a panful of earth and gravel, and, to the youth's astonishment, 'The first trial produced a little piece of gold. "Here it is", I exclaimed; and then washed five pan-fuls in succession, obtaining gold from all but one... "This", I exclaimed to my guide, "is a memorable day in the history of New South Wales. I shall be a baronet, you will be knighted, and my old horse will be stuffed, put into a glass case, and sent to the British Museum".'

Generations of Australian students came to regard Hargraves as Australia's first successful gold discoverer, but this impression needs two important qualifications. First, others had found gold before he did. An amateur geologist named Rev. W.B. Clarke had found some in 1841, but Governor Gipps is reported to have said to him, 'Put it away, Mr Clarke, or we will all have our throats cut'. But when Hargreaves made his discovery the official attitude was different, because the colony had experienced an economic depression. Although there were some misgivings about the effect of the gold find on the convicts, the authorities realised that a gold rush would help to stimulate the economy.

The second qualification is that Hargraves was not so much a gold discoverer as a publicist. After taking part unsuccessfully in the Californian rush of 1849, he had gone to a part of NSW where he knew that traces of gold had been discovered. Instead of continuing to dig after his find, he publicised his discovery in the hope of obtaining a government reward. In this he was extremely successful, receiving two rewards totalling £10 000, a position as Commissioner of Crown Lands, and on retirement a pension of £250 a year.

Hargraves' effective promotion caused thousands of men to flock to the area north and north-west of Bathurst, where large alluvial deposits were found in what became known as the Ophir and Turon fields. Later major discoveries in NSW included those at Gulgong, Hill End and Captain's Flat (now Young).

Meanwhile much richer strikes had been made in Victoria. The resulting rushes almost depopulated Melbourne and Geelong, and attracted such attention overseas that during the month of September 1852 over 10 000 migrants disembarked at Melbourne. The largest Victorian fields were at Ballarat and Bendigo, with others at Ararat, Castlemaine, Chiltern, Clunes, Creswick, Beechworth, Maryborough, St Arnaud, Stawell, Walhalla and elsewhere.

The importance of these finds is shown by the fact that the population of Victoria grew from 97 000 in 1851 to 539 000 in 1861 and 746 000 in 1871, while the total population of all the Australian colonies was 437 000, 1 168 000 and 1 700 000 in the same periods. During those 20 years 50 million ounces (nearly 1.5 million kg) of gold was recovered.

Towns on the goldfields consisted at first of forests of tents, then of slab huts and similar structures. After several years, however, the more permanent and prosperous towns featured impressive stone public and commercial buildings, as can be seen particularly in Ballarat and Bendigo today.

Most of the gold found during the first few years was alluvial, and was won by self-employed miners working singly or in small teams on claims measuring only a few square metres per man. Since the gold was usually in or near creek beds, it could be separated from other

Two north Queensland diggers pose beside their rustic hut late last century. The basic tools of the miner's trade – pickaxe, shovel and gold pan – lean against the wall on the right.

materials by washing the soil in a 'cradle' and then in a dish. As the alluvial gold was worked out, the era of deep-reef mining by companies began, and most miners became employees.

In the early years especially, many spectacular finds were recorded. One digger at Louisa Creek, NSW, washed about 30 ounces (nearly a kilogram) from a single panful of earth. Four men at Mt Macedon in Victoria found 250 ounces (over seven kg) in four days, and at Ballarat one digger earned £1800 (several years' wages for a skilled tradesman) in a single day.

On the whole there was surprisingly little violence and crime, but there were two causes of friction. The first was opposition to the presence of Chinese workers, who came in such numbers that by 1857 there were over 40 000 in Victoria – about one-eleventh of the colony's whole population. There were many attacks on Chinese, and a number of large-scale anti-Chinese riots, of which the worst were on the Buckland River in north-eastern Victoria and at Captain's Flat, NSW. The second cause of friction was resentment against the imposition of licence fees on diggers, which finally resulted in the Eureka Stockade revolt.

In both Victoria and NSW the authorities raised revenue for the costs of administration on the goldfields by requiring miners to pay a licence fee of 30 shillings a month for the right to dig for gold. As the number of diggers increased and the surface gold became scarcer, average earnings fell, and the fee became a crushing

GREAT GOLD RUSHES

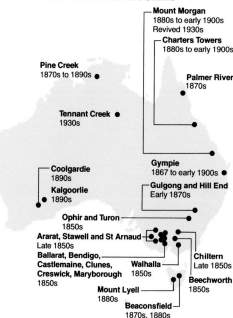

Mount Morgan
1880s to early 1900s
Revived 1930s

Charters Towers
1880s to early 1900s

Pine Creek
1870s to 1890s

Palmer River
1870s

Tennant Creek
1930s

Gympie
1867 to early 1900s

Coolgardie
1890s

Kalgoorlie
1890s

Gulgong and Hill End
Early 1870s

Ophir and Turon
1850s

Ararat, Stawell and St Arnaud
Late 1850s

Ballarat, Bendigo, Castlemaine, Clunes, Creswick, Maryborough
1850s

Chiltern
Late 1850s

Walhalla
1850s

Beechworth
1850s

Mount Lyell
1880s

Beaconsfield
1870s, 1880s

Sites of some of Australia's gold rushes. Major finds were made in the 1850s and 1860s, when thousands of gold-hungry immigrants flocked to this country.

Where to find gold

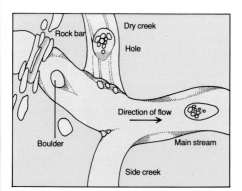

Yellow patches show where alluvial gold will often collect in a stream. Because it is so heavy it is always found in the very lowest layers of gravel.

Specks of alluvial gold – that which occurs in streams – are fairly easy to find once you know where to look for them. Gold is extremely heavy so it tends to settle anywhere where the water current suddenly slows. The best places to look are behind rocks and bars in a stream, around the outsides of bends, in holes in the stream bed and downstream from the junction of a fast-flowing creek and a slower river. Gold in these places will sink immediately to the very lowest level in the river. Stones and gravel must be removed right down to bedrock if possible. There the gold accumulates in cracks and crevices, and these must be carefully scraped clean to catch all particles. This is a difficult operation in a flowing river, but it is easier to do in dry creek beds. Sand and gravel which may contain gold should be washed in a pan (see p 196) or a cradle or sluice.

Relics of old gold mining days are common throughout Australia. They range from ancient machinery left rusting in the bush to the heaps of spoil left by miners. The old poppet head (above) is on the Golden Mile at Kalgoorlie in Western Australia. The excavated hillside (right) is all that remains today of a once busy goldfield at New Chum Hill, Kiandra in the Snowy Mountains, NSW. Almost all traces of the once thriving town have vanished.

burden for most miners. In Victoria especially, there was mounting resentment also against the 'digger hunts' launched by the police in order to enforce payment.

Resentment was brought to a head in Ballarat in 1854 when a miner was murdered near the Eureka Hotel. His mates believed that the publican was guilty, and when charges against the latter were dismissed, they saw this as another act of discrimination against miners. A mob burned down the hotel, the Ballarat Reform League was founded, licences were burned at mass meetings, and several hundred armed miners built a fort called the Eureka Stockade and declared Victoria a republic.

The fort was finally overrun by police and soldiers in a 25-minute battle, the death-toll including an officer, four soldiers and about 30 diggers. However there was such public sympathy for the rebels that the authorities finally dropped charges against those captured,

Everyday life on a goldfield in the 1860s. The site is not identified, but details of the way in which the miners lived and worked must be typical of many areas at that time. Most of the miners were born in Australia or the United Kingdom. In Victoria, in 1861, only just over eight per cent of the population were foreigners.

and Peter Lalor, their leader, later became a respected – and rather conservative – member of the Victorian parliament.

After the Victorian discoveries of the 1850s, by far the most important were those in Western Australia at Coolgardie and Kalgoorlie, where the mines of the 'Golden Mile' made Western Australia for many years the leading gold-producing region of Australia, comparable in production with Victoria in the 1850s. The first discovery at Coolgardie was made in 1892 by Arthur Bayley and William Ford, at a spot now marked by a concrete post and cairn. The first at Kalgoorlie, in 1893, was by Patrick Hannan, a memorial to whom can be seen in Hannan Street.

Other discoveries include those at Mt Margaret and the Murchison field in Western Australia; Charters Towers, Gympie, Mount Morgan and the Palmer River field near Cooktown in Queensland; Pine Creek and Tennant Creek in the Northern Territory; and Beaconsfield, Mount Lyell and Mathinna in Tasmania. South Australia alone had no significant finds.

Famous nuggets found in Victoria include 'Welcome Stranger' (71 kg, Moliagul, 1869), 'Welcome' (68 kg, Ballarat, 1858), 'Blanche Barkley' (54 kg, Rheola, 1871), and five more of 34 kg or over. In NSW two remarkable masses of gold, mixed with impurities and not strictly classifiable as nuggets, were 'Holtermann's Nugget' (93 kg of gold, Hill End, 1872) and 'Kerr's Hundredweight' (39 kg of gold, the Turon field, 1851). The largest in Western Australia was 'Golden Eagle' (35 kg, Larkinville, 1931) and in Queensland the 'Curtis Nugget' (28 kg, Gympie, 1870).

The great number of memorials to be found throughout Australia is a tribute to the public's fascination with the gold rushes. Ballarat has Sovereign Hill, a magnificently recreated mining township, and the Eureka Monument. In Bendigo there are the restored surface buildings and poppet head of the Central Deborah Gold Mine and a Chinese joss house of the 1860s. Hill End, NSW, is a mining museum in itself. In Kalgoorlie visitors are taken underground in the Hainault Gold Mine. Other towns that have museums with relics of gold rush days – and in some cases notable buildings still standing from those times – include Castlemaine and Beechworth in Victoria, Gulgong in NSW, Armadale and Coolgardie in Western Australia, and Gympie and Cooktown in Queensland.

Modern techniques

Many modern prospectors have exchanged their gold pans for metal detectors, and a number of major finds have been made with these machines in recent years, often in areas that were once thought to have been thoroughly worked out.

Modern detectors were developed from machines first introduced during World War II to search for buried mines. There are many types of machines on the market with varying abilities, but generally their price matches their effectiveness. A good detector should be able to find a nugget the size and shape of a 20c coin at a depth of about 250 mm, provided its greatest surface area is facing upwards. If only a small surface area is uppermost then it might easily escape detection at a depth of less than 70 mm. Only gold nuggets can be found using detectors. Fine gold, even in large quantities, cannot be located.

The most useful types of detectors can discriminate between iron-related minerals and objects and gold – an ability that is particularly useful in the heavily-mineralised areas where gold is often found.

How to wash for gold

It is easy to learn how to wash for alluvial gold in a stream. Gold is very heavy and it sinks immediately to the bottom of a pan full of sand and gravel. With a little practice it is impossible to miss finding any gold, even fine particles, that is there.

If possible, get an experienced person to show you how to wash a pan, but the instructions below should be adequate. Do not expect to find gold straight away. Even experienced fossickers can spend an entire day – often several days – searching without success. Old gold mining areas are the best places to start. At least

you know that gold does exist there, even if it may now be difficult to find.

Fossicking areas have been set aside in all states for amateurs to try their luck. Your local department of mines will tell you where they are, and will also let you know whether you need a miner's right to search for minerals or not.

Remember that other heavy minerals, apart from gold, are also revealed by washing. Tin, platinum and some gemstones are all heavy and will sink to the bottom of a pan. Examine any curious finds and check

to see if they may be valuable. It is certain that far more gold exists in the ground than has ever been taken out.

All alluvial gold was originally eroded from rocks, and it is these – the reef – that serious prospectors search for. Sometimes it can be found by working up a stream until no more gold is found. It is then fair to assume that the source may have been located, perhaps on a neighbouring hillside. Sometimes specks of gold can be seen in rocks, particularly quartz. To check, break off a sample of rock and crush it thoroughly with a hammer. Wash the fragments in a pan as before.

 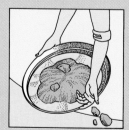   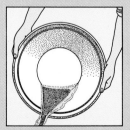 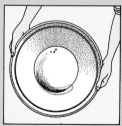

Collect a panful of stones and gravel from a likely place on the stream bed (see box p 195). Immerse the pan in water at the bank and throughly stir the contents with a stick or your hand. Keep the pan tilted at an angle away from you so that any particles of gold will collect in the bottom corner.

Wash large stones throughly over the pan and throw them away. It is particularly important to throughly break up any clay with your fingers because gold frequently sticks to it. Stir the contents of the pan again with a stick when all the large stones have been washed and discarded.

Swish the pan vigorously from side to side – keeping it the same angle as before. Gold is very heavy and does not need much effort to make it sink to the bottom. Coarse particles of gravel and small stones can be washed from the top of the material in the pan as water is allowed to escape over the edge.

Once you are satisfied that the contents of the pan have been thoroughly mixed and agitated, and that any gold has had ample opportunity to sink to the bottom, the first layers of coarse material can be scraped off with your hand. Swish the remaining contents from side to side again with more water.

Continue this process several times until only about a billy-full of fine gravel and sand remains. Dip the edge of the pan in the water and allow it to lap over the material in the bottom, swilling off the surface layers so that they escape over the edge of the pan – a small amount at a time.

Take care not to allow any material that has collected in the bottom corner to escape. Reduce the contents of the pan to only a tablespoon of fine ordinary sand (always), black sand (often) and gold (sometimes). Gently swill the sand around so that a tail is formed around the edge of the base, revealing any gold.

GOLDFISH

Goldfish *Carassius auratus* (to 400 mm) – eastern Asian members of the CARP family – were introduced in 1876 and are now widespread in Australia. They differ from carp in not having barbels, but the two species will interbreed. It is thought that their spread is partly due to the fact that they were widely used as a live bait. They are most common in still or slow-moving water. Wild specimens are more drably coloured than the familiar fish in the goldfish bowl, although they may retain traces of the colour of the aquarium varieties from which they are derived. These wild fish are an example of how a feral population of a highly modified species can revert to the original wild form.

Feral goldfish probably live for many years, but few will reach the record age of Fred, a goldfish from Worthing in Sussex, who died in 1980 aged 41 years.

GORGE

The word gorge is often used loosely for any steep valley, but it should be restricted to a valley that is unusually steep-walled and narrow. During its long evolution a river cuts through the underlying rocks to reach its local base-level and will not excavate below it. When the river is young and well above the base-level, it tends to cut down vertically, producing a valley with steep sides. Later, as the river approaches its base level, more of the sides are eroded.

If the river cuts first through a resistant fault, the walls tend to remain steep, especially in arid or semi-arid regions where the weather has little eroding power.

The impression on looking down into a gorge is usually that it deeper than it is wide, but this is rare. The Torrens Gorge is about 800 m wide but has a maximum depth of only 240 m. The Grose Valley in the Blue Mountains of NSW plunges 300 m in places, but has a width of 800 to 1200 m.

The vegetation within a gorge is often very different from that outside: the valley bottom may contain rainforest, while the plateau above supports only dry woodland. The Finke River in

Ninety-metre-high walls of limestone rise from the floor of Windjana Gorge in north-west Western Australia. It was cut by the Lennard River as it flowed through the Napier Range, east of Derby.

the Northern Territory, which has cut many gorges, has Livistonia palms growing in its bed, yet no others grow within 1100 km.

One of the best known gorges in Australia has been carved by the Katherine River in the Northern Territory, south of Darwin. The sandstone walls there are up to 100 m high and have been cut in the edge of the Arnhem Land Plateau.

There are several spectacular gorges in the south-west of Tasmania, on the Gordon and Franklin Rivers, although they are difficult to reach, except by rubber raft. More accessible, yet just as scenic, is the steeply winding Hellyer Gorge, south of Wynyard in the north-west.

GRANITE

Thousands of millions of years ago the earth was a fiery mass of gas and molten rock. As the earth cooled, the outer skin hardened to a crust while the interior remained molten. This solid outer skin was probably composed of lighter material that floated to the surface in that sea of molten magma – like slag does in a smelter. At intervals throughout the earth's history, huge masses of the lighter molten magma have been forced up into the crust and slowly solidified. These solidified molten rocks are called intrusive igneous rocks, and the most common of them is granite – the basic building block of the continents. Over millions of years, erosion has exposed the granite masses so that they can now be seen on the surface. In Western Australia there are granites 2700 million years old. In south-east Australia granite makes up about one-quarter of the exposed rock.

HOW BOULDERS ARE FORMED

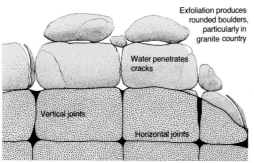

Exfoliation produces rounded boulders, particularly in granite country

Water penetrates cracks

Vertical joints

Horizontal joints

Rounded granite tors are formed by weathering and esosion along regular vertical and horizontal joints in the rock. Thin layers peel from the surface of the rocks as they are heated and cooled each day, gradually rounding off the corners. The best known example are the Devil's Marbles in the Northern Territory.

GOSSAMER

Spiders must get away from their fellows soon after hatching because even small spiders are cannibals. Some simply walk, but many disperse by ballooning, using gossamer – a fine line of silk. The tiny spider hangs on to a perch while paying out a line into the breeze. Eventually this is long enough for the wind to carry the spider aloft. Borne by air currents, ballooning spiders can often 'fly' for hundreds of kilometres before coming to earth. Adults sometimes travel in the same aerial way.

The best known spider aeronauts are the small money spiders. Other kinds of advanced spiders probably travel similarly, and in America some have been caught at a height of 4300 m.

On landing the spiders leave their threads scattered over vegetation, and if there is a dew it is very conspicuous. At times, gossamer clouds are seen in the air.

Granite boulders near Cooma, NSW. Granite is resistant to erosion because it contains a lot of quartz, so it often forms high points in the landscape, such as the Snowy Mountains, which are topped by many clusters of rounded tors. Because it is extremely durable, granite makes an excellent building stone.

Grapes & Winemaking

Riesling grapes produce many styles of wine, but at its best, from cooler parts of South Australia, makes delicate, fruity, aromatic wine. True Riesling vines came from Germany and are often called Rhine Riesling.

Wines were once made mainly in the Hunter, Barossa, Murrumbidgee and Murray Valleys, north-eastern Victoria, and the Swan Valley in the west. But since the 1960s grapes have been planted all over the continent. Australians now drink on average 21 litres of wine each a year. Even mass-produced wines are of high standard, and wine is an important export.

Cabernet sauvignon grapes have proportionately large pips yielding high tannin, so wines need aging or blending. Most come from the Coonawarra-Padthaway area of South Australia, but may be processed far away. Wines are very high quality, dry and fruity.

Grenache, Australia's second most grown red-wine grape, is made into rose or fortified wines, or combined with others in red wines. A hot-climate vine, it can withstand drying winds. Colour varies from pale pink to deep purple; flavour is sweetish, fruity.

G old and wine have gone hand in hand in Australia. One of the oldest continually operating wineries, Craigmoor at Mudgee, began because of the Mudgee-Gulgong gold rush. In north-eastern Victoria there are abandoned mineshafts and mullock heaps in a number of vineyards, and the industry in that region was probably saved by miners. More than one winemaker can relate how a grandfather would load a barrel onto his dray on Sunday mornings and decant its contents into the billies of thirsty diggers at their tents.

Vines were planted in the earliest days of the penal colony. Efforts to export and market Australian wine concentrated at first on fortified wines. Red wine fortified with brandy was sent to London as early as 1822 by Gregory Blaxland, the explorer – and five years on, an improved batch won a gold medal. In wine bars which later proliferated in Australian cities, the favoured drink was a Fourpenny Dark – a cheap port. Australian produces the best Muscats in the world, but those wine bars discredited that glorious drink. Wine drinkers were despised as 'plonkers' (possibly from *vin blanc*).

Several winemakers in Australia are the seventh generation in the industry. Australia was lucky in

Sultana grapes are seedless, so besides being dried, are eaten fresh. About an eighth of the crop is used for wine, often blended or made into sparkling wines. It is Australia's most widely grown grape, nearly all in the Murray irrigation areas.

having representatives of the great wine countries of France, Germany and Italy among its pioneer grape-growers. They imported their own countries' grapes, so Australia has a heritage of all the great wine types. But at the turn of the century, vineyards in Victoria were ruined by the phylloxera blight – a louse *Phylloxera vastatrix* that attacks vine roots. After burgeoning in the gold boom, the industry waned, and many or the original vines were lost.

Re-establishing old traditions

New grapes for Australian conditions, developed by the CSIRO, have not supplanted traditional varieties. Instead, many winemakers have re-imported some of the earlier lost varieties and brought in others new to Australia. Some varieties believed lost have turned up again. The trend is now to look for forms of the traditional varieties that are favoured by the conditions of a particular area. So a Pinot Noir from the High Country of Victoria, for instance, may be a quite different to one from elsewhere.

The industry faltered again in the Great Depression of the 1930s, and re-emerged from the 1950s based mainly on fortified and red wines. It was saved by the post-war influx of large numbers of wine-drinking Eropeans. White wine was suddenly discovered – with such enthusiasm that many vines, decades old, bearing red grapes were pulled out and replaced with white varieties. Wine-producing areas doubled and trebled before a balance was reached.

Popular grape varieties

About four dozen varieties of grapes are grown in Australia. The most widely grown is Sultana, and over 50 000 tonnes are used for winemaking. Shiraz is the most grown red-wine grape. Fortified wines such as Muscat call for particular varieties – such as Muscat Gordo Blanco, the single most popular variety of grape grown in Australia. Over 75 000 tonnes were harvested in 1985–86. Warm areas such as Riverland and the Murrumbidgee Irrigation Area produce highly

Neat rows of vines at Houghton's Oakover vineyard, north-east of Perth in Western Australia. Lupins growing between the vines fix nitrogen in the soil and are eventually ploughed in as fertiliser.

flavoured grapes. Cooler places produce lighter, fresher wines. Wine companies often blend juice from grapes grown far apart.

Vineyards – some of them tiny – can be found from south-west of Hobart to the Atherton Tablelands and Alice Springs. Small makers' wines are finding an increasingly discriminating market. Some growers of high-quality grapes send them long distances to appreciative winemakers. The Cowra area of NSW, for example, has no winery, but is responsible for many of the good white wines that emerge from Hunter Valley wineries.

From vine to bottle

Harvested grapes are taken to a crusher as soon as possible. Stems and stalks are usually removed. The skins and seeds are separated from the juice after an hour, or as much as a week, depending on the wine being made. When red grapes are being used for white wine, the separation takes place as soon as possible. Red wine gets its colour from the skins.

The grape juice sugar is converted to alcohol by yeast, added in fermentation tanks. Fermentation is stopped at a crucial point by cooling the tanks. Filtering removes particles such as remnants of skins, and clarifies the wine. White wines are then usually bottled. Red wines are left to mature further in stainless steel tanks, or in wooden casks which impart certain flavours. Casks are made of American White Oak, and German and French oaks, not English oak which would lend bitterness and a black tinge.

From the middle of the 19th century until World War II, Australia exported enormous quantities of wine to Europe, mostly Britain. Much of it was fortified and sweet. Recently, the nuclear accident at Chernobyl in April 1986 has been a boon to the Australian wine industry as Europeans looked for wines from areas removed as far as possible from contamination. Exports rose sharply, customers liked what they got, and Australian wine-drinkers will from now on have to drink less or pay more.

WINE PRODUCING AREAS

Many new grape growing areas have been established in recent years. South Australia is still the largest producer with nearly 27 000 ha yielding over 295 000 tonnes of grapes for wine production in 1985–86.

Atherton Tablelands

Alice Springs

Riverland
Mildura-Robinvale
Clare-Watervale
Swan Hill
Goulburn Valley
Mudgee
Swan Valley
Margaret River
Barossa Valley
Adelaide Metropolitan
Mt Barker
Southern Districts
Langhorne Creek
Coonawarra-Padthaway
Drumborg
Great Western-Avoca
Roma
Stanthorpe
Hunter Valley
Forbes-Cowra
Riverina
Corowa-Rutherglen
Glenrowan-Milawa
Lilydale
Geelong
Launceston-Tamar Valley
Hobart

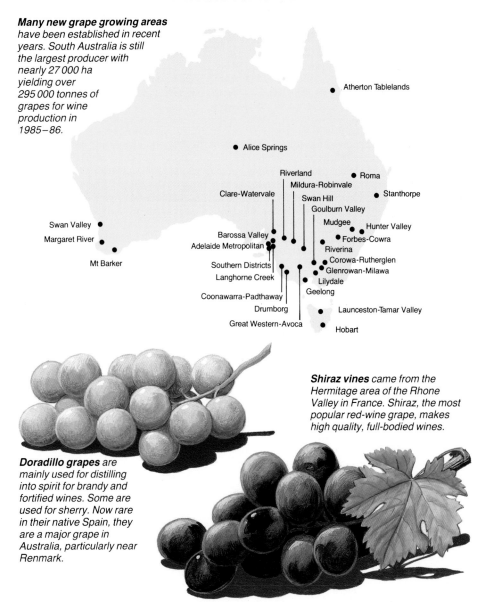

Shiraz vines came from the Hermitage area of the Rhone Valley in France. Shiraz, the most popular red-wine grape, makes high quality, full-bodied wines.

Doradillo grapes are mainly used for distilling into spirit for brandy and fortified wines. Some are used for sherry. Now rare in their native Spain, they are a major grape in Australia, particularly near Renmark.

199

GRAPES, TABLE

Vine cuttings from Rio de Janeiro and the Cape of Good Hope were planted at Farm Cove in 1788 and proudly reported healthy eight months later. They eventually succumbed to humid sea air and a fungus, but it was already apparent that the colony's climate was ideal for vines. The father of the Australian grape industry was James Busby. In 1832, 574 varieties he had collected in France, Spain and the Botanic Gardens at Kew were planted in Sydney and the Hunter Valley. At the end of the 19th century, many vineyards in northern Victoria and around Sydney were devastated by the root louse Phylloxera. Root stocks of American origin were found to be resistant, and grape-growing recovered to develop into Australia's largest horticultural industry. About a third of the total area devoted to fruit crops is occupied by vines. Dessert grapes account for under one-twentieth of grapes produced, but in 1986 $15 million-worth was exported to other countries.

Most dessert grapes (over half) come from Victoria, in particular the Murray Valley from Swan Hill to Mildura. Alice Springs is a new growing area. Queensland's Granite Belt, around Stanthorpe, is well suited to table grapes.

About twice as many white grapes are eaten fresh as red – total consumption is just under two kilograms a person a year. Of white grapes, the fairly small, seedless Sultana variety, marketed for the table as Thompson Seedless, are the most popular, followed by the large greenish-yellow Waltham Cross, and Ohanez or Almeria, which are firm, yellow and tough-skinned. The main red varieties are Red Emperor, large and fleshy; one of the several new seedless red, Flame Seedless; and Cardinal, with a slight Muscat flavour and ripening early in the season which lasts from about January through to June.

From the earliest times of vine cultivation, dessert grapes were distinguished from wine grapes. Of more than 8000 varieties that are found world-wide, Muscat Gordo Blanco and Sultana are among the few that are eaten fresh, made into wine or dried.

GRASS

To a botanist grass means a member of the plant family Poaceae – one of the largest plant families of the world. Other plants such as sedges, rushes or lilies can look like grasses to the untrained eye, but a simple feature of the leaf will reveal in an instant whether a plant is a true grass or not. If the leaf is pulled off, right to its base, a grass leaf is clearly and sharply divided into two parts – a sheathing base which wraps around the stalk or younger leaves, and the flat rolled blade. At the junction of the sheath and blade all grasses have a transverse flap of thin tissue, or sometimes just a band of bristles, which stands out clearly when the leaf is bent backwards. No grasses have flowers with colourful petals, but only tiny groups of stamens or stigmas.

Native grasses are present in all parts of Australia, but are only an obvious part of the vegetation in areas with few trees, such as the far inland. In the tall, wet forests and rainforests of the east they may be uncommon, or at least inconspicuous. Many non-Australian grasses have been introduced, mostly because they are good animal feed, although some that have become weeds were brought in by accident. In cleared grazing land of high to medium rainfall the majority of grasses are likely to have been introduced, as are most grasses in urban areas.

A group of introduced grasses of major importance are the cereals, which account for the greater part of Australia's croplands. The major cereals are wheat, oats, barley, rye, maize, rice, sorghum and millet. Another important grass crop is sugar-cane, grown almost entirely in a narrow strip of the east coast lowlands north of Grafton, NSW.

GRASSHOPPER

Grasshoppers are generally large insects related to CRICKETS. They have thickened forewings, well-developed hindlegs for leaping, and strong chewing mouthparts for eating plants. Many are well camouflaged by colour and shape. Grasshoppers fold their wings like a tent when resting, whereas most crickets keep theirs flat. Nymphs resemble adults. The mainly nocturnal long-horned grasshoppers have antennae at least as long as their bodies, ears on their front legs, and the males sing by rubbing their forewings together. Technically they should be grouped with the crickets. A Swedish species, the Vartbitare *Decticus verrucivorus*, was allegedly used to remove warts; its close relatives are widespread in Australia. Short-horned grasshoppers sing by rubbing pegs on their hind legs against their wings. They have ears on their abdomens and are mainly active in the day. The LOCUSTS are specialised members of this group which has about 580 Australian species.

GRASSTREE

The grasstrees *Xanthorrhoea*, also called blackboys, are peculiar to Australia and, to overseas visitors, are amongst the most striking of the continent's plants. There are about 17 species, most of them found in regions with reliable rainfall, although one species *X. thorntonii* also grows in semi-arid areas.

On some species, a reddish-yellow resin accumulates. This was used by Aborigines to glue spear heads to shafts and has been utilised for a variety of purposes by Europeans. Wood stains and varnishes, a form of incense and the explosive, picric acid, have all been made from it. The straight, light flower stems provided the shafts of Aboriginal fish spears.

Some of the largest grasstrees may be very old – estimates for some species being in the order of 500 to 600 years.

GRAVEL

A modern Australian city uses construction materials at an approximate rate of 19 tonnes per head of population per year. A large percentage of this is gravels, which are used for concrete, dams, roadbase and paving. Gravels are rock

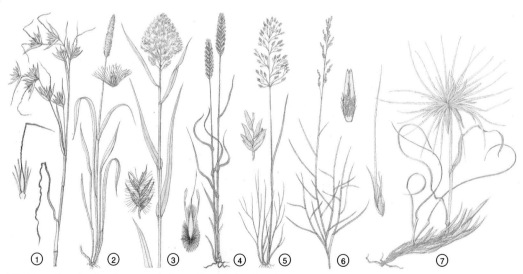

There are hundreds of grasses *in Australia and identification is usually difficult. The common native species above, however, are all easily recognised. They are: **1** Kangaroo Grass Themeda australis; **2** Blady Grass Imperata cylindrica; **3** Common Reed Phragmites australis; **4** Barley Mitchell Grass Astrebla pectinata; **5** Tussock Poa labillardieri; **6** Porcupine Grass or 'Spinifex' Triodia spp. and **7** Hairy Spinifex Spinifex hirsutus.*

Grass trees *provided the Aborigines with both tools – such as spear shafts – and the raw materials to make them. Europeans have also found many uses for the plants, both practical and decorative.*

Heavily forested hills, *precipitous valleys and unscalable cliffs made many stretches of the Great Divide – such as this tortuous area west of Sydney – almost impossible to explore on foot. It took Europeans 25 years to find a way across the mountains from Sydney to the plains beyond.*

fragments greater then 2 mm in diameter and up to boulder size. They are formed by the forces of wind and water eroding rocks into small rounded or semi-rounded fragments. Gravels should not be confused with aggregate used in construction materials, which have been formed by machine crushing of quarried rock. Gravels are formed by natural processes and can be any rock type.

Huge quantities of gravels are found in large river systems such as the Nepean River west of Sydney and the Brisbane River. In many parts of Australia gravel beds give clues to the course of ancient rivers and may reveal sources of alluvial gold or gemstones. In recent years in NSW attention has turned to offshore marine gravels as land-based supplies become more difficult to find and exploit.

GRAZIER

Not long ago the best way to insult a grazier was to call him a farmer. Many graziers thought themselves a class above the 'dirt cockys' who farmed the soil. This class-consciousness probably dated back to early this century when 'grazier' became used instead of 'squatter' to describe those who ran sheep and cattle extensively on unimproved land. Graziers were the new squattocracy, often referred to as the landed gentry, and were usually more wealthy and powerful than their farming cousins. Today, however, the distinction is not so jealously guarded because the financial fortunes of graziers and farmers have become more evenly matched. Also, many former graziers have developed their land for cropping. Australia's main grazing areas are in the Kimberley and Pilbara regions of Western Australia, north and west Queensland, western NSW and some of inland Victoria.

GREAT DIVIDING RANGE

This long stretch of uplands, which runs from Cape York down the east of the continent to the Grampians in Victoria, with an extension in Tasmania, should be called the Great Divide, as it is not, in the geological sense, a range of mountains at all. It has resulted from a tilting of the land in the late Cretaceous period, around 80 million years ago, by movements associated with the break-up of the ancient supercontinent Gondwanaland and the formation of the Tasman and Coral Seas. Later, during the Tertiary period, volcanoes poured out basalt and other igneous rocks at various places along the Divide. Towards the end of the Tertiary there was further uplift which raised the by then somewhat worn-down hills thousands of metres in places.

The eastern side is a steep scarp facing the sea, from which it appears mountainous, while the western side consists of gentle slopes. There are many long stretches of plateaus or tablelands, although these are often deeply cut by erosion. The Divide runs in general parallel to the modern coast, usually from 160 to 250 km inland, although in southern NSW it comes as close as 1 km. The rivers which rise on the eastern side of the Divide run to the sea. Those which rise on the other side flow inland. The land between the Divide and the sea is well watered, but beyond it the country lies in a rain shadow.

GREVILLEA

All but about 20 of the 250 species of grevillea occur only in Australia. Tasmania has just one. They vary greatly, from large trees such as the Silky Oak *G. robusta* (to 20 m) and Beefwood *G. striata*, to the low-growing popular garden plant Laurel Grevillea *G. Laurifolia*. Several shrubs found growing on eastern coastal sandstone have attractive 'spider' flowers.

GROUNDWATER

Groundwater is water stored underground as opposed to surface water which is in rivers, lakes and reservoirs. People living in cities and towns often take the availability of water for granted, but in the more arid regions the presence of groundwater is critical. Perth relies on groundwater to provide 40 per cent of its water needs. Conservation of groundwater is an important consideration in Australia. If too much groundwater is removed in a short time the bores dry up or the water can become too salty.

Groundwater is formed when rainwater or water from rivers soaks through the soil. Contrary to popular opinion, groundwater is not stored in underground rivers – except in limestone caves. Many rocks and sediments – called aquifers – have a remarkable capacity for storing water like a sponge, in spaces between grains or in fractures. Some rock types will not store water, and these are called aquicludes. In large areas of Australia aquifers sandwiched between aquicludes extend for thousands of kilometres deep below the surface. These vast water-bearing sheets are roughly basin shaped and are a very valuable water resource. The best known example of a groundwater basin in Australia is the Great Artesian Basin – one of the largest of its type in the world – and one of 19 major groundwater basins in the country. It underlies 1.7 million sq. km (about 22 per cent) of Australia and is a vital source of water in semi-arid and arid areas for pastoral and town use. Water originates in the high rainfall western slopes of the Great Dividing Range. The aquifers dip below the surface to the north-west, west and southwest so that, in the far west, they are many hundreds of metres below the surface. Ground bores are drilled to tap into the aquifers, and because the level of the top of the bore is usually lower than the source in the Great Dividing Range the water gushes up under pressure.

There are a number of confined aquifers – varying in depth from several metres to several hundred metres. Around the western rim of the Great Artesian Basin, such as at Lake Eyre and Lake Frome, there are many natural springs where groundwater flows to the surface. It is remarkable that this water may have flowed underground from near the east coast. Water soaks through aquifers at a rate of one to five metres per year, which means that some of the water has remained underground for hundreds of thousands of years.

Some bores reach depths of 2000 m, but the average is about 500 m. Water from the deeper wells can be very hot (30°C to 100°C) and has to be cooled before it can be used. There are about 20 000 shallow water bores in the Great Artesian Basin where water is pumped to the surface, usually by windmills. To maintain an equilibrium, drilling of new bores is strictly controlled.

Water gushes from a bore at Clifton Hills, SA, under its own pressure. This water originally fell as rain in the Great Dividing Range, over 1000 km away.

WATER FROM BENEATH THE EARTH

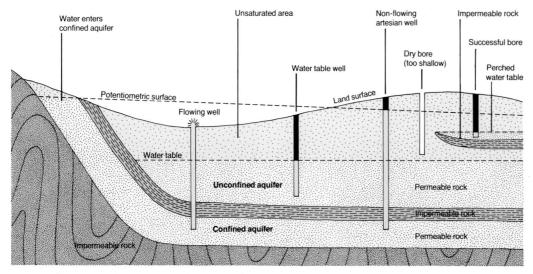

The diagram shows a typical artesian basin, such as occurs in Australia. When the rock above an aquifer – a water-holding layer – will allow water to flow through it vertically then the aquifer is called unconfined. When the rock above is impermeable then the aquifer is confined. Water in a well sunk into an unconfined aquifer will rise to the height of the water table. Water in a well sunk into a confined aquifer will rise to the potentiometric or piezometric surface – the level at which water is entering the aquifer. Often the potentiometric surface is above the land surface and water gushes from wells under considerable pressure.

GUDGEONS AND SLEEPERS

These fish belong to a large family – about 300 species – of mostly small marine and freshwater fishes. Australia, with 40 to 50 species, is particularly rich in freshwater gudgeons. Several have restricted ranges. Gudgeons have no lateral line, and the dorsal fin is in two parts, the first with two to eight spines.

The most remarkable species is the Blind, or Cave Gudgeon *Milyeringa veritas* (to 45 mm), a greyish fish with a scaleless, eyeless head which is found below the coastal plain between North-West Cape and Yardie Creek, WA, where blind cave eels also occur. The gudgeon is thought to be a carnivore.

The widespread Sleepy Cod of northern Australia *Oxyeleotris lineolatus* (to 480 mm) is the largest Australian species. It has a large mouth, a flattened head, a brownish body, spotted fins and a sluggish disposition, although it is a carnivore.

GULL

Gulls are the most familiar of seabirds, and virtually the only ones that can walk well on land. Many species spend as much time inland as near the sea, and very few range great distances from the shore.

Gulls are easily recognised white or grey birds, usually with some black, and with strong bills and webbed feet. They are opportunistic feeders, taking living and dead sea animals, eggs and nestlings of other birds, food bullied from other species, plankton, small fish for which they sometimes dive, insects which they sometimes get by following the plough, and all sorts of rubbish provided by humans.

Many gulls have benefited from their association with humans. Silver Gulls *Larus novaehollandiae* (400–450 mm) often flock at rubbish dumps, particularly when the sea or lakes are nearby. When these are near airports – as in Sydney – the birds are a threat to aircraft landing or taking off, as they can be sucked into jet engines. This danger has led to a small resurgence in falconry, with peregrines and other falcons sometimes being used to scare the scavenging gulls away.

Pioneering work by Niko Tinbergen, at Oxford, on European gulls, showed the importance of the red beak – or red spot on some beaks – of many species. It is used as a target by a pecking, hungry nestling.

Despite the great length of Australia's coastline there are only three species of gulls here, compared with the 11 or so of the British Isles. The most widespread is the Silver Gull which can be found on all coasts and in much of the inland, apart from deserts. The endemic Pacific Gull *L. pacificus* (600–650 mm), a bird with a very strong, red-tipped yellow beak, is largely restricted to southern coasts, like the Kelp Gull *L. dominicanus* (550–590 mm). But the Kelp Gull has been an Australian bird only since the 1940s, having colonised the country, probably from New Zealand. It is very similar to the Pacific Gull, but has white spots along its wings.

GUMS AND RESINS

These are substances secreted by plants, usually from cuts in the bark or wood, which become solid, or at least thick and viscous, when exposed to the air. They are waste products of a plant's metabolism, but are useful in that they quickly cover wounds, preventing infection by decay micro-organisms, and also discouraging attacks by various insects.

Gums and resins are very complex chemically, consisting of mixtures of many different compounds. Gums are exuded as liquids with a watery base in which are dissolved carbohydrates related to sugars and starches, but with larger molecules. Some come under the heading of mucilages – glutinous carbohydrates – while others cannot be classified except by highly technical names. Resins – in contrast – are not water-based, and can be dissolved only in benzene-type solvents. In between are a whole range of alcohol-soluble compounds.

A wide variety of gums and resins are produced by Australian plants. Some were once commercially important, but virtually none is now. The most familiar is probably the dark red 'gum' – also called kino – exuded by some eucalypts, or gum trees. At one time these kinos were used in medicine, mainly as diuretics. Many species of wattle, *Acacias*, produce large globules of almost clear gum from bark wounds such as borer holes. This is a true gum – soluble in hot water – consisting chiefly of carbohydrates, in-

Gum oozes from the damaged trunk *of a eucalypt. Some eucalypts, particularly Manna Gums* Eucalyptus mannifera, *exude a sugery solution which dries into flakes. This is sometimes called manna, and is gathered from beneath the tree. It was used as a laxative by early settlers.*

cluding sugars. They are often sweet to the taste, and were used as food by Aborigines.

The original gum-arabic from North Africa, used for glue, comes from an *Acacia*. A very interesting 'resin' exudes from the leaf-bases of GRASS TREES. It is dark red, very hard and brittle, and is found as globules around the bases of their trunks after fire. This is aromatic, giving off an incense-like odour when burnt or even warmed up. Until quite recently it was gathered commercially as a source of picric acid, used in explosives. Another aromatic resin is found on the leaf bases of the Porcupine Grass in the inland. This was used by the Aborigines as a cement for glueing spear points to shafts. The cut stumps of native Cypress Pines yield a colourless, granular resin called sandarac, at one time used commercially in products such as pill-coatings. In Queensland the giant Kauris were valued last century for their resin, known as 'kauri gum' or dammar. It had a variety of commercial uses and was a component of lacquers, varnishes and oil paints.

GUN

The first firearms seen, and heard, in Australia were probably the match-lock muskets of the Dutch seamen sailing with William Jansz on board the *Duyfken*. Jansz landed on Cape York Peninsula in 1606 and shot over the heads of a group of frightened Aborigines.

A convict, John MacIntyre, was Australia's first sharp-shooter. A week after the arrival of the First Fleet at Sydney Cove he was appointed by Governor Phillip as official hunter with a licence to carry arms.

The guns with the First Fleet were muskets known as *Brown Bess*, and pistols owned by the officers. The supply of weapons to anyone apart from the military and the few free settlers was carefully controlled. However, guns played a major role in the first years of the colony – to control convicts and hostile Aborigines, and to obtain fresh meat.

The most popular rifles in use today range from .22 calibre to .30 calibre – especially the latter which can use a greater variety of bullets. The .30 calibre rifles are used for larger animals such as feral pigs and buffalo.

Shotguns – 12-gauge is the most common – which fire a cluster of spreading pellets, are used for smaller, fast-moving game such as rabbits and ducks.

There is no accurate count of the total number of guns in Australia due to variations in state licensing laws, and because it is normally gun users rather than guns that are licensed. All states require a licence or registration for any concealable arms such as pistols, and these licences are normally restricted to specified groups such as security officers. Most states also require a licence for rifles and shotguns, although Tasmania and Queensland do not.

Licences in all states are issued by the police but in some states farmers using guns to control pests are exempt from holding a licence. Kangaroo shooters, generally using high velocity .22 calibre rifles, need a licence and also a special permit from state wildlife authorities. Shooting is forbidden in built-up areas, on public roads or anywhere it is likely to be dangerous.

H

HAIL

Hail may form within clouds if the temperature is sufficiently low. Once the hailstone starts to grow, water freezes onto its outer surface, creating a layered, almost spherical stone, rather like an onion. If the hailstone remains inside the cloud and in contact with very cold water droplets for a long time, it can grow to a great size. The world's largest recorded hailstone fell in Kansas, USA in 1970. It measured 190 mm in diameter and weighed 0.77 kg. In Australia the largest measured hailstone fell during a storm in Texas, Queensland on 29 October 1970 and had a diameter of nearly 66 mm. Other large hailstones have been collected from storms in Kin Kin, Queensland (45 mm in diameter) and Wickepin, Western Australia (43 mm in diameter), but most hailstones have diameters of less than 10 mm.

Areas of Australia most affected by hail are north-eastern Victoria, central Tasmania and coastal regions of Queensland. In the southern half of the continent, hailstorms occur mostly in winter because of vigorous cloud activity associated with cold fronts moving across the country. For example, Adelaide has three times as many hailstorms from June to September than from December to March. Further north, hail occurs more often in summer where hailstorms are associated with large thunderstorms. Half of Sydney's notable hailstorms have taken place between November and January. The damage caused by hailstones can be devastating, especially to fruit crops, cars and homes. A single hailstorm which struck the south-western surburbs of Sydney on 3 October 1986 cost just one insurance company $57 million as claims were made on damage to 18 000 cars and 8000 houses.

HALO

A halo is a ring of light around the sun or the moon which can be seen from the ground because there is a thin layer of cirrus cloud high in the sky. Cirrus clouds occur where temperatures are far below freezing point, and are therefore made up entirely of ice crystals which have six sides and are prism-shaped. When light from the sun or moon passes through ice crystals, it is bent at certain angles. If the crystals are randomly spaced, light is bent towards an observer creating a circle of light. Often two haloes are seen. This is because the 60° angle of an ice crystal bends light at 22°, while light passing through the 90° angle of the crystal is bent at 46°. A second halo is not as common. Haloes can also be produced in unusual circum-

---

Shooting at clouds

In 1900 in the vinyards of northern Italy 10 000 cannons fired 9 500 000 shots into impending storms. The charges were gunpowder; the 'shot' was smoke and loud noise; the result was hail falling as harmless mush, but also seven deaths and 78 injuries. Shooting at storms has been practised in Europe since the 14th century, but the early 20th-century-cannonades did not survive scientific scepticism and protests about the danger to nearby residents.

New hail cannons, shaped like giant upright megaphones, are now used in large orchards, particularly around Batlow and Orange. Hail-threatening storms are detected by radar weather scanners and the cannons are fired every seven or eight seconds while the danger persists. A chamber filled with acetylene gas is ignited by a spark plug causing an explosion. A funnel-shaped 'chimney' directs the shock wave into the air where it rises to about 10 000 metres. Supporters of the cannons claim that hail falls as harmless mush when they are working. Comparing present losses from hail with previous years, and seeing hail damage at the edge of the cannon's effective radius, orchardists are convinced of their value, despite doubts among scientists. Each cannon protects an area with a radius of about 500 m.

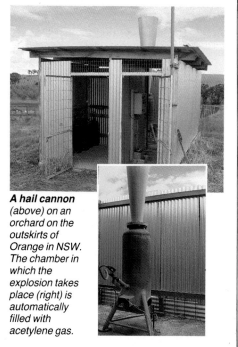

A hail cannon (above) on an orchard on the outskirts of Orange in NSW. The chamber in which the explosion takes place (right) is automatically filled with acetylene gas.

---

stances by fine dust in the air. After the eruptions of Mount Agung in Bali during 1963, a 42° solar halo was seen at Albany in Western Australia and a 30° lunar halo was seen at Canberra.

Haloes around the sun and moon are formed by light refracted through ice crystals which form in clouds that are at the edge of the atmosphere, between 5000 and 14 000 m above the earth's surface.

HAMLET DEVELOPMENT

Since the 1970s an increasing number of groups of people have been pooling their resources and moving out of the cities to buy rural properties, and living on them in varying degrees of communal existance. In many country areas the populations of local communities had been dwindling for decades as farming became more expensive and smaller farmers were forced off the land. The new groups, often disillusioned with consumerism and the pace of modern urban life, sought a communal rural paradise.

For new settlers buying properties was one thing, but setting up multiple residences on each property was another. Many communes began to resemble hamlets or small villages with a communal kitchen, shop, school and other community buildings. This brought them into conflict with the planning and building codes of conservative local councils.

In 1979 the NSW Government introduced multiple-occupancy legislation that allowed more flexibility to local councils. This recognised the many different types of rural community ownership, from total communal ownership, to individually owned house blocks on an otherwise communal property. While providing flexibility for hamlet development the legislation sought to provide maximum levels for the density of dwellings, and standards for such things as fire protection, road access, water supply and site erosion. Although minimum building standards were set, they recognised the use of 'unorthodox' on-site building materials on many communes. The Western Australian and Victorian governments have also brought in special provisions for multiple rural occupancy.

HARDYHEAD

There are about nine Australian freshwater species in this large and widespread family of small, mainly marine fish. Among them is the Central Australian Hardyhead *Craterocephalus eyresii* (to more than 90 mm) which is found in the Murray-Darling River system as well as in the Lake Eyre drainage system, the rivers of which flow inland. Many millions were stranded and died when the lake receded in 1975. They can tolerate a wide range of temperatures and very salt water. Some species, such as the widespread Blackmast *Quirichthys stramineus* (to 70 mm) are kept in aquariums by collectors.

These fishes are distinguished by their two separate dorsal fins – the first of which is rather small – large scales, a silvery band running along their sides, and the absence of a lateral line. Some eat plants and animals, some animals only and several are important prey of larger fish.

HARE

European Rabbits – the ones present in Australia – and Hares *Lepus capensis* belong to different groups. Hares are closely related to the so-called rabbits of America. One consequence is that hares are not susceptible to MYXOMATOSIS. They resemble rabbits but are larger (about 600 mm long with a 80 mm tail) and more rangy in build, with longer ears and hind-legs. Unlike rabbits they spend their day above ground in a 'form' of grass, often in a hollow in the ground. They cannot therefore escape danger by bolting underground, but depend on their fast (50 km/h), swerving run to evade capture.

Hares were first established in Australia in 1862 at Westernport Bay in Victoria and were subsequently widely distributed. They are now found in grass and woodlands, farmlands and some urban areas from south-east Queensland to South Australia and in Tasmania. In Australia does (females) can produce five to six litters a year, each of two to five leverets, compared with three to four litters in Britain. The Mad March Hare refers to the cavorting courting males seen in European countries.

Hares eat mainly grass, but will attack various crops and gnaw the bark from young trees and vines, particularly in nurseries. Consequently they have to be controlled from time to time, mainly by shooting.

Spectacled Hare-wallabies do not drink, even when water is available. Only 5.3 per cent of their total body water changes every day – a much lower proportion than any other marsupial of about that size.

HARE-WALLABY

Hare-wallabies are small kangaroos which got their name from their habit of remaining concealed in a tussock of grass or similar hiding place until almost trodden upon, then dashing away at great speed like a European Hare. Spectacled Hare-wallabies *Lagorchestes conspicillatus* (body 400–470 mm, tail 370–490 mm) of tropical grasslands and open forest, are the only species still common and widespread. They have been studied on Barrow Island, in Western Australia where they spend the day in cool tunnels in spinifex clumps, browsing on shrubs at night. They do not need to drink water. They are mainly brown with white-tipped hairs and orange rings around their eyes.

Rufous Hare-wallabies *L. hirsutus* (330 mm, 375 mm) were once widespread in dry areas, but are now found only on islands in Shark Bay, WA, and in the Tanami desert. Patchy burning by hunting Aborigines once provided the vegetation that the animals needed, but more widespread fires today have reduced the varieties of plants.

Eastern Hare-wallabies *L. leporides*, have not been seen since 1890. Banded Hare-wallabies *Lagostrophes fasciatus* (430 mm, 370 mm), once widespread in south-western Australia, are another species now found only on islands in Shark Bay, living in runs in dense wattle scrub and feeding at night on shrubs and grasses. Central Hare-wallabies *L. asomatus* are known only from a single skull collected in the Northern Territory in 1932, the rest of the specimen having being thrown away by its discoverer. The species name is therefore an academic joke – it means 'without a body'.

HARVEST

Each summer thousands of grain harvesters eat their way through the Australian cereal crops. Harvesting is the culmination of the cropping year – the time when the farmers find out just how much they will get in their pockets for their efforts of the previous months.

The harvest is ready to start when the head-carrying stalks of the cereal plants are dry enough to snap off cleanly. Most areas sown to cereals in Australia will be under harvest by Christmas, and in many regions the harvest will be over by then.

The harvest starts in the northern reaches of the cereal belt – the first cut usually being made in Queensland – and progresses steadily south. Oats ripen first, followed by barley, then wheat. The onset of this busy period sees the farmer call up the biggest, and often most expensive machine in his fleet – the grain harvester. Complex grain processors, these metal monsters cut their way through fields of grain at speeds of up to 15 km/h. Their wide gathering fronts behead the grain plants, an internal rotating drum threshes each grain from its neighbours, and the threshed grain is conveyed to a storage bin atop the harvester. When the storage bin is heaped full of grain, the machine moves out of the crop and alongside a nearby waiting truck, into which it pours its cargo before starting afresh. When the truck in turn fills up, its load is either transferred to a grain silo on the farm, or trucked direct to the nearest town with a grain receival centre.

At these receival points, hundreds of which are scattered throughout the cropping belt, the grain is weighed and classified. It is here that any damage caused by a rain-sodden harvest will become clear. If there is a significant amount of

Hugh McKay's Sunshine harvester revolutionised farming. For the first time grain could be stripped, threshed, cleaned and bagged in one sweep.

A modern combine harvester works its way steadily through a field of wheat near Coonabarabran, NSW. Larger machines have air-conditioned cabs and stereo tape-players, and can cost up to $20 000 each. An estimated 20 000 harvesters are used each summer to gather Australia's crops – all modified and adjusted for different crops and conditions.

sprouted grain present in the farmer's sample his truckload will be downgraded, and his payment reduced by a set amount per tonne. Harvesting is one of the busiest periods in the farming calender. Summer in the grainbelt brings with it not just intense heat, but also an ever-present threat of thunderstorms. Given that the damage caused by heavy rain of hail on a ripe crop can mean the difference between profit and loss, it is small wonder the farmers are keen to harness every available hour to get their crop off the fields and safely under cover.

Half a century ago, the harvesting of a cereal crop was a slow process. Today's modern harvesters can clear an average crop at the rate of around ten hectares an hour, putting much greater pressure on the rest of the harvest chain. As a result, grain receival authorities in each state have had to equip themselves to cope with larger amount of grain over a shorter period.

HOW A COMBINE HARVESTER WORKS

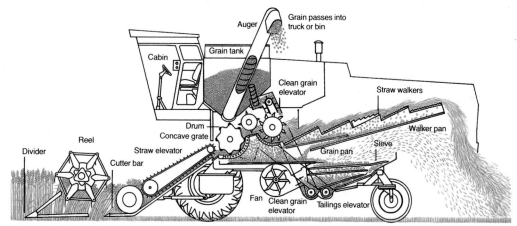

The crop is fed by the reel onto the cutter bar where teeth cut it off, and the auger passes the straw to the straw elevator. The crop comes off the elevator under the drum which rubs it against the grate, removing 90 per cent of the grain. The straw walkers tumble the straw allowing any remaining grain to fall back on to the grain pan. The straw then falls out of the back, together with any chaff and dust. Grain falls through a series of sieves and then travels up the elevator and auger into the grain tank.

Harvesting with horse and man power alone was laborious and time consuming. Before the invention of primitive harvesters – like the horse-drawn one in use here – crops had to be cut by hand using a scythe. Even so, a proficient worker could reap half a hectare per day. After cutting, the stalks were gathered into sheaves and carted off for winnowing.

The arrival of hawkers – these Afghans with their camels trudged the outback tracks of South Australia last century – made a welcome break from the monotony of country life. The range of goods sold by hawkers included clothes, books, tinned food, knives, fabrics and any small items that were easily carried.

HARVESTMEN

Harvestmen look like spiders and are related to them, but they do not have the spider's waist and its ability to produce silk. Their legs are particularly long, and in some species there are additional hearts in the limbs to keep the blood moving. Their eyes are on each side of a small turret on their backs. They are sometimes called daddy-longlegs.

Harvestmen are scavengers and hunters of small animals, and they are usually found in concealed places on the ground, in thick vegetation, or under stones. There are about 60 species in Australia.

HAWKERS AND PEDDLERS

In English cities, from which most of Australia's early settlers came, many of the goods now found only in shops were sold by hawkers and peddlers, loudly calling their wares in the streets. At first there was little opportunity to do this in the convict colony, but in time the practice became common enough for the authorities to see a need for regulating it by law. Thus in 1844 the New South Wales Legislative Council passed a Bill which required hawkers and peddlars to be licensed. An application to join their ranks had to be signed by three respectable householders; and once licensed, hawkers had to display the sign 'Licensed Hawker' and their number, not only on their vehicles, but on every pack, box and other container in which their goods were carried. They must not on any account carry fermented or spiritous liquors. However no licence was required for anyone selling food, water or fuel, or

for manufacturers selling only goods which they had made themselves.

Later in the nineteenth century retail trade was dominated more by shops. However, the Indian hawker, carrying clothing and other merchandise by packhorse, was a familiar sight in the outback. In cities, too, it became traditional for such people as clothes-prop men, knife and scissor sharpeners, 'rabbit-ohs', and Chinese market gardeners to sell from carts in the streets, or to go from door to door. Right up to the 1940s the calls of some of these were a familiar sound in suburban streets.

The Depression also brought a great increase in hawking and peddling. Many manufacturers tried to boost falling sales by relying on door-to-door salespeople, and the unemployed in large numbers tried to eke out a living by selling small everyday items in the streets or at doorways. Some produced goods for sale – pastrycooks baking pies, carpenters making toys or minor items of furniture. Now door-to-door selling is carried on in a more sophisticated manner, so that even the words hawker and peddlar have practically disappeared from use.

HAY

Hay, the most popular form of conserved fodder, is produced in all states. It is fed to livestock, particularly stud and dairy animals, during times of low pasture production and drought.

Hay is made by cutting pastures – such as clover, ryegrass and lucerne – or fodder crops like oats. The quality and nutritional value of hay varies greatly depending upon the crop it is made

from, and the conditions under which it is made. The crops are cut just before maturity and left in the paddock to dry before baling.

Hay is usually made into small rectangular bales which are mechanically tied before being collected and stacked under cover. However, large round bales are becoming more popular because they are cheaper to produce.

HAZE

Haze is a suspension of particles in the atmosphere which reduces visibility. In Australia, dust haze is common because of the dryness of the continent. Particles of soil, small enough to be held in the air, are stirred up, and often carried great distances by the wind. The most severe dust hazes are created by dust storms such as occurred during 1944, when Mascot Airport in Sydney was closed for several days because dust reduced visibility to 500 m. Less hazardous, but common in coastal regions, is sea haze which occurs when large numbers of salt particles enter the atmosphere at the ocean surface. It is estimated that several hundred salt particles are ejected into the air every time a bubble of greater than 2 mm in diameter bursts. The consequent reduction in visibility depends on the size and relative humidity of the particles.

Brown haze is so called because of the brown colour created by scattering and absorption of sunlight by fine particles and gases in the air. About 60 per cent of the reduction in visibility caused by Sydney's brown haze is a result to particles from motor vehicles and domestic and industrial fires.

More attractive is the blue haze which gives many mountain ranges their distinctive colour. It is thought that the blue colour is caused by scattering of light from particles given off by eucalyptus trees.

A familiar tinge of blue colours the rugged peaks of the Warrumbungles in northern NSW. The colour, which is seen in distant views, is thought to be due to particles given off by eucalyptus, although no one has been able to explain exactly how it happens.

HECTARE

The hectare is the metric measurement of land area, equivalent to 10 000 sq.m (abbreviated ha). It has replaced the ACRE as the most widely recognised measure of property size. Most properties are bought and sold for the dollar per hectare price. Many farmers, however, still refer to the acre, which is 2.47 times smaller than the hectare. To convert acres into hectares multiply by 0.405. To convert hectares to acres multiply by 2.47. One square mile equals 2.59 square kilometres or 258.9 hectares, and one square kilometre equals 0.39 square miles.

HEDGE

In Australia this refers to a dense, even planting of shrubs or small trees around a garden. In some of the very long-settled cooler regions, farm hedges are still found, mostly composed of English Hawthorn. Hedges were a feature of 19th-century and early 20th-century Australian gardens. The shrubs most often used were several species of Privet *Ligustrum*, popular for their dense foliage, long life, disease resistance and ability to withstand frequent clipping. Privet hedges were trimmed into severe rectangular shapes, mostly 1.5–2 m high, often incorporating arches over gates, and other embellishments. Also used formerly for hedges were some species of conifer, in particular the Mediterranean Cypress or 'pencil pine' *Cupressus sempervirens* and Monterey Cypress *C. macrocarpa*. A hedge plant that is still popular is the Japanese *Photinia glabra*, with brilliant pinkish-red new leaves, which frequent trimming will stimulate over much of the year. The dwarf hedge used in formal gardens is traditionally composed of 300 mm high Box *Boxus sempervirens*. Few Australian native plants have been used for formal hedges, although occasionally species such as *Grevillea rosmarinifolia* or *Hakea salicifolia* are seen.

HEIFER

Heifers are young, female cattle which have not yet calved, or have had only one calf. They generally have smaller udders and are in better condition than cows which have had many calves. Cattle usually calve for the first time at around two years of age. Heifers are either selected as replacement breeders or are culled for sale or fattening. Criteria for selection as a breeder includes growth rates, fertility, mothering ability – whether they look after their calves and are good mothers – and ease of calving. Heifers are usually put with the bull for one mating and are culled if they fail to conceive or do not rear a healthy calf. Heifers are usually mated with bulls of a small breed to avoid calving difficulties. Culled heifers are sometimes spayed – their ovaries are surgically removed – to speed their weight-gain before sale.

Chinese herbalist *Jan Hin (far left) poses with a group outside his ramshackle hut at Deepwater, NSW, in the 1920s. Herbal cures employed imported plants, rather than native species favoured by Aborigines.*

HERB

Readers of the 1880 *Australian Botanic Guide to Health* suffering from fits, lockjaw, hydrophobia (rabies) or suspended animation, were advised to take a tincture of lobelia seed, cayenne, prickly ash, scullcap, skunk cabbage, valerian and gym myrrh although too much skunk cabbage could cause vomiting, vertigo and temporary blindness. In all its optimistic prescriptions, the book recommends only one native plant, eucalyptus, for its oil. Early settlers learned little from Aborigines who used a wide variety of plants for ailments from colds to rashes, sprains and spear wounds. They did try a few that vaguely resembled European plants, such as peppermint gum (for colic) and native sarsparilla (for scurvy). Later, however, remote bush dwellers found relief and cures in a good many native herbs, although white people and Aborigines often used plants for different purposes. For example, whites took flat spurge for dysentery and kidney disorders, while some Aborigines took it for genital complaints. To most 19th-century cottage gardeners, herbs were plants brought from the old countries, for kitchen use or for prescriptions in the herbals they had brought. Their gardens held horehound, a tonic, and for chest colds; yarrow (to purify the blood); tansy (for hysteria, dropsy and agues); and borage (for catarrh, rheumatism and skin diseases). By the turn of the century, ready-made medicines were widely available. Bush cures were laid aside or forgotten, the medicinal herb garden faded, and herbs became principally aromatics for culinary use.

HERONS AND EGRETS

Herons and egrets – close relatives of the bittern – are long-legged, long-necked birds which wade in water, hunting fishes and other aquatic animals. The vertebrae of their necks are modified so that the birds can dart their dagger-like bills at their prey, and also to ease the prize down their gullets. They stand motionless in shallow water, or wade very slowly, sometimes stirring the mud with their feet. The Intermediate Egret *Ardea intermedia* (620 mm) will sometimes hover and dive into deeper water. The Pied Heron *A. picata* (450–480 mm) walks quickly in search of prey in northern coastal swamps and nearby grassland, and the communal, widespread Cattle Egret *Ardea ibis* feeds on and around cattle and water buffalo in wet pasture, taking insects and parasites.

Egrets are mostly white, although many Eastern Reef Egrets *Ardea sacra* (600–650 mm), coastal birds, are grey, and the white phase is commoner in the tropics. Herons are often pied. Egrets, however, often have beautiful nuptial plumes – the Intermediate Egret's are particularly fine – which were once used, as 'osprey feathers' or 'aigrettes', to adorn women's hats. As egrets and herons commonly nest in colonies it was easy for collectors to kill large numbers of plume-carrying adults, leaving the unfortunate nestlings to starve.

Probably the most commonly seen heron or egret in Australia is the White-faced Heron *Ardea novaehollandiae* (650–690 mm) which ranges throughout the continent and Tasmania. It feeds in fresh water, estuaries and mudflats.

HIBERNATION AND AESTIVATION

In many places there are periods when conditions are unfavourable for the plants and animals that live there, usually because it is too hot or too cold. Animals can escape by migrating or dispersing, or by making changes to the ways their bodies work. Thus some mammals become dormant in cold weather, allowing their heart and breathing rates to drop.

Alternatively, their life-cycle may be arranged so that the unfavourable period is passed in a state where they are unaffected by climate. In winter, for example, food is often in short supply, and the temperatures are too low for 'cold-blooded' animals to be active. Many insects spend this time as inactive eggs or pupae.

To answer the inevitable question about flies in the wintertime in cold climates, some survive as adults, in warm places such as cowsheds, but most overwinter as maggots or pupae, often in fermenting material. If it is very cold, they simply stop developing.

Many insects have a period of suspended development brought on by hormones, and often controlled by day-length. This state is different to dormancy because a temporary return of good conditions does not bring the animal back to active life. More profound changes must occur to break the dormancy, triggered, perhaps, once again by day-length. Many insects hibernate or aestivate – the hot-weather counterpart – in a state of suspended development.

Some land-living vertebrates may go through a classical hibernation. Their body temperature drops until it is little above that of the surrounding air, if at all, and many body processes, such as heart rate and breathing slow down so that little energy is required. Nevertheless the animals have usually prepared by building up large reserves of body fat. If the weather warms up for long enough, hibernating animals will awaken. They will also be roused by extreme cold – otherwise they might freeze and never wake. Needless to say they overwinter in suitable places in which they usually curl up into a tight ball with ears flat and muscles rigid so that a classical hibernator – the European dormouse, for example – can be gently rolled around. The animal's drop in body temperature is not due to a loss of control: on the contrary, the temperature is under tight control, and the animal responds by raising it again if the surrounding temperature drops too much.

Such profound hibernation is rarely needed in Australia, where the temperatures are not often low enough to inconvenience warm-blooded animals severely save, perhaps, in parts of Tasmania or the Alps. They may, however, find it difficult to collect food, particularly if they live on insects. Several Australian mammals and birds do go into a torpor in cold periods. This is similar to classical hibernation, but is not so prolonged. It is the habit of at least some of the insect-eating bats in southern parts of the country and in Tasmania.

Feathertail Gliders *Acrobates pygmaeus*, are usually active at night throughout the year, but during the day they may become torpid when there is a cold spell. Many other small marsupials have the ability to become torpid either daily, or for short periods. Most of these allow their temperature to drop no more than to 15–17°C, even if the air temperature is much lower, but pygmy-possums can undergo longer periods of torpor, and will allow their temperatures to drop lower. While, no doubt, there are many similarities between torpor and hibernation in placental mammals and marsupials, there are some differences. In the arousal phase, for instance, placentals use deposits of brown fat which marsupials do not possess.

In cold weather the body temperature of reptiles and frogs falls, and in cold areas they may become so lethargic that they cannot hunt until their temperature rises again. Some burrow more deeply into the ground to avoid extremely low temperatures. Turtles are known to spend the winter at the bottom of ponds, or more or less buried in damp soil or under leaf litter.

In Australia the ability to survive heat and drought is usually more valuable than the ability to survive cold. There are many ways of doing so. Some ants, for example, store up honey-dew in large workers – called honey-pot ants – to carry the colony over drought periods when they cannot collect food. Water-holding frogs in dry areas retire into a deep burrow after filling themselves with water during rainstorms, and enclose themselves in a cocoon until the next rainfall. Small desert mammals spend the day in relatively cool, humid burrows and produce a very concentrated urine to conserve water.

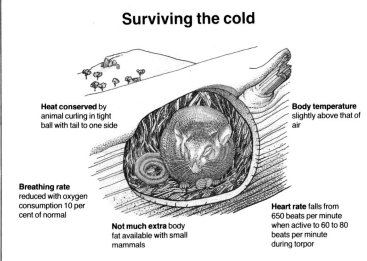

Surviving the cold

Heat conserved by animal curling in tight ball with tail to one side

Body temperature slightly above that of air

Breathing rate reduced with oxygen consumption 10 per cent of normal

Not much extra body fat available with small mammals

Heart rate falls from 650 beats per minute when active to 60 to 80 beats per minute during torpor

Some small native mammals, such as the Eastern Pygmy-possum *Cercartetus nanus* and the Mountain Pygmy-possum *Burramys parvus* go into a state of torpor – similar to that in true hibernation – when the temperature drops very low. This is particularly important for the Mountain Pygmy-possum which is one of only two mammals that live at the summit of Mt Kosciusko throughout the year. Its home is covered by snow for at least three months each winter, although it can move freely around the boulders where it nests.

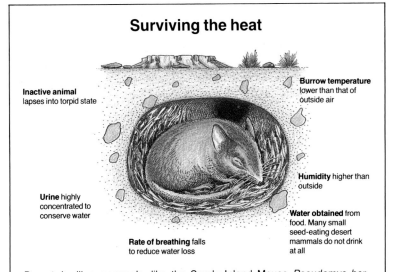

Surviving the heat

Inactive animal lapses into torpid state

Burrow temperature lower than that of outside air

Urine highly concentrated to conserve water

Humidity higher than outside

Rate of breathing falls to reduce water loss

Water obtained from food. Many small seed-eating desert mammals do not drink at all

Desert-dwelling mammals, like the Sandy Inland Mouse *Pseudomys hermannsburgensis* and the Spinifex Hopping Mouse *Notomys alexis* must aestivate to escape the effects of extreme heat in their arid home. Aestivation is the hot-weather equivalent of hibernation, and is aimed at reducing the animal's activity so that it can conserve energy and water during the day. Large animals, which cannot dig burrows, shelter beneath spinifex clumps, sometimes in shallow trenches.

HONEYEATER

The Honeyeater family, with 65 species, is the largest bird family in Australia. In all there are 165, with the most distant representative living in Hawaii. Some biologists believe that this is not a true family descended from a single ancestor, but a composite one whose members resemble each other as the result of convergent EVOLUTION.

The common features of honeyeaters are down-curved bills and long, channelled tongues with fringed ends which can be pushed out to collect nectar. Typical honeyeaters also eat pollen, insects and some fruit. Their digestive system is constructed so that nectar passes straight down to the intestine where it is absorbed, while solid materials pass along more slowly to the stomach. One by-product of the honeyeaters' method of feeding is that they are among the main pollinators of some trees.

The birds are found in almost all places where there are flowering plants. Most of those that hold on to a territory do so only during the breeding season, but BELL MINERS and some others hold territories as flocks.

There are several different groups. The friarbirds, for example, are noisy birds with more or less bald heads. A typical example is the Noisy Friarbird *Philemon corniculatus* (300–340 mm) of eastern Australia, which is also called the Four O'Clock from its call when feeding. Spinebills are small honeyeaters, about 150 mm long, with relatively long beaks with which they probe tubular flowers, restlessly flying from plant to plant. Two of the wattlebirds have red or yellow wattles on their throat, but two do not. The Yellow Wattlebird *Anthochaera paradoxa* (440–480 mm) of Tasmania is the largest Australian honeyeater. The Red Wattlebird *A. carunculata* (320–350 mm) is common in southern Australia.

Most honeyeaters are medium-sized, dull-coloured birds with black, yellow or brown plumage, often with streaks, sometimes through the eye.

Honeypossums are fairly common in the small area of Western Australia where they live. They spend most of the day asleep in an old bird's nest, emerging at night.

HONEY POSSUM

Mouse-sized, nocturnal Honey Possums or Noolbengers *Tarsipes rostratus* (body, 68 mm, tail 83 mm) have long, thin snouts, peg-like teeth, and brush-tipped tongues – all adaptations to their diet of nectar and pollen. Close study of their anatomy and biochemistry has failed to show a close relationship to any other surviving marsupials, so they are thought to be the only living representative of an otherwise extinct group. Their claws are nail-like, apart from the grooming claws, so they hold on to branches with the expanded tips of their fingers and toes. Their prehensile tail helps. Noolbengers live on sandplain heaths in south-western Australia where banksia and similar blossoms grow. In cold weather they become torpid, sometimes huddling together with other individuals, at least when held in captivity.

HONEYSUCKLE

The honeysuckle of England is the hedgerow climber *Lonicera periclymemum* – also known as woodbine – which has cream-coloured flowers that are heavily scented, particularly at night. It is grown in Australian gardens, but is uncommon. A large number of other species, either climbers or small shrubs, are cultivated, one of which, *Lonicera japonica* Japanese Honeysuckle, has become a weed in urban bushland.

The early colonists also used the name honeysuckle for various species of BANKSIA, but this usage is uncommon today. Many species of banksia produce large quantities of nectar and the Aborigines use to suck the sticky liquid directly from the flowers. As a number of species flower in autumn and winter, when bees have fewer sources of nectar, banksias may be useful in supporting hives, although the quality of the honey is poor.

The small Western Australia shrub *Lambertia multiflora* is also sometimes called honeysuckle. Most members of this group of plants produce large quantities of nectar which makes them attractive to HONEYEATERS. All but one species are found only in south-western Australia. The exception is the Honey Flower or Mountain Devil *Lambertia formosa* which is also found in New South Wales.

HOP VINE

It would be fair to describe hops as one of Australia's minor commercial crops – in fact the entire area which is devoted to them would fit comfortably into an average wheat farm. Because of a requirement for a mild, temperate climate, hop-growing is confined to the Derwent, Huon and Channel areas of Tasmania, and the Ovens and King Valleys in Victoria. The crop is planted in early spring and harvested in late summer, after reaching, with the aid of trellises, a height of four to five metres. After picking it is cured in kiln driers – tall sheds which house electric fans to maintain air circulation. The hops are then bleached with sulphur dioxide and pressed into bales.

The best known use for the hop harvest is in the production of beer. About 90 per cent of all available supplies are used for brewing.

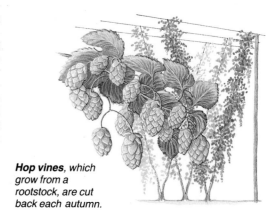

Hop vines, which grow from a rootstock, are cut back each autumn.

HORSE

The first horses brought to Australia were fewer than ten in number in the First Fleet.

Precious draught and transport animals, they were bred as soon as possible. The horse population reached its peak of 2 527 149 in 1918, when there were about one to every two people. Mechanisation then took its hold on roads and farms, and the working horse became largely obsolete. No longer subject to census, Australia's horses probably number about 1.2 million. They represent most of the world's 200 or so breeds, many having developed Australian characteristics. A horse that was strong and had great stamina was of vital importance in the development of Australia. Out of the various breeds that arrived came a hardy, handsome animal called the Waler after its colony of origin. It was used largely for stock work and was exported to India in large numbers where it was popular for sports such as pig-sticking and polo. Over 120 000 Walers served in World War I. The breed has since become extinct.

Many of the Waler's characteristics live on in the Australian Stock Horse, a breed recognised in 1971. Its exceptional strength, reliability and intelligence come from the processes of natural selection and raising by unsentimental blokes who worked their horses hard and seldom molly-coddled them with shoes or fodder, other than that which they found for themselves.

Clydesdales were probably introduced in the 1850s, for agriculture and draught use. They covered the ground quicker than other draught horses, and their shock-absorbing feet made them highly suitable for work on the hard roads. The Carlton and United Breweries' team seen at agricultural shows, are Clydesdales, recognis-

Popular Australian horse breeds

Quarter Horse

Clydesdale

Palomino

Appaloosa

Arab

Australian Stock Horse

THE POINTS OF A HORSE

Poll

Mane   Crest   Atlas

Forelock

Dock   Croup   Loins

Withers

Facial crest

Cheek

Back

Neck

Muzzle

Hindquarters

Shoulder

Throat

Flank   Ribs

Jugular groove

Point of shoulder

Hamstring

Breast

Sheath

Point of elbow

Gaskin

Stifle joint

Brisket

Forearm

Hock

Chestnut

Chestnut

Knee

Back tendons

Cannon

Shank

Fetlock joint

Ergot   Fetlock joint

Coronet

Pastern

Hoof wall

able by their silky, flowing feathers, spats and amenable temperaments.

The Thoroughbred is undoubtedly the most popular of all breeds due to the Australian passion for racing. More than 36 000 horses raced throughout Australia in 1986–87 for prize money in excess of $123 million. Quarter Horses, famed for bursts of speed over a short distance – such as a quarter-mile (402 m) – are used in sprint racing and as stock horses, and for show-jumping competitions.

Horses' heights are measured in hands to the top of the withers (shoulders), one hand being 102 mm. PONIES are usually defined as horses of 14 hands or under.

Wild brumbies

Brumbies are feral horses, *Equus cabellus*. The name is said to be derived from James (or William) Brumby, an ex-member of the NSW Corps, who allegedly let the first horses run wild when he left to join Colonel Paterson's colonisers in Tasmania in 1804. Considering the shortage of horses in the early days of the colony, the story does not ring true. Australia's first horses are thought to have been a stallion, three mares and three colts which came with the First Fleet, although the exact number is in dispute. Early horses in Australia came from the Cape of Good Hope, and were descended from small horses from Java brought there by the Dutch. Many were imported later, and inevitably some must have escaped since fencing was little used in the early days.

Feral horses are found over most of Australia, apart from deserts and intensively farmed areas. Many breeds have contributed to the stock, but those of the plains are considered to be larger with great endurance (height to withers, up to 1.65 m), while those of the high country in the Australian Alps are smaller (1.5 m), but with stronger bones and muscles. It is thought that many draught horses, used in timber-getting, were among their ancestors. An estimate in the late 1970s suggested that there were about 165 000 in the wild.

Each herd consists of about 12 to 50 animals, with a dominant stallion, and all are very wary of human beings. The herd keeps to a territory of between 50 to 150 sq.km. Sometimes they are pests because they destroy pasture, fencing and watering places, and their numbers are kept down by shooting. In the past, when large numbers were killed, hunters devised ways by which they could be fatally wounded so that they lived long enough to move away and die elsewhere, saving the hunters the trouble of disposing of the carcases. During the 1930s two hunters shot 4000 brumbies at Innamincka in one year, and on one outback property, 5000 to 7000 were killed on an outstation in one year. Some are captured for taming, and others are shot for pet food.

HORSE TROUGH

On the immense, arid grazing properties of the Northern Territory, Western Australia and Queensland, the two most important signs of life are the windmill and trough. They mean simply one thing: water – the most essential element for survival in a harsh climate.

The rectangular or circular horse or stock trough holds water pumped to the surface by windmills. This is the grazier's answer to the dam, which is often too difficult to build, or inappropriate, given the low rainfall and higher evaporation rates of arid areas.

However, troughs are also found on smaller, intensive properties, mainly because of the difficulties and dangers of watering stock from dams. Troughs work on a similar principle to the common household flush toilet. A flotation valve – usually made of a large plastic or bronze bubble on a metal stick – is set in a position to allow the water in the trough to reach a certain level. When animals empty the trough below that level, the valve opens to let more water in.

The levels and working parts of the trough have to be checked regularly. Troughs also have to be cleaned of algae, which can cause the water to become 'sour' to stock.

HOT SPRING

Hot or thermal springs are sometimes found in the outback. Water from artesian wells has often travelled many hundreds, or even thousands of kilometres from its source. Sometimes the rocks through which it travels are many kilometres underground, and these are hot because they are closer to the centre of the earth. The water can be close to boiling when it emerges, and it is often rich in dissolved minerals which may be deposited around the outlet.

HUMIDITY

Humidity is a measure of the amount of water vapour in the air. Water vapour is a dry, colourless, odourless gas which may make up between 0 and 4 per cent of a volume of air at any one time. The average for the earth's atmosphere is 1.4 per cent. Water is the most variable gas in the atmosphere because it enters the air by evaporation from oceans and rivers, as well as from soil and plants, all of which are spread unevenly over the earth's surface. The evaporation rate is greatly affected by the temperature of the evaporating surface so that the most humid place throughout the year in Australia is Thursday Island, which is surrounded by warm water.

The amount of moisture that may be held in air is affected by the air's temperature – nearly twice as much water vapour can be held in air at 20°C as at 10°C. For this reason, the term relative humidity is used to describe the moisture content of air. Relative humidity refers to the actual amount of water vapour in the air, relative to the maximum amount that could be held at a specified temperature. At a relative humidity of 100 per cent, no more water vapour can be evaporated into the air unless some of the water condenses, or the air temperature rises.

Although it is the most well-known measure of humidity, relative humidity can be misleading because a drop in temperature of 10°C can almost double the relative humidity, without changing the absolute moisture content of the air. This explains the paradox that, in Perth, the air is about 25 per cent more moist during January than August and yet the relative humidity is 25 per cent greater in August than January. Lower temperatures in August increase the relative humidity.

HUMPY

A humpy was a traditional Australian Aboriginal hut or shelter, but the word has been extended to include any rude outback shelter.

Aboriginal shelters varied seasonally and from region to region. In the north during the wet season Aborigines built water-resistant bark shelters. In the dry, little shelter was needed, but to repell insects platforms were built over smoky fires. In Arnhem Land these platforms were sometimes built in trees.

In the south of the continent the winter cold was more of a problem and Aborigines sheltered in durable domed huts built of wattle and daub, or sometimes stone.

Simple traditional Aboriginal shelters in the north of Australia. Little else is needed in the hot, humid climate of the tropics during the dry season.

HUNTING

The first European settlers, arriving on Australia's seemingly hostile shores in 1788, quickly learnt about hunting. For many years, the convicts, soldiers and free settlers of the First and Second Fleets had to eat wild game when their crop and livestock enterprises failed. In 1806, for instance, a flood on the Hawkesbury River near Sydney forced the expanding colony of Van Diemen's Land (Tasmania) to rely solely on kangaroo meat for several months. In one six-month period, over 1000 kangaroos were slaughtered.

Although very few people now regularly eat kangaroos, the hunting of them and other wild game – including ducks, pigs, foxes and rabbits – is widely practised by many Australians.

Kangaroos are considered to be a pest by most landholders because they eat pasture and crops, and destroy fencelines. Lincensed professional shooters are mainly responsible for controlling

Steam rises from artesian bore water in a pool near the Birdsville track in central Australia. Water rising from very deep underground rocks can often be close to boiling point.

them, usually hunting at night with spotlights.

Kangaroos' meat is sold to pet food manufactures and hides are exported to shoe and handbag makers in Europe. There is much debate about the damage caused by kangaroos and how many of the animals should be killed.

Some conservationists have suggested that a few of the rarer species of kangaroos and wallabies may face extinction. On the other hand, farmers say a large mob can wipe thousands of dollars off a property's income.

Ducks are the second most hunted species of wild animal. There are around 110 000 registered shooters in Australia and many go hunting in the three-month duck season, mainly in NSW, Victoria and South Australia.

HUNTSMAN SPIDER

Huntsman spiders often alarm householders when they enter a house, or are brought in with the washing. They are medium to large spiders, usually about 35 mm long (without legs) and have flattened brown or grey bodies. Their front two pairs of legs are longer than their back two. They are often seen scuttling rapidly sideways across a wall. Most are quite harmless, although the bite of the Badge Spider *Olios diana* and its relatives can injure. Badge Spiders are light yellow-brown and have a dark badge-shaped mark on their undersides. There are two species of huntsmen spiders, and they are found all over Australia. They are sometimes wrongly called triantelopes or tarantulas.

HUON PINE

The most famous of Tasmania's conifers, Huon Pine *Lagarostrobos franklinii* is found only in the rugged south-west of the island where it grows mainly along stream banks. It is an ancient relic of the temperate rainforests which once covered much of the former continent of Gondwanaland, from which Australia split off around 60 million years ago.

Huon Pine is one of the few Australian trees to have annual growth-rings in its wood, and counts of these have shown that many of the larger specimens are of great age, possibly upwards of 2000 years. This means they are likely to be Australia's oldest trees. Growth is very slow, indicated by the very close spacing of the rings, which are often half a millimetre or less apart. In the past Huon Pine was Tasmania's most highly valued timber, especially for boatbuilding. Most accessible stands were felled long ago, and its slow growth means they will take hundreds of years to grow back. However, the construction of hydroelectric dams in remote areas has resulted in the threatened drowning of many old Huon Pine trees. These have been salvaged for timber which has meant that the sawmills have had new supplies. Some is being used for turning and woodcarving, with often very beautiful results.

Moss-covered branches of a Huon Pine tree droop over the banks of the Jane River in Tasmania's southwest. Some of these trees may be Australia's oldest.

HYDATID CYST

Hydatid cysts are the larvae of a small TAPEWORM *Echinococcus granulosus*, which infest the guts of dogs – doing little harm there. They are common in sheep country.

Dogs become infested by eating carrion or uncooked sheep offal which contains the worm cysts. Tapeworm eggs pass out with the faeces and foul pasture, or the fur of dogs. People may swallow them after fondling dogs. Within the victim the egg develops into a cyst – a fluid-filled bag which buds off, internally, many daughter

THE DEADLY TAPEWORM

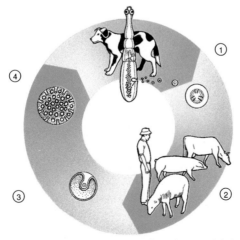

Hydatid tapeworms live normally in dogs, and their eggs pass out of the animals in faeces (**1**). Eggs may be eaten by grazing animals (**2**), or they can be acquired by humans after handling infected dogs. Inside a human the egg hatches into a larva which forms a cyst – a fluid-filled bladder (**3**). Cysts grow, often to a great size (**4**).

cysts containing embryonic tapeworm heads. In human beings cysts usually develop in the lungs, liver or abdominal cavity. If a cyst bursts – during surgery, or, in one Canberra case, in a cycle accident – daughter cysts become established in other parts of the body. The body usually encases cysts in fibrous tissue, but they can still grow to the size of an orange. One Australian woman had a cyst which was 57 litres in volume.

Twenty years ago Tasmania had a higher incidence of cyst infestation in people than any other English-speaking part of the world. A survey showed about 11 per cent of dogs were infested. Strict measures have greatly reduced this incidence and human surgical cases dropped from one a week to nine a year.

The incidence is still high on the mainland and may be increasing. The problem is most serious, for obvious reasons, in rural districts. There dogs should be wormed regularly, and should never be fed raw sheep offal. All town dogs should be wormed after an extended country visit.

There is also a cycle involving Dingoes and wallabies, but it is not known if this has anything to do with the cycle between domestic dogs and sheep. If it does, it will make eradication of the tapeworm very difficult.

HYDROELECTRICITY

The production of energy by allowing water to flow through turbines is non-polluting and does not use fossil fuels – the energy comes from the sun. Nevertheless it has been bitterly opposed by environmentalists who have been particularly provoked by schemes in Tasmania where many beautiful valleys and lakes have been dammed and flooded.

In most of Australia there are more urgent uses for water and, in any case, the country is generally too flat. Consequently the only important hydroelectricity stations are in Tasmania and in the Australian Alps, and these sources contribute only about 14 per cent of the country's electricity.

The Snowy Mountains Scheme, completed in the mid-1970s, includes seven power stations, 16 dams, 80 km of aqueducts and 145 km of tunnels. Each year it produces almost 4 million kw and 2.36 cubic km of water for irrigation. The water falls about 760 m to generate power. The largest storages are Eucumbene, Blowering, Talbingo and Jindabyne lakes or dams, and the largest station is Tumut 3.

In Tasmania there is only one thermal power station. The largest hydroelectric station is underground at Poatina. Water from the Great Lake flows beneath the Western Tiers, then down a hill slope to the turbines.

In 1983, controversial action by the Federal Government stopped the flooding of the Gordon River below its junction with the Franklin River for electricity generation.

I

IBIS AND SPOONBILL

Sacred Ibises *Threskiornis aethiopicus* (680–750 mm) were worshipped by the ancient Egyptians because they arrived with the annual flooding of the Nile. They were the emblem of Thoth, the secretary of Osiris, and were depicted in sculptures and frescoes, and preserved as mummies. The grubby, free-living specimens soliciting food from visitors in Sydney's Taronga Zoo scarcely look divine. The urban population has apparently grown in recent years, and they can sometimes be seen, flying in V-formation, necks outstretched, unlike their relatives the herons, above the city. Their flight, with flaps and glides, is synchronised. They are distributed over most of Australia, apart from some arid zones, and forage in swamps.

Flocks of males find the breeding site, and the females join them later, and after a bowing display by the males, they mate, usually with both holding a twig the male has collected. They do not begin breeding until the site is well flooded. Presumably this is the reason for their association with the annual flooding of the Nile. Their close relative, the Straw-necked Ibis *T. spinicollis* (680–750 mm), has a slightly larger range. The two species are often seen in company, but the Straw-necks will also feed on dry pastures eating locusts and other insects. The Glossy Ibis *Plegadis falcinellus* (490–550 mm) is dark brown with iridescent wings, although it looks black and curlew-like from a distance. It is another widespread bird – both in Australia and elsewhere – which feeds in water and on mudflats. Ibises are nomadic or migratory, and may fly great distances.

The two spoonbills, the Royal Spoonbill *Platalea regia* (750–800 mm), and the Yellow-billed Spoonbill *P. flavipes*, are easily recognised as spoonbills by their flattened beaks. The Royal has a a black bill and face. These long-legged birds stand in water, hold their bills vertically and slightly open, and sweep them from side to side until they feel prey.

IGNEOUS ROCK

Every rock on the planet was of igneous origin – the word means produced by fire or heat. Igneous rocks are formed when molten rock – magma – from deep within the earth moves upwards and cools and solidifies. Sometimes the magma reaches the surface and is spewed out in volcanic eruptions to produce fine-grained rocks like obsidian, rhyolite or basalt. In other cases the magma does not reach the surface and hardens slowly beneath the earth to produce coarse-grained rocks like granite, andesite and gabbro. Thick magma, with the consistency of molten tar, may rise towards the surface at several centimetres per year, while thin magma, with the consistency of honey, may rise at more than a kilometre an hour.

Igneous rocks can look very different to each other, and can have very different chemical compositions. A dark magma, rich in iron, may form beneath the earth's surface at 1000 to 1400°C. If it reaches the surface it will cool rapidly to form basalt, and if it does not it will form gabbro. A light-coloured magma may form trachyte if it reaches the surface, or granite if it does not. Igneous rocks are a valuable source of precious minerals, metals and gemstones.

IMPORTED BUILDING STYLE

In the acute housing shortage of the 1850s and 60s, entire houses formed part of some affluent settlers' baggage. Wooden houses were brought from Germany, America and Singapore, and iron houses from Britain. One elaborate prefabricated iron house is Corio Villa, put up in Geelong in 1855. More commonly, only memories arrived with the newcomers. South Australia, where free settlers were determined to stay, is particularly rich in buildings that betray the identities of the Old Countries from which their makers came. The families of the miners and smelters brought to the copper mines around Burra lived in rows of cottages built by the mining company (of British origins), reminiscent in their monotony of workers' housing in industrial towns of the north of England. The Cornish and Welsh miners imparted their own flavour to many South Australian stone or brick buildings, with white-painted quoins or corner-stones. Lutheran immigrants who founded Hahndorf in the Adelaide Hills built half-timbered cottages and farmhouses in the German style. In the Barossa Valley, Tanunda, Angaston and Nuriootpa have low-spired churches and cottages in the manner of Silesia, now part of Poland. Strathalbyn in the south Mt Lofty Ranges has a Scottish air. Links with India through many ex-military settlers all over Australia produced an essential feature of Australian buildings, the verandah. In tropical Queensland towns like Townsville, houses on stilts with deep-shaded verandahs developed at last into a unique Australian style.

Examples of building styles brought to Australia by settlers can be seen in many country towns. The miners' cottages (above left), similar to many in industrial Britain, were built at Burra in South Australia for Cornish miners. Broken gables (left), a characteristic of German rural architecture, are seen on many buildings in Hahndorf, also in South Australia. Lutheran immigrants settled the area in the 1830s. Beechworth, in Victoria, saw immigrants from many countries during the gold rush of the 1850s and 1860s. The Ovens and Murray Home, with its Flemish facade (above), was opened in 1863.

INSECT

Nearly three-quarters of the known living species of animals are insects. Nearly a million species have been named throughout the world, the largest being the Goliath Beetle *Galiathus giganteus* of West Africa, which is over 150 mm long, and more are discovered every year. In Australia there are more than 54 000 species. The largest Australian insect is the Hercules Moth *Cosinocera hercules* which has a wing-span of 280 mm and a wing area of over 260 sq. cm. The heaviest insect is the Spiny Leaf Insect *Extatosoma tiratum* which can weigh 30 g, and the longest is a stick insect *Acrophylla titan*, which has been recorded at 250 mm.

The name insect means 'in sections', the body being in three parts: the head, thorax and abdomen. On the thorax are three pairs of jointed legs. Some relatives of insects, which are not insects but often confused with them, are the spiders, centipedes and woodlice. They have similar legs but usually more than three pairs.

Most insects have two pairs of wings attached to the thorax. They possess them in the adult stage only, which means there is a sharp transition between the young wingless insect and the winged adult. A few primitive, mostly soil-living, insects have never evolved wings. The bristletails and spring-tails are common examples.

Insect skins cannot stretch much and so growth occurs when an insect sheds or moults its old skin, to reveal a new skin underneath which stretches while it is still soft. In this way growth is not uniform, but takes place in distinct steps. At the final moult a winged adult will appear. Thus insects have a life cycle which involves several stages.

Most insects have a complete four-stage life cycle. This consists of egg, larva in which no wing buds are visible, a resting or pupa stage and then the winged adult.

Butterflies and moths have wings covered with coloured scales. Their larvae are called caterpillars and have extra, fleshy legs on the abdomen. Flies have only two wings and legless larvae. The bees, wasps, ants and sawflies have four wings. Many species live in colonies.

Beetles have the first pair of wings hardened into wing cases which protect the membranous second pair. The moth-like caddis flies and gauzy-winged alderflies have aquatic larval stages.

Many other insects have three stages: egg, followed by a nymph which moults several times and has traces of wing buds, and then the adult. This type of life cycle is called gradual metamorphosis. Some insects which undergo gradual metamorphosis, have aquatic nymphs which spend their lives in water before developing into adults. Examples are dragonflies and damselflies whose adults have all four wings of equal size. The mayflies have large forewings and small hindwings and two or three long tails at the end of the body. Stoneflies have two tails and rest with their wings either folded flat over their backs or rolled round their bodies.

Most of the other insects with gradual metamorphosis have land-living young stages. The grasshoppers and their relatives have hind legs enlarged for jumping. Cockroaches are rather like non-jumping grasshoppers. Earwigs have pincers which are for attack and defence, but also help in folding the wings. The bugs have mouthparts adapted for piercing and sucking, either for drinking blood from an animal or, more usually, sap from a plant.

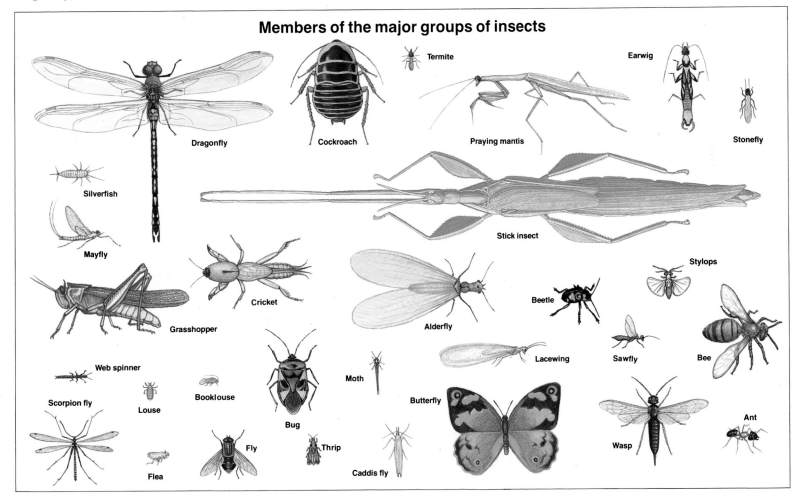

Members of the major groups of insects

Dragonfly

Cockroach

Termite

Praying mantis

Earwig

Stonefly

Silverfish

Mayfly

Stick insect

Grasshopper

Cricket

Alderfly

Beetle

Stylops

Lacewing

Sawfly

Bee

Web spinner

Scorpion fly

Louse

Booklouse

Bug

Moth

Butterfly

Thrip

Caddis fly

Wasp

Ant

Flea

Fly

INTRODUCED ANIMALS

Within days of its establishment at Sydney Cove, the first settlement's seven cattle were reported missing, presumed speared. Seven years later their 70 feral descendants were found at Cow Pastures (now Camden). Since then European settlers have been losing their mammals and birds to the bush, or deliberately releasing them to fend for themselves. Some, such as two rats and the House Mouse, came as stowaways. Now there are 20 exotic mammals, 25 non-marine birds, one non-marine reptile, one toad, and 19 freshwater fish. Some are feral – domesticated species such as the pig, which are now self-supporting – while others were always wild.

Conservationists often complain of the damage done by exotic imported animals, yet proportionately there have been fewer in Australia than in some other countries, such as Great Britain. Most of the British ones, however, have been established since Norman or Roman times and now fit into the ecology of the country, whereas some of the Australian invaders are still causing much damage. They arrived in a country with ample food and without large predators. Some, such as the cat and the fox, are predators themselves, against which native animals have evolved no defences. In the early stages, at least, many of them were free from serious parasites and diseases.

The most dangerous exotic species is probably the feral pig as it breeds so rapidly that it is impossible to control without exterminating the whole population. It damages vegetation, is potentially dangerous to people, and would serve as an almost ineradicable reservoir of foot and mouth disease if it became established in Australia. Rabbits are still troublesome, despite the fact they were almost eliminated in the 1950s by MYXOMATOSIS, but they have not regained their former numbers.

Possibly the most acceptable exotic mammals are deer, although in New Zealand they are counted among the worst pests because of the erosion they cause. A herd is protected in the Royal National Park in Sydney. Introduced birds, with the exception of feral pigeons, are more of a nuisance than a serious pest.

Many of the animals were introduced by Acclimatisation Societies during the last century which, fortunately, matured into the zoological societies of today.

INTRODUCED PLANTS

This general term covers all plants growing in Australia which are not native here, including garden plants, crop plants, trees planted for timber, weeds and other naturalised plants. The number of species included is huge, probably greater than the number of natives, of which there are more than 25 000. As with the natives the great majority are flowering plants, the remainder being mostly ferns and conifers. Only notably successful plants are covered here, most, or all, of which are usually called 'weeds'.

In most of the closely settled parts of Australia, except areas of very infertile soil such as the Sydney sandstone, almost all of the vegetation is made up of naturalised plants. In grazing country, especially in the large areas with 'improved pasture', the grasses are mainly introduced species such as PASPALUM, Ryegrass and Cocksfoot, and these are often mixed with introduced legumes such as clovers.

Outside property fences the roadside plants are mainly rank-growing weeds which benefit from increased rainwater runoff, the absence of grazing, and regular soil disturbance by road machinery, such as graders, which exposes new soil surfaces for seedlings to grow in. Along roadsides in cooler areas a striking feature is the profusion of yellow-flowered 'wild mustards' – a group of weeds closely related to cabbages, turnips, mustard and rape.

In warmer, wetter parts of Australia roadside weeds are often much taller, and can form a barrier difficult to penetrate on foot. One of the thickest is Guinea Grass *Panicum maximum*, a coarse grass up to 2.5 m tall, common in coastal north Queensland.

A group of introduced plants that are causing much concern are the so-called 'urban weeds' which spread through bushland close to housing, taking advantage of nutrients from household effluent. Some of the worst are trees, woody shrubs or climbers, often originally introduced as ornamental plants. Some are also a threat to the surviving remnants of lowland rainforest. Among the worst are: two species of PRIVET; Camphor Laurel *Cinnamomum camphora*, a large tree which is displacing native rainforest trees on the NSW north coast; Japanese Honysuckle *Lonicera japonica*, which smothers native shrubs in urban bushland in NSW and Victoria; PAMPAS GRASS; and Watsonias, bulbous South African plants which form dense infestations on the Western Australian coast near Perth.

Among the most alarming of introduced plants are BITOU BUSH, Rubber Vine and LANTANA. Bitou Bush, or Boneseed, is a yellow-flowered South African shrubby daisy which was planted as an ornamental and to stabilise coastal sand dunes. It is now spreading over large areas of coastal scrub around the southern half of Australia where it is displacing many native species. Rubber Vine *Cryptostegia*, a rampant creeper with milky latex in its stems, is spreading over drier coastal parts of tropical Queensland. In remote areas of western Cape York it is reported to cover many square kilometres.

Agricultural weeds are another major group of introduced plants, too numerous to mention individually. They cause the greatest economic loss when they infest crops, but they can be very abundant and varied on pasture land, especially if it is overgrazed or eroded. Once established and allowed to flower they can rapidly build up enormous reserves of seed in the soil, making eradication difficult. This gives rise to the saying: 'One year's seeding, seven years' weeding'.

IRON

Iron, one of the most abundant elements, makes up five per cent of the earth's crust. Because of its use in the manufacture of steel it is probably the most important metal known to man. The main sources of iron are the minerals haematite, magnetite and goethite. Heamatite is used by Aborigines as red ochre.

The Hamersley Basin in the north-west of Western Australia produces nearly ten per cent of the world's iron ore. The ore is mined from deposits which are literally mountains of iron made up of 200-million-year-old rocks known as Banded Iron Formations, which are layers of quartz and enriched iron. The origin of the iron in the rocks is still something of a mystery to geologists, but it is thought to have been formed by bacteria.

Giant machines *eat their way through a mountain made of iron ore at Iron Knob in South Australia. Most of the ore goes to industrial countries like Japan.*

IRONBARK

This group of about 20 species of *Eucalyptus* is easily recognised by the distinctive hard, furrowed, dark-grey bark which usually covers the whole of the trunk and larger branches. Ironbarks are found only in eastern and northern Australia – from the coast to the semi-arid interior – but not in higher mountain areas. They are most abundant and diverse in Queensland. Some species are valued for their timber, which is among the hardest, densest and strongest of all the eucalypt timbers. It was the main timber used in construction of wooden bridges, and is also the best for electricity poles, railway sleepers and fence posts.

The brilliant green of irrigated fields stands out at Tailem Bend on the Murray River in South Australia (right). Dethridge wheels (above) record the amount of water used by individual farmers to irrigate their crops.

IRRIGATION

Farmers in all Australian states and territories irrigate an estimated 1.5 million hectares of land a year, using several different techniques. The crops and pastures most commonly irrigated include lucerne, rice, sugarcane, cotton, vegetables, annual and perennial grasses, tobacco, oilseeds, grapes and other orchard crops.

Irrigation was first introduced into Australia in the late 19th century in Victoria, NSW and South Australia. However, it was not until the early 1900s that the state governments involved fully mastered the mechanics and administration of the various irrigation schemes.

The first and still most important source of water for irrigation was the Murray-Darling River system, which includes the Murrumbidgee River in NSW. Most of Australia's rice crop is grown under irrigation from this system. In the lower rainfall districts of South Australia, NSW and Victoria, the Murray system, with a total catchment of 30 000 million cubic metres, has ensured the success of many thousands of hectares of crops, vegetables, fruit and pastures. The effectiveness of the system was improved by the NSW Snowy Mountains scheme in the 1950s and 1960s, when water was diverted from the Snowy River to the Murray and Murrumbidgee Rivers.

Since then the Western Australian and Queensland governments, with federal assistance, have established two other large irrigation schemes. These are the Ord River scheme in the north of Western Australia and the Burdekin project, south of Townsville. Both are used in the production of mainly tropical grain crops, fruit, vegetables, sugarcane, mung beans and soybeans.

Farmers use several different methods of irrigation, depending on soil type, farm layout and the crop to be grown. Common methods are:
● FLOOD The most basic system involves flooding of paddocks and is very common in rice growing. It involves raising the water level in several ditches above ground level.
● SPRINKLER This involves applying water in droplet form, usually from above the crop. It is used widely for fruit and vegetables.
● FURROW Water is taken across the surface of the ground by a series of small channels or furrows. It is used mainly in row crops, such as cotton, sorghum and maize.
● TRICKLE This is a relatively new system which allows plants, usually vegetables, to be individually watered via small tubes connected to a main supply pipe.
● CONTOUR This is a variation of the flood system in which water is 'trapped' on the crop or pasture between two banks or contours.

IRRIGATION SCHEMES

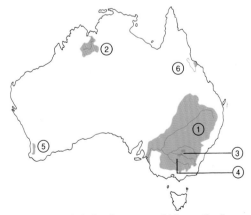

Australia's main irrigation areas: 1 Murray-Darling Basin, which contains three-quarters of the country's irrigated land; 2 Ord River Scheme; 3 Murrumbidgee Irrigation Area; 4 Coleambally Irrigation Area; 5 Preston Valley Irrigation District; 6 Burdekin River Irrigation Area.

ISLAND

Many people find the idea of living on an island – preferably tropical and deserted – to be attractive, although the reality is often much harsher than expected. It is difficult to number the Australian coastal islands as many are nameless and little more than reefs, awash at high tide. There are about 1267 named islands, 866 of them in tropical waters. The numbers within the various state boundaries are: Queensland 593; Western Australia 321; South Australia 115; the Northern Territory 77; Tasmania 70; Victoria 52 and NSW 39.

Many of these are continental islands and when the sea levels were at their lowest during the Ice Ages they were simply hills on the mainland. Consequently both are often similar in form. Some others close to the mainland have been isolated by erosion. Hinchinbrook Island, north of Townsville, is made up of granite and schist, similar to the mainland. The channel separating it is apparently a drowned section of the Tully River which formerly flowed southeast. The islands along the Whitsunday Passage, such as the Molles are also continental.

Fraser and Big Sandy Islands, off the far south coast of Queensland, are composed entirely of sand, and are probably fossil dunes which may have formed on the mainland, before the sea rose to its present level.

Australia has many coral islands but no atolls. Atolls are formed when a fringing reef is left above the water after the mountain peak it surrounded sinks slowly beneath the sea. There are, however, many low sandy cays along reefs where sand collects on a section of reef, and is then stabilised by vegetation, often fertilised by guano (bird droppings). Such islands are surrounded by extensive living reefs. Two of the best known are Heron and Green Islands, off the Queensland coast.

J

Jackeroos were once trainee station managers – with hard work they might one day own or run a property, even marry the boss's daughter. These days the term covers nearly all farm workers, and is losing its original meaning.

JABIRU

Jabirus are now officially called Black-necked Storks. The word is not Aboriginal, as many people believe, but Portuguese, and applied also to other storks in South America and Africa. The Australian species, *Ephippiorhynchus asiaticus* (1100–1300 mm, standing about 1.2 m tall), is also found in southern Asia, and unlike most other storks is not a particularly sociable bird, although family groups are sometimes seen.

The storks feed like herons, wading through shallow water, catching fish, amphibians, some rodents and other creatures, but also eating carrion. Unlike herons they fly with their necks stretched out. To get into the air they must run or hop a few steps, and once airborne may soar to considerable heights.

Family duties, such as building a nest, are shared by a pair. The nest is a bulky mass of sticks with a grass capping, built in a bush or tree.

The birds are found in wetlands and mangroves in the east and north of the continent, sometimes as far south as Sydney or, occasionally, Victoria.

JACANA

Like Jabiru, Jacana is a Portuguese word but this was originally derived from an Amazonian Indian language. The Australian names of Lilytrotter or Christbird are far more evocative of the bird's ability to walk on water, or rather on floating vegetation. To do so they have evolved long hindtoes (75 mm), which help to spread the weight of the 200–240-mm-long birds as they walk, head bobbing, over the leaves. The Aus-

tralian species is the Comb-crested Jacana *Irediparra gallinacea*. Another species, a straggler from Asia, has been seen once in Western Australia. There are seven or eight species in all which live in tropical regions of the world. The Australian species ranges to Borneo and Mindanao and, in Australia, from the north coast to the Hawkesbury River in NSW. They feed during the day on plants, insects and seeds and often, it is reported, lie down on their sides on the leaves to sunbathe. Their nests are rafts of plants within each pair's breeding-season territory. Their eggs are among the most striking of all bird's eggs being glossy tan, covered with dark squiggles. When driven from the nest by predators adults and young can remain hidden below water for 30 minutes or so, snorkelling through their bills.

JACARANDA

One of Australia's most popular ornamental flowering trees, *Jacaranda mimosifolia* is in fact a native of northern Argentina and nearby parts of Brazil and Paraguay. It is a semi-deciduous tree with fine, fern-like leaves and a broadly spreading crown. In late spring the bare branches are covered in a delicate filigree of bright violet-blue flowers which carpet the ground beneath when they fall. Jacarandas thrive only in moist warm-temperate climates, and some of the areas of Australia which suit them best happen to be where the cities are. They do well in Sydney, and in November are visible as filmy blue patches all over the hilly suburbs near the harbour, in fact all over the Sydney region. A town famous for its large, old Jacarandas is Grafton on the NSW north coast – a Jacaranda Festival is held there annually to coincide with their peak flowering. In Queensland, Jacarandas are at their best in the cooler hill towns such as Toowoomba and Atherton. Melbourne is a little cool for them, but there are some magnificent Jacarandas in north-west Victoria, in the irrigation towns along the Murray and also in adjacent parts of NSW and South Australia.

JACKEROO

A jackeroo was originally a farm management apprentice, but now the term is more commonly used for a farm or station worker. The female equivalent is a jillaroo.

As an apprentice farm manager, a jackeroo would be assigned to all the hard work to be done on a property, while at the same time being required to gain social graces from the station manager or owner's family. Often he would be expected to dine with the head family every night, and on those occasions would need to be dressed formally. At one time jackeroos applied for their jobs in England, where many of the owners of large Australian properties lived. Parents often paid for the cost of having their son employed. Only after World War II was an award wage sytem established for jackeroos, based on their labour, but discounted to allow for board, food and laundry. A jackeroo's wage, however, is still low compared to that received by a full station hand.

JADE

Jade has been mined for centuries in upper Burma, Tibet and southern China. It has also been used for a long time by New Zealand Maoris for ornaments and weapons. However, only small quantities of ornamental quality jade have been mined in Australia.

Jade is a general term for a number of tough, nearly white to dark green minerals used as gemstones in jewellery. Usually the name is used for the minerals jadeite or nephrite, but in Australia the green serpentine mineral, bowenite or 'noble serpentine', is also called jade. True jade has been found at the mining town of Lucknow, near Bathurst, NSW.

The rich green colour is caused by tiny amounts of iron, magnesium and sodium. Bowenite is found in the greenstone belts of West Australia and northern NSW. It is used for carving, but is not as tough as jadeite or nephrite and has a greasier feel. Some modern buildings in Sydney use a type of 'noble serpentine' for ornamental stonework.

JARRAH

This is the most common tree over a considerable part of Western Australia's far south-west, from the area north of Perth to a little east of Albany. The best stands are south of Perth on top of the Darling Range, where the trees grow on deep bauxite and ironstone gravel. Further south, in the higher-rainfall Manjimup-Pemberton-Denmark area they are replaced in the better soils by Karri *E. divensicolor*, one of Australia's tallest trees. Jarrah varies enormously in height, depending on the depth of the soil and its fertility. Over large areas of poor, sandy soil it is a low, stunted, often mallee-like tree only two to three metres tall, but on the best sites it becomes a forest giant 50 m tall. The bark is always rough and fibrous – like that of a stringybark – often red-brown but ageing to dull grey. Jarrah is Western Australia's most valuable timber, renowned for its hardness, durability and strength. Compared with most eucalypt woods, it machines well and takes a fine finish. Many beautiful and highly valued items of furniture have been made from it, especially in recent years.

Jarrah is found only in the south-west corner of Western Australia. In recent years many trees have been victims of a soil fungus which attacks and destroys the tree's fine feeding roots, causing Jarrah dieback.

JASPER

Jasper is a brightly coloured variety of flint. It is a rock composed entirely of microscopic grains of quartz coloured by a minute amount of iron oxide. It has a cloudy appearance and can be red, yellow, brown or black. Jasper is the plain cousin of opal, and is sought by gem collectors as an attractive ornamental stone. Sharpened pieces were commonly used by Aborigines for cutting and skinning. Marble Bar in Western Australia was actually named after a famous bar of red and bluish-grey jasper, not marble. Jasper is thought to have formed in the bottoms of oceans from oozes made up of the remains of microscopic marine organisms which have silica skeletons.

Jasper is found in the Atherton region of Queensland; in New England and on beaches near Newcastle, NSW; and around Heathcote in central Victoria.

JUMBUCK

'Waltzing Matilda, Waltzing Matilda,
You'll come a waltzing Matilda with me.
Whose is that jolly jumbuck you've got in your
*   tuckerbag?*
You'll come a-waltzing Matilda with me'.

Banjo Paterson's famous song, *Waltzing Matilda*, has ensured that the early Australian slang word for sheep – jumbuck – is remembered forever. It was originally an Aboriginal word, first used to describe sheep some time in the 1850s. There are two theories about jumbuck's origins. Some say jumbuck or jimbugg was the Aboriginal word for the white mist preceding a rain shower, the only thing with which Aborigines could compare sheep. Others say junbuc or jimbuc was the Aboriginal word for a very hairy wallaby, similar to sheep because of its thick, woolly coat.

K

KANGAROO

Kangaroos are Australia's main grazing and browsing animals. On other continents their niche is occupied by deer, antelopes or similar creatures. Like many other grass eaters, kangaroos have complex stomachs divided into four sections. Bacteria inside their stomachs help to break down plant material such as cellulose.

Many kangaroos have an unusual reproductive cycle. Their sexual cycle is not interrupted by pregnancy, so that they can mate again very soon after giving birth. Their cycle is, however, interrupted by milk production. If a kangaroo gives birth and mates shortly afterwards – but produces milk for the joey in its pouch – the embryo resulting from the last mating becomes dormant. It remains dormant for about 200 days in a large kangaroo, while the joey, or young kangaroo, in the pouch grows. The embryo then starts developing again until the new joey is born and moves into its mother's pouch. The old joey is evicted and follows its mother on foot. Newly born kangaroos are only a few millimetres long and must find their own way through the mother's belly hairs to the pouch and teat.

Researchers once thought that marsupials had difficulty in maintaining a constant body temperature, despite the fact that some of them can survive the heat of the inland without shade. Kangaroos keep cool by tucking their tails into the shadows of their bodies, panting – through their noses, not through their mouths like a dog –

and by sweating and by licking their forelimbs. That particular part of their body has areas very rich in tiny capillaries where, helped by evaporating saliva, the warm blood releases its heat.

Red Kangaroos *Macropus rufus* are perhaps the largest of the group. They are found west of the Great Dividing Range, although they once lived on the Pacific side. They prefer open plains and savannah wherever they can find green grass. They feed at night, and sometimes late in the evening and early in the morning. Adult males are usually pale to brick red, occasionally blue-grey, and females are usually blue-grey – the so called 'blue flyers'. They have a black and white patch on each side of their muzzles, and their noses are naked. Females are sexually mature at 15 to 20 months, gestation lasts 33 days and the joey remains in its pouch for 235 days.

The Eastern Grey *M. giganteus* (male 970–2300 mm, 430–1090 mm, female 960–1860 mm, 446–842 mm) and the slightly smaller Western Grey *M. fuliginosus* are similar species and both live in eastern states, although only the first is found in Tasmania. Two of the kangaroos collected by Captain Cook in Queensland were this species: the other was a Common Wallaroo *M. robustus*. The western species is the kangaroo found on Kangaroo Island.

Eastern Greys are greyer than the browner western species, and both have finely haired noses. Gestation is about 36 days for Eastern Grey Kangaroos.

Boxing and kicking *is common among fighting kangaroos and wallabies. Large claws on the animal's powerful hind legs can inflict fatal wounds on small animals like dogs, and there have been cases in which humans have been attacked and injured by kangaroos.*

Six of the most common *large kangaroos and wallabies. They are: 1 Western Grey Kangaroo Macropus fuliginosus; 2 Common Wallaroo Macropus robustus; 3 Red-necked Wallaby Macropus rufogriseus; 4 Eastern Grey Kangaroo Macropus giganteus; 5 Agile Wallaby Macropus agilis; 6 Red Kangaroo (male) Macropus rufus.*

Common large kangaroos and wallabies

① ② ③ ④ ⑤ ⑥

KANGAROO GRASS

Kangaroo Grass *Themeda australis* (illustration p 200) is one of the most widely distributed native plants in Australia, being found in all states and a great range of habitats – from the arid zone to the Alps and from windswept coastal headlands to forests. It is a loosely tufted plant which grows from long-dormant seeds all year round, normally reaching a height of 600 to 900 mm when flowering.

Young growth is very nutritious and livestock like it, although mature plants are not as popular. In south-east Australia, grazing by livestock has caused Kangaroo Grass to become rarer; it has been replaced there by other native species, and by introduced pasture grasses.

KANGAROO PAW

This is the common name for all 11 species of grasslike plants with colourful flowers which are found only in the south-west of Western Australia. All have long, narrow flowers covered in dense furry hairs on the outside, split deeply down one side and opened out flat with six 'teeth' at the apex. The common name is derived from a fancied resemblance between this unusual flower shape and a kangaroo's paw. The most striking species is the red and green kangaroo paw *Anigozanthos manglesii*, commonest in the area south of Perth. It is Western Australia's floral emblem.

KARRI

The Karri *Eucalyptus oliverrifolia* is the tallest native tree in Western Australia, reaching almost 90 m (300 ft) in height. Among Australian trees this is equalled or exceeded by only two or three eucalypt species of Tasmania and southern Victoria. Karri grows only in a very small area of the far south-west corner, which receives the highest and most reliable rainfall in Western Australia. Most are found growing between Nannup and Denmark. In the Manjimup-Pemberton-Walpole area the most majestic forests are found, with trees 70 to 80 m high, with smooth, shaft-like, blueish trunks, three metres or more in diameter. Karri is Western Australia's second most important timber after JARRAH, which surrounds it on poorer and drier areas. The wood is dark red and richly grained.

NED KELLY

Travellers passing near Benalla, Beechworth, Glenrowan or Euroa in Victoria, or Jerilderie in NSW, should spare a thought for Edward Kelly, the most famous of Australia's bushrangers, born in 1855 and hanged in 1880. Ned lived near Benalla from the age of 11, served two short gaol sentences in Beechworth, was captured in Glenrowan, and carried out his most famous robberies in Euroa and Jerilderie.

It is a curious fact that Ned, a criminal, is so admired in Australia and has been glorified in sayings such as 'as game as Ned Kelly'. A possible reason lies in the tendency to sympathise with the underdog, for the Kellys were clearly in the underdog class. Both of Ned's parents were Irish, his father – who died when Ned was 11 – had been a convict, and they and all their relatives were poor. Like the convicts before them, they distrusted the police, the rich, and authority in general. For the story of the Kelly gang see BUSHRANGERS.

Billed as 'Ned Kelly's portrait – the last as yet taken' this photograph was a fake. It is based on a portrait taken in 1873 which has been pasted onto new shoulders and embellished with more hair and a beard.

KENAF

Of all the crops grown in Australia, kenaf – also known as ambary – is one of the newest and certainly one of the oddest. It is a member of the hibiscus family, the pink and orange flowering shrub found in many Australian gardens.

Scientists from the CSIRO have spent many years investigating the possibilities of using the fibrous kenaf stem to produce paper. However, it is only in the past few years that the Queensland Department of Primary Industry and a private company have started to develop commercially viable crops on the Burdekin Irrigation Scheme, south of Townsville.

After harvest, the stems are processed to separate the different grades of fibre. The paper pulp derived from kenaf can be made into a range of products, from tissues and writing paper to the coarse material used in newsprint.

One jump ahead

The hop of the kangaroo was probably as surprising to early Europeans in Australia as the kangaroo's pouch. A few mammals – the jerboa mice included – were known to travel in a similar way, but they were much smaller.

Kangaroos have two methods of travel: a 'five-limbed' method at slow speeds using legs, arms and tail – sometimes called 'punting', and the familiar hopping motion.

Professor Dawson at the University of NSW has compared the efficiency of punting and hopping in kangaroos, with running in similarly sized mammals by getting them to hop, punt or run for short periods on a moving belt. The cost of moving at various speeds was assessed by measuring the amount of oxygen used per kg of body weight.

Roughly speaking, punting at speeds of up to 6 km/h was about twice as costly as running at the same speed, but as soon as the kangaroo changed to hopping above 6 km/h, the cost dropped and only began to rise at about 20 km/h. It costs a kangaroo hopping at 40 km/h only as much oxygen as it costs a runner to run at 20 km/h. Obviously the kangaroo is well suited to a land of wide open plains.

It is hardly surprising that a kangaroo holds the world record for the highest and longest jumps. One was recorded clearing a height of 3.2 m, and a female Red Kangaroo covered 12.8 m in a single bound during a chase.

THE CATTLE KING

Australian history contains few stories more extraordinary than that of Sir Sidney Kidman. He left home at the age of 13 with only his clothes, a one-eyed horse, a swag and five shillings. Forty years later he owned more land than any other individual in the British Empire, and perhaps the world.

Properties that were at some time owned by the Kidman family, or in which they held a financial interest. At its greatest extent the Kidman family empire encompassed 170 000 sq. km – an area more than twice the size of Tasmania and three-quarters that of the state of Victoria.

Sir Sidney Kidman (left) and two employees. He was an even-tempered man who had a detailed and intimate knowledge of every aspect of his vast business.

The 13 year-old runaway worked for about a year in an Adelaide stockyard, where he heard many drovers talk about the inland and the opportunities it offered. He determined to seek his fortune there, and chose the Barrier Range as his destination because his brother George worked there. George tried at first to persuade him to return home, but soon realised that there was no hope of success, and obtained work for him with a nomadic cattleman. The latter also employed an Aborigine, from whom Sidney learned a great deal about the bush and its resources. He came to admire the knowledge and skill of Aborigines, and in later years seldom made long journeys in the outback without taking one with him.

The fruits of frugal living
Later he worked on Mt Gipps station, where the Broken Hill lode of silver, lead and zinc ores was later to be found, and then at a station near Menindee. All the time he was saving his wages, living frugally and neither drinking nor smoking. After a few years he was able to buy a bullock team, which he used to bring supplies to townships as far apart as Tibooburra,

Wilcannia, Bourke and Cobar in the far west of NSW and Swan Hill in Victoria.

Next he heard of a rich copper strike at Cobar, moved there, opened a butcher's shop, and also bought two bullock teams to transport the mines' output. Then, as the copper boom waned, he sold out his Cobar interests, and moved to Broken Hill. There he bought a one-fourteenth share in the newly-established BHP, sold it at a large profit, established a coaching business, traded successfully in cattle, and became a supplier of horses to the British army in India.

None of these activities, however, helped him to realise his main ambition, which was to become a landowner. Eventually in 1880, aided by a legacy of £400 from his grandfather's estate, he was able to buy a half-share in his first station, Owen Springs, south-west of Alice Springs. However his ambition went far beyond the possession of one, or even several, stations. In buying, droving and selling cattle, he had noticed the poor condition in which beasts often reached the market, after being driven enormous distances. He reasoned that if he owned a string of stations stretching all the way from the Gulf of Carpentaria to

Much of Kidman's land was like this in south-west Queensland. It could only support cattle in some seasons. At other times stock would be moved to areas where the feed was better.

The ruins of Annandale station, one of Kidman's first properties.

South Australia, he would be able to move stock south from one to another, keeping them in good condition. He could also minimise the effects of drought by moving cattle from stations in badly affected areas to others where conditions were better.

Marriage and children
In 1886 he married a school teacher, Isabel Brown Wright, from Kapunda, a small town about 70 km north of Adelaide. They had three daughters and a son, and made their home in Kapunda. However Kidman spent a great deal of time away from there, droving stock, buying cattle and sheep stations and in managing his fast-growing empire.

He finally brought his great design to fruition by acquiring full or part ownership of over 100 stations, including the enormous Victoria River Downs in the Northern Territory. By moving cattle from one to another he brought them in good condition to railheads at Hergott Springs (Marree), Bourke and Charleville for transport to the Adelaide, Sydney and Brisbane markets respectively.

So great were his financial resources that he survived the great economic depression of the early 1890s fairly well. Then came the great drought of 1895 to 1902, towards the end of which he suffered heavy losses, but he was able to restock quickly. A quarter-century later he lost 12 000 cattle, 100 000 sheep and 6000 horses in the drought of 1927 to 1930, but once again was able to recover.

Gifts to the nation
During the World War I he made gifts of fighter aeroplanes and other equipment to the armed forces, and later made valuable donations to the Salvation Army. In 1921 he was knighted, and in the same year gave his Kapunda home to the South Australian Education Department for a district high school. From then on he and his children administered his empire from Adelaide, where he died in 1935.

Today the outback is more closely settled, properties have been improved, land prices are much higher than in Kidman's day, and so are land taxes. It is therefore very unlikely that any single person will ever acquire such a vast extent of territory as that once owned by 'the cattle king'.

KILN

Quicklime for mortar to bond Australia's first bricks was made with oyster shells from Aboriginal middens. A striking kiln in which the shells were burnt remains on the shore at Port Arthur in Tasmania. In the 1830s limestone deposits were discovered, and mortar was made from lumps of lime burned in paired kilns close to quarries. The kilns were built on slopes to increase draught through the grates and to allow carts to unload from above. Limestone and fuel burned for three days, then cooled for three of four more. One kiln was loaded and fired while the other cooled and the lime was collected. Pairs of circular or arched kilns, lined with bricks and sometimes faced with stone, survive in the limestone areas around Goulburn, Mudgee and Blayney in NSW, Mount Morgan in Queensland and Bridgewater in Tasmania. Later, more efficient kilns, loaded from the top, burned continuously. Some large ones can be seen near Capertee, NSW; at Limeburners Point, East Geelong in Victoria; and also at Bridgewater. The lime was also spread on acid clay soil.

A kiln is any curing, firing or drying chamber, such as those used for bricks or porcelain, and the oast-houses that can be seen in the Derwent Valley. Hops spread on the floor above a furnace are cured for about 12 hours at around 40°C. Louvres at the top allow moisture to escape.

KINGFISHER

Only three of Australia's 10 species of kingfisher live near water and catch fish. The others behave like KOOKABURRAS which, indeed, two of them are. Even the widespread Sacred Kingfisher *Todiramphus sanctus* (190–230 mm) only eats fish when it is near water. Often they live in woodland and eat small lizards and invertebrates which they capture – like most land kingfishers – by waiting on a perch until they spot prey, and then flying swiftly and directly to it. Their long straight bills, ideal for grasping, and their rounded wings allowing short dashing flights, are well suited to this method of feeding; their forward toes – joined for most of their length – make walking almost impossible.

Some Australian kingfishers nest in tunnels drilled with their beaks in termite mounds, a habit they share with a few of the PARROTS. The mounds may be those of tree- or ground-living termites. Pairing can be temporary or permanent, and the helpless young are fed, bill to mouth, by both parents until fledging.

KOALA

Doubtless the Aborigines have a story to explain the Koala's missing tail. It is unusual for a tree-dwelling animal, but one possible reason is that it is descended from a tail-less ground-living species, for it is more closely related to the almost tail-less WOMBATS than to any other living marsupial. One of the features Koalas share with Wombats is a backwardly-opening pouch, which sounds quite inconvenient for a tree-dweller, however well adapted it may be to a burrowing life. Both lack canine teeth and have a special gastric gland.

Koalas *Phascolarctos cinereus* (male mean length, 782 mm) range along the eastern side of Australia wherever their main eucalypt food trees grow. They get enough water from the leaves, but have various adaptations to cope with their peculiar diet. Part of their intestine, for example, contains bacteria needed to ferment their food. They also have a special mechanism in their liver which renders the oils and other dangerous compounds in eucalypts harmless.

Koalas have strong claws, and hands that can grip branches firmly. They are usually solitary animals. In the breeding season males mark their trees with scents from a chest gland and bellow at each other. During the day they rest in the fork of a tree, and feed at night. Females are sexually mature at about two years. The gestation period is about one month, and pouch life lasts about five or six months; more than one offspring is unusual. Breeding occurs in summer. One of the first 'solid' meals of a young Koala is the soft faeces of its mother: this probably ensures that it gets a supply of the bacteria it will need for coping with gum leaves. After leaving the pouch, the young are carried on their mother's backs for several months.

Before European colonisation Koalas were common, but were hunted enthusiastically by Aborigines and Dingoes. After settlement their numbers increased and they were hunted for their pelts. In 1924 over two million skins were exported from eastern Australia. In 1927 Queensland declared an open season on Koalas and thousands were killed, but money was set aside from royalties for the protection of native fauna.

Koalas are now strictly protected, and have been reintroduced into many areas from which they had disappeared. With nothing to prey on them, populations have not been limited and in some areas they have destroyed the resources they need to live, and fecundity has fallen off. This may be because of the survival of old, no-longer-fertile females, but a virulent disease related to the organism causing trachoma in human beings may be reducing the fertility of some females by attacking their ovaries. Some populations also suffer from a lung disease, caused by a yeast-fungus.

The future of Koalas depends on proper management. Large enough stands of suitable food trees must be available, and surplus amimals should be removed to new sites to prevent overcrowding. It may even be necessary to kill some animals to keep numbers down, but this will not be a popular course of action with many conservationists.

KOOKABURRA

There are two species of kookaburras – which are large KINGFISHERS – in Australia: the familiar Laughing Kookaburra *Dacelo novaequineae* (400–450 mm) of eastern Australia, and the more brightly coloured Blue-winged Kookaburra *D. leachii* (380–400 mm), of north, north-east and north-western Australia, which lives in wetter forests. Their lifestyles are apparently very similar, and where the territories of two overlap, each treats the other as it would a member of its own species. Much more is known about the Laughing Kookaburra than the Blue-winged species.

One-third of mature males and females of Laughing Kookaburras do not reproduce during a season. Instead they behave as 'auxiliaries' or 'aunts' for the mating birds, helping to rear the crop of youngsters.

Each group defends a territory. When this is next to another group, each family perches directly opposite its opponents. Each morning and evening one group will begin its laughing chorus while one or more members fly around, passing in flight in the so-called 'trapeze' manoeuvre. The other family will watch quietly but, the performance over, it will present its version of the display.

When the territorial boundaries are first being fixed in winter and spring, a member of one group will fly into that of the other, only to be immediately chased out. The chaser then

Visitors to zoos often come away with the impression that Koalas spend most of their lives asleep. They are, it fact, nocturnal and are most active just after nightfall. There is no truth in the story that eucalyptus oil in the leaves that they eat intoxicates them.

Ever-watchful Kookaburras often sit on branches over picnic sites, waiting for an opportunity to fly down and snatch a meal, often disregarding humans nearby. Birds occupy the same territory throughout the year.

– applied to one race – are Pichi-Pichi and Wuhl-Wuhl. These wide-ranging, although apparently rare, long-eared carnivores vary in size from region to region. Their bodies are usually about 70–100 mm long and their tails range from 100–140 mm.

John Gould, who first described them, showed Kultarrs in trees, but they are animals that gallop along agilely in open country on all four feet. They shelter in burrows which they may not dig themselves, but rather take over from true mice and trapdoor spiders. They hunt at night, capturing, it is thought, mainly insects.

Kultarrs are rare throughout Australia, although they are widely distributed. Few, if any, are now found on the east coast where they once lived.

becomes an intruder, which is itself expelled. The result is that a family's territory depends on its size and strength.

Within a family there is a pecking order for each sex. The reproduction rate is naturally low compared with that of more conventional, less altruistic birds. However, because of the division of labour, the survival rate of kookaburra young is correspondingly higher. The help of the auxiliaries also makes it possible for the dominant pair to reproduce more than once in a single season. Kookaburras can sometimes live for 20 years or more.

Like all kingfishers, kookaburras nest in holes, either in trees or in termite mounds. They feed mainly on insects and other invertebrates, but also like small snakes and lizards, and meat scraps from friendly people. Like all kingfishers they wait on a perch, keeping their eyes open for prey, and fly down promptly when they see it.

KOWARI

Kowaris are solitary, brush-tailed, flesh-eating marsupial mice *Dasyuroides byrnei* (body 135–180 mm, tail 110–140 mm) which live on the gibber plains of inland Queensland. They eat insects, small vertebrates and carrion. Like many small desert animals they dig burrows, or take over the burrows of other animals, in which they spend the day to keep cool and conserve water. They mark their home-ranges and burrows with faeces and urine, and by rubbing objects with a gland. They threaten other Kowaris by twitching their tails like a cat.

Mating may last up to three hours – as it does with several other marsupial mice. Their pouch

consists of flaps of skin, but the suckling young eventually hang down from the mothers teats. Adult females apparently have two litters in a year. The mice are greyish in colour, apart from the last half of the tail which is a black brush.

Mulgaras *Dasycercus cristicauda* are similar, and also live in inland deserts in burrows, but their tails are crested.

KULTARR

Kultarrs *Antechinomys laniger* are marsupial mice of the inland. Because they have long hindlegs and long tails, and appeared to be capable of jumping like miniature kangaroos, they were once thought to do so – hence their old name – Jerboa Marsupial Mice. Two other names

Kowaris – once called Marsupial Rats – are active, agile night-time hunters. They have no difficulty killing mice and small chickens, but also eat insects and larger dead animals.

KURRAJONG

This was originally an Aboriginal name for various trees and shrubs with tough bark which was used for cords and nets, but it is now used mainly for the shapely small tree *Brachychiton populneus*. The tree is common on drier parts of the Dividing Range, its western slopes and the nearer plains, and it is also found – although rarely – in coastal districts. It has a stout, straightish trunk with greenish bark, topped by a rounded head of dense foliage. Leaves have long points, and flowers are small white-and-brown bells. Boat-shaped fruiting capsules are packed with floury, yellowish seeds.

Kurrajong is considered the best of all native fodder trees, and in times of drought graziers cut its foliage to feed their sheep or cattle, which eat it with relish. Several other *Brachychiton* species are also referred to as kurrajong at times. Across the far north the rather similar Tropical Kurrajong *B. diversifolius* is found. Less closely related is the Flame Kurrajong or Flame Tree *B. acerifolius* of east-coastal rainforests. This tall tree has scarlet flowers which are borne on leafless branches.

L

LABOUR

At the turn of the century, some smallholders still sowed by hand, used reaping hooks to cut their crops, and threshed with greenhide flails. On larger farms, machines that cut and bound the wheat into sheaves did away with some of the drudgery, but the sheaves still had to be placed in stooks to dry, then pitchforked on to drays to be piled before threshing. The steam- or horse-driven thresher arrived with perhaps a dozen men who bagged the grain and restacked the straw for stock feed. The 110-kg bags were stitched up by a sewer, then lugged on to a dray for stacking in the yard. They were manhauled again for carting to the railway yard where lumpers walked up planks with the bags on their shoulders. The McKay harvester that reaped, winnowed and bagged grain while moving came into wide use 20 years after its invention in 1884. It quartered the cost of harvesting.

Many desperately hard tasks were abolished with the invention of machines, including electric shearing machines (1906), wire strainer (1910s), grain and fertiliser drill with a tyne cultivator (1916), and rotary hoes (1920s). The cost of labour, rather than the pain of the work, provoked change.

LACEWING

Lacewings are beautiful insects with veined wings. Most frequently seen are the medium-sized green lacewings, because they are often attracted indoors by lights. They are green to yellow in colour and have green or golden eyes, long antennae and clear, glassy wings. Their eggs are distinctive as they have long stalks, and are laid in groups, often in gardens. They should be preserved because their active green larvae – with their sickle-shaped jaws – are fierce predators of aphids and a number of other plant pests. Brown lacewings are similar, but smaller.

There are also tiny powdery lacewings – a millimetre or two long – which resemble the aphids on which their larvae feed, although they also attack scale insects and mites. There are 400 Australian species in the group to which lacewings belong.

LADYBIRD

Ladybirds are attractive, small to medium sized beetles with oval, convex bodies. There are about 260 species in Australia, and they are often yellow or red with black spots. Some lay their oval eggs in easily-seen clumps, others lay them singly in crevices. The larvae are, for beetle

Long, narrow coastal lagoons stretch away into the distance at the Lakes National Park, on the south-eastern coast of Victoria. The sand dunes of Ninety Mile Beach separate the lagoon from the ocean.

grubs, long-legged. Most ladybirds – as adults and larvae – feed on aphids, scale insects or mites. Some Australian species have been used to control pests. For example, the red and black, 3 mm-long *Rodolia cardinalis* was used successfully against cottony cushion scale in California. Other ladybirds, however, are pests themselves. In winter vast numbers of some species gather together in such great masses that the temperature within the mass is much higher than that of the surrounding air.

LAGOON

Although this name is applied to many kinds of lakes, a lagoon is strictly one that lies close to the shore. Lagoons are formed by the growth of a sand bar across the mouth of a bay, or by the rising of the coast, leaving a basin between two dunes. In the first type, the bar is often breached by rivers or storms, so that the lagoon is opened to the sea again. Its salinity varies, therefore, with the length of its isolation from the sea, and the amount of fresh water entering it. Residents near some coastal lagoons, such as Smiths Lake – one of the Myall Lakes in NSW – cut through the bar from time to time to allow sea water to enter it and improve the fishing. Lake Macquarie, NSW, is said to be the largest sea-board lake in Australia, but it is a coastal lagoon, 104 sq. km in area. It is separated from the sea by long sand bars and dunes, and is connected to it by one channel about 90 m long.

Threshing was a dusty operation*, and these workers would certainly have been glad of a break and a drink. Despite labour-saving machines, farm work was, and still is, physically very demanding.*

Cradle Mountain towers above the icy waters of Lake Dove, which now fills a basin carved by ancient glaciers. Numerous tarns dot the surrounding countryside.

LAKE

Lakes – geologically speaking – are short-lived features of the landscape, as most of them are slowly being filled by silt and other material carried by the rivers which bring their water. A million years from now a beautiful clear lake will be a marsh or a bog, and later firm, dry land. Others, like Lake Eyre, although once filled with comparatively fresh water, are now rarely full, and more often than not are shimmering expanses of salt.

Lakes, or their basins, can be formed in various ways. Lake George, near Canberra, for example, fills (when there is water) a trough, 48 km long and up to 19 km wide, caused by a FAULT. To the west is the 150 m-high scarp of the Cullarin Range – the local section of the GREAT DIVIDING RANGE – which marks the line of the fault. Much of the basin is filled with silt. Often there is not enough water to fill the lake, although it may sometimes be filled for years at a stretch. Nearby Lake Bathurst – where its discoverer reported seeing a BUNYIP – was formed

relatively recently when Mulwaree Creek deposited gravel in the mouth of a tributary, forming a dam which the smaller stream has not yet breached.

Lake Eyre lies in a depression caused by earth movements which lowered the land surface below sea level. It collects much of the water which formerly flowed southwards to the sea.

In mountainous country, where there were once glaciers, lake basins can be formed by the action of the ice. The bottom of a glacier – carrying debris – sometimes grinds the surface of a mountain to form an armchair-shaped depression with a raised rim. This is called a cirque, cwm or corrie in France, Wales and Scotland – all countries which once had greater ice sheets than Australia. After the disappearance of the ice a cirque fills with water to form a lake called a tarn. There are several such lakes on the Koskiusko Plateau and in Tasmania.

A glacier moving down a valley carries rock debris with it. If the glaciers begins to retreat it drops this rock at its face, where the ice melts.

The resulting mass of debris is called a moraine, and is often massive enough to dam any streams flowing towards it. There are moraines damming Blue Lake and Hedley Tarn on the Kosciusko Plateau, which are at least partly responsible for their existence.

Australia's deepest lake, St Clair in Tasmania (200 m), was formed when a glaciated valley was blocked by a moraine, as was the original Lake Pedder, which existed before dams were constructed which flooded it.

Some lakes form in the craters of extinct volcanoes. The most famous Australian example is the aptly named Blue Lake at Mount Gambier in South Australia.

Oxbow lakes, also known as BILLABONGS, are the shortest-lived lakes of all. They are formed when a loop of a river separates from the main stream as it meanders over a plain usually a floodplain.

Many so-called lakes, such as Lake Macquarie and Lake Illawarra in NSW, are strictly speaking coastal LAGOONS.

Salt lakes, like Lake Eyre, rarely contain enough water to sustain much life. However, a few, such as Lake Corangamite in Victoria, are permanent. Most are only a metre or two deep. Salinity levels vary greatly from lake to lake, and from time to time within a lake. Shallow, small lakes are the most variabale. A saline lake exists where the salinity is greater than three parts per thousand of salt. The open ocean contains 34–36 parts per thousand, and the salinity of salt-saturated water, at an average daytime temperature, is about 350 parts per thousand. In Lake Eyre the question is usually how much water there is in the salt.

The temperature in shallow lakes also varies a lot. It may change by as much as 20° in 24 hours, and 30° in a year. High salinity, and drastic short-term changes in temperature make salt lakes difficult places for plants and animals to live. Organisms must either use a lot of energy to keep their internal fluids constant, or have cells which can tolerate wide salinity ranges. Both strategies are used.

The greater the salinity, the smaller the number of species. In water containing over 200 parts per thousand of salt, the only animal likely to survive is the Fairy Shrimp *Parartemia zietziana*. When the salinity is between 50 and 200 parts per thousand, tiny crustaceans such as some copepods and shell-shrimps, as well as the larvae of some biting midges, can survive in the plankton. Saltwater mosquito larvae *Aedes australis* survives at 125 parts per thousand and the 'freshwater' snail *Coxiella striata* can withstand 112 parts per thousand. Unique to Australia is a creature which belongs to the normally land-living woodlouse group, which lives in salinities from 30 to 159 parts per thousand. One fish, the Central Australian Hardyhead *Craterocephalus eyresii* can live comfortably in lakes with salinities up to 110 parts per thousand. When Lake Eyre dried out in 1975, millions were stranded. The fish began to die when the level of salt rose to 280 parts per thousand.

There are no large underwater plants in very saline lakes, although phytoplankton are found in some where the salinity is over 100 parts per thousand. Salt-loving flowering plants such as fleshy glassworts or samphires and Sea Blight *Suaeda australis*, often grow along the shores of salt lakes.

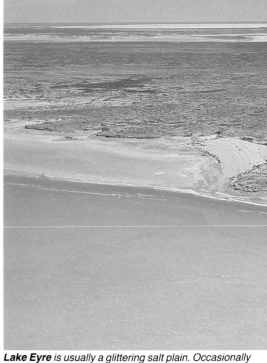

Lake Eyre is usually a glittering salt plain. Occasionally heavy rains in Queensland will supply enough water to fill it, and then life returns in abundance.

Natural freshwater lakes are generally rich in life, although the ecology varies with the lake's shape, volume, geographic position and the amount of food it contains. In summer most Australian lakes are divided into layers – on top there is a layer of warm water, with a colder layer at the bottom, which is low in oxygen. The two are separated by a zone where the temperature changes rapidly with depth. Most life in a lake takes place in the upper layer, where there is enough warmth and light for photosynthesis by microscopic plants – the phytoplankton. Among the plankton lives a variety of animals, many of them tiny crustacea such as copepods and water-fleas, as well as other creatures such as rotifers. Any given lake will contain only a few species at a time. These feed on the phytoplankton, and are in turn food of insect larvae, fish and other animals. Among the animals that live on the bottom of a lake are flatworms, roundworms, true worms related to earthworms, tubifex worms, mayfly and dragonfly nymphs, gnat larvae – including bloodworms which are bright red because they contain a respiratory pigment which helps them to get enough oxygen to survive.

Man-made lakes are created by damming rivers or flooding valleys. The largest artificial lakes are used to supply industrial and domestic water to towns and cities, or for the generation of electricity. Other uses are for the supply of irrigation water for crops, the watering of stock or flood control.

The biology of artificial lakes differs from that of the natural variety for many reasons, but the main difference is that artifical lakes lack the variety of life found in long established bodies of water. Man-made lakes, most of which were created this century, have not had time to become colonised by many of the plants and animals of a region that could live in them.

Large man-made lakes often have a small surface area in relation to their depth – to minimise losses by evaporation – whereas most natural Australian lakes are shallow. Temperature changes therefore lag well behind those of the seasons. Water, when released, tends to cool streams below the lakes, and this has a drastic effect on native fish.

Water levels often vary considerably. In hydroelectric dams, for example, there are changes through the day in sympathy with power demands, and in irrigation areas there are seasonal fluctuations. Consequently few plants can grow at the water's edge because they are alternately flooded or left to dry out.

Some lakes have been stocked with introduced salmon, trout and carp. However, the dams which support the lakes into being provide a barrier to migrating species, unless fish ladders are provided.

Natural freshwater lakes are usually rich in life, provided they have been established long enough. The lake on Moreton Island, Queensland, (left) is in a basin of sand which is sealed by minerals and decaying plants. The Myall Lakes, NSW, (above) are very shallow and covered with vast weed beds.

Man-made lakes *are difficult places for plants and animals to live. Lake Menindee, NSW, (below) was flooded to provide a reservoir for Broken Hill. Blowering Dam, NSW, (above) is part of the Snowy Mountains Scheme. The bare ground at the water's edge is a result of constant changes in the dam's level.*

LAND RIGHTS

When the British established their first colony in Australia 200 years ago, the traditional rights of Aborigines to own and manage their land ceased to be recognised by the new legal system. In 1976, land rights were introduced, now giving Aboriginal people 35 per cent of the Northern Territory. But the issue of land rights is still hotly debated, and other Australian states have yet to go all the way in recognising Aboriginal claims to land, especially when there is a conflict with economic development.

There is a fundamental difference between European concepts of land as an economic resource – to be owned and exploited by individuals – and the spiritual and social relationships which Aborigines share with the land. Galarrwuy Yunupingu, a prominent Aborigine from the Northern Territory said: 'The land is my backbone . . . I think of the land as the history of my nation.' For Aboriginal people, land is not just a piece of real estate that can be bought and sold. Nor is the land just a vast supermarket for gathering food. The land is the basis for ordering their social landscape.

The formation of hills, rivers and gorges are explained as the work of spirit beings who created the land in the course of their adventures. Particular places are related to particular spirit ancestors who have ordained what ritual ceremonies can be held in what places by which people. The social and religious responsibilities of every Aboriginal person is reflected in, and explained by, ties to land. This does not mean that the landscape cannot be altered at all, but that there are constraints on how and where this can be done. Thus traditional Aboriginal landowners have encouraged mining in some areas and diverted or constrained development in others. Further problems are created by the existence of sacred sites, the location of which cannot be revealed by Aboriginal law.

Aborigines generally believe in consultation, but may disagree amongst themselves as to how particular tracts of land are to be managed. Similarly non-Aboriginal Australians are far from agreement on questions of land rights. Conservationists sometimes side with Aborigines when it is in their interests to protect land as a natural heritage area. Mining companies can also find themselves allied with Aborigines who have agreed to their development proposals.

Land rights are seen by most Aborigines as a first step in maintaining and reviving their culture, as well as improving their social and economic conditions. All Australians have much to learn about Aboriginal land management, which has had a dramatic effect on Australia's vegetation during the last 40 000 years. The impact of the new Aboriginal landowners, now recognised by Australian law, has yet to be assessed. But it is likely that the form of land rights will change as national debate over the matter continues.

LAND TENURE

Only about one-seventh of Australia's land is privately owned. Most of the freehold land is in the longest-settled parts of NSW, Tasmania and Victoria. Nearly two-thirds of Victoria, one-third of NSW, and over a third of Tasmania, are privately held, also about one-fifth of Queensland, one-thirteenth of both South Australia and Western Australia, very little in the Northern Territory, and none in the ACT.

About 55 per cent of Australia is occupied under leases or licences from the Crown, administered by the various governments. The rest of Australia's crown lands consist of reserves such as parks, forests and Aboriginal lands, and land that cannot be used commercially, mostly in arid areas.

The laws on land tenure bewilder even the experts. Even freehold land had its complications. For instance, a state government can still take it back (with suitable compensation) for a national park or afforestation, or to allow a city to spread. And there are restrictions on the use of any land – for example, soil conservation authorities can ban clearing of trees on slopes over a certain gradient. Also, governments can have some say when the land is sold, restricting its sale to anyone who already has considerable landholdings. Generally, too, freehold title does not extend to minerals.

Leases and licences from the Crown vary in each state and territory. Types include grazing or pastoral, conditional or unconditional purchase, and perpetual. The principle behind leasehold tenure is to make each property large enough to provide a reasonable living for one person and family, with a reserve for bad seasons. Also, the lease should be for long enough to encourage the lessee to improve the land, The improvements (such as a house) are always the lessee's property; only the land itself belongs to the Crown. The lessee usually has priority when the lease expires, to renew it. State governments usually have to consent to the lease being transferred to someone else.

Governments can stipulate that lessees should put up and maintain fences, or clear some of the land within a certain time. In some areas, leased land is inspected regularly but only very rarely indeed is a lease forfeited because of gross over- or under-stocking.

Rents under perpetual leases are generally low. In Queensland, they are three per cent of the amount bid for the lease at auction. For properties held over a long time, the rent is often nominal.

LAND USE

Australia is a large continent with vast areas of unused land. But much of the country is also impoverished, with poor soils and often constant drought. Thus the effective use of much land is limited. Only a small proportion can be used for crop-farming and – if fertile enough – it is usually because of transport costs that the land near cities and ports is favoured. This, of course, is also the land which is most in demand for urban and industrial development.

Land which is too poor for crops or intensive livestock production may often be used for ranchlike grazing. Much of the semi-arid country found in inland Australia can be used commercially only in this way.

Another use of land that is too poor, or too hilly for crop farming is afforestation, often with exotic softwoods such as Radiata Pine *Pinus radiata*, introduced from the USA.

Finally, of course, land may be used for quarrying or mining. The area directly concerned is often small, but the necessary buildings, processing plants and roads may take up large areas of additional land.

Unfortunately the agricultural, grazing, forestry, urban and industrial uses – or proposed uses – of land often compete with conservation of native plants and animals, scenic beauty, and sites which are important scientifically or historically, or sacred to the Aborigines. These interests also compete with each other. In planning for land use, therefore, all the competing claims have to be considered.

A land-planning scheme may be worked out for a particular region of 10 000 sq. km, but it will rarely be independent, ecologically and economically, of other parts of the continent. An area may be set aside, for example, as a national park for the conservation of certain animals, but if they are migratory or nomadic species they may be completely dependent at certain times on habitats outside the region. Waterfowl in the interior of the country, for example, need coastal wetlands in times of drought.

A conservation area must also be large enough for its purpose. It is pointless trying to conserve Red Kangaroos *Macropus rufus* on 4600 ha, although such an area might be large enough to preserve the population of a Noisy Scrub-bird *Atrichornis clamosus* near Albany, WA. In addition there should be enough large conservation areas scattered throughout the country to preserve examples of all surviving major plant and animal communities.

Since the 1950s, various techniques have been used for planning the use of land in a region. In the simplest version, maps are prepared of the region showing characteristics such as topography, geology and soil types. The areas on one map are graded for their suitability for farming. Another map is used to grade suitability for

The impact of human activity on the surface of the land is clearest when seen from the air. There is very little land around the South Australian settlement of Strathalbyn that is not being put to some use.

forestry, and others for urban development, conservation, road construction and so on. When the maps are completed they are superimposed and the composite map used as the basis for planning future activities.

There is, of course, more to it than that. The planners will have certain objectives in mind before they begin, such as the housing of a certain number of people, and the provision of the necessary services such as roads, shops and schools. At the same time they will try to preserve as much of the beauty of the area, and

its wildlife, as possible. For ecological and aesthetic reasons they will also try to make the region as diverse as possible. Patches of woodland and scrub, for example, could be retained in urban areas for shelter, beauty, as refuges for at least some wildlife, or as corridors for their movements. In many parts of Australia, however, such areas would have to be well managed to reduce the risks from bushfires.

Land can have multiple uses. Although suburbia is often criticised by conservationists, studies in Britain have shown that surburban gardens often support a wider variety of animals than does some of the open country. This probably does not apply fully in Australia, where most gardens are filled with exotic plants that are not attractive to many native species, although planting more native plants would remedy this. But it is improbable that a suburb will become more productive than the farm that it may have replaced, even though some gardeners do grow fruit and a few vegetables.

Farming and conservation have different goals, apart from the preservation of the soil, but the two are not always incompatible. Roland Breckwoldt in his book *Wildlife in the Home Paddock*, for example, has given an account of methods of farming and conserving wildlife at the same time by tree-planting and preservation, and by the establishment of wildlife corridors. He also discusses the management of farm dams so that they encourage waterfowl and fish.

The use of land for both forestry and recreation is common, but forestry and wildlife conservation are often in conflict, even when native species are grown, and even before they are harvested. The ideal forest for a forester consists of stands of even-aged healthy trees, but many species of mammals and birds depend upon old trees, full of holes and fallen logs, to provide cover and nesting sites.

A relatively recent development is the requirement for an environmental impact study to be carried out before any important development is started. The idea is praiseworthy, but the practice is often of little value – as Harry Recher, an ecologist at the Australian Museum points out – because the developer, whose duty it is to provide the report, has to consider only the consequences of the development and not the consequences of alternative uses of the land. Until recently, anyone objecting to the development could not easily do so by taking the matter to court; lobbying government officials or staging demonstrations were the only recourses. In 1979, however, NSW set up the Land and Environment Court to consider all sides of cases brought before it by interested parties.

At present rural establishments – farms, stations and so on – take up about 65 per cent of Australia. About 3.4 per cent of this area is used for crops. National parks and reserves occupy about 4.5 per cent of the country which, while large in terms of hectares, is still below the 5 per cent recommended for all countries by the United Nations. Interestingly, however, Tasmania – much maligned in environmental circles – has devoted 14 per cent of the island to parks and reserves, coming behind only the ACT with its 46.6 per cent.

The rest is urban land, mining leases, unoccupied land which is mainly arid, some land held under grazing licences but not being used for stock, and some fallow land.

Dividing up the face of Australia

GRAZED LAND

Livestock – mainly cattle and sheep – graze over a large part of Australia, although the number of animals per hectare can vary enormously between the lush coast and the arid interior. In 1985 there were 2.82 million dairy cattle, 19.92 million meat cattle, 149.2 million sheep and 2.46 million pigs in Australia. The greatest density of animals was to be found in the south-west and south-east of the mainland, along the east coast, and in the north and east of Tasmania.

CROP LAND

During 1984–85 cash crops were grown on an area of almost 20 million hectares. Wheat was by far the most important crop with about 12 million hectares followed by barley (3.5 million ha), oats (1.06 million ha) and grain sorghum (710 000 ha). Western Australia had the most land under crops (6.72 million ha). The average yield per hectare for wheat growing in Australia was 1.3 tonnes/ha compared with 1.57 t/ha in the USSR, 2.7t/ha in the USA and 4.5 t/ha in the EEC

NATURE CONSERVATION AREAS

National parks and other nature conservation reserves took up 345 304 sq. km (about 4.5 per cent of the continent) at the end of 1986. Western Australia had set aside the largest area – some 146 500 sq. km (5.8 per cent of the state), while the ACT had set aside the largest proportion – 46.6 per cent (1118 sq. km). The largest park in Australia is Kakadu in the Northern Territory, which covers approximately 1.7 million hectares in the Alligator Rivers region.

UNUSED LAND

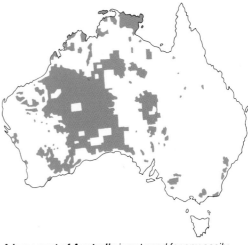

A large part of Australia is not used for any easily identifiable purposes – this catagory includes vacant crown land, commercially unused Aboriginal land and military reserves. Much of this land is taken up by deserts, such as the Simpson, Gibson and Great Victoria, and is really those areas that cannot support agriculture. In all around 36.7 per cent of Australia's 768 284 000 ha was not used for any agricultural purpose in 1984–85 – a rise on 1979–80 (35.5 per cent).

LANDSLIDE

Landslides are catastrophic slides of rock or soil down a hillslope. They can be large and destructive involving millions of tonnes of rock or small slumps in a road cutting. The causes of landslides are usually complex, but they all have one thing in common – they are driven by the force of gravity. Studies around Wollongong, NSW, have shown that occurrences of landslides are related to the steepness of the hillside, local rainfall, the strength of underlying rocks and, to a minor extent, mining activity.

In Australia landslides do not pose the threat that they do in the more mountainous and highly populated countries, but there are some problem areas. Overgrazing in the Mt Lofty Ranges near Adelaide, for example, has meant that landslides there are common. Slips caused by waves undercutting coastal cliffs occur often around the southern coast of Australia. At Port Noorlunga, near Adelaide, it has been necessary to place large quantities of soil and rock in front of eroding clay cliffs.

LANTANA

The rampant shrub *Lantana camara* was originally a native of central and South America, but it has now spread around the world in subtropical areas and has become a weed. In most places it was originally brought in as an ornamental plant, and it is still frequently seen as a neatly trimmed garden shrub.

The plants form dense masses of arching, prickly stems which can spread over high-rainfall country, especially on more fertile soils. Lantana covers valuable grazing country in coastal NSW and Queensland, and some types are poisonous to cattle. Lantana also invades native forest and smothers tree seedlings. The plant will not, however, tolerate drought or more than a very light frost. Nor does it thrive well in the tropical lowlands. Biological control by insects or fungi is being investigated by the CSIRO and state agriculture authorities.

LARVA

The description applied to an insect from the times it leaves the egg until it is transformed into a pupa, the inactive pre-adult form. The caterpillars of moths and butterflies are the most familiar larvae. Sawfly larvae resemble caterpillars, but can easily be told apart because they six or more pairs of legs, whereas caterpillars have five pairs or less. Most other types of insects, for instance beetles and lacewings, have six-legged larvae.

Those insects which provide a store of food for their young or feed them as they grow, such as bees and wasps, have legless, headless, maggot-type larvae. This is also the case among flies whose larvae live surrounded by food in the form of a decaying corpse or plant.

Nearly 60 years have passed since thousands of tonnes of rock crashed down from the cliff at Cyclorama Point, Katoomba, NSW, but the scars are still visible. Warning of the impending landslide was given long before the event, when cracks appeared in the clifftop. People and press gathered to witness the spectacular fall, but were disappointed. The event took place, unseen, one night in June 1931.

Some insects do not have a pupal stage. In these, the egg hatches as a young insect which grows and changes its skin several times until it becomes a winged adult. Unlike true larvae, they develop wing buds. Young stages of such 'no-pupa' insects are called NYMPHS.

LASSETER

Harold Lasseter was born in 1880. He claimed that at the age of 17, while prospecting for rubies west of Alice Springs, he discovered a fabulously rich, gold-bearing reef. He became lost, but was rescued by an Afghan cameleer. Three years later he relocated his reef, but because of faulty watches, its position was was not properly fixed.

It was not until 1930 that Lasseter was able to

Harold Lasseter's death, reported in the Sydney Mirror on 29 April 1931, ended one chapter of the saga and opened a new one. His story of a fabulously rich gold reef fired the imagination of many would-be treasure-seekers. However, argument still surrounds Lasseter's original claims, and even the veracity of the final diary. Some geologists doubt the possibility of, gold-bearing reefs in the Petermann-Rawlinson area.

get backing for a large-scale expedition to search for the reef again. Using Lasseter as guide, the expedition was unsuccessful, and the leader turned back, believing the reef to be a fiction.

Lasseter, however, continued with Paul Johns, a young cameleer, trying desperately to rediscover his old bearings. After six weeks Johns returned for fresh camels and Lasseter was never seen alive again. In 1931 his body and a diary were found east of the Petermann Ranges. The diary records that Lasseter found the reef, that his camels bolted and that he sheltered in a cave in the summer heat waiting in vain for rescue.

Within months of the discovery of the diary Ion Idriess published *Lasseter's Last Ride*, a fictionalised account of Lasseter's quest which became a best-seller and began a legend.

Many attempts have since been made to discover the missing reef, particularly in the 1930s, after the publication of Idriess' book. No trace of it has been found, although the explorer Michael Terry did find a tree blazed by Lasseter at Lake Christopher in 1932, from which he took bearings on the reef.

LEAF INSECT
Leaf insects are a small group within the STICK INSECTS. They are found in New Guinea and south-east Asia, with one species, *Phyllium*, living in the rainforests of north Queensland. Females are said to be uncommon, and males even rarer. Their bodies are flattened from the top to the bottom, and their abdomens and legs have outgrowths so that the general shape is leaf-like. When they change their position they move very slowly. Some species are about 80 mm long. The female of the 130-mm-long Spiny Stick Insect *Extatosoma tiaratum* has leafy outgrowths on its legs and abdomen, although the much smaller, fully-winged male is a typical 'ordinary' stick insect. Some butterflies and moths also mimic leaves when at rest.

LEECH
Leeches are related to earthworms and bristleworms. They can be distinguished from all other worm-like creatures by their two suckers – one at the front and one at the back. There are more than 500 species, some living in the sea, some on land and many in freshwater. Most, although not all, are parasitic blood suckers. The others are predators. Leech bodies, with their 34 segments, are flattened, and usually pointed at the front end which carries a sucker that surrounds the creature's mouth. Some species have a proboscis which is pushed out, and into the victim's tissues. Others have horny teeth within their mouths with which they slice through the host's skins, while remaining firmly attached with the sucker. While sucking blood, many leeches inject an anticoagulant to keep the blood flowing freely. Leeches can move over surfaces with the aid

of their suckers – looping along like some types of caterpillars.

There are about 13 freshwater species in Australia in three families. Hirudinids have large toothed mouths, long thin bodies, red blood, and five pairs of eyes. The commonest is *Limnobdella australis*, a yellow species with longitudinal dark stripes, several centimetres long, found in all states. Glossiphoniids, are shorter, and have a proboscis and colourless blood. *Semilagenta hilli* is a pale green, blind, endemic species. Leeches in this family carry their eggs and young for a time. The leeches of the third family are rare. Australian land leeches belong to the two-jawed leeches, and are found in rainforests east of the Great Dividing Range, along

The black and yellow leech Limnodbella australis *is the commonest species in Australia. The largest Australian leeches are found in the far north of NSW, and can reach a length of 145 mm at rest: 216 mm when fully extended.*

the Northern Territory coast and in Tasmania. They are 20 to 85 mm long, and usually carry longitudinal stripes of gold, yellow or green. They can withstand drought in a dried up condition, and can fast for about a year. They feed on any vertebrate they can reach.

Doctors used to be called leeches because they used medicinal leeches for blood letting – a treatment being explored by modern medicine. Leeches, bred aseptically, are still used to treat, for example, bruising, and there is interest in the commercial breeding of some suitable Australian species for this purpose.

LEGLESS LIZARD
Snake lizards belong to a family restricted to Australia and New Guinea, where there are only two known species. They are completely legless apart from – in the scaly-foot lizards – flaps where the hind legs should be. The differences between them and snakes are explained in the LIZARD entry.

All legless lizards are secretive, living on the ground under cover, and often burrowing. They

eat insects and sometimes other lizards. The largest is the Common Scaly Foot *Pygopus lepidopus*, a variably coloured species which, with a complete tail, can be 750 mm long. They are found in the southern half of Australia. Burton's Legless Lizard *Lialis burtonis*, found throughout Australia in many kinds of habitats, is one of the commonest species. It is variably coloured, and up to 600 mm long, but is most easily recognised by its long, pointed snout. It lives largely on small lizards.

LEPTOSPIROSIS
Leptospirosis is a disease that effects many kinds of animals, including dogs, pigs, cattle and rats. Human beings can sometimes acquire it when urine from animals, containing the bacteria *Leptospira*, contaminates skin with cuts or abrasions. Cases can be mild, but often effects are severe – including jaundice, nephritis and internal bleeding – and may even be fatal. It is, of course, commonest among people who work with animals, but cases are known from various Sydney suburbs. Dogs are probably the carriers on these occasions.

LICE
Lice are hard-bodied, wingless insects. They are external parasites, and die when separated from their host for more than a short time.

There are about 250 species in Australia, although many were introduced on livestock and people. There are two main groups – biting lice with chewing mouthparts, which live on birds and mammals; and sucking lice with piercing mouthparts, which suck blood from mammals. Three types of sucking lice can live on people: the 3-mm-long Head Louse *Pediculus capitita* which glues its eggs or nits on hairs, and which can infest even scrupulously clean people; the slightly larger Body Louse *P. humanus* which lays its eggs on clothes, and the 3-mm-long Crab Louse *Pthirus pubis*, found where hairs are widely separated.

The Body Louse follows wars and catastrophes and spreads typhus and haemorrhagic fever. However, centuries ago lousiness was equated with saintliness. When Thomas a Beckett was murdered in Canterbury Cathedral, the grief of his monks was lightened by the hordes of the so-called 'pearls of wisdom' which poured from his cooling corpse. Head lice can only live on a human head. Flattened bodies and strong, clawed legs enable them to hold on. The nits are greyish white and are just visible to the unaided eye.

Livestock lose condition when badly infested with lice. Pigs carry some of the largest – which can grow to about 5 mm in length – and occasionally brushes made from hog hairs carry 'super-nits'. Birds – and especially feral pigeons – are often badly infested with feather lice.

LICHEN

These small moss-like plants are common on trees and rocks. A lichen consists of a tough, leathery fungus with single-celled algae growing inside its tissues. These two components live together in a state of symbiosis – each depending on the other. The fungus needs the algae's capacity to use sunlight to create organic compounds, and the algae needs the shelter and moisture supplied by the fungus, as well as nutrients it absorbs from it. Although each lichen species consists mainly of a fungus, it is very different from its fungal relatives. Apart from having a different form, lichens are much slower-growing and longer-lived than most fungi, and they can thrive in a dry atmosphere and at low temperatures. During dry periods they become dormant and are able to start growing again when water becomes available in the form of rain or mist.

Lichens can be divided into three easily recognised types. The most common and widespread are the crustose lichens which form hard, crust-like patches on a great variety of surfaces. Their colour varies from greenish-white to dark-grey to yellow, orange or red. They often form circles which increase in diameter at a very slow and steady rate. The size of crustose lichens has been used to estimate the age of surfaces, such as those of brick or stone buildings, because of their predictable growth rate. The two other types of lichens project well above the surfaces they grow on; these are the folios (leafy) and fruticose (branched) lichens. The first has flattened, spreading lobes and the second thread-like branches. Both of these thrive in places where there is high humidity, such as misty mountains, rainforests and oceanic islands. The granite outcrops of the Snowy Mountains are often covered by a rich and varied growth of large foliose lichens, and in mountain forests the dead branches of trees are festooned with masses of a pale-green fruticose lichen.

Lichens are of great importance for their pioneer role in helping plants to gain a foothold on newly exposed rock. Once established they secrete acids which speed the breakdown of rock to soil, and in addition they trap wind-borne or falling dust and organic material, eventually providing a place for mosses and other green plants to grow. Lichens are found almost anywhere, except in places where there is no stable surface, such as on sand-dunes or in creek- and river-channels.

LIGNOTUBER

Some eucalypts seem to grow very slowly at first, but this is because resources are being invested underground in a lignotuber – the plant's insurance in case of a bushfire.

A lignotuber is a large mass of woody tissue which is found where a plant's root and stem join – at or near the surface of the soil. Many eucalypts have a lignotuber, as do a wide range of other plants, such as banksias.

In the event of a bushfire – which may kill all parts of the plant above ground – new buds appear from the lignotuber, which is also a reservoir of food for growing shoots.

Lignotubers can reach an enormous size, and examples have been found which cover an area of 75 sq. m.

Four common lichens

Fruticose, or shrubby lichen growing on the trunk of a tree in forests above Blowering Dam, NSW. This type of lichen takes many forms, depending on where it grows.

Foliose, or leafy lichen growing on rocks high in the Snowy Mountains. Black species, which can absorb heat more readily, are common on rocks above the snow line.

Concentric circles formed by a slow-growing crustose lichen. Their steady growth rates have been used to estimate the ages of structures they are attached to.

A colourful group of crustose lichens growing on rocks near Sydney. Several common types, which can be seen in many parts of Australia, are represented here.

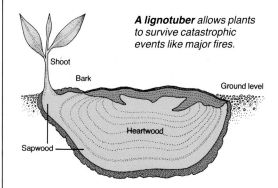

A lignotuber allows plants to survive catastrophic events like major fires.

Shoot
Bark
Ground level
Heartwood
Sapwood

LILY

Many plants have been called lilies, but the word is most commonly used for those in the family Liliaceae. These have grass-like or sword-like leaves and flowers with their parts in threes or sixes, symmetrically arranged. Members of the northern hemisphere genus *Lilium*, grown as garden plants and for cut-flowers, are typical 'lilies'. In Australia a number of widespread small herbaceous plants are called lilies, such as Vanilla Lily *Arthropodium*, Flax Lily *Dianella*, Blue Lily *Stypandra* and Fringe Lily *Thysanotus*, all in the Liliaceae. Less closely related are the strangely coloured and textured Tinsel Lily *Calectasia* of Western Australia and western Victoria, and plants such as the Garland Lily *Calostemma* and Darling Lily *Crinum*, both common in the inland. The largest of all Australian 'lilies' are both found only on the east coast. The Gymea Lily *Doryanthes excelsa* is

Vast caverns are common in the limestone that makes up the Nullarbor Plain. Water trickling slowly down through joints in the rock excavates underground caves.

now confined to the Sydney district, and can send up a flower-stalk to five metres high, with large clustered flowers at the top. The Gigantic Lily *D. palmeri* is found further north. The best known places for seeing it are on Mt Warning in NSW and on the slopes of the Glass House Mountains in Queensland.

LIMESTONE

Limestone is a rock composed mainly of calcium carbonate (calcite), which is a mineral found in seawater and the shells of sea animals. Most limestone deposits accumulated on the bottom of oceans. Very large deposits occur in many areas throughout Australia. There are several different types of limestone, but the most common variety is formed by the accumulation of shells, animal skeletons and corals over thousands of years. Some limestones are composed almost entirely of shells, others of corals, others of large shells and skeletons of animals.

Limestone is being formed today around the coast of Australia. The best example is on the Great Barrier Reef – an enormous structure, comparable in area to a mountain range, composed of limestone with a thin skin of active reef-building corals. The limestone is formed when the corals die and the remains are compressed into rock. In some parts of Australia there are perfectly preserved ancient coral limestone reefs. In Windjana Gorge, near Derby, WA, for example, there is a 400-million-year-old reef.

Other varieties of limestone are formed from calcite, which separates out as a solid from seawater. The crystals of calcite sink to the bottom and are cemented together into rock.

Limestone areas have their own characteristic landscapes, like the Nullabor Plain which is possibly the largest continuous plain of limestone in the world. Below the surface there are many spectacular caves caused by water dissolving the rock. Limestone is used as building stone, for cement, as a flux in steel furnaces and as agricultural lime.

LIMPET

Limpets are marine molluscs, often seen clinging with their muscular foot to rocks and other hard objects. In one experiment a pull of 32 kg was needed to dislodge one which had an attachment area of only 8 sq. cm. Despite their apparent immobility, limpets move around when the tide is in, using their rasp-like radula or 'tongue' to scrape away seaweeds. However, they find their way back to their spot as the tide goes out, recognising it by the crevices into which their shells fit. Some may move as much as one metre from 'home' while feeding.

There are several kinds of limpets on Australian seashores. The largest and commonest 'true' limpet in the south-east is *Cellana tramoserica* (to 50 mm diameter) which is easily recognised by alternating dark and light radiating bands on its shell.

LITCHI

The litchi, or lychee, is a round, red fruit native to southern China where it has been grown for more the 2000 years. Asians consider its sweet, white flesh a delicacy and baskets of the fruit are often given on special occasions, like the Chinese New Year. The first litchis were planted in Australia by Chinese labourers who travelled to north Queensland in the late nineteenth century in search of work. In the early 1980s, a few farmers established commercial litchi plantations, and fruit from northern NSW and Queensland is now sent all over the world. Fresh litchis can be bought in shops from November to February, and the canned fruit is available all year round. Litchi growers pay particular attention to the fruit after harvest to prevent 'browning' and other discolourations which can reduce the crop's appeal and value.

The bright red outer case of a litchi breaks open to reveal soft, white flesh inside.

LIZARD

Lizards, snakes and worm lizards (not found in Australia) are all related. However, lizards differ from snakes in usually having legs, although there are several legless kinds. In addition, however, most lizards have external ear openings, movable eyelids, unforked tongues, and a tail which is longer than the rest of its body. Many lizards can also shed their tails as part of a defence mechanism. When a predator grabs the tail it breaks off, and the predator is distracted by the still-wriggling remnant while the important parts of the lizard escape.

Most lizards eat small animals or insects, although some also eat plants. There are about 420 Australian species, ranging in size from about 70 mm to 2.5 m. Many more species probably await discovery. They are divided into five families – GECKOES, snake lizards, GOANNAS, dragons and skinks.

Most lizards lay eggs, but some produce living young, and some even have a placenta. Like snakes, lizards periodically shed their old skins.

Snakes have deeply forked tongues. The only Australian lizards with similar tongues are goannas, but they have well developed limbs.

A most important difference between snakes and lizards is found in the jaws. In snakes, but not in lizards, the jaws are only loosely connected so that the snake can swallow prey wider than itself. No Australian lizard is venomous, but many snakes are.

LOCUST

Locusts are a group of short-horned GRASS-HOPPERS which migrate and sometimes form swarms. Populations pass through phases which are controlled by the amount of crowding. When the population is low they behave like ordinary solitary grasshoppers, and are often green like the vegetation. As numbers increase, or the breeding area gets smaller as vegetation dries off, the insects change their form, colour and behaviour. Developing nymphs begin to migrate as hoppers, and later take to flight. The crowding apparently synchronises the development of the individuals. A swarm may land in a suitable area, lay large numbers of eggs in the soil, and begin the cycle again.

It has been estimated that the insects may lay as many as 100 000 eggs to each square metre of soil – about one hundred thousand million in a square kilometre. The 40-mm-long Australian Plague Locust *Chortoicetes terminifera* is probably the worst local species. In their solitary phase the insects are generally green, while in plagues they are brown. Hindwings are tipped with black, and hind legs are partly scarlet. A swarm of locusts, which may contain millions of individuals, can do immense damage. In the summer of 1933–34 over 13 million hectares of central NSW were severely affected by a vast swarm of Plague Locusts.

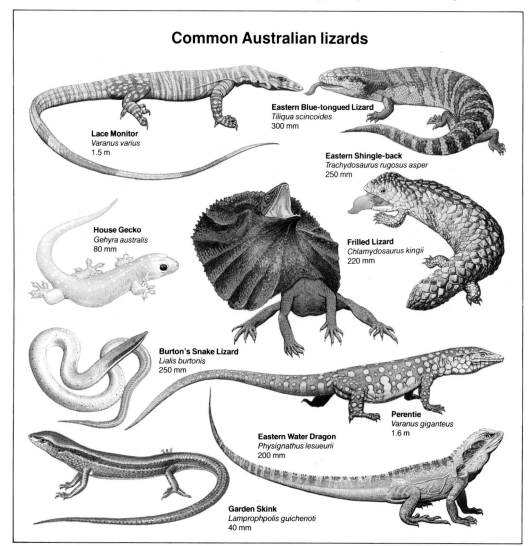

Common Australian lizards

Lace Monitor
Varanus varius
1.5 m

Eastern Blue-tongued Lizard
Tiliqua scincoides
300 mm

Eastern Shingle-back
Trachydosaurus rugosus asper
250 mm

House Gecko
Gehyra australis
80 mm

Frilled Lizard
Chlamydosaurus kingii
220 mm

Burton's Snake Lizard
Lialis burtonis
250 mm

Perentie
Varanus giganteus
1.6 m

Eastern Water Dragon
Physignathus lesueurii
200 mm

Garden Skink
Lampropholis guichenoti
40 mm

A female plague locust Chortoicetes terminifera *laying her eggs. Up to 40 eggs are deposited on each of several occasions during the insect's life.*

LONG PADDOCK

Graziers, especially those in western Queensland, NSW, Western Australia and the Northern Territory, have been using grass that grows wild beside the road for decades. It is one of the cheapest sources of stock feed. In bush parlance, it is known as the long paddock – for obvious reasons – and has helped many landholders to survive a drought.

In most districts, graziers have to obtain permission from the local shire council or pastures protection board, and often have to pay a small fee for use of the long paddock. Sometimes the paddock is used by drovers moving stock over long distances to another property, where feed is available. Grids, made of round iron bars across the road, help prevent stock spreading too far along the road.

LUCERNE

Lucerne, also known as alfalfa, is a lush, leafy summer legume grown mainly in temperate and subtropical areas of Australia. It is also grown under irrigation in Western Australia's north-west and in the Northern Territory. Legumes are high protein plants which fix nitrogen in the soil.

Lucerne is grown in mixed pastures for grazing by sheep and beef and dairy cattle. It is also grown for seed and hay production. Prime lucerne hay is sought after for hand-feeding stud and dairy stock, and also for the horses. Specialist lucerne farmers produce most of the hay grown in Australia.

Before lucerne aphids were introduced in the 1970s, the industry was based only on a few varieties and was mostly unirrigated. Now over 30 varieties are grown for seed production alone, and around 60 000 ha are irrigated.

Lupins growing near Cowra in NSW. Wild lupins contain a bitter alkaloid which makes them inedible, unless treated. The first 'sweet' varieties, without the alkaloid, were developed in Germany in the 1920s and 30s.

Lucerne not only provides valuable feed – both green and as dried hay – but it also improves the quality of the ground by fixing nitrogen in the soil.

LUPIN

To most Australians, lupins are brightly-coloured conical-shaped flowers seen in springtime gardens. To farmers, however, other varieties of lupin are winter growing, grain legume crops which are valued as a high-protein stock feed.

The lupin is a relatively recent addition to Australian agriculture. Around 80 per cent still come from Western Australia, where the crop was first adapted for commercial use in the 1970s. Most of Australia's lupins are grown in the medium rainfall areas of north, south and east Western Australia, although the crop is also popular in South Australia, Victoria and NSW. Varieties have also been developed to suit low rainfall areas.

Like other grain legumes, lupins attract soil nitrogen to their roots and, after harvesting most of this is left in the paddock to be passed on to the next crop.

Lupins are planted between March and May, flower from August to early October and are harvested in November and early December. At around 30 per cent protein, the grain is a valuable stock feed, especially in the intensive pig and poultry industries. A large part of the annual harvest is exported to Japan, the Middle East and Asia, where it is sold as stock feed or for human consumption.

LYREBIRD

Lyrebirds are found only in the forests of eastern Australia. There are two species – the Superb Lyrebird *Menura novaehollandiae* (800–1000 mm, including the long tail) and Albert's Lyrebird *M. alberti* (850 mm). The Superb Lyrebird is found in eucalypt and rainforest from the Dandenongs in Victoria to Ballandean in Queens-land, and the Albert's Lyrebird in subtropical rainforest in northern NSW and southern Queensland. Most of the following details apply to the first species, which has been studied more.

Lyrebirds are unusual in many ways. They are the largest of the perching birds, and although they are not true songbirds, they can sing at least as well as any of the many species which they mimic. Males maintain territories of two to three hectares in which they scratch several display mounds of earth, each one usually on a ridge, with light shining on it from above. During the breeding season the male visits his mounds to display and attract females. The display includes song (with mimicry) and dances during which the lyre-shaped tail is raised and pointed for-wards. Nearby females are attracted to the male, and mate. The females maintain their own feeding territories which overlap – or may be within – that of the male. There may be more than one female territory within the male's. The females build large, domed nests independently of the males, and raise their young alone.

Lyrebirds use their long legs and toes to turn over leaf litter to find insects and other food. Outside the breeding season small groups of both sexes and young may forage together. They have short wings, but do not fly very much.

M

The shells of macadamia nuts are particularly tough and need a hammer to crack them.

MACADAMIA NUT

Macadamias are one of the few native crops grown commercially in Australia. They are native to the subtropical rainforests of the continent's east coast, and are sometimes known as 'Queensland nuts'. Varieties selected from native and Hawaiian species are grown by about 350 producers in southern Queensland and northern NSW. The small, round, hard-shelled nuts are valued for their high oil content and delicious flavour. Most producers supply a few, large companies which grow, buy and process macadamias. Australia cannot satisfy world demand for its macadamia nuts and around three-quarters of annual production is exported.

Macadamia plantations – which take over 10 years to come into commercial production and have high establishment costs – represent a long-term investment and need careful management. Annual yields from mature trees range from 20 to 40 kg. Trees produce for up to 40 years.

MAGPIE

Australian Magpies *Gymnorhina tibicen* (380–440 mm) are found almost throughout Australia. The differences between various groups are only in the colour of their backs, which may be white, grey or black. They have been described as butcherbirds that have become communal and have taken to feeding on the ground, on insects, so that they have evolved longer and stronger legs than their relatives. Social organisation is complex, and apparently differs from region to region, but females usually predominate.

Nesting magpies are aggressive to human intruders – particularly, it is said, to strangers in an area, or to people who have offended them in the past. They dive-bomb the neck of the victim and one recommended defence is to wear a peaked cap and sunglasses – both pointing to the rear. Many schoolchildren wear ice cream containers as protective helmets.

Magpies are sometimes confused with the widespread, similarly coloured but smaller, Australian Magpie-lark or Peewee *Grallina cyanoleuca* (260–300 mm) which also feeds on the ground, but which belongs to a different family. While their call is loud and strident in alarm on warning, the magpie's song, an organ-like fluted carolling, is one of the best loved sounds of the Australian bush.

MAHOGANY

This name is used in Australia for several eucalypts which are found only on the east coast and in nearby ranges. Early settlers named trees such as *Eucalyptus resinifera* 'Red Mahogany' because of their red-brown, close-grained wood which is like the original mahoganies of tropical America, but in no way related. To the same group as Red Mahogany, and with a similar range in Queensland and NSW, belong the Large-fruited Red Mahogany *E. pellita* and Swamp Mahogany *E. robusta*. These are large forest trees with a thickly fibrous, dark reddish-brown bark on both trunks and limbs. Southern Mahogany or Bangalay *E. botryoides* is found only on the NSW coast and in eastern Victoria. White Mahogany *E. acmenoides* is quite unrelated, and is in fact a close ally of the stringy-barks.

THE MAHOGANY SHIP

Some writers claim that the first Europeans to sight the Australian coastline were not the Dutch, but the Spanish or Portuguese. Among the evidence cited for this view is the story of a mysterious wreck, with dark mahogany-like timber, which a number of people claimed to have seen among sand hummocks west of modern Warnambool in Victoria, almost exactly south of the famous extinct volcano, Tower Hill. Reported sightings occurred between 1837 and 1880, after which the remains were most likely buried under the drifting sand dunes.

Digging and drilling by members of the Monash University Archaeological Society in 1969, and by scientists from the Warrnambool Institute of Advanced Education in later years, have found no trace of the wreck, and its origin remains a matter for conjecture.

MAITLAND PANTHER

Maitland, NSW, is only one of several places from which sightings of large cat-like creatures have been reported. In early 1987, for example, a television news item reported the evidence for such animals in Gippsland, such as tracks and stock that had been slaughtered. The suggested explanation was quite mundane – an American army unit stationed in the area during World War II was said to have released their mascots rather than kill them on the orders of the Australian authorities. Some people believe that this is an example of a rural 'urban myth', akin to the one about alligators living in the sewers of New York.

If the Maitland Panther is a cat then the candidates could be a leopard (about 2.1 m total length), an (American) puma (to 2.4 m), or a feral cat (to 950 mm). Feral cats can, however, get larger. 'Himmy' of Cairns topped 20.7 kg although he was probably useless as a bushcat. It is, however, possible that an exceptionally large feral cat, which avoids human beings, could appear even bigger in the gloomy distance, and feral cats occur almost everywhere in Australia. Author Bernard Heuvelmans in his book *On the Track of Unknown Animals* ignores feral cats and suggests a marsupial cat. He quotes Ion Idriess's accounts of two encounters with such an animal in north Queensland. One had just killed, and been killed by, Idriess's staghound. There are certainly several reports of such a predator in Queensland, and earlier generations of Australian mammalogists included it in their books, despite the lack of museum specimens.

Giant cats in the wrong places are reported from other countries. There was, for example, the Surrey Puma in England a few years ago, which also remained unidentified.

MAIZE

Maize, known by farmers in the United States as corn, is Australia's second most important summer-growing cereal crop after SORGHUM. However, its popularity among growers has dropped in recent years due to poor prices.

Around 200 000 tonnes of the yellow grain are produced annually, mainly in northern NSW and on Queensland's Atherton Tablelands. The annual crop is worth around $30 million.

Nearly all of the crop is used on the domestic market to feed stock or to make cornflour, starches and breakfast cereals. Field or dent maize is the main type grown, although some farmers produce sweetcorn or popcorn for human consumption. Maize can also be cut before it matures, when it is used as green fodder or turned into silage.

The crop is planted from August to January, depending on the area. Mature plants are very tall, growing up to three metres in hot, humid climates. Despite its preference for tropical and subtropical localities, maize is sometimes grown under irrigation, notably in the Murrumbidgee Irrigation Area in NSW.

Unlike other cereal grain crops, maize has separate positions for the male and female flowers involved in pollination on the same stalk. The male flowers are produced at the very top of the plant, while the female flowers are borne where the leaves meet the stalk lower down on the plant. The flower organs, and later the grain kernels, are enclosed in several layers of papery tissue, called husks.

Typical mallee vegetation in Little Desert National Park, Victoria. Vast areas of mallee were cleared around the turn of the century, but it was marginal land and settlers were lucky to get one good crop every ten years.

A maize crop in flower. As the seed heads ripen, the plants shrivel and die. Maize is the world's third most important cereal crop, after wheat and rice.

MALACHITE

Green malachite, and its blue relative azurite, were the first minerals mined in Australia at Kapunda, 80 km north of Adelaide. At nearby Burra, mining in the past has disclosed magnificent specimens of malachite, equal to the finest in the world. Malachite and azurite have the same composition but are different colours. Azurite more often forms crystals.

Both minerals are mined as valuable sources of copper throughout the country, and are formed by the weathering action of water and air on other copper minerals like chalcopyrite and bornite. They are usually found close to the surface. The brilliant green of malachite and rich blue of azurite make them some of the most sought – after minerals. Malachite, with concentric bands in different shades of green, is valuable as an ornamental stone used for making vases and jewellry, for which compact, deep-coloured stones are used.

MALLEE

The name is used both for a particular growth form of some eucalypts, and for stands where most of the trees are mallees. Mallee eucalypts are small, multi-stemmed trees, with the stems arising from a subterranean LIGNOTUBER. Many eucalypts can adopt this form when growing in marginal country, but some species are only found on mallees. Mallee eucalypts grow in heathland, but stands dominated by mallee are usually found in semi-arid areas.

Mallee communities are uniquely Australian, and as well as being very rich in plants, they also support many animals – of which the MALLEE-FOWL is probably the best known member. Malleefowl are a member of the small group of species, the megapodes, which construct large mounds of earth and leaf litter in which eggs are incubated. Large areas of mallee have been cleared for wheat farming in the areas where they were once abundant – south-west Western Australia, north-west Victoria, South Australia and south-west NSW. Remaining areas of mallee have been broken up and little of this type of vegetation is found in conservation reserves.

MALLEEFOWL

Malleefowl *Leipoa ocellata* (600 mm) still exist in fair numbers in the dry areas of southern Australia in patches of scrub such as MALLEE, where they can feed on *Acacia* seeds on the ground, and on other vegetable matter and insects. Like other Australian MOUNDBIRDS they incubate their eggs in mounds of decaying vegetation, but take more care in ensuring that the temperature remains at a constant 33°C during the breeding season. In autumn a pair dig a large hole in the centre of an old mound and fill it with new vegetation which they kick in from the surrounding land. An egg chamber is prepared, and after rain has fallen it is covered with sand to allow fermentation to progress. All this takes about four months. The female lays her large eggs – which can range in number from 5 to 33, depending on the season and the rainfall – at intervals in holes made ready by the male, and later filled in by him. When the fermentation has run its course, the mound is heated by the sun.

The male regularly checks the temperature by pushing in his opened beak, and keeps it constant by piling on more sand, opening the mound during cool periods if too hot, or during sunny periods if too cool. If the female arrives to lay when he judges that opening the mound would change the temperature too drastically, she is sent away. The chicks emerge unaided – from as deep as one metre – after about 49 days and are self-sufficient. They may not ever see either of their parents.

MAMMAL

Mammals are animals with backbones and hair, which suckle their young. Even whales and Mexican hairless dogs have hairs, although they may not be easy to find. Whales, for example, have moustaches. All mammals evolved from mammal-like reptiles about 190 million years ago, before the rise of the dinosaurs. Mammals therefore existed at the time of the dinosaurs, but they were tiny creatures which kept out of the way and only came out at night, otherwise we would not be here today. It is, of course, usually impossible to tell if a fossil millions of years old once had hair and suckled its young, so there is another technical definition. In mammals the jawbone is a single bone, whereas in reptiles there are additional bones where the lower jaw hinges with the upper. Two of the bones on each side, which were used in the hinge in reptiles, became two of the chain of three tiny bones which conduct sounds within a mammal's ear.

The success of mammals is due to several developments. They can maintain their body temperature at a reasonably steady level which allows them to be active, even when it is very hot, or very cold. Their hair, of course, helps in this, as it acts as an insulator. Their heart, like that of a bird, is four-chambered so there is no mixing of oxygen-poor, carbon dioxide-rich venous blood with arterial blood – an arrangement which also helps the animal to be very active if it needs to be. Swallowing and breathing arrangements are so 'designed' that a mammal can chew and breathe simultaneously, and the teeth are almost always divided into incisors, canines, premolars and molars to carry out different tasks. Reptiles, on the other hand, must swallow their food whole, or in big lumps. They cannot chew it much before swallowing, or they will suffocate – crocodiles excepted. A mammal's method is a far more efficient way of dealing with food, and once again helps the animal to be very active and to maintain and a constant body temperature. Other features are a diaphragm, which helps in efficient breathing, and the placing of the legs vertically below the body instead of sprawling to the sides as in reptiles. Finally of course, there is the great development of the mammal's brain.

There are about 4000 living species of mammals. This may seem not very many compared with the insects' millions, but mammals are clearly the dominant animals, even if *Homo sapiens* are discounted.

The smallest mammal, the Bumblebee Bat of Thailand, has a wing span of 160 mm which suggests a length of about 37 mm, and the largest – the biggest Blue Whale recorded – is 33.58 m long. Insects range from 0.2 mm to about 330 mm in length, and the largest dinosaur, *Diplodocus*, was about 26.6 m long. Excluding marine mammals, introduced mammals, and man, there are about 243 species in Australia – 2 monotremes, 130 marsupials, and 111 placentals, mainly rodents and bats.

Further research may well show that some species are composed of several different ones, and that the members of some groups, now regarded as separate, belong to one species. Some may still await discovery, including, perhaps, BUNYIPS and YOWIES.

THE MAN FROM SNOWY RIVER

'Banjo' Paterson's poem of this name, which tells of the exploits of a young mountain horseman in rounding up a mob of wild horses, and so recovering the runaway 'colt from Old Regret', is perhaps the best-known piece of verse in Australian literature. After its publication in 1895 there were several claims regarding the identity of the man on whom Paterson based his story. However, in a letter to the *Sydney Mail* on 28 December 1938, he claimed that both the character and the incident were fictitious. *The Man from Snowy River*, he stated, 'was written to describe the cleaning up of the wild horses in our own district. To make any sort of job of it, I had to create a character, to imagine a man who would ride better than anyone else, and where would he come from except the Snowy? And what sort of horse would he ride except a half-thoroughbred mountain pony?' The popular film of the same name (1982), based partly on Paterson's poem, was made around Merrijig in Victoria, and on nearby Mount Buller.

MANGO

The mango is considered the king of tropical fruits. Its sweet, orange flesh has long been enjoyed by the people of northern Australia, particularly in Queensland where large mango trees are common in most coastal towns and cities. But in most other states it used to be a rare delicacy. However, the establishment of several large mango plantations in Queensland, the Northern Territory and, to a lesser extent, West-

Kensington Pride is the most common variety of mango grown in Australia, although others are being planted in small numbers.

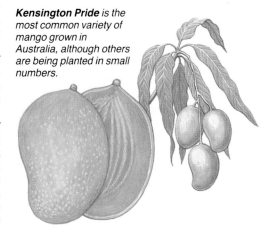

ern Australia, will change this. By 1990, when most of the trees planted will reach commercial production, around 600 000 trees will yield up to 40 000 tonnes of fruit a year. Apart from encouraging increased domestic consumption, it is expected that mangoes will be exported to the United States, Japan and the Middle East. Most of the commercial mangoes are the Kensington Pride variety, often called Bowen mangoes after the Queensland town famous for the fruit.

MANGROVE

Mangroves have traditionally been viewed with suspicion, as unhealthy, mosquito-ridden swamps, impenetrable areas of soft stinking mud. Old attitudes die hard, but there is increasing recognition of their fascination and importance as a habitat.

The term mangrove is used both for a community of plants which grow between the tide marks, and for a type of vegetation.

Australia has some of the most extensive and diverse mangroves in the world. Mangroves are found in all states, except Tasmania, with a total area of approximately 11 500 sq. km. Few other countries have such a large area. Over 20 per cent of Australia's 47 000-km coastline is fringed with mangroves.

There are about 40 species of mangrove in Australia. It is difficult to tell exactly how many there are because the boundaries between them and nearby land plants are indistinct. Most species are found only in the tropics, with the greatest variety living in north-east Queensland. In temperate regions there are very few species of mangroves, with many stands containing only the single most widespread species – the Grey Mangrove *Avicennia marina*. Grey Mangroves even grow in Victoria, which makes them the most southerly mangroves to be found anywhere in the world. Not only are there fewer species the further one moves south, but those that grow there are also smaller. In north-east Queensland, mangroves form magnificent forests, with canopies up to 30 m high. At their southernmost limit, stands of mangrove are made up only of patches of low shrubs.

Mangroves grow in places that would be impossible for other plants to live in. Regular flooding with salt water results in sediments which are waterlogged and salty. Many mangroves have modified root systems which allows their underground portions to obtain enough oxygen. These modifications include the spectacular stilt roots of *Rhizophora* species, and the stalagmite-like pneumatophores of *Avicennia*. While these modified root systems may make progress on foot through mangroves difficult, their appearance adds to the mystery of a mangrove forest.

Mangroves also have various adaptations to enable them to resist the harmful effects of a lot

PLANT AND ANIMAL ZONES IN A NORTHERN MANGROVE SWAMP

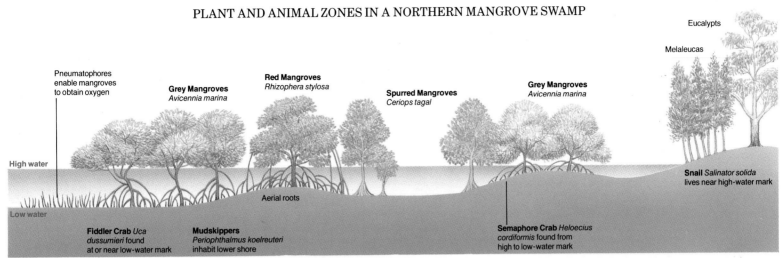

Eucalypts

Melaleucas

Pneumatophores enable mangroves to obtain oxygen

Grey Mangroves *Avicennia marina*

Red Mangroves *Rhizophera stylosa*

Spurred Mangroves *Ceriops tagal*

Grey Mangroves *Avicennia marina*

High water

Snail *Salinator solida* lives near high-water mark

Aerial roots

Low water

Fiddler Crab *Uca dussumieri* found at or near low-water mark

Mudskippers *Periophthalmus koelreuteri* inhabit lower shore

Semaphore Crab *Heloecius cordiformis* found from high to low-water mark

of salt. Some species have special glands on their leaves which excrete salt. Although they usually grow in conditions where there is a lot of salt in the water, mangroves do not need salt for survival, and they can be grown satisfactorily under non-salty, non-tidal conditions – in botanic gardens, for example.

Some species of mangroves produce seedlings instead of seeds. In most plants, after the flowers have been fertilised, a seed forms, but further development is halted until the seed has found a suitable place for germination. In some mangroves, however, there is no waiting period and the embryo develops into a seedling while it is still attached to the parent. Instead of seeds being dispersed, the plant sheds seedlings.

As they live between the land and the sea, mangroves are able to support both land and water animals. The lower trunks of the trees may be covered with oysters and other marine animals that are permanently attached, while crabs, marine snails and worms live in the mud. At high tide, fish are able to enter the community, while in the tropical north crocodiles live among mangroves. The canopy provides a home for land animals such as birds, insects and spiders.

Apart from the dominant trees, other plants are less obvious. The aerial roots and stem bases

Different species of mangroves and other coastal plants have different tolerances to salt and other environmental factors, and each therefore grows in the zone that suits it best. The cross-section shown above is of a typical coastal swamp in northern Australia.

may be covered with algae, while higher on the trunks lichens may be common. EPIPHITES and vines are not normally found on temperate mangroves, but they are moderately common in some tropical areas. In north-east Queensland, ANT-HOUSE PLANTS are common among mangroves in some areas.

In south-east Asia, mangroves are heavily used as a source of firewood, wood chips and building timber. Within Australia there is at present no large-scale commercial forestry of mangroves, although in the past there was some harvesting for boat-building timber and oyster stakes. Mangroves have also been used as a source of tannin, while some species may be a valuable source of nectar for honey bees. In the early nineteenth century, large areas of mangroves in south-eastern Australia were felled and burnt to yield a potash-rich ash which was used for making soap.

In southern Australia, but only to a very local extent in the tropics, many mangrove areas have been reclaimed to provide sites for industry, housing or recreation. Reclamation of mangroves was viewed as a public service, removing sites which were the source of disease and biting insects. Attitudes have changed and conservation of mangroves is now given high priority. As well as being fascinating and beautiful places in their own right, mangroves are now regarded as productive habitats, with a valuable role in maintaining fisheries. Mangrove creeks are important nurseries for young fish – including many that are commercially valuable – while the leaves of mangroves may, after they have fallen from the trees, provide food for many creatures that live in the mud.

Tangled, stilt-like roots help Rhizophora *mangroves to obtain enough oxygen. Much of Queensland's coast is lined with mangroves – these are on Lizard Island.*

Grey Mangroves are the most common species found in temperate areas around Australia. The spiky pneumatophores obtain oxygen from above the mud.

241

MANTIS

Mantises are fierce, predatory insects. Many of the 130 or so Australian species are large – a female *Archimantis latistyla*, for example, is about 90 mm long. They have huge eyes, triangular faces, extremely flexible necks, and spiky forelegs which snap shut – like a penknife – on their prey. As they are ambushers rather than hunters, they wait motionless for their victims, poised in an attitude of prayer, using both colour and form as camouflage. The camouflage may also protect them from birds and other enemies. Like their relatives the cockroaches they lay eggs in a 'purse', but they form theirs from rapidly hardening froth, and glue them to trees, fences or other supports. Young resemble adults, apart from their smaller size and the fact that they are wingless. Most live in foliage, some on tree trunks, and a few hunt on the ground. When disturbed some will rear up in threat, often displaying bright patches of colour.

MAP

Australia has roughly four million place names. About two-thirds are Aboriginal. Place names are a rich repository of cultural links, so rich that investigating them is a new science – toponymy. Place names committees from the various federal and state mapping bodies meet regularly to add to or subtract from the lists. They also standardise spellings, since Commonwealth and state bodies produce maps covering the same areas, although at differing scales. Very broadly speaking, the Commonwealth – through the Surveying and Land Information Group (formerly Natmap) – produces *small-scale* maps, showing large areas in a *small* size, while the states produce *large scale* maps that show small areas in a *large* size, with much detail of roads, creeks, hills and towns.

The largest scale maps covering the whole of Australia are Natmap's 544 sheets at a scale of 1 250 000. One centimetre on the map equals 250 000 centimetres on the ground, i.e. 2.5 kilometres. Natmap has published 1640 sheets of the 1 100 000 series (1 centimetre = 1 kilometre).

Much of each state has been mapped by the respective state mappers at a scale of 1:50 000 (1 centimetre = 0.5 kilometre). Smaller proportions of each state have been covered by 1:25 000 maps (1 centimetre = 250 metres). The areas covered by 1:25 000 sheets vary from state to state, but are usually about 12 by 15 kilometres or about 180 square kilometres. They give enough detail to be useful to walkers, particularly in areas where there are no roads.

Topographical maps, with contour lines showing hills and valleys, best convey an impression of landscape. Orthophotomaps (aerial photographs overlaid with contour lines, some roads and names) and cadastral maps (showing property and district boundaries) are used mainly by property developers, planners and conveyancers.

Forestry, mining and national parks authorities bring out large scale maps that are useful for touring, fossicking, walking and camping trips. It may be necessary to visit government departments or specialist map shops to get them. Outdoor shops often carry many large scale government maps, maps of National Parks, and also very large scale sketch maps compiled specifically for walkers.

MARBLE

The cool, white shine of polished marble has intrigued people since ancient times. Throughout the centuries numerous cities have been adorned with marble statues and buildings. Strictly speaking marble is a rock formed when limestone is subjected to intense heat and pressure. The best quality stone is found where limestone has been baked by heat from molten rocks such as granite. Calcite grains in the limestone are recrystallised to produce a very hard, smooth texture. In industry, however, the term marble is sometimes used to include limestone.

In Australia in recent years there has been a strong demand for the colourful swirls and mottled stains of local marble. Buildings using marble can be seen in most Australian cities and they include the Reserve Banks in all state capitals, NSW Parliament House, the AMP Centre in Brisbane and Melbourne's Rialto.

Pure marble is white to pale greyish-blue, but small amounts of impurities, notable iron and magnesium, can give the rock various tints of green, yellow and golden brown. The best known quarries are at Wombeyan in NSW, Angaston in South Australia and Ulam in Queensland.

Marble at the Wombeyan quarry is cut from the ground using a wire saw – a 1000-m loop of steel wire which is dragged through the stone with a mixture of sand and water. In 1986 around 2000 tonnes of marble were removed from this single quarry. Unfinished, it fetched up to almost $100 per sq. m.

MARCH FLY

These flies – also called horse flies or clegs (see illustration p 179) – can range in length from 6 to 20 mm. They have large eyes, often banded, moderately long antennae, and a strong beak. Both sexes of most species are vicious blood suckers which attack humans and other mammals. Blade-like sections of their mouthparts draw blood which is then sponged up. In some countries they transmit human diseases, but are not known to do so in Australia. Some species feed on nectar. Their predatory larvae are found in damp soil, swamps and holes in trees. Some species with northern hemisphere relatives probably originally came to Australia with their rodent victims.

MARRAM GRASS

Marram Grass *Ammophila arenaria* has been widely planted in Australia to stabilise and restore coastal sand dunes damaged by overgrazing, excessive clearing, off-road vehicles, or other human use.

The grass is native to Europe, but has been used widely around the world for sand dune stabilisation. In Australia the native dune-forming grasses are *Spinifex sericeus* in the south and *Spinifex longifolius* in the north. *Spinifex* has long horizontal stems on, or just below, the sand surface producing an open system of upright shoots. Marram Grass on the other hand produces dense tussocks which are more efficient sand trappers than the shoots of *Spinifex*. In general, under the disturbed conditions where stabilisation becomes necessary, Marram Grass is more effective than *Spinifex*. The shapes of dunes produced by the two grasses differ – *Spinifex* produces a low rounded form while Marram Grass dunes develop into conical hillocks over a period of time.

MARSHES, BOGS AND SWAMPS

Wetlands – country that is covered with water, or where the land is saturated with water for at least long enough for characteristic water-loving plants to grow – include marshes, bogs and swamps. The three are often confused by the general public, but ecologists strive to distinguish between them. Unfortunately the ter-

Swamps (above) are covered with stagnant or slowly-flowing water and sometimes, as here, are home to trees such as paperbarks. This swamp is in Edmund Kennedy National Park, between Ingham and Tully on the Queensland coast. Bogs, such as this example (below) in Kosciusko National Park, NSW, form in cool, wet places where sphagnum mosses and other plants grow. Dead plants do not rot, and often form peat.

minology is confusing: in 1942 one writer found 90 different English-language words used for peatlands alone, and since then the Americans have added more. Recently the old word 'mire' has been revived to include all peaty wetlands.

Australia, a relatively dry, flat country, does not have the vast tracts of bogland which cover large areas of Ireland, northern Britain, America and Finland. They are formed in cold, humid climates where the ground is constantly wet, drainage is poor and conditions favour the growth of *Sphagnum* and other related mosses. The mosses and other plants die and build up layers of acid peat, with little mineral matter mixed with it.

A bog may spread as a layer over flat land or on a slope as blanket bog so that its surface is above the water table and the mosses growing there depend on rainfall and the atmosphere for water and minerals. Bogs, often built up into domes, can form on the sediments in old lake basins and those also depend on rain. Sometimes, however, bogs may form in shallow depressions where the water table reaches the surface. If peat is formed where the water is alkaline or rich in silt, a fen is the result.

Clearly the Australian climate does not favour bogs except on high, rain-soaked mountains, or in places near the coast. Australia has only 15 000 ha of peatland – 0.002 per cent of the country – compared with Finland's 10 million (33.5 per cent) and Eire's 1.18 million (17.2 per cent). Most bogs are relatively young – they only began to form a few thousand years ago when the climate began to change.

Marshes are wetlands where the water table is

The soil in marshes – this example is near Cooktown – is saturated with water, but it is not peaty. When the water is fresh the vegetation consists of water-loving grasses, sedges and rushes. Saline marshes carry succulent plants such as glassworts in coastal areas, and salt-tolerant plants such as saltbushes inland.

at or just below the surface long enough for plants such as grasses, reeds and sedges to grow. The surface is squelchy and boots sink in. The soil – which is richer in minerals than that of bogs – is neither very acid nor very alkaline. Peat is not formed. Generally marshes are a stage in the transition between a wet area, such as a lake, and dry land. The water which drains into a marsh carries silt which, together with decaying vegetation, builds up soil. A marsh can be salt – there are often mudflats which support succulent glassworts lying inland from coastal mangrove swamps in many areas.

In swamps the plants grow in shallow, stagnant or slowly-moving water, and peat is often formed. Reed swamps, which surround many lakes and border slow-flowing rivers, are the most familiar examples. Trees such as paperbarks *Melaleuca* and River Gums often grown in or near swamps. American biologists often use the term swamp to describe only wetlands dominated by trees.

In the Australian high country, and in Tasmania, there are several types of mires which are homes to tussock grasses, mosses and sedges. Even the arid zone has its wetlands, some of which are permanent. They depend for their survival on water brought by rivers from many hundreds of kilometres away. Characteristic plants of the inland swamps include the floating fern *Azolla* and the rooted fern *Marsilea* which was used by the Aborigines for food, cumbungi, cane grass and lignum. The Coolibah Tree, as the poem suggests, is often found in swampy places.

MARSUPIAL

The outstanding difference between marsupial mammals (such as kangaroos, possums and koalas) and placental mammals (such as cows, human-beings, dogs and whales) is their method of reproduction. Young marsupials are born after a short gestation period in a very undeveloped state. Despite their tiny size they find their way to a nipple – usually inside a pouch or 'marsupium' – and hang on to it firmly while they continue to grow until they reach a stage of development similar to that at which placental young are born.

Placental mammals develop further than marsupials in the uterus. They grow by obtaining nourishment and oxygen – in a parasitic fashion – from the blood system of their mother through a placenta. The term 'placental mammals' suggests that marsupials do not have a placenta. This is, however, quite wrong. Several marsupials have placentas, but they generally have a less intimate connection with the mother's tissues. In placental mammals, the placenta is formed early in pregnancy, whereas marsupial embryos retain an egg membrane – which is never found in placental mammals – for much of the pregnancy, and form a placenta at a relatively late stage. In addition the eggs of marsupials are more yolky than those of placentals – they have a bigger inbuilt food supply.

The marsupial method of reproduction is not necessarily less efficient than that of placentals. Marsupial females are committed to only a short period during which they carry offspring in their uterus, so they use relatively small quantities of resources in this phase. The sexual cycle is not interrupted by pregnancy, so that they can mate shortly after giving birth. It is interrupted by milk-production, but starts again if the suckling is lost. It is a system which can be adapted to opportunistic breeding, which is particularly useful in a country with an unpredictable climate. Marsupials are also able to bear more young without mating again, through the natural phenomenon of delayed embryo implantation. Placental mammals must go full term, or abort – and in drought conditions, for example, this may put great stress on both mother and foetus.

Other differences between marsupials and placentals are relatively minor; were it not for the differences in reproduction, biologists would probably not set the two groups so far apart.

Some of the other differences between placentals and marsupials are as follows: in marsupials the bones of the pelvic girdle are not fully fused, and there is often an extra pair of bones which help to support the pouch when it is present. Marsupials only have one set of teeth and none, apart from one premolar, are replaced. Marsupials (like MONOTREMES) have a cloaca – a common chamber into which the gut, the reproductive system and the urinary system all lead – and one sphincter (a circular band of muscle) that closes them all. The vagina and the uterus are double, and the scrotum is in front of the penis. The metabolic rate of marsupials is generally lower than comparable placentals, and often their body temperature is 2° or 3° lower.

Many features of the marsupials led biologists to argue that they were more primitive and less efficient than placentals, but since the 1950s this view has been challenged by Australian zoologists who have shown how many of the features are superbly adapted to the Australian environment. Large KANGAROOS, for example, can withstand extreme midday temperatures, despite their lower metabolic rate, which might suggest that they would be less able to keep their body temperature constant. The hopping motions of kangaroos over open plains, once they get going, is at least as economical, and probably more efficient, than an antelope's run.

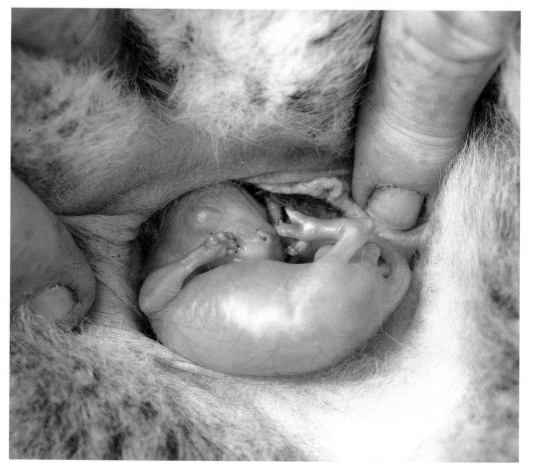

Young Marsupials complete far more of their development outside their mother's bodies than placental mammals do. The tiny Parma Wallaby (right) is only two months old. It has spent only 35 days in its mother's womb, but will spend 212 days in her pouch. The young Red-necked Wallaby (above) is very close to being ejected by its mother.

MARSUPIAL MOLE

The Marsupial Mole of Australia, the common European Mole and the Golden Mole of Africa provide one of the most remarkable examples of convergent evolution. The last two are placental mammals, although in different families, yet, externally at least, they all look much alike. The Australian species and the African are, in fact, difficult to distinguish. Both are blind, their eyes being covered by skin, they have no external ears – merely a hole leading to the inner ear – and their front legs are powerful and modified for burrowing, each with two spade-like claws. The European and African animals evolved from shrew-like mammals, and the Australian probably from a possum-like species. As a result of their burrowing lives they have all evolved to end up looking very much alike.

Marsupial Moles *Notoryctes typhlops* (body length 121–159 mm, tail 21–26 mm) live in sandy areas of the arid inland from South Australia westwards. They 'swim' below the surface through the sand, rarely emerging except after rain. In soft sand their tunnel fills in behind them. Sometimes they burrow vertically for more than two metres. They apparently feed on insects and larvae but – not surprisingly – little is known about their behaviour and social organisation. Females have a backward-opening pouch, and males also have a rudimentary pouch.

Marsupial moles are burrowers, rarely seen on the surface – usually emerging only after rain. They are blind, although they do have traces of lenses underneath their skin.

MAYFLY

Mayflies have short adult lives of only a day or two, devoted just to mating. They are often seen in swarms above streams. Adults do not feed and have two pairs of triangular wings – with the second pair often very small – fairly short

antennae, and two or three long 'tails'. Feather models of mayflies are often used as lures by anglers. Nymphs have two or three tails, gills on their abdomens, and are plant-eaters or scavengers. Mayflies are unique in having two fully winged stages. Having acquired wings they once more cast their skin. There are more than 120 Australian species, mostly found in the highlands of south-east Australia, and along cool sections of coastal streams.

MECHANICS' INSTITUTE

The peeling facades of many Mechanics' Institutes and Schools of Arts can still be seen in outback towns. These establishments had their origins in early nineteenth century Britain, where there was an intense interest in science and technology, and also a demand for education to be extended to the working class. These two drives produced the adult education organisations known as either Mechanics' Institutes or Schools of Arts. The two titles were interchangeable, the word 'mechanics' meaning an artisan or skilled tradesman, and 'arts' meaning the 'useful arts', which were considered to be of greatest use to mechanics. The first of these institutions, the Edinburgh School of Arts, was founded in 1821, and was closely followed by the London Mechanics' Institution (1823), with several hundred more being founded by 1850.

Australia soon followed the English lead. The Van Diemen's Land Mechanics' Institute was founded in 1829, the Sydney Mechanics' School of Arts in 1833, the Melbourne Mechanics' Institute in 1839, and hundreds more before the end of the century. Some of them developed well-attended classes in technical subjects, but most concentrated on offering lectures and providing libraries and reading rooms.

The original objective of the Sydney Mechanics' School of Arts was stated to be 'the diffusion of Scientific and other Useful Knowledge', by the provision of a library and reading room, the purchase of 'apparatus and models illustrating the principles of Physical and Mechanical Philosophy', and 'engaging teachers and lecturers in the above'. However in time the intention to keep to 'useful knowledge' was abandoned, and literature, history, art, music and other subjects were added to the range of study. Meanwhile, however, most of the smaller institutes, finding it difficult to organise courses of lectures, had tended to concentrate on their libraries, and on social and recreational amenities such as meeting and billiards rooms.

Eventually other institutions took over the functions of Mechanics' Institutes and Schools of Arts. Their technical classes became technical colleges – that of the Sydney Mechanics' School of Arts, for example, becoming Sydney Technical College in 1883. The Workers' Education Association and University Tutorial Classes competed

Kalgoorlie Mechanics' Institute library appears to be freshly painted, and may still be in use. In most towns both Mechanics' Institutes and Schools of Arts closed down years ago, as the need for them declined.

in general educational work; Institute libraries were superseded by municipal and other public libraries, and clubs offered better recreational activities. Nevertheless a few have survived as subscription libraries, these including the Sydney Mechanics' School of Arts, which has dropped 'Mechanics'' from its title, but still conducts a library on its original site in Pitt Street.

MEDIC

Along with subterranean CLOVER, medics are a common pasture legume in Australia's temperate or winter rainfall farming regions. They are particularly suited to the heavy, alkaline soils, found in many parts of Western Australia, South Australia, Victoria and NSW.

Like clover, medic has an annual growth cycle, starting with germination in autumn, growth through winter and spring and seed-setting in summer before the soil dries out. Stock, mainly sheep, are able to graze medic seeds during summer. The seeds are usually found in the top few centimetres of soil. Thus, an otherwise barren-looking paddock may sustain large numbers of sheep during the hot months of December, January and February.

In the past 15 years, plant breeders have developed new varieties of medics which are resistant to the pest, lucerne aphid. These varieties – which are normally named after the shape of the seed – include barrel, snail, disc, cutleaf and burr medic. Other less popular varieties include gamma and black medic.

MEDICINAL PLANTS

For most of human history people have treated their ills with medicines from plants, animals, microorganisms or minerals. It has been only in the last four or five decades that new drugs have been synthetically manufactured rather than extracted from some natural source. The main advantages of these chemicals include easier administration, increased availability and storage life and more predictable efficiency and specificity. Certainly, the new drugs are more convenient, but the search still continues for natural compounds which could improve the action and range of application of existing medicines.

Every society has had its folk medicines, and in Australia the Aborigines knew a range of treatments for any complaints they might have. Aborigines still remember and prefer bush cures to combat familiar sicknesses, and only resort to modern drugs for the more virulent diseases brought by Europeans. Some bush first-aid treatments were even found for those, but often a complete cure was even beyond the medicine men who knew the powerful remedies using wild medicines, as well as invoking powers from the spirit world. Perhaps all medicine is a mixture of pharmacology and magic, with a cure requiring the patient's faith in the recommended treatment. However, scientists are discovering pharmacologically-active chemicals in some 'magical' Aboriginal bush medicines.

One of the most obvious features of Australian landscapes are the gum trees, or eucalypts. Oils from the leaves of many species were extracted by the first settlers, and eucalyptus oil was probably one of the first natural products exported from the colony. The oils contain aromatic compounds and one of these, cineole, which also occurs in paperbark trees (*Melaleuca* spp.) has been noted as active in treating the symptoms of the common cold. Aborigines crushed and bruised the leaves and inhaled the vapours, or made an infusion with water and drank the liquid for the relief of headaches. Species which exhibit low levels of cineole, but high amounts of a compound called terpinen-4-ol, have an even greater pharmacological value. Tea-tree oil, extracted from *Melaleuca alternifolia* has recently enjoyed a resurgence in popularity. This oil is now distilled from the foliage, and is used as an anti-microbial agent. It penetrates unbroken skin and is useful in the treatment of all types of cuts and infected wounds including tinea, ring-worm and mouth ulcers. During World War II the oil was added to machine cutting oils to reduce the infection of skin injuries from metal filings and turnings.

Eucalypts have other uses in bush medicines. The orange-red exudations on the trunks of gum trees are kinos (not gums). These are astringent and contain tannins which constrict blood vessels. This property may explain the Aboriginal use of kino preparations for mouth and eye washes, liniments and to reduce fever. Dilute solutions of kino were also drunk as a cure for dysentery and diarrhoea by both Aborigines and later by white settlers.

Many Australian species of wattles also exude mucilages, properly called gums, which can be used medicinally. Non-astringent wattle gum can be softened in water and eaten as a high-fibre food. Some gums are extremely sweet and are called bush lollies by Aboriginal children. The soluble fibre in wattle gums may have played a protective role against diabetes and other 'diseases of civilisation' becoming common in Aborigines. The water absorbing qualities of gums can be used to treat two extremes of digestive disorders; constipation and diarrhoea. Eaten with adequate water the gums will swell in the gut and assist in curing constipation. This was one ailment not often recorded amongst

Just three of hundreds of bush remedies known to the Aborigines. Cycad seeds (above), which are highly toxic, were used to combat infections. Leaves of the widespread sword bean Canavalia rosea *(left)* were placed on burnt skin to act as a bandage and relieve pain. Caustic bush Sarcostemma australe *stems (below)* exude a milky sap which was painted over bleeding wounds, sores and ulcers by both Aborigines and white settlers.

Many of the gums exuded by plants are too astringent to eat, but those from some wattle species are sweet, and are known as bush lollies by children. Other gums were used as remedies for digestive disorders.

Aborigines living on bush food, but today may be more prevalent. In apparent contrast, tannins also in the gums would have the same use in treating diarrhoea as eucalypt kino. In addition, gum soaked in water forms a mucilage which is easily applied to the skin as a soothing gel for burns and irritations.

Another plant which contains a mucilage is the Native or Long Yam *Dioscorea transversa*. The tuber has always been a staple food of many northern Aborigines and the soluble fibre in the yam is mucilaginous. This may be another protective food against diabetes, but an additional isolated use of the yam has been recorded in the Tully district of Queensland. There the local Aborigines used the yam in the treatment of skin cancer. Perhaps it was simply the soothing coolness of the tuber which allayed symptoms, or perhaps the local species produced active steroid compounds, as do many non-Australian species.

Whereas modern pharmacology has largely forgotton aromatic oils, mucilages and tannins from natural sources, plant alkaloids are still of some interest and have not yet been fully investi-gated. This group of varied compounds contains many pharmacologically active chemicals such as cocaine, strychnine, digitalis, caffeine, morphine, quinine and nicotine to name only a few.

From Lismore in NSW, across the 'Top End' of northern Australia and down to around Geraldton in Western Australia a type of sword bean called *Canavalia rosea*, has a well established place in Aboriginal medicine. As a first-aid treatment for burns, the leaves of this beach creeper were picked and warmed on hot stones. The softened leaves were placed onto the burnt skin and acted as a bandage, a pain killer and in promoting healing. The roots were also mashed and an infusion applied externally for aches and pains from rheumatism, colds, broken bones and even leprosy. The active components causing these effects have not been identified, but the whole plant contains several alkaloids related to canavaline.

Two very potent bush medicines which also contain alkaloids, the effects of which have not been fully researched, are gidgee-gidgee seeds from *Abrus precatorius* and several parts of the palm-like cycads. Gidgee-gidgee seeds are commonly used as beads for necklaces and other decorations, but it is well known that they are extremely toxic. The seeds have been used as homicidal poisons by native populations throughout the plant's range in the tropics, and Australian Aborigines have found another application for this toxicity. Unwanted pregnancies could by terminated by careful use of gidgee-gidgee. A single seed was selected by the pregnant woman using critieria that have not been recorded. Perhaps seeds which floated in water, or were malformed and unlikely to germinate were chosen, or immature seeds may have been found suitable. Eating the seed was sufficient to accomplish the task, although occasionally the treatment killed the mother as well. The seeds have also been used in western medicine in the treatment of eye problems such as ophthalmia and trachoma.

The palm-like CYCADS have male and female plants which produce cones which bear pollen or seeds, respectively. Both of these cone structures have been used medicinally by Aborigines against infection of injuries. Traditionally the male cone was reserved for serious male injuries, such as spear wounds, but the seeds of the female plants have been shown to be strongly antibiotic. The seeds contain a mixture of toxic glycosides – two common ones are cycasin and macrozamin. These are complex molecules which, if eaten, release cyanide after being partly digested by enzymes in the gut. The residual compounds are also potently carcinogenic and one, an aglycone, becomes toxic after further digestion in the intestinal tract. Interestingly, in most non-arid areas of Australia, Aborigines ate the seeds of most species of cycads and the related zamiads after a lengthy processing.

All food plays an important role in preventative medicine, and Aborigines all over Australia were aware of the tonic properties of some foods. In the tropical north, Aboriginal women have always collected a species of marine borer (*Teredo* spp.) from mangrove swamps. This mangrove worm was eaten by pregnant or menstruating women and mineral analysis of the worms has revealed that they contain very high levels of iron, calcium and zinc. This provided a valuable mineral supplement at a nutritionally critical time for the women.

The list of Australian natural products and Aboriginal bush medicines which have been added to the pharmaceuticals of western medicine is growing. An important project started in Australia's bicentennial year – the systematic recording of the Aboriginal pharmacopoeia – should contribute even more. Unfortunately, important natural environments are continually being threatened and degraded, and unless these areas are protected many valuable resources may be lost forever.

Three of 12 meteorite craters at Henbury in the Northern Territory. The largest is 18 m deep and 180 m across. Australia's largest intact meteorite weighs 12 tonnes and is in the Western Australian Museum in Perth.

MELALEUCA

There are about 150 species of *Melaleuca*, both trees and shrubs, and most are found only in Australia. The scientific name is derived from two Greek words: melas meaning black, and leukois meaning white, and refers to the blackened patches on the white papery bark after fire. Several of the trees in this group are known as paperbarks, other species are referred to as tea trees (sometimes ti-tree).

Flowers vary from white through yellow, pinks and purples to red. Many species produce large amounts of nectar and are an important source of food for honeyeaters.

Melaleuca are related to *Eucalyptus, Callistemon, Leptospermum* and other familiar Australian plants. Like these, they contain oils in their foliage and at various times these oils have been extracted for medicinal, germicidal and cosmetic uses. However, this interest has never developed.

The Swamp Paperbark *Melaleuca quinquenervia*, a widespread species of tree in eastern Australia, has become a major noxious weed in the swamps of Florida in the USA.

METAMORPHIC ROCK

Some of the most attractive and intriguing rocks to be found are those that have been changed by great heat and massive pressure deep within the earth's crust – the metamorphic rocks. The process is similar to that involved in taking a piece of clay and compacting and heating it in a kiln until it becomes a brick. In the same way a piece of sandstone can be subjected to great heat and pressure until it is changed into quartzite, or limestone into marble. Metamorphic rocks take millions of years of form, rather than a few days. In most cases the chemical composition does not change as clay turns into a brick, but in metamorphic rocks exotic new minerals can be created. For example, a piece of clay can change into GARNET or MICA.

There are two main types of metamorphism – regional and thermal. Regional metamorphism changes rocks that are deeply buried. At a depth of 10 kilometres the temperature reaches 300°C and the overlying rocks exert enormous pressure. Large areas of Australia are covered by regional metamorphic rocks, particularly in Western Australia, South Australia and the Northern Territory. Slate is a typical regional metamorphic rock.

Thermal metamorphism also occurs deep in the earth where molten volcanic rock comes into contact with existing layers and bakes them. Exotic minerals and large mineral deposits are often formed in these conditions.

Much of Australia's mineral wealth is extracted from metamorphic rocks.

METEORITE CRATER

Meteorites – rocks from space – are travelling very fast when they reach the earth's atmosphere – up to 74 km/sec. If a large piece reaches the surface the impact digs a large crater. Each year about 100 tonnes of material – ranging in size from dust to large rocks – lands on earth. Over 1000 separate falls of meteorites are known to have occurred in Australia. Most meteorites are small pieces of rock but there are many craters in Australia produced by the impact of large meteorites. The best known are at Wolfe Creek in Western Australia and at Henbury, about 120 km south-west of Alice Springs in the Northern Territory. Wolfe Creek is a single crater 850 m wide and 50 m deep, with a rim raised 18 to 30 m above the surrounding surface. At Henbury there are 12 craters, the largest of which is about 200 m wide and 15 m deep.

In both cases the force of the impact was so great that the meteorite was melted and shattered into small pieces. Large craters are rapidly destroyed by erosion, making it sometimes hard to recognise old structures. However, at Gosses Bluff, west of Alice Springs, there is part of a crater 4 km in diameter, surrounded by a disturbed area 25 km across. The huge meteorite that fell to earth there might have weighed many thousands of tonnes and would have caused a huge explosion when it arrived about 130 million years ago.

MICA

Mica has some remarkable properties – it is transparent, it bends, and it is found in 'books' that can be separated by a knife point into wafer-like sheets. Micas are common rock-forming minerals that are found mainly in granitic and METAMORPHIC rocks. There are a number of different varieties, but the most common are muscovite mica and the black biotite mica. Single crystals up to three metres in diameter have been mined in Canada. Small bronze-coloured flakes of mica are often seen in creek beds, and are sometimes mistaken at first sight for flecks of gold.

Mica is an electrical insulator and is also heat resistant. Large sheets are mined and used to make electrical, radio and aircraft components. It is commonly used in the front windows of wood-burning stoves, and to support the heating coils of electric toasters.

MICE

The terms rats and mice do not correspond with any scientific classification. One group of Australian rodents, *Pseudomys*, for example, contains some species which are called rats and some which are mice. Generally speaking, rats are larger than mice, but even this rule is broken sometimes.

All Australian mice belong the family Muridae, and all but the introduced House Mouse *Mus musculus* (body length 60–95 mm, tail 75–95 mm) are peculiar to this country. Most are very similar to the House Mouse, which is now probably the most common Australian mammal, and the most widespread mammal in the world apart from *Homo sapiens*. A House Mouse can be distinguished from *Pseudomys* mice (with difficulty) by a notch on the inner side of the upper incisors, and if a female by counting teats. There are five pairs on a House Mouse – three on the chest and two in the groin – and two pairs in pseudomys, in the groin.

The group *Pseudomys* contains about 17 native mice (and two rats). Some are rare or may be extinct, and many are found in small areas.

Possibly the most attractive Australian mice are the hopping-mice which have bodies like miniature kangaroos. Most are found in arid zones and the north, but some are found in more settled areas. The arid zone species will drink water but can survive easily without it. They produce the most concentrated urine of any rodent. Like most small desert animals they are active at night and spend the day in burrows. Mitchell's Hopping Mouse *Notomys mitchelli* (115 mm, 150 mm), a long-whiskered creature, is the largest and lives in the MALLEE in southern Australia on seeds, insects and green plants.

Plains Rats Pseudomys australis *were once widespread, but are now found only in the Lake Eyre basin. The rats dig complex burrows which are sometimes connected to one another by surface paths. One colony near Charlotte Waters, NT, covered an area of over 50 sq. km.*

MIDDEN

Other people's garbage can tell us a lot about the way they lived and what they ate. Aboriginal middens – often seen along the coast or beside inland waterways – are rubbish heaps, the mounds of debris left behind after innumerable meals. They usually contain vast masses of shells, bones, charcoal from fires and sometimes stone tools.

Some middens are huge, forming mounds over 10 m high and nearly 50 m across. Groups of Aborigines used to return each season and actually camp on top of the middens, high above the surrounding wetlands.

Middens are most commonly seen along the coast where patches of white shells spill from the eroded flanks of weathered dunes. These middens are younger than the dunes, which were formed less than 6000 years ago, when the sea rose to its present level. Ancient middens – some over 30 000 years old – have been found in the inland beside the shores of dried-up lakes, such as those at Lake Mungo in western NSW.

An Aboriginal hunter (below) crafts a boomerang while sitting on top of a coastal midden near Port Macquarie, NSW, in 1927. The litter of objects around him – shells, fragments of tools and charcoal – build up over thousands of years into vast mounds. The eroded remains of middens (above) are often seen beside rivers, lakes or beaches.

MIDGE

There are two groups of midges – biting and non-biting. Non-biting midges look like mosquitoes, and are about the same size. They often gather in large mating swarms near water and they can cause severe allergic reactions in susceptible people. Most are brownish but there are yellow, red and green species. Their larvae usually live at the bottom of ponds. Some of them – the blood worms – which live in stagnant water and drains, have haemoglobin in their bodies to cope with low oxygen levels.

Biting midges are commonly called sandflies in Australia. They are small to minute, vicious bloodsuckers whose larvae live in mud and debris in wet places, and in rock pools. In some countries they spread human diseases, but they do not often do so in Australia. Some species are potential carriers of the devastating blue-tongue virus of sheep.

MIGRATION

Migration has been most studied in birds, but it is also well documented in certain mammals, fishes and insects.

The reasons for migrations are usually simple. At times of the year, for example during winter, food becomes scarce and animals must migrate or starve. This is a satisfactory explanation when the distances covered are only a few hundred kilometres, or from the high country to low country. It is also satisfactory for explaining why seabirds, such as Short-tailed Shearwaters, make a huge figure-of-eight migration from southern Australia into the north Pacific. It is not, however, convincing for many land birds which migrate over oceans. One possible explanation is based on climatic changes, the other on continental drift.

The first explanation suggests that originally these birds had to migrate only short distances because the rate of change in climate as they travelled was rapid. They therefore did not have to travel far to reach suitable areas. However, now that the climate has altered, the rate of change has become less abrupt and the birds must travel further.

The second theory is that breeding areas and overwintering areas were originally close to one another, but that with the break-up of Gondwanaland, and the subsequent slow separation of the present continents over hundreds of thousands of years, the two areas gradually became further and further apart. Nevertheless the birds have kept to their original areas, although they have had to travel a few centimetres more each year.

Australian mammals do not migrate in the way that African herbivores of the Serengeti do.

However, some insect-eating bats migrate rather than hibernate. The common Bent-wing Bat *Miniopteris schreibersii*, for example, is known to travel many kilometres to hibernation and maternity sites.

Many freshwater fish migrate long distances. Trout and salmon, for example, migrate to the sea then return later to fresh water to spawn. Eels, on the other hand, spawn in the ocean but mature in fresh water.

Among the insects, dragonflies and butterflies are the most important migrators. The outstanding species is the large, orange and black Monarch or Wanderer Butterfly *Danaus plexippus* which has established itself in Australia. It does make migrations here, but they are not as far-ranging as those it makes in north America.

The magnetic mystery

To get from one place to another, when homing or migrating for example, birds must have some means of judging direction. In other words they need a compass and a map. The compass can be based on the direction of the sun and stars, with an inbuilt clock compensating for the their changing position, or it could be a magnetic compass. In some birds at least, and in some animals, there seems to be a magnetic sense. In experiments in which small ceramic magnets were fitted to the heads of young gulls, and pieces of non-magnetic ceramic to others, the 'magnetised' birds did not navigate as well, at least on overcast days when they could not get reliable sightings of the sun or stars. In other experiments birds, completely enclosed in cages which shielded them from the earth's magnetic field, lose their sense of direction.

MILESTONE

A century or more ago, when travel was slow and arduous, milestones were very important in providing guidance and reassurance for travellers. Governor Macquarie ordered the first, and for many years they were actually of stone. In the twentieth century, however, they were superseded by wooden or concrete posts, often with two sloping surfaces visible from the road – one for the distance from the last town passed, and the other for the distance to the next town. As travel became faster, and signposting better, travellers had less need of guidance every mile or kilometre, and the small kilometre posts of today are useful mainly as reference points for surveying. A few of the old milestones have been preserved as historical relics, but the most accessible reminder of early road measurement is the obelisk in Macquarie Place, Sydney, which Macquarie had erected to mark the point from which all road measurements out of the future city were to be calculated.

A few battered milestones still exist, reminders of days when travel was more leisurely. A man on foot took perhaps 15 minutes to reach the next stone.

MILL

The 40 iron hand-turned mills brought by the First Fleet soon became blunt. Day and night labour with them and pestles and mortars was needed to produce enough flour for the colony. Two treadmills proved too slow.

The first of Sydney's 19 windmills began work in 1797. It was a tower mill – one of the three types of windmill – with a revolving top to its stone tower. Smock mills – usually wooden – also had moving tops. In post mills, the entire millhouse turned so the sails faced the wind. Water mills were common by the 1830s. A few were powered by seawater released through sluice gates from ponds filled by the tide. A few mills used horses; at Stroud, NSW, a team of 16 bullocks drove a wheel when water was low. The hateful treadmill at Port Arthur in Tasmania used men; it operated from 1845 to 1855 although steam had been applied to milling in Australia since 1815, and steam mills were numerous by the mid 1840s. All these mills rotated an upper millstone, the runner, by a spindle through the lower, the bedstone. Wheat and flour ran through channels in both runner and bedstone.

As settlers pushed inland, mills went up in almost every town. Roller mills that ground finer and whiter flour were adopted rapidly in the 1880s and their cost and capacity brought centralisation to milling. Hundreds of country mills became derelict or were converted, many to warehouses and, a few to museums.

Victoria's only surviving tower mill (right) stands at Kyneton, north-west of Melbourne. It was built in 1854 and is now only an empty shell. The splendid Mt Gilead windmill (above) near Campbelltown, west of Sydney, gives an idea of how the Victorian mill must have looked in its heyday. Nothing now remains of the NSW mill or, indeed, any of Sydney's other 19 mills.

MILLIPEDE

Millipedes look superficially like CENTIPEDES, but they have cylindrical bodies, two pairs of legs on each apparent leg-bearing segment, and are vegetarians. They have between 11 to 40 segments on their bodies, antennae and usually groups of tiny eyes. Some are short and tufted, some are short and roll up like a WOODLOUSE, but most are long and wriggly. Many defend themselves by oozing or squirting irritating fluids from pores along their bodies. They are often found in soil and litter, and some are crop pests. Recently the introduced black Portuguese Millipede *Ommatoiulus moreletti*, which is about 40 mm long, has swarmed in houses and gardens in and around Adelaide and Melbourne.

MIN MIN LIGHT

Long since burned down, the Min Min grog shop stood by a bore-head near Lucknow station, east of Boulia in north-west Queensland. The name lives on in the 'ghost' light first seen there and later reported in western Queensland, southeast Northern Territory, and northern South Australia. Several observers believed that car headlights were approaching, but they faded away. One man thought a car was keeping pace with his own, but its beam slowly vanished. Drovers have supposed another drover was camped a short way off. One man described a table-sized glow at a distance of 50 m. In 1953 two men on the Barkly Tableland watched

Millipedes were once grouped with centipedes, but researchers no longer think that they are closely related. None of the 130 or so Australian species is dangerous, although some found in other countries are.

for ten minutes as a white light, fading and brightening, spiralled to about 300 m above the ground and down again, before it disappeared.

No satisfactory explanation has been put forward. Theories have ranged from spontaneous combustion of methane gas from bores – although the light wanders over the ground – to night-time 'mirages' as coach or car lights bounce from low cloud. Aborigines do not seem to have seen the light before white men arrived.

MINE

Lonely chimney stacks, rusting ore stampers, crumbling engine houses, lumpy hillsides and poppet heads that once held winding mechanisms above shafts are echoes of mining activity throughout the continent. Between 1861 and 1909 each colony or state by itself was – at different times – the world's largest producer of gold, silver-lead, copper, tin or coal. Australia's 1500 or so modern mines have little romance but great importance, bringing in about one-twentieth of its income. Coal, first mined by convicts in Newcastle in 1801, accounts for over one-third of mineral export earnings. Of some 130 mines, roughly one-quarter are open cut. Mining goes underground when the seam is about 60 m below the surface. Exported coal is largely the high quality coking coal – black coal heated to expel gases and liquids. Brown or steaming coal is mostly used near the mines for making electricity. Two-thirds of its weight is moisture, so it is uneconomic to transport it far.

Australia has 20 iron ore mines and is the

world's third biggest producer. Iron ore was first mined in Australia in 1848 at Mittagong, NSW. From 1915 to the 1970s the main source was the Middleback Ranges of South Australia. Now it is the Pilbara region of Western Australia; the Mt Tom Price and Mt Whaleback mines are two of the world's largest. The hugely rich copper deposits at Kapunda and Burra in South Australia, found in the 1840s, and later at Walleroo and Moonta, brought wealth and people to the struggling colony. The miners were nearly all immigrants from Cornwall. The biggest of the 10 modern fields is at Mount Isa in Queensland.

Engine houses at Burra, in South Australia, were built by Cornish miners in the 1860s to hold machinery that pumped water from the mine. The mine, known as 'The Monster' yielded five million pounds worth of copper.

251

Common Australian minerals

Minerals are naturally occuring chemical compounds. From them are extracted many of the materials that we use, such as copper, lead, zinc, iron, calcium, phosphorous and sulphur. Minerals are also the building blocks of rocks. Granite, for example, is made up of the minerals quartz, feldspar, biotite and hornblende.

There are 2500 known minerals in the earth's crust, made from combinations of 92 elements. However, only 34 minerals make up 98 per cent of the earth's crust. The common rock-forming minerals are composed of a mixture of only eight elements – oxygen, silicon, aluminium, iron, calcium, sodium, potassium and magnesium. Each

has a unique set of characteristics which can be distinguished in a laboratory by chemical methods or by using a microscope. Amateurs can differentiate between them by examining six simple physical properties – crystal shape, colour, lustre, density, hardness and cleavage (how the mineral splits). Some minerals have properties which make them easy to identify – such as magnetite which is magnetic, halite which tastes salty and kaolin which smells like wet earth.

The 29 minerals shown here are some of the most common, attractive and important to be found in Australia.

Gypsum
(Lake Gillies, SA)

Chrysotile Asbestos
Used as an insulator
(Beaconsfield, Tas.)

Augite
(Allynbrook, NSW)

Chalcopyrite
Ore of copper
(Cobar, NSW)

Calcite
Flawless crystals used
in optical equipment
(Kandos, NSW)

Quartz
Sometimes used
as a gemstone
(Torrington, NSW)

Plagioclase Feldspar

Native Copper
(Broken Hill, NSW)

Principal uses are given for
some minerals. Locations in
brackets show where specimens
illustrated were found.

Muscovite Mica
Used as an insulator
(NT)

Biotite Mica
(Broken Hill, NSW)

Cinnabar
Ore of mercury
(Lionsville, NSW)

Pitchblende (black) and Carnotite (yellow)
Sources of uranium and radium
(Nabarlek, NT)

Graphite
Used in 'lead' pencils
(Wilsons Downfall, NSW)

Cassiterite with Quartz
Ore of tin
(Emmaville, NSW)

Malachite (green) and Azurite (blue)
Both copper ores
(Burra Burra, SA)

Olivine
(Warrnambool, Vic.)

Apatite
Source of phosphates

Sphalerite
Ore of zinc
(Broken Hill, NSW)

Scheelite
Ore of tungsten
(Hillgrove, NSW)

Rhodonite
Sometimes used as an
ornamental stone
(Tamworth, NSW)

Rutile
Ore of titanium
(Southport, Qld)

Molybdenite
Ore of molybdenum
(Kingsgate, NSW)

Bauxite
Ore of aluminium
(Weipa, Qld)

Orthoclase Feldspar
(Thackaringa, NSW)

Galena
Ore of lead and silver
(Booroolong, NSW)

Hematite
Ore of iron
(WA)

Magnetite
Ore of iron
(Gulgong, NSW)

Hornblende
(Carcoar, NSW)

Pyrite or Fool's Gold
Source of sulphur dioxide
(Leadville, NSW)

253

MIRAGE

A mirage is an image produced when light is bent as a result of large changes in air density. As light travels through the atmosphere, it slows down when it encounters dense air and speeds up when air is less dense. Bending of light in this manner always occurs in the atmosphere, but at angles too small and variable to be really noticeable, except when differences in density are great. Variations in air density great enough to produce significant bending of light may occur when the ground is very hot. Then, air near the surface becomes much hotter and less dense than the air even a few metres higher. If the decrease in temperature with height is greater than about 0.3°C per metre, then light rays will be bent in a direction opposite to that of the earth's curvature, causing an object in the distance to appear lower than it is in reality, and thereby producing a mirage. Thus, the sky may appear to be lower than the horizon on a hot summer's day and – when accompanied by the shimmering of heat waves – may give the illusion of water. Mirages are most common in desert areas, and over bitumen highways on hot days.

Mirages are a common sight, especially in summer on hot bitumen roads in the outback. They are formed when light from a section of sky is bent passing through hot, less-dense air near the ground, forming an image below the horizon.

MISTLETOE

There are many species of mistletoe in Australia, and all of them rely on a host plant for water and mineral nutrients. However, they do have green leaves and are capable of providing their own nutrition, using the sun's energy by the chemical process called photosynthesis.

Most mistletoes are shrubby plants attached to the branches of their hosts. There are also a small number of root parasites, which at first glance appear to be free-living, but are attached underground. The Western Australian Christmas Tree *Nuytsia floribunda*, which grows up to 10 m tall, is probably the biggest parasitic flowering plant in the world, and when covered with orange flowers is one of the most spectacular plants on the continent. It is widespread in the south-west of Western Australia.

Many Australian mistletoes are pollinated by birds – particularly honeyeaters. Seeds are also dispersed by birds which eat the fruit, and in most cases the Mistletoebird *Dicaeum hirundinaceum* – found everywhere on the mainland but not in Tasmania – is responsible.

Australian mistletoes live on a very wide variety of hosts, including some introduced species. If infestation is high, the growth rate of the host may be reduced, and it may even die. In many cases, however, there appears to be no obvious effect. The incidence of mistletoe may have increased this century.

Mistletoes – recognised by their different foliage – are often seen on trees in the Australian bush. They are parasites, drawing water and nutrients from their hosts, although often without causing any apparent harm.

MITE

Mites are related to spiders and scorpions. There are about 20 000 known species in the world and about 2000 have been identified in Australia. However, it has been estimated that there may be up to 40 000 species living here. No mites (apart from TICKS) are more than two or three mm long, and many cannot be seen with the naked eye. Most adults are eight-legged, but their larvae are six-legged. Some mites live in soil, recycling organic matter, or living as predators. Two-spotted (Red Spider) mites *Tetranychus urticae* are major pests which attack most plants. Hundreds of species are parasites of animals. Virtually everyone – apart from new-born babies – has the microscopic mites *Demodex folliculorum* living in the sebaceous glands on their chins, and at the bases of their noses. A related form causes serious mange in dogs, but the human variety rarely does any harm.

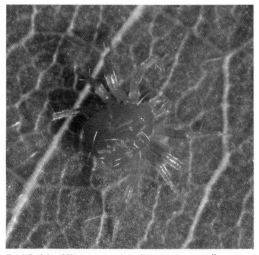

Red Spider Mites – a major plant pest – usually escape undetected because they are so small. There are several species, some of which were introduced into Australia, and that live on plant sap.

The vast bulk of Ayers Rock, and its position in the centre of a plain, make it one of the most impressive monoliths. It is, of course, attached to strata beneath the surface.

MOLE CRICKET

These large, elongated CRICKETS, which grow to about 35 mm long, live in tunnels underground, but sometimes they fly to light and may enter houses at night. They have a large thorax, but their wings and antennae are relatively short. Forelegs are spade-like, for digging. Most are dark brown or grey in colour. They are common insects and may be heard singing at the entrances to their burrows after rain. They live on roots and may sometimes be pests in a garden. There are about 50 species in Australia.

MOLOCH OR THORNY DEVIL

The Moloch *Moloch horridus* (200 mm) is a frightening looking, but quite inoffensive and harmless dragon lizard. Its fat body is covered with many large conical spines which are not, however, hard or sharp. It has curved spines over its eyes, and a large hump on the back of its neck which may be used for storing food. Its spiny tail is short. Background colour is brownish with numerous darker markings. Molochs live in arid country in the western half of the continent where they feed during the day exclusively on ants. Some people have claimed that during storms rainwater collects on the moloch's body and is channelled to its mouth.

MONOLITH

Monoliths – or inselbergs as they are also known – are gigantic, generally rounded, bare blocks of rock which stand above the surrounding countryside. Australia boasts some of the world's finest examples. The most famous is Ayers Rock, but to the east and west of it are two other imposing monoliths – Mt Connor and the mysterious Olgas. There are many other examples in the Gawler, Everard and Mann Ranges and on Eyre Peninsula. Mt Connor is composed of quartzite, Ayers Rock is a variety of sandstone with an abundance of the mineral feldspar, and the Olgas are coarse conglomerate. Most of the other prominent monoliths in Australia are made of granite.

MONOTREME

Monotremes are the only surviving egg-laying mammals in the world, and there are only two examples – the PLATYPUS and the ECHIDNA. They are classed as mammals because, among other more technical details, they have hair and they suckle their young on milk.

Monotremes lay large, yolky, shelled eggs, which is a characteristic of reptiles. The young take milk from grooves which hold glands as there are no nipples. Monotreme limbs also have a tendency to splay out at the side, rather than being set vertically below their bodies. This is also characteristic of reptiles such as lizards.

The two surviving forms, Echidnas and Platypuses, are highly specialised. This makes it difficult to relate the monotremes to extinct groups of mammals. The fact that adults have no teeth adds to the difficulties. Teeth are the most durable parts of a mammal's skeleton and are often the only fossil remains. New species of primates, for example, have been deduced from teeth sold in a Chinese pharmacy. Consequently the classification of mammals, and particularly of ancestral mammals, is largely based on teeth. Until recently fossil monotremes – found only in Australia – all resembled modern forms in having no teeth. However, in 1984 the 15-million-year-old fossil teeth of a platypus were found at Riversleigh in Queensland. In the following year an almost perfect skull was unearthed there. These remains – and any other parts of the skeleton which may be found – will help to unravel the problem of the origins of monotremes. Studies show that echidnas and platypuses are related to one another, but that they have been developing separately for perhaps 50 million years. It is possible that monotremes originated on the Australian part of Gondwanaland and never reached the other regions before the super-continent broke up.

ECHIDNA BIOLOGY

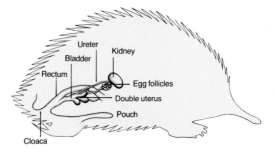

Monotreme means single hole, and refers to the cloaca – a common opening in the pelvic system for the gut, the excretory system and the genital system – all closed by a single ring of muscle. Marsupials have the same arrangement.

MONSOON

Monsoon means season in Arabic, and refers to the large-scale seasonal shift of winds which dominates the climate of many tropical countries. The best known monsoon occurs in India, usually by late June, when south-westerly winds bring a steady flow of warm, moist air across the Indian subcontinent, causing life-giving monsoon rains. However, by September the south-westerly monsoon begins to retreat and it has left the subcontinent by November. Similar seasonal wind shifts are felt in most south-east Asian countries, as far north as China, but to a lesser extent on the continent of Africa.

Although monsoons are very complex, they may be understood in terms of a response by the atmosphere to seasonal shifts in the zone of maximum heating by the sun. As the sun moves progressively poleward towards its summer solstice, it is followed by a region of low pressure called an equatorial trough. South-east Trade Winds from the southern hemisphere, and north-east Trade Winds from the northern hemisphere converge towards the equatorial trough, which is an area characterised by moist air and plenty of cloud. When the equatorial trough extends well into either hemisphere, Trade Winds from the other hemisphere are deflected as they cross the equator and become westerlies, known as monsoon westerlies. Thus, the south-west monsoon in India originates as a south-east Trade Wind in the southern hemisphere, and is deflected to the right as it crosses the equator. The strength of the Indian monsoon is also influenced by the high temperatures of much of the Indian subcontinent and by the height of the Himalayas. A similar monsoon occurs during the southern hemisphere summer when the equatorial trough lies over northern Australia. North-east Trade

THE AUSTRALIAN MONSOON

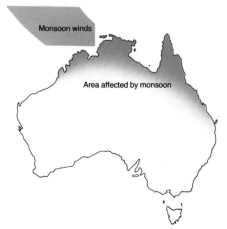

Monsoon rains fall over northern Australia between December and March when prevailing easterly winds change to westerlies. Darwin in the Northern Territories averages 19 rainy days in January.

Winds cross the equator as they converge towards the equatorial trough and are deflected to the left to become north-westerlies which bring summer rains to southern Indonesia, Papua-New Guinea and northern Australia.

The Australian monsoon is similar to monsoons elsewhere in the world, but has lower average wind speeds and does not extend as far poleward as does the northern hemisphere monsoons, mostly because there is less land area in the southern hemisphere and because the Australian continent is much lower. Nevertheless, the Australian monsoon coincides with a well-defined wet season at the northern edge of the continent. The onset of the monsoon is heralded by a change from prevailing easterly to westerly winds, accompanied by rain which accounts for 80–90 per cent of the December to February total for northern Australia. There is often a transition period of eight or so days between the onset of the wet season and the arrival of monsoon winds, during which time considerable rain may fall. A decrease in the strength of westerly winds during the monsoon marks a 'break' in monsoon.

The Australian monsoon usually occurs by December and retreats sometime during March. However, the fact that the monsoon is connected to other, global-scale atmospheric circulations means that its arrival is not always regular. For example, during the summer of 1982–83, widespread drought occurred in northern Australia because the first good monsoonal rains did not occur until March. The failure of the monsoon was linked to high water temperatures in the eastern Pacific Ocean.

DANIEL 'MAD DOG' MORGAN

Not all of Australia's bushrangers were brutal. Ben Hall, for example, had a reputation for chivalry, good humour, and for avoiding unnecessary violence.

'Mad Dog' Morgan was the opposite. From 1862 to 1865 he terrorised parts of the Riverina and Monaro districts, holding up coaches and travellers, raiding homesteads, burning haystacks and farm buildings, and even shooting cattle. Among his victims were two policemen, one shot during a chase, the other murdered while in a tent.

At times he treated captives with joviality, but if he suspected danger he was liable to turn on them in fury; and he took great joy in seeing suspected informers suffer. For example, he once tied a station owner to a fence, gave him five minutes to choose between being shot in the sight of his wife and children, or having the woolshed set on fire. During this time he kept placing the muzzle of his revolver against the captive's forehead. He finally fired the woolshed.

In 1865 Morgan crossed the Murray River, and after several robberies took captive all the

people on a station near Wangaratta. However a nursemaid managed to send for help, and by the next morning the homestead was surrounded by armed men. As he began to leave, a station hand shot him down, wounding him mortally (see photograph p 109).

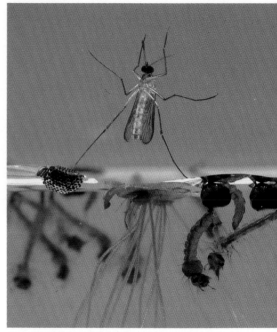

Four stages in the life of Culex annulirostris, a mosquito responsible for transmitting several viruses. Eggs (left) are laid in rafts and hatch into larvae (wrigglers), which usually hang head down by their breathing tube from the surface. Larvae develop into comma-shaped pupae (tumblers), which eventually split open to reveal the fully developed insect .

MOSQUITO

Mosquitoes are all too-familiar blood-sucking, longhorn flies, of which there are about 230 Australian species. Their larvae are wrigglers, which are often seen in water, rising to the surface to collect air through a breathing pore. One group however, breathes through a spike pushed into water plants. Air is drawn out from between the cells. Their active pupae resemble commas. Each species has its preferred breeding sites. Ponds, creeks and lakes are used by many, but 'container' species such as the black and white *Aedes aegypti* and *Culex fatigans* breed in tin cans and discarded tyres. Some species became widely distributed by using the open water butts on sailing ships for breeding. The native *Anopheles australis* breeds in very salty rock pools near the sea.

Adults have scales on their wing veins and margin, and most males – although no females – have bushy antennae. Only females suck blood, which they need for developing eggs. Males prefer nectar. Females specialise in their victims, some preferring people, for example, others cattle, and yet others birds. In some countries *Anopheles* species transmit malaria, *Culex* passes on elephantiasis and *A. aegypti* carries yellow fever. In Australia various species transmit DENGUE FEVER, MURRAY VALLEY ENCEPHALITIS, Ross River virus and other viruses such as MYXOMATOSIS and dog heartworm.

MOSQUITO AND AQUARIUM FISH

The familiar mosquito fish *Gambusia affinis* and *G. dominicensis*, belong to an American family of small fish which produce living young rather than eggs. Males have a special structure – the gonopodium – for transferring packets of sperm to the female's genital opening.

Females of the two species reach 60 mm in length, but males are only half as big. They have been introduced into many countries – often by the American armed forces – in an attempt to control mosquitoes carrying malaria and other diseases. Often the introductions have been fruitless, but some countries have reported limited success. Many countries, however, have native species which would be more effective if properly managed.

The second species prefers warmer waters, and has been introduced into Australia several times since World War II. They are found near Alice Springs. The first species, which compete with CARP for the title of the world's most widespread freshwater fish, was first introduced in 1925 and is now abundant in many parts of Australia. In parts of the south-west they are a great pest, crowding out native species. According to author Eric Rolls in his book *They All Rain Wild*, one of the fish's Asian names means 'useless' – a reference to its value as food and its bitter taste.

Some other species of fish imported for fish-hobbyists are also now well established in the wild, including the guppy *Poecilia reticulata*, and several swordtail species which are found near Brisbane, and the one-spotted live bearer *Phalloceros caudimaculatus* which is found in south-western Australia. The 'sword' of the swordtail refers to the gonopodium.

A second group of fish commonly kept in aquariums, and with species now established in the wild in Australia, is the Cichlids, also called mouth-brooders. These aggressive, strongly territorial fish are originally from central and South America and Africa. Three species are found in power station cooling ponds in Victoria – where the temperatures are higher than in nearby natural waters – and a fourth occurs in some reservoirs and other waters in Queensland and south-western Australia. The last, the Mozambique cichlid *Sarotherodon mossambica* (to 360 mm), has destroyed many native species in similar habitats in other countries.

MOSS

Mosses are overlooked by many casual observers in the bush, but if examined closely they are plants of great diversity and beauty.

Mosses always have a stem and leaves, and produce capsules on stalks from the side or tip of a leafy stem, usually in spring. The capsules contain spores and are covered by a little hood, the calyptra.

There are two alternating generations in the life cycle of moss. The plant itself carries male and female organs. After fertilisation, these produce a capsule. Stalk and capsule together form an asexual, spore-bearing generation. The spores produced are capable of germinating into new plants. Mosses also reproduce vegetatively, by small pieces breaking off and growing into a new plant.

Mosses do not have roots, and for the most part lack any internal system for transporting nutrients or water. Nutrients and water necessary for growth are absorbed directly through the whole surface of the plant. Although many mosses can survive for long periods completely dried out, growth is only possible under moist conditions. In addition, as in the ferns, mosses have to be covered by a film of water for successful reproduction. Mosses are therefore most abundant in rainforests or in sheltered gullies. However, a surprising variety of mosses live in the semi-arid zones, although they are dry and shrivelled for much of the time.

Although the lack of roots limits the range of places in which mosses can live, they can grow to a surprisingly large size on very limited resources. The dangling skeins of moss, which are such a characteristic feature of rainforests, get all their water and nutrients from rain, mist and droplets falling from the branches of trees.

Although mosses are not of direct value to humans, as very few large animals eat them, they can be an important part of a plant community. Sphagnum mosses in bogs act as sponges, absorbing water, helping to regulate the flow of streams as well as providing a store of water to draw on during dry periods. In rainforests, the dense growth of mosses on tree branches may intercept much of the rain, reducing the risk of erosion in heavy storms, and again providing reserves of water for dry periods.

Mosses are one of the groups of plants that make up the bryophytes. The other major group is the liverworts, superficially similar to mosses, but differing in many details.

Four common mosses

Campylopus introflexus, *which grows on rock surfaces and on soil, is very common all over Australia.*

Members of this moss family – *the polytrichaceae – are often found growing on disturbed soil in open areas.*

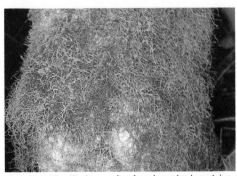

Species of Papillaria *are often found growing in curtains that festoon tree branches in dense rainforests.*

Hypnum cupressiforme *is common in cool wet forests, where it grows on logs and on the bases of trees.*

MOTH

The differences between moths and BUTTERFLIES are only very small. Together they make up the insect order Lepidopera, and have as a characteristic feature a covering of scales on their wings, and often over most of their bodies. The name of the order means, in fact, (little) stone wings because the scales on their wings are arranged rather like the tiles on a roof. Most collectors identify moths and butterflies by their colours and patterns, although this can be unreliable. In some moths large parts of the wings are without scales, and are therefore transparent. These species are often excellent mimics of wasps and bees. Mouthparts are almost always made up of a double tube coiled, except when in use, like a watch spring. Adult

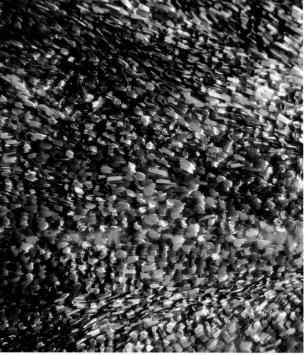

A glittering carpet of tiny, overlapping scales cover a small section of the wing of a White-stemmed Gum Moth Chelepteryx collesi. *These scales are the fine 'dust' that comes off on human hands after a moth has been picked up.*

moths and butterflies usually feed on liquids such as nectar, fruit juices or fluids oozing from dead animals.

The life cycle of a moth or butterfly consists of an egg, a larva (caterpillar), a pupa or chrysalis and an adult. Most caterpillars are vegetarian and usually eat living plants, but some will attack stored products such as flour or dried fruit.

There are 75 families of moths and butterflies, and the moths are divided into four groups based on largely technical differences between such

details as the veins in their wings and the structure of their mouthparts. Two groups contain only a few very small moths.

The first group of seven families contains – among others – the swift moths. They range from small to very large and are often beautifully coloured, with somewhat pointed or bent forewings. Their larvae often live in vertical holes in tree-trunks, feeding on regenerating bark around the mouth of the hole, under the cover of silk webbing. Some burrow in soil and are pasture pests, or eat the roots of eucalyptus trees. Great swarms of these often appear after rain in inland areas. Some swift moths drop their eggs onto vegetation as they fly. As this is a hit and miss method few survive, so some species can lay more than 18 000 eggs. One of the largest is the Bent Wing Swift Moth *Zelotypia stacyi* which has a wingspan of 180 mm. Its caterpillar is a tree borer on the north-east slopes and central coastal regions of NSW.

Most of the moths and all of the butterflies belong in the second group. Some of these moths are both colourful and interesting.

The goat moths contains several large, swift, greyish insects with wingspans up to 180 mm, whose larvae bore into the heartwood of plants. A well known example is *Xyleutes leucomochla*, the WITCHETTY GRUB. The tortrix moths on the other hand, are all small with an average wingspan of about 10 mm and are often better known as larvae than adults. The introduced Codling Moth *Cydia pomonella* is the cause of maggoty apples. The light-brown Apple Moth *Epiphyas postvittana* is very unusual because it is a native pest that has flourished overseas.

The case or bag moths have larvae which live in bags made of sticks, sand, bits of lichen and silk, which are often seen hanging from plants. Many Australian species are unusual in having fully-winged females. In a typical case moth the adult female is wingless, has short legs and remains in her bag. There she is fertilised by the males which have wings with few scales. They are sometimes minor pests. The closely related tineid moths can be much more harmful. There are many native species which live on trees and shrubs, but the family includes the case-bearing Clothes Moth *Tinea pellionella*. Their cases are often seen behind furniture on house walls.

The pyralid family contains moths whose larvae shelter in ugly masses of webbing on native trees, but on the credit side it also contains *Cactoblastis cactorum*, the introduced devourer of PRICKLY PEAR. Many, however, are pests of growing plants, or stored food, and one that is often seen in the kitchen is the Indian Meal Moth *Plodia interpunctella*, which has a wingspan of 14–20 mm. The outer half of its forewings are dark, the inner half white, and its hindwings are light, with dark margins. Its caterpillars are the most common culprits when

dried fruit is found to be covered with silk threads and debris.

The ermine moths are so-called because many are white, spotted with black. They include the Diamond Back Moth *Plutella xylostella*, which eats away the leaves of vegetables such as cabbages, leaving only a skeleton. This is said to be the most widespread moth in the world. It often comes indoors to light, and can be recognised by its small size and a row of light diamonds along the ridges of its wings. Some native species feed in groups on native trees. The caterpillars of the small *Ogmograptis scribula* are the phantom graffiti writers on SCRIBBLY GUM.

Cup moths have brilliantly coloured but unpleasant larvae which are armed with tufts of retractable stinging spines. Those of *Doratifera* are called Chinese Junks because of their shape. Adults have a wingspan of about 45 mm. Cocoons resemble small cups, and are often found on gum tree bark.

The geometrids are almost the only moths famous in song – in Danny Kaye's *Inchworm*. The family name means 'earth measurer' and refers to the caterpillar's appearance as it loops along (thus the other common name, looper).

The emperor moths include one of Australia's best-known moths – which is also well established in New Zealand – the Emperor Gum Moth *Antheraea eucalypti*. Like most of its relatives this species has conspicuous eye spots on its wings, and the males have feathery antennae, used to detect the scents (pheromones) released by nubile females. The males have a wingspan of about 130 mm. The bluish-green larvae and cocoons are covered with hairs which can be irritating. Another famous species is the Atlas or Hercules Moth *Coscinocera hercules* (wingspan 250–350 mm), which has four eyespots and tailed hind wings. Its large larvae feed on rainforest trees in north Queensland.

The hawk moths are also unmistakable. They are quick fliers and have long, pointed wings. Several species can hover in front of a flower, feeding from it like a humming bird. A well-known species, at least in the green and white caterpillar form, is the Australian Privet Hawk *Psilogramma menephron* which has a wingspan of about 110 mm. Hawk moth caterpillars have a spine near their tail which has earned them the American name of hornworms. The tussock moths, in contrast, are not so easily recognised as adults. They are medium to large moths with hairy bodies, and broad wings, although females are often wingless. The caterpillars have a dense covering of hairs, often in tufts.

The BOGONG MOTH is an example of the cutworms which emerge from the soil and 'ringbark' several plants in a crop row during the night. The caterpillars of some species are known as 'army worms' from their habit of advancing through a crop on a broad front.

Common Australian moths

Goat Moth
Xyleutes leucomochla

Painted Apple Moth
Orgyia anartoides

Emerald Moth
Praesynocyna semicrocea

Geometrid Moth
Oenochroma vinaria

Emperor Gum Moth
Antheraea eucalypti

Codling Moth
Cydia pomonella

Bent Wing Swift Moth
Zelotypia stayci

Cup Moth
Doratifera vulnerans

Clothes Moth
Tinea pellionella

Cactoblastis Moth
Cactoblastis cactorum

Bogong Moth
Agrotis infusa

Privet Hawk Moth
Psilogramma menephron

Saunder's Case Moth
Metura elongatus

Old Lady Moth
Dasypodia selenophora

MOUND BIRD

The mound birds or megapodes – big feet – are related to barnyard hens and pheasants but are quite unlike any other birds. They do not use the heat of their bodies to incubate their eggs, but rely on warm earth or decomposing vegetation to bring out their chicks. They are found from Australia to Indonesia, New Guinea, the Solomons and Polynesia. There are three species in this country.

One widespread species, the Orange-footed Scrubfowl *Megapodius reinwardt* (400 mm), sometimes merely makes a hole in unshaded sand, lays her eggs then leaves them. When available the birds use soil warmed by volcanic steam. In Australia, however, they make huge mounds – 7 m wide and 3 m high – of sand mixed with vegetation. They are, indeed, so large that early explorers believed them to be Aboriginal burial mounds. Before the hen lays her 3 to 13 very large eggs – they measure 90 by 52 mm, almost a quarter of her length – the pair dig test pits in the mound. They insert their heads into one of these, apparently to check the temperature. The eggs are laid at intervals of 9 to 20 days. The parents do not care for the young when they emerge – they are self-sufficient as soon as they leave the mound. Several pairs may use one mound. In Australia this species is sometimes found in northern coastal forests.

The second species, the Australian Brush Turkey *Alectura lathami* (700 mm), reproduces in a similar way, but the mounds are smaller. They live in damp, warm, eastern coastal forests north from Sydney. The MALLEEFOWL has the most complex behaviour.

Mound birds live on seeds, fruits and insects raked up from the forest floor.

A Malleefowl on its mound in the Mallee district of South Australia. The birds take about four months to build the mounds in which they incubate their eggs, and these can be 5 m across and 1.5 m high.

MOUNTAIN

Mountains have always been a source of fascination for humans. Every great river in the world is born in a range of mountains and they are formidable barriers which can control the weather systems of entire continents.

Some mountains are formed by volcanic action, where molten material from deep within the earth builds a mountain on the surface. The largest single mountain on earth, Mauna Loa in the Hawaiian Islands, has grown in this way. The Warrumbungle and Glasshouse Mountains are the eroded stumps of volcanic peaks.

Most mountains, however, are formed by FOLDING and FAULTING in the earth's crust. For a thousand million years or more large slabs of the earth's crust, called plates, have been moving about relative to one another. Where the plates collide the rocks are folded, faulted and uplifted to create mighty mountain ranges. Even though mountain ranges seem to be permanent natural monuments, whole ranges are actually on the move. They are being uplifted by the forces of collision, and at the same time constantly worn down by erosion. The Mt Cook area in the New Zealand Alps, for example, is being uplifted at a rate of about 5 mm a year, while it is being aroded at about 2 mm a year. The highest mountains of the world – the Himalayas and the Andes – are also some of the youngest. The Himalayas were formed by the Indian plate colliding with the Asian plate and the Andes by the Pacific plate colliding with the American.

Massive faults in the earth's crust can also produce mountains like the Sierra Nevada of North America and the Hamersley Ranges in Western Australia.

On a world scale Australia has no large mountain areas. This is because this continent is one of the oldest on earth and is free of plate boundaries. However, hundreds of millions of years ago it was a mountainous land. In the west there were large ranges that have since been eroded by the forces of wind and rain. The Great Dividing Range, on the east coast, was also once much larger than it is now, but it has been worn down and then lifted up again only a few million years ago.

MOUSE PLAGUE

In 1917 at Brim in north-western Victoria, 96 barrow loads containing about 65 000 mice each – over six million animals – were caught in one night beside a railway wheat stack. The mice poured into a pit trap 'like a stream of water'. The record weight that year was at Brim too: ten tonnes in one night. The culprit in rodent plagues is often the introduced and misleadingly named House Mouse *Mus musculus*, especially in the wheat belt of south-east Australia and in neighbouring areas. The phenomenon also occurs among native rodents such as the Spinifex

The first rays of dawn sunlight touch the peaks of the Snowy Mountains in NSW (above). This view from the summit of Mount Tate looks south-west along the main range to Mount Twynam on the horizon. Despite its lack of mountains, Australia's mean elevation (below) is 340 m, the same as that of Europe.

HEIGHT OF THE CONTINENTS

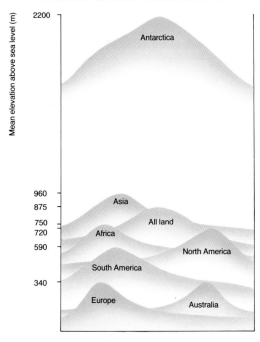

MUDSKIPPER

Mudskippers are GOBIES found in mud flats and mangroves in the warmer parts of the world, including northern Australia. A typical example has eyes on turrets, and stiff pectoral fins by which it moves over the surface of the mud, often at some distance from the water's edge. While out of the water they keep their respiratory chambers full of water to allow breathing through their gills. They can also leap with the help of their tails. The commonest species in Queensland is probably *Periophthalus koelreuteri*, a rather dull-coloured fish about 150 mm long. The larger Great Mud-hopper *P. barbarus* (to about 300 mm), a green spotted fish, extends as far south as Moreton Bay. At Thirsty Sound, in May 1770, the naturalist Joseph Banks found them to be 'a very singular Phaenomenon' and 'of . . . great abundance'.

MULESING

Mulesing is one of Australia's most controversial sheep farming practices, causing much heated debate between farmers and the animal welfare movement. It involves removing two V-shaped folds of skin from the upper areas of the sheep's back legs, around the tail and anus. A pair of sharp shears is usually used to carry out the operation, first developed by farmer Mr J.H.W. Mules. Mulesing stops blowflies laying their eggs on the sheep, and thus prevents blowfly strike. If 'struck', sheep can be literally eaten alive by several hundred maggots hatched from the blowfly's eggs. This is both painful to the sheep and costly to the farmer. Most farmers say mulesing – which leaves a dry, smooth area around the sheep's backside, largely unattractive to blowflies – is the only way of preventing flystrike. On the other hand, some sectors of the animal welfare movement believe mulesing should be banned, or that farmers should at least be forced to anaesthetise sheep.

Hopping-mouse, the Dusky Rat and, in particular, the inland-dwelling Plague or Long-haired Rat *Rattus villosissimus*. Armies of plague rats can root up the ground like pigs, and sometimes advance in bands 80 km wide and 200 km deep at five to eight kilometres or even 15 to 30 km a day, nibbling cattle and horses' hooves, eating harness, biting people camped out, and often devastating crops. Mice too can cause great crop losses. Moving carpets of mice can make driving at more than 30 km/h dangerous for risk of skidding. They are a highly expensive nuisance, gnawing shoes, invading food stores, even chewing rubber fridge door seals. They cause great distress, even mental breakdown, among meticulous householders.

Plagues begin when three to five months of heavy summer rain soften the soil so it is ideal for burrowing, coinciding with abundant grain. Plague rats and mice can multiply rapidly, starting to breed when only about two months old. The rats produce up to seven young every month; House Mice generally have litters of from four to eight. Knowing the cause of plagues holds no promise of prevention or control. Starvation and cannibalism bring plagues to an end after as long as four years.

MUD BRICK

Buildings made from unbaked clay bricks may once have been common in Australia, although few examples survive today. The technique could have come from the USA, possibly with Californian miners in the 1850s, or with English settlers. Both countries have a long established tradition of building with this material, which is called adobe in the USA and cob in Britain. As with PISÉ, the secret of a building's survival lay in giving walls good footings, providing overhanging eaves and a waterproof outer coating.

A mountain of mice. The 500 000 mice in this pile were estimated to weigh about eight tonnes. They were trapped by a double fencing system over a period of four nights during a mouse plague at Lascelles, western Victoria, in May 1917.

CONTROVERSIAL OPERATION

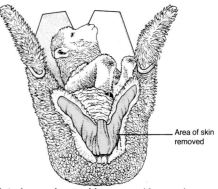

Area of skin removed

The tinted area shows skin removed from a sheep during mulesing. Those in favour of the technique claim that opponents have never seen a sheep that has been 'struck' by flies.

*Colourful **Murray Crayfish*** *are the second largest aquatic crayfish in the world. They are highly prized by fishermen and are reckoned to be excellent to eat.*

MULGA

Mulga *Acacia aneura* is the most widely distributed wattle in arid and semi-arid parts of Australia, where it forms low woodlands. It is a major species over some 130 million hectares, and is also found scattered over a much wider area. Leaves are often cut from trees in times of drought to feed stock.

Although it is only a small tree, mulga is one of the mainstays of the tourist souvenir trade – items such as ashtrays, book ends and napkin rings are made in large numbers from mulga wood. It is popular because of the contrast between the dark heartwood and the light sapwood, and also because it is easy to work and can be given a high polish. Mulga trees are also used for fence posts, and enormous numbers must have been cut for that purpose.

MURRAY COD

Australia's largest freshwater fish is claimed to be the Murray Cod *Maccullochella peeli* (to 1.8 m and 113.5 kg) although the River Whaler Shark and the Small-toothed Sawfish can be longer. The cod belongs to a widespread family of freshwater basses and cods, of which eight or nine species are found only in Australia. The members all have small scales, with one or two spines on their gill covers, a single dorsal fin with the front part spiny, and a lateral line. Murray Cods have rounded snouts, heads with concave profiles, and large mouths. Colour varies, but is often brownish above, white below with white tips to the fins. They will eat other fish, ducks, molluscs and even possums. The fish begin spawning at about four years old, and females lay their eggs in hollow logs or shallows. The species occurs widely in the Murray-Darling River system, but is less common than it formerly was, possibly because of commercial fishing and the amount of silt in the river.

MURRAY CRAYFISH

The Murray Crayfish *Euastacus armatus* is the second largest aquatic crayfish in the world, reaching a length of 450 mm, excluding its claws, and weighing up to 2 to 7 kg. The group it belongs to contains about 27 species, most of which live in cooler rivers, although they sometimes wander on land. Unlike the smooth, dull YABBIES, they are colourful, and well supplied with spines on their claws and abdomens. A Queensland species, *E. sulcatus* – the Lamington Spiny Cray – is bright blue, white and scarlet. The Murray species is usually brown with touches of green, and has white spikes and claws. They are so striking they were once on display in a sideshow at the Royal Melbourne Show.

The largest aquatic crayfish is a Tasmanian species *Astacopsis gouldi*. One has been recorded with a claw-to-tail length of 760 mm, and some have been known to weigh 4.5 kg, although 3 kg is a more common weight. Despite their great size they can live in extremely small streams. They are blackish-green and often covered with parasites – certainly not as esteemed as the greatly prized Murray species.

Queensland boasts the smallest of all crayfish, which, at 25 mm, is shorter than its name, *Tenuibranchiurus glypticus*.

MURRAY VALLEY ENCEPHALITIS

Murray Valley encephalitis is a disease caused by one of several viruses spread by insects. Many have virtually no symptoms and have been called 'viruses in search of a disease'. It is closely related to Japanese, St Louis and West Nile encephalitis. Many birds have the antibody for the virus, and it is believed that these are the reservoir for the disease in northern Australia and New Guinea.

The viruses are spread by mosquitoes, and humans are thought to be intruders in a bird-mosquito cycle. Outbreaks occur when bird numbers build up during wet periods in southern parts of Australia.

In human beings the disease is often mild, but sometimes the illness may be severe with neck stiffness, vomiting, drowsiness, stupor, coma and – in some children – convulsions and even death. Severe cases who recover may be found to suffer from brain damage.

The disease is not confined to the Murray Valley so the name is incorrect, and is resented by tourism promoters in the area.

MYNAH

The Common Mynah *Acridotheres tristis* (230–250 mm) is one of the successes of the Victoria Acclimatisation Society whose object was to establish exotic organisms in Australia, and Australian organisms in other countries. Two others were the House-SPARROW and the European STARLING. In 1862 the Society introduced 42 'Indian myno birds' to help to control caterpillars attacking market garden crops around Melbourne. There was some sense, for once, in the idea. A related species had been taken to Mauritius at the end of the 18th century to counter locust plagues with some success. It was the first known case of biological control in which a control agent was introduced from one country into another. There were further releases in eastern Australia. In 1883, for example, mynahs were established in north-east Queensland to combat beetle grubs in sugar cane. Mynahs have proved to be urban birds, however, much happier in streets, parks and rubbish tips scavenging anything edible, than hunting for insects in crops. There may be some competition with native birds for food and nesting sites in outer suburbs. They pair for life, and nest in holes. Their populous roosts can be very troublesome.

Jaunty Mynahs are so common in city gardens along the east coast – particularly in Sydney – that urban Australians tend to think of them as widespread. In fact they have not become established in the country at all.

MYXOMATOSIS

Myxomatosis is a virus disease of RABBITS which was first observed in laboratory rabbits in Montevideo, Uruguay, in 1896. There were several other outbreaks in European rabbits which almost invariably died. It was thus realised that the European rabbit was an 'unnatural' host for the virus, and consequently extremely susceptible. In 1942 it was found that native American rabbits – more closely related to European HARES than European rabbits – were the true hosts. In them the disease caused no more than a swelling at the site where the transmitting mosquito bit the animal. In European rabbits large tumours form in connective tissues, especially around their mouths and eyes which are soon permanently closed.

Dame Jean Macnamara – a polio specialist – lobbied strongly for the introduction of the virus into Australia. Research was conducted at Cambridge University in England, by an Australian scientist Sir Charles Martin in 1933 and trials were carried out in semi-arid areas of South Australia between 1936 and 1943, but the disease did not become established because of the lack of mosquitoes. Their role was not known at the time. The CSIRO and the Victorian government tried again in 1950, at Gunbower on the Murray River and later at Albury.

The virus seemed to disappear but, after a few weeks it flared up unexpectedly, and within nine weeks had spread over an area of one million square kilometres. Not everybody was happy with the results, however, and Jean Macnamara began to get threatening telephone calls from people involved in hunting and selling rabbit meat and skins.

By 1953 Australia was virtually free of rabbits and it has been estimated that the additional agricultural products made available in the first year without rabbits were worth $100 million. The wool clip alone increased by an astonishing 32 million kg in one year.

The virus was at first so effective that it was subjected to strong natural selection – extremely virulent strains killed their hosts before having a chance to be transmitted by mosquitoes. Less virulent strains, on the other hand, survived. There was also some selection of resistant strains of rabbits. Consequently the impact of the disease on rabbits decreased year after year, and although they have not regained their former high numbers, they remain a serious pest.

The initial success should have been followed by other measures such as the destruction of warrens, and poisoning to get rid of the last few animals over large areas. The CSIRO has continued the work by importing new virulent strains, and other possible carriers of the disease, such as the European Rabbit Flea. These were important in British outbreaks of the disease, where mosquitoes were relatively scarce.

Skin tumours caused by myxomatosis close an infected rabbit's eyes. The disease, spread by mosquitos and fleas, can kill within 13 days.

The mosquito, incidentally, acts as a 'flying needle'. It merely carries some of the virus on its piercing mouthparts.

At the time of the original epidemic in Australia there was an outbreak of MURRAY VALLEY ENCEPHALITIS which many people attributed to the rabbit virus. Three Australian scientists, including Sir MacFarlane Burnet and Dr Ian Clunies Ross, stifled public fears by injecting themselves, without harm, with the myxoma virus.

CYCLE OF DEATH

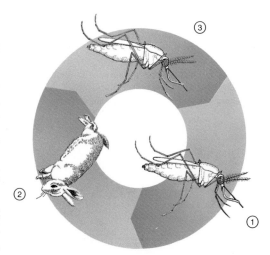

A mosquito (1) carrying the virus on its mouthparts feeds on a healthy rabbit (2). The rabbit develops the disease and mosquitoes that feed on it subsequently (3) pick up the virus with their meal of blood and transmit it to other rabbits in turn.

N

Nabarleks are only seen out in the open during the wet season when they will bask on rocks or feed for several hours after dawn and before dusk. In the dry season they stay under cover during the day and feed at night.

NABARLEK

Nabarleks are a type of rock-wallaby – the Little Rock-wallaby *Peradorcas concinna* (mean body length 319 mm, tail 297 mm). Although marsupials do not have milk and permanent teeth like placental animals, some can replace worn molars to some extent. Nabarleks, however, can apparently produce an unlimited number which is fortunate because in the dry season their diet consists largely of Nardoo *Marsilea crenata*, a strange fern used by Aboriginies to make flour. When dried, 26 per cent of its weight is silica. In the wet season the animals live on grasses and sedges which also have a high silica content. Nabarleks are more active in daylight than most kangaroos, basking in the sun and feeding for a few hours in the mornings. They live in sandstone country in the Northern Kimberleys, and in the north of the Northern Territory, including Arnhem Land, but are reported to be rare.

NAILTAIL WALLABY

These medium-sized wallabies have a fingernail-like horn hidden in the fur at the tip of their tail. Its function is unknown, but little credence need be given to the story that the animal pivots on it when changing direction.

Bridled Nailtail Wallabies *Onychogalea fraenata* (male body 510–700 mm, tail 380–540 mm; female smaller), once widespread in inland eastern Australia, were thought to be extinct since the 1930s, but in 1973 a fencing contractor at Dingo in central Queensland noticed a mob of unusual wallabies which he reported to wildlife authorities. They proved to be the missing species, and with the cooperation of two graziers they are now being conserved. Nailtails spend the day on a patch of bare ground near a tree or bush, and emerge to feed at night at the edge of the scrub. Crescent Nailtail Wallabies *O. luneata*, formerly found in the Centre and south-west Australia, are presumed extinct, although there were reports of some from the Northern Territory in 1961. Sandy-coloured, tropical Northern Nailtail Wallabies *O. unguifera* (600 mm, 570 mm) are still common in savannah, long-grass woodlands and floodplains. They are sometimes called the Organ-grinders after their hopping gait. There are accounts of Bridled and Crescent species escaping from pursuers by climbing up inside hollow trees.

NATIONAL PARK

In 1879 Australia became only the second country in the world to dedicate a national park. That land, only 30 km from the centre of Sydney is now the Royal National Park and attracts over a million visitors each year. Early parks such as the Royal were established purely for recreation – forests were felled to create lawns areas for picnickers, sports grounds were built and exotic animals like deer released into the parks. More recently the need to conserve species and environments has become a major reason for setting up parks.

National parks are only one of many types of reserves dedicated for nature conservation in Australia. Altogether these nature conservation reserves occupy 4.5 per cent of the continent of which the 500 or so national parks make up half. The other reserves include such classifications as NATURE RESERVES, historic sites, Mutton Bird reserves, Aboriginal sites and game reserves. Over 30 million people visit parks each year.

It is only because of the pressures of economic growth and the impact of humans on the natural environment that there is a need for national parks. Without park protection many more plants and animals would become extinct or rare.

A national park today is best defined as an area, preferably relatively large, set aside for the conservation of plants and animals, dedicated for public enjoyment and education, and managed so that its natural attributes are retained.

National parks, despite their name, are set up and managed by the states and territories. The only two mainland parks administered by the Australian National Parks and Wildlife Service are Kakadu and Uluru. Policies and practices vary from state to state: some states have more, but smaller, parks. For example over 60 per cent of all national parks are in Queensland, but the state has the lowest proportion of its area (two per cent) dedicated to nature conservation reserves of any state.

Some parks have been listed by UNESCO as World Heritage sites – Kakadu, Uluru, the Great Barrier Reef, the northern NSW rainforest parks, Mungo National Park and the south-western Tasmanian parks join the Grand Canyon and the Pyramids on a list of the world's most important natural and cultural sites.

Specimens of the Northern Nailtail Wallaby were first collected by naturalists on board the Beagle *at Derby, in Western Australia, in 1838.*

Australia's greatest national parks

There are over 50 national parks in Western Australia, and almost six per cent of the state's total area is in nature conservation areas of some kind.

Geikie Gorge National Park cuts through a fossilised coral reef left from a time when the sea reached the Kimberleys. Mangroves, sawfish and stingrays live here – 350 km from the nearest ocean. Bungle Bungle National Park is a spectacular wilderness of extraordinary rock formations. Nambung National Park is a coastal park which also contains bizarre rock formations. The Stirling Range National Park contains an unparalleled diversity and richness of flowers and shrubs, while Hamersley Range National Park includes many oases of pools and waterfalls in the otherwise arid, iron-rich mountains.

Queensland has over 300 national parks, but most are minute. Lamington National Park is covered with sub-tropical and temperate rainforest – containing red cedar, hoop pine and Antarctic beech. Hinchinbrook Island National Park on Queensland's biggest and highest island has dense tropical rainforest, while Wallaman Falls National Park, north of Ingham, contains a waterfall with the longest clear drop (279 m) of any in Australia. North of Cairns, Cape Tribulation National Park contains a section of the beautiful coastal rainforest that stretches northward from the Daintree River.

The Great Barrier Reef Marine Park is not strictly a national park, but it is the largest area of planned conservation in the world.

NSW has doubled the area contained in national parks over the last decade. The most important additions have been the north coast rainforest parks such as the Washpool, which now have World Heritage status. Blue Mountains National Park borders Sydney and contains magnificent walled sandstone valleys. The spectacular spires, domes and pinnacles of the Warrumbungle National Park are on a western spur of the Great Divide.

Kosciusko National Park contains Australia's highest mountains with ski resorts and massed alpine flowers in spring. In the arid western region Kinchega National Park is reclaimed grazing land to which plants and animals that have not been seen in the region for decades are gradually returning.

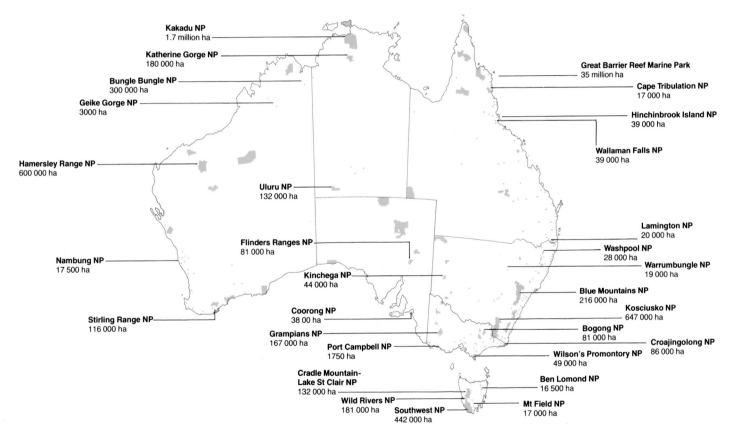

South Australia has 12 national parks and almost seven per cent of its land is nature conservation areas. Flinders Ranges National Park covers a section of this fertile ancient range that rises dramatically out of the arid outback. Coorong National Park stretches south along the coast from the mouth of the Murray River, and is a wetland of international importance.

The Northern Territory has Australia's largest and biologically richest park, Kakadu. It stretches from the Arnhem Land escarpment across the Alligator River floodplain to the sea. Uluru National Park contains Australia's most famous rock and the Olgas. In Katherine Gorge National Park the Katherine River winds between sandstone walls up to 100 m high.

Tasmania has dedicated, sometimes unwillingly, a far greater slice of its area to nature conservation areas than any other state – almost one-seventh – and over 80 per cent of this is contained within three great continuous World Heritage parks in the south-west – Wild Rivers, Southwest, and Cradle Mountain-Lake St Clair. Wild Rivers was born out of the battle over the damming of the Franklin River, and also contains the huge quartzite peak of Frenchmans Cap.

Mount Field National Park is more accessible, and includes an astonishingly wide range of plant communities in a small area. Ben Lomond National Park in the north-east has the unforgettable 'organ pipe' dolerite columns of the central massif.

Despite being the most densely populated and intensively farmed state, Victoria has over six per cent of its area in nature conservation areas. About two-thirds of this is in 30 national parks.

Six large peaks dominate Wilsons Promontory National Park, overlooking dense eucalypt forest, rainforest, grassland, swamps and sandy beaches. Croajingolong National Park in the far south-east is thought by many naturalists to be the most interesting. Bogong covers the state's largest section of alpine country, and is a mecca for cross-country skiers. Port Campbell National Park is a maze of gorges, arches, and islands, while the Grampians National Park covers the western heights of the Great Divide.

NATURALIST

Australia has always attracted naturalists, starting with Joseph Banks and Daniel Solander on Captain Cook's first visit. Before Cook there were observers on some Dutch, Portuguese and British vessels. Even earlier were the Aborigines whose existence depended upon the accurate identification of, and understanding of, the biology of Australian plants and animals. Many of the first settlers, such as Governor Phillip himself and Captain Watkin Tench, combined natural history with their other duties. French visitors in the early days included the notable naturalists Francis Péron and Charles Lesueur in 1801, and Pierre Lesson in 1824.

The first naturalists after settlement were essentially economic biologists whose main duty was to collect plants and animals, unknown in Europe, which might be useful for cropping, domestication, medicine, or ship building, or as garden and zoo novelties. Banks sent out several of his protégés, the best known of whom were George Caley, superintendent of Parramatta botanic garden and collector from 1800 to 1808, and Allan Cunningham, the 'King's botanist'. At that time, 1816, there was also a 'colonial botanist', Charles Frazer. Allan Cunningham was followed by his brother, David, some years later. Caley was an irascible man, of whom even his sponsor, Banks, wrote that 'Had he been born a

A page from naturalist Ludwig Becker's notebook describing a gecko he found at Paine's Hotel at Menindee. The entry is dated 1 November 1860, during the Burke and Wills expedition, six months before Becker's death.

gentleman, he would have been shot long ago in a duel'.

Allan Cunningham joined exploring parties – and led some – in order to collect. This became the practice for later naturalists and several died on expeditions. Ludwig Becker succumbed to scurvy with Burke and Wills, John Gilbert – an ornithologist – was speared to death, and Ludwig Leichhardt disappeared. Gilbert came as an assistant to John Gould whose books on Australian birds and mammals now command high prices. Contrary to common belief Gould was more an entrepreneur than artist, and most of the illustrations were painted by his wife Elizabeth and others such as Edward Lear, the poet, author of nonsense verses.

Among the successful naturalists were Baron von Mueller – the 'Father of Australian Botany' – the colourful Ludwig Krefft, once falsely accused of selling dirty postcards in the Australian Museum, and members of the wealthy Macleay family, important in Australian palaeontology, entomology and museums.

A trained pharmacist – and consequently herbalist – von Mueller established Melbourne's botanical gardens and during nine years collected more than 9000 new species of Australian plants. He also introduced exotic species such as watercress, and encouraged the spread of bramble to supply wreath makers with leaves.

The names of many naturalists who worked in Australia are remembered in the names of plants and animals. John Lewin (of Lewin's Honeyeater), for example, produced some of the finest and earliest plates of Australian birds and moths. Charles De Vis (of De Vis' Banded Snake) was an example of that common British eccentric – the parson turned naturalist. He worked in Queensland from 1870 to 1915.

In the early days Australian naturalists regarded themselves as merely aides to the scientists of Europe. Many, for example, supplied Sir Richard Owen – Darwin's antagonist – who became the authority on extinct Australian animals such as the diprotodont, although he never visited Australia. Eminent naturalists who did visit the country included Charles Darwin and his 'bulldog', T.H. Huxley. In time, however, people such as Krefft began to show their independence, and even to question European opinion. Australian naturalists had begun to break away from the European yoke.

NETTLE

These stinging plants are found in most temperate parts of the world. Two common nettles grow in Australia, one native and one introduced from Europe. The native species, *Urtica incisa*, is a scrambling plant which can develop arching stems up to two or three metres long, sparsely armed with stiff, sharp-pointed hairs which can deliver a severe sting at the

slightest touch. Its narrow leaves also have stinging hairs, but not as fierce as those on the stems. Each hair is made up of a tubular upper part – like a hypodermic needle – and a swollen, poison-containing base which reacts to any pressure on the hair by forcing poison through the tube. The native nettle is mainly a forest plant which grows in wetter areas of Australia. The smaller annual European Nettle *U. urens* has broader leaves and grows in open pastures. It is particularly abundant in spots where cattle or sheep gather and enrich the soil with nitrogen. The plant is widespread and is found in moist spots in the far inland.

The stinging hairs on a nettle have a pointed single cell above a bulbous base holding a poisonous liquid. The hairs are brittle and, after piercing the skin, break off, allowing the poison to enter the wound.

NEVER-NEVER LAND

A vague region in north-west Queensland and neighbouring parts of the Northern Territory was called the Never-Never Land or Never-Never Country. The term began to appear in print in the 1880s but was probably coined in the 1860s, for remote parts from which pioneers thought they were never likely to return, or to which, once they had been there, they never wanted to return. The name may have come from repeated failures by pastoralists to take sheep across this harsh territory. In *We of the Never* Never (1908), about Elsey station near Mataranka in the Northern Territory, Mrs Aeneus Gunn sadly offered yet another meaning: like her dead husband, some pioneers were never able to leave. The name is now used loosely for any sparsely populated desert area, or even for an imaginary region.

Just four of hundreds of newspapers that have served the residents of country towns. Amalgamations resulted in wonderfully complex titles such as the Kaniva and Lillimur Courier and Servicetown Gazette.

NEWSPAPER

In proportion to population, Australia is one of the main newspaper-reading nations of the world. Besides the main metropolitan newspapers, there are many suburban ones, including more than 50 in Sydney alone, while newspapers published in country towns are even more numerous, NSW, for example, having over 140.

This varied press enjoys a freedom which is in marked contrast to the situation in early colonial times. The first newspaper in NSW was the semi-official *Sydney Gazette and New South Wales Advertiser* (1803). Then came two fully independent papers, the *Australian*, owned by William Charles Wentworth and Robert Wardell (1824), and the *Monitor*, both of which had to contend with efforts by Governor Darling to censor their criticism of him. The *Hobart Town Gazette and Southern Reporter* was similarly harassed by Governor Arthur.

As settlement spread, newspapers were established in great numbers, in small country towns as well as in the larger centres of population. Many, however – including ones with such intriguing titles as the *Boggy Camp, Tingha and Bora Miner*, the *Binalong Bugle* and the *Boggabri Budget* – failed, and others underwent mergers, so that today's papers represent only a fraction of all those which have been founded at various times.

Circulation is dominated by the main metropolitan dailies and Sunday papers, with total sales of over seven million. In spite of the wide circulation of the city press, hundreds of country newspapers continue to flourish. From dailies with circulations of 20 000 or more down to humble weeklies selling fewer than 1000 copies, they fulfil a real need by giving information on crop prospects, livestock sales, and a range of other local trends and events which affect their readers' welfare. For visitors too, reading a local newspaper is a good way to gain an understanding of life in a particular town or district.

NIGHT BIRD

Most people think only of owls, and perhaps nightjars and other nocturnal hunters, when night birds are mentioned. Many other birds, however, are active at night. Masked Lapwings *Vanellus miles* (330–380 mm), for example, can often be heard calling at night in eastern Australia and Tasmania as they fly from feeding grounds to their roosting sites. Two parrots habitually drink and feed at night. They are the closely related Ground Parrot *Pezoporus wallicus* (300–310 mm) and the Night Parrot *P. occidentalis* (230–240 mm). Bitterns are also birds of the night.

Owls are, however, *the* nocturnal birds. They are not closely related to the eagles and hawks: the powerful talons and hooked bills of the two groups are the result of their similar lifestyles. Owls have large eyes pointing directly forwards so that they have excellent binocular vision, even in dim light. They also use their extremely keen sense of hearing for detecting prey. Their plumage is soft so that they fly silently, and they are often camouflaged. There are two groups: the masked owls and the hawk owls.

Masked owls have a more definite circular face and relatively small eyes. Best known is perhaps the Barn Owl *Tyto alba* (300–400 mm) which is thought to be the world's most widespread bird, being found in all continents except Antarctica.

The smallest and commonest Australian owl is one of the hawk owls, the Southern Boobook *Ninox boobook* (250–350 mm). It is also called the mopoke because of its call, and is more often heard than seen. These birds are found in wooded areas, even in trees in towns, throughout the mainland and Tasmania where they feed on birds, mammals, and invertebrates.

The other night hunters are the frogmouths; the insect-hunting Australian Owlet-nightjar *Aegotheles cristatus* (210–250 mm), and the three nightjars. Owlet-nightjars are found only in Australia and New Guinea, and are a mixture between frogmouths and nightjars. The Australian species hunts by hawking in flight, by pouncing from a perch, or even by running along the ground. They are found all over the country, but are rarely seen. Spotted Nightjars *C. argus* (290–310 mm) hunt on the wing, with an erratic, jerky flight, in the dim light of dusk and dawn, and roost on the ground during the day. They are widespread on the mainland.

Hunting at night

The ability of owls to see in the dark is proverbial: their eyes are reputed to be hundreds of times more sensitive in the dark than are human's. Recent work by Graham Martin in Britain on the Tawny Owl *Strix aluco*, one of the most thoroughly nocturnal of the owls, throws doubt on this belief. The owl hunts at night in dark woodlands, yet Martin's measurements showed that it performed only two and a half times better than the average human being. There may, indeed, be some people with better night eyes than the average Tawny Owl! Furthermore he found that the owl's sensitivity was close to the theoretical maximum for a vertebrate eye. Owls do hunt by hearing and some can detect – and catch – a mouse in total darkness. Nevertheless the Tawny Owl's hearing is little better than that of a healthy, young human being and, once again, close to the theoretical maximum. How, then, does a Tawny Owl survive in a dark woodland full of obstacles such as twigs and tree-trunks? One clue is the small territory (up to 12 ha) used by such nocturnal woodland birds. As Martin says, they go nowhere. It seems that the owl builds up a very detailed knowledge of its small territory by which they navigate.

NINGAUI

Ningauis – tiny marsupial mice – have only been recognised since 1975, but they are apparently common. Since the first ones were discovered they have been found over a very large part of inland Australia where the average rainfall is less than 350 mm a year. They have been found in sandy habitats in the eastern goldfields, the Gibson Desert and in spinifex country. They are nocturnal creatures which resemble small DUNNARTS, but with relatively wider hindfeet. Ningauis' heads are pointed, and their tails are lightly covered with hair.

There is some doubt about how many species there are. The Wongai Ningaui *Ningaui ridei* has a body length of 57–70 mm and a tail length of 60–70 mm. It, and similar ningauis, seem to be scattered over suitable inland country in all mainland states and the Northern Territory. The slightly smaller Pilbara Ningaui *N. timealeyi* is a bristly little animal of semi-arid grassland on the Hamersley Plateau in Western Australia. It eats a range of insects, some of which are larger than it is. In this species at least – and probably in the others – the adults rarely survive from one breeding season to the next.

NOCTURNAL ANIMAL

Most of Australia's mammals come out only at night, or at least they are most active in the twilight of dawn and dusk. Tourists are often disappointed if they come expecting a wildlife show to compare with that still to be seen in some parts of Africa. It is, perhaps, surprising, that some of the larger kangaroos are not active during the daylight hours as there are no large predators – like cheetahs or lions – to hunt them by sight. They do, however, escape the heat of

Large and aggressive insects pose a problem for the tiny Pilbara Ningaui when it tries to overcome them. These 50-mm-long predators live on the Hamersley Plateau, in the north-west of Western Australia.

Seeing in the dark

Animals clearly differ in their ability to see in the dark. None can see in complete darkness, of course, but some are more efficient than others in dim light. Nocturnal animals generally have larger eyes than those which spend most of their time in daylight. In addition, the distance between the lens and the retina in 'night eyes' is relatively short so that all the available light is concentrated on a small area of the retina.

There are two types of light-sensitive cells in the retinas of most eyes – rods and cones. Rod cells are very sensitive, and cone cells are less sensitive, but are able to detect different colours. Some nocturnal animals, such as cats, have almost no cone cells, but many rod cells. This means that their vision is very acute at night, but that their colour vision is poor. In human eyes the rod cells are concentrated at the edges of the retina which explains why it is easier to detect movement at night 'out of the corner of your eye'.

Nocturnal animals in flash photographs sometimes appear to have red eyes because light is reflected back to the camera from a mirror-like layer behind the retina.

the day by remaining in cover, and may come out during daylight in the winter months or on dull days. Small desert animals, particularly those which never drink, must spend the day in relatively humid, cool burrows in order to maintain their water balance.

Some completely nocturnal animals – and particularly those which also live in dark caves such as many bats – find their way and catch prey by using echolocation. Other nocturnal animals rely on their acute sense of hearing, smell and sight. Many which rely on sight have very large eyes with great light gathering power. Some also glow in the dark. This is not phosphorescence, but the reflection of light from a mirror-like layer – the tapetum – behind the retina. Any light that passes through the retina without stimulating it has a second chance on its return journey. This glowing is put to use by kangaroo hunters with spotlights, or biologists searching for possums. Some animals, such as cats, have a vertical iris rather than a round one and this allows their eyes to close right down to slits in bright light and to open very wide in poor light.

Nocturnal animals must also rely on their sense of touch. Whiskers are often long, and may be used to judge the width of a gap. Many animals, such as rats, tend to keep to definite routes, and these can often be detected by streaks of grease left where they habitually rub past objects as they go by. They also have a kind of mechanical memory, making precisely the same movements each time they make a journey. Experienced pest control workers realise this, and set their traps accordingly.

NUMBAT

Numbats or Banded Anteaters *Myrmecobius fasciatus* (mean body length about 245 mm, tail about 490 mm) are one of the most attractive marsupials, with their reddish-brown bodies, several white transverse bars, black stripes through their eyes, and long faces. A numbat's tongue is about half the length of its head and body, and is used to lick up termites which it uncovers with its clawed front feet. Although they have many teeth, they apparently swallow the insects without chewing them. The animals are active during the day and sleep at night.

Numbats formerly ranged from south-west Australia to north-west NSW, living in the woodlands which provided the hollow logs both they and their prey used for shelter. Now they are found only in a few wandoo *Eucalyptus wandoo* and jarrah *E. marginata* forests in the south-west of Western Australia. Their gradual decline is due to foxes, frequent fires – which destroy their log homes on the ground – and possibly recent droughts.

Numbats are the only member of their family, and are one of the few marsupials without a pouch. Young numbats cling to the four teats of their mother, but are later left in a nest in an underground chamber, and are carried, when necessary, on their mother's back.

NUT

Many kinds of nut trees take time to reach full potential, and some are dependent on air currents for pollination, so the crop is variable from year to year. But nuts have become attractive to growers, seeing that Australia needs to import about half its needs. Average consumption is about 4 kg a person every year. Large numbers of most kinds, particularly MACADAMIAS and chestnuts, have been planted in recent years. Almonds *Prunus amygdalus* are already an important crop; about 5000 tonnes are harvested yearly, mostly on the Adelaide plains and in irrigation areas of the Murray Valley. The Murray Valley also suits pistachios *Pistacia vera*, originally a desert plant from Iran. Cashews *Anacardium occidentale* have been planted re-

Numbats – *also known as Banded Anteaters – use their long, pink, sticky tongues to pick up termites. Because they lack strong digging claws, they expose only the most shallow underground termite galleries when hunting for food.*

cently to the east of Darwin and on the Ord River. The shell contains a chemical which, although a skin irritant, is valuable, being used in corrosion-resistant paint, among other products. Walnuts *Juglans regia* are grown commercially,

mostly near Myrtleford, Bright and Dargo in Victoria. Hazelnuts *Corylus avellana* – sometimes erroneously called filberts – grow in the Dandenongs; about 30 tonnes a year are harvested. Spanish or sweet chestnuts *Castanea sativa* are grown near Bright and Beechworth in Victoria. The harvest of some 65 tonnes a year is likely to increase thirtyfold in a few years' time. Pecan trees *Carya illinoensis*, native of the southern United States and northern Mexico, can grow to 20 m. One of the largest plantations in the world is near Moree in NSW.

NYMPH

Nymphs are the immature stages of insects such as cockroaches and grasshoppers. Unlike a LARVA, a nymph resembles the adult but it is smaller, sexually immature and wingless, although wing-buds are visible in the later stages. Land-living nymphs lead lives similar to those of adults, eating much the same food. Nymphs of dragonflies, mayflies and some other insects which develop in water obviously have adaptations such as gills which do not occur in adults, and they are often called naiads (from the Greek *naias*, water nymph). Insects with nymphs have no pupal stage while larvae, on the other hand, undergo complete metamorphosis (as when a caterpillar changes into a butterfly).

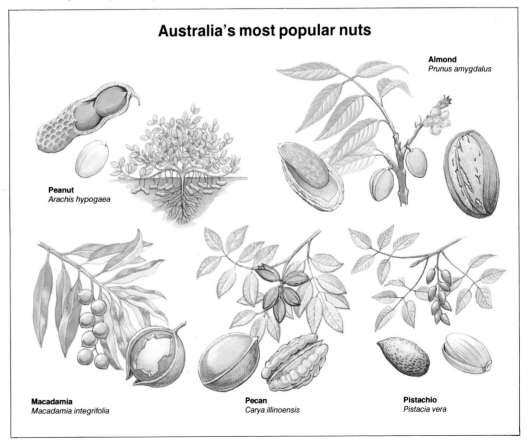

Australia's most popular nuts

Peanut
Arachis hypogaea

Almond
Prunus amygdalus

Macadamia
Macadamia integrifolia

Pecan
Carya illinoensis

Pistachio
Pistacia vera

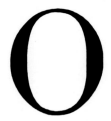

OAK

This English name was originally used for a group of trees which have a characteristic fruit called an acorn. A number of true oak species, including the English Oak *Quercus robur* have commonly been planted in temperate areas of Australia since the earliest days of white settlement. But the settlers also bestowed the name 'oak' on various native trees they encountered, purely because their timber looked like that of the true oaks. The most obvious point of resemblance is the presence in the wood of large medullary rays, giving it a coarsely flecked grain. The earliest trees so named were the SHE-OAKS, which are common around Sydney, as well as most other parts of Australia. Their pine-like foliage could hardly look less like that of a true oak. Apart from she-oaks, the most important group of trees to be called oaks are various rainforest trees which are mainly found in Queensland. Earliest known was Silky Oak *Grevillea robusta* which is common around Brisbane and extends into northern NSW. It yields a valuable joinery timber. Most other 'oaks' in this family are found only in north Queensland rainforests.

Tasmanian Oak is a timber trade name for wood from some of the tallest species of eucalypts, including Mountain Ash, Alpine Ash and Messmate. These trees do not have conspicuous rays in their wood, but in other respects the timber is similar to that of the true oaks.

Ruins of the oil extraction plant at Newnes, to the west of Sydney. In the early years of this century oil was recovered from vast oil-shale deposits in the area.

OATS

Oats are Australia's third most important grain crop, after wheat and barley. They are grown for grazing, hay or grain production.

If oats are grown for grain, the farmer allows the crop to mature fully, and harvests it with a combine harvester. Hay and grazing oats are not allowed to mature, and are often cut or used at least one month before the crop reaches the height where grains emerge.

Nearly all of Australia's oats crop is used within the country. Small amounts, however, are exported to Japan, south-east Asia, South America and Europe, mostly to West Germany. In these countries oats are fed to cattle.

Oats are grown in most temperate, mid to high rainfall grain-growing regions. Small areas are planted in the more subtropical, humid parts of northern NSW and southern Queensland. The main growing areas are Western Australia's south and east, central NSW and Victoria's Mallee, Wimmera and western regions. Oats were at one time restricted to cool, high rainfall districts, but scientists have bred varieties to suit most conditions.

Australia's annual oats production is highly variable, depending on prices and the availability of pasture feed. The prices received for oats are generally several dollars less per tonne than those paid for wheat and barley. In good, high rainfall years, when there is plenty of pasture around, farmers may plant other grain crops.

OIL

Oil is vital in maintaining the way of life of developed nations. Oil fields are formed from the remains of microscopic plants and animals, just as coal is. However, while coal is formed from the remains of land plants only, oil can be formed from land plants or the remains of untold millions of microscopic organisms that once lived in the oceans of the earth.

Over millions of years these remains are buried beneath thousands of metres of silt and sand to form rocks containing between one and five per cent of organic material.

Oil in oil shale gathers in pores between sand grains. When the pores are joined together the oil can travel through the rock to form reservoirs containing up to 25 per cent oil and gas by volume. It is these richer oil fields that are mined all over the world today. Australia is about 70 per cent self sufficient in oil, with most of it coming from the Bass Strait fields.

The drooping seed heads of oats are distinctive. Some of the harvest ends up on the nation's breakfast tables as porridge or muesli.

OLEARIA

This group of shrubs and small trees is part of the daisy family, and its members are sometimes known as Daisy-bushes. Although species are found in most parts of Australia, the ones from cooler south-eastern areas are the most attractive. Their mostly toothed leaves are often felty or scaly on the underside and the white, pink or violet daisy flowers usually grow in loose clusters at the branch tips. The largest species is the Musk Daisy-bush *O. argophylla* of south-eastern mountain forests, known simply as 'Musk' in Tasmania where it can be a 15-m tree. Its broad oval leaves are silvery on their undersides. In subalpine areas several low shrubby species with dazzling white flowers can make a spectacular show in summer. On the NSW coast Wooly Daisy-bush *O. tomentosa* is an attractive shrub of sandstone headlands, with densely furry leaves and large white to pale pink flowers, the petals being darker pink on their undersides.

OLIVE

Branches from the evergreen olive tree have traditionally symbolised peace. The trees are valued by many Australian farmers, however, as windbreaks and for their small, round fruit. One species is native to Australia, but those grown commercially originated from around the Mediterranean. Olives grow in a wide range of climates – even running wild in some parts of of the country – but produce best in regions free of extremes of heat and cold. The trees are drought

A maze of shafts and heaps of earth dot the landscape around the Lightning Ridge opal fields in the far north of NSW. Chips of opal can be gathered from spoil heaps.

resistant, but require at least 450 mm of rain each year, or irrigation, to produce a commercial crop. The trees come into full production at eight to ten years, yielding up to three tonnes of fruit per hectare.

Although olives grow in most states, commercial orchards are centred along the Murray River in South Australia and Victoria. Olives are harvested in autumn, either when green and unripe, or black and ripe, for pickling. In some other countries ripe olives are also pressed for their highly-prized oil.

OPAL

This gemstone, with its dazzling fire, is distinctly Australian. The names of the towns where it is found – Coober Pedy, Lightning Ridge and White Cliffs, with their underground houses and secretive miners, are part of folklore.

Surprisingly, opal has a similar chemical composition to common quartz, but a different, more random, arrangement of atoms. It is the fiery flashes of colour against a white, cream, grey or black background which gives precious opal its value, and these are due to minute, tightly-packed spheres of silica crystals that can only be seen under an electron microscope. The relative size and arrangement of these spheres, which reflect light waves, governs the colour of a stone. Larger spheres give a red flash, medium ones show green and the smallest ones blue. Black opal is regarded as the most valuable. Opal

without the internal flashes of colour is called potch, which is worthless.

The best opal is found in the arid sandstone regions of western Queensland, western NSW and South Australia. Most opal is recovered from

OPAL MINING AREAS

Australia's major opal areas are: *1* Lightning Ridge, first discovered in the 1880s; *2* White Cliffs; *3* Coober Pedy; *4* Andamooka and *5* the Queensland region, where many scattered finds have been made since the first stones were discovered in the early 1870s.

less than 20 m below the surface, but only about one per cent is classed as precious.

Opal is thought to have formed from the slow evaporation of a gel rich in silica. This gel becomes concentrated in water circulating through the ground, not far beneath the surface. Sometimes the gel replaces organic material, such as fossilized shells, bones and twigs, but the shape of the original organism is perfectly preserved – in opal.

OPEN-CUT MINING

When minerals of economic value occur close to the surface they are extracted using open-cut mining methods. Firstly the top layer of valueless soil and rock – the overburden – is removed using bulldozers or large ripping machines called draglines. Then the ore minerals are excavated by strip or bench methods. The strip methods – which expose a series of parallel strips – is commonly used in Australia to mine coal and iron ore. Bench methods excavate a large crater by digging circular benches which spiral into the ground. The largest man-made excavation in the world is an open-cut copper mine at Bingham Canyon, Utah, in the USA, which is over one kilometre deep.

The ore is removed using explosives if the ground is hard – as it usually is in gold and copper mines – or by digging directly into it with mechanical shovels if the ground is soft, as is the case with coal.

ORCHARD

Orchards are often associated with romance They are the place where, according to many poems and songs, young couples go to be alone.

But in the less romantic world of fruit production, orchards are the enclosed area where trees are planted, protected from pests and diseases, and their crops are harvested. The most common orchard crops are apples, pears, stone-fruit (such as plums and cherries) and citrus.

The introduction of machinery, such as misters and other sprayers, has greatly increased the size of orchards. The one-acre apple orchard may still exist at the back of some colonial estates, but the modern orchard is usually 10 ha or more in size. Some commercial apple orchards may have 100 ha or more of one variety of fruit. Varieties are grown separately to avoid cross-pollination to fruit species. Most orchards are rectangular, allowing the farmer to manoeuvre machinery between the rows.

ORCHID

There are 30 000 members of the orchid family – one of the world's largest groups of flowering plants. Their flowers are usually colourful and often have elaborate shapes, usually featuring a prominent centeral 'lip' which may be blotched or spotted. Orchid seeds are minute, containing no stored food, and millions of them may be produced in each fleshy pod. In order to become successfully established, the seedling depend on being infected with a symbiotic fungus which enables them to absorb nutrition from decaying vegetable matter. Living in the outer layer of their fleshy roots, this fungus remains a lifelong part of the orchid plant.

The 700-odd species native in Australia are in two major groups, which grow in different ways. Epipytic orchids, which are found mainly in the wet tropics, have swollen stems, leathery leaves, and fleshy aerial roots which cling to trees or rocks. Well known examples are the Cooktown Orchid (Queensland's floral emblem) and the 'Rock-lily' of the south-east. The other group, found mainly in temperate regions, are the ground-dwelling orchids. Most of these small plants have underground tubers and thin leaves which are renewed each year. They are found in grassland and forest areas.

OSPREY

Ospreys *Pandion haliaetus* (500–630 mm) are magnificent fish-hawks which are found almost all over the world, and they can be seen around most of the coast of mainland Australia. In pairs, or singly, they maintain territories stretching along 5 to 20 km of coasts and inlets, fishing by either snatching prey from the water, or by dropping bodily into the sea, feet first. There is an old European belief that the birds use magic to bring the fish to the surface, belly-up. When

Ostriches on a farm at Port August, SA, in 1888 (above) sacrifice their tails so that they may be used to decorate the hats of fashionable ladies (below).

the plumage pattern cannot be seen Ospreys can be distinguished from other fishing birds-of-prey by their bowed wings. Fishing eagles have upswept wings. Ospreys appear to be holding their own in Australia, but numbers have dropped drastically in some other parts of the world. Some of this decline can be attributed to fish contaminated by persistent pesticides, PVCs (industrial solvents which were once widely used) and mercury used in paper making.

OSTRICH FARMING

In the late nineteeth and early twentieth centuries, when the tail feathers of ostriches were widely used in ladies' hats, boas and fans, a number of ostrich farms were established in Australia. The first one was probably at Murray Downs, near Swan Hill in Victoria, which was started in 1875. In later years the leading producer among the states was South Australia, which in 1912 had 1345 birds, mostly around Port Augusta. In NSW the largest ostrich farm was that owned by Mr. J. Barracluff near South Head, Sydney, which in 1901 had 100 birds. The total number of ostriches in the state reached a grand total of 606 in 1916.

For a while the industry's prospects seemed bright, for the ostriches adapted well to Australian conditions, and the feathers produced by each bird annually were worth several times as much as the wool from a sheep. Ostrich farming therefore became a subject for research and study in agricultural colleges. In 1901 Hawkesbury Agricultural College imported two birds from South Africa, and by 1914 its flock numbered 14. Yanco Experimental Farm in the Murrumbidgee Irrigation Area had 76 birds in 1917. From about that time, however, the popularity of the feathers fell rapidly as fashion moved on, and during the 1920s ostrich farming came to an end in Australia.

OUTBACK

The origin of the term outback is unclear, but it most probably derives from the colloquial expression 'out back of beyond'. Alternatively, it could be a derivation from 'out the back'. Like the name, the area covered by the term outback is equally unclear, but for most Australians in covers the arid interior of the continent. The outback is pastoral country, where there is little or no agriculture without irrigation. Sheep and cattle populations are measured in terms of one beast to every two to three square kilometres. Sheep dominate the bottom half of the agricultural outback, while cattle dominate the northern half. The human population is also sparse. Less than one per cent of Australians live in the outback, in an area that occupies at least 75 per cent of the continent. Neighbours are separated by hundred of kilometres and rely on special services such as the FLYING DOCTOR and the SCHOOL OF THE AIR.

THE OVERLAND TELEGRAPH

Before 1872 Australia's fastest means of communication with Europe was a monthly mail steamship service. In that year, however, the completion of a telegraph line from Adelaide to Darwin (then named Palmerston) transformed the situation. The construction of such a line was first suggested in 1859 by Charles (later Sir Charles) Todd, South Australia's Director of Telegraphs. At that time explorers had not yet even reached the centre of the continent, but by 1862 John McDouall Stuart had succeeded in travelling from Adelaide to the north coast, and so had helped to make Todd's suggestion a practical possibility. In the following year the administration of the Northern Territory was transferred from NSW to South Australia, which then had a strong interest in the construction of a telegraph line, since it would help in the development of the territory. Britain was already linked to Java by telegraph, and in 1870 the British-Australian Telegraph Company agreed to lay a cable from that island to Port Darwin, provided the South Australian government finished construction of a land line between Port Darwin and Port Augusta by 1 January 1872.

Todd was appointed general supervisor, and since about 2990 km of line had to be constructed in a mere 18 months, he divided the route into three main sections, in which work was carried on simultaneously. Nevertheless the whole project was fraught with difficulty, especially since provisions and construction materials – including iron poles to resist termites – had to be transported great distances through difficult country which had been barely explored.

Materials were brought from Port Augusta, largely by camels, for the southern and central sections, and these were both completed on time. However, work on the section from the north coast to Tennant Creek was hampered because of the difficulty of bringing supplies in by sea through Port Darwin, and by severe flooding during the wet season. It was completed in August 1872, and in October, after a fault in the submarine cable had been repaired, Australia's link with the outside world was complete.

A LINK WITH THE WORLD

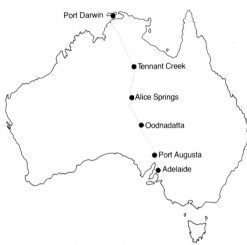

The Overland Telegraph (above) snaked its way across some of the continent's most inhospitable land. Charles Todd, third on the right from the gangplank in this view of the construction party waiting for suitable weather at the line's northern end, (below) was appointed general supervisor of the entire venture.

OVERLANDERS

When new settlements were founded in the Port Phillip district (now Victoria) and South Australia, the quickest way to provide them with sheep and cattle was by droving stock from the settled districts of NSW. Men who did this became known as colourful characters. As one Adelaide resident wrote: 'The gentlemen overlanders affected a banditti style of hair and costume. They rode blood or half-bred Arab horses, wore broad-brimmed sombreros trimmed with fur and eagle plumes, scarlet flannel shirts, broad belts filled with pistols, knives and tomahawks, tremendous beards and mustachios'.

The first to reach Melbourne were John Gardiner, Joseph Hawdon and John Hepburn – a monument to whom can be seen beside The Boulevard, above Yarra Bend National Park – in 1837; and Joseph Bonney arrived later in the same year. Hawdon was also the first to reach Adelaide, and Patric Leslie was the first to overland sheep from New England to the Darling Downs in 1840.

OYSTER

Sydney people are convinced that their oyster, the Sydney *Crassostrea commercialis*, is the finest in the world. It grows along rocky coasts and in estuaries from northern Queensland to eastern Victoria, but near the cities it is foolish to sample 'wild' oysters because of the danger of pollution. Unlike most bivalves they vary a lot in shape, which depends on the surface they are clinging to and the degree of crowding. Shells are purplish blue on the outside, and white inside. The left shell is attached, and convex to contain the oyster's body, while the right is flatter. A single, large, central muscle closes the shell.

Rock oysters grow best in estuaries because the water there contains more organic particles on which the oysters feed, drawing the material in with their gills. Consequently most oyster leases are in estuaries, mainly on the NSW coast. Stones, tiles, or mangrove sticks are set out by the growers for young larvae to settle on. Spawning by adults can take place at any time, with a peak in late summer.

About 16 days after hatching from the fertilised egg the 0.5-mm-long shelled larva settles, and having found a suitable site, loses its foot. After three to five years the oysters are ready to harvest, but they must be cleaned.

Oysters are attacked by many creatures, including seastars, and oyster borers – snails with black, knobbly shells resembling a hand-grenade or mulberry.

On southern coasts another species, the Mud Oyster *Ostrea angasi*, is collected. It was a favourite food of the Aborigines.

None of these belong to the same family as the pearl oysters, although they can sometimes contain inferior PEARLS.

P

Red-necked Pademelons are common in the dense forests of eastern Australia. They are usually seen at the forest edge in the evening when they emerge to graze on grass and green shrubs.

PADDOCK

Outside Australia a paddock is a small field close to the farmhouse, or a small area used for exercising horses. Australian paddocks, however, can range in size and use from the small home paddock to grazing paddocks of many thousands of hectares. Paddocks are areas of land enclosed by fences. Their shape can be determined by natural factors, such as a hill and bushland. Their size is usually determined by their use – a weaning paddock, for example, is likely to be much smaller than a grazing or fattening paddock. Farms are usually divided into paddocks according to soil types and other factors which affect management. Paddocks in northern and inland Australia can cover vast areas and take days to muster, whereas in more intensive operations they can be less than one hectare in size and easily covered on foot. All stock paddocks contain at least one watering point. Paddocks are usually named according to their size, purpose, position or other distinguishing characteristic. Weaner, milker, holding, airstrip and top paddock are common names on many properties.

PADEMELON

The two Australian pademelons are small wallabies which live in thick cover, even dense rainforest, and emerge at night into more open country to graze and browse. The very common Tasmanian Pademelons *Thylogale billardierii* (male body length 630 mm, tail 417 mm; female smaller) are often a pest in forestry plantation and crops, consequently many are killed each year in pest control without, apparently, reducing the population permanently. They were, however, brought to extinction on the mainland many years ago, but some survive on the larger Bass Strait islands.

Red-legged Pademelons *T. stigmatica* (492 mm, 463 mm) are still common in suitable areas along the east coast, north from central NSW. They eat fallen leaves and fruit, including figs, some ferns and grasses, from late afternoon until early morning. They then sleep, sitting on their tail, leaning back against a tree, head drooping forward onto their chest.

PALM

These are popularly thought of as tropical plants, and indeed this is true of the vast majority of the world's palms. True palms are all members of one plant family, and are different from other palm-like plants such as the CYCADS and

Pandanus. Australia has 50-odd native palms, of which all but a few are confined to the tropical north. Only on the moist east coast do several extend into temperate regions, with four in NSW and one just getting into far eastern Victoria. North-eastern Queensland is home to the largest number of species.

Most important in Australia are the *Livistona* or Cabbage-tree Palms, with their fan-like 'fronds'. Most of the 16 species are scattered across northern Australia, some being confined to remote areas. The Central Australian Palm *Livistona mariae* occurs in the oasis-like Palm Valley near Alice Springs, about 800 km away from any other naturally occurring palms. In coastal NSW the rather similar *L. australis* is the most common palm, found near beaches, even in Sydney suburbs. In the Northern Territory, close to Darwin, the very small *Livistona humilis* is seen in large numbers in flattish sandy country. Bangalow or Piccabeen Palms, an elegant, feather-leaved species, are common in moist valleys in many parts of northern NSW and southern Queensland.

PAMPAS GRASS

As the name implies, this giant grass, *Cortaderia selloana*, is native to Argentina, but it has commonly been grown in Australia as an ornamental. Plants form large, dense clumps about 1.5 m high of narrow, rather tangled, raspy-edged leaves; above these rise many taller, plume-like seeding heads, either cream or pinkish, which bend and ripple in the wind. In gardens the plants are long-lived and very hardy, their only disadvantage being the work involved in removing dead leaves and seed-heads. But in recent years there has been growing concern in parts of Australia about the way this plant is invading native bushland. Its small seeds are blown long distances, and the resulting plants can survive in undisturbed bush on very poor soils. In New Zealand Pampas Grass has already formed dense infestations, displacing native vegetation. In 1987 it was proclaimed a noxious weed in NSW, which means that landowners are legally obliged to remove it from their property.

PAPAYA

The palmlike papaya tree – also known as papaw – is grown in the tropics and subtropics for its elongated yellow-orange fruit. The smooth, soft flesh of the fruit is eaten and the small, round, black seeds are discarded.

Coastal Queensland – particularly around Yarwun (near Gladstone), Maryborough, Rockhampton and Cairns – dominate papaw production. There are also plantings in northern NSW. Around 90 per cent of the crop is frozen, canned, dried or processed into tropical fruit salad which is then canned.

Papaya trees may be male, female or bi-sexual.

When bi-sexual species are used, about 10 per cent of plantings are of male trees, to enable pollination. Usually four to six crops are taken from one tree, with most fruit being produced between August and November. The trees prefer warm, sheltered positions, and are usually planted on north-east slopes to minimise wind and frost damage. Nutrition and the control of insects, diseases and weeds are more important for papayas than most other tropical and sub-tropical crops. The fruit, which is soft when ripe, is susceptible to blemishes and bruising.

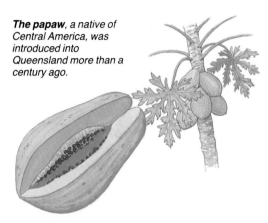

The papaw, a native of Central America, was introduced into Queensland more than a century ago.

PARASITE

Organisms can live very closely together. Sometimes the association is mutually beneficial, as with fungi and algae which together make up LICHENS, or the protozoa within TERMITES. Often, however, the association harms one of the pair and benefits the other, which is called a parasite.

In the most familiar cases parasites live permanently, for at least one stage of their life-cycle, either in or on their victim, the host, at its expense. It is not in the best interests of a parasite to destroy its host because in doing so it is threatening the livelihood of itself, or at least of its offspring. Evolutionary processes ensure that in time the two species come to a form of accommodation. Therefore a severe illness resulting from a parasite generally indicates that the particular association is recent in evolutionary terms. The European rabbit was, for example, the 'wrong' host for the MYXOMATOSIS virus which normally lives in – but does little damage to – American rabbits, which are more closely related to hares. On this time scale typhus and AIDS are relatively recent and deadly diseases of humans.

It is probable that there are more species of animals that are parasitic than animals that are not. Virtually every mammal, for example, is a potential host of dozens of different parasites, and many of these can survive only on, or in, one particular type of host.

PASPALUM

This grass, *Paspalum dilatatum*, originally from South America, was introduced into Australia as a pasture grass for dairy farms. It is mainly found on the subtropical east coast. The majority of people in this region, however, regard it as a weed because of the way it infests lawns, or forms tangled masses of stems, 300 to 600 mm high, on waste land. Its most unpleasant feature is the way the narrow seed-heads are almost always infected with a sticky, blackish fungus – one of the plant-parasitic *ergots* – which comes off on clothes or leaves bare legs spotted with what feels like contact glue. This ergot also contains poisonous alkaloids which can affect livestock, sometimes causing deaths. One of its components is lysergic acid. Other *Paspalum* species, some of them native, are found in warmer parts of Australia.

PASSIONFRUIT

Passionfruit is a type of passion flower – a woody vine with unusual blossoms which originated in South America. In the late 1500s Roman Catholic priests named the passion flower for the Passion – or suffering and death of Jesus Christ. They believed parts of the plant and its flowers symbolised those events.

Australia is one of the world's largest producers and consumers of passionfruit. One of the country's national dishes, the pavlova, is traditionally decorated with it.

Passionfruit are a small, round hard-skinned fruit with yellow, pulpy flesh containing hundreds of small, hard seeds. The hardy passionfruit vine is supported by trellises and the fruit are picked by hand. About three-quarters of the country's crop is grown in Queensland, mostly in the state's south-east. The other major plantings are on the NSW north coast, and there are minor areas in Victoria and Western Australia. Altogether, about 300 ha are planted commercially. Passionfruit is a popular fruit in gardens, perhaps because it thrives with little attention.

Passionfruit originally came from Brazil. The hardy vines are now often seen trailing over sheds in Australian backyards.

PARROT

Brilliantly plumaged parrots are possibly the birds which are most evocative of the Australian countryside. They can be seen – and often heard – in all kinds of habitat, from rainforest to the arid centres. They are also easily recognised by their strong, hooked bill with its fleshy cere, their short necks and often long tails, and their zygodactyl feet – the second and third toes point forward and the first and fourth toes point back.

Of the 340 species of parrots and cockatoos in the southern hemisphere, 51 are found in Australia. These include the large black or white COCKATOOS, the green lorikeets, the tiny fig-parrots, the broad-tailed rosellas, the ever present pink and grey GALAHS *Cacatua roseicapilla* and the familiar little BUDGERIGAR *Melopsittacus undulatus* (175–185 mm).

Although the Australian parrots include some of the most striking species, there are certain interesting groups which are absent: the hanging parakeets, which range from India to the Philippines, and pass the night hanging by their claws from branches like bats, braced by their stiff tails; the small parrots of New Guinea which vary their diet of insects and seeds with slimy fungi and algae they scrape off tree bark; and the keas of New Zealand, which land on the backs of sheep and may take flesh from them when they are sick or dead.

All Australian parrots share some traits and abilities. They are fruit-, seed- and nectar-feeding birds, and they habitually use their beaks for climbing, and one foot – usually the left – to hold food to their mouths. All have distinctive calls. Most are gregarious and flock, and mating is often permanent. They nest mostly in hollows in trees and their plain white eggs are incubated by the female, or by both sexes in white cockatoos. Both parents feed the young. Although known to mimic the human voice, they are not unique in this. And there is no doubt that they have no understanding of what they are saying, despite an abundance of stories about embarrassing comments made at the wrong time.

The first report of 'talking birds' seems to have been given by the Greek Ctesiphon who was the personal physician of Ataxerxes in the 5th century BC and who had heard of the *bittakos* from Indian merchants. Alexander's generals brought some back from India to Greece, including the species now known as the Alexander Parrot (not to be confused with the rare Australian Alexandra's Parrot *Polytelis alexandrae*). Classical Greeks and Romans took a great

Galahs are found all over Australia, and they can gather in flocks of up to 1000 individuals. Farmers regard them as pests because of the damage they do to crops and many are killed.

interest in parrots, and Diodorus and Pliny the Elder discuss methods of speech training.

Although their human vocabulary may be meaningless to parrots, many of them make great use of their own. Studies have found that the Crimson Rosella *Platycercus elegans* (320–360 mm) and White-cheeked Rosella *P. eximius* (280–320 mm) have at least 21 and 25 distinct calls, the Galah has 11, the Cockatiel *Leptolophus hollandicus* (320 mm) and the Budgerigar eight, and the King Parrot *Purpureicephalus spurius* (360–370 mm) has only four.

There seems to be a correlation between vocabulary and habitat. The parrots of tropical rainforest and those of arid areas seem to be less verbose than those of intermediate habitats. And there is also a correlation with other aspects of behaviour. Researchers believe that where the resources are neither as abundant as in the rainforests, nor as sparse as in the arid zone, the most varied behaviour patterns develop, thus the need for the most complex communications system between birds.

The eastern race of the White-cheeked Rosella (280–320 mm) was extensively studied by one researcher, John Brereton, in open woodland near Armidale, NSW. He found, in an area of 320 ha, a population of about 100 birds: a core population of more or less sedentary pairs, and a subsidiary population consisting of groups of

Budgerigars are widespread in Australia, and have been taken to most of the rest of the world. Probably the most popular domesticated bird, there are societies devoted to them in most countries.

four to six parrots which ranged widely and could form and break up.

They fed almost entirely on vegetable matter, largely seeds, and as specific seeds are available for only short periods, the parrots needed relatively large areas to support themselves. In the spring the birds began to search for nesting holes, and aggression within the larger subsidiary groups increased so that they often broke up. After nesting, the juveniles began to spend less time with their parents and started to form groups, consisting of birds from different nests.

By autumn the birds had formed loose flocks which eventually broke up into the new subsidiary groups, usually with young adults from the previous year as 'leaders'. These groups interspersed throughout the area of the established pairs, thus there were various groups arranged according to status, and with a ranking within each group.

Parrots have made popular domestic pets for centuries and many Australian parrots bring high prices overseas. This is not surprising with a rare species, such as Alexandra's Parrot, but it seems odd with such common birds as the Galah. Some of the most sought after species, such as the corellas, the Cockatiel and the Sulphur-crested Cockatoo *Cacatua galerita* (450–500 mm) are often, in fact, pests of grain crops and many are legally captured and killed in this country. But while it remains illegal to export any parrot, the high prices paid for the very few smuggled birds which survive the journey will continue.

There is, however, one danger in keeping parrots in domestication: the risk of contracting psittacosis, a disease caused by a natural parasite of all Australian parrot species. In 1929 and 1930 there were outbreaks of the disease in north America, north Africa and Europe, with 750 known cases and 143 deaths. It is now known, however, that many other birds, and in particular pigeons and finches, can carry the disease which is, consequently, also called ornithosis.

The organism responsible is *Chlamydia psittaci*, closely related to the agents of trachoma and lymphogranuloma venereum. The people most at risk are those working with birds in large numbers. The disease can be contracted by handling infected birds – which often show no symptoms – or by inhaling the germs from droppings or from dust in feathers. It is rarely transmitted to other people and is, fortunately, very uncommon. Most cases have probably been misdiagnosed as pneumonia (the feverish symptoms are similar in both cases) and successfully treated as such.

A pair of Double-eyed Fig Parrots Cyclopsitta diophthalma *feeding on wild figs in north Queensland. Dark spots near the eyes of some races gave the bird its strange name.*

PASTURE GRASS

From the arid interior to the temperate regions of southern Australia, pastures form the basis of more than 90 per cent of livestock production. Despite the increasing importance of pasture legumes, such as subterranean clover, grasses are still the most widespread type of pasture, responsible for the improved pasture revolution.

Most of the sown pasture grasses are introduced from overseas, although native species, such as MITCHELL GRASS are also used. However, native pastures are generally high in fibre and low in nutritional value. They typically have short active growing seasons with abundant green feed, followed by long periods of dry, low quality fodder. Some native pastures have been improved, however, by grazing management and aerial topdressing with fertiliser.

Introduced species, such as buffel grass, have been sown, often aerially, to improve many extensive pastures. Others, together with legumes, form the basis of more intensive pastures. Unlike practices in most other countries, intensive pastures – especially those used for dairy, prime lamb and vealer production – are often irrigated. Pasture grasses are also sown in rotation with cereal crops and legumes. Hence the rye pasture grass of one year becomes the weed in next year's grain crop. Pasture grasses such as buffel, perennial rye, green panic and phalaris also are grown for seed production.

Other important pasture grasses – among the dozens that are grown – are paspalum, particularly suited to NSW's coastal regions; phalaris, a winter/spring growing plant; cocksfoot and perennial ryegrass.

PATERSON'S CURSE

This introduced plant, *Echium plantagineum*, is a native of the Mediterranean region. In South Australia and parts of Victoria it is known as Salvation Jane, but in the south-east as Paterson's Curse after the owner of a garden near Albury from which it was said to have spread. The plant has bristly leaves and spikes of purple-blue flowers. When densely infesting pasture land it is unmistakable, appearing as a haze of purple over the countryside. It is most abundant in a belt from the central and southern tablelands of NSW west through the Riverina and northern Victoria into South Australia.

PEA

The pea family – the legumes – is one of the larger families of flowering plants. There are three major groups in the family, and although their flowers are very different, they all produce the characteristic 'pea pod' fruit. The first includes the Acacias, the second the Cassias and the third the well-known pea flowers. Varieties of the latter group are found in most habitats, and range from small herbs to climbers, creepers, shrubs and even massive rainforest trees.

Most members of the pea family have root nodules which contain bacteria capable of 'fixing' atmospheric nitrogen – taking up nitrogen and using it to synthesise nitrogenous compounds. This ability allows many legumes to grow on comparatively poor soils. In Australia species of legumes have been of great importance in pasture improvement. Not only do they thrive in Australian conditions, but they also improve the soil and provide good fodder for livestock. In temperate areas the most important species used for this purpose has been subterranean clover *Trifolium subterraneum*. In recent years there has been a major effort to develop forage legumes for use in the tropical savannas of northern Australia. A number of species have become established, of which the best known is Townsville Stylo *Stylosanthes humilis*.

However, while legumes are economically very valuable as soil improvers and directly as crops such as peas, beans and peanuts – a number of the Australian species are also toxic to grazing animals. This was a serious problem in south-western Australia where a number of poisonous species are widespread. Until researchers realised that these species were poisonous, the unexplained death of stock had been a major problem in developing land.

PEACHES AND NECTARINES

Peach trees were growing in Sydney by 1800. Australia now has about 1.7 million trees in orchards producing nearly 60 000 tonnes of fruit each year. Peaches need warm to hot summers, and, to develop buds properly, winters with some hundreds of hours of temperatures below 7°C. Conditions are ideal around Shepparton in Victoria, in the Murrumbidgee Irrigation Area and around Bathurst in NSW.

The Romans brought peach trees to Italy from Persia, hence the scientific name *Prunus persica*, but the trees first came from China where the fruit was a symbol of immortality – despite the fact that the trees only lived for 20 to 25 years. Nectarines are a subspecies of peach, *Prunus persica nectarina*, probably first occurring centuries ago. They differ from peaches only in having smooth rather than downy skins. Peach seeds can produce nectarine trees without warning and vice versa.

The fruits have yellow or white flesh that clings to, or comes away from, the stone. The yellow-flesh freestone variety Golden Queen is the one that is usually canned. J.H. Hale is a dessert peach, also with yellow flesh and a freestone. The most grown nectarine is the white-fleshed Goldmine.

Fields stained purple by Paterson's Curse are a common sight in early summer. The plant is controversial, being declared a noxious weed in some states, although much of Australia's honey harvest depends on it.

PEANUT

Queensland is known as the peanut state. The industry, which dates back to the 1920s, thrives in the red soils around the state's south-eastern town of Kingaroy – also well known as the home of politician Sir Joh Bjelke-Petersen. Peanuts are also grown in the state's Central Burnett region and the northern Atherton Tablelands. Smaller areas are planted in the north of Western Australia and in NSW.

Peanuts, a member of the pea family, are an annual summer legume. Grown between mid October and January, they take up to 20 weeks to mature. The bushy plants grow to about 500 mm tall and the peanut pods form under the ground. Peanuts are susceptible to diseases and may require irrigation.

About 750 growers produce over 50 000 tonnes of Virginia and Spanish peanuts annually and achieve yields ranging from 1.5 to 3.5 tonnes per hectare. The Peanut Marketing Board in Queensland is responsible for cleaning, storing, grading and selling the crop. Peanuts are sold on domestic and overseas markets whole or for processing into confectionery, peanut butter and edible oil. The main overseas markets are the United Kingdom, Japan, New Zealand and some Asian countries.

PEAR

Like apples, pears are known as pome fruit – they have a centre core instead of stone. Pears probably originally came from around northern Afghanistan. The Australian industry was founded on French saplings.

Pears are grown in the cool to warm temperate regions of most states. They are usually irrigated and must have cool weather if the fruit is to set. Most of Australia's pears are grown in the Goulburn Valley in Victoria. Other growing centres include the southern, central and northern table-lands of NSW and the Murrumbidgee Irrigation Area; Tasmania's Huon and Derwent Valleys; South Australia's Adelaide Hills, Barossa and Murray Valleys; and Stanthorpe in Queensland's Granite Belt. Among the best known varieties are Packhams Triumph, Winter Cole, Winter Nellis and Beurre Box.

Pears are picked while green and hard and immediately placed in cold storage. Their cold storage life varies from three months for early varieties, to six months for late maturing varieties. If picked too soon, the fruit will not ripen after storage, and later picking can reduce storage life.

Pears are sold on domestic or export markets fresh, canned or as juice. Around eight million 8-kg cartons of pears are harvested annually. Exports to the traditional United Kingdom and European markets have steadily declined over the last ten years. However, new markets are being developed in south-east Asia.

Popular pear varieties

Packham's Triumph

Beurre Bosc

Josephine

William's Bon Chretien

Winter Nelis

PEARL

Although pearls are associated with oysters, many kinds of bivalve molluscs – such as mussels – can produce them. Indeed pearls in some European mussels are a nuisance because they make them unfit for consumption.

Pearls are formed when a parasite or some foreign body lodges between the animal's mantle and its shell. The mollusc responds by encasing it in layers of calcium carbonate. In some species this has the iridescent appearance which is characteristic of pearls. The best and most valuable pearls are obtained from tropical oysters of the *Pinctada* genus.

Pearling in Australia began in the 1850s. At first Aborigines were used as divers, then Indonesians and finally Japanese. At one time Thursday Island was the largest pearling centre in the world. In 1904 there were 403 luggers in Western Australia, mainly at Broome; 378 on Thursday Island and 50 at Darwin, collecting pearls and trochus shell for buttons and other uses. The demand for trochus shell has since vanished, and most Australian pearls are now cultivated, with Australian-Japanese firms dominating the market. Young oysters are collected, seeded with a nucleus – usually made from an American freshwater mussel – and placed in a cage. If successful the pearl is large enough for harvesting in two to three years. Shell (mother-of-pearl) is also harvested.

The largest Australian pearl was the 'Star of the West' from Broome in 1917, which weighed 6.48 g and was sold in London for £6000. The world's largest is probably a giant-clam pearl, the 'Pearl of Laotze' from the Philippines. It weighed 6378 g, was 140 mm in diameter and 240 mm long, and was valued at over four million (US) dollars in 1971.

NATURAL TREASURE

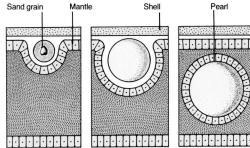

Sand grain   Mantle   Shell   Pearl

Natural pearls are formed when a foreign object, often a grain of sand, lodges between an oyster's shell and its mantle. Gradually thin layers of calcium carbonate are built up around the grain, encasing it.

PELICAN

There is a reason for the slightly prehistoric look of pelicans. The oldest known fossils of ancient pelicans found in Australia are 30 to 40 million years old. Study has shown that the bird then, *Pelecanus tirarensis*, was closely related to the six modern species.

Australian Pelicans *P. conspicillatus* (1600–1800 mm, with bill) are seen in flocks or singly on fresh or salty water. Groups cooperate in fishing, driving the fish before them and dipping their bills simultaneously. They do not dive like some species found elsewhere in the world. They breed at any time of the year if water levels allow them to. The young take food from their parent's pouched bills then go into convulsions and collapse for a short time. This is interpreted by human observers as a way of asking for more. Possibly the adults see it this way also. The huge bill is also used in display. Despite their bulk, pelicans fly gracefully and sometimes use their great wings to flee to New Zealand or Indonesia to escape from a drought in this country.

Little Penguins – sometimes called Fairy Penguins – are quite common around the southern coast of the mainland and Tasmania. They may even occasionally surprise swimmers and surfers at beaches around Sydney as they bob up unexpectedly.

PENGUIN

Penguins are supposed to be Antarctic birds but three – Galapagos, Peruvian and Blackfoot Penguins – are tropical, and one, the Little Penguin *Eudyptula minor* (330 mm tall: the smallest penguin), breeds in New Zealand and along the coasts of Tasmania and southern Australia. Three other species – one subantarctic, one from islands south of New Zealand, and one from New Zealand itself – are washed up from time to time, living or dead, on southern Australian shores.

Penguins, unlike most flightless birds, have large pectoral muscles and a strong keel on the breast bone because in a sense they do fly, although only under water. Their wings, which they cannot fold and which lack quill feathers, are used as paddles, and their legs, which are set well back, are used for steering. Their oily outer feathers make a completely waterproof covering for the downy layer below.

Little Penguins are the only species to come ashore after dark to roost, and at some places – such as at Phillip Island in Victoria – they do not seem to mind spotlights, electronic flashes and tourists. In groups they walk to cliffs and dunes where they roost in burrows under grass tussocks, or in crevices. Egg laying starts in July, and the pair share duties, with one in residence while the other feeds at sea on fish and squid, possibly many kilometres away. A shift can last as long as ten days so, not unexpectedly, there is a ritual to be observed at change-over during which the partners lean forward, dangle their flippers and growl at each other. It is tempting to wonder if one is asking the other why he or she had been out so long. This ends when the two eggs have hatched for then the shifts last a day each. When the chicks are bigger both parents have to go out at once to fish. They regurgitate their catch into the mouths of their offspring.

PEPPER TREE

This small to medium-sized tree was introduced into Australia from subtropical South America – it is a native of northern Argentina – and is widely planted as an ornamental in some areas. Its botanical name is *Shinus malle* and it belongs to the same plant family as mangos and cashews. Like most members of that family it has resinous, caustic sap. Its leaves are fern-like – making this an attractive tree for its foliage – and its flowers are small and greenish in profuse sprays, followed by numerous small, bright pink berries which have dry flesh. These are hot to the taste – hence the name pepper tree – but they should not be eaten. Pepper trees have run wild in some dry subcoastal areas, for example in the Upper Hunter Valley Region of NSW where thickets infest eroded gullies. Closer to the tropics the Brazilian Pepper Tree *Schinus terebinthifolia* is more common. This mostly smaller tree has broader, dark green leaves and dense bunches of crimson berries. It has become a bad weed in south-east Queensland and on Norfolk Island.

PERCH

European perch or redfin *Perca fluviatilis* (to 500 mm) were only introduced once into Tasmania and Victoria, in 1862 and 1868, but are now common in many places in south-east and south-west Australia and in Tasmania. The fish belongs to a northern hemisphere family and has strong spiny scales, and a long, spiny first dorsal fin (see illustration p 177).

Perch feed on molluscs, insects and other fish, including small trout. They prefer still water or streams with a slow current, preferably with weeds, and with temperatures below 31°C. In suitable conditions – some farm dams, for example – populations build up so quickly that individuals are stunted.

PERIPATUS

A peripatus is a peculiar creature with characteristics of two groups of animals – the arthropods (insects, spiders, centipedes etc.) and the annelids (earthworms, leeches etc.). There are about 75 known species and they are found in Australasia, Africa, Asia and the Americas. Five species are known to live in Australia and they are found in the east and south-east of the continent, with one species living high in the Australian Alps.

The peripatus has been described as a squat, velvety earthworm about 50 mm long with 15

The caterpillar-like peripatus may have been one of the first life forms to have emerged from the sea around 400 million years ago. The intricate patterns on their bodies have been likened to a Persian carpet.

pairs of unjointed, stumpy legs. It has a pair of flexible antennae with a small eye at the base of each. Internally and externally it is a mixture of annelid and arthropod features. The respiratory system, for example, resembles that of an insect, but the legs are not jointed. Peripatus species live under logs and stones, emerging at night to hunt and scavenge. They capture prey by spraying it with a quickly hardening slime and then suck out the contents.

An almost identical animal has been found as a fossil 550 million years old, so biologists have been tempted to regard these creatures as a 'missing link'.

PESTS

A pest is any organism which harms people or their property although, by convention, internal parasites of human beings and animals are excluded. Pests thus include, for example, insects and mites which attack humans, crops and domestic animals, fungi and bacteria which attack crops, and weeds which compete with them. Furthermore the damage that they cause must be of significant economic importance, or cause disease or discomfort to humans or animals when they are attached.

The damage can be direct, as when it is caused by the pest's exploitation of the victim's tissues – for example, by cabbage caterpillars or aphids – or indirect, as when mosquitoes transmit a disease, ants husband aphids, or weeds compete with a crop for light, water and food.

In Australia most of the worst pests were introduced by humans. When such pests leave their country of origin they leave behind them the parasites, pathogens and predators which held them in check. Often in the new country they have few of their traditional enemies so if there is food and a suitable climate, there is often a population explosion. Classic Australian examples of this phenomenon are rabbits and prickly pear.

PETRIFIED WOOD

Wood can be turned into stone in certain special circumstances. Firstly it must be buried very quickly before it deteriorates in the air. This may occur when a river is in flood, or when a tree floats into a lake. As the tree is buried the surrounding sediments – sand or silt grains – are squeezed by the weight of material above until silica-rich fluids in the form of crystalline silica, chalcedony or even opal are squeezed out of them like juice from an orange. These fluids slowly penetrate pores and cells in the wood, like oil penetrates a wooden fence. Every feature of the wood, such as growth rings, knots and bark are preserved as the fluids eventually harden. Sometimes iron stains the petrified wood so that it may have the same colour as the tree.

Petrified wood is common throughout Australia, particularly in the east, and in parts of Western Australia. Opalised wood, which is very rare, is the most valuable.

The appropriately named Brush-tailed Phascogale spends most of its life in trees. These creatures have no pouch – only an area of soft, folded skin to offer protection to developing young.

Picnic race meetings may appear to be casual affairs, but they are certainly taken seriously by the organisers and participants. Horses are raced by local people and their children, for often substantial prizes.

PHASCOGALE

There are two phascogales: the Brush-tailed Phascogale or Tuan *Phascogale tapoatafa* (male mean body length 202 mm, tail 196, female a little smaller) which is still fairly common, and the Red-tailed Phascogale or Red-tailed Wambenger *P. calura* (113 mm, 141 mm, female a little smaller) which is endangered and is now only found on a few reserves in south-western Western Australia. Curiously, its range coincides with areas where certain plants grow containing fluoracetates – poisons related to the commercial product 1080. These plants are very toxic to sheep and cattle, although many native marsupials can eat them without ill effects.

Brush-tailed Phascogales are found in northern Australia, along much of the east coast and in south-west Western Australia. They are grey, mouse-like creatures with big naked ears, and a black 'bottle brush' on their tail. They live in trees and when alarmed drum on the wood with their forefeet, possibly as an alarm signal. They spend the day in a nest in a tree-hollow and feed at night on small animals. Red-tailed Phascogales, which also live in trees, but feed mainly on the ground, are usually found in dense woodland.

PICNIC RACES

Most picnic race meetings are registered and controlled by racing bodies, and sometimes the prize money adds up to several thousand dollars. But these are social events, and during the lengthy lunch breaks the racing can seem a side-show. There is fierce competition to provide the most elaborate meal, often in a family tent or marquee. For many small communities this is the year's social focus. At some of the larger picnic races, attendance is by invitation of committee members only.

The day often includes a race for grass-fed horses – which entails all the runners being corralled in a paddock for some time before the race to give them all equal chances on the same feed. Races for 'gentlemen riders' are for non-professional jockeys, male or female.

The day always ends with a dance or a ball – black tie, please. In remote districts, with racegoers travelling great distances, revellers sleep over, camping at the racecourse – probably in the tent of their party's host. Invitations say 'Bring your swag'.

Its all a curious blend of horse racing, competitive hospitality and dancing.

PIG

There around 11 000 pig farmers in Australia and 2.5 million pigs. The average farmer has around 190 pigs, although some have several thousand. Compared to the cattle and sheep industries, pig farming is small and localised. It produces around 250 000 tonnes of pigmeat a year, valued at around $400 million.

Each Australian eats around 16 kg of pigmeat a year, including six kg of pork and 6.5 kg of bacon. The remainder is canned meat and offal. Australians do not eat much pigmeat compared to other nationalities. Germans, for example, eat on average 50 kg a year, while North Americans eat on average 30 kg.

In Australia pigs have traditionally been farmed in conjunction with dairy cattle or cereal crops because they were the ideal animal to eat waste, or second-grade cereal and dairy by-products. But in the late 1970s, in line with the trend in other industries, specialist pig farms increased.

Pigs are usually fed high protein, grain-based diets and are housed in stalls. Most farms are still found in the cereal areas of Western Australia, Queensland, northern NSW and Victoria, due to the availability of good feed.

One of the problems of intensive piggeries is waste disposal. As pigs produce around one litre of waste for every 10 kg of bodyweight every day, farmers have to install large slurry storage systems. The slurry is often emptied onto crops and pastures as fertiliser.

Sows usually have two litters a year, each with around ten piglets. At least one piglet in every litter usually dies in the first few weeks of life. At between three and seven weeks of life most piglets are weaned, and are then fed on high protein diets for up to 22 weeks, depending on whether they are to be sold early as young 'porkers' or later as 'baconers'. Female pigs before their first mating are called gilts.

Most intensive piggeries are based on crossbred pigs from three breeds – Landrace, Large White and, to a lesser extent, Berkshire. Other breeds include Large Black, Duroc, British Saddleback and Pietrain.

Pigs, however, face one problem they never seem to be able to overcome – their image. Despite opinions to the contrary, they are one of the cleanest of farm animals if kept properly.

PIGEON PEA

Pigeon peas are one of several grain legumes to have taken their place on farmers' 'crop menus' since the late 1970s. Others in this group include LUPINS, CHICKPEAS, lentils, cowpeas, guar and field peas. Grain legumes contain a higher amount of protein – usually around 15 per cent – than other field crops.

Pigeon peas – which produce round, brownish grain – are mainly exported to Asia or India where they are used as a non-meat protein. They

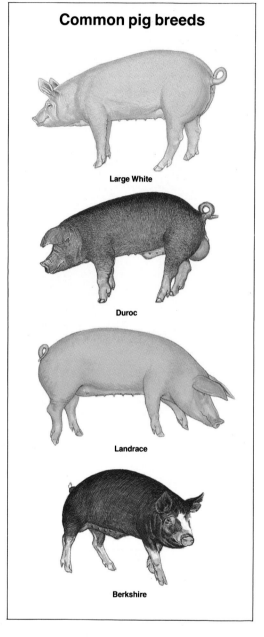

Common pig breeds

Large White

Duroc

Landrace

Berkshire

are often ground up to form a meal, or the dried split peas are cooked into a thick soup – called dhal in India. They are also used whole in other non-meat meals and food products. In Australia pigeon peas are mainly fed to cattle, or are occasionally sold as split peas or as a meat substitute for vegetarians.

The crop was first grown in Queensland in the late 1800s. Then it was sown in pineapple and banana plantations and was used as green manure – to be dug in as a fertiliser.

Pigeon peas are a winter crop, suited to medium to high rainfall areas and clay soils. The main growing areas are in northern NSW,

around Moree and Northern Star, and in southern Queensland, particularly on the Darling Downs, west of Toowoomba. Many farmers are turning to crops like pigeon peas to provide some diversity and 'insurance' against fluctuations in world wheat prices and uncertain markets for traditional products. Despite their promise, pigeon peas remain a minor crop and secure, long-term markets are still being developed here and abroad.

Pigeon peas are sold either as dried seed, or sometimes as canned or frozen green seed.

PIGEONS AND DOVES

There are no real differences between pigeons and doves, and all could be called by one name or the other. They do differ, however, from other birds in two ways. Pigeons feed their nestlings for the first few days on 'pigeon's milk', which is a curd-like material secreted by the linings of their large crops, and many drink water by immersing their beak and sucking through it as though it were a straw. The only other birds which drink in a similar way are sandgrouse and button quails. All pigeons and doves are plump birds with relatively small heads, and they feed mainly on seeds and fruits. There are about 300 species in the world. In Australia there are 22 native species and three that have been introduced.

The most familiar, at least in cities, is the Feral Pigeon *Columba livia*, a descendant of the Rock Pigeon found in Europe and the Mediterranean region. This was first domesticated by the Egyptians about 3000 BC and as a wild bird it is a great pest. The native species have been placed in two groups on the basis of the way they live. One consists of birds living in rainforest, and other densely forested country in northern and eastern Australia, and the other of birds found in more open, drier country where they often feed on the ground. Many of the rainforest species are brightly coloured. The Torres Strait Imperial-Pigeon *Ducula bicolor* (350–400 mm), which migrates to northern Australia from New Guinea to breed, was probably the first Australian animal to be reported by a European. It was recorded by Diego de Prado on the Torres expedition of 1606.

PILLIGA SCRUB

Anyone lost in this great triangle of forested plain between Pilliga, Narrabri and Coonabarabran in north-eastern NSW can find the right direction by looking at mosses and lichens that grow on the southern side of the trunks of the numerous White Cypress-pines *Callitris glaucophylla* found there. About half of New South Wales' floorboards are cut from the Cypress Pines of the Pilliga every year, and about 100 000 railway sleepers from the Narrow-leaf Ironbark *Eucalyptus crebra*. About half the area is state forests – there are ten sawmills – and another tenth is nature reserve. Beehives are a common sight; some 100 tonnes of honey a year are obtained from the flowers of the Mugga Ironbark *E. sideroxylon* and various species of box.

Until they collapsed in the 1930s, salt caves in the heart of the Pilliga stretched 30 m into a rocky outcrop. Hanging columns of salt were licked by kangaroos, feral horses and cattle, and pulled off by locals and used for curing meat. Apart from the horses, feral pigs and goats also roam the Pilliga.

There are patches of dangerous quicksands in some creeks, and surface water is often too salty to drink.

The name Pilliga comes from an Aboriginal word for casuarina. Belah *Casuarina cristata* are common in the area.

PINE

Both native and introduced pines are common in Australia. The term 'pine' is rather ambiguous. It could refer just to trees of the genus *Pinus*, none of which are native to Australia, but many are planted here for timber. In a broader sense it can mean almost any conifer, and in Australia has been applied particularly to cypress-like trees of the genus *Callitris*, and to the much taller *Araucarias*.

Cypress-pine is the standard name for *Callitris*, but bushmen know the common inland species simply as White Pine *C. glaucophylla*, Black Pine *C. endlicheri* and Mallee Pine *C. verrucosa*. The first of these, White Cypress-pine, is found right across Australia in sandy soils and on rocky central ranges. It forms fine forests in the PILLIGA Scrub of northern NSW, and in inland southern Queensland. The attractive, aromatic timber is known particularly for its resistance to termite attack.

The genus *Araucaria* has two Australian mainland species. In addition to the well known Norfolk Island Pine *A. heterophylla*, Bunya Pine *A. bidwillii* is a majestic tree which grows naturally only in the Bunya Mountains, north-west of Brisbane, and in the upper Brisbane River valley. Its giant cones contain seeds which were roasted and eaten by Aborigines. Hoop Pine *A. cunninghamii* is a tall rainforest tree with a crown made up of separate clumps of dark green

Mature plantations of Monterey Pines Pinus radiata *ring the shores of Blowering Dam in Bago State Forest, west of the Snowy Mountains. This native of California, USA, is the most widely grown species in plantations.*

foliage. It is common in parts of coastal Queensland and is also found in northern NSW. It has soft whitish timber.

In Tasmania there are a few conifers that are found only on the island, including HUON PINE *Lagarostrobos*, Celery-top Pine *Phyllocladus* and King Billy Pine *Athrotaxis*.

Pine plantations in Australia consist almost entirely of *Pinus* species, with Monterey Pine *Pinus radiata* being the most widely planted. The largest plantations are in cooler areas of the south-east, especially the Tumut-Albury district of southern NSW and nearby parts of north-eastern Victoria.

PINEAPPLE

One of the most memorable sights in Queensland, especially on the drive north from Brisbane along the Bruce Highway, is the nation's pineapple crop. Row upon row of the knee-high, spiky-leafed plants can be seen for most of the year in subtropical coastal regions. The south-east corner of Queensland is the heart of pineapple country. More than 80 per cent of the nation's crop is grown within a 400-km radius of Brisbane. Indeed, the town of Nambour is home of the 'Big Pineapple'.

Pineapples are not native to Australia, but came originally from the tropical countries of central and South America, including Mexico, Brazil and Honduras. They are also an important crop in countries such as Taiwan, Malaysia and South Africa.

In Australia around 85 per cent of the crop is

grown under contract for canning and processing into chunks, slices and juices. The industry is now worth around $30 million a year to the Australian economy.

Soil erosion is one of the biggest problems faced by pineapple growers. Rain and wind can remove many tonnes of unprotected top soil from between the pineapple rows, especially from the thousands of plantation hectares on sloping land. Queensland researchers have estimated that 105 tonnes of soil per hectare can be lost in the first year of a crop grown on a 17 per cent or steeper slope.

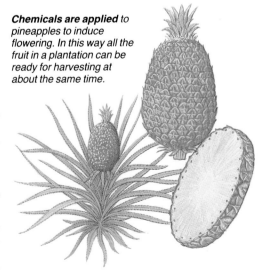

Chemicals are applied to pineapples to induce flowering. In this way all the fruit in a plantation can be ready for harvesting at about the same time.

The Perils of Pioneer Life

Many of Australia's pioneering settlers found it very difficult to establish smallholdings in the virgin bush. Some of the hardships that faced them were described by Edward Sorenson in his book *Life in the Australian Backblocks* which drew on his experiences as a selector near Grafton, NSW, at the end of the nineteenth century.

'Most of our neighbours were married men, and many of them brought their wives and families with them on horseback, in buggies and carts, and on top of the dunnage... In some instances the houses had been built before the family appeared, but mostly only a rough hut, used afterwards as a kitchen, was there to receive them. In a few cases not even the site for the camp had been picked, and when the dray pulled up on a rise and all got down, there was an inspection of the ground, and much discussion and walking about. The woman wanted to be as near as possible to the water, but the man was afraid of floods and preferred the high ground. She was tired, night was coming on, the dray had to be unloaded, supper cooked, tents pitched, and beds made, so he had his way – which accounts for so many selectors' huts being a mile away from water.

'The first evening on a new selection under such circumstances is not as cheerful as one could wish. It is the beginning of a new life – a hard one, with nothing done and everything to do. There is no house in sight, no sign of life but that of wild birds and animals, and the freed horses feeding out into the wilderness of trees. Boxes, furniture, tools and camp-ware are strewn about the dray, a fire burns under a tree, and a tent or two is erected nearby. This is home. The children enjoy it; it is new and strange and novel, and they race about, climbing trees, gathering wild flowers, rooting hollow logs and hunting goannas and possums...

An uncertain future

'To the mother, seated on the ground by the fire, and watching the sun go down as she eats her first meal,

Camp ovens were an indispensible part of any pioneer's kitchen equipment. The cast iron pot was simply placed in the ashes of a fire and the food in it was allowed to bake. Even the toughest meat would eventually be rendered edible.

A well established bush hut and its rustic owner in Gippsland, Victoria, probably photographed late last century. Despite the apparent clutter most items have been tidily stacked, or are hung up out of the way.

and listening to the croaking of frogs and chirruping of crickets, the groaning of interlocked trees, and the wailing of curlews, it is a wretchedness that brings tears to her eyes.

'Her husband is full of hope, and fairly bristles with ideas and schemes... What he plans that first night usually takes him about ten years to carry out...

'A rough two-roomed house, with walls of split slabs, earth floor, and a shingle roof, was the first improvement. A fence across the bight, enclosing part of the scrub, followed months later. Timber was plentiful, but farmers built sparingly in those days, being content with the roughest habitations imaginable. Doors were made of split pine palings, having plenty of daylight over the top; shutters of the same material; both being fastened with wooden pegs which, when not in use, hung to the doorpost by a strip of hide or a piece of cord. Beds were also made of pine battens. Some of the more fastidious settlers went in for spring mattresses – made of round timber and fencing-wire. Chairs were unknown, the universal seats being rough stools, made with a slab and four round legs...

'Mosquitoes came in swarms from the holes at night, necessitating the burning of cow-dung in our bedrooms; possums were other nocturnal visitors. They scampered about the roof of our house, purred down the chimney, and sometimes got inside. Snakes, centipedes and scorpions were the only things we had to fear, and a careful inspection of our bedding was made every night before turning in.

Clearing the land

'The first work was to clear the undergrowth and vines with brush-hooks. All the small growth is brushed in the jungle, low branches are lopped, the vines that twine into the tops and lace the trees together are cut at the root and severed where they cross near the ground. The brushing is about the easiest part of the work. It is clean and light, though subject to many annoyances. When it is done one can walk comfortably through the scrub, and the way is clear for the swing of the axe.

'Felling the scrub is slow and laborious work, and at times attended with considerable risk. The small trees are merely nicked, the larger ones are cut partly through. Perhaps half an acre or more will be done like this, then a big tree is cut down and carries the lot crashing to earth in one tangled mass...

'Very little timber is consumed in the first burning off, and the blackened logs lie thickly across each other all over the ground. A road is cut down the centre, wide enough for a dray to pass through when the time comes to bring in the crop. Cross-cutting the huge, black logs, and even levering them aside is heavy work, and takes weeks to accomplish.

This stockman's cottage offered few creature comforts to its inhabitants. Not that men exhausted by a hard day's work would have had much time to savour their surroundings.

Planting the first crop

'Then the crop is put in. With a bucket of seed soaking on the road, and a bag-pouchful in front of him, and a long, narrow-bladed hoe, the farmer starts along his first row, running it as straight as possible from road to river, digging the hoe in at every stride and dropping four grains behind it so that the earth will drop back...

'They had heroic hearts, those early farmers, to face the prodigious pioneering work that confronted them on every side. They were unconventional people for the most part. So much so were some of them that I have seen men dressed in pants of soojee-bag, and shirts made of flour bags, the brand in broad letters still visible across the back in cases where it could not be hidden conveniently on the tail. Hats were home-made, cabbage-tree and calico forming the principal material. As for boots, one member of the family wore them regularly – 'the old man' – and his clod-squashers were patched with hide and wire as long as anything remained to hold by. The overcoat was a bag, having a head-hole at the top and arm-holes at the sides...'

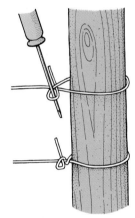

The Cobb and Co. hitch is the bushman's way of fastening things together. A length of wire is simply bound around the objects to be joined and twisted with a convenient spike. The joint is strong, easy to remove or remake and more convenient than anything made with nails.

A comfortable station homestead was the dream and goal of many settlers. Few achieved it, and those who did often had to spend years of their lives in backbreaking labour to build some kind of future for their families.

PIPI

Pipis *Donax deltoides* (called ugaris in Queensland and Goolwa cockles in South Australia) are common on beaches from southern Queensland to Cape Leeuwin in Western Australia. They are bivalves, with smooth, whitish shells that can grow to 75 mm. They live in sand or mud at the water's edge, using their powerful digging foot to bury themselves rapidly when exposed by a wave. Some people prefer their taste to mussels. Others use them for bait.

A pipi uses its 'tongue' to bury itself in wet sand. These shellfish will disappear from sight with astonishing rapidity if released on a beach.

PISÉ

When Governor Phillip's band of settlers landed in 1788 one of their greatest difficulties was to find local materials suitable for building. They lacked the skilled labour and equipment to quarry much stone; lime was obtainable only by heating and crushing oyster shells and the local

Tantallon, on the outskirts of Dubbo in NSW is a fine example of a pisé house. It was built in 1887, and has 430-mm-thick walls and Italian marble fireplaces.

PITCHER PLANT

There are two insect-eating plants in Australia which capture their prey in pitchers.

In south-west Australia, around Albany, *Cephalotus follicularis*, the Albany Pitcher Plant, grows in peaty swamps and is one of the botanical curiosities of the continent. It has a thick, branching rootstock which bears clusters of pitchers and conventional oval-shaped leaves. Its flowers are small and inconspicuous and grow on a stout stalk 500 to 600 mm tall.

The pitchers are like jugs with half open lids, and are about 50 mm deep. In the shade they are green, but in the sun have deep red or purple pigment. During the early development of the pitcher its lid remains closed, but as the pitcher reaches full size, it opens and acts as a canopy. The lid is not 'hinged', and is not capable of rapid movement, but it does have a tendency to close up slightly in dry conditions and to open wider in humid weather.

When mature, the pitcher is partially filled with fluid and the remains of numerous insect prey. Crawling insects, such as ants and small beetles, apparently fall into the pitchers, but exactly how flying insects are first attracted and then captured is not clear.

Australia's other pitcher plant, *Nepenthes mirabilis*, is found only in north-east Queensland. It is a variable species, and the pitchers can be many shapes and sizes.

The plants are climbing vines and the pitcherwood was extremely hard, except for Cabbage Tree Palm logs which rotted within a few years. It was also some time before clay suitable for baking bricks was found. For a time, therefore, most buildings were either made of WATTLE AND DAUB or pisé.

The latter is common in many parts of the world, especially in dry climates. It consists of earth, placed between wooden formwork, rammed down hard, and usually whitewashed after the formwork has been taken away. Buildings made of it by experts can last for several hundred years, but the settlers had no skill in judging the proportion of soil to clay or sand, and in times of heavy rain their pisé walls were often washed away. As settlement spread, however, many farmers mastered the art of pisé construction, and used it especially for buildings such as storehouses, where thick walls helped to maintain a uniform temperature. Even when other materials were used for the main structure of a house, pisé was sometimes used for the chimney. As late as December 1901 the *New South Wales Agricultural Gazette* had a lengthy article on its use, and more recently still artists and others have used pisé and other colonial building methods in the Warrandyte and Eltham districts east of Melbourne.

leaf is made up of a blade with a very long tendril. The tendril finishes in a pitcher, which is held in an upright position and is partly filled with fluid. The pitchers are up to about 200 mm long and have partially raised lids as a canopy at the entrance. On the underside of the lid, and around the rim of the pitcher, are glands which produce nectar to attract insects. On the inside of the pitcher, below the rim, is a waxy zone. Insects are unable to get a foothold on the waxy surface and any that venture on to it fall into the fluid below, where they drown and are subsequently digested.

PITTOSPORUM

The 150 or so species of plants in this group are widely distributed around the world. In Australia there are about ten species which are all trees and shrubs.

Most of the Australian species are found in the wetter forests of the eastern states and in sheltered parts of some drier forests. However, one species, *Pittosporum phillyreoides*, is widespread in semi-arid regions of all the mainland states. It is a small tree with an attractive weeping appearance.

Several species of *Pittosporum* are widely grown for their heavily-scented cream coloured flowers, colourful orange fruit and often attractive dark green foliage.

One species, *P. undulatum*, is a good example of a native species which has become a weed. Native to wet sclerophyll forest along the east coast, it has recently invaded the bush around Melbourne. Originally planted in gardens, its seed has been distributed widely, largely through the efforts of the introduced European Blackbird. Around Sydney *P. undulatum* has become much more common in urban bushland, and now forms dense patches in many places. This spread may be a result of nutrients (particularly phosphorus) running off from houses and gardens on surrounding developed land.

PITURI

This Aboriginal name – which originated in central Australia and has also been recorded as 'pitchery' or 'bedgery' – is used for a narcotic drug made from dried plants which was once traded extensively over a large area of the inland. The best known plant used in this way is the shrub *Duboisia hopwoodii*, belonging to the same group as the east-coast Corkwood *D. myoporoides*, from which medicinal drugs are extracted. However, in some parts of central Australia the most important ingredient in pituri has been found to be native species of tobacco.

Pituri was reported to consist of dried leaves and flowers, usually carried in a small bag of animal skin or woven fibre, and either chewed or smoked. In small quantities it was said to have a stimulating effect, preventing hunger and in-

Early settlers who tried Pituri Duboisia hopwoodii when their tobacco ran out were disappointed – they only received half of the nicotine they were used to.

creasing endurance. *Duboisia hopwoodii* is a shrub which grows up to about three metres tall with narrow, willow-like leaves, small white bell-shaped flowers with dark stripes on the inside, and small blackish berries. It is found over a wide area of inland Australia on sandy ridges and dunes, although nowhere is it common. It contains the alkaloids nicotine and nor-nicotine, and is poisonous to livestock.

PLACE NAMES

To a tribal Aborigne, the idea of naming a place, even a street, just to give it a convenient label, is inconceivable. Each place name is part of a people and a myth. A large proportion of Australia's four million or so place names are Aboriginal, many of them melodious, none able in translation to fully convey their associations.

Early settlers, squatters and their employees, used and recorded Aboriginal names, and Surveyor-General Thomas Mitchell took trouble to perpertuate them. Benalla, Illawarra, Tumbarumba, Walcha and Quirindi are all Aboriginal, and many went through several European spellings, and have suffered indignity in pronunciation with illogical stresses: Eungella is YUNGella; TalLANGatta but WangaRATa; GUNnedah, though Goonoo Goonoo is GunnaganOO. Repetition, as in Wagga Wagga, Min Min and Mitta Mitta, is for emphasis.

The banality of so many European names is not the fault of mid-19th century surveyors who, passing quickly through the land, noted descriptions that were later taken as names. Hence, in the gazetteer of the 1:250 000 maps of Australia there are a total of 38 Sugarloaf Mountains, 58 Bald Hills, 180 Oaky Creeks, and 379 Sandy Creeks.

The flood of settlers from the 1850s sprinkled Australia with Old Country names such as Gloucester, Ashbourne, Heathcote, Hahndorf, Klemzig and Hapsburg. Many Germam settlers' names were changed in and after World War I, some pointedly. Both Mt Bismarck in Victoria and Kaiserstuhl in South Australia became Mt Kitchener, and Germantown Hill in South Australia became Vimy Ridge.

PLANIGALE

One of these nocturnal marsupial mice – the Long-tailed Planigale *Planigale ingrami* – is the smallest Australian mammal, and after the Bumblebee Bat and a shrew, the smallest mammal in the world. The average body length of these tiny creatures is 59 mm, and they have a 59-mm tail. Their mean weight is 4.2 g (males) and 4.3 g (females).

The skulls of all planigales are flattened, and in this species they are not more than 3 mm deep. Most planigales, of which four species are known in Australia, push into small cracks in clay soil, presumably searching for food, and the flattening of their head makes this easier. Long-tailed Planigales live on grass plains and savannah woodland in the north. Common Planigales *P. maculata* (body mean length about 80 mm, tail 79 mm) live in many kinds of habitats in the north of the Northern Territory and along the east coast from Cape York to near Sydney. Their head is less flattened than those of the other species. Planigales live on insects, often as large as themselves.

Common Planigales are aggressive, despite their tiny size. They live in a range of different habitats, and some even survive on the outskirts of large cities.

PLATYPUS

There is a good case for the Platypus to replace the kangaroo as Australia's national mammal, for there is no animal anywhere else in the world like it. They are found along the east coast, from Cooktown to Tasmania, mainly east of the Great Dividing Range, and have been introduced onto Kangaroo Island. They are still common over much of this area. They live in mountain and lowland streams, feeding on aquatic invertebrates.

Their scientific name is *Ornithorhynchus anatinus*, which means bird-snout and refers to the animal's most characteristic feature, its bill. It looks like a duck's bill but is, in fact, soft and richly supplied with nerves and sense organs, and has nostrils near its tip so that the animal can breath while almost completely submerged. Eyes and ears lie in grooves which are tightly closed – as are the nostrils – when the animal submerges. Thus the snout becomes the main sense organ.

The animal's front feet have webs extending beyond its toes, and are used for propulsion. The partly-webbed hind feet and the broad tail are used for steering, but the tail is also used for storing fat. A dense underfur keeps the animals dry. Platypuses are usually solitary, and are most active around dusk and dawn, but can be busy in daylight. At other times they live in small tunnels with hidden entrances on the stream bank. Females, however, nest at the end of a long tunnel in a chamber lined with vegetation. After mating in the water the female lays two eggs, incubates them for one or two weeks between her belly and her tail, and suckles the young for four to five months.

Young females and males of all ages have spurs on their back legs. In an adult male this can inject venom from a sac in its groin. The venom is most copious or potent during the breeding season and may be used in quarrels over females, or, it has been suggested, to subdue females. It is also very toxic and very painful for human victims who may be sick for several days after being stung.

The size of platypuses varies with locality, and the males are larger than the females, but average measurements are: head-body, 500 mm; bill 58 mm; tail 125 mm.

When the first specimens of Platypuses reached Europe scientists spent hours looking for the stitches that would reveal this animal as a hoax.

The intricate patterns formed by ploughing are striking from the air. Most ploughing is done at about 7 km/h, and the hours spent in an open tractor, particularly in hot windy conditions, can be very uncomfortable.

PLOUGHING

The plough is one of the grain farmer's most important machines. It is the tractor-drawn implement used for primary cultivation, and has played a dominant role in the development of much, if not all, of Australia's cropping land.

There are several types of plough, but all make a furrow, gutter or slit-like cut in the soil. The main pupose of ploughing is to kill weeds and to aerate and break up hard soils. The furrows also allow water and rain to penetrate the soil and enable further tilling by finer implements before seeding. The basic type is a mouldboard plough. The forward passage of the implement cuts out a continuous piece or sod. A furrow opens to the left of the plough, while the soil falls to the right. Such ploughs are still very popular in Europe and some parts of the United States, but in Australia's larger paddocks, where speed is important, other types of plough are more popular. Nevertheless, in some parts of the country, farmers who appreciate the art of mouldboard ploughing take part in annual competitions.

The most famous plough in Australian history is the STUMPJUMP plough, invented in 1876 by Robert Bowyer Smith in Adelaide. The plough allowed the development of wooded country for cropping, a process which was previously extremely costly and frustrating. Settlers in many states, particularly South Australia, Victoria and NSW, could now clear land in the low rainfall areas which had once been considered suitable only for grazing cattle and sheep. Together with Ridley's harvester (invented in 1843), it was responsible for the development of the Australian wheat industry. The plough's weighted and hinged body was designed to fall back into the furrow after riding over stumps or rocks. No longer did the primitive, wrought-iron plough-shares break up so easily.

The most common modern ploughs in Australia are the disc and chisel. Disc ploughs are suited to paddocks covered with large amounts of weed or rubbish. They cut and turn the soil through the movement of several angled, circular blades. One tractor may pull up to 12 discs, mounted in groups.

The chisel plough is probably the most popular variety in grain-growing areas. It is made up of rows of tines, perhaps as many as 18, which open up the soil without turning it over. This allows air and water into the earth, without exposing the topsoil to wind or water erosion.

PLOVER

The word plover has had a confusing history because what were called lapwings elsewhere were called plovers in Australia, and plovers were called dotterels. It is true that these were book names, and that the book convention has changed. The solution in Australia has been to consider one family of waders – the Charadriidae – as plovers, although what were once plovers are now lapwings!

Many waders – including plovers – breed in the northern hemisphere and spend the northern winter in Australia on mudflats, seashores and, sometimes, inland plains.

Best known is perhaps the Red-capped Plover *Charadrius ruficappilus* which, as its name suggests, has red-orange patches on the crown of its head and the nape of its neck. These small birds are common around beaches, estuaries and the shores of both fresh and salt lakes all over Australia. When disturbed, brooding birds run from their nests, stopping every so often to display their white fronts. If this does not distract the intruder they will sometimes feign injury.

Popular varieties of plums

Mariposa Plum

Narrabeen Plum

Santa Rosa Plum

Wilson Plum

Angelina Plum

President Plum

PLUM

The only plums that most plum puddings see are prunes – plum was once a catch-all term for dried fruit. In Australia, prunes are a variety of plum, mostly D'Agen. The fruit has dark purple skin but golden-yellow flesh, and can also be eaten fresh. Like peaches, apricots and cherries, plums are members of the rose family. The two main species grown commercially in Australia cannot pollinate one another. Japanese plums *Prunus salicina* were probably introduced to Japan from China around 1500 AD. They include Santa Rosa; Narrabeen, of Australian origin; and Mariposa, a 'blood plum'. European plums *P. domestica* originated from near the Black Sea. They have broader, more coarsely serrated leaves and need a cooler climate than Japanese plums. Among hundreds world-wide, important Australian varieties are Angelina, President, Greengage and the prune varieties. Another popular plum is Wilson, probably a hybrid between Japanese and Cherry Plums *P. cerasifera*. Wilson plums have bright red skin, yellow flesh, a round shape and almost free stone. Other cherry plums tend to have small, tart fruit. Damsons *P. institita*, so popular in Britain, are little grown in Australia. Annual production of plums and prunes is about 21 000 tonnes, roughly one-third being prunes from Young and the Murrumbidgee Irrigation Area, NSW, and one fifth being Japanese plums from the Darling Range and Dwellingup regions of Western Australia.

POISONOUS PLANT

The vast majority of poisonous plants are, for practical purposes, poisonous only to introduced livestock. Their leaves and stems are unlikely ever to be eaten by humans. Poisoning of native animals by native plants is rarely if ever recorded, and probably seldom happens. The reasons for plants being poisonous have been much debated. In many cases it is likely to be a means of discouraging browsing, but in other plants it seems probable that it is accidental. Chemical by-products accumulate in the plant, and they just happen to be poisonous.

The most common group of poisonous substances in plants are the alkaloids – organic compounds of nitrogen – the best-known example of which is nicotine. The plant family Solanaceae is especially rich in alkaloids, some of which are used medicinally. A well-known poisonous member of the family is Thornapple *Datura stramonium*, a common weed of richer soils, the seeds of which are the most toxic part. Another large class of plant poisons are glycosides – substances related to sugars. One group release hydrocyanic (prussic) acid, among the fastest-acting of all poisons, when the plant is chewed or digested. A well-known poison plant of this type is the introduced Cherry-laurel *Prunus laurocerasus*, the foliage of which is usually fatal to

stock. Some fodder grasses can also sometimes develop dangerous levels of toxic glycosides.

One group of poisons which act directly on heart muscles are the cardiac glycocides, the best known being digitalis which is present in foxgloves. Oleander *Nerium oleander splendens* is a common ornamental shrub which also has a high level of deadly cardiac glycoside in its stems and bark, but fortunately these are unlikely to be eaten either by humans or livestock. The worst cases of Oleander poisoning have occurred when its twigs have been used as skewers to grill meat, or to stir hot drinks. There is another type of glycoside found in CYCADS. These are present mainly in the large seeds, and are powerful liver toxins which have often poisoned humans. Aborigines ate the starch-rich seeds of cycads only after washing them for a long time in running water.

Saponins are a group of plant poisons that foam in water, and some are used as fish poisons in various parts of the world. The large seeds of Queensland Black Bean *Castanospermum australe* contain saponins, which have poisoned people. They have also proved poisonous to pigs. Saponin poisoning is less fatal than other types.

Other groups of plant poisons involving organic molecules are too numerous to include here, but there are also some relatively simple inorganic poisons in plants. These include nitrates and nitrites, which may be accumulated by many plants, especially when grown in soil which contains a lot of nitrogen. A weed commonly involved in poisoning is the large Variegated Thistle *Silybum*, which may be grazed by stock, often with fatal results. In Western Australia native members of the shrubby *Gastrolobium* group are notorious stock poisons, because they contain the highly toxic compound fluoroacetic acid, which is similar to sodium fluoroacetate, or '1080', used for poisoning rabbits. Occurring over large areas of land potentially useful as grazing country, the various species are known simply as 'Poison' with various prefixes, for example Heartleaf Poison or River Poison. In far western Queensland and the Northern Territory the low-growing Georgina Gidgee *Acacia georginae* contains this same poison, and has also caused considerable stock losses.

Hardly any native plants produce fruits, nuts or roots which are at the same time both poisonous and palatable to humans. Most fleshy fruits found in rainforests are non-poisonous, or only mildly poisonous, although in the latter case they are generally unpleasant to eat. Birds regularly eat a large range of fruits inedible to humans. The Finger Cherry *Rhodomyrtus macrocarpa* of north Queensland rainforests is one of the few really dangerous fruits which is at the same time palatable. The poison in it is reported to destroy the optic nerve, resulting in permanent blindness.

Deadly plants

The white trumpet-shaped flowers and spiky green seed pods of Thornapple are a common sight.

Oleander, a bush that is seen in suburban gardens, has been responsible for poisoning of humans.

The Finger Cherry, restricted to north Queensland, can damage the optic nerve and cause blindness.

Agricultural chemicals are the pollutants which give the most cause for alarm in rural Australia. Concern has been expressed about aerial spraying (left), when sprays can drift across populated areas. Dumping (above) is a problem, as is water pollution (below).

POLLUTION

Pollution is not always caused by human activity. Masses of rotting vegetation in lakes sometimes cause fish deaths, and the gas from a volcanic lake killed hundreds of people and animals in Africa in 1987. However, natural pollutants like these are less of a problem than some of those introduced by humans.

Many pollutants are chemical substances. Over the millions of years which passed before modern industrial society developed, plants and animals encountered thousands of toxic compounds and were often able to evolve to deal with them. Recently, however, organisms have been faced with the appearance of new compounds at a much greater rate than before, and many cannot cope. However, there is encouraging evidence that there may be natural solutions to many pollution problems. Strains of bacteria are developing, for example, which can break down some poisonous substances that were thought to be impossible to deal with a few years ago.

Artificial pollutants are introduced into the environment in sewage, waste from industry and from homes, in industrial accidents or through carelessness, in car and machinery exhausts, and from agriculture.

Sewage includes a lot of organic matter, and if it is discharged untreated into a river it will be attacked by micro-organisms whose activity will rob the water of its oxygen, killing fish and insect larvae. A related problem sometimes occurs when fertilisers run off from agricultural land into waterways. These stimulate the growth of plants which eventually decay, using up the oxygen in the water as they do so. Sewage and industrial waste released into rivers can also contain oils, heavy metals such as mercury, which are very difficult to remove, and various other chemicals. Formerly detergents were very troublesome, producing rafts of foam where waste water was discharged, but modern products break down rapidly.

There have also been improvements in motor engines which have reduced the amount of lead in the atmosphere, as well as carbon monoxide and nitrogen compounds which formed smog over large cities in some weather conditions.

Possibly the most notorious examples of pollution in the country have been caused by pesticides, although the problems may have been exaggerated. Although some people condemn all pesticides, the main culprits have been the chlorinated hydrocarbon insecticides, such as DDT and dieldrin. The dangers to human beings are probably negligible – DDT is about as toxic as aspirin – but they cause ecological problems.

Being extremely stable and soluble in fat, they enter food-chains becoming more concentrated at each level, so that some predatory birds, at the top of a food-chain, can accumulate lethal amounts. While it would be impossible to do away with pesticides altogether, modern pest control uses compounds which break down – such as organophosphates and pyrethroids. There are also continual attempts being made in the industry to find effective non-chemical methods of dealing with agricultural pests.

POND

Naturalists have long been fascinated by ponds, and since the invention of the aquarium in 1850 have often reproduced them in their homes and laboratories. They provide excellent examples of ecosystems, with plants and animals living together in communities.

Ponds vary greatly with area, depth and the nature of the soil that underlies them. All, however, contain primary producers – plants which capture the energy of sunlight and use it to make sugars and other carbon compounds which, in turn, provide various animals with their food. These, in their turn, are preyed upon by other animals. In addition, there are organisms, such as fungi, bacteria and some minute animals, which break down and decompose organic matter, finally releasing simpler compounds which are used by the plants.

The plants range from relatively large flowering plants or ferns to microscopically small floating plankton. The latter include diatoms and other algae which often have intricate coats of silica and other substances. These are found only in those levels to which light can penetrate. The larger plants may be rooted to the bottom, in which case they are restricted to the edges of the pond when the centre is deep, or are floating freely, like the troublesome, introduced weeds Water Hyacinth *Eichhornia crassipes* and the fern *Azolla*. Some poke out of the water, while others are completely submerged.

There is often a great range of animal life in a pond. Some, like the planktonic protozoa – the rotifers or wheel animalcules, hydras and the nematodes – are microscopically small. Others include freshwater fish, molluscs, arthropods and sponges. Among the arthropods many insects, such as ALDER FLIES, CADDIS FLIES, WATER BEETLES and DRAGON FLIES live in ponds in larval or nymphal stages, and some – certain BEETLES and BUGS – also as adults. Various crustaceans, such as water fleas and the microscopic cyclops – so-called because of its single eye – are often common. There are also many molluscs, particularly water snails which feed on plants and algae, and freshwater clams which are filter-feeders. A pond can quite often be the home of frog tadpoles, turtles and such mammals as water rats and the platypus.

PONY

The Australian Pony became recognised as a breed in its own right in 1931, although the foundation of the breed began in 1802 when the first Thoroughbred arrived at Sydney Cove. A year later the first Timor Pony arrived. This, plus the general intermingling of other imported breeds including the Welsh Mountain Pony and the Exmoor Pony, culminated in the Australian Pony, a tough horse with a sturdy constitution and robust nature.

Apart from the Australian Pony, two of the most popular pony breeds are the Welsh Mountain Pony and the Shetland Pony. Others include the Welsh Cob, Manipur and Batik Ponies, the Hackney Pony and the Connemara Pony. The Shetland and Welsh Mountain ponies both have reputations for tireless work, but are more widely known as ideal horses for children. They are well represented at shows, pony clubs and gymkhanas. Ponies are generally classified as HORSES of 14 hands or under (a hand is 102 mm, and the height of a horse is measured from the top of its withers, or shoulders).

POPPY

Poppies, Australia's only commercial pharmaceutical crop, are grown in Tasmania in a strictly controlled industry.

About 500 growers produce poppies, the source of the opium derivatives morphine and codeine, under contract to two international drug companies. The annual harvest of dried poppy heads produces nearly 20 per cent of the world's medical supplies of these drugs. Poppy seeds are also sold for use in cooking.

The industry has developed on the state's north coast and in the south-east regions to produce one of the world's highest yielding and quality crops. Poppies are sown in early to mid winter, flower in late November and are harvested in late February.

They are grown under strict conditions and with federal government licensing. This is partly because the immature poppy heads are much sought after by the illegal drug trade as a source of high-grade heroin. People have been arrested in Tasmania for stealing poppy heads, and for planting opium poppies illegally.

Opium poppies growing in fields at Dickson, in the ACT, during World War II for the production of morphine and codeine. Now the poppies are grown only in Tasmania under strict control by the federal government.

POSSUM

There are four families of marsupials called possums in Australia. The most familiar, including the Common Brushtail Possum, the CUSCUSES and the Scaly-tailed Possum, are called phalangers. The second family includes ring-tailed possums, four GLIDERS, Leadbeater's Possum and the Striped Possum. The third family is that of the PYGMY-POSSUMS and the fourth contains only the HONEY POSSUM, which recent research suggests is not a possum at all.

Phalangers are the possums most familiar to Australians, mainly because of the Common Brushtail *Trichosurus vulpecula* (body length 350–550 mm, tail 250–400 mm) which is often seen in suburbs as well as the bush, and frequently mates noisily in attics. They have probably become more common since the arrival of Europeans because gardens provide fruit and flowers to supplement a diet of gum leaves. Common Brushtails have pink noses and large ears, but size and colour vary a lot from place to place. The tail is bushy except for the naked tip and can be used to grip branches. Brushtails are active at night and live mainly in trees, but unlike cuscuses they bound with apparent ease through the branches. Scaly-tailed Possums *Wyulda squamicaudata* (400 mm, 300 mm) of northernmost Western Australia have a tail which is hairy at its base, but mostly naked and

Common Brushtail Possums are all too familar to many householders, particularly along the east coast. The red stain on the animal's chest is from a gland used to mark territory.

scaly like a cuscus's. In other respects they resemble a Brushtail.

Ringtail possums have tapering, prehensile tails which are often curled at the tip into a spiral. They use them to grip branches and carry nesting material. Three species are found only in small areas of Queensland rainforest, and one among rocky outcrops in northernmost Western Australia and the Northern Territory. However, Common Ringtails *Pseudocheirus peregrinus* (300–350 mm, 300–350 mm) are found from Cape York to South Australia and in Western Australia and Tasmania.

Leadbeater's Possum *Gymnobelideus leadbeateri* (150–170 mm, 145–180 mm) resembles a Sugar Glider, but lacks the gliding membrane. They were thought to have become extinct in about 1909, but were rediscovered in Mountain Ash forest not far from Melbourne in 1961.

Striped Possums *Dactylopsila trivirgata* (263 mm, 325 mm) are striped black and white like a skunk, and also smell. They are noisy, agile, erratically-moving hunters of woodborers and other insects in rainforest and woodland in eastern Cape York and New Guinea. They drum on the bark with their hands, possibly to detect insects underneath.

POTATO

Potatoes are an important part of the diet of most Australians. Indeed, the average Australian eats around four tonnes of potatoes in a lifetime.

Potatoes are Australian's largest vegetable crop, and are grown in all states. Because they will grow in a wide range of climates and soils, potatoes are found from the south-west of Western Australia to the Atherton Tablelands in Queensland and the Dorrigo Plateau in NSW. Victoria is the largest producer, however, accounting for just over one-third of the annual one million-tonne harvest.

POTOROO

Potoroos are small, cat-sized KANGAROOS which look like BANDICOOTS. They live in tussock and dense grass in woodlands and rarely, if ever, come out into open country. Furthermore they only emerge at night and are therefore rarely seen by casual observers. Only one of the three known species is common, but it is restricted to limited areas along the east coast from the NSW-Queensland border to Victoria and in Tasmania, in areas with more than 760 mm of rain a year. It has not been seen in Western Australia for about 80 years. This species, the greyish-brown Long-nosed *Potoroo Potorous* tridactylus (male body length, 380 mm, tail 235 mm, females a little smaller) was noted by Governor Phillip in 1789.

The Long-footed Potoroo *P. longipes* (400 mm, 320 mm) is found in east Gippsland, Victoria, but only a few specimens have been collected. Both feed on soft invertebrates, tubers and roots.

Long-nosed Potoroos are common in south-eastern Australia and Tasmania although they are rarely seen because they only emerge from cover at night.

POULTRY

The modern poultry industry is far removed from the backyard chicken coop with a collection of hens scattered across a farmyard. Although there are a few free-range egg and chicken meat producers, the vast majority of poultry products eaten by Australians these days are grown under intensive conditions.

The Australian poultry industry produces around 190 million dozen eggs a year. It turns out around 4.7 million table-ready birds a week, with NSW supplying around two million, Victoria 890 000 and Queensland 660 000 birds. An average Australian eats more than 20 kg of poultry each year and the total value of the meat industry alone is estimated at $890 million annually. The meat industry is dominated by two large companies – Inghams and Amatil – which have refined and mechanised chicken production.

Many practices have been automated in the past ten years, leading to enormous cost savings. In 1962 a typical 6000-bird-an-hour processing plant employed around 3000 people. Today, the same plant would need to employ only a total of about 160 workers.

Chickens grown for the table are not kept in cages, like their egg-producing counterparts. They are grown on the floor of large sheds and have their beaks and wings clipped to make them easier to manage and to prevent cannabilism.

The egg industry is also dominated by large intensive producers and companies, usually regulated by a statutory marketing board in each state. Some egg boards are making moves to privatise the industry. The boards license egg producers who are allowed to keep only a certain number of hens. Most eggs are sold domestically, with small amounts of shell, pulp and dried egg being exported. There are around 2000 egg producers in Australia, most having up to 1000 hens. There are, however, a small number of growers with 20 000 hens each.

PRICKLY PEAR

This name is used in Australia for cacti of the genus *Opuntia*, which all originally came from the Americas, but were introduced into Australia at various times over the last 200 years. They are succulent plants with stems divided into regular joints, mostly flattened into oval pads. Distributed over their surfaces are small hair-tufts, from which spring small barbed bristles and frequently also fierce spines. Decorative flowers emerge from the edges of the pads, followed by red or yellow fruits with juicy flesh.

The earliest prickly pears in Australia came with the First Fleet in 1788, brought as host plants for dye-yielding cochineal insects. Others were introduced for ornament and hedges in the 19th Century. By the beginning of this century farmers in south Queensland became alarmed at the way several species were spreading. Various methods of eradication were tried, including slashing machines and poisoning with arsenic compounds, but by the outbreak of World War I about 25 million hectares of land – extending from around Mackay in Queensland to Singleton in NSW – was densely infested. In 1916 the Commonwealth Prickly Pear Board was set up to investigate possible control methods using insects or fungi. Their investigations centred on various cochineal insects and the moth *Cactoblastis cactorum*, brought from Argentina. Large numbers of eggs of the latter were released in 1925 with spectacular success. By 1929 the major infestations had been eradicated and much of the land returned to productive use.

Despite Cactoblastis, a number of prickly pear species are still common, mainly in drier subtropical areas and in the semi-arid interior. In parts of Queensland, for instance between Rockhampton and Toowoomba, the Velvet Tree Pear *Opuntia tomentosa* forms a tree to 10 m tall, common in eucalypt forest. The Common Pest Pear *O. stricta* is a shrubby plant scattered widely through eastern Australia, while the Tiger Pear *O. aurantiaca* – a very unpleasant plant with vicious spines that can cripple horses – is still common in the Hunter Valley and other parts of northern NSW. A species often cultivated for its edible fruits is the Indian Fig *O. ficus-indica*.

Because of the prickly pear problem, the cultivation of all members of the cactus family was made illegal in Queensland, and that of all Opuntia species illegal in NSW.

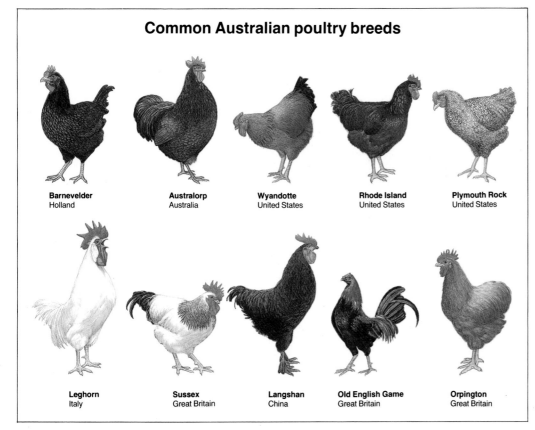

Common Australian poultry breeds

Barnevelder	Australorp	Wyandotte	Rhode Island	Plymouth Rock
Holland	Australia	United States	United States	United States

Leghorn	Sussex	Langshan	Old English Game	Orpington
Italy	Great Britain	China	Great Britain	Great Britain

Caterpillars of the moth Cactoblastis cactorum *(inset)* and an example of their efficiency in eating prickly pear. The top photograph was taken in October 1926 at Chinchilla, Qld; the bottom three years later.

PRIVET

Several shrubs and small trees of the genus *Ligustrum* are called privet. They are mainly natives of subtropical and temperate Asia. Vigorous growers, they bear sprays of small white flowers with a rather pungent smell. The variegated California Privet *Ligustrum ovalifolium*, actually a native of Japan, was one of the most popular hedge plants in former decades, and the only European species, *L. vulgare*, is still used for hedges in cooler parts of Australia. However, it is two Chinese species, Small-leaved or Chinese Privet *L. sinense* and Broad-leaved or Glossy Privet *L. lucidum*, which have adapted best to Australian conditions and have become serious weeds.

PROSPECTING

Prospecting conjures up colourful images of 'old timers' scouring the parched Australian interior for minerals with packhorse, pick and shovel. The fabulous lodes of Broken Hill, Mt Isa and Kalgoorlie were discovered by these skilled pioneers. But the major rich deposits, which were literally sticking out of the ground, have probably all been discovered by now so that modern mineral prospecting usually involves searching below the ground.

In recent years many new mines have been developed as extensions of traditional mining areas, while large new lodes, such as the massive copper-uranium deposits of Roxby Downs, north of Port Augusta in South Australia, have been discovered. Prospecting for these finds began in the research departments of mining companies, often with the help of satellite photographs. When an exploration licence is granted to the mining company by one of the state governments, the potential of the land is investigated in a three-part programme.

Firstly a geological map is prepared. A geologist walks over the ground recording all the rock types or minerals he finds. This enables him to concentrate on potential mineral-bearing rocks. These are examined in detail by taking samples of soil or rock for chemical analysis, or by using geophysical methods such as seismic, radiometric or resistivity surveys to investigate the physical properties of rocks below the surface of the earth.

Chemical and geophysical methods are particularly useful in areas covered by deep layers of soil. Economic minerals have a characteristic 'signature' which can be recognised in the soil or rocks around them. Mercury, for example, is often concentrated in soils around gold-bearing rocks, while sulphide deposits have a characteristic response to an electric charge.

The third phase is to drill below the ground to investigate promising areas. Samples of drill cores or chips of rock are analysed chemically. If valuable minerals are found there will be a detailed drilling programme to determine the extent of the deposit, so that an accurate, three-dimensional picture of the entire area can be produced for examination.

Petroleum exploration methods are similar to those used in the search for minerals, but geophysical methods, particularly seismic surveys, are more commonly used. This involves generating a shock wave in rocks by explosive or mechanical means. The speed at which the shock wave travels through the ground varies from rock to rock so that an 'X-ray' view of rock formations below the ground can be produced.

A modern exploration programme commonly takes five years, and it may take another five to ten years to develop a working mine. The cost of developing a mine is commonly between $100 and $1000 million.

Some environmental damage can be done to vegetation during large scale prospecting programmes, particularly by seismic surveys. The major impact is from access roads, but with careful planning most of this damage can be avoided or repaired.

PUNTS, FERRIES AND FORDS

River crossings caused much of the difficulty and danger of travel in 19th-century Australia. Even if a river was shallow enough to ford, its banks were often as steep as a house roof and many a dray overturned and its horses and bullocks were drowned. After rain a river might not be fordable for days or weeks. Enterprising publicans often set up shop at crossing places, forming the nucleus of many Australian towns.

Merely getting wet contributed to the delays and discomforts of the journey. A day might have to be spent drying goods after a crossing, such as that on the Nepean River at Emu Ford, before a punt was installed. Many cattle drowned swimming over, and sometimes sheep sank, weighed down by their waterlogged wool.

Wide rivers had to be crossed by ferry or punt. The first ferries were rowing boats or less. One at Albury in the 1830s consisted merely of a dug-out canoe attached to a rawhide rope stretched across the Murray. Flat-bottomed punts came later, and those taking drays and draught animals became quite elaborate. Some were steam-driven, and one launched at Echuca in 1868 was able to take 1000 sheep at a time. By the end of the century, government authorities had taken the operation of most punts out of the rapacious hands of private operators. Some had gleefully raked in scandalously huge fares during the gold rushes. Dray owners wanting to cross the Goulburn River at Seymour in Victoria in the 1850s were charged one pound ($2), the value of quarter of an ounce of gold.

New South Wales' ten car ferries are the sole relics of the 137 punts and ferries that were being operated in the state in 1888.

PYGMY-POSSUM

Pygmy-possums are tiny marsupials, about as large as mice, with prehensile tails which they curl in a spiral at rest. There are five species. Mountain Pygmy-possums *Burramys parvus* (body about 115 mm, tail about 148 mm) are unique animals because they were first described in 1895 from fossils discovered in deposits in Wombeyan Caves, NSW. In 1966 a living example turned up in a ski-hut on Mt Hotham in Victoria. Since then they have been found to range over two areas, totalling less than 70 sq. km, in the Australian Alps, including the summit of Mt Kosciusko. They are Australia's only known exclusively alpine and subalpine mammal. In cold conditions they can become torpid for some time. They eat insects and vegetable food and they may store seeds like a squirrel.

Eastern Pygmy-possums *Cercartetus nanus* (70–110 mm, 75–105 mm) live in coastal regions from southern Queensland to eastern South Australia and in Tasmania. They feed largely on nectar and pollen from native trees – using their brush-tipped tongue – and may be a pollinator. They also eat insects. In winter they spend much time in nests in tree holes in a torpid state with their body temperature scarcely higher than that of the outside air. The slightly smaller Western Pygmy-possums of South Australia, western Victoria and south-west Australia are agile, nocturnal creatures which include insects in their diet.

PYLON

Stalking for thousands of kilometres over the country, pylons, or in modern parlance, power transmission towers, carry electricity to ever more consumers. The Electricity Commission of NSW alone runs over 16 000 km of power lines. People in the Australian Capital Territory use most electricity – it is a severe climate and they are better off. Perth people use least.

Towers carrying the maximum voltage of 500 000 kilovolts (kV) are usually about 55 m high and 400 m apart. Those carrying the more usual 330 000 kV are about 40 m tall and 375 m apart. The electricity authority has to obtain the use of a strip of land along the line – an easement – between 45 and 70 m wide, depending on the type of line and tower. Landowners and electricity authorities generally manage to negotiate a fee to compensate for the loss of land on which the towers stand, and for disturbance during the building stage. However, sometimes

Geological maps are essential to prospectors. This group of surveyors at Southern Cross in 1911 were part of an expedition preparing geological maps for the Western Australian government.

Eastern Pygmy-possums feeding on nectar from a banksia blossom. These tiny animals generally only come out at night, and are therefore rarely seen by casual observers. During the day they rest in nests in tree holes.

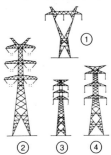

Electricity transmission towers march across the Snowy Mountains. Easements beneath the wires, rather than the towers themselves, are an eyesore in timbered areas. Four typical towers (right) are: (**1**) 330 kV single circuit; (**2**) 500 kV double circuit; (**3**) 132 kV double circuit and (**4**) 330 kV double circuit.

PYTHON

The snakes of this family, of which there are about 13 Australian species, are non-venomous and kill their prey by constriction. A victim's body is encircled by loops of the snake, and when it exhales, the coils tighten, eventually suffocating the animal. They tend to be bulky, slow moving snakes.

Black-headed Pythons *Aspidites melanocephalus* (to 2.5 m) have a jet-black head and neck and the rest of their body is lighter, and striped. They live in the northern half of Australia, although not in very arid regions. Green Pythons *Chondrophython viridis* (to almost 2.0 m) live only in New Guinea and rainforest areas of Cape York, but they are familiar to most Australians from photographs of them winding their way along tree branches.

There are two subspecies of *Morelia spilota*. One is the Diamond Python (illustration p 339), and the other the Carpet Python, names which describe their patterning. The species occurs in a horseshoe band from northern Western Australia through Queensland and NSW to south-western Western Australia; they are not found in southern Victoria. They sometimes live in trees, sometimes in burrows made by other animals and sometimes in outside lavatories and the barns of countrymen who value their ability to catch rats.

the authority has to resort to a court to resume (force) an easement. Normal use of the land below the wires can return after they are put up – the electro-magnetic field around the wires reaches the ground at a lower intensity than is usually found in homes being generated by appliances like microwave ovens, television sets and personal computers.

The galvanised steel structures are not beautiful, and any plans for new lines usually have to undergo an environmental impact study. Many Commonwealth and state bodies have to be consulted, for example pastures protection boards and education authorities – in case schools, with potential tower acrobats, are planned along the line. Nowadays pylons are sited so that as few as possible are silhouetted against the sky, and after construction they are often painted dark green to harmonise with bushland. The wires are treated to reduce their shine. Putting lines underground costs about 16 times as much as conventional installation, and the heat build-up means the lines have to be brought to the surface at intervals for inspection.

Q FEVER

The Q of Q Fever stands for query, not the state, although it is commoner in Queensland than elsewhere. It is a disease that humans acquire from animals, in this case cattle, sheep, and goats, although bandicoots also suffer from it. It is transmitted between animals by ticks, but those do not appear to spread it to people. Humans catch it by inhaling dust from animals (which show no symptoms) infected by the organism *Coxiella burnetii*. Consequently people working with livestock, and particularly abattoir workers, are the commonest victims as the organisms responsible are often concentrated in the placenta of infected animals. It is rarely transmitted from person to person, and has a low death rate even when untreated.

QUANDONG

This small native tree, *Santalum acuminatum*, belongs to the sandalwood family, and like other members of that family it is partially a parasitic on the roots of other plants. The trees are found on the dry plains of inland Australia, and have the distinction of producing the best edible fruit of any tree in those regions. It is small and crooked, with drooping, willowy, pale green foliage. The almost spherical to slightly pear-shaped fruits are up to about 30 mm in diameter and a bright glossy red. The crisp, juicy flesh tastes slightly acid and contains a spherical, deeply-wrinkled stone. The stones were at one time collected as curios and used for beads, or as marbles in board games such as Chinese Checkers. Although valued as a fresh fruit by the Aborigines, quandongs were, and still are, used mainly in the form of jams and jellies by white settlers. Attempts are being made to grow them commercially, but their cultivation presents problems. They are nowhere very common in the wild state.

QUARRY

The man-made scars of quarries are often seen on the sides of valleys or the tops of hills. Most are mined for non-metallic materials like building stone, road aggregate, limestone and various types of clay.

Sites for quarries are chosen so that they are as close as possible to the point where the material will be used, usually on the sides of valleys or hills so that the material can easily be moved downhill to a treatment plant. The scale of mining is small, employing only a handful of people compared to the large scale open-pit mines such as the La Trobe coal fields and Hamersley iron ore deposits. Mining methods used in quarries depend on the material being extracted. The famous Wombeyan marble quarry in NSW uses rotating wires to cut marble slabs which are delicately toppled using pneumatic jacks. The numerous limestone quarries use explosives to break up the rock. Many local councils operate small quarries to provide aggregate for road construction while there are large private operations providing road base for cities and clay for bricks.

QUARTZ

The ancients believed that quartz crystals were solidified water. The Greeks called the mineral krystallos or 'ice' and the Aborigines believed that the water-like clarity was due to a supernatural origin, a link between humans and the spirits. It is the most common of all minerals, being a compound of the two most abundant elements to be found in the earth's crust – oxygen and silicon.

Quartz crystallises from molten magma deep within the earth's crust, or from silica-rich solutions in veins, into sizes which vary from several meters for one crystal, down to those not visible to the naked eye. Given room to grow, quartz crystals have a characteristic six-sided shape. They are usually colourless or clear, but small amounts of impurities such as titanium, chromium, iron and manganese give rise to the delicate colours of gemstone varieties of quartz, such as purple amethyst, yellow citrine and brown, grey or black smoky quartz. The milky white variety often occurs in veins which criss-cross rocks in a complex latticework, varying from a few millimetres to many meters across. Such veins sometimes contain gold.

Quartz is one of the most durable substances on earth and is present in all major types of rocks. The forces of erosion have concentrated quartz grains on many brilliant white beaches for which Australia is famous.

QUARTZITE

As the name suggests, quartzite is a rock composed mainly of quartz grains. It is formed when sandstone is heated and compressed at great depths within the earth's crust. Quartzite is hard, and was used by the Aborigines to make stone implements. It is also a valuable and durable building stone.

During the transformation from sandstone to quartzite, quartz grains literally become welded together. If there are any impurities in the rock, such as iron, the quartzite can have orange-brown to golden-yellow hues, otherwise it will be white. In the sapphire fields of central Queensland quartzite blocks are called 'sapphire boulders' because of their common association with the gemstone.

QUEENSLAND LUNGFISH

Lungfish have much in common with amphibians, but are no longer thought to be their direct ancestors. Most fishes have fins supported by rays, but Queensland Lungfish *Neoceratodus forsteri* (to 1.5 m) have fleshy outgrowths containing within them a skeleton. The appendages have tasselled fringes. In their surviving relatives – the African and South American lungfish – the appendages are long, rayless filaments. Lungfish have gills which are used in the normal fishy way, but they also have a lung – a pair in non-Australian species – which corresponds to the swim bladder of other fishes, opening into the gut. The Australian species is far less dependent upon lungs than are its overseas cousins which come to the surface more often, and may, indeed, have to use their lungs from time to time. Queensland Lungfish live in waters which may become stagnant, making an ability to breath air useful, but they do not have to aestivate in dried mud, as the African and American species must often do.

Internally a Queensland Lungfish is different from other fish. Its skeleton is made up largely of cartilage (a tough elastic tissue) although its skull is made of bone. Its stomach does not hold food, but is a spirally-arranged tract through which its food passes. Food – which mostly consists of small animals – is broken down by the grinder-like teeth rather than by the stomach. Its body is covered by a series of large, bony, overlapping scales.

When the species was first described by Ludwig Krefft in 1870 it was found only in the Burnett and Mary River systems in south-east Queensland where, in suitable habitats, it was apparently reasonably common. Since then it has also been introduced into several other river systems, such as the Brisbane and Pine Rivers, where the temperature is suitable, and where this sluggish fish would not become an easy meal for a predator.

Lungfish have a long fossil history, stretching back more than 350 million years. They were once widespread, being common, for example, in the northern hemisphere.

Queensland Lungfish normally breathe through their gills, like any other fish, but they can gulp air from the surface if the water is particularly foul. Their single lung is attached to their alimentary canal by a tube.

QUICKSAND

The belief that quicksand will actually suck in men and animals until they drown is something of an old wives tale. It is true, however, that it presents a danger because it is not easily recognised and a panicking animal or person can be drowned.

Quicksand is simply plain sand which is mixed with water and trapped in a pool so that the individual grains are pushed apart and flow over one another. The liquefied mass will not support a heavy weight, but if the water is drained it will revert to a normal sand bed.

Quicksand usually occurs near the mouths of large rivers and on flat shores underlain by stiff clay or other impervious material, or in streams fed by underground springs. Water flows through the sand from a spring, river current or ocean tide but cannot drain away due to the impervious layer. Quicksand often develops a thin, dry crust.

It is not surprising, perhaps, that the first Europeans to see Quokkas thought they were cats or rats. Most of the animals live on Rottnest Island, off Perth, WA.

QUOKKA

'A rat as big as a cat' was among the surprising discoveries made by Dutch explorer Willem de Vlamingh when he landed on the West Australian coast in 1696. He named the island where he found these strange creatures Rottenest (later to become Rottnest Island) from the Dutch for 'rat nest'. An earlier Dutch visitor, Samuel Volchertzoon, in 1656 or 1658 (the date is not certain) had described the creatures as 'civet-cats'. In fact what both men had seen were not cats or rats at all, but Quokkas.

Male Quokkas – really small wallabies – have a mean body length of 487 mm and a tail of 289 mm; females are a little smaller. They are stocky animals with relatively short tails, very short ears, and long, grizzled fur.

Quokkas were once common on the mainland of south-western Western Australia, but their numbers fell drastically. Now they seem to be recovering. On the mainland they prefer dense vegetation and moist conditions. On Rottnest – which they share with tourists and visiting biologists – the environment is far harsher, and very dry in summer. Then the Quokkas assemble at seepages near salt lakes and the beaches, each local group keeping to its own water supply. There is a well developed social organisation, with a hierarchy among the adult males. On Rottnest the breeding season is short (oestrus January, later if the season is hot; gestation 27 days; young in pouch till August) but on the mainland Quokkas breed throughout the year.

Because they are so easily seen on Rottnest, and are easily reared in captivity, Quokkas have been the most intensively studied wallabies. Much pioneering work on the physiology, ecology and behaviour of marsupials has been carried out with them.

QUOLL

Quolls are commonly called Native, Marsupial or Tiger Cats although their long, pointed snouts are not in the least feline. Cat is really short for polecat – the wild ancestor of the domestic ferret – no doubt familiar to many of the convicts who claimed to have been transported for poaching a few rabbits. They are one of the largest members of a family of animals that includes the TASMANIAN DEVIL, the KOWARI, and ANTECHINUSES. All quolls have white spots on a brown or grey-brown background. These help to camouflage the animals against a sun-and shadow-dappled background. In *the* TIGER-CAT the spots extend to the tail, so it is now officially known as the Spotted-tailed Quoll.

Eastern Quolls *Dasyurus viverrinus* (male, mean body length 370 mm, tail 240 mm, female a little smaller) were once widespread in south-east Australia, but died out on the mainland at about the beginning of the century, possibly as the result of an epidemic. They feed on insects, including pests, smaller vertebrates such as bandicoots, and carrion, as well as some plants. Females can produce 30 young but have only six nipples. Survival is presumably a case of first come, first served.

Western Quolls *D. geoffroii* (347 mm, 251 mm) are also known by their Aboriginal name *chuditch* which imitates its call. They are now restricted to south-western Australia and New Guinea, but were formerly found in all states other than Tasmania.

Northern Quolls or Satanellus *D. hallucatus* (123–310 mm, 127–308 mm), the smallest of the group, live along the northern edge of Australia. Females have no pouch, but flaps of skin develop by the teats when young are born.

It was once thought that marsupials did not play like placentals, although play is an essential process for a young carnivore learning its trade. Quolls are, however, noted for social play among their young. They are also expert climbers.

Western Quolls are now found only in the south-western corner of Australia. In towns they raid rubbish bins, and will occasionally take poultry.

R

RABBIT

Rabbits *Oryctolagus cuniculus* came with the earliest European settlers to Australia – including five with the First Fleet – and some escaped. However, either because they were 'hutch' rabbits, or because the sandy soils and conditions around Sydney were unsuitable (or both), they did not become established. Most, if not all, of Australia's modern wild rabbits are descended from 24 introduced by Thomas Austin of Barwon Park, near Geelong, Victoria on Christmas night, 1859. Some this homesick settler probably released at once, while others, or their descendants, escaped in the months that followed. By the end of the century, the population had reached plague proportions.

Their spread in Australia has been described in great detail by Eric Rolls in his book *They All Ran Wild*. Within 60 years they filled the southern half of the continent, bypassing or scrambling over the thousands of kilometres of rabbit fencing and turning thousands of square kilo-metres of pastureland into dustbowls. They are still spreading, especially in favourable years.

Rabbits are grazers, preferring to eat protein-rich plants and thus encouraging their replacement by valueless weeds. They also prevent many trees from regenerating by eating their seedlings. In dry conditions they can get enough moisture from tree bark and roots. Rabbits live in burrows, usually grouped in warrens, and come out at night to graze.

They are extraodinarily prolific – each doe can produce from 11 to 25 kittens a year, with the larger litters in the more favourable feeding areas. Many infants die, however, but those that survive the first three or four months – when they become sexually mature – often live for two or three more years and produce up to six litters a year of their own.

Rabbits suffer from various parasites which can slow down their rate of reproduction in wetter areas, but their main disease is the introduced MYXOMATOSIS. At first this killed 99.9 per cent of its victims, but within a few months less virulent strains evolved so that now the death rate of infected animals is about 40 per cent. Populations fell dramatically at first, but have risen since, although they have not reached their former levels. Rabbits are also attacked by FOXES and feral cats. In wetter areas all these enemies can keep the rabbit population in check, but in more arid regions the population fluctuates violently with conditions.

In Elizabethan England the Warrener – the person who looked after the groups of tunnels in which colonies of rabbits lived and produced their litters – was an important man, and gentlemen of fashion set up warrens within their parks. The Normans probably introduced rabbits into Britain – it is a species that is native to some Mediterranean countries – and the warrens came to be guarded as carefully as the deer parks. In the 18th and 19th centuries Englishmen were allegedly transported for merely emptying a warren of a few occupants – usually by the introduction of ferrets.

How 24 rabbits took over Australia

The 24 European rabbits imported in 1859 by Thomas Austin for sport on his property near Geelong, Victoria, had become thousands by 1862. In 1868 rabbits were reported as a calamity in the Western District of Victoria. Five years later they had spread to the Murray River, and in 1878 were seen at the Murrum-bidgee. During the 1880s they poured into NSW. By 1886 the flood had arrived in southern Queensland and South Australia. In 1894 they reached South Austra-lia's northern and western borders, and were established in the south of Western Aus-tralia by 1900. A few short years later they had crossed the desert and had begun to take over the agricultural land on the west coast.

Grey areas show distribution and approximate density of rabbit population

Spread of rabbits from release sites

Rabbits colonised most of southern Australia in a few short years. Only heat and humidity keep them from repeating their success in the far north of the continent.

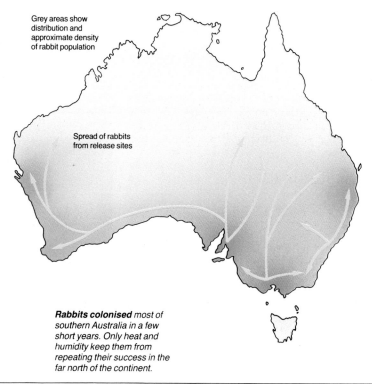

By crowding into a corner and hopping on top of one another, rabbits can soon scale a fence. None of the so-called 'rabbit-proof' fences ever worked for long.

RAILWAY

Australia's first steam railway began its three-kilometre service in 1854, between Melbourne and its port. By 1861, Australia had 400 km of track, about half of it in Victoria. In the 1880s – the boom decade for railway building – 8834 km of track were laid. The peak was reached in 1941, with 43 829 km altogether, since when about 4000 km have been closed. In 1917, Western

Australia's isolation ended with the completion of the trans-Australian line. A traveller could get from Brisbane to Perth in six days, but had to change trains no fewer than six times. Through bureaucratic bungling, NSW built lines 1.43 m apart (standard gauge) while Victoria and most of South Australia used a broad gauge (1.6 m), and Queensland, Western Australia and parts of South Australia adopted a narrow gauge (1.1 m) to minimise construction costs for lines where traffic would be slight. Only in 1962 were the east coast capitals linked by a standard gauge line.

Trains transformed farming, trade and social life, and opened up vast new areas for settlement. Victoria and NSW claimed that no farmer was more than a half-day's journey from a station. Perishable crops could now be grown inland. No longer did farmers have to pay exorbitant sums to carters, or leave their properties for two or three months to take wool or grain to cities. Towns lobbied frenziedly for lines. The station became the hub of the town and its new prosperity. The station master shared the social status of the bank manager.

RAIN

Clouds are composed of water droplets which fall as rain – if they are large enough to overcome updrafts in the cloud. Once a liquid droplet forms in a cloud by condensing onto a nucleus of airborne dust, salt or bacteria, it grows by colliding with other droplets. However, growth by collision is slow and produces only relatively small droplets, except when nuclei are larger than about 30 micrometres. Larger droplets initially form as ice crystals which attract water molecules from surrounding droplets and grow quickly. As they fall towards the earth, the ice crystals collide with other droplets and grow larger still, until they eventually encounter warmer air near the earth's surface, and melt. Most rain therefore occurs as liquid droplets, usually 0.5 to 5 mm in diameter.

Rainfall in Australia is highly seasonal. North-ern Australia receives most of its rain between November and April from clouds associated with monsoon rains during the 'wet' season, or from occasional tropical cyclones. Tully, on the eastern coast of Queensland, has the highest long-term

SEASONAL RAINFALL

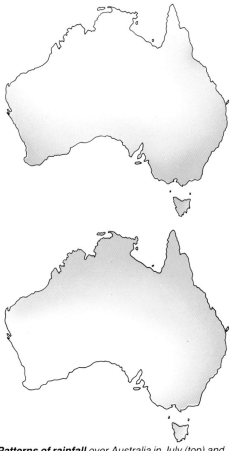

Patterns of rainfall over Australia in July (top) and January (bottom) are markedly different and reflect the paths of prevailing winds over the continent.

annual average rainfall in Australia – 4203 mm. High annual falls of rain also occur near Lake Margaret, Tasmania (3575 mm on average) but mostly during May to October from clouds associated with cold fronts. However, much of Australia is arid. Large parts of central Australia receive no more than 100 mm rain per year on average, making Australia the driest continent in the world after Antarctica.

RAINBOW

A rainbow is an arc of light which is separated into different colours because of raindrops in the air. When a ray of light enters a spherical raindrop it slows – because water is denser than air – and bends. The amount of bending depends on the wavelength of light so that red light bends most (42° 18′), followed by orange, yellow, green, blue, indigo and violet which bends the least (40° 36′). The separated light rays are then reflected from the droplet, bent once again as they enter the air, and travel towards an observer with each colour forming a complete arc. If one rainbow – the primary rainbow – is visible, then light has been reflected just once in the droplet. A secondary rainbow occurs above the primary rainbow when light is reflected twice in the raindrop. The separated colours leave the droplet at greater angles than those of the primary rainbow. For example, red light travels towards the observer at an angle of about 50° as well as at 42°. The secondary rainbow is fainter than the primary rainbow because light is lost when it is reflected twice.

HOW RAINBOWS FORM

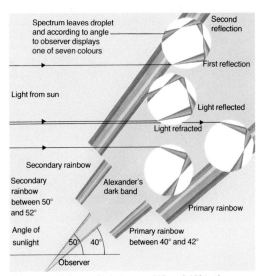

Primary rainbows lie between 40° and 42° to the angle of sunlight, and secondary rainbows between 50° and 52°. Because the light in a secondary rainbow has been reflected one more time, the colours are reversed – red appears on the inside, instead of the outside, of the bow.

Attempts at making rain

In one of the world's driest continents, it is understandable that scientists would spend considerable amounts of time and money trying to make rain. Cloud seeding is the best attempt to date to create rainfall, although there has been considerable debate about the technique's success.

At intervals between 1955 and the early 1980s, scientists from the Commonwealth Scientific and Industrial Research Organisation (CSIRO) took part in cloud-seeding experiments. This involves spraying clouds from an aeroplane with chemicals such as silver iodide and carbon dioxide. The scientists hoped the chemicals would form nuclei within suitable clouds (those with temperatures of at least −8°C, and with ten ice crystals and 1 mg of

water droplets per litre) to attract and bind particles together, thus forming raindrops.

However, extensive trials recorded no immediate increase in rainfall, and the experiments were abandoned in 1981. Recent reappraisals of the results have indicated that rainfall did increase in some areas over a number of months. It worked best over Tasmania and the Snowy Mountains where rainfall increased by around 20 per cent.

Scientists are still unsure whether the silver iodide increased rainfall directly, or whether the seeding operation itself set in motion a chain of events which indirectly increased it. Despite the results, the experiments have not been restarted, partly due to cutbacks in CSIRO funding.

RAINFOREST

A forest-type of great antiquity in Australia, rainforest covers less than one per cent of the land surface, but is home to an enormous number of unique plants and animals. Originally 'rain forest' was used in a rather vague way to refer to any forest growing in a very wet tropical or subtropical climate. In Australia, rainforest has come to be used in a slightly more specialised sense, taking in even some vegetation types in rather dry areas. In this sense it coincides with the term 'closed forest' which is used by vegetation scientists for a forest in which the tree crowns are hard up against one another, forming a near-continuous mass of foliage which prevents between 70 and 100 per cent of sunlight from reaching the ground. In this respect rainforest differs from all forests dominated by eucalypts, in which less than 70 per cent of light is blocked by tree crowns.

Another obvious feature of many rainforests is the large number of vines or lianes which form dense masses of foliage over the tree crowns, with many thick, flexible, looping stems – 'jungle ropes' – hanging below. There are also numerous EPIPHYTES which grow on the tree trunks and branches. Most abundant are mosses and lichens, but in the wetter tropical and subtropical rainforests these are joined by a great variety of ferns and orchids, often forming large masses high in the limbs of big trees.

Many species of trees live in tropical rainforests and 100 or more per hectare have been recorded, compared with the one to five which usually dominate eucalypt forests.

In Australia rainforests are found only in the east, far north and north-west. Plotted on a map they show as a broken-up pattern of small

RAINFOREST REMNANTS

Much of the rainforest in Australia has been cut down to clear land for agriculture, or for timber. Now the few remaining patches are under threat.

Most of Australia's rainforest stretches along the east coast, from north Queensland to Tasmania. Those in the tropical north, such as at Bellenden Ker, south of Cairns (above) contain a far greater variety of plants and animals than sub-tropical forests which extend south to near Sydney at Minnamurra (left). Epiphytes (below) are a feature of all rainforests.

patches, most running down the east coast from Cape York to Cape Otway and into Tasmania.

Rainforests can be divided into types according to two sets of environmental factors: warm-cool and wet-dry. Whether a forest is warm or cool depends on its distance from the Equator and its height above sea level. Whether it is wet or dry depends on rainfall and humidity. The most luxuriant rainforests are those in the highest-rainfall coastal areas of tropical north Queensland. From there to the southern tip of Tasmania there is a steady change towards a simpler type of cool-temperate rainforest with

fewer species. Trees are of a more even size with smaller leaves, and there are far fewer lianes and large epiphytes. A similar progression is found going from sea-level to the highest mountains (about 1500 m) in north Queensland. Moving from wet to dry areas, there is a steady decrease in height of rainforests, from well over 30 m to only about 5 m. In the tropical north there are still many drier rainforests, and the term 'vine thicket' or 'vine scrub' is often given to them. Further south, the most extensive type of dry rainforest is 'Bottle-tree scrub', which is found scattered over a large area of inland south-east

Queensland. Here again the forest is growing on fertile soil, and most of it has now been cleared for grazing or cropping.

In the southern half of Australia rainforests are classified as subtropical, warm-temperate or cool-temperate. Subtropical rainforests are found mainly on the south Queensland and northern NSW coastal lowlands, such as the famous 'Big Scrub' of the Lismore district which was cleared almost entirely long ago. They reach their southern limits on basalt soils in the Illawarra district. These forests are moderately rich in species, usually with no single one being dominant. Warm-temperate rainforests are found in mountain gullies of NSW, extending into far south Queensland and far eastern Victoria. They are dominated by few species of trees, the chief ones being Coachwood, Lilli-Pilly and Sassafras. Cool-temperate rainforests are most extensive in Tasmania and the mountains of east Victoria, with some patches on higher mountains of northern NSW, as far as the Queensland border ranges. The characteristic trees there are Myrtle Beech *Northofagus cunninghamii* in Tasmania and Victoria, and Antarctic Beech *N. moorei* in Queensland and NSW.

There is now a lot of scientific evidence to suggest most Australian rainforest plants and animals are very similar to the ancient forms which lived in parts of Gondwanaland – the southern supercontinent – which progressively broke up into the present Africa, India, South America, Australia, Antarctica and New Zealand, between 135 and 50 million years ago. Biologists believe that Australian rainforests contain a richer collection of primitive forms than are found anywhere else in the world.

RAM

Choosing the right ram can mean the difference between profit and loss for the sheep producer. Rams – mature uncastrated male sheep – are used in breeding either for wool or meat production. Merino are used for wool, and British breeds, such as Border Leicesters, for meat.

With roughly 200 ewes per ram, the ram has a significant effect on lambing rates, wool clips and growth rates. Rams are selected for their fertility – which is directly related to their testicle size – wool production and growth. Farmers have traditionally based their selection of rams from their own flock on the recommendation of a qualified wool classer. Most farmers also buy in rams from studs – sometimes taking shares in a ram worth up to $250 000.

Rams between the ages of one and a half and six years are put in with the ewes for around eight weeks in either summer or winter, depending whether the farmer wants a spring or autumn lambing. There is some evidence that a ram's libido is greatest in late summer or autumn. The rams may be put back with the ewes for a second mating with those which did not conceive the first time around. It is important to feed rams well prior to mating and to avoid heat stress to maintain sperm production.

Australia has a world-wide reputation for its rams, and merino rams are exported to Argentina, China, the USSR and New Zealand.

RAPESEED

Rapeseed is a member of the oilseed group of crops, along with SAFFLOWER, linseed and SUN-FLOWER. It is used in a wide range of products. Highly refined oil, extracted from the plant's seeds, is used to lubricate heavy industrial machinery, while less refined rapeseed oil is mixed with other fats to make table margarine.

Rapeseed belongs to a plant family which also includes cabbage, cauliflower, broccoli and Brussel-sprouts. Its closest relative is the turnip, and the word *rapum* is Latin for turnip.

Rapeseed is the third most popular oilseed in Australia after sunflower and soybean. Each year farmers in the mainland states, but mainly NSW and Victoria, produce around 75 000 tonnes. The plant produces distinctive yellow flowers during late spring and early summer.

Yellow fields of flowering rapeseed (above) are a colourful sight on sunny days. An oil extracted from the seeds (left) is used for lubrication and in margarine.

RAT

Rats and mice have a bad reputation because of some of them are pests and are guilty of spreading disease. Most native rats and mice are attractive, often unique to Australia and as worthy of protection as any marsupial. There is no clear-cut distinction between rats and mice, and the common names cut across the formal classification. In general large species are called rats, small ones mice. Superficially many resemble marsupial mice, but the latter are carnivores.

The rats can be divided into two groups – the 'old endemics', and the 'new endemics' and introduced species.

The old endemics include the mosaic-tailed rats which have naked, or largely naked, tails with scales. Among them is the White-tailed Rat *Uromys caudimaculatus* (male mean body length 341 mm, tail 336 mm; female smaller) which is one of Australia's largest rodents. They are found in north-east Queensland where they live on the ground or in trees, sometimes attacking crops such as green coconuts, and also tin cans, which they can penetrate with their teeth. The suckling young are dragged along on elongated teats as the mother moves. Its four relatives are called Melomys, among them the Grassland Melomys *Melomys burtoni* (130–140 mm, 130–140 mm) of the north and east coasts, which is sometimes a pest in canefields.

All species of the new endemics are related – and therefore similar in appearance, though not necessarily in colour – to the introduced Black and Brown Rats. The Canefield Rat *Rathus sordidus* (180 mm, tail variable but shorter than head and body) lives in north-east Queensland including Cape York, and is a pest of cane, but also lives in tropical grassland. The Swamp Rat *R. lutreolus* (164 mm, 113 mm) lives in riverside swamps, river flats, heaths and grassland, but swims only if it must. It is a coastal species of central Queensland, south-east Australia and Tasmania. The Long-haired Rat *R. villosissimus* (187 mm, 167 mm) is found in arid regions and its numbers can multiply rapidly in good years. Predators such as kites gorge themselves, but the populations tumble with the return of dry conditions. The old common name Plague Rat refers to this periodic abundance. There is no connection with the disease bubonic plague, which is usually carried by the Black Rat *R. rattus*.

RAT-KANGAROO

There are three species of rat-kangaroos, although one has been extinct since European settlement. However, brown Musky Rat-kangaroos *Hypsiprymnodon moschatus* (mean body length 230 mm, tail 145 mm) are so different from all other kangaroos that they probably deserve a family of their own. They do not hop, but gallop like rabbits, and have five hindfoot toes where all other kangaroos have only four. They live in a small region of rainforest in north-east Queensland, eating seeds, fruits and small animals. The arrangement of their teeth differs from that of all other kangaroos, and they have simple stomachs and small caecums. They feed in the mornings and later afternoons, resting in nests of fallen leaves at night and midday. Finally, they regularly give birth to twins, a rare occurrence with other kangaroos. A closely-related, 15-million-year-old fossil has been found recently.

The more common Rufous Rat-kangaroos *Aepyprymnus rufescens* (385 mm, 360 mm) are sometimes called Rufous Bettongs, and they live in eastern Australia, in open forest with grass. They sleep during the day in cone-shaped nests of grass. Their hind legs are longer than those of Musky Rat-kangaroos, and they hop. They are reddish-brown with hairy noses and feed on grass, roots and tubers.

The smaller Desert Rat-kangaroos or Oolacuntas *Caloprymnus campestris* (268 mm, 314 mm) lived in the most arid parts of Australia with only a small, above-ground nest for shelter. They have not been seen since 1935, and are presumed extinct. They could hop for kilometres at the speed of a horse, with the right hindfoot always leading the left, which was splayed out at 30°. There appear to be no left-footed Oolacuntas.

RAVEN

Ravens are the three largest crows. Most widespread are the Australian Ravens *Corvus coronoides* (480–540 mm) which are found in south-west, south and eastern Australia. Their range includes that of Little Ravens *C. mellori* (480–500 mm) of south-eastern Australia, which have only recently been recognised as a separate species. Australian Ravens have distinct hackle feathers at their throats which they spread when cawing. Little Ravens also have them, but they are less distinct. Forest Ravens *C. tasmanicus* (520–540 mm) are the only crows found in Tasmania, but this species also lives in small areas of Victoria and NSW.

All ravens eat both plants and animals. They have been accused in the past of killing lambs, but close studies show that healthy lambs are rarely killed, although sick and dead ones are attacked. Lambs may be pecked as a test of healthiness. On the other hand, they remove carrion and destroy insects. Established pairs of Australian Ravens and Forest Ravens defend large territories against their own species and also against other crows, but Little Ravens defend only a small area around their nests, and forage elsewhere. They are nomadic, flocking birds. Australian Ravens have a wailing caw; the other two have deeper calls.

REDBACK SPIDER

The widespread Redback Spider *Latrodectus mactans hasselti* is closely related to America's Black Widow and New Zealand's Katipo. Females are glossy black or brown with usually a broad red or orange stripe on top of their pea-shaped and -sized abdomens, and with a red, often hourglass-shaped, area below. Males are much smaller, and are sometimes seen on females' webs waiting to mate and be eaten. The untidy snares, almost always connected to the ground, are spun under rubbish, electricity meter covers, lavatory seats and so on. Females are not aggressive, but will bite when guarding their white egg sacs, or if squeezed or sat upon. The bite is painful and can be dangerous, but is easily treated with antivenene. The silk is strong and was once used for the cross-hairs in gun sights.

RED-BELLIED BLACK SNAKE

Red-bellied Black Snakes *Pseudechis porphyriacus* (average length 1.5 m, but sometimes over 2.0 m) are one of the most commonly seen venomous snakes in eastern Australia. They range from north-east Queensland to south-eastern South Australia, although they are not found in all places. They are commonly seen near creeks and in swamps and other wet areas, and feed during the day, mainly on frogs, although they will also eat reptiles and small mammals. They often live under rocks, or in rabbit holes.

The snakes' upper parts are iridescent black, but this changes to bright red or pink along the sides, and to a duller red below, apart from under the tail where it is black. Although venomous, they are not thought to be mortally dangerous to healthy adults. However, children can be killed by their bite. The snakes are not aggressive except when cornered, and even then a strike is often just a bluff.

Red-bellied Black Snakes are one of the many Australian species which produce living young. They emerge – between 8 and 40 at a time – enclosed within membranous sacs which are discarded within minutes, or at most an hour.

Musky Rat-kangaroos are usually seen on rainforest floors in north Queensland where they search among leaf litter for food. They are common, but only emerge at the beginning and end of the day.

RESERVE

Apart from NATIONAL PARKS, there are reserves or parks that are set up with greater emphasis on conservation and scientific research than on public recreation. In most states these are called Nature Reserves, but in some states they are known as Fauna Reserves, Fauna Refuges, Conservation Parks or Conservation Reserves.

The largest land park or reserve of any kind in Australia is the Great Victoria Desert Nature Reserve in Western Australia – at two and a half million hectares it is over a third the size of Tasmania.

Some nature reserves, such as Queensland's fauna reserves, are totally closed to the public to protect endangered species or fragile habitats. Many nature reserves have restrictions on public access – such as bans on camping, or entry only at certain times of the year. Generally, public access is not encouraged or provided for.

Nature reserves are important for scientific research. In order to manage national parks and to ensure that they are not harmed by human activity, it is important to know how communities of plants and animals live together.

LAND IN NATURE RESERVES

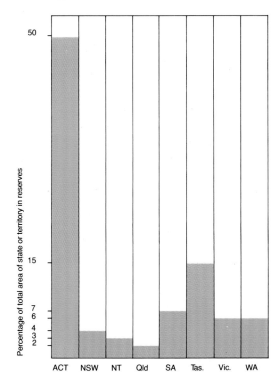

The graph shows the proportion of each state and territory set aside in public reserves, including national parks, nature reserves, aboriginal sites, historic sites and special purpose scientific reserves. While the ACT has set aside the highest proportion of its land (47 per cent), this only represents 2400 sq. km. Western Australia's six per cent represents 146 487 sq. km.

Rice probably originally came from east Asia. It is the staple diet for millions of people throughout the world.

RICE

It may sound like taking coals to Newcastle, but Australia is one of the few countries to consistently sell rice to Asia. Rice was first grown in Australia in the late 1920s near Leeton in southern NSW. A handful of farmers, inspired by developments in the United States, believed that the expanding Murrumbidgee Irrigation Area was ideal for 'paddy rice', although they were not sure how to plant or harvest the crop. From these pioneering days, one of the world's most efficient rice-growing areas has developed, producing up to 800 000 tonnes of medium and long-grain rice a year. The industry supports around 2300 farmers in the Murrumbidgee, Coleambally and Murray Valley Irrigation Areas, and is the mainstay of several towns, including Griffith, Leeton and Jerilderie. The farmers grow soft rice varieties, which are particularly suited to the Asian style of cooking. The rice is also sold to Mediterranean and Pacific countries. Several thousand tonnes of long, hard-grain rice – the type favoured by the people of India – is grown in the Burdekin district, south of Townsville in northern Queensland. Most of this rice is sold locally in Australia.

After sowing, the ground is flooded and drained at intervals until the seedlings have two or three leaves. Then the plants, *Oryza sativa*, stand in 5 to 15 cm of permanent water until two or three weeks before harvesting. In NSW the crop is harvested between March and June. In north Queensland, the dry-season crop is harvested in December–January, and the wet-season crop in April–May. Sometimes the crop is rotated with legume pasture or other cereals.

Harvested rice is called paddy rice. Once the husks have been removed, it is brown rice which cannot be kept indefinitely because of its oil content. Removal of the brown outer layer to the grain, and polishing, produces white rice.

The oil is edible, and a small proportion of the husks can be used in stock feed. Broken rice is used in food processing.

RINGBARKING

This method of clearing forested land for grazing was widely used by white settlers in Australia. It consists of cutting a notch through the bark of a tree and just into the wood, completely encircling the trunk. This cuts off the downward flow of the sap through the inner bark, starving the root system of essential carbohydrates and so causing the death of the tree. By this means even the largest trees could by killed with only a few minutes' work by one man with a sharp axe, while felling could possibly take hours when only axes and saws were available. The dead, leafless trees were left standing, the resulting increase in light reaching the ground allowing good growth of grass, which benefited also from removal of competition by tree roots for soil nutrients and moisture. Ringbarking was clearly wasteful in that no use was made of the often valuable timber, but it was the only means by which poor settlers, such as selectors and soldier-settlers, could rapidly bring their blocks of timbered land into a productive state. In some regions the ringbarked trees have stood for decades, representing a dismal picture which was evoked in Dorothea Mackellar's famous lines: 'The stark white ringbarked forests, all tragic to the moon....'

Ringbarked trees are not seen as often as they once were. Chemicals have been developed that kill trees just as effectively, and with much less hard work.

RIVER

Australia was unfortunate when the rivers were allocated. The country has relatively few, and many of those that do exist flow only seasonally or intermittently, often draining uselessly into the dry interior. More than 2.5 million sq. km of the continent has no waterways at all, save for empty beds which fill only occasionally.

The Murray-Darling, with a length of 3833 km, is the fourth longest river in the world and has the sixth largest catchment area but, because of the dryness of the continent, delivers only 14.8 cubic km of water on the average to the sea each year – in comparison with the Danube which unloads about 281 cubic km. All of Australia's rivers together discharge only some 440 cubic km. In addition, the amount of water flowing in the Murray at a given time is inconstant. At Morgan in South Australia, it has varied about 35-fold between 1902 and 1956.

The poor performance of the Murray River system is due to two factors: the relatively low average rainfall in its catchment area, and to the fact that it runs for much of its length through semi-desert where evaporation losses are far greater than gains – direct or indirect – from rainfall. Around Lake Victoria, for example, the average potential loss by evaporation is about 1500 mm a year, and the rainfall is only roughly 260 mm. The eastern coastal rivers, on the other hand, carry relatively far more water because they rise in the Great Dividing Range and run throughout in well-watered country. The Burdekin, for instance, is only about 680 km long and has a catchment area of only 130 500 sq. km, but

Placid waters of the Darling River near Bourke in central NSW. The river here has almost no 'fall' as it meanders across flat country on its way south-west to join the Murray River at Wentworth.

Precipitous gorges in the Blue Mountains west of Sydney – some over 300 m deep – are a striking testament to the erosive power of the rivers and streams that flow through them.

discharges on the average 7.6 cubic km – about half as much as the Murray.

Rivers and creeks are often ancient features: some of them are far older than the mountains through which they run, although their courses may have been changed during the formation of those mountains. They are constantly evolving, so that some may be regarded as young while others, which may have flowed for millions of years, have become mature.

Most rivers and creeks have their sources in mountains where the rainfall is often heavy. Some of the rain, or melting snow, runs over the surface, but is eventually channelled by the rough ground. The water collects loose particles or breaks them off and carries them down with it. Smaller fragments are held in suspension, but bigger ones bounce along the bottom. All these fragments are known collectively as the stream or river load. In time the stream's bed is deepened, and the headwaters cut further back into the hills. At this stage the slopes are steep, and the water and its load rapidly cut down into the underlying rocks, forming narrow, steep-sided valleys or, if it has cut through a hard surface layer to softer rocks below, steep-sided gorges. At places along its course the young river is joined by other rivers – its tributaries – so that its power and volume is increased. Typically the river passes over rocks of different degrees of hardness, so that in places the water is shallow

and the river becomes a rapid. When the river leaves a stretch of resistant rocks to run over softer strata it cuts down into the latter to produce a waterfall. As time passes, the hard rock itself is eroded so that the waterfall moves slowly back up the river.

In the northern hemisphere the great ice sheets of the last ice age scoured the mountain valleys that rivers had earlier carved, changing their profile from a V shape to that of a U. Side valleys which carried tributaries of the earlier rivers were left hanging above the main valley, their streams entering as waterfalls or cataracts. Such glacial forms are rare in Australia.

As the river approaches lower land, and the slopes become less steep, the valley becomes wider and its slopes gentler. The volume of water has been increased by tributaries, but its force is no longer enough for boulders and large stones to be carried along, except in times of flood, although the water may still be laden with large amounts of sand and silt.

In its lower reaches the river passes through the plains and thus the valley widens. Over thousands of years the river often changes its course, depositing on its floor some of the material brought from the higher levels. If the fall of the land is only slight, as with much of the courses of the Murrumbidgee and the Murray, the river meanders in smooth loops. When the river makes a bend, the water current is faster on the outer curve than on the inner, so that the outer bank is steeper, often undercut, and the water is deeper. Sand and gravel are often deposited in the shallower, more gently-sloped curve on the other side.

Meanders in rivers are common. One of the reasons suggested is the Corialis force, caused by the spin of the earth, which is responsible for the winds in depressions (and, theoretically, the water down plug-holes) going in opposite directions in the northern and southern hemispheres.

Sometimes a river will cut a new channel, or reopen an old one, bypassing a loop. Such a loop, called in Australia – but apparently not elsewhere – an ANABRANCH, may remain connected to the main course of the river at each end, with an island between the two. The most striking example is the Great Anabranch of the Darling which leaves the river at Menindee and, after flowing about 480 km, rejoins the Darling – now united with the Murray – near Wentworth. Sometimes cut-off meanders lose their connections with the main river to form a BILLABONG.

Throughout their development, rivers continue to cut into the underlying strata but eventually they reach their base level below which they will excavate no further. This slopes gradually down from the source to the sea. Few long rivers reach this extreme maturity; more often there is a series of local and temporary base levels resulting from the river's flow over areas of rocks of different degrees of hardness. Long before the ultimate base level is reached, geological changes – such as the uplifting of new mountains or earth movements – rejuvenates the river or forces it to cut a new bed.

Warburton Creek meanders across flat country near Cowarie Station in the arid north-east of South Australia.

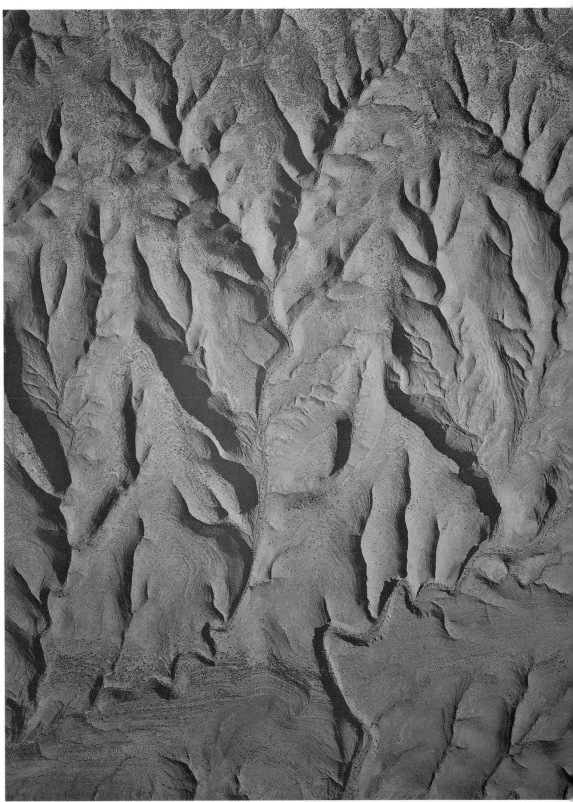

The extraordinary power that rivers and streams have to change and shape a landscape, even in the arid interior, is revealed near Hermannsberg in the Northern Territory, on the edge of the Macdonnell Ranges.

RIVERBOAT

In the nineteenth century small ships were used on several of Australia's coastal rivers, for carrying goods rather than passengers. However it was on the Murray and Darling Rivers that riverboats made their main contribution to the colonies' development. The beginning of steam navigation on these long inland rivers was encouraged by an offer made by the government

RIVERBOAT ROUTES

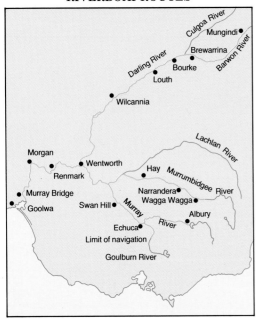

In the 1870s nearly 6500 km of the Murray-Darling River system (above) was open for navigation – more than double the navigable length of the Mississippi. Boats and barges like these at Wilcannia in 1893 (below) carried produce from riverside properties.

of South Australia in 1850 to pay £2000 to the owners of the first two steamers, of specified dimensions, to go from Goolwa to the Murray-Darling junction. In 1853 the *Lady Augusta* and the *Mary Ann*, did this, but the latter was too small to qualify for the full prize, and received only a bonus grant of £750. From then on paddlewheelers became very popular for supplying stations along the two rivers, and for transporting their wool. Normally, however, they did not venture beyond Wilcannia on the Darling, and Echuca on the Murray.

The peak in river traffic was reached in the 1870s and 1880s. Then the competition of railways and the unreliability of the rivers' flow brought a sharp decline, and by 1914 there were few boats left. Today old disused paddlewheelers are preserved as tourist attractions at Swan Hill, Wentworth, Mannum and Echuca – the last-mentioned having three, including the *Philadelphia*, which was featured in the television series *All the Rivers Run*. Tourist trips are also available from various towns on the Murray, including Goolwa, Murray Bridge, Renmark, Echuca and Swan Hill. However, of the boats used, only the *Mary Lou* is a genuine paddle-wheeler.

ROACH

This European fish, *Rutilus rutilus*, belongs to the carp family, which has no native representatives in Australia. Individuals can grow to 450 mm, although rarely, and are often seen in schools. Their head and mouth are small, and they have an olive to silvery body with brown or reddish fins. Eyes are red.

Roach were introduced between 1860 and 1880, but only became established in parts of the south-east, particularly southern Victoria. They prefer still or gently flowing water.

ROBIN

As the first European settlers came from Britain many Australian birds were given the names of British birds which resembled them, even though there were often no close relationships. There are therefore 17 so-called robins in the 'thick-head' family and the Rock Robin *Origma solitaria* (120–140 mm).

The various plump thickhead robins come in various colours – some even have red breasts although the females often do not have the same breast colour as males. They feed on insects, mainly caught by darting from a perch to the ground. They have an upright posture, with tails and wings slightly drooping. The Eastern Yellow Robin *Eopsaltria australis* (145–155 mm), which resembles the European Robin, is probably the most familiar species.

ROCK-WALLABY

Rock-wallabies live in rocky outcrops, from where they rarely move far. However, in the past some species must have made long journeys to get from one rocky outcrop to another. Among the rocks they leap as sure-footedly as mountain goats, but using half the number of feet. To aid their agility their feet have thick pads, rough granulation – which can eventually wear away the rocks – and fringes of hairs. Males are generally larger than females. There are nine species, although the smallest is sometimes called the WARABI.

The barred-tail Yellow-footed Rock Wallaby *Petrogale xanthopus* (body up to 650 mm, tail to 690 mm) is the most attractively coloured member of the group, a prettiness for which it has paid. Once fairly widespread in inland south-eastern Australia it is now common only in the Flinders Ranges. The Black-footed Rock-wallaby *P. lateralis* (495 mm, 540 mm) is the most widespread, being found from western Queensland to south-western Australia.

Black-footed Rock Wallabies are now rare, although at one time they were common in many parts of Australia. Very agile, they will climb trees as well as rocks on occasions.

Common Australian rocks

IGNEOUS ROCKS

SEDIMENTARY ROCKS

Rhyolite

Siltstone

Conglomerate

Diorite

Sandstone

Gabbro

Trachyte

Limestone

Shale

Basalt

Dolorite

METAMORPHIC ROCKS

Slate

Schist

Granite

Marble

Gneiss

ROCKS

The formation of rocks is on a time scale almost beyond human comprehension. Near the time of its birth, about 4400 million ago, the earth was an inferno of molten lava and gas. Gradually the surface began to cool and form a skin or crust which was made up of the first solid rocks. These are called igneous rocks because they came from fire, and examples are granite, basalt, diorite, dolerite, gabbro, trachyte and rhyolite. As the earth continued to cool, large blocks of lighter granite rock began to form the continents while the heavier basalts settled into the oceans. The vast array of complex and colourful rocks

that can be found all over the planet today developed from these beginnings.

As the earth evolved, the forces of wind and water began to erode the first primitive rocks, breaking them down by chemical and physical action into small fragments – silt, sand and pebbles – which were moved under the force of gravity into hollows in the earth's crust such as seas, valleys and oceans. Over millions of years vast quantities of these fragments were deposited until, under its own weight, the sediment began to change. The fragments at the bottom were subjected to intense pressure which squashed the individual grains together, cement-

ing them into sedimentary rocks like sandstone, shale, siltstone, limestone and conglomerate.

Throughout this process the earth's crust started to heave and stretch, and the continents began to move about. If the sedimentary or igneous rocks remained buried during the movements of the continents they were subjected to even greater pressures and temperatures so that new minerals grew. These are the metamorphic rocks like slate, schist, gneiss and marble.

Igneous and metamorphic rocks are composed of minerals like quartz, feldspar and mica, whereas sedimentary rocks are composed of fragments of other rocks or minerals.

Country rodeos are still enormously popular events, and organisers can always count on there being a big turn-out of locals as well as visitors. Any events involving local riders are anticipated with great relish.

RODEO

Although Australian rodeos have been taken over by American-style cowboys in ten-gallon hats and loud shirts, it is still possible to find a traditional event which celebrates the skills unique to Australian stockmen.

There are two types of men and women who ride, rope and bulldog in rodeos, sometimes also known as bushmen's carnivals. There are the professional rodeo riders who follow the circuit from town to town in huge caravans, and the locals, who usually pluck up courage to enter an event on the day.

Rodeos are far from fun for the hardened full-time cowboys who accept bruising and broken bones from rogue bulls and wild horses as an occupational hazard. The locals usually save themselves for events like the steer or poddy ride, or perhaps even the second division bronc (bucking horse) ride. The professionals compete in events like the saddle bronc, bareback bronc, bull riding, calf roping and bulldogging. Finer skills are displayed in the barrel and flag horse racing events.

The HORSES and bulls – usually Brahman or Santa Gertrudis – are encouraged to buck by a rope tied around their flank. In bulldogging, the competitor jumps from a galloping horse to wrestle weaners to the ground. Bulldogging and roping competitors race against the clock, whereas in the riding events they aim to cheat time and stay on the required eight seconds.

The rodeo clown, who must have the skill of a matador, plays a vital role in distracting angry bulls' attention from injured or fallen riders while they are rescued.

In traditional rodeos, such as the annual New Year's Day event at the small NSW country town of Tumbarumba, the skills of the bush are on display. Pickup men, who pluck competitors off broncs at the end of their ride, are still recruited from the cattle properties around the town. They are immaculately turned out in moleskins, white shirts and ties, very different to the colourful attire seen in the more Americanised events. Whereas Americans say ROdeo – with the stress on the first syllable – the Australians say roDEo, with the stress on the second syllable.

RUBY

Deep red rubies are second only to emeralds as rare and valuable gems. They can be distinguished from all other minerals, except diamond, by their great hardness. Ruby is actually the red variety of sapphire – the mineral corrundum – having a simple chemical composition of aluminium and oxygen. The rich colour is due to small amounts – up to 4 per cent – of chromium oxide in the crystals.

Even though Australia provides about 50 per cent of the world's sapphires, rubies are not mined commercially here. There have been rare

RODENT

The rodents – with an estimated 1600 to 2000 species – are the largest order of placental mammals. They are burrowing, tree climbing or aquatic creatures. Their teeth are one of their distinguishing characteristics. In their upper jaw they have only two incisors (chisel-shaped front teeth) – humans have four – which grow continuously and which are very often yellow. Their canines and their front premolars are missing, leaving a gap, and the remaining premolars and molars form a grinding surface. Their feet usually have five digits and claws. Rodents are mainly vegetarian and are often scavengers.

There are three major divisions: the squirrel and beaver group; the porcupine and cavy group; and the rat, mouse and jerboa group. Only the last is found in Australia, where there are about 58 species, including three that were introduced. All are in the one family, the Muridae. Australian and New Guinean rodents came from Indonesia and Asia by a process of 'island hopping'. The ancestors of most of the so-called 'old endemics' arrived about 15 million years ago. Those of the 'new endemics' – seven species of native RATS – came no earlier than one million years ago.

Hares and RABBITS are not rodents: they belong to another order of animals, the lagomorpha, none of which are native to Australia. Their most characteristic feature is the arrangement of their two incisors on each side of the upper jaw. One lies directly behind the other.

finds of tiny stones, and sometimes rubies occur as very fine clusters in some metamorphic rocks, but they have no commercial value. Some have been found at Mt Painter in South Australia and at Rubyvale in Queensland.

Ruby and sapphire can be manufactured synthetically so that the only way of distinguishing between a natural stone and a synthetic one is by microscope. The world's best natural rubies come from Burma.

RURAL INCOME

Farmers' incomes depend on many factors. Drought, fire, interest rates, outbreaks of diseases, falls in commodity prices and increased farm costs can all reduce rural incomes. Of all occupations, farmers' and graziers' incomes are by far the most dependent on largely uncontrollable factors. During the 1982–83 drought, for instance, most of Australia's 170 000 farmers and graziers suffered a 75 per cent drop in income.

Over more recent years, regular falls in the world market price of commodities such as wheat, sugar and oilseeds have had an enormous effect on farming communities throughout Australia. The wheat downturn, in particular, devastated communities in the Western Australian wheatbelt, the central west of NSW, and Victoria's Mallee and Wimmera regions.

The health of a farmer's bank balance is also important to the prosperity of the broader rural community, and – as the 1984–87 wheat crash indicated – to the nation as a whole. Economic researchers have found that every dollar generated on a farm can be worth between three and four dollars in the wider community. This flow-on effect also creates jobs in rural service industries, such as transport, retail and banking.

The two most important factors relating to a farmer's income are commodity prices and farm costs. Farm costs are either variable or fixed. Variable costs can be related to a specific crop or livestock enterprise and may include fertiliser, sprays and seed. Fixed costs are spread over the total farm and include interest rates, council charges and depreciation on machinery and buildings. Variable or operating costs are subtracted from the gross income of a particular enterprise to find the per hectare gross margin. The gross margin gives an indication of the likely return of an enterprise, and allows farmers to compare the gains from various livestock and cropping operations.

Over the past few years, the rate of increase of farm costs has been several percentage points below the national inflation rate. However, the rapid increase in interest rates and low commodity prices have combined to keep the average farmer's income well below that of most city dwellers.

World commodity prices have an enormous impact on rural incomes because around 80 per

A mining dredge works through deposits near Newcastle, NSW. Several minerals, apart from rutile, are extracted, including zircon (zirconium silicate), ilmenite (iron titanium oxide) and monazite (a phosphate of rare earths).

cent of rural commodities produced in Australia are exported. Thus, the trading policies of large economic forces such as the United States, the European Economic Community and Japan, can have an immediate effect on the incomes of farmers at Bourke, in western NSW, for example.

In an effort to help stabilise incomes, some larger commodity groups have established grower-funded price or market support schemes. The Australian Wool Corporation and the Australian Wheat Board administer such schemes for farmers. Unlike other nations, successive federal governments have avoided direct income support for farmers.

RUTILE

Rutile – titanium dioxide – is the major constituent of the black beach sand deposits which are found on the Australian east coast between Broken Bay in NSW and Wide Bay in Queensland, and also in the far south-west corner of Western Australia.

These beach sands are among the largest sources of titanium in the world, and Australia has been a leading producer of it for many years. The mining of beach sand deposits are a controversial environmental issue because of the damage done to beaches and dunes. Mining companies claim, however, that they restore areas to their original condition, and that after a few years there will be no sign of their activities. The mineral is exported and is turned into metallic titanium, which is used in the manufacture of aircraft parts.

Originally the east coast rutile came from rocks in the New England region of NSW. Over millions of years it has been washed to the coast by RIVERS and then concentrated on the beaches by wave action.

RYE

This winter grain crop is usually referred to as cereal rye, in order to distinguish it from rye grass, a common pasture species. Cereal rye is not as important in Australia as in other parts of the world, particularly Europe. Production, prices and import levels fluctuate widely from year to year. However, the popularity of rye has increased in recent years, partly due to the increased consumption of health foods. The grain – and dark coloured rye flour – are used in high-fibre wholemeal and wholegrain cereals, crispbreads and breads. Some coffee substitutes are also based on rye.

Most rye plantings in Victoria and South Australia are for grain, while those in NSW are mainly for fodder. The crop is not suited to hay making. Rye may be planted from late February through to April. Yields are lower than for other cereals, but rye does have an advantage in less fertile, poor rainfall regions. It is often planted to help bind soil and prevent wind erosion.

Rye has gained in popularity with recent interest in health foods.

S

SACRED SITE

Sacred sites are places of special religious and social significance to Aboriginal people, and their existence is often kept secret. Only properly initiated people can disclose their location and true meaning. Aboriginal people have a complicated set of rules which govern their responsibilities to each other and to the land itself. Responsibilities to the land are usually concerned less with survival and conservation, than with the maintenance of ritual ceremonies and the observance of regulations governing who can visit particular places. This is not to say that Aborigines have had a deleterious impact on the Australian countryside – although their impact on vegetation has been dramatic – but to emphasise the spiritual and intellectual importance of land to Aboriginal people.

Thus land rights and sacred sites have been intimately related. But whereas land rights basically involve claims to whole tracts of land, sacred sites are usually smaller, well-defined places such as water holes or caves, often associated with particular clans and spirit ancestors. These associations are specified in myths, ceremonies, paintings and decorative art.

Places may be sacred to particular communities, clans or individuals. In a broad sense all of Australia might be thought of as a sacred site because the entire landscape is criss-crossed with the paths of spirit ancestors, sacred water holes and conception sites where the spirits of children enter the wombs of pregnant women. A site may be sacred to particular Aboriginal people because there are prohibitions which restrict who can visit places. Very well defined places which are regarded as dangerous for uninitiated people to visit have been termed secret-sacred sites.

On the other hand, a site may be sacred in the same way that a church or temple is sacred – a place of religious importance which may be visited with appropriate respect.

There is such a wide range of meanings and degrees of significance associated with Aboriginal sacred sites, that it is little wonder that legislation dealing with these issues has not been satisfactory for Aboriginal and non-Aboriginal people alike. The first Australian legislation to refer to sacred sites is the 1976 Aboriginal Land Rights (Northern Territory) Act. Sacred sites are defined according to what Aborigines think. Traditional beliefs may define land that is sacred and the site may have paintings or be totally devoid of archaeological evidence of human occupation. Thus a rock, a painted cave or a billabong may be a sacred site.

Because a natural feature of the countryside may be a sacred site and unknown to all but a few Aborigines, it is difficult for non-Aborigines to recognise these sites, and to respect their religious significance. Guidelines for mining companies and protection of sacred sites are thus contentious issues and the best way to appreciate Aboriginal viewpoints is to listen to what they say.

An intriguing example of Aboriginal perceptions of the landscape was provided by Frank Gurmanamana, an Arnhem Land tribal elder, who visited Canberra with prehistorian Rhys Jones. Gurmanamana wanted to know the meaning of street patterns mapped out over the city. What were the relationships between the streets and people in the houses? Who carries out the appropriate rituals which embodied religious and social ties to the landscape? It was inconceivable that these relationships did not exist. Thus it is a common charge that white people have lost their Dreaming. White people, in Aboriginal perceptions, do not care for the land, and, as Gurmanamana says, they breed indiscriminantly like camp dogs breaking all the rules of an ordered social landscape.

Sometimes Aboriginal perceptions of what is sacred are similar to European views – as with some places which mark important historical and mythological events. In other situations, the sacred places are so charged with ritualistic and cosmological significance that intrusion or disturbance will threaten the very fabric of Aboriginal society. Respect shown by non-Aboriginal people for these sites is a common courtesy and vital for harmonious relationships with the traditional Aboriginal owners.

Sacred sites are generally secret and not publicised, although some places of special significance are described in literature of Aboriginal heritage organisations, and these sites may be visited.

A burial ceremony photographed by scientist Sir Baldwin Spencer in the 1920s. A grave site, with no permanent marker, is one example of a sacred site that it would be impossible for non-Aborigines to know about.

Uluru *– Ayers Rock – and the Olgas beyond are places which now have a special sigificance for all Aborigines, not just those from central Australia.*

SADDLE

Saddles were invented about 3500 years ago with the principle then, as now, being to give the rider comfortable control over the horse. The original saddle was probably just a blanket or light covering between the rider and the horse. It took time for the more sophisticated saddle – the forerunner of today's type – to appear. Stirrups, for example, were not invented until 1500 years later. Today there are a number of special saddles with different cuts designed to help the rider adopt the correct seat for any particular activity. Among the most carefully designed is the Australian stock saddle which has taken over 100 years to perfect. It is comfortable both for the rider and, because it does not allow the rider to sit incorrectly, for the horse. Jumping saddles are a variation of the old stock saddles and they bring the rider well forward over the mount, while dressage saddles, with their straight flap, short seat and straight tree, give the rider complete freedom to use the lower part of his or her legs to contact the horse. Show saddles are also straight cut, but in this case to show off the horse. Racing saddles are in use for only a short period of time, with the rider rarely remaining seated for long. The saddle point can therefore be thin, and would quickly give the horse a sore back if used for any length of time. For children there is a special shape designed to give maximum aid to achieving a balanced seat.

A TYPICAL SADDLE

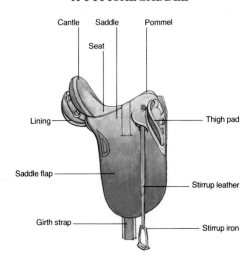

A typical Australian stock saddle. This design has been evolving for over 100 years, and many different versions with minor differences are available.

SAFFLOWER

Safflower is a member of the oilseed family of crops. Although it is gaining in popularity, it is still of relatively minor importance. SUNFLOWER, SOYBEAN and cotton seed all outstrip the crops' yearly production of 49 000 tonnes of oil.

Safflower, distinguished by its thistle-like leaves, is mainly grown in the subtropical climates of northern NSW and southern Queensland during winter. It is a spring or summer-growing crop in north and central Victoria, where it is often produced under irrigation.

Like other oilseeds, it is used in the manufacture of cooking oils, margarines, paints and varnishes. In fact, its high percentage of polyunsaturated fats makes it very suitable for making high-quality margarine. The crop, due to its chemical composition, also suits soap, cosmetic and textile production.

Sometimes the plant's leaves are also dried to yield a red dye, used to make rouge. The same dye is used extensively in the textile trade for colouring yarns.

Safflower is sown by farmers in May or August in winter growing areas, or November in summer ones. In warm, temperate climates, it takes from five to seven and a half months to mature. In most agricultural areas, safflower is included in a five-year rotation. It is used to break the 'disease cycle' associated with the persistent cultivation of grain crops like wheat or barley.

Several countries around the world make Australia's 70 000 hectares a year of safflower look insignificant. The USSR, Argentina, Romania, Bulgaria and Yugoslavia all grow several million hectares of safflower annually. The main safflower-importing countries include Italy, Japan and East and West Germany.

Safflower's bright yellow, thistle-like blooms are easy to recognise. It is one of the world's oldest crops, being grown originally as a dye.

SALEYARD

The shouting auctioneer stands on the top rail. Graziers and farmers, in their best working clothes, lean on the dusty wooden rails looking at the pens of stock. Conversation is about the weather, the bank manager and, of course, the price of stock. They may be there to bid for store cattle for fattening, or to sell ewes. Whatever the case, saleyards are an important part of rural life.

Regular livestock sales are held at most large rural centres. Among the best known are those at Gunnedah and Wagga Wagga in NSW; Horsham and Portland in Victoria; Midland in Western Australia; Toowoomba in Queensland; Burnie in Tasmania; and Gepps Cross in South Australia.

The saleyard is usually located at or near the local showground as it is also the scene of frantic bidding during the annual show stock sale. The most important people there are the auctioneer, the stock buyer and the producer. The auctioneer is often a well-known local identity who accepts the bids and coaxes the prices as high as possible. The buyer, on the other hand, is concerned only with paying the lowest possible price for the best stock. Whether the buyer is a farmer or meat processor, he or she must be aware of the state and 'feel' of the market.

The results of the larger sales are reported widely to enable the industry to assess the market. The price of store stock at Gunnedah may affect the decisions taken by a grazier thousands of kilometres away. However, new

technology – in the form of computers – is bringing the market even more up to date. A system called Computer Aided Livestock Marketing, or CALM, enables producers to sell and buy stock via a computer or telephone link-up. The stock and grazier do not have to physically attend the sale, which is conducted by CALM centre staff and a centralised computer.

Bids are taken over the phone, by direct computer link or by a system of reserve prices. However, CALM still has a long way to go before it replaces, or even makes a significant impact on, the importance of the saleyard.

SALMON

Salmon belong to a northern hemisphere family, but several species have been introduced into southern hemisphere countries. Like trout, salmon – given the opportunity – mature in the sea and re-enter freshwater to spawn. Two species have been introduced into Australia.

Atlantic Salmon *Salmo salar*, a species which lives in the cool rivers of Europe, North America, Greenland and Iceland, have been introduced into Australia and Tasmania at various times since 1864. One attempt at colonisation in 1963 hoped to establish land-locked populations in Lake Jindabyne, NSW, but it was not successful. In 1864, a Tasmanian company started farming the fish in 'sea cages'; several companies are now involved in this thriving – and growing – industry. In some countries, Atlantic Salmon can reach

Most graziers prefer to sell their stock at a saleyard, rather than make private deals with neighbours. In that way any problems with stock that has been purchased do not lead to bad feeling between buyer and seller.

1.5 m in length and weigh up to 38 kg, but in Australia they are harvested at about 5 kg.

Quinnat Salmon *Oncorhynchus tshawytscha* are also a smaller fish here than they are in their native homes in North America and north-east Asia. Few if any specimens exceed 890 mm and 11.4 kg. They do not spawn out of captivity in Australia so their presence – and survival – in the wild, like that of the Atlantic Salmon, depends on continuous releases.

SALT
See entry p 314

SALTBUSH

Saltbushes and BLUEBUSHES are the most important plants over large areas of arid inland southern Australia.

Although many species of saltbushes are found in different regions, and under different conditions, two particularly important ones are the Old Man Saltbush *Atriplex nummularia*, which is the tallest growing species (up to 3 m) and one of the longest lived – some specimens are known to be at least 100 years old, and some individuals may be very much older – and the Bladder Saltbush *A. vesicaria*.

Saltbushes are particularly drought tolerant and are important as a source of fodder for the pastoral industry. However, as the name saltbush indicates, the leaves may have a high salt content which limits their value unless stock also have plenty of water to drink. Several species are susceptible to overgrazing, and in the early years of the pastoral industry large areas of perennial saltbush were stripped from the land, particularly in western NSW.

SALT LAKE

Many Australian rivers flow – when they do flow – into the dry inland. If their waters accumulate for a time in a depression they may dry out to form a claypan or salina, or a dry salt lake. Lake Eyre (9300 sq. km when full) is the centre of an inwardly flowing system covering about 1.3 million sq. km, but water reaches it only when there have been at least two consecutive years of exceptionally heavy rain over the area. Its lowest point is 14 m below sea level. In the last 20 000 years about five metres of silts rich in gypsum and layers of salt have accumulated on the old lake bed.

The origin of the salts in this lake and others in the region is uncertain. Some may have been brought when ancient seas covered the area, but most workers believe that the bulk has been carried from the surrounding country by the

Pink lakes in the 'Sunset Country' of western Victoria contain saltwater. A commercial operation harvests salt from two of them for domestic and industrial use.

intermittently flowing rivers, or that the salt is blown in by winds from the sea. Lake Eyre lies in the driest part of the continent, and the evaporation rate is about 2.4 m a year. In the wettest conditions this, and the neighbouring lakes, are only four metres deep at the most, and usually much less, so they dry up quickly.

Victoria's largest lake, Lake Corangamite, although only two metres deep on average, is permanent. The water in shallow lakes varies greatly in the amount of salt it contains, but deep ones, such as Bullenmerri (Victoria, maximum depth 64 m) are less variable with about 8 to 9 parts of salt per 1000 parts of water. Salt waters are considered to be those with over three parts per thousand.

Very salt lakes have their own peculiar animal life whose members, strangely, are derived from freshwater species, not marine ones. Fish have not been recorded from lakes with salinities greater than 70 parts per thousand, but crustaceans, rotifers, sandfly larvae and even a jellyfish may be common.

SAND

Australia is well endowed with sand. Fraser Island, off the Queensland coast, is the largest sand island in the world. Sand is produced by the weathering of rocks and is concentrated by the forces of erosion. White sand is made up mostly of quartz grains which range from 0.06 mm to 2.00 mm in size, whereas coloured sands contain small amounts of garnet, cassiterite, magnetite and monazite. Sand is used mainly for making concrete, mortar and plaster and for glass-making, ceramics and paint. The very pure sand used for glassmaking is found on coastal dunes in Queensland, NSW, Victoria, South Australia and Western Australia.

SALT

The increasing salinity of soil is a widespread problem in dry areas of Australia where the land is often irrigated. If water which is applied to the land does not drain away, sooner or later it rises again, drawn up by evaporation from the surface, or by the transpiration of plants, and brings with it dissolved salts from lower levels. Alternatively, heavy applications of water without drainage may bring the WATER TABLE to within a metre or two of the surface, so that ground water can rise to the area where plant roots are growing, and this water too is often salty. Eventually the salts brought to the surface can form an encrustation on the surface.

Dryland farmers also have their problems. In Western Australia there are 167 000 salt-affected hectares, and in Victoria, 85 000 hectares.

Even if the water does drain away, it may carry salts with it to a stream or river which, in turn, becomes salty. The lower Murray River has been badly affected by salt, and water drawn from it in irrigation areas is pumped onto crops. The water then drains back to the river, carrying still more salt with it. Lower down the river, the water is removed again for irrigation, and once again collects even more salt from the soil. For most of its middle and lower course, the river loses more from evaporation than it gains from rainfall, and this too aggravates the problem. Some of the salts are 'native' to the soil through which the irrigation waters percolate, and some are brought by wind and rain from the sea, or from SALT LAKES. About 33 per cent of Australian soil is salt-affected and could be (or has been) made saline by unwise irrigation.

In the Darling Range, which supplies water for Perth and irrigation water for the plains below, and where the valued timber Jarrah grows, each hectare has 50 to 100 kg of salt deposited on it each year. In drier areas the soil and the clay store about 1000 tonnes per hectare. On forest-covered land, measurements have shown that the intake and output of salt is more or less balanced, but when the land is cleared water passes through more quickly, taking with it larger amounts of salt – up to 21 times as much in one cleared area where measurements were taken. Land clearance for agriculture in the range has thus increased the salinity. So too has the die-back of the Jarrah, caused by the fungus *Phytophthora cinnamomi* which came with European settlement. Trains used to stop at the Blackwood River, south of Perth, to pick up water, and in 1904 regular measurements of its salinity were begun. At that time the level was usually below the allowable limit for locomotives – 430 parts per million (ppm). By 1975 the levels ranged from 1000 to 5000 ppm and above. For comparison, seawater contains 30 000 ppm, saline waters more than 3000, and brackish water, 1000 to 3000 parts per million.

Saline soil contains salts in solution. The main ones in Australia are common salt (sodium chloride), and salts of magnesium and calcium. In alkaline soils the sodium ions in the irrigation or ground water change places with other ions on the soil particles so that the water contains

The differences between vegetation growing around bodies of salt water, as at Pink Lakes in South Australia (below), and around fresh water, as at Edmund Kennedy National Park in Queensland (above), clearly show salt's effects.

Why plants do not like salt

A small number of plants are able to flourish in salt conditions, such as mangroves and salt-marshes. These species are called halophytes (halo = salt). The vast majority of plants, however, are adversely affected by exposure to salt and are called glycophytes ('glyco' referring to sweet, as in sweet water).

The distinction between halophytes and glycophytes is not clear-cut, and among those species which are regarded as glycophytes there is a range of responses to the presence of salt. Some plants, such as avocadoes, are extremely sensitive, while others have moderate tolerance.

Salt kills glycophytes in three ways: it may be directly toxic; large quantities may interfere with the uptake of nutrients; and salt may affect a plant's ability to absorb water.

The biochemical mechanisms of all plants are sensitive to the presence of salts – this is not a specific property of sodium chloride, any salt would have the same affect in high enough concentration. In halophytes the salt is contained so that it does not come into contact with the physiologically active parts of the cells. Glycophytes can survive limited concentrations of salt by executing it altogether, but above certain concentrations this is no longer possible. Glycophytes do not have the ability to isolate the salt internally so that it comes into contact with the cell contents, and death follows.

At one time the high salt content of halophytes was exploited. In early 19th century Australia the ash obtained from burnt mangroves was used in soap manufacture.

White encrustation of salt covers bare red earth beside the lower reaches of the Murray River. Many thousands of hectares are now threatened by increasing salination.

little free sodium. On riverine plains, for example, where heavy clays contain such sodium, it is difficult to get water to run through the soil, and for seedlings to become established.

These plains are also regarded as ideal for rice-growing because, it is believed, the heavy clay soils allow the water to form into ponds in which rice can grow. Tests have shown, however, that a lot of water escapes, and that the water table is rising each year. It is not only rice growing, however, that is causing the problem. Seepage from unlined irrigation canals, wet years and excessive irrigation of other crops have all aggravated the trouble.

Saline soils are usually easy to work, but the high concentration of salt makes it difficult for the plants to get the water they need. They have to draw their water from a highly concentrated solution which is stronger than the pull of the sap (see box). This is the main mechanism which

inhibits plant growth, but sometimes the soil water may also contain toxic substances such as the element boron.

Plants with low salt-tolerance include most fruit trees, beans, celery and radishes. Some which are tolerant are barley, cotton, sugar beet, table beets, kale, asparagus, spinach, tomato, and several grasses.

If soil is likely to become saline under irrigation, it is wise to arrange good sub-soil drainage to prevent the water table from rising, although this will probably only transfer the salts to streams and rivers. When drainage allows it, extra irrigation water can be applied to leach out the salts as they accumulate in upper layers. If too little water is applied, the salt will rise. Sometimes gypsum – hydrated calcium sulphate – is applied to the soil to reduce its salinity. In the riverine plains it is put into the irrigation water when annual pastures are being established. It

was also widely used in the Netherlands after disastrous inundation by the sea in the 1950s.

Another approach is to use the 'natural pumping action of plants'. Most plants that grow on severely affected soils are of little value, but breeding work is now in progress with River Red Gums *Eucalyptus camaldulensis*, some of which are very salt tolerant. During land reclamation they could provide a valuable crop, so Lex Thomson, of the University of Melbourne, tested collections of seeds, and grew some seedlings in water that was half as salty as the sea. However, it takes many years for eucalypts to produce seeds, and they are well-known for being difficult to grow from cuttings. New tissue-culture methods are therefore used to grow salt-resistant strains of the trees which can be produced in their millions using these techniques. The resulting trees are now being tested on saline soils in Victoria, and also in Israel.

SAPPHIRE

Sapphires are the next hardest natural substance to diamond. Clear sapphires – particularly blue ones – are very valuable gemstones and have the same chemical composition (aluminium and oxygen) as RUBIES. Clouded sapphires, however, are considered worthless. A sapphire may vary in colour from a deep golden yellow to a pale, almost lime green and sometimes blue. The colour is due to minute traces of titanium. Synthetic sapphires, coloured with small amounts of chromium and titanium, have been manufactured since the turn of this century.

Sapphires are found in large numbers at several places in Australia. Central Queensland – notably in the Tomahawk Creek area – has possibly the most consistent gem-quality sapphire fields in the world.

SAWFLY

Sawflies are related to bees and wasps but, unlike them, they do not have a narrowly constricted waist. Their name comes from the saws in their egg-layer, which are used to make the slits in plants in which eggs are placed. The larvae are usually caterpillar-like, but with more false legs. However, the larvae of the introduced pear and cherry sawflies, *Caliroa cerasi*, are slug-like. The familiar larvae – often called spitfire grubs – of the native Steelblue Sawfly *Perga dorsalis*, feed separately on eucalypt leaves at night, and cluster in the daytime, flicking their tails in unison and discharging a yellow liquid when disturbed. The group, which has about 160 species in Australia, also contains the introduced SIREX WOODWASP.

Sawfly larvae gather in clumps and deter potential enemies by flicking their tails in unison. Large groups can strip vegetation from a plant amazingly quickly.

Seven pupils and their teacher pose outside their tiny one-roomed school, some time early this century. For teachers, strangers in a tiny community, the isolation meant that they were often keen to get a city posting.

SCALE INSECT

Scale insects are bugs which form scales on plants and are often very destructive. Nymphs crawl on to the host plant and feed through their sucking mouthparts. Females become sexually mature while still in the nymphal form. They are virtually limbless and attach themselves permanently to a plant. Males moult once more, and are more or less 'ordinary' mobile insects, and may even have wings. Some species reproduce without mating. Young nymphs – the crawlers – may be born alive or hatch from eggs. Hard scales have a hard covering: soft scales do not, but may produce masses of wax or threads for protection. Many native scales form GALLS on native plants. Mealybugs are closely related insects, but their females are more mobile. Scales and mealybugs are of immense economic importance, both in Australia and in other countries. The Australian Cottony Cushion Scale *Icerya purchasi* (a hermaphrodite) nearly destroyed the Californian citrus industry after it was taken there accidentally on wattles in the 1880s, but it was controlled biologically (see LADYBIRDS). There are more than 500 species in Australia, but many of them were introduced, often attached to their host plants.

SCAT

Two meanings of scat are a group of Australian fishes, and animal faeces. Scatalogy is the study of animal faeces or obscene literature. This entry deals with faeces.

A skilled biologist or Aborigine can tell from the presence of scats that a certain animal has been there, and from their condition, how recently. Fresh scats will be damp and will have kept their shape: older ones will be dry if there has been no rain, and still older ones often have coatings of fungus, and probably signs of insect attack. The scats and trails of many nocturnal animals are often seen more frequently than the animals themselves. Mice and rat droppings, for example can be distinguished as follows: mice droppings, cylindrical, pointed ends, about 5 mm long and often left on otherwise clean surfaces; rat droppings similar, but larger (10–15 mm), with those of the brown rat in piles, and those of the black species scattered.

Biologists have another use for scats. Carnivorous animals pass out the hard parts of the skeleton of their prey, and an examination of the scats can reveal what they are living on in a particular district. The method must be used with discretion, however, because different kinds of prey are digested at different rates, and to different degrees. In Europe, for example, it has been found that the digestive system of foxes breaks down the molar teeth of Short-tailed Voles more quickly than those of the slightly smaller Field Mice. A simple extrapolation from the ratio of the remains of the two found in scats to give the proportion of mice to voles in the diet would therefore give an inaccurate result. It is even possible to detect the skins of some insect larvae in remains, and very easy to find the hard outer skins of insects like beetles. In some cases microscopic examination has revealed – by the presence of their bristles – that foxes will even sometimes eat earthworms.

Microscopic examination will even help a biologist to get some idea of what plant-eating animals have been living on because the indigestible parts of plants are often easy to recognise.

Owls and some other birds often vomit indigestible parts of their prey from the gizzard in pellets which may be found beneath their roosts. These are examined in the same way as scats.

SCHOOL

Many bush schools stood in isolation, unfenced, with paths to their doors through the trees. Along these the children came, carrying dinner bags and, in summer, waterbottles. Some ran the kilometre from home, some rode three or four to a horse, some led tiny brothers or sisters, sent along out of parents' way. Some walked six or eight kilometres, in winter starting at sunrise and getting home at dusk. Latecomers straggled in, flushed from having despatched a snake along the way, or having had trouble catching the pony. Banjo Paterson in *My Various Schools* said the standard excuse for lateness was, 'Father sent me after 'orses'. He distributed different excuses among his schoolmates but to his disgust the familiar formula came out and the boys, as usual, took two cuts of the cane on each hand. It was a common myth that resin hardened the palm. Alan Marshall in *I Can Jump Puddles* said his infusion of wattlebark, supposed to do the same, earned him many marbles and cigarette cards.

Rarely were all a school's pupils present. Children were often needed at home, harvesting corn, picking fruit, digging potatoes – short backs supposedly bent without aching. When primary schooling became compulsory, it took some time for parents to renounce their children's labour, and teacher and family struggled for the young minds and hands.

Free, compulsory and secular education for children between 6 and 14 was promised in all colonies' education acts between 1872 and 1895. But threepence to one shilling and threepence a week was charged, a heavy burden on some parents. Attendance was not constantly required – in NSW, for instance, children had to attend on merely 70 out of 120 school days a half-year.

'Secular' allowed for religious instruction of a general kind.

Hundreds of schools were built at this time, many of which are still being used today. Many were single rooms to be presided over by one teacher. At one time, in NSW alone, there were 1066 single-teacher schools. With eight or nine pupils – the minumum for a teacher to be appointed – the quality of teaching could be high but when a teacher had to manage over 100 youngsters, little attention could be given to even a potential intellectual.

The rural teacher faced special problems over how the syllabus should relate to the hard realities of country life. Arithmetic and the virtues of hard work were stressed. Many schools organised young farmers' or project clubs, and had gardens that earned money from eggs or produce. Nevertheless, the would-be rural teacher was still examined on the geography of the red areas on the world map that hung on every schoolroom wall, and on such history as 'How England's sea-power grew in Tudor times'.

In some sparsely populated areas, itinerant teachers reached the children of boundary riders, timbergetters or railway fettlers. In Queensland in 1925, ten such teachers, with average districts of 79 000 sq.. km each, travelled an average of 6700 km and visited about 100 children. Correspondence teaching began in Victoria in 1914, and itinerant teachers' numbers declined.

Country school teachers enjoyed considerable prestige, but then as now, isolation often provoked almost yearly moves. Modern education departments try to make remote area postings attractive with special allowances, or the right to return to the city, or, in NSW, merit points towards promotion – a school in the Sydney suburb of Manly rates one, Tibooburra eight.

SCHOOL OF THE AIR

The radio network that grew around the Flying Doctor Service plays another important role. It is opened every day for the 'galah' or chat session among neighbours, perhaps hundreds of kilometres apart. Another use of the network is the School of the Air. There are in fact a dozen schools, run by state education bodies, in NSW, Queensland, the Northern Territory, Western Australia and South Australia. Some of them reach children from other states, and lessons may have to be planned according to two or three state syllabuses. The three or more hours of lessons every day supplement correspondence courses for primary school-age children; nearly 1400 are enrolled. They manage the radio equipment themselves, while the teacher sits in a classroom-studio linked to the Flying Doctor Service operator in case the radio is needed for a medical emergency. The first School of the Air opened in 1951, owing to the efforts of Miss Adelaide Miethke of the Flying Doctor Service.

Lessons are broadcast from all of the towns shown above. For many children who live in the remote outback contact with others of the same age, and with teachers, is almost as important as the lessons.

SCLEROPHYLL FOREST

Much of Australia's vegetation is described as sclerophyllous – a term that refers to the tough, hard leaves of many species of native plants. Originally, the word was used particularly for shrubs in the understorey of a forest whose leaves are often stiff and frequently small with spiny tips. Over the years, however, usage has changed and now the term sclerophyll forest is used for a whole community of plants, including the tallest ones, which are usually eucalypts. While eucalyptus leaves are certainly tough, they are not as rigid as many of those from plants in the understorey.

The canopy of most eucalypt forests is fairly open, with the lower levels getting plenty of light. The openness is due both to the arrangement of branches, and to the fact that eucalypt leaves often hang vertically from their stems. In contrast, closed forests (most of which are called RAINFORESTS in Australia) have dense canopies which allow less than 70 per cent of sunlight to penetrate and the forest interior is very dark.

Many of the adaptations shown by the leaves of sclerophyll plants may be aimed at reducing water loss. However, many groups of sclerophyll plants are found in regions of comparatively high rainfall, while many arid zone plants are not particularly sclerophyllous, even though they are clearly drought-tolerant.

The fossil record of sclerophyllous leaves extends back to periods when most of Australia was much wetter than it is at present. It is now generally accepted that sclerophylly evolved mainly to make maximum use of scarce nutrients from the soil – particularly phosphorus, rather than primarily as a response to drought.

Small mottled scorpions such as Cercophonius squama *here are not known to have dangerous stings. Two fatalities have been blamed on Australian scorpions – both babies – and in each case one of the forest scorpions was blamed. The largest Australian scorpions, up to 160 mm long, come from the Flinders Ranges, SA.*

SCORPION

Scorpions are the oldest surviving land arthropods: they have inhabited the earth for about 400 million years. They may indeed have been the first of all land animals. A scorpion's body is divided into a head-thorax, which is covered by a shell or carapace, and a two-part abdomen. The narrower hind part of the abdomen carries the sting. Scorpions have four pairs of walking legs, and the head carries a small pair of pincers, for handling food, between a much larger pair which are used for mating and catching prey.

Scorpions hunt by night and hide under stones during the day. In Mexico more people die from scorpion bites than from snake bites, but the 30 or so Australian scorpions are credited with only two deaths – both babies. The commonest species found is the small, widespread marbled scorpion, *Lychas marmoreus* which is 25–50 mm long. The largest species are about 160 mm long. Scorpions have elaborate courtship dances and produce living young.

SCORPION FLIES

These are long-legged, two-winged or wingless, small to medium sized, fly-like insects. They usually have a horse-like head, and the males of some species have a tail resembling a scorpion's

sting. They do not, however, sting. The larvae are usually caterpillar-like. The adults are often found in cool, damp areas where they feed on nectar and often on other insects. The larvae are predators. There are about 20 Australian species, in five families.

SCREE

Scree (or talus) is the pile of rock fragments which accumulate like a flared skirt around the bottom of cliffs and rockslopes. Screes are usually sloping surfaces without any vegetation or soil. The size of the rock fragments depends on the nature of the rock in the cliff face. Scree of shale, for example, will be in small pieces that erode rapidly, whereas granite scree will be made up of larger blocks. Scree indicates a rapidly eroding cliffline. Despite their appearance they are usually a thin veneer of rubble, less than 10 m thick, but can be unstable as fragments fed from above steepen their slopes.

They are most frequent in hot, dry climates and in cold mountain regions, particularly where there have been glaciers, or where there are severe frosts which break up rocks. Screes occur in central Tasmania and the Snowy Mountains. In the Ben Lomond area of Tasmania some scree slopes are thought to be 80 000 years old.

SCRIBBLY GUM

The name is used for a group of five closely related eucaltptus species of temperate eastern Australia. Their smooth whitish bark is marked here and there by peculiar 'scribbles', almost as though someone had been aimlessly drawing on it with a pen. The scribbles are in fact made by the larvae of a small moth *Ogmograptis scribula*, which burrows through and feeds on the tender new inner bark at the time it is first formed. About a year later, when another bark layer has grown from beneath, the old bark is shed, revealing the meandering burrows of the larvae. This insect only attacks one group of trees, which includes snow gums, blackbutt and mountain ashes. Scribbles can be formed on the smooth barks of these eucalyptus as well.

The most widespread species is Inland Scribbly Gum *E. rossii*, which is found in sandy soils in drier parts of the great Dividing Range and its western slopes, from the far north of NSW to the far south. Around Sydney, Broad-leaved Scribbly Gum *E. haemastoma* is a common small tree on barren sandstone ridges. Northern Scribbly Gum *E. signata* takes over from northern NSW to the south Queensland coast.

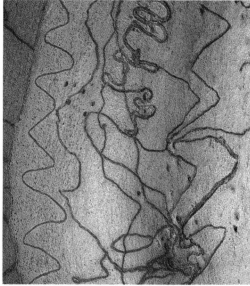

Patterns traced on the trunk of this eucalypt were caused by the larvae of a tiny moth Ogmograptis scribula. *The insects leave their mark by burrowing beneath the surface of the tree and eating a track in newly-forming bark.*

SCRUB

The word was a 16th century variation of shrub, but when it migrated to Australia 'scrub' came to be used interchangeably with bush for a wood with little grass. Its most noble sense – for a large forest with tall trees – survives in the Pilliga Scrub. Its aura degenerated as it came to mean

318

tracts of stunted trees and shrubs, with the word 'miserable' appended, or lurking in the speaker's mind. Now it can mean any area of vegetation except open forest (bush), or anywhere far from civilisation, or where a person can avoid other people. Someone might 'take to the scrub'. Some speakers, botanically more particular, might 'head for the mallee', or 'for the mulga'. Others, for rather uncertain obscurity, head 'for the tall timber'. Scrubbers, in rural parlance, are cattle that have run wild.

SCRUB ITCH

Mites that attack native mammals occasionally bite people who wander through their habitats, sometimes causing dermatitis.

Trombiculid mites are among the worst offenders. The adults are often relatively large, velvety, figure-of-eight-shaped mites, sometimes bright red. They are predators or scavengers, but the tiny six-legged larvae (0.2–0.3 mm) climb foliage and attach themselves to the skins of passing animals and feed there for several days before dropping off and developing into an eight-legged nymph, which matures into an adult. When attacking people they usually gather where clothing constricts the skin, producing a line of weals. Often such mites transmit diseases, but the only one of any importance in Australia is SCRUB TYPHUS.

People swimming in lagoons and billabongs often develop a severe itch. This is usually caused by the larvae of tapeworms, which normally infest waterfowl, trying to penetrate the skin, and dying in the attempt.

SCRUB TYPHUS

Scrub typhus is a disease which normally infects animals, but which human beings sometimes acquire. It is caused by an organism *Rickettsia tsutsugamushi* which is closely related to the one that causes classical or louse-borne typhus. Normally it infects small forest mammals, and is spread from host to host by the larvae of the mite *Leptotrombidium deliensis*. The mites can carry the organism from generation to generation, passing it on with their eggs. Human beings can become infected when they enter the scrubland home of the mites and the mammals. The first symptoms are headaches, fever, swollen lymph glands and a hard scab where the bite was. If untreated the disease can lead to complications such as encephalitis and death from cardiac failure. It responds well to tetracycline antibiotics. It is not directly transmissible from person to person.

In Australia the disease occurs in certain parts of coastal Queensland, but is uncommon. During World War II, however, it incapacitated more allied soldiers than did the Japanese in the Pacific area. It is also known by the Japanese name of tsutsugamushi disease.

SEABIRDS

Seabirds are those birds which get most of their food from the sea, and so the seabirds *par excellence* are those which never come to land, except when nesting. At the other extreme are birds which merely feed on the seashore – the waders and similar species. In between are the birds which sometimes feed at sea, sometimes on land or inland waters, birds such as the GULLS, terns, sea-eagles and most CORMORANTS. The seashore feeders are not included here.

Seabirds get water from their food, and by drinking seawater. Excess salts are then excreted by the nasal glands which lie in grooves above the bird's eyes. The salty solution – saltier than seawater – drips from their beaks. Some seabirds apparently have a good sense of smell, a most unusual characteristic in birds.

Albatrosses are truly oceanic birds which come to land only to breed, and this may not occur every year. They soar and glide for hours, with scarcely a wing beat, and land on the water to feed on fish and squid. One of the eight species that can be seen around the southern coasts breeds in Australia – the Shy Albatross *Diomedea cauta* (810 mm, wing span, 2.1 m). They nest on three islands off Tasmania during the summer, each pair raising only one chick. They do not appear to travel far, unlike the Wandering Albatross *D. exulans* (1.35 m, wing span to 3.25 m, average weight 8.2 kg), the world's largest flying bird. They are most common off the coast of south-east Australia in winter. They breed, laying one egg every other year after reaching maturity, on subantarctic islands including Macquarie. Wandering Albatrosses can live to 40 years.

Petrels, fulmars and related birds have their nostrils united in a single tube above their beaks (albatrosses have two tubes). Two species of giant petrels (900 mm long) visit southern Australian waters in winter, and breed on a few southern islands.

Shearwaters are dark-coloured petrels which nest in burrows. They fly and glide gracefully just above the water, frequently flipping so that their wing tips shear the water. Five species nest on Australian coasts – the most famous being the Short-tailed Shearwater or Muttonbird *P. tenuirostris* (400 mm). They nest along southern coasts, particularly on and near Tasmania. On their return in the last week of September from a 30 000-km figure-of-eight migration to the north Pacific they clean their burrows and mate. They lay between 20 November and 3 December and rear the single chick, which hatches out after 52–55 days. The chicks get very fat – much heavier than adults – and for many years they have been harvested for food on the Bass Strait islands between Tasmania and the mainland.

Frigate Birds, which neither walk nor swim unless forced to, are superb fliers. Males have naked red patches on their throats which can be

Two Brown Boobies Sula leucogaster *conducting a conversation on the shores of Raine Island, on the Great Barrier Reef. These birds are common throughout tropical seas, and they breed on several offshore islands along the northern coast.*

inflated like balloons in display. They pick up fish and squid from the surface of the sea, and rob other birds in flight of their food. Two species are found along northern coasts, and they nest on some Australian islands.

Tropicbirds are white birds with long tail streamers, found in tropical and subtropical waters where they plunge-dive for prey.

Gannets and boobies are diving birds which look like Ws as they plunge from great heights to catch fish. The Australasian Gannet *Morus serrator* (840–920 mm) fishes and feeds in southern Australian waters.

Terns resemble gulls, but are more lightly built, and generally have black heads, finer bills and forked tails. In Australia 14 or 15 species can be found, 11 of them nesting, often in huge colonies on the ground. Some are found on inland waters, as well as at sea.

LIVING ON SALTWATER

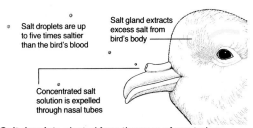

Salt droplets are up to five times saltier than the bird's blood

Salt gland extracts excess salt from bird's body

Concentrated salt solution is expelled through nasal tubes

Salt droplets *ejected from the nose of a petrel are excreted by a salt gland in the bird's head. In this way the bird can rid its body of the excess salt it accumulates from drinking seawater.*

SEAL

There are three groups of seals, and they may each have evolved from different kinds of terrestrial carnivores. One group, which contains just the Walrus, is found only in Arctic regions. The other two are found in both hemispheres. The first is the sea-lion and fur-seal family, and their most obvious characteristic is their small external ears. They can also bring their hind legs forward under their bodies when on land so they are more agile than the true seals. Their fore-limbs and necks are relatively long, but they have no claws. Sea-lions are the seals usually seen in circuses. The second group is the true seals, which do not have external ears.

Southern Elephant Seals *Mirounga leonina* (males to 4.2 m long, and to 3800 kg in weight) are the largest of the true seals, and they once bred in large numbers in Bass Strait, but were

IDENTIFYING SEALS

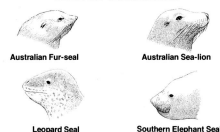

Australian Fur-seal

Australian Sea-lion

Leopard Seal

Southern Elephant Seal

Only the Australian Fur-seal and the Australian Sea-lion are commonly seen. The others are occasional visitors to Australia's southern shores.

exterminated by sealers. The nearest large breeding colony is now on Macquarie Island, although females have pupped in Tasmania in 1958 and 1975. Some other stray true seals, such as the predatory Leopard Seal *Hydrurga leptonyx* (female 3.6 m, 450 kg, larger than male) sometimes reach Australian shores but they are rare.

All of Australia's breeding seals are either fur-seals – so called because of their commercially valuable pelts – or sea-lions. Australian Fur-seals *Arctocephalus pusillus* (male 2.16 m, 279 kg) are the largest and the most abundant (20 000–25 000), and have colonies around Tasmania, and on the Victorian and southern NSW coasts. Pupping – with single births – and mating take place over six weeks in November or December, with oestrus occurring about a week after the birth. Maned bulls come ashore and establish territories in October, but they do not herd the females into harems. This species can dive to 130 m, and may use echolocation. They feed on fish, squid and crustaceans.

New Zealand Fur-seals *A. forsteri* (males 1.5–2.5 m, 120–185 kg) breed mainly in New Zealand and its islands (about 40 000–50 000 individuals and increasing), but there are some colonies on Kangaroo Island and nearby coasts, and on the Recherche Archipelago and nearby islands in Western Australia. The total population is about 2000 according to some authorities, 7000 according to others. Males come ashore in October, establish territories, and gather pregnant females into small harems as they arrive.

Australian Sea-lions *Neophoca cinerea* (males

1.85–2.35 m, 300 kg) are found only in Australia, on islands from Houtman Abrolhos off Western Australia, to Kangaroo Island of South Australia. In 1979 it was estimated that there were between 3000 and 5000 individuals. Pupping has been recorded from August to January, and researchers have suggested that the breeding cycle may be 18 months long.

Whaling and sealing were among the earliest Australian industries and led to great destruction among seals. Populations now, however, seem to be stable or even increasing.

SEASHORE

The edge of the sea is one of the most variable places on earth in which plants and animals can exist, yet an enormous range of living things are found there. This is most obvious on a rocky shore, where the animals and plants are on the surface, but it is also true of sandy shores and mud flats, where many of the animals are below the surface, at least when the tide is out.

Variable conditions are due to the rise and fall of the tide, which covers the shore with water once or twice a day. The tides rise and fall according to a strict timetable so that within the normal tidal range there is only a limited period during which the surface is uncovered. Living creatures can adapt to such a cycle, although they may not be able to cope with unpredictable wet and dry periods. There is, however, some variation in the heights by which the tides rise and fall, so that some parts of the shore are covered only at extreme high tides, and other parts – above the high tide mark – are dampened only by spray. On suitable shores there are rock pools which are filled only from time to time, and they can therefore become difficult places to live as the water evaporates making it saltier, and temperature rises. Even so, some organisms can survive in these conditions. Within the normal tidal range, conditions can be just as extreme when the tide is out. One day the sun may beat down on the surface, producing very high temperatures, and the next day it may be rain-lashed and bitterly cold.

Many shore-dwelling plants and animals can withstand short exposure to the air, but there is intense competition for space at the lower levels. Some organisms avoid this competition by adapting to, and colonising, areas where the exposure to the air is longer. In doing so they usually lose the ability to live at lower levels. Consequently many shores – rocky ones in particular – have a series of zones extending from the extreme low tide marks to the spray zone, well above the high tide mark, where particular plants and animals live. The variety of life in a particular zone varies from place to place, although similar patterns are found in many parts of the world. On cold British shores, for example, the zonal organisms are seaweeds.

Australian Sea-lions at Seal Bay on the coast of South Australia. About 500 animals live here, in what is the largest-known breeding colony of this species. There are perhaps 5000 individuals in Australia altogether.

Giant seas *crash into cliffs to the north of Sydney (above and below). Waves are the most striking manifestation of the sea's awesome and immense power. They constantly wear away rocks and move sediments over great distances.*

In some areas the zones extend below the extreme low tide level, and the organisms that live there vary according to the amount of light that reaches each layer.

The following description of zones on rocky shores applies mainly to the most populated parts of the east coast of Australia, although much of it is also true of coasts around other parts of the continent.

The cunjevoi zone is the lowest, and it extends below the level normally exposed at extreme low tide. The most characteristic organism of this zone is the large sea squirt, CUNJEVOI. It normally lines up to about 450 to 600 mm above extreme low tide level, although at Eden, NSW, it has been found extending to 1.2 m. Cunjevoi is rare west of Cape Otway in Victoria and north of Caloundra in Queensland. On southern shores its place is sometimes taken by seaweeds. The cunjevoi zone often contains specimens of the largest Australian barnacle, *Balanus nigrescens*, which can be about 65 mm tall. Its outside is dark blue to black, and the flesh just inside the opening is bright blue. Barnacles are not molluscs, but crustaceans, enclosed in a shell or valves, within which they live in an inverted position and kick food into their mouths with their feet.

Above the cunjevoi is the galeolaria zone which is dominated by a small worm *Galeolaria caespitosa* which lives in hard, white, limy tubes. Although the worms can live at other levels, this zone suits them best so that their tubes form a dense encrustation which is sometimes called, quite wrongly, coral. When they are covered with water the worms extend their crown of 36 filaments through the tiny openings, although any disturbance, such as a shadow, makes them withdraw immediately. The width of the galeolaria zone is about 450 mm.

Many kinds of molluscs live in the barnacle zone, but they can move. The fixed animals are barnacles which are cemented to the rocks. At one time there was interest in the cement that they used because it was thought that it might make a good material for securing false teeth. The zone is uncovered about half the time, and extends from the mid-tide to the high tide level. The most common species is the small *Chamaesipho columna* which is almost always less than 25 mm tall. They can be very crowded and densities of 13 per sq.cm have been recorded. On more exposed surfaces, and often on more or less vertical surfaces where waves break over the rocks, two larger species, the surf barnacles *Catophragmus polymerus* and *Tetraclita rosea*, take its place. At the top of the zone, near the high tide mark, a fourth species, larger than *C. columna*, may be common. This is *Chthamalus antennatus*.

Above the barnacle zone is the supra-littoral belt which is wetted, if at all, only by spray. Some molluscs live here, among them tiny periwinkles, the grey or white *Nodolittorina pyrimidalis* which has a knobbly shell, and the smooth,

Rhythm of the tides

Some parts of the Australian coast receive two tides a day, while other have only one. Even where two tides a day are usual, they may arrive at uneven intervals, and reach different levels on the shore. The height of the tide also varies considerably at different places around the coast. In the north-west the water level sometimes rises and falls by as much as 12 m, changing the look of the coast beyond recognition in a couple of hours. In Darwin, wharfs and other seaside fixtures must be designed to cope with this huge variation. In other areas, such as along the coast near Perth, the daily variation in water level is only about 600 mm at its greatest.

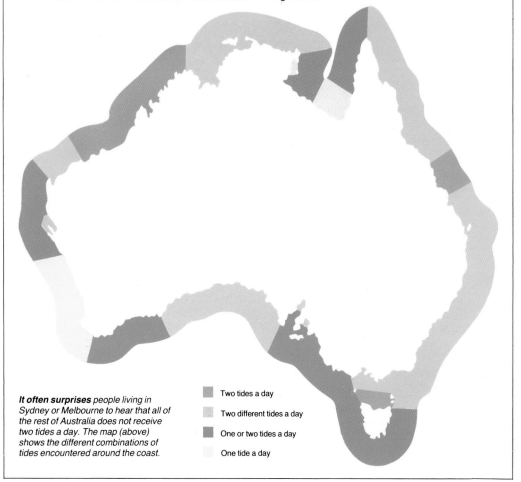

It often surprises people living in Sydney or Melbourne to hear that all of the rest of Australia does not receive two tides a day. The map (above) shows the different combinations of tides encountered around the coast.

- Two tides a day
- Two different tides a day
- One or two tides a day
- One tide a day

plankton – drifting plants and animals – which are usually too small to be seen with the naked eye.

The organisms attached to the rock will usually include some weeds such as Neptune's Necklace *Hormosira banksii*, which looks like a string of beads, and encrusting pink coralline seaweeds which have so much lime in them that they feel gritty to the touch. There may also be encrustations of colourful sponges which are little more than colonies of cells, and of sea-mats and sea-mosses which are also colonial, but in which the individuals are much more complex animals. Sea anemones are very conspicuous, particularly *Actinia tenebrosa* which has a dark red body and brighter red tentacles. Less common is the larger *Oulactis muscosa* whose beauty, however, is obscured by the pieces of gravel and shell grit it carries on its tentacles.

The most common seastars in rock pools, at least along the NSW coast, are species of *Patiriella*, pastel-coloured creatures with short arms – sometimes so short that their body is almost a perfect pentagon.

Most of the molluscs in rock pools will be gastropods, though the odd chiton will be seen, clinging to the rocks like a huge woodlouse. One of the most easily recognised gastropods is the carnivorous black oyster-borer, *Morula marginalba*, which drills holes into other molluscs. It is covered with black knobbles so

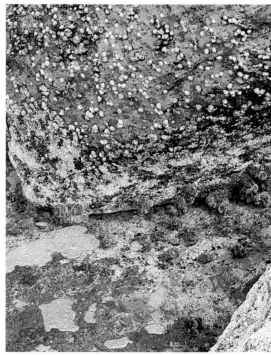

Obvious zones stand out in this view of a rocky shore on the coast of NSW. They range from the cunjevoi zone through the galeolaria and barnacle zones to the supra-littoral zones.

bluish-purple *Melarapha unifasciata*. These are often found huddled together in any crevice which retains moisture and provides shade. The first species has been found 12 m above sea level, and experiments have shown that some stay there for at least a year.

This zone may also have some lichens clothing the rocks, but these are invaders from the land, not from the sea.

Although these zones – or similar ones on other coasts – are often quite obvious, the simple pattern is frequently broken by gullies and rock pools, or large, separate rocks with damp sand and growths beneath.

For those who browse along the shore, rock pools are particularly fascinating. Those that are covered by each tide often 'capture' mobile animals which would normally retreat as the water dropped. They therefore contain a miniature version of the community which normally lives permanently below the surface of the water.

The retreating tide may leave behind, for example, small fish, BLUE-RINGED OCTOPUSES, and various shrimps and crabs. The pools will also contain a variety of animals and weeds that are permanently attached to the rocks, as well as some mobile animals such as limpets and other gastropods which move around, but tend to remain in the pools. The water will also contain that it looks like a miniature hand grenade and is often found in clusters. Just as obvious are groups of the grazing periwinkle *Austrocochlea*, which have zebra stripes on their largest whorls. The more conical *Bembicium* shells, also with stripes, are usually common, as are the matt black *Melanerita atromentosa* shells which have a white interior.

In the sand at the bottom, or in the damp sand beneath the rocks, there will probably be various kinds of worms which are related to the *Galeolaria* worms, but without their tubes. There may also be brittle stars, close relatives of the seastars, but much more active, and with their legs sharply distinct from their central disc. They belong to a group of creatures which are found only in the sea, called echinoderms – the name means spiny skin – which includes sea urchins.

Higher on the shore the rock pools are more variable – sometimes they are extremely salty, and sometimes very diluted by rain. The most frequently found inhabitants are often the larvae of salt-tolerant mosquitoes.

The animals of sandy shores and mud flats are not so easy to find, and must be dug for. They only emerge, if at all, when the tide is in. They include a variety of worms, some with tubes, some without, crabs, and molluscs – particularly burrowing bivalves and some gastropods such as whelks. These shores are also divided into zones, but again the zones are difficult to see.

Harvest of the sea

Seaweeds are some of the larger algae found on rocky shores around the coast. They are divided into three major groups according to their colour – green, red or brown.

Attitudes towards seaweeds vary. On the one hand they are regarded as objects of interest and beauty on the shore, while on the other hand when large amounts of algae are washed up onto beaches by storms, the resultant decaying heaps are viewed with distaste.

Seaweeds have been used for various purposes. Agar – which is a jelly – is extracted from algae; at various times, but particularly during World War II, a red algae was collected in Australia for agar extraction. Alginates – used as stabilisers in the food industry – can also be extracted from a number of seaweeds. On King Island, in Bass Strait, Bull Kelp *Durvillaea potatorum* is still collected for the alginate industry.

In other parts of the world, most notably in Japan, seaweeds are an important part of the national diet. A number of Australian species are edible, but to date there have been no serious attempts to exploit them.

There are many different types of algae on Australian shores, particularly in cooler temperate waters. The rocky coasts of southern Australia probably have a greater variety of seaweeds than anywhere else in the world.

A vast range of seaweeds can be found on temperate Australian coasts. Some typical varieties include: *1* Corallina *sp.*; *2* Padina *sp.*; *3 Dead Man's Fingers* Codium *sp.*; *4* Colpomenia *sp.*; *5* Sargassum *sp.*; *6* Phyllospera *sp.*; *7 Neptune's Necklace* Hormosira *sp.*; *8 Sea Lettuce* Ulva *sp.*; *9* Dictyota *sp.*; *10* Pterocladia *sp.*; *11 Kelp* Ecklonia *sp.*; *12* Porphyra *sp.*; *13* Cryptonemiales *sp.*

SEASON

A season is a period during a calendar year which has a distinctive and recurring weather pattern. However, the idea that a year is made up of four seasons of equal length is inappropriate for a continent the size of Australia. In northern Australia, two major seasons occur each year – the 'wet' season, from October to March, and the 'dry' season from April to September. In the south, weather patterns change more through the year and summer, autumn, winter and spring can be identified.

Seasons occur chiefly because the amount of radiation received from the sun varies throughout the year, although the extent of the variation depends on latitude. The earth's axis is tilted at 23.5° from the vertical, and that part of the globe which receives most sunlight changes during the year as the earth revolves around the sun. When the sun reaches its December solstice it appears to be overhead at the Tropic of Capricorn – 23.5°S, about the latitude of Alice Springs and Rockhampton. More radiation is received from the sun in the southern hemisphere at this time of year. As the earth continues on its way around the sun, the sun lies overhead at progressively higher latitudes and eventually reaches the Tropic of Cancer, 23.5°N, in June. Least radiation is, therefore, received in the southern hemisphere at that time. Changes in the amount of sunshine received at different latitudes at different times of year affect the movement and location of weather systems and, in turn, seasonal weather patterns.

In northern Australia, the summer weather pattern is dominated by monsoonal winds from the north-west, thunderstorms, and occasional tropical cyclones, all of which combine to produce uncomfortably hot and humid conditions. Rainfall is high. Darwin, for example, has an average rainfall of 262 mm during wet season months, November to March, with rain falling on 10 to 20 days each month. In the southern part of the continent, summer weather is dominated by high pressure systems which bring clear skies and more settled weather. High pressure systems move eastwards at a latitude of about 35°S, bringing easterly winds to much of southern Australia. As a result, south-western Australia experiences hot, dry summers as easterly winds blow across arid inland Australia, whereas south-eastern Australia has a wetter and more humid summer because easterlies come across the vastness of the Pacific ocean.

Winter in northern Australia is a dry season because south-easterly winds come from inland regions as high pressure systems move north-

The rhythm of the year

Spring, summer, autumn and winter (left to right, top to bottom) at Bowral in NSW. It is the introduced trees and shrubs that demonstrate seasonal changes most dramatically. The area is noted for its similarities with England, both in scenery and climate. Other areas may show little change from season to season.

ward in response to the seasonal shift of the sun. Darwin receives a meagre 6 mm of rain at the height of the dry season, from June to August. By contrast, southern Australia has a much colder, cloudier and wetter winter because of the frequent mid-latitude frontal depressions which move eastwards at a latitude of about 40°S.

SEDIMENTARY ROCK

More than 75 per cent of the exposed surface of the earth is made up of sedimentary rocks, although they only make up 5 per cent of the bulk of the crust. The rock are obviously spread out in a very thin layer. But in this thin layer there is a wealth of economic material. Coal, oil and gas are formed in sedimentary rocks, as is much of the world's supply of iron, salt and building materials. As the name implies, sedimentary rocks are layered or stratified rocks formed from compacted sediments. Sandstone, shale, limestone, conglomerate, chert and coal are all sedimentary rocks. The sediments come from the breakdown of any other, older rocks. Since the first winds blew and the first rain fell on earth, the relentless forces of erosion have been breaking down rocks and depositing the

The alternating layers of shale and sandstone in this cliff near Sydney were deposited during the Triassic Period, between 180 and 230 million years ago.

pieces in low-lying areas of the earth's crust, such as valleys, lakes and oceans. Over many millions of years the layers of sediments change under their own weight. The water is squeezed out of them and the grains are cemented together in a process called lithification, or 'rock making'.

SEED INDUSTRY

Australia has a small, but thriving rural industry dedicated to the production of seeds for Australian and overseas farmers, and also for the use of private companies.

The range of climates and the isolation of many rural areas makes Australia one of the world's best places to produce disease-free, pure seeds – the 'basic stock' of all pastures, crops, flowers, fruit and vegetables.

The industry produces around $40 million worth of seed a year. The main seed crops are pasture varieties, such as clovers, medics, ryegrass, lucerne, kikuyu, phalaris and cocksfoot. In a typical year, around $10 million worth of pasture seed is exported.

Most of the 100 000 ha planted each year to seed crops are in Western Australia. There are also small, but expanding, pockets of seeds being produced for other crops, including vegetables, in Victoria and Queensland. Tropical grain crops and pastures are produced for seed in the Northern Territory, as are cereal grains in NSW.

Most farmers produce the seeds on a strict contract basis for a handful of private companies, which then re-sell the seeds for widespread commercial use. Producers must be very careful not to mix seed crops or allow contamination by pests, disease and weeds.

Australia is also very popular with overseas companies wishing to produce large amounts of seed. By producing seed in the southern hemisphere, European and North American companies can effectively enjoy two growing seasons in one year.

In the past, the lack of Plant Variety Rights (PVR) legislation has discouraged many foreign seed companies from investing in Australia. PVR, introduced in 1987, gives the company ownership of seed produced on its behalf. Farmers must pay the companies royalties for use of the stock. The legislation thus protects companies against 'poaching' of varieties by other companies or farmers.

SELECTION

In 1860 several million hectares of Australia were occupied by a few hundred pastoralists, running sheep on land that could often bear crops. The decade saw each colony except Western Australia attempting radical land reform. Idealists dreamed of a land dotted with farmhouses beside every creek, with crops tended by a yeomanry formed from the strong, independent and now unemployed gold diggers. NSW acted

'Some trouble with the steer.' This illustration is from an early edition of On Our Selection by Steele Rudd, a sardonic tale that told of the misadventures of Dad and Dave Rudd on their Queensland selection.

first, in 1862 making it possible for any person to select a block of Crown land, from 40 to 320 acres (16 to 130 ha), before survey, whether or not it was leased by a squatter. The price was £1 an acre, a quarter to be paid as deposit, and meeting certain conditions the selector could get freehold title in three years. The other colonies' Acts were on similar lines. Districts were declared open for selection. At midnight, selectors would rush to peg out their claims. Furious, the squatters saw 'their' land being fenced off, huts erected and trees cleared. Contemptuously they and their stockmen dubbed the settlers 'cockatoo farmers' – cockies – either because they scratched the earth for a living or after the nuisance birds. It often proved to be a desperate living. Many farms were too small to provide a living. Few selectors had capital to clear and equip them. Many, town-bred, chose land unwisely and knew nothing about farming. Backbreaking labour and debt were cruel rulers of many lives. Often the men had to take outside work such as shearing or fencing, leaving wives and children, housed in tents or shacks, to run the farms.

The squatters were given some protection, in NSW, for example by being allowed first option to buy one-twentyfifth of their stations and the areas were improved with dams, shearing sheds or fences. But generally they retained control of their holdings by such tactics as 'dummying' – getting a nominee to select land which was later transferred to the squatter – and 'peacocking' – buying up land along both sides of a creek or around a waterhole so the surrounding land was useless. Their strategies defeated the Acts. Only a few selectors prospered, notably in South Australia and the more fertile parts of Victoria. Ironically they often expanded their farms and ceased to be the smallholders the parliamentary reformers had envisaged.

SEWAGE

In 19th-century Australia, Chinese market gardeners put human excrement on vegetable gardens, as is done in Asia today. Vegetables grow on sewage farms in France. At Werribee in Victoria, cattle and sheep graze on pasture where raw sewage runs in furrows and is purified by organisms in the soil. Most sewage in Australia is treated by filtering to remove oil and grease, the resulting sludge being broken down by bacteria to give a solid material. Around the coast most sludge is discharged into the sea. Inland it is usually broken down furthur by bacteria, and the effluent is then discharged into watercourses. Sludge has not generally been put on the land in Australia because it can harbour viruses, bacteria and worm eggs and, being a mixture of household and industrial waste, contains heavy metals and salts. Until recently it was feared that these might affect plant growth and human health. Now it seems that sludge does not make most plants toxic in metals such as zinc, nickel and copper, although cadmium can accumulate in leafy vegetables like spinach. Disease organisms can be killed by heat. So, with some precautions, such as leaching out of salts, and selection of crops, sludge may become a common fertiliser.

SHALE

Shale is a soft fine-grained rock with distinct layers which is formed from the sediments that are often seen clouding the waters of seas, lakes and rivers. The tiny particles – most less than 0.06 mm in diameter – can be carried for hundreds of kilometres by even gentle ocean currents. It can take thousands of years for just a few centimetres to build up on the ocean floor, where they are gradually compacted into rock.

The main components of shale are quartz, clay and mica, and it varies in colour from black to red, green, blue or olive. Black shales are best known because they are rich in organic matter and can yield from 4 to 50 per cent oil. Oil shales were mined in some parts of the Sydney basin, notably at Newnes near Lithgow, in the early years of this century.

SHE-OAK

This name was given by the earliest white settlers in Australia to the casuarinas, the common native trees. They were so named because of the grain of their wood, which is marked with large medullary rays, like the wood of the European oaks. She-oaks are somewhat pine-like in appearance, lacking normal leaves. A close examination of the 'needles', however, shows that they are in fact fine twigs, marked with longitudinal grooves and encircled at regular intervals by rows of minute teeth. These teeth represent the tips of their leaves, which are fused to the twig surface. The small flowers are in spikes of all male or all female, and are pollinated by wind. The female spikes develop into small woody fruiting cones, which open to release winged seeds.

There are about 50 species of she-oak, of which five belong in the genus *Casuarina* and 45 in *Allocasuarina*. Some of the largest belong in the former, including River She-oaks *C. cunninghamiana* which are common along freshwater streams the whole length of the east coast and Dividing Range. They reach a height of about 30 metres. *Allocasuarina* species are mostly small trees or shrubs which grow on poorer sandy or rocky soils. Few become large trees. Forest She-oaks *A. torulosa* grows to about 25 m tall in eucalypt forests on steep coastal ranges in NSW and Queensland. In the south-west the main species of she-oak is *A. fraseriana*, common on the coastal plain around Perth and reaching a height of 15 m. In the far inland, Desert Oaks *A. decaisneana* grows into large, shapely trees on deep sands in the very arid country around the borders of the Northern Territory, South Australia and Western Australia.

SHEARER

The shearer – the prince of Australian itinerant workers – maintains an important place in the country's history. It is a shearer who is the hero in Australia's unofficial national anthem, *Waltzing Matilda*. It was the shearers who formed one of the country's first – and still one of its strongest – unions, the Australian Workers' Union (AWU). Shearers have been the only workers in Australian history to be killed in clashes with the police and strike-breaking militia. There is even an item of clothing named after a shearer – the Jacky Howe singlet.

Itinerant shearers grew with the spread of the wool industry towards the end of last century. They would spend months 'on the track', as they followed the shearing cycle from station to station across the pastoral country. In the days before the union, hopeful shearers would gather at a station having travelled perhaps hundred of kilometres on foot, pushbike or horse in the hope of a pen – the right to shear sheep – at a station. The station overseer would make his selection from the gathering and, as often as not, there would be police on hand to see the unsuccessful ones off the property and back onto the track again. In those early times shearers worked very long days under terrible conditions. However, a number of bitter strikes that saw wool sheds destroyed, wool barges on the Darling River burnt to their waterlines – and sometimes the death of striking shearers – resulted in the birth of a strong union and a well ordered, well paid and skillful industry.

A shearer is the only man in a SHEARING SHED who is paid according to the rate at which he

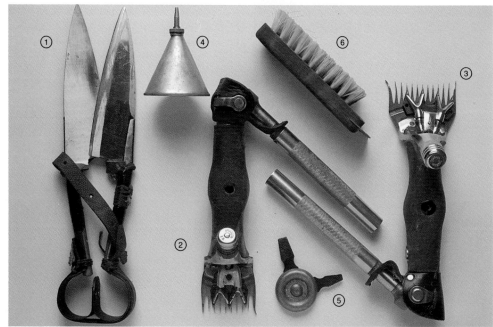

Tools of the shearer's trade

1 Hand shears are now only used for shearing stud rams – because there is less chance of an expensive accident. More wool is also left on the beast afterwards, to help keep it warm in cold weather. The technique involves pushing the blades through the wool, rather than a clipping action; 2 hand piece with narrow comb; 3 hand piece with wide comb, now used by almost all shearers; 4 oil can; 5 screwdriver; 6 brush.

The tools may have changed slightly, but shearing today is every bit as hard as it was in 1901, when the workers in this shed were photographed.

works. He is paid by the number of sheep he shears, and it is matter of great personal pride – and widespread fame – to be thought of as the 'gun' shearer, and the 'ringer' of the shed – literally the fastest shearer in the team.

The ringers in the big sheds – some of which in the old days would employ as many as 100 shearers to shear perhaps 300 000 sheep – were treated in much the same way as modern sporting heroes. They lived the part, dressing in silk shirts and fancy waistcoats for a celebration drink at the 'cut out' at the local pub, where the drinks flowed freely and fables were born.

Following the loss of manpower in the bush after World War II, and the break up of many of the big stations for SOLDIER SETTLEMENTS, the nature of the shearing industry changed. Now, shearers will very often be young farmers from the district earning extra money to finance their own properties and, instead of following the work from shed to shed, they will shear in their own area for a couple of months and then go back to farming. The big sheds in pastoral – as opposed to farming – areas are still shorn by travelling professionals, but the shearing team will usually be put together by a contractor who will undertake to manage the shearing.

The number of shearers employed in a shed determines the number of shed hands or rouseabouts to be employed. The award under which shearers are employed stipulates that there must be a certain number of employees to pen the sheep, and a certain number to keep the shorn wool away from them. The award also stipulates that in any shed employing more than six shearers there must be a pen set aside for a newcomer to learn his trade in.

Shearers work from Monday to Friday, starting at 7.30 am and finishing at 4.30 pm. The day is divided into four 'runs', with a 'smoko' – a rest – between the first and second and the third and fourth runs. There is a meal break of one hour between the second and third runs.

The shearer's pen of shorn sheep is counted out at the end of each run by 'the boss of the board' and each shearer's tally is written up for all to see. He will be paid according to the number of sheep he has shorn, with rams counting as double. Just how many he gets through in a day will depend very much on the type of sheep. One hundred average Merinos – the usual wool sheep in Australia – is a reasonable tally, but a 'gun' shearer can manage twice that, and 150 of the less wrinkly cross-bred sheep is quite common.

The owner of the shed, or the contractor, is required to supply the shearer with a handpiece or 'bogeye' – the machine that shears the sheep. The shearer, however, is responsible for supplying his own combs and cutters (see box), the moving, replaceable parts of the machine that do the actual shearing. These need to be replaced a couple of times during each run and again, it is the owner's responsibility to supply the 'expert' to sharpen them again for the shearers. Sometimes, however, shearers – especially those who work only for short periods in farming districts – will own their own handpieces and sharpen their own cutters.

Shearing Sheds

A shearing shed can be anything from a primitive structure with rough timber walls and a bark roof to the vast 'corrugated iron cathedrals' that were built on some of the larger properties last century. Dunlop shed on the Darling River at Louth, NSW, is typical of the grand old sheds. The board – the area where the shearers worked – is 100 m long and there was room for 7000 sheep inside the shed.

No matter what size it is, a shearing shed will follow a predictable pattern. Around the outside are a series of yards into which the sheep are mustered. There they will be separated into groups. Ewes will be drafted from their lambs, and sheep of one age-group from those of another.

Inside the shed, a series of pens, progressively smaller in size, will lead up to the individual shearer's 'catching pens' at the board. Each of these pens may hold from 20 to 30 adult sheep.

The shearer gains access to his pen through swinging doors. He catches his sheep, drags it onto the board and shears it. The shorn animal is then usually pushed down a chute leading back under the catching pen into a small 'counting out pen' outside the shed. Each shearer's sheep are kept separate until the end of a 'run'.

Set at right angles to the shearing board is the wool-rolling table. Long and wide, it has a slatted top to allow small pieces of wool to fall through. A shed hand or 'rouseabout' will pick up the fleece after it had been shorn. Like everything else, there is a knack to the job. He walks into the fleece on the floor. His feet go under the shorn wool and the fleece is pulled back against his shins. He takes hold of the back legs of the fleece, one in each hand, and then folds them around the bundle picking the whole lot up in a ball. He walks to the table and, still holding on to the back legs, throws the fleece gently up and away from him. If this is done properly the fleece will then open out and fall, shorn-side down, onto the table.

Skirters then attack it. They remove any substandard wool from around the outside of the fleece, turning the edges in as they go. Again the fleece is rolled into a ball. This time the shoulder wool – considered a fair sample of the fleece – is left on top. The wool classer, a trained tradesman, inspects it and grades it into any one of a number of catagories.

The fleece is then removed to the wool room – a large open area with portable bins erected to hold the various types of wool.

The greasy wool is pressed into jute, or possibly polythene bales, about 30 fleeces, or 120 kg to a bale. These are then branded with the name of the property and the grade of the wool.

8 Wool classer judges quality of fleece before putting it in the appropriate bin. The fleece is thrown on to the table, "skirted" to remove any burrs and stains, then rolled up, folded and classed.

9 Wool press — electrically powered — presses one bale while the other is loaded. Three, pointed rods pass through the pressed down wool to hold it in place. The press is elevated and more wool put on top. A second pressing begins and the rods are relocated so that more wool can be put in. A third pressing usually achieves the required weight, and the bale is secured with metal clips and removed by a door in the side of the press.

Bins for classe fleeces before baling

10 Counting-out pens, usually take 35 to 40 sheep, allowing a tally of each shearer's output to be taken at each "smoko", or at the end of the day. The tally is recorded on the tally board.

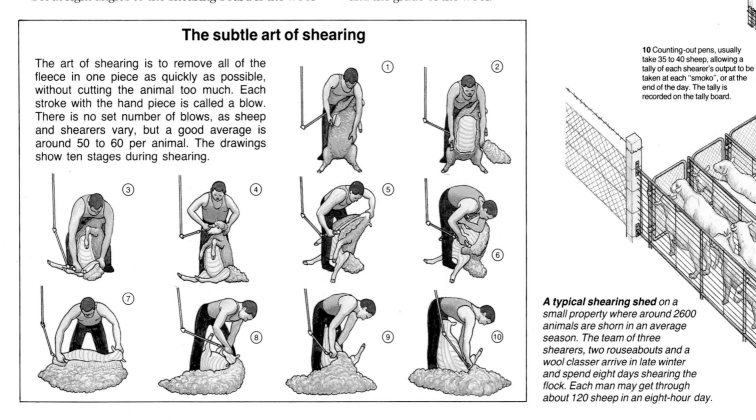

The subtle art of shearing

The art of shearing is to remove all of the fleece in one piece as quickly as possible, without cutting the animal too much. Each stroke with the hand piece is called a blow. There is no set number of blows, as sheep and shearers vary, but a good average is around 50 to 60 per animal. The drawings show ten stages during shearing.

① ② ③ ④ ⑤ ⑥ ⑦ ⑧ ⑨ ⑩

A typical shearing shed on a small property where around 2600 animals are shorn in an average season. The team of three shearers, two rouseabouts and a wool classer arrive in late winter and spend eight days shearing the flock. Each man may get through about 120 sheep in an eight-hour day.

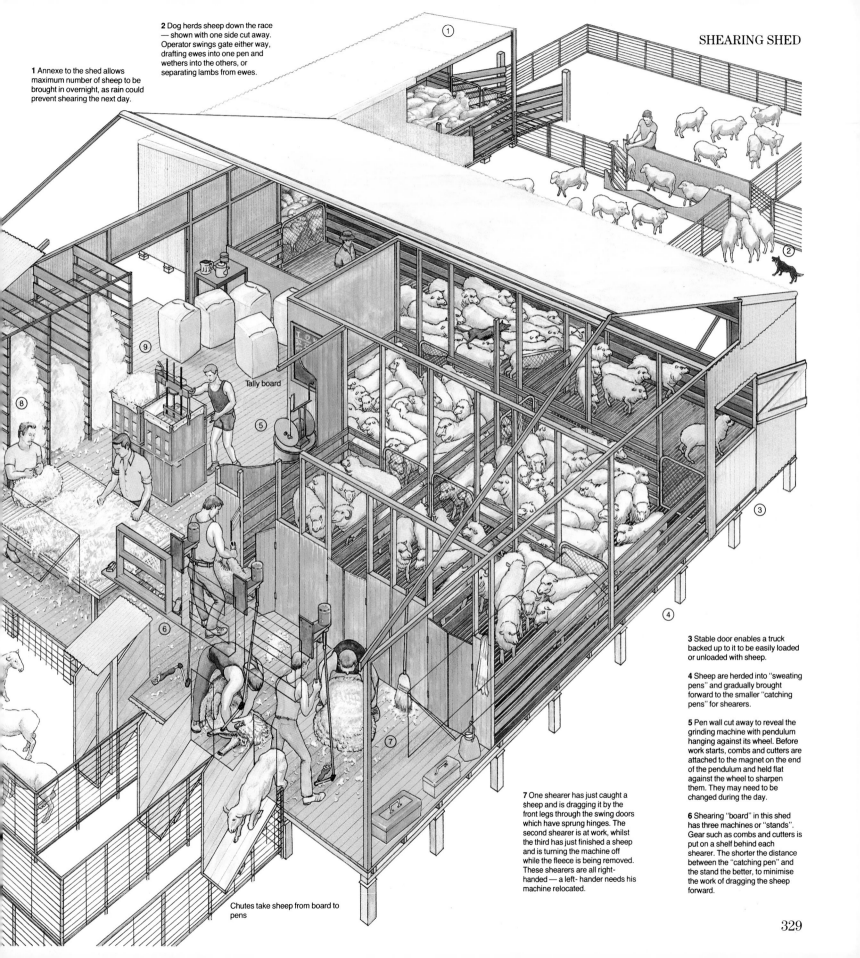

SHEARING SHED

1 Annexe to the shed allows maximum number of sheep to be brought in overnight, as rain could prevent shearing the next day.

2 Dog herds sheep down the race — shown with one side cut away. Operator swings gate either way, drafting ewes into one pen and wethers into the others, or separating lambs from ewes.

Tally board

Chutes take sheep from board to pens

3 Stable door enables a truck backed up to it to be easily loaded or unloaded with sheep.

4 Sheep are herded into "sweating pens" and gradually brought forward to the smaller "catching pens" for shearers.

5 Pen wall cut away to reveal the grinding machine with pendulum hanging against its wheel. Before work starts, combs and cutters are attached to the magnet on the end of the pendulum and held flat against the wheel to sharpen them. They may need to be changed during the day.

6 Shearing "board" in this shed has three machines or "stands". Gear such as combs and cutters is put on a shelf behind each shearer. The shorter the distance between the "catching pen" and the stand the better, to minimise the work of dragging the sheep forward.

7 One shearer has just caught a sheep and is dragging it by the front legs through the swing doors which have sprung hinges. The second shearer is at work, whilst the third has just finished a sheep and is turning the machine off while the fleece is being removed. These shearers are all right-handed — a left-hander needs his machine relocated.

329

SHEEP

'In this branch of rural economy...the greatest and most decisive improvement has taken place, since to this object the whole attention and energies of the most wealthy and intelligent men in the colony have been for several years directed...'

Thus wrote the NSW grazier and author James Atkinson in 1826, about Australia's rapidly developing sheep industry. Along with other settlers and administrators, such as James Macarthur, James Ruse and John Thomas Bigge, Atkinson realised that sheep of both Merino and British origins were naturally suited to conditions in the newly-settled continent. Just 23 years after Atkinson published his opinions, there were about 16 million sheep in Australia.

The Australian sheep industry – made up of the wool, meat and livesheep trades – is one of the nation's largest money earners. It regularly brings in more than $5 billion a year in export income alone.

Since 1950, the number of sheep in Australia has not fallen below 115 million and has reached more than 160 million a number of times. Around 30 million lambs and older sheep are slaughtered every year to supply both the domestic and export sheepmeat trade. The price of wool tends to determine the number of sheep in Australia. Over recent years, the national flock has grown in size in line with the rapid increase in world demand for woollen garments.

Sheep can be classified into wool, meat and dual-purpose breeds. The Merino, derived from Spanish and other European stock, is the most popular wool breed. It accounts for more than 110 million head of the national flock. Corriedale and Border Leicester are considered dual-purpose breeds, being able to produce both wool and meat. Sheepmeat breeds include Dorset Horn, Suffolk and Southdown, all British-derived sheep. Many graziers also run crossbreeds, such as Border Leicester-Merino cross, to gain the advantages of both breeds. A 'comeback' is a crossbreed which has been bred in subsequent matings towards the Merino type. They usually suit high rainfall areas, and are noted for their high wool yield and mothering ability. Most popular for meat breeding are Dorset Horn, Poll Dorset, Suffolk, Southdown and South Suffolk.

Apart from the wool industry, sheep are the backbone of several other rural sectors, notably sheepmeat, livesheep and skins. Sheepmeats can be divided into two types: lamb meat from sheep less than one year old; and mutton meat from older stock. Every year, the average Australian eats around 7 kg of mutton and 15 kg of lamb. A further large amount of lamb and mutton – usually around 50 000 tonnes – is exported to a range of countries in chilled, fresh or frozen form. These exports earn the nation around $300 million a year. Sheepmeat is produced in most

Popular breeds of sheep

Fine Wool Merino
Wool

Corriedale
Wool and meat

Polwarth
Wool and meat

Border Leicester
Long wool and meat

Romney Marsh
Long wool and meat

Lincoln
Long wool and meat

Suffolk
Meat

Southdown
Meat

Dorset Horn
Meat

states, notably in the high to medium rainfall districts of NSW, Victoria and Western Australia.

In most states, lamb is sold largely during the late winter or spring months of July, August, September or October. This is because most graziers prefer summer-autumn mating. However, there is a trend towards the production of lambs between January and April to cash in on high prices in Australia and overseas. In northeast Victoria, lambing is also carried out in the autumn months, as the hot spring weather can kill more lambs than does the cold. The gestation or pregnancy period for sheep is 150 days.

Mutton is a lower-priced sheepmeat from animals over two years old. It is usually considered to be a by-product of the wool industry when graziers sell off older ewes at the end of their productive life. Mutton is commonly used in pies, sausages and canned meats.

Another option for the disposal of older sheep is the live export trade to the Middle East. The trade, which developed in the late 1970s and early 1980s, involves the export of live wethers, ewes and rams to Muslim countries.

The final facet of the sheep industry is the developing market in skins. Australia is the world's largest supplier, exporting around $250 million worth every year.

The age of a sheep is indicated by its teeth. A two-tooth is between one year and 18 months old; a four-tooth is between one and a half and two years; a six-tooth is between two and a half and three years; and mature, full mouth (eighttooth) sheep are between three and four years old. At around five years, the two middle teeth start to wear down, and the beast is often sold soon afterwards. Most ewes are therefore culled by the time they reach six years of age, while wethers are usually slaughtered at five.

Sheep are found in all states, from south of Hughenden in western Queensland to north of Geraldton in Western Australia. Over one-third of the national flock is in NSW, which is the largest producer of both wool and sheepmeat.

SHELL

Shells are produced by molluscs to protect and support their soft tissues. They are secreted by the animal's mantle, which surrounds its body, and are made up largely of calcium carbonate and horny material.

There are more than 65 000 living species of molluscs, and about half that number are known as fossils. Many live in the sea, and a smaller number live on the land or in fresh water. Most molluscs fall into one or other of four classes. The chitons or coat of mail shells, often found in rock pools, are regarded as being most like the ancestral mollusc. They are more or less oval, and their shell is made up of eight plates, one behind the other. The mantle protrudes at the sides. They graze on seaweed using their radula – a rasp-like strip which is drawn backwards and forwards over a hard boss, rather like a rag being used to clean a shoe. As it wears out at the front it is replaced from behind.

Gastropods are the largest class of molluscs which is made up of all those species with a single shell. These are often spiral-shaped as in snails, or may be conical as in limpets, or ear-shaped as in abalone. The soft parts consist of a head-foot – with one or two pairs of tentacles which often carry eyes – and the mass of the body. In some gastropods the shell has dis-appeared, or is reduced and is concealed inside the animal's body, as is the case with sea slugs, nudibranchs and some snails. Most gastropods use a radula for feeding, but the diets of the various members vary from carrion to plants. Cone shells have a harpoon-like radula on a flexible proboscis with which they stab prey and inject venom. Those which prey on fish have a venom which is dangerous to humans, and some have killed people. This is unfortunate because cone shells are among the most attractive to be found on coral reefs, and many fetch high prices from collectors. Other collectable families include volutes, balers – which were once used for that purpose by boating Aborigines – and the familiar cowries.

Bivalves are the second largest class of molluscs, all of which live in water, most of them in the sea. In this group are such familiar animals as oysters, clams and mussels. The body is enclosed by two shells – or valves – which are hinged and are opened and closed by muscles. The foot, if there is one, is hatchet-shaped. Some bivalves, such as clams, use their foot for burrowing into sand and mud, but some like oysters, are firmly cemented to the rock. Mussels and some other bivalves use fine threads as anchors. This attach-ment is called the byssus – from a Hebrew word translated in the Bible as fine linen – and that of the species *Pinna menkei* was once used for making expensive robes in Mediterranean countries. This species is the razor shell of Sydney mud flats, so-called because the edges of its fan-shaped shells are extremely sharp.

In general, bivalve shells are not as attractive as gastropod shells, but everyone knows the scallops whose flesh makes fine food, and shells excellent ashtrays. The bright yellow, orange or silvery jingle shells, which have roughly the same shape as scallop shells but are smaller (50 mm), are commonly washed-up on the shore.

One of the commonest shells on eastern coasts is that of the PIPI *Plebidonax deltoides* (50 mm), a wedge shell. They live below the sand surface on ocean beaches. They were once a favourite food of the Aborigines.

Sometimes the rubbish on the beach may contain the remains of cephalopod shells. The cephalopods are octopuses, squids and their re-latives, and their shells are usually inside their bodies or are absent altogether. But the por-celain-like ram's horn shell is the coiled, external house of *Spirula spirula*. Only one or two have been found on Australian beaches with living animals inside. Occasionally the paper 'shell' of the pearly nautilus *Argonauta* may drift ashore – it is not a true shell, but a loose shelter made by the female for her eggs.

Common shells on Australian beaches

SHELLS FROM COOL TEMPERATE SEAS
(from about Sydney to Perth, including Tasmania)

Triple Murex
Murex triformis

Chiton
Rhyssoplax jugosa

Blue-tinged Dosinia
Phacosoma caerulea

Painted Lady
Phasianella australis

Kelp Shell
Phasianotrochus eximius

Pacific Yellow Cockle
Vasticardium flavum

Pink Tellin
Albinella sp.

Frilled Venus
Callanaitis disjecta

Paper Nautilus
Argonauta nodosa
(The egg case of an Argonaut, a relative of the octopuses)

Brown Cowry
Cypraea angustata

White-ribbed Horse Mussel
Modiolus albicostus

Mud oyster
Ostrea angasi

Much Desired Volute
Amoria exoptanda
(rare)

Lightning Volute
Ericusa fulgetrum
(uncommon)

Turban shell
Ninella torquata

Common shells on Australian beaches

SHELLS FROM WARM TEMPERATE SEAS
(between about 25°S and 35°S)

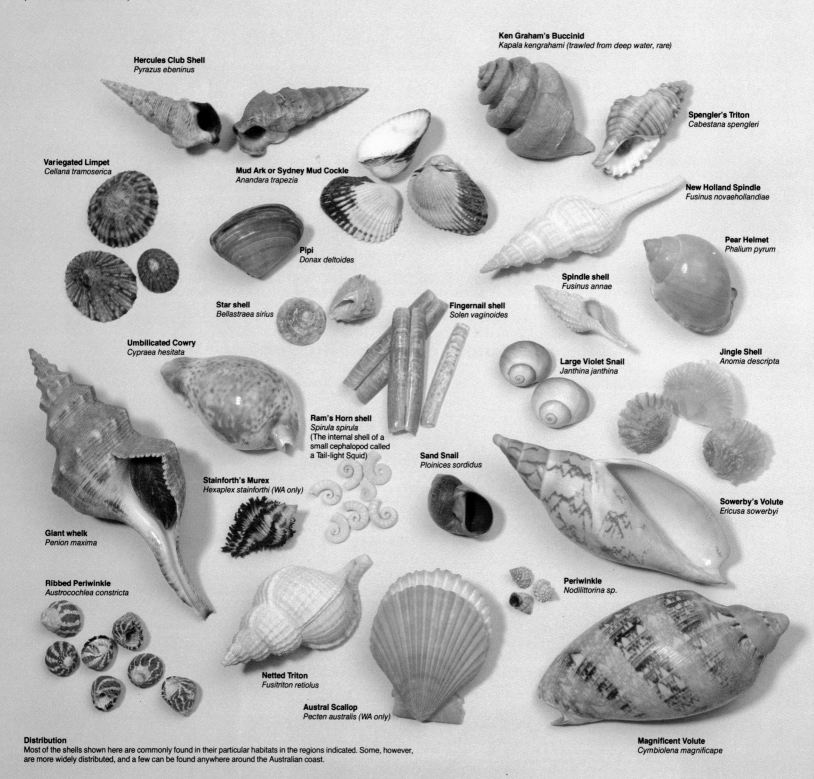

Hercules Club Shell
Pyrazus ebeninus

Ken Graham's Buccinid
Kapala kengrahami (trawled from deep water, rare)

Spengler's Triton
Cabestana spengleri

Variegated Limpet
Cellana tramoserica

Mud Ark or Sydney Mud Cockle
Anandara trapezia

New Holland Spindle
Fusinus novaehollandiae

Pipi
Donax deltoides

Pear Helmet
Phalium pyrum

Spindle shell
Fusinus annae

Star shell
Bellastraea sirius

Fingernail shell
Solen vaginoides

Umbilicated Cowry
Cypraea hesitata

Large Violet Snail
Janthina janthina

Jingle Shell
Anomia descripta

Ram's Horn shell
Spirula spirula
(The internal shell of a
small cephalopod called
a Tail-light Squid)

Sand Snail
Ploinices sordidus

Stainforth's Murex
Hexaplex stainforthi (WA only)

Sowerby's Volute
Ericusa sowerbyi

Giant whelk
Penion maxima

Ribbed Periwinkle
Austrocochlea constricta

Periwinkle
Nodilittorina sp.

Netted Triton
Fusitriton retiolus

Austral Scallop
Pecten australis (WA only)

Magnificent Volute
Cymbiolena magnificape

Distribution
Most of the shells shown here are commonly found in their particular habitats in the regions indicated. Some, however, are more widely distributed, and a few can be found anywhere around the Australian coast.

SHELLS FROM TROPICAL SEAS
(north of about 25°S)

Carrier shell
Xenophora sp.

Strawberry Cockle
Fragum unedo

Murex shell
Chicoreus cornucervi

Asses's Ear (Abalone)
Haliotis asinina

Long-spined Thorny Oyster
Spondylus wrightianus

Campbell's Stromb
Strombus campbelli

Volute
Voluta peristicta

Elliot's Volute
Amoria ellioti

Volute
Voluta pulchra

Zebra Volute
Amoria zebra

Diana's Stromb
Strombus aurisdianae

Orange-lined Auger
Terebrata dimidiata

Tun shell
Tonna dolium

Fly-spotted Auger
Terebra areolata

Distaff Spindle
Fusinus colus

Episcopal Miter
Mitra mitra

Snake's Head Cowry
Cypraea caputserpentis

Lynx Cowry
Cypraea lynx

Textile Cone
Conus textile (venomous)

Venus Shell
Periglypta chemnitzii

Milk Spot Cowry
Cypraea vitellus

Map Cowry
Cypraea mappa

Arabian Cowry
Cypraea arabica

Clam
Tridacna fossor

Giant Triton
Charonia tritonis

SHIELD BUG

Shield bugs look like beetles, but they are easily distinguished from them by their beak – sucking mouthparts – and by their forewings, which are only partly hardened. Some – the stink bugs – also produce an unpleasant smell. Many are brightly coloured. Most are plant feeders but some are predators, and one has a liking for bedbugs. A familiar example is the 25-mm long Bronze Orange Bug *Musgraveia sulciventris*, a notorious widespread, smelly pest of citrus trees which distorts the growth of foliage (see illustration p 96).

SHINGLE-BACK LIZARD

Shingle-back Lizards *Trachydosaurus rugosus* (to 450 mm) are closely related to BLUE-TONGUED SKINKS. They are very common, dark coloured creatures whose surface has been likened to a pine-cone. This resemblance is due to the greatly enlarged, rough dorsal scales. Both legs and tail are short. These slow-moving lizards are active during the day amd eat small animals and some plants. They are found over much of southern Australia, although not in the highlands and coastal districts of east or west Victoria. They produce living young – usually one or two, and only rarely three, and shelter under ground litter, logs, tussocks of grass and similar cover (see illustration p 236).

SHIRE

Relics of old England, hundreds and parishes live on in surveys in South Australia, Tasmania and NSW. The term shire also flourishes, remote in every way from the leafy lanes and village greens of the English counterpart. Australia's largest shire is almost three times the size of the whole of England: East Pilbara in Western Australia covers 377 647 sq. km.

Early governors of the Australian colonies tried to split them into counties, hundreds and parishes, as in England, but it was naturally the cities and towns that first had cause and means to set up formal local government. By about 1850, much of settled rural Australia was divided into districts formed primarily to build and keep up roads and bridges. Gradually central governments imposed local government systems on rural areas. South Australia led, creating district councils in 1852.

Not all states call the rural unit of local government a shire. Tasmania calls them, oddly, municipalities. South Australia retains its district councils. About 85 per cent of that state is unincorporated – has no local government at all. Western Australia clung to its road districts until 1961 when it created shires; 114 of them cover the entire state. Queensland has 134 shires, but as in NSW the rural distinction has dimmed, with some shires on the fringe of, or actually in, city areas, such as Logan in Queensland, and War-

ringah and Sutherland in NSW. NSW has 112 shires, and about 12 per cent of the state is administered by the Western Lands Commission. Victoria, all of it incorporated, has 133 shires. Its country centres with 4000 people can be boroughs or, with 1000 people more, towns. Other states, and the Northern Territory, have either towns or municipalities only.

Voting for local councils is voluntary in South Australia and Tasmania and for some councils in Victoria. By another verbal throwback, electoral units in NSW and Victoria are ridings, a word borrowed from Yorkshire which was divided by its Viking rulers into thridings, or thirds.

SHOW

No matter how small the country town, it will have a showground and will manage to organise itself each year for 'the Show'. Shows – the Australian version of rural fairs – are undoubtedly one of the highlights of a country town's social and business calendar, as farmers take advantage of a few days in town to catch up on friends and business. Shows, whether they be in country towns or capital cities, bring farmers and townspeople together to have a look at one another and to compare skills. Farmers display commercial and well-groomed stock for judging and, sometimes, sale. All forms of local agricultural produce – from bags of wheat and sorghum to cotton and bales of hay – are put forward for judging. Town produce, such as fruit and vegetables are also cultivated for the big event, where crocheted garments, flower arrangements, cake-icing, preserves, and photographs compete for blue ribbons. Many country shows also feature exhibits from local school children and special interest groups, such as rotary clubs. In the often dusty show-ring, equestrian skills are tested in hacking, jumping and dressage events, while sheep dogs are also put through their paces. One of the most popular events at shows is undoubtedly the woodchop where burly axe-wielding men and women race to fell timber posts. And of course a good deal of business – as well as gossip – is talked in the public bar. It is at shows that studs build reputations and farmers catch up on the latest agricultural machinery and practices. Some farmers and stock owners travel thousands of kilometres every year to exhibit their wares at Australia's major shows, held in the capital cities. It is not uncommon for stud animals to be sold for hundreds of thousands of dollars after winning grand champion prize at Sydney's Royal Easter Show. Of course no show is complete without some form of sideshow alley, fairy floss and hotdogs.

SILAGE

Silage, a type of preserved fodder, is used to maintain livestock through the year's lean periods and for survival during droughts. It is mainly

produced in Australia's temperate regions for dairy and feedlot cattle.

Silage is made by mowing young, growing pastures, cereals or forage sorghum, and leaving them in the paddock for a short time to wilt, or reduce in moisture content. The material is then chopped by a forage harvester, compressed and stored under oxygen-free conditions in a silo or plastic-covered pit.

The success of silage-making depends largely upon the type of organism which thrives in the stored silage. Good quality silage is made when bacteria produce lactic acid, preserving the fodder and its nutritional value for up to six months after it is stored. The wrong type of bacteria can putrify the silage or make it acidic and unattractive to animals.

Silage making is more common in Europe and the United States than in Australia, where

weather conditions favour hay making. Silage generally provides better quality feed than hay because of its high protein levels. However, silage making requires greater skill and more machinery and equipment.

SILO

Silos are concrete or metal cylinder-like constructions for storing grain and other products. Also known as bins, they are a familiar sight on farms and in towns throughout Australia's grain-growing regions.

However, Australian farmers do not rely upon on-farm silos to store the annual harvest as extensively as their American and European counterparts do. It is common, particularly in America, for farmers to withhold their harvest to take advantage of price fluctuations. But most Australian farmers deliver their harvest im-

Silos are the most prominent features of many towns in the wheat belt.

mediately to the appropriate authority's bin at the nearby town or railway siding. Some larger farmers, wishing either to avoid lengthy queues at grain delivery points during harvest or to wait for better prices, do have silos capable of storing vast quantities of grain. These represent a substantial capital investment of up to $60 000. They hold between 500 and 1000 tonnes of grain. However, most farmers find it more economical to have a number of smaller silos for the different grades and types of grain.

Silos also house grain which is to be used for feeding livestock or as seed. These usually sit above the ground on a stand and taper at the bottom, allowing them to be emptied by gravity.

Large silos, storing up to 10 000 tonnes of grain and standing up to 30 m tall, are found at grain delivery and export points around the country. They are filled and emptied by complex elevator systems, and owned by statutory authorities such as the NSW State Rail Authority. Large tin sheds are also used as central grain storage points. In many country towns, the grain bin is the most outstanding landmark, as well as being the site of seasonal employment.

Maintenance and construction of silos is very important because of the high load they have to bear – one cubic metre of wheat weighs about 750 kg. Silos are emptied and filled from the centre to spread the stress evenly.

Some farmers also use silos for making and storing SILAGE. They are both more effective and expensive than storing silage in pits or under plastic. These silos are usually tall and thin because of the need to compact silage and exclude air. Although still not widespread in Australia, this last type of silo has become more common over the past decade.

The pride that rural people take in exhibiting their wares is as strong today as it was in 1906, when this display (left) was assembled. Pavilions around the main arena at the Royal Easter Show in Sydney (above) house elaborate displays of produce and handicrafts ranging from cakes to needlework.

SILT

Silts can cloud rivers and dams, form huge dust plumes over desert country and even get blown around the world in the aftermath of violent volcanic eruptions. Silt is made up of fragments of rock or mineral less than 0.6 mm across, that can only just by seen with the human eye. Silting is a problem in many man-made dams because streams carry the fine particles into the dam where they settle in thick deposits. Silt is so fine that it can be carried thousands of kilometres by ocean currents, eventually settling to the bottom to form siltstone or shale. Because silt will only settle in very still conditions it often forms a natural burial ground for animal or plant remains, which eventually become fossils after millions of years beneath the surface.

SILVERFISH

Silverfish are among the most primitive surviving insects. They are wingless, as were all their ancestors. Their body is torpedo-shaped, although somewhat flattened, their antennae are usually long and they have three conspicuous tails. Many are silvery, and can slip easily through fingers and wriggle along quickly, so they deserve their common name. They are nocturnal, secretive creatures, but during the night domestic species sometimes fall into sinks and baths from which they cannot climb out. Five widespread species are pests, eating materials such as paper, glue and size. One, the brownish Firebrat *Lepismodes inquilinus* (about 10 mm long), likes to live in warm kitchens and bakeries. Native species live in litter, under bark or in caves, but some are 'guests' in ant and termite nests although it is not clear why they are tolerated or how the ants or termites benefit from their presence.

SIREX WOODWASP

Woodwasps belong to a family of SAWFLIES whose larvae are woodborers. The 25-mm-long Eurasian *Sirex noctilio* was introduced into Australia, probably in the 1940s and 50s, from New Zealand, and is now widespread in the south-east. Females lay eggs in holes they bore in *Pinus radiata* and related introduced pines. At the same time they introduce the spores of a fungus which are stored in abdominal pockets on the insects. The tunnelling larvae feed largely on the growing fungus, which can kill the tree. Adult females automatically pick up the fungus as they emerge from the wood in which they developed.

The wasp is being biologically controlled by introduced parasitic wasps, and by a worm which will multiply in the grubs when present, but which can reproduce on the fungus. Females are steely-blue, and have a conspicuous 'sting' – really the egg layer – which accounts for their alternative name of horntails. Males are blue with a red abdomen (see illustration p 379).

SKELETONWEED

This plant from the Mediterranean region, *Chondrilla juncea*, has become one of the worst weeds of wheat crops in southern areas of Australia. Skeletonweed is so called because of the tangle of wiry, almost leafless stems formed by older plants. These bear scattered, stalkless yellow flowers like small dandelions. Another feature of the plant is its very strong root system which can send up additional suckers to aid its spread. If the root system is broken up, each piece can send up new shoots, so that the cultivation of land by farm machinery causes it to spread. In wheat and other cereal crops it not only competes very effectively for moisture, but its tough, wiry stems foul harvesting machinery. The worst infestations of Skeletonweed are in southern NSW, western Victoria and the southeast of South Australia, and its control in these areas costs millions of dollars annually.

Skeletonweed *is a severe problem in wheat crops in the eastern states where it gets tangled in machinery. Each plant produces about 15 000 seeds.*

SKY

The seven rainbow colours which combine to form the white light of the sun have different wavelengths. Red and yellow waves are the longest; blue, indigo and violet are the shortest. Anyone looking at the sky is seeing sunlight scattered by air molecules and further deflected by dust particles. The sky appears to be blue since the shorter wavelengths are scattered rather than the longer waves, and the human eye is less sensitive to violet light.

The intensity of the blue depends on the quantity and size of the dust particles. Most are large enough to scatter all the wavelengths of sunlight so that the colour of the sky is lightened. This is why skies appear to be darker blue when seen from places that are relatively free of dust, such as a mountain top, or when the wind is blowing from the sea.

SLAB CONSTRUCTION

One of the greatest difficulties which Australia's first European settlers encountered was the lack of softwood trees for building. Eucalypts were hard to fell, even more difficult to shape into planks, and did not even provide many regularly-shaped logs. In time, however, methods of slab construction were devised, and came into wide use, particularly in the bush.

Logs were split into roughly-shaped slabs, usually about 50 to 80 mm thick and 150 to 180 mm wide. Grooved corner posts were then erected, and in one method of construction – examples of which can be seen at Old Sydney Town in Somersby, NSW – the slabs or logs were dropped in from the top, in horizontal position, with their ends fitting the grooves. In another method, which became more common, the slabs were placed upright, with their lower ends fitting into another grooved sleeper at, or a little below, ground level. The top ends fitted into another grooved beam known as a wall-plate. Sometimes clay or plaster was applied to the inside of the walls to block the gaps between the slabs, but this often washed away in heavy rain. The roof was usually made of large sheets of bark placed on top of sloping beams, with thin logs on top to stop the bark from curling or blowing away.

SLATE

Slate was once shale or clay, changed by heat and pressure deep within the earth's crust. Usually black or bluish-grey, slate can be tinged green by chlorine left by water, or brown, red or yellow by iron oxides. Besides being able to be split into the thin sheets used for roofing and in bygone schoolrooms, slate, though strong, is soft and is easily cut into building blocks. The 'bluestone' of several old public buildings in Adelaide is slate from Mitcham and Glen Osmond, and the creamy pink stone of the Government Buildings in both Kalgoorlie and Coolgardie is also slate. It was often the only building material in areas with few trees, as at Beltana homestead (1860s) in the north Flinders Ranges. Before rich deposits, particularly at Delabole near Willunga in South Australia, began to be exploited from the 1840s, Australia imported roofing slate from Wales.

SLUGS AND SNAILS

Slugs and snails are gastropod molluscs which are adapted to living on land or in freshwater. Most of those likely to be seen on a casual stroll, or on a damp-night safari in the garden with a torch, are introduced species. Many have invaded the bush. Snails have a shell in which the body can be hidden, but slugs have no external shell, or only a small one. Most breathe by means of a 'lung', not a gill.

Many native snails are tiny – 1 mm long or less – and have yet to be named and described by scientists. They are found in a wide variety of

A fine slab hut built at Lithgow, NSW, in the 1890s by a miner. A major problem with this method of construction was the gaps between planks, which were difficult to seal.

places, but have been forced out of some former habitats by introduced species. One of the largest native snails is the Giant Panda *Hedlyella falconeri* (to 100 mm in height and diameter) of mountain rainforests in Queensland and northern NSW.

Most snails eat plants or decomposing vegetation, but the native paryaphantid snails are carnivores, and *Strangesta capillacea* of NSW attacks introduced snails. It has a thin, flattened, circular shell with a diameter of about 25 mm. Melon snails are so called because of their glossy, globular shells.

An introduced carnivorous species is the Garlic Snail *Oxychilus alliarius*, which has a flattened, circular shell about 5 mm across and smells like garlic.

The destructive European Garden Snail *Helix aspersa* has spread to many parts of the world and is the commonest species in Australian gardens. It is not the *escargot* of the gourmets,

but it is edible, and used to be sold as 'wall fish' in markets in England. Another world traveller is the Sand-dune Snail *Theba pisana* which is a major pest from time to time in South Australia.

There are very few native slugs. The best known is *Tribonophorus graeffei* (to 150 mm) which has a red triangle surrounding its breathing pore. There are, however, many introduced species, some of which are serious pests. They hide in the soil during the day and emerge at night to feed. The yellow slug, *Lehmannia flava*, which leaves a trail of iridescent slime, is probably the commonest.

There are many species, in about ten families, of snails living in inland waters, some of which are three times saltier than the sea. Many of them are important as intermediate hosts of FLUKES, and in particular the liver fluke. Unfortunately, new species are introduced from time to time with exotic fish, many thousands of which are imported annually from Asia.

The native slug Triboniophorus graeffei *is common from Sydney along the east coast to north Queensland. It is found in many different colours, and often bears a red triangle on its back. The breathing holes are clearly visible in these specimens from northern NSW.*

SNAKE

Snakes are closely related to LIZARDS, from which they are believed to have evolved. An important difference between the two groups of animals is the attachment of the lower jaw to the skull. In snakes the connecting bones are looser so that the mouth can open widely. The two halves – the right and left – are not firmly fused, but are attached to each other by an elastic ligament. Consequently a snake can swallow very large prey. As snakes often swallow living animals which may struggle as they are being eaten, the bones of their skulls have grown to give the brain full protection from below.

Snakes, unlike lizards, are virtually deaf and have no ear drums. They are, however, sensitive to some vibrations. They do not have eyelids, but a transparent part of the skin covers the cornea.

A snake's most important sense is chemical. The tongue is long, and forked, and slides into a sheath. When a snake is active its tongue is continually being flicked in and out. Each time it retracts, the tips are pushed into two pits near the front of the palate. Any particles picked up by the tongue from the surroundings are 'tasted' by

sensory cells in the pits. The tongue itself has few taste buds.

Many snakes appear to be sensitive to heat, and they may use special areas of thin skin, underlain by nerves, to detect it. Most pythons have organs on the scales of their upper lips which enable them to sense the presence and direction of warm objects – such as mammals – in front of them.

A snake's internal organs are, as would be expected, long and thin. There are few loops in the alimentary canal, and the stomach is a simple sac. The liver is long and narrow. The left lung is missing in almost all snakes, but the respiratory surface of the remaining lung extends into the windpipe in compensation. The urinary bladder has disappeared in adult snakes. Many snakes are, of course, venomous.

There are 13 families of snakes, with about 3000 species, of which about 250 are venomous to humans. In Australia there are about 160 species, in seven families, but 32 are sea snakes. Three families are completely non-venomous and the rest are either composed entirely of venomous species, or contain some that are

venomous – although relatively few of them are very dangerous.

The most primitive of Australia's snakes are the blind snakes – burrowing species which live on ants, termites and worms. Their heads are blunt, their mouths small and their eyes are reduced to a pair of dark spots under their scales, but the animals are not completely blind. Blind snakes are harmless, and their only defence seems to be the release of a foul smell, which may also help the sexes to find each other. They may be seen on the surface on warm nights.

There are about 28 species of blind snakes in Australia, with none in Tasmania, and most districts have one or more species. The largest reaches about 500 mm, although most are much smaller. They are generally pinkish or greyish.

Snakes of the python and boa family – which has about 13 Australian species – are non-venomous and kill their prey by constriction. All Australian species are pythons, although there are some boas in the Pacific islands.

There are only two species of wart or file snakes, and both occur on the north coast of Australia. They live in water and have loose and

What to do if bitten by a snake

The chances of being bitten by a snake are not very great, but the risk is there nevertheless. Modern techniques for treating bites are very effective, and even those attacked by highly venomous species stand a good chance of surviving the experience.

Essentially the approach is to delay the spread of the venom as much as possible. This is achieved by pressure bandaging, which shuts down small blood vessels and lymph channels near the surface of the skin, and stops them transmitting the poison to the rest of the body.

A victim should be kept as still as possible from the moment he or she is bitten. Vehicles should be brought to the site of the incident if at all possible. If

the victim must be carried, then the operation should be performed with as little disturbance to the bitten area as possible. Only in extreme cases should the victim walk to get help, although this may be unavoidable if he or she is alone. All victims must be taken to the nearest doctor or hospital.

The pressure technique is obviously ideal for use on limbs, where most bites occur, but it can also be used on the trunk, provided it does not constrict the victim's breathing.

Do not interfere with the bite or try to suck venom from the wound. Do not apply a tourniquet and do not try to catch the snake responsible – the result may simply be another victim.

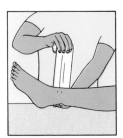

Place one end of a broad, flexible bandage over the fang marks and wind it around as firmly as you would with a sprain. If you do not have a bandage, tear a towel or some clothing into strips.

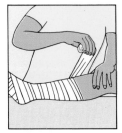

Wind the bandage as far up the bitten limb as possible. Keep the victim still and move him or her as little as you can – any disturbance will allow venom to enter the bloodstream. Be calm.

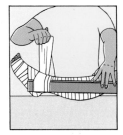

Place a piece of flat wood, or some other rigid object next to the affected limb. Bind the limb to it so that it is as immobile as possible. The bandages and splint should be reasonably comfortable.

Treat an arm in essentially the same way, using the best method available to immobilise it. Keep the victim lying down, and get him or her to help as quickly as you can. Do not remove the bandage.

MOVEMENT WITHOUT LEGS

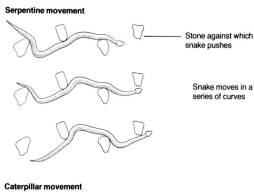

Serpentine movement

Stone against which snake pushes

Snake moves in a series of curves

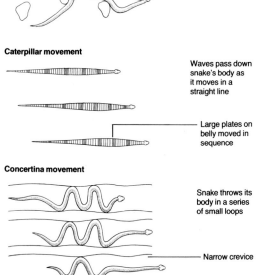

Caterpillar movement

Waves pass down snake's body as it moves in a straight line

Large plates on belly moved in sequence

Concertina movement

Snake throws its body in a series of small loops

Narrow crevice

baggy skin with a rasp-like texture which enables them to hold fish within their coils. The Colubridae family contains more than two-thirds of the world's snakes, but there are only about ten species in Australia. The Common Tree Snake *Dendrelaphis punctulatus* (to 2 m) is a common member of this group and is found from north-east Western Australia to just south of Sydney. It is active in the day and lives mainly in trees, but can often be seen on the ground. It swims well. In NSW it is usually green above and yellow below, while in the north-west it is often golden. It eats birds, frogs, some reptiles and small mammals.

The remaining families of snakes, which many workers regard as one – the Elapidae, or front-fanged land snakes – contain all of Australia's dangerously venomous snakes with hollow, front fangs, together with many species which, while venomous, are relatively harmless to humans. See VENOMOUS SNAKES, TIGER SNAKES, BROWN SNAKES, BLACK SNAKES and TAIPANS.

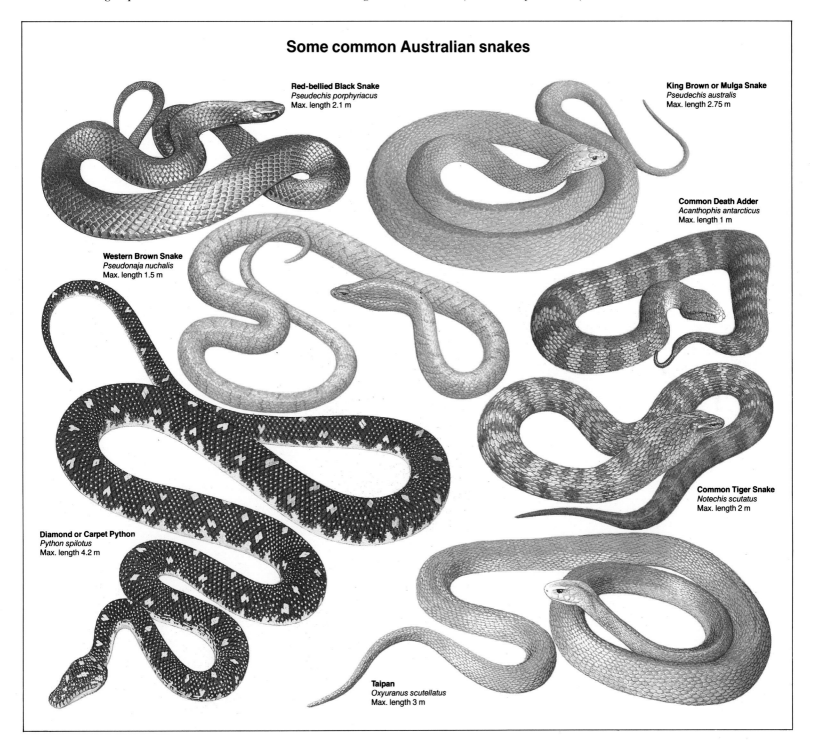

Some common Australian snakes

Red-bellied Black Snake
Pseudechis porphyriacus
Max. length 2.1 m

King Brown or Mulga Snake
Pseudechis australis
Max. length 2.75 m

Common Death Adder
Acanthophis antarcticus
Max. length 1 m

Western Brown Snake
Pseudonaja nuchalis
Max. length 1.5 m

Common Tiger Snake
Notechis scutatus
Max. length 2 m

Diamond or Carpet Python
Python spilotus
Max. length 4.2 m

Taipan
Oxyuranus scutellatus
Max. length 3 m

SNOW

Snow forms at low temperatures when water vapour changes directly into a solid without first becoming a liquid. A snowflake initially forms as a small, six-sided ice crystal which grows fastest at the six points of the crystal where exposure to additional water vapour in the air is greatest. Australia has no permanent snowfields, but winter snowfalls are frequent at high altitudes where conditions are sufficiently cold. The Snowy Mountains regularly receive snow during periods ranging from late autumn until early spring. Locations such as Spencers Creek and Charlotte Pass have annual average maximum snow depths of greater than two metres.

SNOW FIELDS

Visitors are incredulous when told that Australia has more extensive snowfields than Switzerland, if only for a short time each year. Compared with the vastness of the country however, they are little more than a dot on the map.

Snow lies continuously for at least one month each year on about 11 700 sq. km of high country. The snowline – the limit of this subalpine area – lies at about 900 m in Tasmania (6500 sq. km), at 1400 to 1500 m in Victoria (2250 sq. km), and at 1500 to 1700 m in the ACT and NSW (360 and 2600 sq. km). Enclosed within this is the alpine region at 1800 m and above, where the snow lies for four months or longer. The 1800-m contour is also the tree line, above which no trees grow. In sheltered places the snow may lie for more than eight months of the year, but there are no extensive permanent snowfields like those of Europe. The area differs also, in that much of it is high plain, with Snow Gums replacing the fir trees of other countries.

Skiing was probably introduced to Australia by Norwegian gold miners in the 1850s. Australia is said to have been the first country to form a ski club – at Kiandra in 1861 – and to introduce competitive skiing, in 1862. In NSW the resorts include Thredbo (1676 m), Perisher Valley (1676 m and often recording the state's lowest temperature) and Charlotte Pass (1750 m). In Victoria there are Hotham Heights (1862 m) and Mount Buller (1800 m). The season is from June to October. Unfortunately all ski resorts are a long way from the large cities, other than Canberra and Hobart, and few urban Australians can enjoy skiing after a day's work.

SNOW GUM

This species of eucalyptus, *E. niphophila*, grows at higher altitude in the Australian Alps than any other eucalypt, in country which is snow-covered for four to five months in winter. It usually only grows to about four to ten metres tall, and is divided at ground level into several short, sinuous trunks which have a smooth bark that is attractively streaked in shades of cream, olive-green and orange-tan. Its umbrella-like crown is made up of small, shiny, leathery leaves on bright red or yellow twigs. Like trees in other parts of the world which survive in snow, its branches and twigs are very tough, and are not easily broken by the heavy snow that can accumulate on them. The trees reach altitudes of around 1800 m on steep hillsides and ridges in the Mt Kosciusko and Bogong High Plains areas, although the broad valleys below are treeless because of the cold air that drains into them. In Tasmania the highest eucalypt is *E. coccifera*, which is also known as a Snow Gum in that state.

A cold, mid-winter's morning on the barren summit of Mt Kosciusko, Australia's highest mountain (2228 m). In the distance is Mt Townsend (2210 m).

SOIL

From the earliest times, the survival of humanity has depended on the soil. Even before humans learned the art of cultivation, they were closely related to the soil through hunting and gathering. Without soil the world would at best be covered with mosses and lichens, and there would be no humans or large animals.

But what exactly is a soil and how is it formed? There is no universally accepted definition of soil, other than the earthy material that covers land surfaces. Soils are composed of five main components: mineral particles; organic materials from dead and decaying plants, animals and animal products; water, which is the 'soil solution', containing dissolved nutrients; air which fills the spaces between particles; and living organisms, ranging in size from small animals to viruses. Soils are different from one another because they have different proportions of these components, and because their constituent particles have been affected by weathering to different degrees.

The basic building blocks of soils are created by the action of natural physical, chemical and biological forces on the rocks and minerals of the earth's surface. As rocks are weathered they split along planes of weakness, and their mineral components react chemically with water, oxygen and organic carbonic, nitric and sulphuric acids, that are formed in the atmosphere or by living organisms. Over thousands of years the rock fragments are broken down into smaller and smaller pieces and eventually all that is left is a mixture of sand, silt and clay, each with a chemical composition which depends on the minerals from which the original rock was formed. Clays are probably the most important constituent of soils, and they are formed by the weathering of crystals of the mineral Feldspar.

Eventually the sand, silt and clay are mixed with organic matter, which is the second most important constituent of soil. Weathering and other processes transform it into humus which is chemically-stable, finely-divided organic matter, like that which eventaually forms in a garden compost heap.

Soil types vary enormously, not only from place to place across the surface of the land, but also according to depth. A hole dug in the ground to reach bedrock will reveal a number of horizontal layers, each of a different soil type. This is called a soil profile, and it is often best seen in road cuttings. There are up to three main layers – also called horizons – at any place, and these have been labelled (from the surface downwards) A, B and C by soil scientists. The A layer contains organic material and plant nutrients, and it is the most weathered and leached. The B layer is moderately weathered, and it is the place where the chemicals removed from the A layer, like sodium, silicon, iron,

A SECTION THROUGH THE SOIL

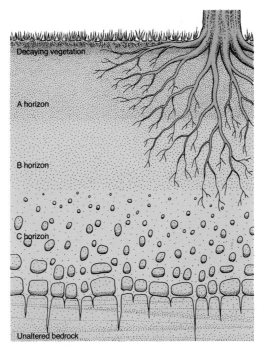

A typical soil profile showing the A, B and C layers above unaltered bedrock. The thickness of the profile can vary greatly from place to place, and three well-defined layers are not always present.

manganese, potassium and aluminium, accumulate. The C layer is a transition to the underlying layer of weathered bedrock.

The division of soil into layers is helped by water which drains down, washing chemicals with it as it goes. This process is called leaching. In higher rainfall areas, such as in the tropical north of Australia, or along the coastal ranges, the soils are generally more leached – their chemical components have been drained away by the rain over millions of years.

Australian soils are generally very old in world terms, most having been formed between one and 50 million years ago. In contrast, much of the landscape of the northern hemisphere is the result of changes that took place in recent glacial periods, less than one million years ago. In many instances Australian soils were formed under conditions that were vastly different to those that are found today. Perhaps the best example of this is provided by the widespread lateritic soils. These are soils rich in iron oxide fragments which were formed in high rainfall areas. They are found throughout Australia, even in areas which are deserts today.

Because soils are formed as the result of many complex processes, it is impossible to make any generalisations about them in Australia. Soil

depth varies enormously across the country, from a few millimetres to about 15 metres for the oldest soils. In some parts of Australia, such as the Darling River Valley, bedrock may be covered by 100 m of loose sand, gravel and clay, and the forces of erosion have often weathered the bedrock to a depth of another 100 m or more.

Deep sands are found over more than 30 per cent of Australia. The land surface in these hot, dry regions often has a protective layer called duricrust. It is formed by the precipitation of lime (calcrete), silica (silcrete) or iron (ferricrete) which makes the surface resistant to erosion. The eastern coastal ranges generally have richer soils than most of the rest of the country, but soils on steep slopes are not usually as deep and productive as soils on gentle slopes. Where soils have developed from sandstone they tend to be less fertile than those which were formed from rocks such as shale. As a general rule, alkaline soils are more common in dry regions, while acid soils are more usually found in wetter areas.

The red colour in some Australian soils is due to the chemical ferric oxide which is a strong colouring agent. Sometimes it may mingle with organic pigments to form brown or chocolate soils. Gilgai are another common feature of Australian soil, particularly in the east. These are roughly circular mounds – a metre or two across – or sometimes long parallel ridges and depressions, which form on clayey soils when the climate alternates between wet and dry seasons.

In Australia there are many areas where inferior soils give low crop yields and poor pastures, particularly in the arid central and

SIMPLIFIED SOIL MAP

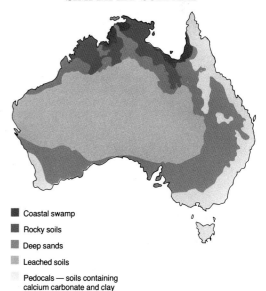

■ Coastal swamp

■ Rocky soils

■ Deep sands

■ Leached soils

□ Pedocals — soils containing calcium carbonate and clay

A simplified soil map of Australia. The continent's great age means that much of its surface is covered by very poor soils or desert sands.

western regions. Fortunately there are also areas where fertile soils give better yields, such as in southern Western Australia and on the slopes of the Great Dividing Range. The widespread poverty of Australian soils has been recognised for a long time, and perhaps no other large country has quite so many different soils which are lacking such a variety of important trace elements. Cattle fed on pastures where the soil is deficient in copper, for example, soon become unhealthy, and sheep grow a steely wool. Stock

A soldier settler, his wife and daughter, at Amiens, Queensland, in about 1920. Few men made a success of the formidable task of settling virgin land.

can become anaemic in coastal areas because the soil does not have enough cobalt in it. Different soils also suit different crops. A good soil for clover will not grow strawberries, and the ideal soil for a tea plantation is not the best for cultivating wheat.

A jungle beneath our feet

A few of the larger inhabitants to be found in a teaspoon of soil. A high-powered microscope would reveal many more.

Thirty grams of soil may contain 4000 million tiny organisms – more separate living things than there are people in the world. Just as a town is a collection of buildings filled with people, so the soil is a complex structure filled with life. One hectare of soil contains up to 10 tonnes of living organisms.

Infinitesimally small viruses, bacteria, complex protozoa, slime moulds and fungi are all active in breaking down organic matter such as decaying plants. Fungi are especially energetic in breaking down matter like decaying wood. As different fungi attack at different stages of decay, there is usually a predictable sequence in which fungi occur. Toadstools and mushrooms are the most conspicuous species of soil fungi.

There is vigorous animal life too. A hectare of soil may contain 250 million small animals. Among them are likely to be thread-like eelworms, mites, springtails, millipedes, centipedes, woodlice, hordes of fly larvae, beetles, caterpillars, ants, earthworms, slugs and snails. Some feed on decaying plant and animal material, some on the roots of living plants,

and many prey upon each other. Many spend their lives in restless movement, seeking food or mates, or searching for more favourable living conditions. The smaller animals, such as the mites, are much more numerous than the larger animals, and decompose much more soil matter. Some animals are continually migrating up and down in the soil in response to changes in temperature and moisture and the availability of food. One thing that most soil animals have in common is their dependence on moisture. If it is not available, many die. On the other hand, if the soil becomes flooded, many animals are killed while others manage to survive for a time by keeping in the little pockets of air.

The amount of life in the soil varies with the season. Many organisms most active in the spring and autumn are dormant in the extreme temperatures of winter and summer. In severe weather their numbers fall dramatically, as generally they live in the top few centimetres of the soil, close to supplies of moisture and food. Soil organisms are not evenly distributed, but congregate in colonies.

SOIL CONSERVATION

The destruction and disappearance of millions of hectares of soil is one of Australia's toughest conservation problems. The first few centimetres of soil – known as topsoil – contain many of the nutrients that plants need to germinate and grow. Over vast areas of Australia, topsoil is being blown or washed away because the ground has become bare as a result of overgrazing or overcropping. In many cases the land that is being degraded was never suitable for farming in the first place. Soils can be rebuilt, but it is a slow and costly process. Government authorities have been set up to assist farmers in preserving their land. Measures include contour ploughing, building soil banks on steep slopes, keeping land under pasture for longer periods, reducing stocking rates and planting trees and permanent pasture wherever possible.

SOLDIER SETTLEMENT SCHEME

The most ambitious scheme for settling ex-soldiers on the land was launched after World War I, operating mainly in irrigation areas along the Murrumbidgee and Murray Rivers, but also in wheat-growing areas of Western Australia, South Australia and Victoria, and in south-east Queensland. Towns and districts that were settled as part of the scheme, or at least had their development significantly boosted by it, include Barmera, Berri and Waikerie in South Australia;

Kerang, Merbein, Red Cliffs and the Mallee in Victoria; and the Murrumbidgee Irrigation Area in south-western NSW.

The federal and state governments cooperated in financing the scheme, but unfortunately it was marred by some very bad planning. In particular, many of the land blocks were too small to be profitably farmed, some were on marginal land, they were under-capitalised, and most of the soldier settlers had little or no farming experience. Consequently, of the 31 561 men who had been settled by 1929, nearly 30 per cent had already left their holdings, and another 25 per cent were in financial difficulties. Nevertheless there were many successes, particularly among wheat farmers in the Mallee. After World War II a much smaller scheme was better planned and had a higher success rate.

SORGHUM

Sorghum is Australia's most popular summer grain crop. In the past few years, farmers in subtropical areas of Queensland and northern NSW have planted up to one million hectares. Annual production is around two million tonnes.

The three sorghum types each have a particular use. Grain sorghum is grown for grain stock feed; sweet or fodder sorghum is mainly fed to cattle as silage; and broom millet – a

All sorghum contains poisons which can kill stock. Most dangerous are young crops, less than 500 mm tall, or those with fresh shoots after cutting or grazing.

member of the sorghum family – is used in the heads of brooms and brushes. The waxy-grained types of grain sorghum are also grown for their special high-quality starch, which is used in canned products like soups and stews.

In Queensland sorghum is mainly grown on the central highlands, in the Darling Downs region, west of Toowoomba, and in the Wide Bay-Burnett area between Kingaroy and Maryborough.

Each type of sorghum contains the poison cyanogenetic glucosides. This is particularly dangerous in the young, growing crop and has been known to kill grazing sheep and cattle.

SPARROW

The House Sparrow *Passer domesticus* (140– 160 mm) was introduced into Australia in the 1860s by the Australian Acclimatization Society, allegedly to control caterpillars attacking market garden crops. It was a pity that members of the society did not seem to know the difference between House Sparrows and Hedge Sparrows or Dunnocks. The latter, *Prunella modularis*, is a European insect-eating bird, while the House-Sparrow likes to eat seeds, fruit buds and some fruit, as well as insects.

The birds can certainly be pests, although it is easy to make biased estimates of the damage they do, because, being close associates of humans, they attack most vigorously those parts of a grain paddock that are nearest the house.

So far, the West Australians have been successful in excluding sparrows, but they are thriving in the eastern half of the mainland, and in Tasmania. The similar Tree Sparrow *P. montanus* (140–150 mm) which was released in Melbourne at the same time, has spread only to Gippsland and the Riverina.

SOYBEAN

Like other oilseed crops, soybeans produce oil used in margarine, salad dressings and other table oils. However, the seed's peculiar properties also enable the crop to be used in the manufacture of paints, detergents, plastics, adhesives, synthetic fibres and alternative 'meats' and 'milk'. Soybean 'milk', a common drink in Asia, is gaining popularity in Australia. It is often used instead of cow's milk by people allergic to butterfats. Similarly, soybean 'meat' is often eaten by vegetarians as a meat substitute.

Soybeans are a summer crop, grown mainly under irrigation in northern NSW and Queensland. The Darling Downs, west of Brisbane, is a major producing area, as is the Dawson-Callide region in central Queensland and the Burnett district around Kingaroy in the state's south-east. The crop's susceptibility to frost damage and its high water requirements exclude it from most other farming areas, although soybeans have been grown on the Ord River Scheme, in the far north-east of Western Australia, and in irrigated farming areas around Katherine in the Northern Territory. Soybeans are the most common oilseed crop after SUNFLOWERS. Australia's total production exceeds 90 000 tonnes. Nevertheless, Australia has to import around $25 million worth of soybean seed, oil and meal a year, mainly from the USA and South America.

The United States regularly supplies more than 50 per cent of total world soybean production. The size and quality of its crop is therefore a major factor in determining world prices for soybeans and other oilseeds.

An added incentive for farmers to produce soybeans is the plant's ability to fix nitrogen in the soil, in a similar way to leguminous crops. Like other oilseeds, the crop is also valued for its high protein meal, produced in the process of oil extraction. The meal, which is fed to stock, can contain as much as 50 per cent protein.

Soybeans, originally from Asia, have become a major crop in many western nations during this century.

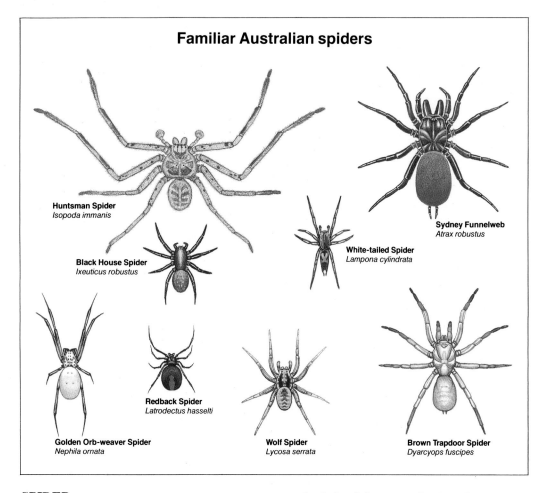

Familiar Australian spiders

Huntsman Spider
Isopoda immanis

Black House Spider
Ixeuticus robustus

White-tailed Spider
Lampona cylindrata

Sydney Funnelweb
Atrax robustus

Redback Spider
Latrodectus hasselti

Golden Orb-weaver Spider
Nephila ornata

Wolf Spider
Lycosa serrata

Brown Trapdoor Spider
Dyarcyops fuscipes

SPIDER

There are more than 30 000 known species of spiders in the world, with 1400 identified so far in Australia. It is certain that many more await discovery in the future.

A spider's body is divided into two parts connected by a narrow waist. The front part carries eight legs, fangs, and the pedipalps, which are sensory feelers, and are also used by males when mating. He places a packet of sperm on the ground, takes it up with the bulbous end of the pedipalp, and inserts it into the female. On the abdomen are the spinnerets which feed out threads of silk and which are used by some spiders to make webs. Other spiders use silk as life-lines for security when hunting, or pay out long lengths to be caught by the wind which carries them away. The gossamer which is sometimes seen on grass on damp mornings is formed from these parachute lines.

Spiders usually have eight eyes, but some have only six. Their arrangement is a useful guide to identifying different species. Males are often smaller than females, and usually have swollen tips to their pedipalps.

Spiders use book lungs – light patches underneath their abdomen – for breathing. These resemble the leaves of a book, inside a cavity opening to the air.

There are three groups of spiders in Australia. The first is made up of funnelwebs and related species which are usually robust spiders with four book lungs and huge, parallel fangs which strike downwards. These spiders are thought to be the closest in form to the first spiders. FUNNELWEB, mouse and trapdoor spiders, usually found in tunnels in the ground, are typical members of this group which is made up of about 140 species in Australia, many of them dangerous to humans.

The Tasmanian cave spider and its relatives come between the last group and the next. Their fangs are crossed at the tip and they have four book lungs. There are two Australian groups.

Advanced spiders are the 'typical' spiders with crossed fangs, and either two book lungs or none at all. There are many families, most of them with different habits. They include the familiar orb spiders and many, such as the REDBACK SPIDER, which make tangled snares. The short-legged jumping spiders, which are often piebald or brightly coloured, stalk their prey and leap on it,

using silk as a life-line. They are rarely more than 20 mm long. Ogre-faced spiders hold a rectangular net in their four front legs and drop it onto prey. They can often be found in suburban gardens under bushes, but must be looked for at night, which is the best time for spider-watching. Ogre-faced spiders, some of which are 60 mm long, are so-called because they have two very large eyes, framed with 'whiskers', staring forwards. The 5-mm long spitting spider sprays gum from its pincers over prey. The angler spiders of eastern Australia twirl a long thread with a sticky drop at the end until they catch flying insects. It is believed that the drop contains a chemical lure which resembles sex attractant chemicals which are released by the moths they prey on. The golden orb web spiders, make huge webs in forest, often across bushland trails. They are so strong that small birds sometimes get caught in them. The moderately large wolf spiders emerge from burrows to hunt on the ground, often with a brood of spiderlings hanging on.

Many spiders have painful bites. Two common species – the Sydney Funnelweb and the Redback – have caused deaths.

SPINIFEX

Australia has no direct equivalent of great natural grasslands such as the prairies, the pampas or the African savannas. However, vast areas in semi-arid regions are grasslands, but grasslands dominated by plants commonly called spinifex, which look very different to most other grasses. These plants form dense, hummock-shaped tussocks of stiff, rigid stems. In some species, as the hummock ages, the centre dies, producing a ring of smaller tussocks.

Resin is exuded from the base of leaves and forms sticky globules which harden as they dry. This resin was highly valued by Aborigines, who used it to fasten spear blades to shafts.

Spinifex species are highly inflammable and burn fiercely. Most are unpalatable to stock, although the seed heads of some species provide

Clumps of spinifex *or porcupine grass,* Triodia *and* Plectrachne *species, cover the red soil of the remote Hamersley Range in Western Australia.*

useful fodder. However, new growth is more palatable, and regular burning of spinifex in north-west Australia by graziers produces young growth which is the mainstay of the local pastoral industry.

The name 'spinifex' is a great source of confusion. The grasses described above belong to two genera – *Triodia* and *Plectachne*. Another important group of grasses, some of which are familiar because they grow on coastal sand dunes, belong to the genus *Spinifex*.

SPRING

Nothing tastes quite as refreshing and invigorating as cool, clear water flowing from a natural spring, and nothing is quite as rejuvenating as a bath in a hot spring. For centuries mineral springs have been claimed to have almost magical powers for prolonging life and bringing good health, to the point where bottled 'mineral water' has become widely accepted for daily consumption throughout Australia.

A spring is a place where underground water emerges in a stream, or where a pool of water is replenished from an underground source. In some cases there is an obvious point of emergence, but in others water simply seeps from rock. The term spring does not apply to artificial openings, such as bore holes, but in many cases artificial means are used to improve the flow of water from natural springs.

In Australia's arid outback, spring water is essential for the survival of many farms and small towns. In the Lake Eyre, Mt Isa and Roma

WATER FROM THE GROUND

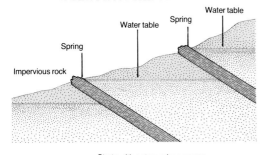

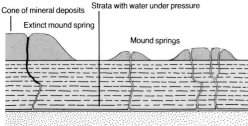

Typical hillside springs (above) and mound springs, showing how they are formed. Mound springs, which are found in the arid interior, are fed by artesian water and are more reliable than other types which can dry up during a long spell of dry weather.

regions, for example, there are many springs in which the water has travelled deep underground from a source in the Great Dividing Range. The rate of flow may vary from more than a million litres per day to a small trickle, and in many instances the water issues from the ground at up to 100°C. These hot, or thermal, springs are created when water travels for many kilometres underground through hot rocks. The water often contains dissolved mineral salts which have been leached from the surrounding strata. Sometimes these salts are deposited at the surface, building up a mound spring which resembles a small volcano on an otherwise flat desert. The mounds can be up to 40 m high and may cover several square kilometres.

However, springs do not only occur in the outback. They are very common in rolling countryside, where rocks carrying water come to the surface. Then fractured and faulted rocks serve as pipeways. The best known natural spring water is the bottled variety, misleadingly called 'mineral water'. This is, in fact, very pure water which is low in mineral salts. The purity is due to the water having travelled for short distances underground, through rocks which effectively filter the salts from it.

SQUATTER

Originally this name was applied to anyone who occupied Crown Land illegally in order to graze sheep – a practice which became very common in the 1820s and 1830s. In 1829 Governor Darling decreed that settlement would not be allowed outside the Nineteen Counties, which extended about 200 km from Sydney. However, the squatters took no notice of such restrictions. They simply set off into the wilderness, chose land, and developed it as if they owned it.

The British Colonial Office urged Governor Bourke (1831–37) to deal firmly with them. However by 1831 nearly half the colony's sheep were beyond the official boundaries, and Bourke soon realised that the colony's prosperity depended on wool from their sheep. Moreover, he pointed out in his despatches, the squatters were generally not from criminal backgrounds, in fact they included many ex-officers and young men from well-to-do English families, who were just the type of enterprising settlers the colony needed. Finally, they were so numerous and widespread that 'not all the armies of England . . . could drive back our herds within the Nineteen Counties'. These arguments were finally accepted, and in 1836 Bourke was allowed to intruduce a licensing system, by which a squatter could retain the use of his run by paying an annual fee of £10 a year. As a result of this step, and later measures by which licence-holders gained the right to buy parts of their runs, the name squatter lost its original meaning and was applied to any rich rural landowner.

SQUATTOCRACY

In colonial times, as the term SQUATTER began to mean simply any large landowner, so too the term squattocracy came to be applied to squatters as a class.

For people to think of themselves as a class they need to have common interests and a common outlook, and this was clearly the case with the squatters. Their main social contacts were with one another, they had a common style of living, and they had common economic interests, which were under threat. They had gained control of most of the best grazing land in eastern Australia, and naturally wanted to keep it. On the other hand, the authorities wanted to make land available for new immigrants, and many laws were passed to help small farmers, or SELECTORS, to buy parts of squatters' leases.

Squatters also saw that the wool which they produced was the main basis of the colonies' prosperity. They saw themselves as an upper class, an aristocracy, and the grandeur of their houses and their general life-style reinforced this view. In recent years, when the rural industries have become less important in the economy, the term squattocracy has lost much of its meaning for the mass of city-dwelling Australians, but in the predominantly pastoral regions of Australia the old class links remain strong.

STAGHORN

This large fern grows high on the trunks and branches of rainforest trees in east coastal Australia. This name, and Elkhorn, are used somewhat interchangeably for two different species, and there is a long-running debate about which should be called by which name. Both have fronds of two different types on the one plant – sterile fronds which build up in layers to form a spongy body – which can reach one metre in diameter – and fertile fronds which are straplike and forked, and carry on their undersides large, dark-brown patches of spore cases. The most common species is *Platycerium superbum*, which is most appropriately called Staghorn. Its sterile fronds die quickly, turn pale brown, and form a ball-shaped mass, while the many fertile fronds have few forks. The rarer *P. bifurcatum*, which most deserves the name Elkhorn, is a more striking plant with a basket-like mass of sterile fronds which remain green much longer, and have lobes on their upper edges. They usually only have one very large fertile frond, which hangs down, is repeatedly forked and may be up to two metres long on a large specimen. Staghorns and Elkhorns have been popular as garden plants for many years, usually being grown on a slab of wood attached to a wall, fence or tree. Their fronds are often disfigured by the native Staghorn Beetle. Plants have traditionally been removed from native forests, but wild plants are now protected.

STARLING

The love of an eccentric millionaire for birds and the words of William Shakespeare are the reasons for the presence of Starlings *Sturnus vulgaris* (210–230 mm) in the USA. He imported every European bird mentioned by the great writer. The Australian Acclimatization Societies in the 1850s were stimulated by a more down-to-earth motive – pest control.

When in small numbers, starlings can be useful because they probe pasture for insects. In Lancashire, England, they are called shepsters because they land on sheep to take ticks. When numbers are high, however, they will eat grain and attack fruits. They nest in holes, including roof spaces, and compete with native birds for nest sites, where they often congregate in large, noisy, messy roosts at night. Starlings nesting in houses will introduce bird lice and other vermin.

The Indian MYNAH is often called a 'starling' and is, indeed, the third member of the starling family in Australia.

STEER

When the First Fleet arrived in Botany Bay in 1788, its meagre livestock supplies did not include a steer. The Fleet's cattle herd – one bull, one bull-calf and four cows – escaped captivity soon after. When the expanded herd was later found along the banks of the Nepean River, it still did not contain any steers. But this situation was not remarkable – a bull could not become a steer without some human interference.

Steers are castrated male cattle between about one and three years of age. Steers of all breeds are extremely common in the modern cattle industry, and most of the steak on Australian barbecues has come from steers.

Steers are castrated to enable them to be mixed in groups or pens with other cattle. Castration also allows producers to control the characteristics that are reproduced in the herd through breeding.

Many beef producers buy steers to be fattened for resale. This enables graziers to make full use of the property's feed capacity. Young or weaner steers are usually purchased when they weigh 150 to 200 kg, and are slaughtered at 400 to 500 kg in weight.

STICK INSECT

These long-legged insects look like sticks or twigs, a deception they enhance by their surface detail, the way they stand, their colour and behaviour. Usually they are immobile, but sometimes they will sway slowly. When disturbed they fall to the ground and may stay motionless for hours. Most Australian species – there are 140, including LEAF INSECTS – are wingless. When winged, males usually have larger wings than females. The forewing is thickened. The eggs, which have little caps and are characteristic of

the species, are dropped on the ground, and the emerging nymphs crawl up any nearby plant. Stick insects chew the foliage of herbs, shrubs and trees. A few species can reach plague numbers, and then they sometimes change colour, as LOCUSTS do. The largest, the Regal Phasma *Acrophylla titan* of northern Queensland, is said to reach a length of 300 mm. It has been claimed as the world's longest insect, but a well-known record book gives that honour to an Indonesian species at 330 mm.

STINGING TREE

Some native rainforest trees belong to the same family as stinging NETTLES, and have similar stinging hairs, although they produce much more severe effects. There are three common species, all of them found only in rainforests on the east coast and ranges, although each has its own areas. The most southerly is the Giant Stinging Tree *Dendrocnide excelsa* which is a large, buttressed tree up to 30 m tall which grows from south Queensland to the far south-coast of NSW. Its large, heart-shaped, pale-green leaves are thickly felted with stinging hairs which can produce agonising and long-lasting pain from the slightest contact. The Shiny-leaved Stinging Tree *D. photinophylla*, found from the NSW north coast to north Queensland, is a medium-sized tree which sometimes has very few stinging hairs, although it is capable of causing great pain. The most notorious species, however, is Queensland 'Gympie', often hardly more than a shrub with large, crinkly, heart-shaped leaves. The slightest contact with these causes agony, accompanied by swollen, painful lymph nodes in armpit or groin, and an area of sensitised skin, painful to touch, which persists for months. There have been reports of deaths where this plant has made contact with large areas of the bodies of people or animals.

The toxin-laden hairs on Gympie Bush Dendrocnide moroides *leaves can inflict excruciating pain. Deaths have been reported in the past.*

Stick insects *can reach great lengths. The Australian record is held by a tropical species at 300 mm.*

STOCK AND STATION AGENT

This advertisement appeared in a 1935 directory: *Cobar and Jack Le Fievre. A leading town with a leading salesman. Your gain, if you connect. Your loss, if you miss. Write Him . . . Box 11. Phone Him . . . 20 (day or night). He resides on the premises. Livestock, station property, insurance, merchandise, motor cars, motors, refrigerators, Raycophone radio, station requirements. Anything required. Whatever you require, he will endeavour to acquire for you. Stock lists on application.'* Mr Le Lievre could have saved money and given only his box and telephone numbers because this was, and is, the part played by all stock and station agents. But the advertisement does not convey the power an agent can wield. He knows all the properties in a wide radius. He knows their owners, he knows their animals. He quite possibly owns the saleyard. Almost inevitably he is an auctioneer. He lends money to graziers and pastoralists. Thus he can influence, even control his clients' disposal of stock. It is at times an unpopular role. His premises, scene of many lengthy conversations every day, holds sacks of lucerne seeds and hay; saddlery, sheep dips and jetters; pumps and windmill parts. But his most valuable asset is his local knowledge.

STOCKMAN

See BUSHMAN p 106

STOCK ROUTE

As new settlements were established throughout Australia, the only convenient way to stock them was often by droving sheep and cattle long distances from the older settled areas. The DROVERS naturally looked for easy terrain, good grass, and well-spaced supplies of water, and soon regular routes, satisfying all these needs, developed. Then police stations were established, shops and saleyards built to capture the passing trade, and soon the routes became even more firmly established. A good example is the route through Yass, Gundagai and Albury to the Port Phillip district.

As the south-east became more closely settled and was serviced by railways, stock routes became less important there, but others were established for the movement of cattle in northern Australia. These included the Murranji Track from the Victoria River in the Northern Territory through Newcastle Waters and across the Barkly Tableland to Camooweal in Queensland; that from Birdsville in Queensland to the railhead at Marree in South Australia; one from the Gulf of Carpentaria through Bourke, Wilcannia and Hay to Wodonga in Victoria; and the Canning route in Western Australia, from Halls Creek to the railhead at Wiluna. Along all of these, or parts of them, government bores were provided to ensure regular watering of the stock. In more recent times the spread of railways, the establishment of meatworks in northern Australia, and increased use of motor transport have almost ended the importance of drovers and the stock routes along which their herds travelled. Particularly important has been the federal policy, initiated in 1961, of providing funds for 'beef roads', along which road trains consisting of a prime mover and up to four trailers take cattle to markets and railheads.

STOCKYARD

Stockyards are places where stock – sheep, cattle, horses or goats – are confined to be worked. That might mean anything from drenching to drafting – separating one type of stock from another.

It was in the most basic type of stockyard – an enclosure made from saplings in the bush – that Australia's unique horse sport, campdrafting, began. A skilled stockman rides into a mob of cattle held in a crude yard and separates out the types that he wants – taking calves away from

Stockmen must work long, hard hours, often in hot weather. The busiest time of year comes when animals have to be mustered for checking, drenching or selling, or when young animals are branded and castrated.

mothers, for example – and, one by one, pushes them away from the mob and into another yard. It is a job that calls for a tremendous amount of skill, both from the horse and the rider.

More complicated yards are usually built close to a shearing shed, on a sheep property, or in a central point on a cattle property. They will have a 'wing' fence which will force stock to move towards the yards. Yards are designed so that a large holding area leads to successively smaller enclosures. Gates always close behind animals to help push them on.

Central to any set of yards is a 'race' – a very narrow yard. This is only wide enough for one animal at a time, and will vary in length. The race is used for drenching stock and other simple veterinary procedures. At the end of the race will be a drafting gate, or gates, which open into small yards that lead off the race. By opening and closing the various gates, a stockman can split up a herd of animals, separating cows from calves or wethers from ewes. A stockyard on a cattle property will also have a 'crush', in which animals can be restrained while they are marked (castrated) or branded. There will probably also be a loading ramp attached to the yards so that animals can be moved directly into a truck.

The site of a stockyard must be carefully chosen. Stock confined in them are 'under pressure', so it is important to have shade trees nearby. A race is never positioned so that it runs east-west – no one wants to look into the rising or setting sun while they are working animals. Water should also be available in the yards if stock are to be kept there for any length of time.

Looking down the 'race' into an old set of stockyards in outback NSW. Years of use have provided the seeds and fertiliser needed to clothe the dusty ground with a carpet of green weeds.

STONE, BUILDING

The first durable structures in the white colonies of Australia were made from stone, and some of them are still standing today. In the last 50 years there has been a resurgence in the use of stone for building. Modern skyscrapers often have a central core of steel and concrete with a thin cladding of polished stone, particularly marble and granite. Older buildings, on the other hand, were frequently constructed from solid, sawn or rough-hewn blocks.

Many ROCK types are used as building stone, some of the most common being sandstone LIMESTONE, MARBLE, GRANITE, dolerite, BASALT, trachyte, gneiss and schist. They all have qualities of great hardness, strength, resistance to weathering, ability to be cut or shaped, resistance to damp and often beautiful internal patterns.

Sadly some stone structures are being eaten away by the acids in polluted urban air.

Many Australian cities are characterised by their beautiful stone buildings – Melbourne for its basalt or 'bluestone' (St Patrick's Cathedral), Adelaide for limestone (University and Museum) and Sydney for its famous Hawkesbury sandstone and Bowral trachyte (the GPO, Central Railway station and St Andrew's Cathedral).

Trachyte columns and arches frame the main entrance to Sydney Technical College.

Sandstone blocks in an old wall on the outside of Berrima gaol, southwest of Sydney, NSW.

Limestone – used here in the customs house at Robe, SA – often contains fossils.

Marble slabs in black and white make up this splendid floor at the old Supreme Court in Sydney.

Gneiss – sometimes known locally as granite – is used in many buildings in Bungendore, NSW.

Granite is a common around Beechworth, where this court house was built in the 1850s.

STONE FLY

Stone flies are sluggish insects, 4 mm to 50 mm long, found near streams and lakes, usually in high country. The abdomen of an adult is soft, rather flat, with parallel sides, and two, many-segmented 'tails'. The insect's wings are moderately well-veined, and are folded flat over their body. Hind wings are usually larger. They have rather weak biting mouthparts and long, thread-like antennae. Adults have an irregular, sluggish flight, and often run rather than fly when disturbed. Nymphs, which prefer clear water with a gravelly bottom, resemble wingless adults, but have gills on various parts of their body. Some are apparently carnivores, and some are vegetarians. They are an important food for fish. Stone flies were first mentioned in an English angling book 500 years ago which gave instructions for making an artificial one.

STONEFRUIT

Stonefruit – including PEACHES, APRICOTS, PLUMS, nectarines and CHERRIES – are grown in orchards around the country's temperate and subtropical regions. Main growing areas are: Victoria's Goulburn Valley, the Murrumbidgee and northern Tablelands around Armidale in NSW; the Murray Valley in South Australia and Victoria; South Australia's Barossa Valley; and Stanthorpe in Queensland's south-east. Cherry production is centred around the Adelaide Hills, and Young and Orange in NSW.

Most stonefruit are grown under irrigation, are mechanically harvested and must be chilled during growth – they need low temperatures in order to set fruit. However, they are susceptible to frosts and extreme temperatures. Fruit is usually harvested at the firm, near-ripe stage. Although storage ability varies, it is generally not long enough to supply the fresh market year-round. Apricots, for instance, which probably originated from western China, can be stored for 10 to 14 days, while nectarines and peaches can be stored for up to eight weeks. Some varieties of plums will store for up to nine weeks.

Stonefruit are sold fresh and for processing into juices, jams and glacé fruit. They are also canned and dried. Varieties such as Tilton apricots and clingstone peaches have been developed for canning. Of course, cherry and peach brandy are also popular – as is one of Australia's most famous desserts, Peach Melba.

STONE TOOL

Aborigines used stone tools for many everyday tasks such as woodworking, butchery and cleaning animal skins. Flakes of stone are easy to make, very sharp and durable. A small cutting blade or scraper only takes an expert a minute or so to fashion, and the cutting edge can be re-worked easily when it becomes blunt. Bearing in mind the fact that Aborigines have lived in Australia for at least 40 000 years, it is hardly surprising that some parts of the country are littered with many thousands of lost or discarded tools, and the numerous waste flakes produced during their manufacture.

However, most casual observers only recognise as tools highly finished articles such as edge-ground hatchet heads or spear points. Scrapers, blades and points used for everyday chores look to an untrained eye like any other scraps of stone. In fact many of the highly finished tools were intended for trade, rather than everyday use. There is little point lavishing a lot of time and effort on a scraper when it is only to be thrown away after it has done its job.

It is often very difficult – even for experts – to tell at a glance whether a tool is old or new. An efficient blade made 100 years ago looks very much like one made 10 000 years ago. Some tools are peculiar to a particular time and place – such as Bondi Points which were made mostly in southern Australia, particularly in the south-east, between 5000 and 500 years ago. Apart from the introduction of a few new types, there is a remarkable similarity between stone tools made throughout Australia over the past 40 000 years. However, these and other changes in size and the way tools were made indicate different techniques of collecting food at various times.

Tools that are found are best left where they are. Once moved they are of little value to scientists who must know *exactly* where they came from – even a matter of centimetres can make a difference. If a tool must be moved to preserve it – from a road or a ploughed field for example – then make an exact note of its position and report the find to a local museum or National Parks officer in case it is important.

STORM

Storms usually have strong winds, and are often accompanied by heavy rain, thunder, hail and – in coastal areas – high seas. Local storms occur often in Australia and take a number of different forms, including TROPICAL CYCLONES, THUNDERSTORMS, TORNADOES, WILLY WILLIES, squalls, gales and southerly busters. Severe weather associated with storms is usually experienced on a local scale, but may be part of a larger weather system. In southern Australia storms may be associated with cold fronts or intense depressions, and with thunderstorms or tropical depressions in northern Australia. Damaging storms occur most frequently in summer: nearly 40 per cent of storms in southern Australia and 50 per cent of storms in northern Australia take place during the three months from November to January. Wind speeds in Australian storms rarely exceed 200 km/h.

STRIKE

Many rural workers, particularly in the pastoral industry, belong to the Australian Workers' Union, which is some 120 000 strong. Being dispersed, they have seldom gone on extended or widespread strikes, although in 1956 Queensland shearers struck for ten months over a cut in pay – and won. A more famous strike was the shearers' strike in Queensland in 1891. The itinerant workforce was difficult to organise, but unity was achieved because of the cruel and insanitary conditions in which they often had to work on outback properties.

In the 1880s, shearers might have to sleep in three-tiered, tightly packed bunks without mattresses. Their employer dictated hours of work. Once a man had signed on, he could not leave a property before shearing was over without forfeiting all his wages. The general wage, 17s 6d for 100 sheep, could be reduced to 15 shillings if the employer considered the job badly done. Shearers formed a union in Ballarat in 1886. Within a year, after winning against squatters who wanted to reduce wages, it had 16 000 members. Between 1886 and 1889 over 3000 strikes were called, most of them minor. The defeat of a maritime strike of August and September 1890 emboldened the pastoralists to repudiate an agreement with the Queensland shearers' union on the use of non-union labour. On 6 January 1891, shearers at Logan Downs in Queensland struck. By March, shearers were gathered in camps across the state. Those at Barcaldine and Clermont were organised on military lines, and the squatters' forebodings of revolution and anarchy seemed to have been realised. Although a few militants did terrorise some of the most hated squatters and set fire to a number of woolsheds, in general the shearers were careful not to provoke attack. But militia and police raided the main camps. At their trial in Rockhampton before a blatantly biased judge, the leaders were convicted of conspiracy under a long-disused statute. Non-union labourers who flocked to Queensland met some hostility, but by June the strike had petered out. Despite the bitterness, no lives had been lost.

Between July and September 1894, shearers struck again when pastoralists reduced wages because of the rural slump. Conflict was more violent, although again no one was killed. It culminated in the burning of the steamer *Rodney* bringing scab labourers up the Darling River. Once more the ready supply of workers weakened the shearers' position and the strike eventually collapsed.

STRINGYBARK

This kind of eucalypt has bark that is thick, shaggy and fibrous over the whole trunk and at least the larger branches. The true stringybarks are a close-knit group of about 30 species found only in higher rainfall areas of eastern Australia. Apart from the bark, they can be recognised by their tight clusters of hemispherical to almost spherical woody fruits, and seedling leaves and twigs with scattered small hair tufts – a unique feature among eucalypts. In some lower mountain areas on poor stony soils, stringybarks are the commonest trees, often forming forest with other rough-barked eucalypts such as peppermints. Most yield a high-quality, durable timber, although the trees are often too small for milling and are used chiefly for fence posts on farms. The thick bark can be removed when green and unrolled into large, flat slabs. Aborigines used it for making shelters and canoes, and early white settlers frequently built the walls and roofs of their houses from it. Darwin Stringybark *E. tetradonta* is an unrelated species found across the far north of Australia, although again the Aborigines used it for similar purposes. Stringybarks are very fire-resistant, their thick, spongy bark insulating the living inner bark and sapwood from the heat of bushfires.

STUD

To the casual observer, stud animals may appear as no more than pampered pets which are groomed and trotted out each year to compete and parade in the local country and major metropolitan shows. Depending on the colour of the prize ribbon collected, they are often then sold for seemingly exorbitant sums of money.

However, stud animals represent far more than expensive showpieces. Livestock industries – whether sheep, cattle, deer, horses or goats – rely upon studs to develop and improve the breed and supply superior parent stock. Sires are most commonly sold because they have the potential to have a widespread effect on a herd's progeny. Hereford bulls led around the show ring are most probably the fathers of hundreds, if not thousands, of stud and commercial stock. It has been estimated, for instance, that about one-third of the nation's Merinos can be traced back to a leading, long-established Merino stud, Collinsville in South Australia.

Studs must register with the appropriate breed society. About 2000 studs Australia-wide are registered with the Poll Hereford Society, for example. Careful records and identification of all registered stock must be maintained by the stud's owners. Such stock usually carry the stud's name as a prefix to their own. *Mandalong Duchess*, for instance, was the name of a cow registered at the Mandalong Stud in NSW.

Traditionally stud stock have been bred and selected according to comments made by the judge at a local show, or subjective visual appraisal. However, new technology like artificial insemination and embryo transfer is having a significant effect on many studs' operations. Whereas one ram traditionally sired about 300 lambs, artificial insemination has increased this figure to a potential 100 000. Similarly, stud cows traditionally had only one calf a year, but now can be 'mother' of many more calves in a year through embryo transfer which involves flushing several fertilised eggs out of a cow and surgically implanting them in recipient cows. New technology can thus spread superior genetic qualities over vast numbers of animals – or can lead to a genetic defect having a serious widespread effect through many generations.

Aboriginal stone tools from around Australia. They are: **1** adze flake for wood working; **2** hammerstone for making stone flakes; **3** edge-ground hatchet; **4** Kimberley point made from beer bottle; **5** slab for grinding hatchet heads; **6** flake chopping tool; **7** spear tip; **8** spear tip; **9** spear barb; **10** spear barb; **11** horsehoof core.

STUMP JUMP PLOUGH

Before early farmers could set a plough to their land, years of back-breaking labour had to be performed clearing and grubbing it – hidden rocks or roots could break a plough or injure horses. The preparation could cost between two and seven times as much as the land itself. A farmer called Mullens invented a way of scratching the land by dragging a spiked, V-shaped log over the ground, but it was a poor alternative to ploughing. In the 1870s, a selector on the Yorke Peninsula, Robert Bowyer Smith, when ploughing rough ground one day broke a bolt holding the ploughshare. To his surprise, the plough went on working and, moreover, rode over stumps and stones. Smith, formerly an engineer, and his brother Clarence developed the concept of a pivoting ploughshare. On meeting an obstacle, the blade tipped back and slid over it, and was pulled back into the furrow by a weight. A prototype won first prize at the Moonta Show in November 1876, but farmers were sceptical. When Robert was unable to afford to renew the patent in 1878, Clarence perfected the idea, and thousands of the ploughs were soon in use. The invention radically altered the economics of settling virgin land, and enabled vast areas of the Mallee to be put under wheat. Adaptations of the principle are still in use today.

Stump jump ploughs are still in use today, and many farms have an old one (above) at the back of the shed. The 'Vixen', three-furrow plough (below) was made by the Smith Brothers in 1876.

ACCIDENTAL INVENTION

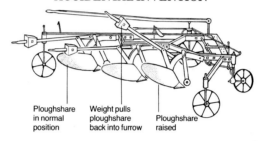

Ploughshare in normal position

Weight pulls ploughshare back into furrow

Ploughshare raised

STURT'S DESERT PEA

One of the most spectacular wildflowers of the Australian inland, this distinctive plant, *Clianthus formosus*, is South Australia's floral emblem. It grows as an annual or biennial with woolly-surfaced stems radiating from a deep taproot and lying flat on the ground. The leaves consist of five to eight pairs of leaflets with white-fringed edges, and clusters of bright scarlet flowers are held well above the stems on erect stalks. The elongated flowers are about 80 mm long, and all face outwards. Each has at its centre a shiny, convex 'boss', which may be black or in some plants merely a slightly darker red. Sturt's Desert Pea is closely related to the Darling peas *Swainsona*, but appears to have evolved its large red flowers to attract nectar-feeding birds, which transfer pollen between plants. They are found in sandy or stony ground in all arid regions of Australia, from western NSW and Queensland to the drier parts of the Western Australian coast, but in many areas have almost been eliminated by grazing animals.

The flowers open progressively over several months, from about August to November. Although highly ornamental, Sturt's Desert Pea has proved to be difficult to cultivate away from the inland. It needs a very hot, sunny position and deep, loose, sandy soil, and the seeds need to be thoroughly soaked before planting.

SUGARCANE

In coastal areas from northern NSW to north Queensland, the tall green cane stalks grow up to five metres high, overshadowing their surroundings. Around 6500 farmers grow sugarcane in a 2100-km stretch from Grafton, NSW, to Mossman in Queensland.

Cane is harvested between June and December, depending on where it is grown. Some of the crop is still burnt, or 'fired', before harvest to remove excessive leaf matter. But the introduc-

Emerald green fields of cane in north Queensland. About three-quarters of the crop is produced north of Rockhampton. The average Australian consumes 45 kg of sugar each year in food, drinks or crystals.

tion of new machinery in recent years has enabled farmers to harvest green cane. After harvest, the cane is either trucked or carted by rail to one of around 30 mills spread along the sugarbelt. The milling process removes raw sugar from the cane and produces several by-products. These include molasses, filter mud, boiler-ash and bagasse – remains of hard fibrous stalks used to fire the mill's gas boilers.

Despite low world prices over recent years, sugar is still one of Australia's most important rural exports, earning around $800 million a year. The Australian industry produces around three million tonnes of raw sugar a year, 80 per cent of which is exported.

As sugar cane grows back after harvest, farmers do not need to replant a new crop every year. In fact, over the past few years, some farmers have been able to take up to five harvests from the same crop.

SULPHUR

In the latter half of the twentieth century sulphur has become an infamous chemical because it is associated with sulphur dioxide, industrial pollution, exhaust fumes and acid rain. It is perhaps the most widely used industrial chemical, as the source of sulphuric acid, and for its use in the manufacture of fertilisers, insecticides, paper, rubber, detergents and pharmaceuticals.

Sulphur is the second most abundant non-metallic element in the earth's crust after oxygen, and it occurs in nature in combination with a group of metals which are fundamental to industrial societies. These minerals – the metallic sulphides – are exploited in the great mines of Mt Isa, Broken Hill, Cobar and Kambalda. They are the source of lead from galena, zinc from sphalerite, copper from chalcopyrite and nickel from pentlandite.

SUNDEW

Sundews are insect-eating plants which have leaves covered with tentacles, each tipped with a red gland and a drop of sticky liquid which gleams and glistens in the sunlight.

When an insect lands on the leaf it becomes trapped by the gluey liquid of the tentacles. As it struggles, the tentacles curve over and enfold the victim. In some species, the whole leaf may roll up with the victim inside.

The glands on the tentacle then secrete a digestive juice which reduces the soft tissues of the prey to a fluid which is absorbed by the plant. This process takes a number of days – the exact time depends on the size of the prey – after which the tentacles unfold and the hard parts of the insect either drop off, or are blown away.

Sundews are found world-wide, but over half the total number of species live in Australia, with the greatest concentration in the south-west. They vary considerably in size from tiny rosette-forming plants to species which scramble over other plants. In Europe, sundews are characteristically plants of bogs. Some Australian species also live in wet habitats, but the majority are found in places which may be dry for much of the year. Sundews are perennial, but may stop growing during hot, dry periods, when many species die back to a tuber which re-sprouts in the next wet season.

In their method of capturing prey, sundews are like flypaper, although the tentacles move actively to secure the prey after it has been ensnared. Another group of plants, superficially similar to sundews, also live in the south-west and north of Australia. These are covered with glands to which insects stick, but unlike sundews, they do not move to enfold their prey.

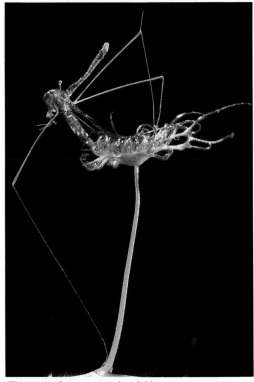

The tentacles on a sundew fold over to secure a newly-snared prey. Soon the process of absorbtion will start, which can take up to ten days to complete.

SUNFLOWER

Sunflowers are one of the most spectacular crops grown in Australia. The two-metre high plants, complete with large yellow flowers, present a familiar and picturesque scene in many parts of Queensland and NSW during October and November.

Sunflowers are a summer crop, grown mainly for their seeds, which contain oil. The high quality oil, containing polyunsaturated fats, is used to produce margarine and cooking oils. The meal left over from the oil extraction process is a valuable high-protein stockfeed, mainly sold to intensive poultry, pig and cattle producers.

Sunflowers are a very quick growing crop, taking only around four months to reach maturity. Most farmers plant the crop in late August or early September and, when necessary, use irrigation to supplement natural rainfall.

Sunflowers are the most important of the so-called oil crops grown in Australia. The main growing areas are the Darling Downs and Central Highlands of Queensland and NSW's north-west. Small areas are also planted in Victoria, South Australia and Western Australia.

The area planted to sunflowers often varies greatly between seasons depending on their market price in comparison to other summer crops. In the past few years, poor returns have resulted in sunflower plantings falling from 260 000 ha to 180 000 ha.

Fields of brilliant yellow sunflowers make an attractive sight during October and November.

SUNSHINE

The earth intercepts only one two-billionth of the sun's radiation, but it is sufficient to sustain life and to provide enough energy to maintain the circulation of the earth's atmosphere. Sunshine is made up mostly of visible light and infra-red radiation, but also contains lesser quantities of X-rays and ultra-violet rays. The latter are mostly absorbed high in the atmosphere, which is fortunate because they can penetrate human skin and cause sunburn. Even so, people should not expose themselves to too much sunshine for fear of damaging skin tissue.

Australia is aptly called 'a sunburnt country' because it receives more sunshine than most countries in the world. Its location in the subtropical belt of high pressure gives it clear skies and intense sunlight when the sun is high in the sky. Over 75 per cent of Australia has more than eight hours of sunshine per day. The sunniest parts of the country are south and western Australia, some areas of which receive an average of more than 11 hours of sunshine per day in summer. Less sunshine is received in cloudy areas such as the coastal regions of northern Australia during the wet season and in southern Australia during winter. Highland areas also receive less sunshine because of a greater frequency of cloud. The west coast and highland regions of Tasmania, for example, receive approximately five hours of sunshine per day, about 40 per cent of the maximum possible.

SEASONAL PATTERNS OF SUNSHINE

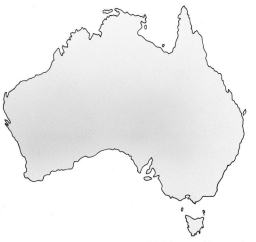

January brings over ten hours of bright sunshine each day to much of inland and western Australia. The far northern coast receives less than six hours.

July brings an average of less than three hours of sunshine to the west coast of Tasmania, and over ten hours to the north-western corner of the continent.

SUPERPHOSPHATE

Phosphate, along with nitrogen and potassium, is one of the three essential nutrients for most crops and pastures. Phosphate is removed from the ground in 'rock' form, treated with an acid and then processed into superphosphate granules. Eventually 'super' is spread on many millions of hectares of Australian crops and pastures, where it is essential for plant grown by countering nutrient deficiencies in the soil. Australia's 170 000 farmers use around three million tonnes of superphosphate every year. In an average season they spend upwards of $60 million on fertiliser.

Superphosphate was first used in Australia at South Australia's Roseworthy Agricultural College in the 1880s, when the college's first principle, J.D. Custance, realised that the fertiliser could make soils more fertile and thus improve productivity. However, it was not until the 1900s that scientists discovered the potential importance of phosphate to Australian agriculture. They found that many farming soils, especially the clay loams, were deficient in phosphorus. Trials in South Australia, Victoria and NSW showed 70 kg per hectare of super increased average yields from 540 kg to 900 kg per hectare. This led to the establishment of what are now known as the wheat belts, large tracts of medium to low rainfall country in all states except Tasmania. However, even though scientists were aware of super's importance, many farmers – either through a lack of will, funds or knowledge – did not readily accept superphosphate until the 1950s and 60s. During this period, farmers received a federal government subsidy to encourage super usage. Rapid acceptance of super followed, culminating in 1968 with a record wheat crop.

For many decades Australian farmers' supplies of super came from Christmas Island, an Australian territory in the Indian Ocean. But in late 1987, the mine was closed, leaving mainland fertiliser companies with the domestic market. Australia does have rock phosphate deposits, both in North Queensland and in Western Australia. In many remote areas of Australia superphosphate is delivered to the farm in bulk, either by truck or rail. Many farmers also make a 'super run' in their own trucks to cities and rural centres to pick up the year's supply. This job is usually carried out in the summer months between the end of harvest and crop planting. Super is usually sown along with seed, thus ensuring a healthy start for the plant.

SWAGMAN

'The old battler can usually tell at a glance what State a man belongs to by the way he carries his swag. The swags, too, are different. Matilda [Waltzing Matilda, the original phrase, meant travelling with a swag], of Victoria, has the most

Life for a swaggie was a constant battle to get work and enough food. Few, however, were willing to swap their freedom for a more secure life in the city.

taking figure. She is five or six feet [1.5 to 1.8 m] long, neat and slim, and tapering at the ends. Her extremes are tied together, and she is worn over the right shoulder and under the left arm – much in the way a lubra wears a skirt. The Bananalander's pet is short and plump. She is carried perpendicularly between the shoulder-blades, and held in position by shoulder-straps. Getting into this, to a new chum, is like putting on a tight skirt. The cornstalk [the young countryman in NSW] doesn't much care how he rolls his; merely objects to bulk and weight. Generally it is borne on a slant from right shoulder to left hip, his towel doing duty for shoulder-strap'. So wrote Edward Sorenson, from first-hand experience, in *Life in the Australian Backblocks* (1911).

The swag was a waterproof sheet – groundsheet or roof – or calico bag. Inside were blankets – dark blue so not to show the dirt, hence 'humping bluey'. There was a change of clothes, needle and thread, perhaps a billy for meat, and odds and ends of another life – a tattered book or limp dog-eared photographs. A tomahawk – precious item – was stuck in the strap of the swag. The 'nose-bag', usually a former sugar-bag, hung from the top of the swag and dangled in front on the chest. It held rations and tobacco, a tin mug and the traveller's mixing bowl for damper – a square of canvas or calico to be laid over a hollow in the ground. Most travellers carried their water-filled billy in their right hand as they walked, sometimes wrapping it in a bag to keep it cool and to stop soot rubbing off on their trousers.

Swagmen were respectable if eccentric, offer-

ing labour for rations and a little money. 'Sundowners', on the other hand, would turn up at a station at dusk, get fed, but take themselves off before dawn the next day. Itinerant workers were essential to squatters. A station at shearing time might need 100 casual hands. A swaggy could be a rouseabout for two weeks, a drover for three, pull thistles for five days and cut timber for ten. He might call at a dozen homesteads and find no work, but in the backblocks particularly he was given meat, flour, sugar and tea enough to take him to the next property, perhaps 50 or 80 km away. Squatters found it preferable to hand out supplies than to have their sheep disappear.

Journeying could be hard in the heat. The length of the journey was the distance to the next waterhole, bore or tank. Those with 'cigarette' swags, slim and light, often walked 60 km a day. After a couple of weeks' work in one place, legs would stiffen up so it was unwise to sit down until leaves had been gathered for a bit of a bed and the billy set to boil.

Many of these travellers simply loved the bush and the freedom of the life. Others were cranks, refugees from genteel society or possibly the law. A very few were women, pushing their belongings in front on a barrow or box on wheels. Some took to 'the wallaby' (track) for adventure, like the farmer-poet whose *Diary of a Welsh Swagman* (1869–1894) recounts experiences in the western half of Victoria. In 1873 he wrote: 'They have finished with the harvest so I shouldered my swag and I am tramping the road again in search of another job. I rejoin a threshing team, and work sixteen hours

Unfortunately, the only facts known about this photograph are that it was taken in 1901, somewhere in NSW. At that time many property owners relied on the labour of men like this for seasonal jobs such as harvesting or fruit picking.

a day, even threshing by moonlight. The wages are at the rate of 2d an hour...I have never received a wage in excess of 5s for a day of fifteen hours, that is at the rate of 4d an hour. The swagman's labour is required for only three months in the year, the harvesting lasts four weeks on an average, threshing for only a limited period of a week or so, and the seeding season for some seven weeks...'

At some farms, food was good and plentiful, and the family kind. Sometimes the swaggy slept with a shepherd in his hut, or in a stable with the work horses, or with a calf in a shed, its mother bellowing all night nearby. Sleeping company could be rowdy. 'It is a common custom in the Colony for hoteliers to own an adjoining farm on which swagmen are engaged for a small wage. They are expected to spend this on drinks at the hotel, and of course they do this.'

The nomads took to bicycles in the early 1900s, and the advent of the telephone meant they could fix up jobs through agents in the towns. The swagmen's ranks began to thin. But in the Great Depression, thousands 'hit the track' once more, prepared to take any work for merely their keep. A man arrested in Melbourne for begging, begged again for compassion – he had walked 1770 km for his last job. With so many competitors for the scarce rural jobs, the old-time, fiercely independent swagman finally disappeared from outback roads.

Ambrose Dyson, *The Clarion*, 1909

The swaggie: 'You might have stretched a point, and given a starving man a job!'
The cockie: 'What! a starving man – and be eaten out of house and home.'

SWALLOWS AND MARTINS

Gilbert White of Selborne, the 18th century English naturalist, could not decide whether his beloved Barn Swallows and swifts migrated, or spent the winters in suspended animation in mud-bottomed ponds. He would have been astounded to learn that some Barn Swallows *Hirundo rustica* (140–160 mm) – north Asian, not Hampshire, breeders – reached northern Australia each southern summer. Their close Australian relatives, Welcome Swallows *H. neoxena* (150 mm), breed in spring and summer in the wetter parts of Australia, to as far north as Cairns and Derby. Their familiar mud and vegetation cup-nests are often seen under over-hangs and road culverts or in hollow trees. Some migrate north after breeding, travelling as far as New Guinea. Like other swallows and martins, they are superb catchers of flying insects.

Widespread Fairy Martins *H. ariel* nest in colonies in bottle or pear-shaped mud nests, and Tree Martins *H. nigricans* (120–130 mm) nest in holes, often in tall eucalypts. Their nests are made from leaves, feathers and grass. A tree, or group of trees, will often support a colony of the birds. They are found throughout the country and migrate to New Guinea, the Solomon Islands and Indonesia.

Endemic White-backed Swallows *Cheramoeca leucosternum* (140–150 mm) roost communally in burrows in sand and gravel banks, and place their nests at the ends of their burrows. They are found in most of the southern three-quarters of Australia – not in Tasmania and the extreme south-east. In the winter time, when the weather is bad, a group may enter a torpid state for several days.

Welcome Swallows *and their cup-shaped nests are a common sight throughout most of Australia.*

SWAMP WALLABY

Swamp or Black Wallabies *Wallabia bicolor* (male mean body length, 756 mm, tail 761 mm; females smaller) differ from typical *Macropus* WALLABIES in many ways. They have, for example, fewer chromosomes and different teeth, behaviour and reproductive methods. Their upper parts are dark brown to black, and their underparts are lighter. They have a yellow cheek-stripe, but it is difficult to see on animals from the south. They hop with their head low and their tail stretched out behind. They live in thick cover in forests and heath from Cape York to Victoria, emerging to feed on grasses, herbs, and shrubs during the night. They sometimes attack crops near to their cover, but will also eat weeds such as bracken which contains cancer-causing chemicals, and the poisonous, introduced hemlock. Despite these strange tastes, they are common along the east coast.

Swamp Wallabies *– also called Black Wallabies – are common along the entire east coast of the mainland. Their small size and coarse fur makes them unattractive to shooters, so they are generally left alone.*

Black swans with their downy cygnets. Explorer George Bass thought the birds' call '... exactly resembled the creaking of a rusty ale-house sign on a windy day.

SWAN

The natural-history historian, Colin Finney, suggests that a Black Swan was the first Australian animal to be illustrated by a European – in a sketch in 1697 by Victorszoon showing the Dutch navigator Willem de Vlamingh's sailors chasing the birds in Western Australia. None of their captives reached Holland alive.

Black Swans *Cygnus atratus* (male 1300 mm, female 1200 mm) need a clear stretch of about 40 m to get airborne so they prefer larger waters. When breeding, a pen (female) encourages a chosen cob (male) to challenge another, and if she is satisfied with the outcome they approach each other, calling, necks outstretched and wings raised. After further displaying, including head dipping, they mate. Black Swans are far from mute, but then neither are Mute Swans *C. olar* (1300–1600), a European white swan, which is established in Western Australia. Their large nests of vegetation are made on reeds, small islands or bushes. Cygnets are at first brownish-grey. After moulting the birds are unable to fly

for several weeks, and often congregate in large flocks. When flying they often take up a 'V' formation in the air.

Black Swans feed on water vegetation which they gather by dipping their head, or even up-ending, but they will also graze on pasture near the lakes or marshes where they live.

SWIFT

Despite their resemblance to SWALLOWS AND MARTINS, swifts are not closely related to them – the similarities are due to convergent evolution. The family name means 'without feet', which is misleading since they do have them, small though they are. They scarcely need them, however, because everything, save caring for the nest and young, and occasionally roosting, is done in flight. They feed, mate, drink, collect nesting material, even sleep, on the wing. Some swiftlets nest in total darkness in caves in south-east Asia, and navigate by sonar. Among them are some which use saliva to make their nest – the basis for birds-nest soup. An old writer

believed that the material used was the sperm of whales and other sea creatures, and was accordingly disgusted with the cuisine.

Three species are Australian. Fork-Tailed Swifts *Apus pacificus* (160–180 mm, wing span 380–430 mm) breed in Asia and move across Australia in the summer, often following eastward-moving low pressure systems, and veering northwards along the Great Dividing Range. White-throated Needletails *Hirundapus caudacutus* (200–220 mm, wing span 500 mm) migrate from their breeding grounds in the northern hemisphere to eastern Australia and Tasmania. They can cruise at 50 to 130 km/h. Their spiny tail helps to support them as they cling to vertical surfaces. White-rumped Swiftlets *Aerodramus spodiopygius* (110–115 mm) breed in colonies in caves in north-eastern Australia, and have recently been found to be a species that uses sonar to navigate. They emit a series of sharp clicks inside their dark breeding cave. Their small cup-shaped nests consist of moss, grasses and feathers held together with saliva.

T

TADPOLE

Tadpoles – as every schoolchild knows – turn into frogs, although some in the northern hemisphere turn into newts or salamanders.

A 'normal' female frog lays her eggs – frog spawn – in water after mating. These are usually gelatinous spheres with the small round embryo in their centre. They eventually hatch to release the tadpole, a creature with a globular head, a body and a tail. At first there are external gills, but these disappear, and the animal takes in oxygen-containing water through its mouth, and passes it out through an opening on its flank – the spiracle. In time, hind legs appear just in front of the tail. Forelegs also develop, but cannot be seen externally at this stage.

The tadpole's mouth is furnished with horny lips and horny teeth with which it feeds, first on algae, and later on a wider range of food, including small animals.

The final metamorphosis to a small frog is usually quite rapid. The front legs appear, the tail is resorbed, and the animal leaves the water.

Many Australian frogs do not have a free tadpole stage: small froglets hatch out from the eggs which are often laid in burrows rather than in water. In two curiosities, the male Pouched Frog broods its tadpoles in external pouches, while those of the female *Rheobatrachus* frog develop in her stomach.

TAIPAN

Taipans *Oxyuranus scutellatus* (commonly 2 m) are probably Australia's most famous snakes, although they are rarely seen. Before the introduction of antivenom, recovery from a bite was rare. Fortunately Taipans avoid people if possible, but if cornered they strike rapidly and repeatedly. They are usually active in the day, except in very hot weather when they may hunt at night. They range from the Kimberleys, through north and east Queensland to northern NSW. They can live in a wide variety of habitats, ranging from wet tropical forests to savanna woodlands. They have a long, narrow head and a delicate neck, and relatively large eyes. Upper surfaces are light to dark brown. Fangs are very long (to 13 mm). Taipan usually feed on small mammals, and are an egg-laying species.

The Small-scaled or Fierce Snake *O. (Parademansia) microlepidota* (to 2.5 m) was, until a few years ago, confused with the Taipan. It is an inland snake, ranging from the Queensland-Northern Territory border to the Victorian-NSW border. The colour of the snake's upper body is a rich brown, and the smooth scales often have darker leading edges which may form faint cross-bands. Lower surfaces are cream. Like the Taipan, Fierce Snakes feed on small mammals and lay eggs.

Their venom is the most toxic of the venoms of all the land snakes.

TALLOW

Most people probably do not realise, as they stand under the shower, that they are in fact washing themselves with the refined remains of dead animals. Many soaps are made from tallow, ιch is, in its pure form, a tasteless, odourless, solid fat extracted from the carcases of sheep and cattle after butchering. It is also used in the manufacture of some lubricants, while edible tallow is used to make some margarines.

Tallow was first made on a wide scale in Australia in the 1840s when falling wool prices and drought resulted in sheep and cattle being boiled down for their fat. Today the 'rendering' or extraction of tallow from carcase remains is a lucrative enterprise for abattoirs throughout the country. Much of the production is exported and the material that remains after extraction is sold as meatmeal to poultry and pig producers.

TAPEWORM

Most tapeworms live as adults in the guts of animals. They are, in a sense, colonial animals. Their body consists of a head which is attached to the gut wall of their host, and one to thousands of segments behind. The segments have common nerve cords and excretory canals.

***Sheep tapeworms** cause less concern than beef tapeworms in Australia. The only certain way to avoid infestation is to cook all meat thoroughly.*

Young segments are budded off behind the head so that those furthest from the head are the oldest. When mature these may burst, releasing eggs, or the ripe segment containing eggs may be voided with faeces. The segments have no gut and absorb food through the body wall. Hence a tapeworm trap patented in the USA – a silver baited container with a spring-loaded lid attached to a string long enough to reach down from the mouth to the intestine – was ingenious, but useless for catching worms.

The larvae of tapeworms vary greatly. Some live in insects, some even in soil mites, and some a variety of vertebrates. Thus the larvae of the Beef Tapeworm *Taeniarynchus sagatinus*, which infests humans in Australia, live in the muscles of cattle as bladder worms. The cattle become infested by grazing on pasture contaminated with human faeces. People become infested by eating insufficiently cooked beef, although it is rare for this to escape the eye of an inspector at the abattoirs. Adult worms can reach a length of 22 m, and many may be made up of thousands of segments, but this is uncommon. Tapeworm often cause surprisingly little inconvenience – usually only symptoms of dizziness, abdominal pain, localised sensitivity to pain, nausea and, oddly enough, loss of appetite – but sometimes the intestine is obstructed. The HYDATID tapeworm is far more dangerous, particularly to humans, although not to the dogs which harbour the adults.

Some tapeworms have been proposed as control agents for rabbits.

TASMANIAN DEVIL

Tasmanian Devils *Sarcophilus harrisii* (male body length 652 mm, tail 258 mm, female smaller) have been treated unjustly, both by their name and in their depiction in an American cartoon series. They will kill animals, but much of their food is carrion and they are said to find it difficult to kill a rat. They also eat many corbie caterpillars, a pasture pest. Furthermore they have been described as delightful pets when reared in captivity – clean, fond of bathing and sun-baking, frolicsome and affectionate. On the other hand they are black, stocky, big-headed animals with impressive teeth and a whining growl followed by snarling cough. Their nature, like their white-marked pelt, is not entirely black.

Devils are now found only in Tasmania but, like THYLACINES, they were once common on the mainland. A popular theory is that they were displaced from there by the DINGO, which was introduced by Aborigines, but which did not reach Tasmania. They are certainly easy prey for dogs, but their mainland disappearance would have been due to competition from, not predation by, dingoes. They appear to be secure on the island, and have probably increased since European colonisation.

Devils are solitary animals, although apparently not strongly territorial. They deal with carrion very efficiently, often in company with others with whom they quarrel noisily, but rarely attack. Their powerful jaws leave nothing of the carcase, not even the skull of a kangaroo.

The gestation period is about 31 days, and the young remain at the four nipples in the backward-opening pouch for about 15 weeks, after which they are left in the den by the mother.

Tasmanian Devils are not as fierce as their name suggests. They eat mostly carrion, and are easily killed by a dog if forced into a fight.

TEA

Every year Australians drink their way through 20 million kilograms of tea – an annual brew-up of around 2.5 kg of leaf for every man, woman and child. Until the mid 1980s, Australia imported around $45 million worth of tea annually from India and Sri Lanka. But a few companies have since established a flourishing tea industry on the Atherton Tableland in far north Queensland, including local company Nerada, which sells tea in distinctive orange packs across the country. Unlike growers on the Indian sub-continent, Australian farmers plant and harvest by machine. The bushes, which yield roughly 3000 kg of leaf per hectare in full production, take four years to produce a commercial crop.

The high cost of the specialist machines used by tea growers has restricted the number of farmers able to enter the new industry. Nevertheless, it is not unrealistic to expect that by the end of the twentieth century 100 farmers on the Atherton Tablelands will supply around 70 per cent of Australia's brewing needs.

TEA TREE

This name is used for native shrubs or small trees belonging to the genus *Leptospermum*, but is sometimes also used for members of the genus *Melaleuca*. Both belong to the myrtle family, which includes the eucalypts as well. Like most members of that family they have aromatic oils in small cavities, or 'oil dots', in the leaves.

Leptospermum consists of about 80 species of small-leaved shrubs that are found over a large part of Australia, but they are most common and diverse in the higher-rainfall areas of the east. The few Western Australian species are found mainly in the far south-west.

The name Tea Tree goes back to Captain Cook, who in 1770 had his crew prepare tea from the leaves of *Leptospermum* in the belief that it would help prevent scurvy. The name is sometimes spelt Ti-tree, but this arises from confusion with a quite unrelated New Zealand plant called Ti (a Polynesian name).

Leptospermum species are recognisable by their small, simple leaves arranged spirally on the twigs. Flowers are produced singly and are stalkless, or very short-stalked, with five circular, white, pink or red petals arranged around the rim of a nectar-filled cup. Fruits are conical or hemispherical to almost spherical, often woody, and last for years. The flowers are often massed and showy. One of the best known species in southern Australia is Coast Tea Tree *L. laevigatum*, which grows mainly on coastal dunes and headlands, often in the front line of seashore vegetation, forming a small, gnarled tree which grows to about 6 m tall, with thick, flaky bark on its trunk.

The name Tea Tree is also used loosely for some species of *Melaleuca*, a larger genus, which lacks any satisfactory common name of its own.

Tea Tree oil is obtained from species of *Melaleuca*, mainly *M. alternifolia*, which is found on low, swampy ground in coastal river valleys of northern NSW. It is a small tree with thick, papery bark and very narrow, crowded leaves, rich in oil which can be obtained by steam distillation of the foliage. Tea Tree oil has valuable antiseptic properties which were recognised at least 50 years ago, and in recent years there has been a great revival of interest in its commercial potential.

TEKTITE

Tektites are small, usually black, buttons and beads of natural glass that are found in a number of scattered areas over the earth. They are found in Czechoslovakia, the Ivory Coast, south-east Asia, in the states of Texas and Georgia in the USA and over large areas of southern Australia. The Australian variety – called australites – are the most interesting because of their extraordinary regular and symmetrical shapes. These curious little objects are still a mystery to geologists and astronomers. They usually weigh between 1 and 20 g and are shaped like small buttons or dumbbells. On the average they become larger as one moves westwards across Australia. In arid country they can be found in sandhills and claypans, where they stand out as striking black objects. They are generally found in clusters. Several thousand have been found around Charlotte Waters in the Northern Territory. All the australites larger than 100 g are found in a north-south zone in the wheat belt of Western Australia. About 25 000 are known to be held in private or government collections.

Australites are about 700 000 years old, whereas tektites from other parts of the world are older. Originally it was thought that they were from volcanoes, then they were thought to have come from the moon. Now it is thought that they were formed when large meteorites hit the earth and melted on impact. The drops of molten material were sprayed over huge areas.

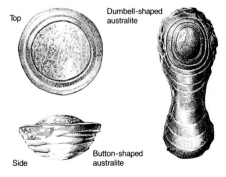

Top

Dumbell-shaped australite

Side

Button-shaped australite

Two typical australites (above) and a specimen lying where it was found at Port Campbell in Victoria. Theories that they came from the moon were discarded when astronauts brought back the first samples of moon rock, and found their composition to be quite unlike that of tektites.

TELEPHONE

The importance of telephones for Australia, with its wide scattering of population, was realised as soon as the instrument was invented. The first trunk line calls, from Adelaide to Port Augusta and from Maitland to Sydney, were made in 1878, only two years after Alexander Graham Bell had carried out his first demonstration. Exchanges were established in Brisbane, Sydney and Melbourne in 1880, and in the other capitals within several more years. Today most people take the telephone for granted, and few city dwellers realise its special importance to people in remote country areas, or the difficulties to be overcome in obtaining access to it. Some families in the far outback still make contact with their neighbours

Until coaxial cables carrying telephone lines were routed underground in the 1960s, large telegraph poles such as these near Yass in NSW carrying about 200 lines, were a familiar sight along main roads. Gangs of linesmen 10 to 20 strong maintained sections of about 80 km. The hardwood poles lasted for about 30 years. The original telegraph route between Melbourne and Sydney, built in the 1860s, had iron poles and iron wires. The line on the left was a railway signalling line.

through the Flying Doctor radio network, many others rely on radio telephone, and a smaller number have expensive services via Aussat satellites. It is also common for people to go to the expense of erecting their own line to within a specified distance of an exchange, and to rely on a 'party line' shared by several subscribers.

TEMPERATURE

Temperature is a property which varies in degree according to the flow of heat to and from a body, Thus temperature is expressed in 'degrees' on a relative scale. Several temperature scales are in common use, but Australia has adopted a version of the scale devised by Anders Celsius (1701–44) called the centigrade scale, where 0° is fixed at the freezing point of water and 100°C is the boiling point of water. (Celsius' original scale had 0° as the boiling point of water and 100° as the freezing point.) Even though temperature scales are arbitrary, they allow useful comparisons between things such as air temperatures at one place and another. For example, Australia is the world's hottest continent in terms of duration of high temperatures. Marble Bar in Western Australia experienced the longest sequence of maximum temperatures exceeding 37.8°C (100°F): 160 days, between 31 October 1923 and 7 April 1924. Likewise, the world's longest sequence of maximum temperatures above 33.2°C (90°F) was 333 days, at Wyndham, Western Australia in 1946. The highest air temperature recorded in Australia was 53.1°C (127.5°F) at Cloncurry, Queensland on 16 January 1889. By contrast, the lowest air temperature in Australia was measured in the Snowy Mountains at Charlotte Pass, near Mt Kosciusko, on 14 July 1945, when the thermometer fell to −22.2°C (−8°F).

TENCH

Tench *Tinca tinca* (to 700 mm) are thick-bodied, blunt-nosed fish of the CARP family, with orange eyes and grey or pinkish fins, which were introduced into Tasmania before 1876, and in 1876 in Victoria. They are now found in the Murray-Darling River system and in Tasmania and the south-east of the mainland. They are carnivores which, while feeding, often muddy the water. Their most characteristic feature, however, is the copious slime on their bodies to which medicinal properties were once ascribed. The tench is the 'doctor fish': other fish species are reliably reported to rub against it. Even wounded pike were believed to cure themselves by this contact and consequently, it was said, the pike, voracious though it is, would never attack its benefactor. Izaak Walton retold a story of 'a great cure done by applying a tench to the feet of a very sick man...done after an unusual manner, by a certain Jew'. The tench has good flesh, but many small bones.

TERMITE

Termites are social insects which organise their colonies in a way that is remarkably like that used by ants. Despite this similarity their nearest relatives are cockroaches. It follows that termites and ants are *not* descended from a common ancestor which was a social insect, and that this kind of behaviour and organisation has arisen and evolved independently for the two groups. It is one of the most remarkable cases of convergent evolution – as it is called – that has been discovered.

A typical termite colony contains individuals belonging to four distinct castes: primary and supplementary reproductives, workers and soldiers. The primary reproductives are the kings and queens which founded the colony. Originally they had two pairs of wings, with their forewings very similar to their hindwings, but these are lost, apart from tiny remnants, in later life. They have thick, brown cuticle over their bodies. Supplementary reproductives, which succeed the original king and queen when they die, either have no wings, or rounded wing buds. Their cuticle is not as stout as that of the primaries. In some species they may develop among a group of nymphs that has separated from the main colony to form a new one.

Worker termites are blind, sterile and wingless, and, in contrast to true ants where all workers are female, termite workers can be of either sex. Their cuticle is thin and pale, except on the jaws. They, and the reproductives, have typical biting and chewing mouthparts. Workers do the foraging, nest building and repair, egg tending and feeding of the other castes and the nymphs. In some families there are no true workers: their place is taken by nymphs called pseudo-workers, which may later become reproductive or soldiers, or remain as pseudo-workers throughout their lives.

Soldiers are sterile, and may be male or female. Their head is well developed and armoured, and may be bigger than the rest of their body. Some have heads which fit into breaks in the defences, like the brave Dutch boy's finger in the leaky dyke. Usually soldiers are blind. Some soldiers are called nasutes and specialise in a kind of chemical warfare: their heads are pear-shaped and carry a pore at the front that is linked to a large gland which makes a sticky fluid that quickly incapacitates an enemy. Sometimes a species has two kinds of soldiers, presumably each with its own duties. Soldiers are often so bizarre in their shape that they cannot feed themselves, and have to depend on the workers to help them.

Colonies also contain large numbers of eggs and nymphs. It is believed that a newly hatched nymph has the potential to develop into any caste, according to the colony's needs. Its development is probably determined by chemical

Giant termite mounds are a feature of many parts of northern Australia. Only about 15 of Australia's 300 species of termites are troublesome to humans.

A queen and workers of the notorious pest Coptotermes acinaciformis which often nests in buildings and trees. A queen may produce up to 1000 eggs per day after some years.

substances (pheromones), quantity and quality of food, and various other stimuli provided during development.

Most termites found new colonies by releasing their winged reproductives, usually after rain in warm, humid weather. Often there is synchronisation between many colonies of a particular species, as in ants, so that there is a good chance of interbreeding between colonies. The winged termites land, discard their wings and then, male following female, find the site for a new colony. Each successful pair seals itself in a small chamber and mates. The first small brood is cared for by the king and queen.

Termites feed on vegetable matter such as wood, grass, fungi and herbivore dung. Some non-Australian species make compost heaps within their nest on which they grow fungi – their food. This 'mushroom farming' has also developed among the true ants, but, once again, not in any known Australian species. Many termites harbour single-celled animals in their guts to digest cellulose since they do not have the necessary enzymes, although the termites of the largest family use bacteria, as cattle do. Inside the nest termites exchange food, *via* their mouth or anus.

Termite nests vary from species to species, and often from area to area within a species. The simplest is a system of tunnels and chambers within the wood upon which they feed. Some make an underground nest with galleries or covered runways leading to their food supplies, often many metres away. Many others make complex nests above the ground – 'ant' hills – or in trees or posts. These are very hard outside and soft within, and contain galleries and chambers – such as the royal chamber – for the various activities of the occupants. Some use the nests of other species. Within the colony the climate is remarkably stable and humid. Termites use soil, chewed wood and faeces as building materials. Often one kind of termite will use part of the mound made by another. Some mounds are believed to be over 150 years old and must have seen many dynasties of kings and queens. Some parrots often, or always, live in tunnels in large mounds.

Australia suffers from the unique, giant, 17 to 18-mm long *Mastotermes darwiniensis*, whose anatomy and biology link the termites and the cockroaches. This is a very destructive species found in the tropics, although not in high rainfall areas. Its nests are usually underground or in logs and tree stumps, and may contain over one million individuals, but the termites attack wooden buildings if they are not built on a concrete raft. The colonies lack true workers. Recently they have invaded New Guinea, but otherwise they are known only as fossils in other parts of the world.

The drywood termites, another group without true workers, live in decayed or dead wood in tree stumps, with their nests not necessarily in contact with the ground. The family contains the introduced West Indian Drywood Termite *Cryptotermes brevis* (soldiers 4 to 4.5 mm long), said to be the world's worst termite pest, because it will colonise even the smallest wooden article.

The dampwood termites, the second group of workerless termites, are found only in wood, usually in standing trees or fallen logs. *Porotermes adamsoni* is a typical example, attacking timber in contact with the ground, especially around Melbourne. They form pipes filled with mud within the timber, but do not make exposed runways across the surface.

Rhinotermitids are mainly wood-eating, subterranean species making runways, but some make mounds. Several *Coptotermes*, which are members of this family, are serious pests. The soldiers have a pear-shaped head with a pore through which they exude milky drops when disturbed, and large mandibles. Some colonies contain more than a million individuals, and the genus contains the worst pests of standing and structural timber. Most have subterranean nests, but some build mounds. The widespread, 3.5 to 6.5-mm-long *C. acinaciformes* builds mounds in the north and south-west of Australia, and only subterranean nests in other regions.

In this family the primary queens (and to a smaller extent, the secondary queens) have grossly swollen abdomens, so much so that they can scarcely move, and they are merely egg-laying machines. Their white, membranous 'skin' is stretched like a balloon with little brown islands of thicker cuticle on the surface.

The termitids make up the largest Australian termite family, and they include many types. The soldiers have either rounded or rectangular heads with stout mandibles, or nasute heads with vestigial jaws. Probably the most famous species

Dozens of termite mounds dot country in the far north-west of NSW. Studies carried out in parts of the Northern Territory estimated that the total weight of termites within a given area was almost twice that of the cattle.

is the Compass Termite *Hamitermes meridionalis* of the Northern Territory which makes three-to four-metre-tall mounds which are much longer than they are wide, and which always point north-south. The midday sun thus shines on a narrow face, so that temperature regulation in the nest is made easier. The soldiers are about 6 mm long, and the colony lives on grass and debris. The many species of the widely distributed 7-mm-long *Nasutitermes* are recognised by their relatively small nasute soldiers with rather spindly legs. Most feed on grass and debris, but some will attack timber. *N. walkeri* often makes dark nests on trees: these were once commonly called niggerheads.

Some termites obviously cause much damage to buildings and to growing timber. A survey in 1982–83 in NSW showed that 20 per cent of houses either harboured termites or had been infested before. Termite control is a task for the specialist, but regular inspections will help, as will taking care that wood does not lie around in contact with the soil for long periods. Chemical soil barriers are valuable, although environmentalists oppose the persistent insecticides which are needed for long-term protection. Some timbers are naturally resistant to some extent to most termites, such as American Redwood *Sequoia*, for example. Some other timbers are resistant to some species and not to others. JARRAH *Eucalyptus marginata* is susceptible to *Nasutitermes exitiosus* but not to *Coptotermes acinaciformes*. On the other hand termites replace the earthworm in many areas, ensuring that plant debris are buried and recycled. In some parts of the Northern Territory it was found that the biomass (total weight) of subterranean termites was 20–25 kg/ha, while that of cattle was 10–15, and kangaroos, 0.16 kg/ha. The annual consumption of the termites was 50–100 kg/ha – about the same as the cattle.

Termite trails snake their way across a tree as the insects continue their relentless quest for food. Irate soldiers rush out to defend any break in the wall.

THISTLE

This common name is used for various weedy annual, biennial or herbaceous perennial plants in the daisy family, although their flowers are not obviously daisy-like. They fall into two distinct groups, not closely related. The Sow or Milk Thistle *Sonchos oleraceus* and *S. asper* are softer plants with prickly-toothed leaves, bitter milky sap and small, yellow flower heads. They are common weeds of home gardens and waste ground and are often gathered for feeding to pets such as rabbits and canaries.

The true thistles are related to cornflowers and artichokes, and mostly have fierce, needle-like spines on their leaves, stems and flower heads. Originally coming from Europe or west Asia, most are serious weeds of grazing and crop land, and can cause great economic loss to farmers. The most common is the Black or Spear Thistle *Cirsium vulgare*, which infests grazing land and vegetable crops, mainly in higher rainfall areas. It has hairy, very spiny leaves and round heads of mauve flowers, and is often wrongly called 'Scotch Thistle'. The true Scotch Thistle is a much larger plant, *Onopordum acanthium*, which grows to about two metres in height, is less spiny and has broadly winged stems. It is common in cooler parts of Australia, in paddocks and on roadsides. Several other, more slender thistles are of importance in slightly drier areas, including St Barnaby's Thistle, Star Thistle, Saffron Thistle, Nodding Thistle and Maltese Cockspur. All are viciously spiny and have either yellow or pink flowers. A very distinctive thistle is the Variegated Thistle *Silybum marianum*, a coarse plant often seen growing on moist, fertile soil disturbed by livestock – beside farm dams, for example. Its broad shiny leaves are veined paler green and it has large mauve flower heads. It accumulates nitrates from the soil, which can poison grazing stock.

Flower heads of Spear Thistle – best unopened – can be eaten either cooked or raw. The soft interior is scooped out with a spoon after being cut open.

THRESHING

Threshing, which involves separating grain from the straw or husk, was carried out by hand well into the 18th century, although a primitive threshing machine was made in England as early as 1636. Workers made their way slowly across a barn, beating the harvested crops with sticks.

The end of this back-breaking task came in the early 1800s when steam-powered threshing machines were introduced. In Britain the first portable steam threshing machine was exhibited in 1841. These first machines were mostly too expensive for individual farmers who relied on contractors. The sheaves were fed into the threshing machine, where the seed heads were rubbed between beaters on a revolving drum. Apart from being very noisy, the whirling grain from the first powered threshing machines also damaged many farm workers' eyesight.

Now threshing is just one part of the larger mechanical operation of grain harvesting. The

A traction engine-driven threshing machine at work in 1905. Before the introduction of combine harvesters, the crop had to be cut, stacked by hand and driven to the thresher which removed the grain and bagged it.

introduction of multi-purpose harvesters in the 1940s signalled the end of the thresher. Nevertheless, they are still used in some parts of Australia – but not for their original purpose. They are now used by contractors to turn immature grain crops, usually oats, into chaff for stock feed.

Modern HARVESTERS are based on the same basic principles as the early threshers. After the crop is cut, an internal rotating drum threshes each grain from its neighbour. The threshed and cleaned grain in then conveyed to a storage bin, either on the harvester or on a nearby truck.

THRIP

Thrips are tiny, elongated insects with two pairs of strap-like wings fringed with long hairs, although *Idolothrips*, found on fallen, decaying eucalypt branches, is about 12 mm long. Their mouthparts are asymmetrical, and are used for scraping and sucking. On some plants this allows air into the plant, producing characteristic silvery streaks. Many species, such as the cosmopolitan 1.3-mm-long Onion Thrips *Thrips tabaci*, are serious pests of crops and fruit blossom. Some, which are found only in Australia and Indonesia,

form galls on such plants as sheoaks and wattles. In Britain they are sometimes called thunderflies because they seem to be attracted to sweaty skin and eyes in sultry weather. Their nymphs look like the adults, but are unusual in having two or three stages during which some metamorphosis takes place. Some even form a cocoon.

THUNDEREGG

It would be easy to imagine the colourful swirls inside a thunderegg as a drop of solid thunder. Their origins are not quite so romantic, but nonetheless fascinating. When molten lava flows from a volcano it contains a lot of gas which bubbles to the surface, just as it does in boiling mud. When the lava hardens the gas bubbles leave cavities in the rock. In lava rich in silica the cavities can fill with fluid, which in time hardens to form thundereggs. They are usually almost spherical, and are covered with a solid, thin shell of the surrounding lava. Cutting them open can reveal delicate fine horizontal or concentric bands of a variety of minerals, but usually of silica minerals like quartz, agate, chalcedony, amethyst and calcite. Often the central cavity is filled by agate in the shape of a crude star.

THUNDERSTORM

About 44 000 thunderstorms occur around the world each day, either as isolated storms, as a sequence of storms organised along a squall-line, or as a large group in multicell thunderstorms. Thunderstorms occur because moist air is lifted rapidly to altitudes usually greater than 3 km and sometimes as high as 20 km. This lifting takes place when the ground is heated by intense radiation from the sun, causing hot air to rise; when a front passes; or when moist air travels over mountainous areas. As the moist air in a thunderstorm moves upwards, it cools, forming a cumulus cloud which may grow rapidly if it is sufficiently buoyant. As further upward motion lifts water droplets above freezing levels, ice crystals form, leading to a build-up of positive electrical charges at upper levels.

In global terms, Australia has relatively few thunderstorms, largely because of the dryness of the continent. Nevertheless, warmer, more humid parts of the country do have more thunderstorms than other places. The number of days each year on which thunder is heard is about 70 in Darwin, 35 in Brisbane, 15 in dryer places like Alice Springs, Perth and Adelaide, and only 5 in colder places like Hobart. Lightning killed 126 unlucky people in Australia between 1939 and 1968.

THYLACINE

There is no doubt that there would be more rejoicing over the return of the Thylacine or Tasmanian Tiger than for all the sheep that it may – or may not – have killed. Almost every year there are reports of possible sightings, of the finding of kills that may have been their work, and even of possible lairs but, unfortunately, no specimens, living or dead, have been secured. There are even reports from time to time of fleeting glimpses of a barred animal from various parts of the mainland.

Thylacines *Thylacinus cynocephalus* (body 1.0 to 1.3 m, tail 50–65 mm) were the largest modern carnivorous marsupials. Like MARSUPIAL MOLES they provided a remarkable example of convergent evolution because they looked very much like wolves or dogs – their only claim to tigerishness were their stripes – and their skull, in particular, was very dog-like.

At the time of European settlement Thylacines were found only in Tasmania, although they once lived on the mainland and in New Guinea. Bones found in the north-west of Western Australia some 13 years ago gave an estimated age of up to about 80 years, but no other finds have been less than about 3000 years old. This evidence fits the theory that dingoes – whose oldest remains date back 3000 years – displaced Thylacines from the mainland, but that they survived on Tasmania, which dingoes did not reach.

Thylacines hunted alone or in pairs at night for wallabies and kangaroos, finding their prey, like dogs, partly at least by scent. They lived mainly in forest and open woodland where their prey was found. When white settlement became denser they turned to sheep for food and consequently a bounty was placed on their heads and they were hunted to extinction. Graziers cannot be condemned because, despite the recent claim by an English environmentalist that as Thylacines were marsupials and therefore vegetarians like kangaroos, they were efficient predators. Nevertheless there were probably few who wished to see them disappear completely, and the Tasmanian government protected them by law in 1936. Unfortunately, the last known Thylacine had already died in captivity in a Hobart zoo in the mid-1930s.

A description may help to prevent some spurious reports in the future. Thylacines were (are?) dog-like, but their long tail was thick at its base and semi-rigid. Their coarse fur was sandy brown and there were about 17 dark, parallel bars across their back and rump. Their mouth had a very wide gape. The animal's movements were rather stiff, and they did not run fast. Their pouch opened backwards.

BOLTS FROM THE BLUE

Lightning occurs when different charges (positive + and negative −) build up on different parts of a thundercloud, between one cloud and another, or between a cloud and the ground. The six most common types of lightning are shown above, in order of frequency of occurrence.

Very few photographs of living Thylacines exist. Most, like the one above, are of animals that were killed by hunters before the species became extinct.

TIDAL BORE

In some funnel-shaped estuaries, especially on coasts with great tidal ranges, the force of the incoming tide, compressed by the banks of the estuary, may be so great that it overwhelms the water flowing in the opposite direction. For a moment the meeting water-masses pause, then a wave rears up from shore to shore and travels rapidly up the estuary and, sometimes, its rivers. Such waves are called tidal bores or eagres.

Even a small bore, such as those which run up some British rivers, can be frightening: 'Equally terrible', wrote Thomas Fuller in 1662, 'with its flashings and noise to the seers and hearers, and oh, how much more then to the feelers thereof'.

There are about 60 known tidal bores in the world. The Severn bore of England has reached a height of 2.8 m but that on the Ch'ient'ang'kian of China reaches 7.5 m, and can be heard 22 km away. In comparison, Australia's only well known bore – which runs with spring tides up Broadsound, south of Mackay in Queensland – disappoints with its wave only being about one metre tall. It is possible that in some of the more remote estuaries in areas with great tidal ranges, such as on the coast of the Kimberleys, there are other Australian tidal bores waiting to be reported by travellers.

The word 'eagre' is probably related to a Saxon word for flood, while 'bore' is derived from the Old Norse for wave or billow.

Bores have even been ridden by surfers. The longest ride – on the Severn bore – was 4.73 km made in May 1982 by C.K. Wilson.

TICK

Ticks are large mites that suck the blood of animals through a tube which has harpoon-like barbs to anchor it. Hard ticks have a hard plate over part of their bodies, while soft ticks do not. Soft ticks commonly attack birds, resting in the nest between meals. The native Paralysis Tick *Ixodes holocyclus* of eastern coastal Australia, is a three-host, hard tick. The one-mm long, six-legged larva – or seed ticks – hatch from eggs laid on leaves, climb vegetation and cling to passing mammals, usually native species such as bandicoots. They feed, drop off, moult to become nymphs, attach to a second mammal – which need not be a native – feed again, drop off, moult to adult, and attach to the final host, which is often a human or a dog. If the tick is female it swells to the size of a 12-mm long pea as it swallows blood from its host. Males get some of their food from animals, and some by feeding on female ticks.

The one-host, introduced *Boophilus annulatus* of cattle spreads a disease called tick fever in northern Australia. The Cattle Tick costs Australia tens of millions of dollars annually, and is resistant to almost all pesticides.

THE DEADLY TICK

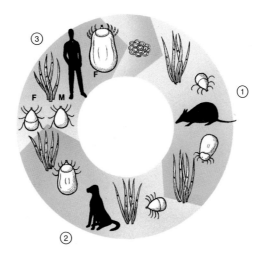

The paralysis tick has a complex life-cycle which goes though four basic stages. Egg hatches into six-legged larvae which attach to host number one, drop off and moult. Eight-legged nymph of attaches to host number two, drops off and moults again. Adult attaches to host number three, engorges and lays eggs.

TIGER-CAT

Tiger-cats are now known among biologists as Spotted-tailed QUOLLS: a sensible change because Tiger-cats and their relatives are marsupials, and do not even resemble cats. They do, however, resemble Polecats superficially, but, over the years, the 'pole' part of the original settlers' name has gone out of use.

All quolls are spotted, but this species, *Dasyurus maculatus* (male body length 380–759 mm, tail 370–550 mm, female smaller), the largest of the quolls, is the only one on which the spots extend to the tail. The background colour is reddish-brown. The animals are found in north-east Queensland, south-eastern Australia and Tasmania, mainly in rainforests and sclerophyll forests. They are carnivores which eat birds and mammals, and can kill animals as large as PADEMELONS. Captain Phillip first reported their existence, having seen them near Sydney, and called them spotted martens. He described them as very ferocious and exceedingly stubborn. They are said to have lived in the Sydney suburb of Vaucluse into the 1960s, but have generally become much scarcer since European colonisation. This is due to the loss of their habitats, shooting – since they sometimes raided poultry yards – and competition from cats and foxes.

TIGER SNAKE

Tiger snakes are found in many parts of Australia. Mainland Tiger Snakes *Notechis scutatus* (mean length 1.0 m to 1.2 m) of south-east mainland Australia are the most common cause of serious snake bites in Australia, although they are rarely aggressive if left alone. Their colour varies, but is often brownish with lighter bands, and with a light coloured belly. Unbanded specimens have been confused with brown snakes. Their main prey is frogs.

Black Tiger Snakes *N. ater* are found in south-western Australia, on islands off South Australia, including Kangaroo Island, and on Tasmania and adjacent islands.

On the Bass Strait islands the snakes often share burrows with mutton bird chicks, on which they often prey, and chick collectors are sometimes bitten. They also feed on small mammals.

Both species produce living young. They are active during the day and around dusk and dawn, but in warm weather they hunt during the night.

TIGER'S EYE

Tiger's Eye is a mysterious gemstone which looks like frozen fibres of light. It is well known at Cowell in South Australia and Wittenoom Gorge in Western Australia. It is an exotic form of blue asbestos, crocidolite. The asbestos fibres have been hardened by solutions rich in silica, as if they were covered with a hard transparent glue, but in fact the silica has penetrated into the asbestos fibres.

Harvesting the forest

One of Governor Phillip's many disappointments in 1788 lay in the fact that the trees around Sydney were practically all hard-wooded eucalypts. Compared with the softwoods of England these were difficult to fell, and even more difficult to cut into planks. However, it was not very long before the colonists discovered, growing along the coastal rivers of their new homeland, a softwood with very beautiful and valuable timber. This tree, *Toona australis*, became known as Australian Red Cedar. For about a century it was widely used for furniture and house fittings, and for a while it provided the struggling colony with a valuable export.

The trees were found mainly between the coastal ranges and the sea, from about Ulladulla in NSW to the Bloomfield River, a little south of Cooktown, in Queensland.

Phillip himself was probably the first to notice the Red Cedar, for his description of trees along the Hawkesbury fits it well. Writing to Lord Sydney early in 1793, he noted that 'the wood of some of these trees is very light, they are about the size of large walnut trees, which they resemble, they shed their leaves'.

Within the next several years many cedars were being felled in that area, and in January 1795 the ship *Experiment* left Sydney for England with a cargo which, according to the colony's young Judge-

Advocate, David Collins, included 'sixty large logs of the tree which we had named the cedar'.

Before long the high value of cedar was causing problems. Sawyers on government work were found to be falsifying their returns, so that they could keep some of the timber. Convict labourers on the Hawkesbury were said to be spending half their time looking for cedar, and men were felling trees on crown land, so depriving the government of a valuable resource.

Meanwhile the discoverers of the Hunter River in 1797 had noted an abundance of cedar trees there, and by the time a convict settlement was founded at Newcastle in 1804 a vigorous cedar trade had already developed. This provides an early example of the way in which cedar cutters often preceded permanent settlement, and indeed they were the first to explore some of the more remote districts.

A hardy, dissolute and lawless people

During Governor Macquarie's term of office (1810–22) the Illawarra region, and especially the Shoalhaven River, became the main source of cedar. From January 1812 there was frequent mention in the *Sydney Gazette* of ships arriving from there with cargoes of it.

It was in the Illawarra region too that cedar cutters gained a wide reputation as hardy, dissolute and in some cases lawless people. On 1 July 1826 the *Sydney Gazette* claimed that they often felled trees on other people's private property as well as on crown land, and

A pair of cant hooks *were used for hauling logs. Although apparently simple, they had to be made very precisely. The ends had to grip the log, but they also had drop out easily and quickly if the log started to roll.*

A team of bullocks *drags a log up a steep forest track, some time late last century. The demand for timber meant that roads had to be built to reach more and more inaccessible areas.*

'it was stated that vice of the most abominable kinds was practised among these cedar hordes, to the total annihilation of every correct principle'.

The cedar workers' wild carousing was recorded by Alexander Harris, who visited the Illawarra in the 1820s, in the book *Settlers and Convicts*. He described a small bay – very likely the boat harbour at Kiama, a main port for the shipping of cedar – which: 'presented a scene more like what may be imagined to belong to a pirate isle than anything else. On this green sward might be seen sometimes half a dozen groups, each gathered round a keg of rum, often of ten, seldom less than five gallons... A more unlicensed and reckless mob than was thus sometimes gathered at that lonely beach, prolonging day into night in their carousal until all the liquor was gone, it would be impossible to find anywhere. The bushrangers often mingled with the boisterous assembly, and took their tithe of the revelry'.

In spite of these and other unfavourable descriptions, many observers noted that there was a strong sense of honour among cedar cutters. If one group discovered a good stand of cedar, others would leave it alone; but on the other hand it was understood that one pair of sawyers should not claim the ownership of more trees than they could cut at a single pit. The surveyor and explorer John Oxley, after travelling through the Illawarra, reported that he did not hear of a single dispute between parties of cedar cutters during his journey.

Methods of extracting the timber

Cedar trees grew to a great size, and were found scattered through large areas of thick brush. Therefore transporting them either to a port for shipping as logs, or, more commonly, to places where saw-pits could be dug and the logs cut into planks, was a major problem.

The tendency was for each district to be worked through in three stages. First, trees growing close to river banks were felled and rolled into the water by manpower alone. On major rivers they were then commonly formed into rafts, with men travelling on them, living in tents and equipped with cooking facilities. Next came felling of trees close to creeks which in flood-time carried enough water to float the logs. Finally, trees far from streams were felled, cut into logs of manageable size, and moved by bullock teams. This involved the laborious cutting of tracks through the brush, and the destruction of many trees besides the precious cedars.

In general the life of the timber-getters was fraught with hardship. They led lonely, itinerant lives, were largely at the mercy of the weather, had little chance of maintaining a balanced diet, and were in constant danger from falling branches and trees, and from accidents with axes and saws.

By the early 1820s the industry was also well

established in the Port Stephens area and along the Hastings River inland from Port Macquarie. From then on the timber cutters kept moving gradually up the coast, with particularly large amounts of cedar being cut along the Manning, Nambucca, Bellinger, Richmond and Tweed Rivers. From the late 1830s, steam-powered saw mills became more numerous, and the long two-man handsaws gradually went out of use for cutting logs into planks.

In Queensland, which did not contain as much cedar as NSW, the search reached the Daintree and Johnstone Rivers by the mid-1870s. Large stands on the Atherton Tablelands were also worked from 1882, but the difficulty of getting the timber to the coast caused a great deal of it to be spoiled.

By the end of the century there was little accessible cedar left in either colony. Today many trees can still be found in dense bush, even quite close to large cities. Some cedar is still cut, but the timber now commands very high prices.

Cedar getters and their sawpit, near Dorrigo, northern NSW, in 1898. Logs felled in forest, where transport was difficult or impossible, were cut into planks on the spot by two men with a long saw. One worked on top of the log and the other underneath, in a pit.

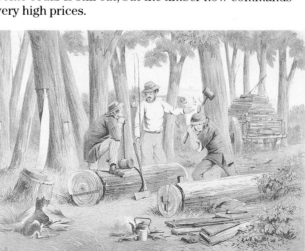

Lengths of straight-grained timber could be split using either a broad splitting axe or, as here, wedges and a maul (mallet). Fence posts, slabs, planks and shingles could all be made using this method.

TIN

Tin is the metal familiar to most people as the silvery coating on tin cans, but in its natural state it has a very different appearance. The main source of tin is the mineral cassiterite (tin dioxide), but it can also be won from stannite, or tin pyrites, which contains a mixture of copper, iron, tin and sulphur.

Tin has been mined extensively in Australia since the 1850s in all states except South Australia. Most of the mining has been in alluvial deposits which are old river gravels in which the tin is concentrated because of its considerable resistance to weathering.

Cassiterite looks like dull, red-brown pellets or sand grains in alluvial deposits, but in granitic rocks, from which it originally comes, it can be found on rare occasions in delicate and characteristic crystal shapes.

TOBACCO

The tobacco industry is one of the smallest sections of the Australian rural economy. Around 800 authorised growers produce about 12 000 tonnes, or $70 million worth of tobacco leaf a year. The industry supplies roughly 55 per cent of the tobacco required by Australian cigar and cigarette companies. The rest is imported from north and South America.

Tobacco used to be grown in several country towns in NSW, Victoria and Queensland, but over the past 20 years the industry has contracted into two main areas – north-eastern Victoria and north Queensland. Around 6000 ha are planted each year in either the King, Ovens, Kiewa or Buffalo Valleys in Victoria, or near Mareeba, Dimbulah and Mary River in north Queensland.

The Australian Tobacco Board strictly controls the area of tobacco grown under a quota system. This maintains price levels and grower returns against cheaper imports.

Tobacco is planted in rows at around 500 mm

Only one of two species of tobacco, Nicotina tabacum, is grown in Australia.

spacings. This enables machines, such as crop sprayers, to be used without damaging the precious leaf. The crop is harvested from late summer to early autumn, usually by machine. After harvest the leaf is dried by a process called 'flue-curing' which involves high pressure processing in a large 'smokeroom' or flue. The cured leaf is sold at official Australian tobacco board auctions, which run from March to September in Mareeba and Melbourne.

TOPAZ

Topaz is a delicately-coloured, popular gemstone which has the brilliance of a diamond when cut by a jeweller. It resembles quartz, but is much harder and therefore more useful. It is made up of a combination of silica, aluminium and fluorine and varies in colour from pale yellow to white, green, blue and red. Good stones are transparent or translucent.

In Australia, topaz is found mainly as small rounded pebbles among gravels in streams that cut across granite country. However, it is also found with other minerals in seams of coarse granite, or in cavities in some lavas.

Most Australian topaz comes from New England and Lightning Ridge in NSW; Beechworth in Victoria; Flinders Island in Bass Strait; north-east Tasmania; and the Mt Surprise area, West of Ingham, in north Queensland.

TORNADO

Tornadoes are the most violent of nature's storms. A tornado initially forms as an updraft in a large, rotating thunderstorm, typically 30 km in diameter. In a severe thunderstorm as much as 8000 tonnes of air travels upwards every second, creating an area of low pressure at the base of the updraft which develops into a rotating vortex. The tornado becomes evident as air rushes into the vortex and extends from the cloud base, increasing in rotational speed as it grows towards the ground. The vortex becomes visible when a funnel-cloud forms and eventually 'touches down' at the surface, bringing wind speeds as high as 480 km/h. A typical tornado stays on the ground for 10 km and carves a path of destruction 150 m wide.

While tornadoes are most prevalent in the USA, it is thought that Australia has tornadoes of comparable severity, although they are not reported as often because there are fewer people to see them. The most tornado-prone areas of Australia are south-western Australia, western Victoria and along the eastern highlands in Queensland and NSW. Most Australian tornadoes occur in remote areas. However, tornadoes do touch down in residential areas on occasions and then they cause considerable damage. A tornado struck Adelaide on 17 July 1958 and caused havoc as 200 km/h winds swept along a path 50 m wide through houses.

TORTOISES AND TURTLES

Tortoises and turtles are reptiles. Their most characteristic feature is, of course, their shell which protects them so effectively from predators. The upper, convex part is the carapace; the flatter, bottom section is the plastron. The outer surface is horny, but beneath this lie the large bony plates. These correspond to the bony structures found in the skin of many other reptiles, but in this group they are enlarged, and are joined together. The ribs are immovable, so cannot help in breathing. This is achieved by a system of bones and cartilages which move the throat and the floor or the mouth up and down. Modern species do not have teeth, but their jaws are covered by a horny beak with cutting edges.

In Australia, ocean-living species are called turtles, and all but one of the others are popularly called tortoises. In other countries they would also be called turtles, and should be called so in Australia because of their association with water. Tortoises, in the strict sense, have little to do with ponds and lakes, and this has led to some confusion in Australia among pet-owners who do not realise their 'tortoises' need water, and will wander away to find it.

All tortoises and turtles eat mainly insects, crustaceans, molluscs and small fish, but also some plants.

There are two families of non-marine turtles on the mainland, but none in Tasmania. The first contains only the Pig-nose or Pitted Shell Turtle *Carretochelys insculpta* (700 mm), which differs from all other Australian species in having flippers. They also have a fleshy snout, and their shell is covered with a thin skin.

The remaining 16 species belong in the second family. They can all draw their head back under their carapace, which they do by folding their neck once or twice, unlike, for example, Grecian tortoises which draw their head straight back. All have long necks, jointed legs which are not paddle shaped, four or five claws, and webs.

In the long- or snake-necked turtles the creatures' extended head and neck is at least as long as its shell. There are five species, the best known being probably the Eastern Long-necked Turtle *Chelodina longicollis* (shell length 250 mm) which is found from eastern Queensland to south-eastern South Australia. They live in swamps, still waters and some slow rivers, and lay ten or more eggs in a hole in the bank. Hatchlings are orange and black, but the adults are dark above and white or cream below. The largest is the Broad-shelled River Turtle *C. expansa* (500 mm) which is distributed from coastal southern Queensland to northern Victoria, mainly in the Murray-Darling River system. Oblong turtles *C. oblonga* (400 mm) of the south-west of Western Australia are so-called from the shape of their shell.

Northern Snapping Turtles *Elseya dentata*

(350 mm) are found in a broad band across northern Australia in large rivers, lagoons and oxbow lakes. They snap viciously, in one case damaging a child's finger so severely that it had to be amputated. The carapace is usually black and the plastron usually yellowish. Related Saw-shell Turtles *E. latisternum* (200 mm) are dark above, pale below and the back of their shell is serrated, except when worn away in very old animals. They range from Cape York to northern NSW, in rivers.

Western Swamp Turtles *Pseudemydura umbrina* (150 mm) are probably the country's rarest and smallest species, being found in only one or two swamps near Perth. They are regarded as Australia's most endangered reptile, and were not seen between 1839 and 1954. They have a short neck and head, the neck being covered with tubercles. They are adapted to living in waterholes, which sometimes dry out for months at a time. The swamps in which they live now form a nature reserve.

TRACKS AND TRAILS

Everyone must have seen a television naturalist minutely study the ground, approach a rock and proclaim that a certain animal is hiding below it. Invariably it is there, and it had not been placed before the cameras started rolling.

Unfortunately for Australia's tourist industry many of the country's vertebrate animals come out only at night and are timid, and often the only clues that they are in a particular area are their tracks or other 'signs', such as kills, skeletons, tufts of fur or feathers, or their SCATS.

Modern biologists, although rarely as skilled as nomadic Aborigines, often make use of animal tracks in their studies and can often reach surprisingly complicated conclusions from the signs that they find. Much of the population work on Dingoes in arid regions carried out by the CSIRO, for example, was based on tracks.

Mammals and birds leave their best tracks in mud or soft ground, and such sites provide the best examples for learning how to recognise the various kinds. A knowledge of the foot anatomy of the animals is a great help. Kangaroos and wallabies, for example, have extremely long feet. The central toe with its large claw and the somewhat shorter one beside it, also clawed, usually leave a clear print, but the others often do not. The impression, therefore, is of a long, two-toed track. If only these can be seen, then the animal was probably hopping. If five-toed 'hand' prints can be seen, then it was moving slowly on all four legs and tail. The size of the prints, and the region, will narrow the species down. Adult kangaroos obviously leave bigger prints than wallabies. If hand and foot prints are visible it is often possible to determine the sex of the animal because males have relatively larger hands than females.

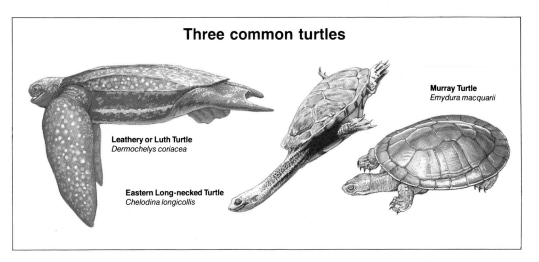

Three common turtles

Leathery or Luth Turtle
Dermochelys coriacea

Eastern Long-necked Turtle
Chelodina longicollis

Murray Turtle
Emydura macquarii

Tracks in the sand

Kangaroo hopping quickly

Emu

Goanna

Dingo

Seagull

Heron

TRACTION ENGINE

Even the largest modern farm tractors are tiny beside the vast steam-powered traction engines which served farmers until after World War I.

The first steam-powered road vehicles were designed by Nicolas Cugnot in 1769, but they proved impossible to steer and only ran for 15 minutes at 5 km/h. His project was dropped. On Christmas Eve 1801 Richard Trevithick's steam carriage achieved 15 km/h on a level stretch of road near Cambourne in Cornwall, England, but frightened horses and damaged roads restricted further development. However the potential use of steam power on the land was quickly seen and in 1854 Worcestershire iron-master James Boydell designed and made a traction engine (from which the modern term 'tractor' comes).

However, these six and ten-tonne monsters still frightened farm animals. When smaller, more nimble tractors, using the newly reliable petrol engine, were manufactured around the turn of the century, the magnificent traction engines became obsolete.

Traction engines *were used both for ploughing fields and as a source of power for agricultural machinery used in the fields, such as threshing machines.*

TREE

Trees are woody plants, generally with an indefinite life span. Throughout their lives they add new layers of wood to their trunks, and their growing points continue to be carried higher and higher above the ground. This is one of the main differences between trees and herbaceous plants and shrubs. As a tree increases in height, and spreads, its root system must also increase in size, mainly so that it can obtain enough water for the leaves in its crown, but also to obtain mineral nutrients from the soil. Trees can send their roots to a great depth, often penetrating cracks in the bedrock, and thereby obtaining an assured water supply. For this reason they are frequently the only permanent elements in the vegetation of many arid inland areas. However most Australian trees seem to be incapable of going into a completely dormant state, so that when this source of water dries up during a long drought, the tree must die.

Over much of Australia the native trees have relatively little foliage, with thick harsh-textured leaves. This is thought to be an adaptation to very hot, dry conditions – such leaves lose water at a lower rate than the thin-textured leaves of trees in high rainfall areas. The leaves are often greyish in colour because they have a thick, waxy surface layer to keep water in. Frequently the leaves also hang vertically, thereby mini-

mising the amount of heat absorbed from the powerful midday sun.

Australian trees are often short-lived, putting on rapid growth in their early stages, but soon decaying. This is particularly true of trees from semi-arid region. In some coastal and mountain areas, with high and reliable rainfall, trees seem to have much longer life spans. The age of some eucalypts has been calculated at 800 years or more, and some rainforest trees probably live much longer than that.

The great majority of Australian trees are evergreen. This contrasts with the situation in the northern hemisphere. Some deciduous species are found in hotter parts of Australia, but there are hardly any in the coolest southern mountain areas. Possibly the only exception is the deciduous beech of Tasmania, *Nothofagus gunnii*. In far-northern monsoonal vine thickets, most species of trees may be deciduous, losing their leaves in the long dry season.

Evergreen species do, of course, lose their leaves. Each leaf has only a limited life span, usually of between two and ten years (in the case of rainforest species). As new leaves are formed at the ends of twigs, the old leaves die and are shed further back.

The most important product of trees is wood which consists of countless cells, the basic structural material of which is cellulose. This is a

complex carbohydrate formed entirely from water and carbon dioxide from the air. The mineral nutrients from the soil go mainly into green tissues. One of the most amazing phenomena that takes place in all trees is the constant flow of water from the roots to the leaves, where it is lost to the air through the countless minute pores. There has been much debate about how this is achieved in very tall trees, as the lifting of water that high seems to defy the laws of physics. The answer is still uncertain.

Like all green plants, trees use up carbon dioxide from the air and photosynthesise it to form organic molecules, giving off oxygen in the process. The world's forests may be an important source of oxygen in the atmosphere, but most is thought to come from the oceans.

Trees are found in nearly all parts of Australia. Even in the far inland it is hard to find a spot where no tree is visible, although in some regions they may be only four to six metres high. The greater part of Australia is covered by forest or woodland, but being largely an arid continent, this is often rather sparse and stunted except in small areas of high rainfall near some coasts. In the drier areas trees are found only where there is likely to be moisture in the soil, such as in the beds of streams and st the bases of cliffs, rocky ravines, and sand dunes.

Of the 25 000 or more species of flowering-plants native to Australia, a considerable proportion grow to tree size, probably at least 2000. The EUCALYPTS account for a very large number of these, as nearly all of their 700 or so species can become trees given enough water and fertile soil. *Acacias* – the wattles – are an even larger group, but most of them are shrubs rather than trees.

TREE FERN

These are true ferns, but have stems which, instead of growing as a creeping or underground rhizome, make a straight, strong, erect trunk, up to 10 m or more tall in some species. The fronds are very long – uncoiling from a bud at the top of the trunk – and are arranged symmetrically around it like a green umbrella. Each frond is divided into thousands of small leaflets, giving it a lace-like pattern when seen against the sky. On the undersurface of a mature frond large numbers of brown spore-cases are found, their size and arrangement being important clues to the fern's identification. Also significant are the brown, woolly hairs or chaffy scales which clothe the thick bases of the fronds. Lower down on the trunk there is usually an interesting spiral pattern of scars left by thousands of fallen fronds, but this is often covered over by a dense mass of aerial roots.

In Australia tree ferns are found only in high-rainfall areas of the east, either in the wetter coastal rainforests or the cooler moist eucalypt forests and temperate rainforests of the Dividing

Tree ferns are found only on the east coast of the continent. Aborigines once obtained large quantities of starch from the tops of the trunks of some species which were roasted or eaten raw.

Two Lumholtz's Tree Kangaroos, *their eyes reflecting the flashlight. The idea of kangaroos in trees may seem incongruous, but they are efficient climbers, although rather less elegant when clambering down.*

Range and its foothills. In the south the most abundant tree fern is *Dicksonia antarctica*, the Soft or Brown Tree Fern, notable for its very thick trunk (up to half a metre in diameter) with masses of velvety brown hairs at the top. In damp ground in Tasmania and southern Victoria it can form an almost pure understorey to tall wet forest. Tasmanians call it 'man fern', a name which originally applied to an English fern. Most other Australian tree ferns belong to the genus *Cyathea*, these being mostly taller and more slender than *Dicksonia*. The greatest number of species is found in tropical rainforest in the coastal ranges of north Queensland. In the Blue Mountains near Sydney *Cyathea australis*, the Black Tree Fern, is a common tall species on more fertile forested slopes. It survives major bushfires and is among the first plants to put out new green growth.

TREE KANGAROO

Australian tree kangaroos are descendants of kangaroos which crossed Torres Straits when sea levels were lower. The two Australian species are peculiar to this continent, and there are five more species living in New Guinea and on adjacent islands. The group probably evolved from land-living kangaroos in New Guinea, pos-sibly to exploit the foliage of rainforests. They will, however, move over the ground, hopping and walking. Their arms are relatively long for kangaroos, and their legs relatively short and broad, and unlike those of other kangaroos, can be moved independently. Their tail is long and cylindrical, and not as tapering as those of many other species.

Lumholtz's Tree Kangaroo *Dendrolagus lum-holtzi* (male body 555 mm, tail 668 mm, females smaller) and Bennett's Tree Kangaroo *D. ben-nettianus* (635 mm, 850 mm) live in rainforests in north-east Queensland, where the former is common in patches, while the latter is sparsely distributed over an area of 70 by 50 km. Both eat fruit and leaves, and the first species also eats introduced wild tobacco. Both are active at night, spending the day curled up in trees.

TREE RING

This feature is seen in the wood of trees that have a pattern of growth in which there is a dormant period. This applies mostly to trees from cold climates of the northern hemisphere. In late spring and early summer they grow rapidly, adding a layer of wood to their trunks. As growth slows down in late summer, the wood being added becomes denser, with smaller, thicker-walled wood fibres, until finally growth stops altogether in autumn and does not resume again until spring. The denser wood laid down forms a distinct ring in a cross-section of the trunk. Because only one ring is produced each year, an obvious result is that the number of rings corresponds with the age of the tree – adding the few years it takes for the seedling tree to reach the height at which the trunk happens to be cut. In Europe and North America the ages of very old trees have been accurately measured in this way. The greatest ages established are over 3000 years for the Giant Sequoias of the California Sierras, and over 4000 years for the far smaller Bristlecone Pines of the Rocky Mountains. Ring counts are done on pencil-like cores of wood running from the bark to the centre of the trunk, which are obtained with a special drill which does not harm the tree.

In Australia, with its mostly warmer climate, few native trees show a pattern of growth with complete dormancy in winter, and hence they do not have well-developed growth rings. Many introduced trees such as pines and oaks, how-ever, still develop growth rings even when planted in moderately warm areas. Except in the coldest mountain areas, all the native Eucalypts make repeated flushes of growth, often most vigorously in autumn and winter, and the same goes for many other native trees. In the moun-tains of southern Tasmania some of the unique conifers such as Huon Pine and King Billy Pine do form clear-cut annual rings, allowing their ages to be measured. These are very slow-growing trees, with successive rings sometimes only half a millimetre apart. The largest Huon Pines measured have been found to be over 2000 years old, and are believed to be Australia's oldest living trees.

Annual rings *can be counted on the trunk of this Norfolk Island Pine. This is not possible on many native species, which do not have regular growth patterns.*

Trees of the Australian countryside

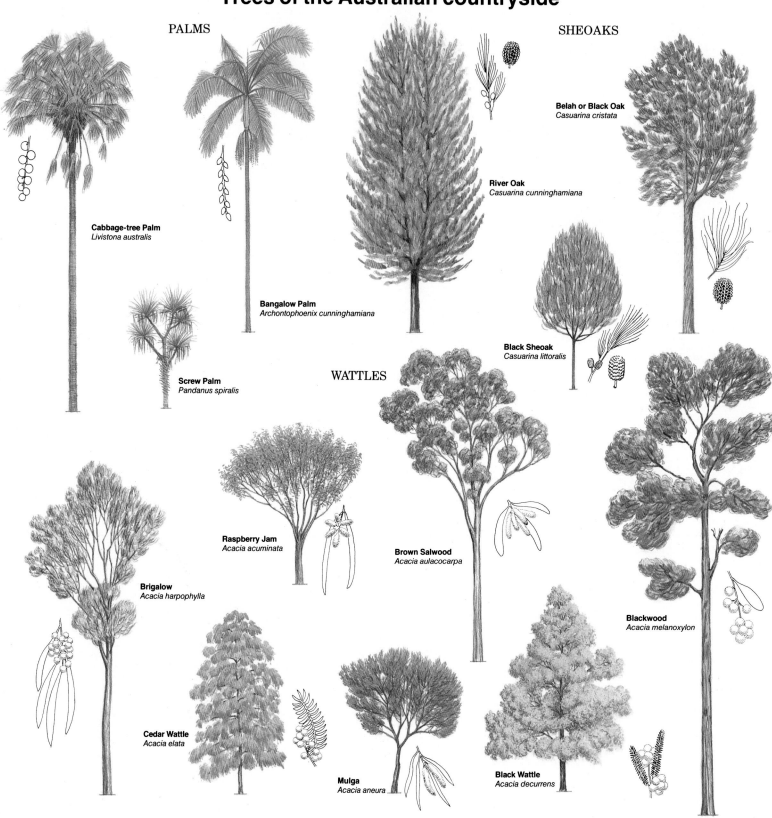

PALMS

SHEOAKS

Cabbage-tree Palm
Livistona australis

Bangalow Palm
Archontophoenix cunninghamiana

Screw Palm
Pandanus spiralis

Belah or Black Oak
Casuarina cristata

River Oak
Casuarina cunninghamiana

Black Sheoak
Casuarina littoralis

WATTLES

Raspberry Jam
Acacia acuminata

Brown Salwood
Acacia aulacocarpa

Brigalow
Acacia harpophylla

Cedar Wattle
Acacia elata

Mulga
Acacia aneura

Black Wattle
Acacia decurrens

Blackwood
Acacia melanoxylon

RAINFOREST TREES

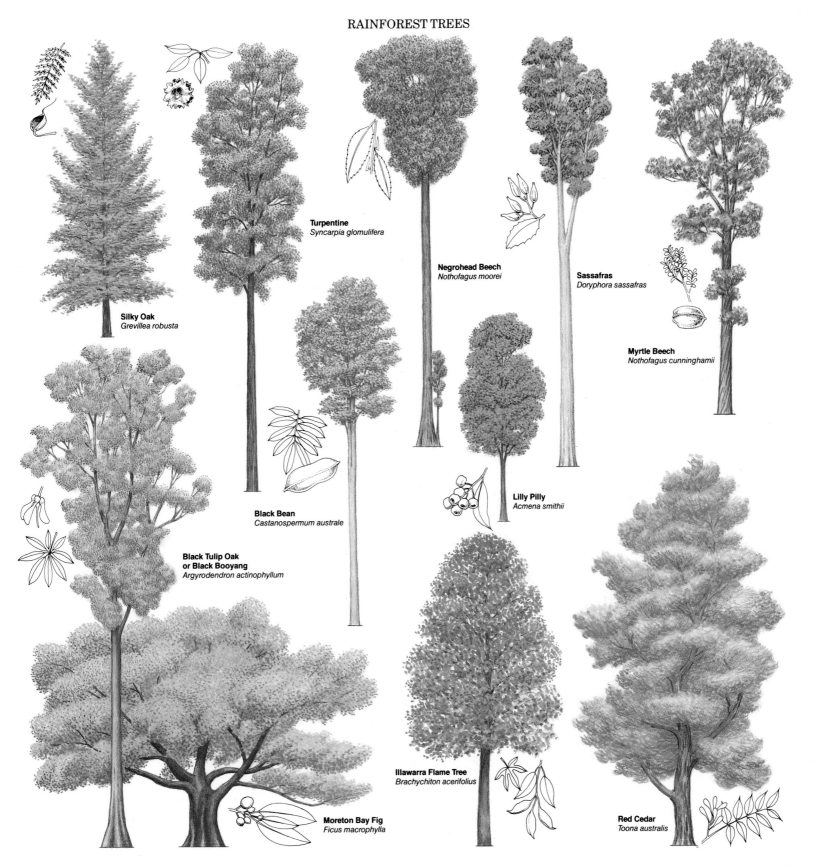

Silky Oak
Grevillea robusta

Turpentine
Syncarpia glomulifera

Negrohead Beech
Nothofagus moorei

Sassafras
Doryphora sassafras

Myrtle Beech
Nothofagus cunninghamii

Black Bean
Castanospermum australe

**Black Tulip Oak
or Black Booyang**
Argyrodendron actinophyllum

Lilly Pilly
Acmena smithii

Moreton Bay Fig
Ficus macrophylla

Illawarra Flame Tree
Brachychiton acerifolius

Red Cedar
Toona australis

EUCALYPTS

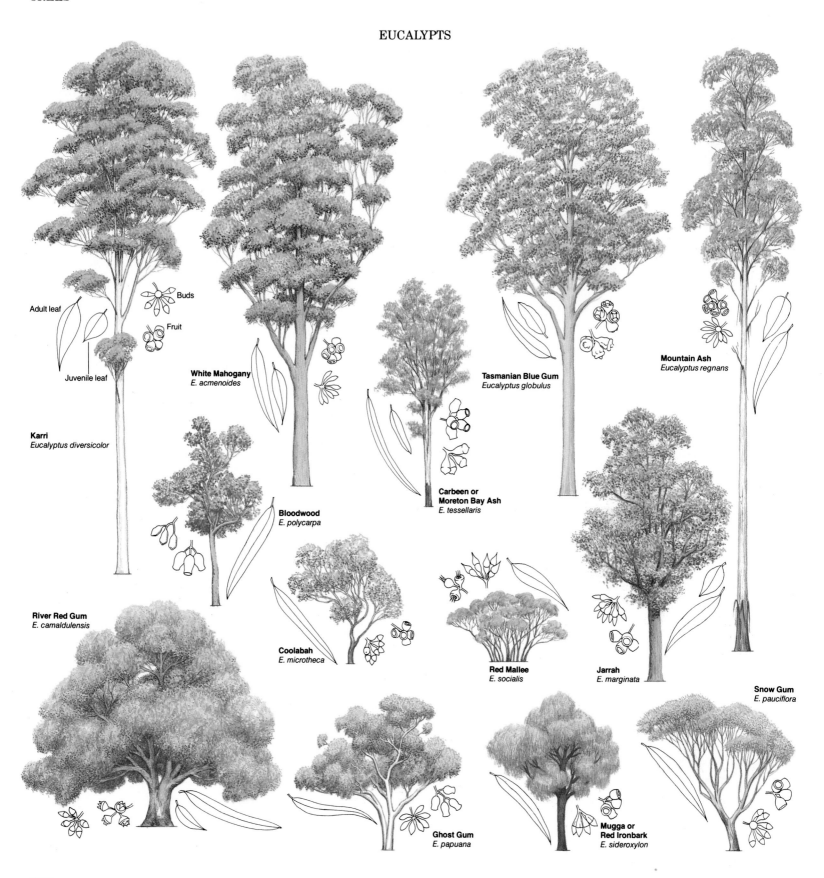

Adult leaf

Buds

Fruit

Juvenile leaf

Karri
Eucalyptus diversicolor

White Mahogany
E. acmenoides

Bloodwood
E. polycarpa

River Red Gum
E. camaldulensis

Coolabah
E. microtheca

**Carbeen or
Moreton Bay Ash**
E. tessellaris

Tasmanian Blue Gum
Eucalyptus globulus

Mountain Ash
Eucalyptus regnans

Red Mallee
E. socialis

Jarrah
E. marginata

Snow Gum
E. pauciflora

Ghost Gum
E. papuana

**Mugga or
Red Ironbark**
E. sideroxylon

CONIFERS

OTHER TREES

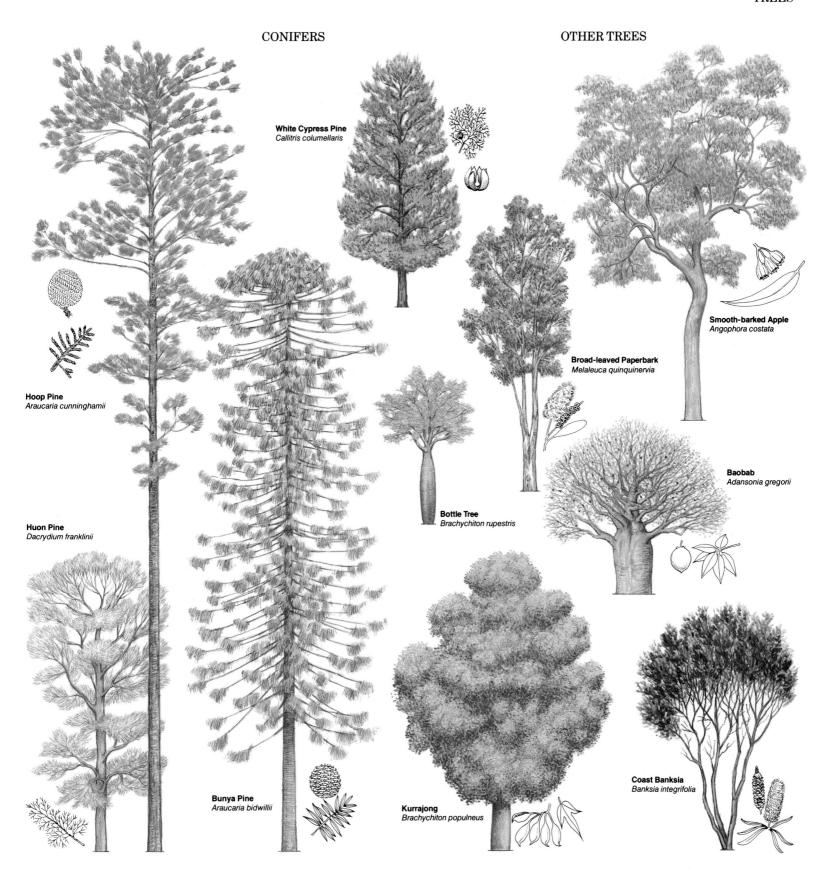

White Cypress Pine
Callitris columellaris

Hoop Pine
Araucaria cunninghamii

Huon Pine
Dacrydium franklinii

Bunya Pine
Araucaria bidwillii

Bottle Tree
Brachychiton rupestris

Kurrajong
Brachychiton populneus

Broad-leaved Paperbark
Melaleuca quinquinervia

Smooth-barked Apple
Angophora costata

Baobab
Adansonia gregorii

Coast Banksia
Banksia integrifolia

TRIGGERPLANT

Triggerplants are well known for their unique method of pollination. A 'trigger' or column rises from the throat of the flower and is bent downwards, below the petals at most times. When stimulated by an insect visitor to the flower – or by a curious observer with a grass stalk – the trigger moves rapidly through an arc, so that the top of it strikes the insect. Both the anthers and stigma are situated at the top of the trigger. If the anthers are mature when the trigger is tripped then pollen is deposited on the insect. The stigma normally matures after the anthers. If the anthers have already discharged their pollen then, when the top of the trigger strikes an insect visitor, pollen, deposited on visits to other flowers, may be transferred from the insect to the receptive stigma, thus achieving cross-fertilisation. After each tripping of the trigger, it returns to the cocked position ready for further visitors.

Triggerplants take many forms, from tiny ephemeral herbs, to quite large plants. Often they are found in vast numbers so that large areas may be carpeted with flowers.

Most of the roughly 140 species are found in Australia, although a handful are found outside the continent. Although triggerplants can be seen in most regions of Australia, the greatest variety – more than 90 species – grow in the south-west.

A REMARKABLE TRAP

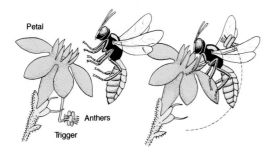

Petal

Anthers

Trigger

An unsuspecting insect visitor springs a triggerplant's *extraordinary trap. Each insect either takes a dab of pollen away with it on its back, or leaves a sample of pollen on the plant to cross-fertilise it.*

TROPICAL CYCLONE

Tropical cyclones – called hurricanes or typhoons elsewhere in the world – are intense low-pressure weather systems occurring in the tropical regions of Australia. They are characterised by strong winds, a spiral cloud band which may be 400 to 800 km in diameter, and a calm, cloudless eye in the centre of the cyclone. About 70 tropical cyclones occur around the globe each year. In Australia an average of about nine cyclones form off the northern coast annually and, of these, about five or six cross the coast. Most tropical cyclones occur between January and March, but the 'tropical cyclone season' extends from November to April. The paths of tropical cyclones can be quite erratic, some crossing the coast more than once before finally petering out.

A tropical cyclone forms initially with a lot of cloud growth. Air pressure continues to fall if conditions such as ocean temperature and upper air patterns are favourable, and eventually air starts to swirl around the low pressure centre causing strong winds. At this stage, the cyclone is called a tropical depression and, by convention, is not considered a fully-fledged tropical cyclone until sustained wind speeds exceed 63 km/h. In a mature tropical cyclone, surface winds swirl towards the centre of the cyclone and are swept upwards in the eye-wall clouds, sometimes to heights of 20 km where they flow outwards. It is estimated that two million tonnes of air are transported upwards every second in the eye-wall clouds of a mature tropical cyclone. By contrast, in the eye itself – which may be 10 to 50 km in diameter – there is dry, subsiding air – a stark contrast to the devastating winds and torrential rain elswhere in the storm.

The most destructive cyclone in Australia's history was Cyclone Tracy which struck Darwin on Christmas Day 1974. The cyclone started as a cloud mass 500 km north-east of Darwin, but it intensified and started to move until by 10 pm on Christmas Eve it was 40 km away and travelling directly towards Darwin at a speed of about 6 km/h. Cyclone Tracy struck Darwin in the early hours of Christmas Day and winds of up to 217 km/h battered the city for five hours. The combination of destructive winds and torrential rain (estimated at 100 mm per hour as the cyclone passed) almost totally destroyed the city, killed 65 people and injured another 140. Tropical Cyclone Tracy eventually dissipated as it travelled across the Gulf country of northern Queensland.

TROPICAL FRUIT

The northern coastal regions of Australia suit the production of a wide range of tropical fruits. But until recently, the only areas in which large scale developments had taken place were along the Queensland coast, in northern NSW and around the Gascoyne River in Western Australia (near the town of Carnarvon).

However, the introduction of new irrigation technology and an increasing availabilty of transport have led to the development of new areas. These include far north Queensland, including some of Cape York Peninsula, The Ord River in WA, and near Darwin and Katherine in the Northern Territory. The Burdekin Dam scheme, south of Townsville, has, like the Ord before it, made several thousand hectares of land suitable for tropical fruits.

The main exotic fruit area is the triangle from Townsville to Cooktown to the Atherton Tablelands in far north Queensland. More than one million mangosteen, sapodilla and jackfruit trees have been planted there, and the fruit will be sent to the main markets in the southern states over the next few years.

The main tropical fruits are BANANAS, PINE-APPLE, AVOCADOES and MANGOES. Other exotic fruits include PAPAYS, LYCHEES, guavas, custard apples, mangosteens, persimmons, carambolas, and rambutans.

These fruit have been chosen by a small, but ever-growing number of farmers eager to find riches from 'the right crop at the right time'. However, with just 16 million people, the Australian market is comparitively small and unable to absorb large quantities of new varieties of fruit. Nevertheless, the country's immigrant population, particularly those from Asia and South America, are potential buyers for many of the newer fruits.

TROUT

Trout and salmon belong to a family whose natural range is restricted to temperate parts of the northern hemisphere, although various species have been introduced into other regions. The fish have small scales, a lateral line, a dorsal fin placed high on their back and, most characteristically, a small, dorsal, fleshy, rayless fin just in front of their tail.

Brown trout *Salmo trutta* are *the* trout – the one that British fly fishermen rhapsodise and lie about. In Europe they can reach 1.4 m, but Australian species only occasionally reach 900 mm and 14 kg. A native of Europe and western Asia, they first arrived in Australia in 1864. The fish breed in cool, clear waters with, if possible, a gravelly bottom in which females hollow out depressions for egg-laying (the area of gravel with its cavities is called a redd). In many European populations with access to the ocean the young trout migrate downstream to the sea, returning when they are mature. In most of mainland Australia where they occur, trout remain in the upper reaches of rivers, and do not migrate down through warmer lower waters. However, breeding fish do migrate upstream. Some Victorian and Tasmanian populations do, however, run to the sea.

'The troughte...is a right deyntous fyssh and also a right fervente-byter' (Dame Juliana Berners, 1496) and will eat many kinds of animals, including GALAXIAS and other native fish, and may be partly responsible for their decline in some districts.

Two other trouts, both American in origin, are also well established. Rainbow Trout *Salmo gairdneri* (to 775 mm and 10 kg in Australia, introduced in 1894) resemble the Brown, but their spots extend onto the tail fin. (see illustra-

TURKEY

The turkey population of Australia is roughly 1 200 000, and considerably less on Boxing Day. Increasingly, however, small turkeys are being bought all year round, and turkey meat is now available in about 60 different forms such as hams, steaks and sausages. Turkeys of 30 kg have been recorded, but most meet their end when they weigh 2.5 to 5 kg, at between 10 and 12 weeks old. Females (hens) are much smaller than males (toms or, when older, gobblers). Nowadays nearly all turkeys produced commercially are white hybrids, to avoid the risk of carcases being discoloured by any particles of dark feathers. Fanciers breed the iridescent green and bronze Australian Bronzewing.

Turkeys *Meleagris gallopavo* originated in North America and were domesticated by the Mexicans. They reached England in 1549. There the name turkey cock – used for guinea fowl, which came from Africa by way of Turkey – was mistakenly transferred to this much larger, naked-headed bird. Mere similarity in size led to the Bustard *Ardeotis australis* being called the Plains or Wild Turkey. The mound-building Brush Turkey *Alectura lathami* does at least have a similarly red head, although without the fleshy red ornament over its bill.

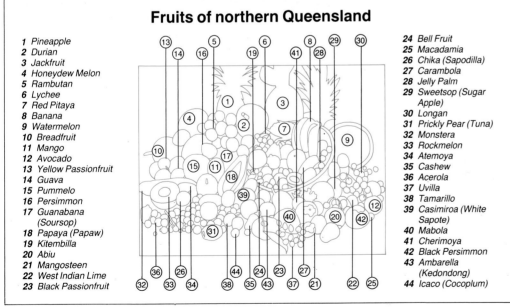

Fruits of northern Queensland

1 Pineapple
2 Durian
3 Jackfruit
4 Honeydew Melon
5 Rambutan
6 Lychee
7 Red Pitaya
8 Banana
9 Watermelon
10 Breadfruit
11 Mango
12 Avocado
13 Yellow Passionfruit
14 Guava
15 Pummelo
16 Persimmon
17 Guanabana (Soursop)
18 Papaya (Papaw)
19 Kitembilla
20 Abiu
21 Mangosteen
22 West Indian Lime
23 Black Passionfruit
24 Bell Fruit
25 Macadamia
26 Chika (Sapodilla)
27 Carambola
28 Jelly Palm
29 Sweetsop (Sugar Apple)
30 Longan
31 Prickly Pear (Tuna)
32 Monstera
33 Rockmelon
34 Atemoya
35 Cashew
36 Acerola
37 Uvilla
38 Tamarillo
39 Casimiroa (White Sapote)
40 Mabola
41 Cherimoya
42 Black Persimmon
43 Ambarella (Kedondong)
44 Icaco (Cocoplum)

tion p 176) The fish become more reddish at spawning time. Brook Trout *Salvelinus fontinalis* sometimes reach a weight of 4 kg in Tasmania and 2 kg in the Snowy Mountains, but Australian specimens are much smaller than those of eastern north America. They are slender, large-mouthed fish and are coloured brown with red spots encircled by blue haloes.

Trout are now being farmed for the table in the Snowy Mountain region. Further importations have been banned because of the danger of introducing an infection called whirling disease.

Turkey breeds

Australian White

Bronzewing

U V

UNDERGROUND ORCHID

Orchids are one of the largest and most diverse of all flowering plant families and are represented in Australia by many varieties, from small, soft tuberous plants to large tough-leaved epiphytes, climbers and semi-parasitic plants. Mostly their flowers are colourful and complex, with elaborate mechanisms for achieving cross-fertilisation with the aid of insects. Perhaps the most bizarre members of this family are two species discovered in Australia which go through their entire life-cycle almost completely underground. The first was found in 1928 near Corrigin in Western Australia and named as a new genus *Rhizanthella gardneri*. Only three years later a different underground orchid was found at Bulahdelah in NSW and named *Cryptanthemis slateri*. Apart from the original preserved specimens, both became lost again to science until quite recent rediscoveries. They have fleshy white rootstocks which seem to be associated with the roots of certain shrubs, probably obtaining nutrition from them via a symbiotic fungus. The small pink or reddish flowers are in dense heads. The flower-head pushes upward, causing slight cracks in the soil surface which probably allow small insects to enter to assist with pollination. Seed-pods rise higher into the soil litter and the seeds may possibly be scattered by the scratching of birds or animals. Both species have now been classified under the one genus, *Rhizanthella*.

URANIUM

Uranium was created at the birth of the planet, when many of its constituents were undergoing nuclear reactions and transformations. But while most other elements are now stable, uranium has remained radioactive, which means it continuously emits small amounts of energy which are harmful to the human body in high enough doses. Uranium is a metal, approximately as common as tin or zinc. It is even present in seawater. Australia has about 17.5 per cent of the world's low cost uranium, mainly in deposits in the Alligator River area of the Northern Territory. Australia produces uranium for export from several open-cut mines in that area, such as those at Ranger and Nabarlek. At the mine site the rocks are concentrated into yellowcake, which is a slightly radioactive uranium oxide. The three other steps needed to produce nuclear-reactor fuel are carried out in other countries.

The main uses of uranium are for power generation, nuclear weapons and medical therapy.

The first Holden utility. This and subsequent models were sold from 1951 to 1985 when the company stopped making utilities in the face of competition from cheaper Japanese pickup trucks.

UTILITY

In 1928 Lew Bandt started work as a draughtsman at Ford's Geelong factory. In August 1932 Ford released a range of vehicles using a new and powerful 3.3-litre side-valve, V8 engine. Developing 63 kw of power, the sedan, roadster, tourer and coupé range was an instant success.

Soon after the V8 was released, a Geelong farmer chatted enthusiastically to Lew Bandt about the new range. He asked why Ford did not design a vehicle with the comfort and performance of the coupé, but one which could carry a farmer's smaller loads.

Lew Bandt immediately set to work and within months the prototype was built. It broke new ground with the side panels, tray and rear of the cabin all pressed from the same metal sheet, and then assembled around a wooden frame.

The vehicle was called a coupé utility. It was the world's first and proved an instant success – to the extent that General Motors-Holden's (which had been Holden's Motor Bodies until 1931 when it merged with the giant US car builder) released a Chevrolet closely copying the same ideas the following year, 1934.

In 1948 Holden announced the model 48/215, and by 1951 a utility version was released. Like the Ford it was light, powerful and comfortable proving a huge success in successive models until the late 1970s.

Bandt retired from Ford in 1972. He located his original prototype coupé utility and restored it. While returning from making a television documentary in which he was driving the fully-restored utility on 18 March 1987 he was involved in an accident with a sand truck. Eighty year-old Lew Bandt was killed, and the irreplacable utility was destroyed.

VALLEY

Most valleys are produced by flowing water, although the water may flow only occasionally, or may now flow underground, or may have ceased flowing long ago. Rift valleys, or Graben, however, are the results of earth movements when land subsides between two parallel FAULTS. The depression containing Lake George, NSW, the Fortescue River valley in the Pilbara, the Fitzroy River-Christmas Creek valley in Western Australia, and the Latrobe valley in Queensland, are all rift valleys but, since their formation, rivers have also added to their character.

In the hills, near the source of a river, a river-formed valley usually had a V-shaped cross section. In alpine areas former glaciers have converted their valleys into ones with a U-shaped cross-section, uncommon in Australia.

In the lowlands a valley typically widens out, and its slopes become less steep. If the gradient of the river is small it may form meanders, widening the valley even more, and there are often wide alluvial flats of good agricultural land.

In places there are valleys within valleys, where a river has cut a deeper trench in a wider shallow valley. The Murray valley above Mannum is an example.

VEGETABLES

Although seeds for vegetables such as potatoes, peas and turnips were introduced into Australia with the First Fleet's arrival in 1788, commercial vegetable production did not really commence until the gold rush years of the 1850s. The Chinese were Australia's first market gardeners, offering many consumers the first alternative to home grown supplies. They dominated the industry for more than 50 years until the advent of new immigration requirements. The area planted with vegetables was at its greatest during World War II because of the armed forces' demand for processed vegetables. Although the area has since almost halved, improved yields and management mean that the industry now meets almost all of Australia's requirements for fresh and processed vegetables, as well as an increasing export demand from Asian and European countries.

Vegetables, from the traditional potatoes to the more exotic kohl rabi and okra, are grown in all states, from the Atherton Tablelands in northern Queensland to Tasmania. A thriving industry also exists in the Northern Territory. Production is largely confined to good soils in the coastal and sub-coastal regions, close to capital cities. However, urban sprawl and the increasing value of urban land have led the industry to expand into more remote regions, such as the NSW tablelands and the south-east zone of South Australia.

About 7000 vegetable enterprises, mostly owned by family partnerships, produce around two million tonnes of fresh vegetables annually. The major growing states are NSW, Victoria and Queensland, with the most important crops being potatoes, tomatoes, onions and carrots. Vegetables are mostly sold through central city markets for retail distribution, although a significant proportion are sold for processing into canned, quick-frozen and dried products.

VENOMOUS SNAKES

It is difficult to decide which is the most dangerous SNAKE in Australia. Obviously the toxicity of the venom is of great importance, and its quantity, but the distribution and habits of the snake help to determine the threat. The most venomous snake may well be a timid species living in an area rarely visited by people, but it is not as dangerous as a less-venomous, aggressive one living in populous districts. Fortunately, most snakes prefer to escape from people rather than to attack them. Their venom has evolved for subduing prey, not killing people.

Snake venoms are complex mixtures of proteins which can have various kinds of actions. Neurotoxins disrupt the passage of impulses from nerve-endings to muscles and can produce paralysis; other components can prevent blood from clotting, break up red blood cells or act as spreading factors which help the venom to travel through the body. Closely related snakes tend to have venoms with similar actions.

The following snakes are the most important dangerous species.

The mainland Tiger Snake *Notechis scutatus* is the snake most commonly responsible for serious bites in Australia. It has the fourth most toxic venom in the world – the average yield of 35 mg would kill almost 8000 mice. It contains three neurotoxins and a blood clotting factor, and it can also damage muscles.

The Eastern Brown Snake *Pseudonaja textilis* is the second most common snake causing serious bites in Australia. Its venom (mean yield 4 mg) is neurotoxic, but does not seem to harm muscles, and it contains anticoagulants. Paralysis develops slowly and sometimes the effects on the blood are more serious. The venom (on a weight basis) is the second most toxic among the world's land-dwelling snakes.

The Mulga or King Brown Snake *Pseudechis australis* should not be confused with true brown snakes as their venoms are quite different, and brown snake antivenom is not effective. It is a light-brown, small-headed, heavy snake found throughout the mainland apart from the south-east and the south-west. The average yield of venom is 180 mg, the highest in Australian snakes, but is of relatively low toxicity. It is an aggressive snake if provoked.

There are three death adders in Australia, all similar in shape, and between them they 'cover' nearly all of the mainland, apart from Victoria.

Their venom is very toxic: the average yield of the Common Death Adder *Acanthophis antarcticus* is 85 mg. The main symptom is severe paralysis, and before a specific antivenom was released about half the bite victims died.

The TAIPAN *Oxyuranus scutellatus* is probably Australia's most infamous snake. Before the introduction of antivenom, recovery from a bite was rare. The venom (mean yield 120 mg) is very neurotoxic and also has effects on the blood. It is the third most toxic Australian venom. The related Small-scaled or Fierce Snake, *Oxyuranus (Parademansia) microlepidota* has a mean venom yield of 44 mg – enough to kill 100 000 mice. This neurotoxic venom is thus the most toxic of the venoms of all the world's land snakes. Only one human bite (at least up until 1981) has been recorded, and the victim recovered. Taipan antivenom was used.

VOLCANO

Volcanoes are a direct link between the molten inferno that is the earth's core and the apparently stable surface. Fortunately there are no active volcanoes in Australia at present, and the last volcanic eruption probably took place about 4000 years ago at Mount Gambier in South Australia. Throughout the country, however, there is abundant evidence of an active volcanic past, such as hundreds of small 'cinder cones' scattered across western Victoria and south-eastern South Australia. These are made up of layers of ash, lava and mud flows, and are small relatives of the classic Mt Fuji or Mt St Helens type of volcano. Along the east coast there are remains of many large volcanoes, at places such as Orange, the Warrumbungles, Nandewar, Tweed and Nebor. In northern Australia there were long volcanic fissures on the Antrim Plateau, from which over 35 000 sq. km of basalt spilt onto the surrounding land.

The cone of Mt Schank, the best preserved of several volcanoes near Mt Gambier, SA. It is composed mainly of ash and other material thrown out during eruptions.

WALLABY

The so-called 'typical' wallabies belong to a group which also includes the great KANGAROOS, EUROS and the other WALLAROOS. There are eight species, ranging from the small Tammar Wallaby *Macropus eugenii* (body 643 mm, tail 586 mm) to the large Western Brush Wallaby *M. irma*. (about 1.2 m, 720 mm), a grazer that lives in the south-west of Western Australia.

Wallabies tend to be smaller than kangaroos because many live among much denser vegetation. They are also often browsers as well as grazers. In general they have suffered more than the great kangaroos from European colonisation because of the destruction of their habitats. (Red Kangaroos have even extended their range.) The extinction of Toolache Wallabies (pronounced TOO-LAY-TSHI) *M. greyi* (810 mm, 730 mm), formerly of south-eastern Victoria, was due partly to hunting, a unfortunate consequence of their attractive pelts.

Tammar Wallabies live on several southern islands, including Kangaroo Island, on and near the Eyre Peninsula, and in the south-west of Western Australia. They live in short dense vegetation, emerging into open land at night to feed. On some of the islands, fresh water is unavailable for long periods. Studies of Tammar Wallabies in laboratories have found that they are able to maintain weight and suckle their young on a diet of dry food and salt water. In the wild they have been seen drinking sea water.

Red-necked Wallabies *M. rufogriseus* (body to about 820 mm, tail 780 mm) are abundant in the south-east of the mainland, on Tasmania and on adjacent islands. They live in eucalypt forest and tall heathland, emerging to feed at night on grasses and herbs. They will live in cleared areas, provided that there are some patches of forest or wooded creeks for cover. They also live in the Peak District and Sussex in England. They may graze in company with others, but are not particularly sociable. Agile Wallabies *M. agilis* (800 mm, 770 mm) are also abundant, but in northern coastal regions. Whiptail Wallabies *M. greyi* (924 mm, 941 mm), perhaps more affectionately known as Pretty-face Wallabies, are also still fortunately common, from northern NSW to Cape York. They are grazers, and are more active in daytime than most wallabies or kangaroos. Parma Wallabies *M. parma* (482–528 mm, 489–544 mm), which live in wet and dry forest, preferably with a dense undercover, were long thought to be extinct until a thriving population was found in 1965 on Kawau Island,

New Zealand, where they and Tammars had been established by Sir George Grey in the 1800s. At the time of discovery the New Zealanders were trying to eradicate them in order to establish forests. Specimens were quickly brought to Australia to found colonies for future re-establishment, but soon afterwards they were found in the wild near Gosford in NSW. Since then they have been found to be widespread, although rare and scattered.

WALLAROO

Wallaroos are large KANGAROOS with large, bare, black noses. When standing, their shoulders are held back, their wrists are raised and their elbows are pulled in. Common Wallaroos are covered under the EURO entry.

Antilopine Wallaroos *Macropus antilopinus* (mean body length 1.064 m, tail 815 mm, female much smaller) are found in open eucalypt woodland, with perennial grass cover, in monsoonal areas of the north of Western Australia, the Northern Territory and Cape York, where they lead a life similar to Grey and Red Kangaroos of more southern regions. They will also venture out on to the plains. They are more slender than other wallaroos, and more gregarious. Males are reddish, as are some of the females, but the latter can be partly or completely grey. In hot weather they rest during the day, but on cool or rainy

Specimens of Common Wallaroos *were collected by members of Captain Cook's expedition near Endeavour River, Qld, in 1770. They are abundant over much of the continent.*

days they may be active. Adults have been reported grooming each other, an unusual activity for kangaroos.

Very little is known about Black Wallaroos *M. bernardus* (683 mm, 609 mm) which are found on rocky hillsides in Arnhem Land in the Northern Territory. They are usually found in pairs, resting in caves or in the shelter of boulders during the day, and feeding on grass and herbs at night. They were first described by Lord Rothschild.

WARABI

In 1978 a newly discovered tiny ROCK-WALLABY, the Warabi, ousted the NABARLEK as the smallest member of the kangaroo family. Warabis *Petrogale burbidgei* (mean body length 322 mm, tail 276 mm) are found in the rugged King Leopold sandstone country of the Kimberleys in Western Australia, a region where Nabarleks are also found, and they were therefore not recognised as a different species, although they have shorter ears. Warabis also live on some islands of the Bonaparte Archipelago. Little is known so far about their biology.

WARATAH

There are four species of waratahs, all of which are only found in south-eastern Australia. The generic name *Telopea* comes from the Greek word 'telopos', meaning 'seen from afar', a reference to their spectacular crimson flowers, which are some of the most striking to be found on any Australian plant.

The four species are: *T. truncata*, the Tasmanian Waratah, a small shrub found only in Tasmania; *T. oreades*, the Gippsland Waratah, a small tree found in eastern Victoria and southern NSW; *T. mongaensis*, a large shrub with a very limited distribution from Braidwood in NSW; and *T. speciosissima*, a tall shrub – the floral emblem of NSW – which is found in the central coastal region of the state.

Waratahs are members of the same family as *Banksia* and *Grevillea*. All four species have been cultivated. Although the flowers of all species are normally bright red, other colours are sometimes seen: white flowers on *T. oreade* and *T. speciosissima* and yellow on *T. truncata*. Attempts are being made to develop these forms for horticulture. Although *T. speciosissima* blossoms are already important to the cut-flower trade, an active research effort is being made to develop forms of the species which can be cropped regularly.

WASP

Wasps are related to bees and ants. Social wasps, such as the introduced 15- to 20-mm-long European Wasp *Vespula germanica*, have an organisation like that of honey bees, with queens, drones and workers, but they are largely carnivorous, and do not make any honey. In Australia colonies survive mild winters, and consequently become much larger and more dangerous than in Europe. The native 20-mm-long *Polistes* make small colonies in a suspended, stalked comb of 'paper' which is chewed, weathered wood mixed with saliva. Solitary wasps in many families show the beginnings of social organisation by making a burrow or mud cell, stocking it with paralysed caterpillars or spiders (each kind of wasp specialising) and laying eggs on their victims. The larva is thus left with a living larder. Many related insects in other families are called parasitic wasps. They lay their eggs in or on caterpillars, sawflies and beetle grubs, but do not place these in a nest. They are immensely important in the regulation and control of pests. There are about 280 species of social and solitary wasps in Australia. Others in the parasitic families run into thousands, and many are still unknown to science.

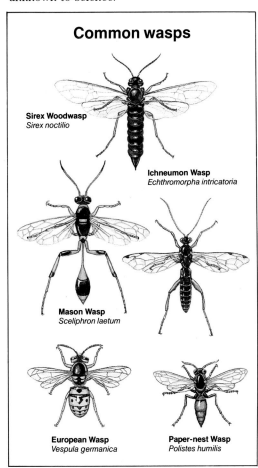

Common wasps

Sirex Woodwasp
Sirex noctilio

Ichneumon Wasp
Echthromorpha intricatoria

Mason Wasp
Sceliphron laetum

European Wasp
Vespula germanica

Paper-nest Wasp
Polistes humilis

WATER

See entry p 380

WATER BEETLE

Several families of BEETLES live in water, both as larvae and as adults. The adults have no gills and need oxygen which they take down as a bubble under their wing covers, or as a silvery coat called plastron held to their body by a dense pile of short hairs. They often have flattened limbs or hair fringes for swimming. Larvae usually use gills to obtain dissolved oxygen from the water. Most water beetles are flesh-eaters, both as adults and as larvae. Some larvae in the large Dytiscid family pump digestive enzymes into captured prey, then suck out the resulting liquid. The commonest Australian dytiscid is the 12-mm-long, yellow *Eretes sticticus*, a worldwide species. Some dytiscids are 25 mm long. Prey includes small fish and insects. Adult whirligig beetles live on the surface – often in groups – gyrating in small circles.

WATER BIRD

Many Australian birds live on or by the water, and live largely on water plants and animals. Some of these have their own entries in this book, although in some of these groups not all members are aquatic. This section deals with some of the other birds which are associated with water.

Moorhens and their allies belong to the rail family, which contains several birds that are rarely seen because of their secretive nature, and the moorhens, swamphens and coots so often seen in public parks. They are usually slim and long-legged so they can easily slip through thick reeds and grasses.

Moorhen really means merehen. Dusky Moorhens *Gallinula tenebrosa* (340–380 mm) will feed on land and in the water on vegetable matter and suitably-sized animals. They are territorial, sedentary birds which form small groups in which males may outnumber females. The group incubates and tends the young. Black-tailed Native Hens *G. ventralis* (340–350 mm) live in loose flocks in lignum swamps in the inland. The closely related Tasmanian Native-hen *G. mortieri* (450–480) is much bigger and cannot fly, although it can run swiftly. The Purple Swamphen *Porphyrio porphyrio* is the same size but can fly. It rarely swims but runs well. It lives in reed beds and is common in public parks. The Eurasian Coot *Fulica atra* (320–390 mm), easily recognised by its 'baldness', tends to keep to open water, often in large groups.

Grebes are diving fishing-birds, with their legs set so far back that one of them – the widespread Great Crested Grebe *Podiceps cristatus* (500 mm) – is called 'arsefoot' in parts of England. In the breeding season there is a crest on each side of the face in both sexes, which the birds use to great effect in courtship displays. In the other two species there are no crests, but the Hoary-headed Grebe *Poliocephalus poliocephalus* (270–300 mm) has breeding plumes on its head. The smallest and most commonly seen species is the Australasian Grebe or Dabchick *Tachybaptus novaehollandiae* (350–270 mm). All grebes are shy and will dive and swim away when disturbed.

Grebes making floating nests of vegetation, and eat their feathers and regurgitate them to feed to their young, possibly to protect them from hard fish bones.

Most, although not all, waders find their food in water, mud flats, estuaries and swamps and therefore often have long legs and beaks. Many species breed in the northern hemisphere and come to Australia for the summer. Only a few are mentioned here.

The most widespread of the stilts and avocets is the Black-winged Stilt *Himantopus himantopus* (360–390 mm), which is a bird with proportionately the longest legs. They are so long that it cannot swim and must wade for its food, which is composed of minute water animals. Red-necked Avocets *Recurvirostra novaehollandiae* (400–450 mm), which breed only in Australia, are also long-legged, but they swim well. Their most characteristic feature is their upcurved bill which they sweep, open, through the water to collect small animals.

None of the 27 species of sandpipers and their allies which visit Australia breed here. Most arrive from north and central Asia, and spend the summer on Australian shores and lakes. They include birds with names for crossword-puzzle enthusiasts such as dowitchers, knots, godwits, tattlers, ruffs, phalaropes and snipe. One of the most commonly seen – and heard – is the Eastern Curlew *Numenius madagascariensis* (580–620 mm including 180 mm bill) which arrives from north-east Asia in August and September, and feeds on worms and crabs which it catches by probing on mud flats and sandy beaches and in estuaries. Another common visitor from northern Eurasia is the Greenshank *Tringa nebularia* (320–350 mm) which spends the summer on coasts and in much of the inland, wherever there is water.

Some waders of this family do remain in Australia – usually in the north – during the winter. These are usually immature birds which will probably leave the following year.

Oystercatchers are pied or black birds with strong, chisel-like, scarlet bills. They open mollusc shells by hammering or stabbing them. The Pied and the Sooty Oystercatchers *Haematopus longirostris* and *H. fuliginosus* are about the same size (480–520 mm) and are found around all mainland and Tasmanian coasts, but the former prefers sandy shores and estuaries, and the latter, more rocky habitats. They are noisy birds with piping calls.

WATER

Water is a strange liquid, with qualities that have made our kind of life – based on carbon chemistry – possible. It is the only liquid in which most biochemical reactions can take place. It has unusual physical properties, an important one being the relatively large quantity of heat that must be applied to a given amount to raise its temperature by a degree or two. It can, therefore, shield living things and the earth from excessive and harmful temperature changes. Large quantities of heat are also needed to change water into its vapour, and conversely, much energy is released when water vapour condenses. When sweat evaporates, our bodies are cooled. Finally water is probably unique in that its solid form – ice – is less dense than liquid water a degree or two warmer. Consequently lakes freeze from the top downwards, and once a 'skin' of ice forms on the surface it protects the water below from the cold air above – which is fortunate for fish and other living things.

Much of the water in the world is in circulation although some – such as that in the polar ice sheets – may have been immobilised for tens of thousands of years. The great reservoir is the sea, but an estimated 333 000 cubic km evaporates each year. Approximately the same amount reaches the sea in the same time as rain or snow, or run-off from the land which receives about 100 000 cubic km annually. A rough estimate for Australia – based on rainfall maps – is 2800 cubic km, which is about half the average for land over the whole of the planet.

Water which evaporates is held in the atmosphere, at least for a time. The rate of evaporation depends on energy arriving from the sun, and the condition of the air above the surface. If this is saturated and still, there will be no evaporation. As the air temperature rises, however, it can contain more water (about 5 g/cubic m at 0°C, 25g at 26°C, 50g at 38°C). Air movements can sweep away saturated air from above the surface, replacing it with drier air, and thus increasing evaporation. The type of surface is also important. The surface of a lake or the sea will lose water continuously as vapour, as long as the air above it is not saturated, but bare soil will continue to lose water quickly from the surface only as long as the topmost layers remain wet or at least damp.

Land surfaces also lose large amounts of water by the transpiration of plants, and some through respiration of animals. Plants can, and must, drag up water from the soil, and this escapes as vapour from their surfaces.

When air is cooled to its dew point – the temperature at which the amount of water it contains is just enough to saturate it – the water begins to condense, releasing, as heat, the energy which had been needed to change it into vapour. This is the energy which is responsible for the power of storms. Dew – and sometimes hoar or ground frost – is formed when cold ground or vegetation lowers the temperature to the dew point and below. If the ground is cold enough to cool a considerable depth of air, and the air is stirred only slightly, mist or fog appears. The water droplets form, but are too small (0.02 to 0.05 mm in diameter) to fall to the ground.

Clouds are the results of condensation at higher levels. When a volume of air – with or without water vapour – rises, it expands because it is passing into air of lower and lower pressure. An expanding gas cools, so the rising air cools as it ascends – by about 10 C° each 1000 m if dry, and by about 6.5 C° at lower levels if it is saturated, although the figure approaches 10 C° at great heights. Sooner or later its temperature falls to the dew point and condensation can begin. The water vapour will not always, however, form droplets unless there are surfaces for them to form upon. Otherwise the air remains supersaturated. The nuclei for cloud-formation are tiny particles of various kinds such as dust, crystals of salt blown from sea spray, industrial pollutants and, once formed, other water particles. This phenomenon is the basis of attempts to produce rain from clouds by seeding with

A 'wet season' storm breaks over Elcho Island, off the north-eastern tip of Arnhem Land. The area's rainfall is high, but seasonal. In summer no rain falls.

Water was extremely important to Aborigines, particularly in the arid interior. The cairn placed on top of this prominent hill indicates a stream or spring.

SURFACE WATER

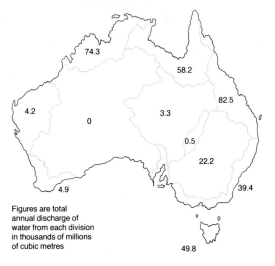

Figures are total annual discharge of water from each division in thousands of millions of cubic metres

74.3
58.2
82.5
4.2
0
3.3
0.5
22.2
4.9
39.4
49.8

Over most of Australia average annual run-off is less than 25 mm a year. However, in areas where run-off is much higher, only a tiny proportion is put to use.

silver iodide. Once formed, droplets may join together so that they are heavy enough to fall as rain, hail or snow.

There are several ways by which air with vapour may rise far enough to form clouds. The sun may heat the ground which warms the air above it so that convection cells are formed. Cumulus clouds are the common result. Winds blow air up the side of a mountain, and clouds, often releasing rain, form on the windward side. On the other side, however, the air sinks again and the clouds dissolve. This is often seen in eastern Australia where rain may be falling heavily between the Great Dividing Range and the sea, while the skies are clear on the other side of the mountains. Weather fronts also push air upwards. A moving mass of cold air may push under warm air (a cold front) or moving warm air may ride over a mass of cold (a warm front).

Finally turbulence, resulting from gusty winds blowing over rough country, can force volumes of air upwards. All of these processes can result in cloud formations of various kinds and, depending upon prevailing conditions, rain, hail, sleet or snow.

Rain, once it lands, tends to move downwards towards the sea or, in Australia, towards the arid interior. One-third of the Australian land mass drains to the sea, the rest to the interior. Large quantities soon evaporate, of course, and some enters the soil, but a large part of this eventually finds its way into creeks and rivers. Some soil-water binds strongly to soil particles, while some moves freely up or down by capillary action, in the spaces between. A large quantity enters water-holding rock strata called aquifers. If the strata are covered by impervious ones, and the land surface in the centre of the basin is lower

than the water-table where the rain falls, artesian wells can be drilled and the water gushes out, although it is often hot and brackish. Nevertheless GROUND WATER is a more important resource than surface water over about 60 per cent of Australia. The amount used each year is estimated to be 2.5 cubic km, compared with about 15 cubic km of surface water. The last quantity excludes water used for hydroelectric power, as that is reusable.

Australia is the world's driest inhabited continent. Its river systems discharge only 440 cubic km of water into the sea each year. Europe's Danube, alone, discharges 280 cubic km annually, although its catchment area is only 80 per cent of that of the Murray-Darling River system. At the same time Australia is the lowest continent, and much of its flatness is due to the erosive power of water over hundreds of millions of years.

A tranquil billabong in the dry east of South Australia. Water is the key to survival here – for humans and for animals – as it is in much of inland Australia.

WATER BUFFALO

Water Buffalo *Bubalis bubalis* (height at shoulder to 1.8 mm) was probably first domesticated in India, and it is said that there they show a dislike towards Europeans, although small Indian boys can handle them with ease. The first in Australia were 16 animals from Timor which were taken to the Melville Island outpost of Fort Dundas in 1825 or 1826. Further stock were imported to Raffles Bay and Port Essington between 1827 and 1849. When these outposts were deserted the stock was set free and multiplied quickly in the surrounding country. It suited them, with its numerous swamps and lagoons, rich with water plants. In the dry season they keep to the northern rivers and nearby swamps, but in 'the wet' they spread more widely, and have reached Wyndham, WA, Nutwood Downs, near Newcastle Waters, NT, and Burketown, Qld. In the dry, and in drier country, the groups of bulls are separate from the females with calves, but in the wet season they join the females for mating. Each group tends to keep to the same district for years, provided that conditions remain favourable. Each area contains a grazing zone, a sleeping area usually in woodland, wallowing and drinking places, and trees to rub on.

Buffalo damage native vegetation to some extent. In some places they have grazed out water rushes, and eroded swamps so that salt water has seeped in, killing stands of paperbark *Melaleuca*. Swamps have been reduced to quagmires which have deprived many Magpie Geese of their refuges. The animals also suffer from various parasites and diseases, including tuberculosis and contagious bovine pleuropneumonia, which could threaten domestic cattle. They could also serve as reservoirs for exotic diseases and parasites such as rinderpest, foot-and-mouth disease and blue tongue.

Water Buffalo *have caused havoc in many coastal swamps in the far north of Australia. Many are harvested each year for export, and this has kept numbers in check to some extent.*

Wallaman Falls, *near Ingham in Queensland, plunge 278 m in a single drop – the longest uninterrupted waterfall in Australia, and the third highest in the world. Australia's highest waterfall is Wollomombi, 455 m.*

WATERFALL

Waterfalls in creeks and rivers can be formed in various ways, but the commonest is probably by the river excavating a gorge as it passes from a surface of resistant rocks to a softer one. Other waterfalls are formed when there is a geological uplift in the upper stretch of a river. The rejuvenated river carves a so-called 'nick-point' which slowly migrates back towards the headwaters. In limestone regions, where creeks or rivers often flow into extensive caves, they may do so as waterfalls.

The highest waterfall in Australia is the Wollomombi Falls, where the river tumbles from the New England Plateau to the bed of a gorge 455 m below. The longest 'free fall' is 200 m. These take sixteenth place in the world, and second in the hemisphere, but the volume is negligible, not surprisingly in this dry continent. The Boyoma (Stanley) Falls on the Congo drop 535 cubic km of water a year – more than the total discharge of all of Australia's rivers.

WATER HOLE

The survival of Aborigines in Australia's dry lands depended upon an intimate knowledge of waterholes and sinks, although in an emergency they could extract drinkable water from some roots, tree cavities or waterholding frogs. Many of the animals which they hunted also needed surface water.

Much of the rain that falls into the desert soaks into sand or evaporates, but some finds its way into holes with more or less impervious sides. If these cavities are large and sheltered, they can retain water during severe droughts, particularly if a large flat stone is placed over them to prevent evaporation.

WATER LILY

Water lilies are water plants with flat floating leaves and easily recognised, many-petalled flowers. They are found in relatively shallow, still waters or very slow-moving streams.

True water lilies *Nymphaea* spp. are widespread except in southern Australia. However, various other types are grown in ornamental ponds throughout the continent, and populations of these have become established in local natural water bodies. Scientists are still not sure how many native species there are living in the remote parts of northern Australia.

The very large water lily of tropical Australia, with showy pink flowers, is *Nelumbo nucifera*, the Sacred Lotus Flower of India. In this species the leaves are normally above the water surface.

Plants with floating leaves very similar to those of water lilies – but with smaller flowers and fewer petals (normally five), each with a characteristic fringe around its margins – are species of the genus *Nymphoides*. About twelve are found in Australia, but again the exact number and their distribution is still not clear.

WATER PLANT

While it is difficult to produce a single satisfactory definition to cover all water plants, it is easy to recognise the following different types:
● submerged species that are rooted in the mud of a lake or river bottom, with foliage that does not break the water surface
● floating plants with leaves which can be divided into two types – those with roots in the mud, but with floating leaves – such as water lilies – and free floating species. The second group includes duckweeds and two of the world's most successful and widespread weeds – Water Hyacinth *Eichhornia crassipes* and the aquatic fern *Salvinia molesta*.
● plants with roots in the mud, but with leafy stems extending above the surface of the water. This group includes various species found in the centres of shallow ponds, and plants which look like reeds and are characteristically found fringing lakes and rivers.

It is difficult to draw a firm dividing line between this last group and the plants found in swamps, which may be partially submerged for brief periods, but which live in waterlogged soils for most of the time.

Water plants are members of many different plant groups, and are not necessarily closely related. The ability to live in water appears to have evolved independently several times. Most water plants are flowering plants, but there are also a number of ferns and bryophytes.

While the majority of water plants are found in fresh water, there is a small group of species – called sea grasses – which are found submerged in the ocean. Sea grasses are an important, highly productive part of many estuaries and coastal bays around the coast.

Although Australia is, overall, a dry continent, there are many water bodies, both permanent and ephemeral, which provide places for water plants to live. Most water plants are found in still waters or in slowly moving rivers, there are very few species which can survive in rapid torrents.

WATER-RAT

Australian water-rats have no relationship to any of the water-rats or water-voles in Kenneth Graham's famous book *Wind in the Willows* – they do not even belong to the same family of rodents. The two Australian water-rats belong to a group of about ten species that are found only in Australia, New Guinea and adjacent islands. True Water-rats *Hydromys chrysogaster* (male mean body length 310 mm, tail 275 mm, females smaller) are found in all states near permanent fresh and brackish water, and sometimes on the seashore. They are active at sunset, and to a smaller extent during the day, and are almost entirely carnivorous, eating any insects, crustaceans, mussels, fish, and other small vertebrates that they can get. They are said to leave shellfish in the sun until the muscles that close the valves slacken. Their hind feet are partly webbed, and their fur is thick and waterproof. Colour varies with the region, but is usually dark above and white to orange below. The tail usually has a white tip. The animals have been hunted for their pelts.

In good conditions a female can breed in the season in which she was born, and can produce up to five litters in a year, although one or two is the usual number. The animals' nests are tunnels in stream banks or in logs.

False Water-rats *Xeromys myoides* (115–127 mm, 93–99 mm) are far rarer, and may have disappeared from some of their former areas, unlike true Water-rats. They were not seen from 1901 up to the 1970s, and only about 17 specimens have ever been collected. Some are now known to live in two areas of coastal Northern Territory, and one in southern Queensland. Despite their name, the animals do have waterproof fur and a streamlined body, so their affinity with water is probably not false. Their teeth are similar to those of the true Water-rats – both have fewer molars than other Australian rodents – but their feet are not webbed. Their fur is dark slate-grey above and white below. Recently one was seen attacking and eating a crab in Arnhem Land.

WATER SKINK

Despite its name, the Eastern or Golden Water Skink *Sphenomorphus quoyii* (300 mm or more) of east and south-east Australia, is not a truly aquatic lizard. It has no adaptations for swimming, such as a tail that is flattened from side to side, or webbed feet. Nevertheless it often lives near streams and if disturbed while it is sunning itself it often dives into the water and swims efficiently to the opposite bank. Some of its food – small frogs and tadpoles, for example – is taken from or near the water. It sometimes lives in suburbs of towns near water drains.

Eastern Water Dragons *Physignathus lesueurii* (900 mm) are semi-aquatic, tree climbing lizards. Often the only indication of their presence is a splash as one drops into the water from an overhanging branch when disturbed. They often have a bright orange patch on their breast. In at least some populations, males establish territories along stretches of river bank in which live one or more females.

WATER SPIDER

The true water spider, which carries a bubble of air below the surface and lives in a bell attached to weeds, does not occur in Australia, but several other species live near water, and will scurry across the surface. Some wolf spiders do so to catch flying insects, and the widespread, 20-mm-long *Dolomodes* spiders will plunge briefly to catch beetles, tadpoles and fish. Spiders of the genus *Desis*, which are about 10 mm long, are found on many southern hemisphere coasts, including those of the west and east of the mainland and Tasmania. They live in silk-lined holes in coral and rock, emerging at low tide to feed on small crustacea and perhaps small fish. When the tide rises they retire and seal their holes with silk. Several other spiders live in the spray zone on Tasmanian beaches.

WATER TABLE

Even in the desert it is possible to find water if the hole is deep enough. The water table at any locality is the depth below which the soil or the rock is saturated. This depth varies from place to place, and at any locality it will change with recent weather and the season. It also depends on how far water must penetrate before it encounters impervious rocks. In some soils a hard 'pan' is formed after the land has been cultivated, as water percolates down and deposits material as a hard, cement-like layer. In such areas crops suffer in wet weather when the water table is high, and they dry out quickly when rain does not fall. Irrigation may raise the water table locally, but the soil may also become salty as a result.

Erosion gullies, on the other hand, lower the water table in surrounding land. Near the sea or beside a permanent river the water table is naturally near the surface, and in the desert it is usually far down, unless there have been recent flooding rains. In wetlands, by definition, the water table is at the surface, or above, at least at certain times of the year.

WATER TANK

Most farmhouses have at least two nearby water tanks, made out of either concrete or corrugated iron. One stores precious rainwater, collected when it rains by the roof guttering of the house and other buildings. The rainwater tank is usually the farm's only source of drinking water – and is also often home to frogs! The second tank holds water from either a nearby dam or artesian bore, for general use in the home and outside. A small engine or windmill pumps the water into this tank. Both tanks are sometimes raised on a high platform to provide some water pressure. Water tanks are also usually found near artesian bores, where they store water pumped up from deep under the ground for use in drinking troughs for stock.

WATTLE AND DAUB

This type of housing construction is one of the oldest known to mankind. It uses thin rods or stakes – called wattles – interwoven with twigs or thin branches, in the style of basketry. This is covered – daubed – with soil, preferably containing a good deal of clay mixed with straw, and may then be whitewashed with a material such as pipeclay.

In the very early stage of European settlement, wide use was made of this building method, and since various species of acacia provided suitable material, they became known as wattle trees. Because wattle walls would not bear the weight of a roof, it was necessary first to construct the framework of the house with logs and poles. Then the spaces between were filled with panels of wattle, which were finally covered with daub. The roof might be of thatch, shingles or bark, depending on what was available.

In Sydney the whole process was at first fraught with uncertainty, for there were very few men with building skills, and choosing soil with sufficient clay in it was a matter of trial and error. Not only did the daub tend to wash away, but buildings frequently collapsed. Today visitors to Old Sydney Town, at Somersby near Sydney, can see modern examples of successful wattle and daub buildings.

WATTLEBIRD

The four wattlebirds are HONEYEATERS. Two of them do have wattles – fleshy appendages hanging from the necks of both sexes – presumably as an indication to prospective mates that they have found the right species. All of them feed in forests, but will often enter gardens. They feed on nectar, pollen and insects – at least two species feed their young almost exclusively on insects, protein-rich food. Yellow Wattlebirds *Anthochaera paradoxa* (male 480 mm, female 440 mm), which have thin, pendulous, yellow wattles, are the largest of the honeyeaters, and live in forests in eastern Tasmania and on King Island. They feed in loose groups, usually in the forest canopy. Sometimes they attack fruit. On the mainland their place is taken by Red Wattlebirds *A. carunculata* (320–350 mm). After breeding they form nomadic bands which may contain about 100 birds. The songs or calls have been described as coughs and gurgles interspersed with pleasanter noises.

The two wattleless wattlebirds have only been recognised recently as separate species. Little Wattlebirds *A. lunulata* (270–300 mm) have chestnut-red eyes, a clutch of only one egg, and live in heaths, woods and forests in the south-west of Western Australia. Shrub Wattlebirds *A. chrysoptera* (270–320 mm) live in heaths and forests on the coast and ranges of south-eastern Australia. Their eyes are blue-grey, and their clutch contains two or three eggs.

WEANING

Calves which have been weaned, or taken away from their mothers, are known as weaners. Generally they are held and fed in stock yards or small holding paddocks for a short time after being weaned, to prevent them finding their way back to their mothers' milk. The age at which calves are weaned varies according to the enterprise – dairy calves are weaned as soon as possible to allow milk production to resume, but on a large pastoral property calves may be a year old before being weaned. Young pigs are also known as weaners, and are separated from their mothers at between three and eight weeks of age. Cows and sows put on condition, and are ready to breed again after their offspring have been weaned. Weaned lambs, instead of being called weaners, are generally referred to according to their sex, as either hoggets (females) or wethers (males).

WEATHER

Weather is the term used to describe the condition of the atmosphere on the scale of hours and minutes. By contrast, climate refers to atmospheric conditions in the long term, usually 30 years or more. The weather at a place is made up of a number of elements including temperature, pressure, humidity, windiness and visibility of the air, but also includes the presence or otherwise of clouds, rain, snow, dew and hail. Weather changes hour by hour because weather systems, such as anticyclones (high-pressure systems) or mid-latitude depressions (low-pressure systems) move eastwards around the globe. Much of Australia's weather is dominated by the eastward movement of anticyclones which bring clear skies and dry conditions to inland and northern regions between April and September, and to southern parts of the continent from October to March. Less settled weather occurs when rain-bearing cold fronts cross southern Australia during winter, and when monsoons and tropical storms affect northern Australia. More localised atmospheric phenomena, such as sea and land breezes, thunderstorms, tornadoes and southerly busters can bring about rapid changes in weather.

WEATHER LORE

Weather lore is an accumulation of people's sayings about the weather. Much of our existing weather lore originated from sailors, shepherds and hunters, whose livelihoods depended on correctly anticipating good or bad weather. These people were often unable to write down their observations and so expressed them in easily remembered rhymes or couplets that passed from one generation to the next. Some sayings about the weather have no basis in fact, but others have a scientific explanation.

Perhaps the best-known piece of weather lore is 'Red sky at night, sailor's (or shepherd's) delight'. This relates to the presence of dust particles in the air which impede all but the red wavelengths of sunlight, and give the sky a reddish colour. Dust is raised to considerable heights usually during warm, dry weather and, since weather systems move from west to east, it is reasonable to expect that warm, dry weather might be approaching. However, the behaviour of the atmosphere is too complex to be encapsulated in a sentence or two, and predictions based on saying can be expected to be right only about 70 per cent of the time. A body of weather lore takes a considerable time to amass, so almost all of that used in Australia by Europeans was brought with them from their own countries. No attempt seems to have been made to gather Aboriginal sayings about the weather, which would be based on at least 40 000 years of accumulated wisdom and observations.

The familiar red evening sky is supposed to foretell fine weather. Such folk beliefs can be expected to be correct about 70 per cent of the time.

WEATHERBOARD

The ubiquitous weatherboard cottage was not an Australian invention. The method was brought to a fine art in clapboard houses in the USA. Some of New Zealand's finest colonial architecture also used weatherboard construction, which was originally a centuries-old English style.

Australia's first weatherboard houses went up in the very early days of settlement. Timber was used only reluctantly for building at first – stone and brick were the 'proper' materials. But the bricks were of such poor quality that water, and thieves, easily worked their way in. So the settlers resorted to the old 'brick nog' method. They put up a timber frame, filled the spaces between the uprights (studs) with bricks, and faced the outer walls with weatherboards – overlapping planks that were about 150 mm wide and 25 mm thick tapering to about 6 mm thick at

Australia has been carved by the force of wind. But water is the most powerful weathering force. Rivers wear away rocks, as do waves on the coast, and even rainwater. Rain is slightly acidic because it contains small amounts of carbon dioxide from the atmosphere. Over long periods of time it eats into rocks, breaking them down into small grains.

A fine weatherboard house in Maryborough, Queensland. Some of the country's best examples of weatherboard are to be seen in that state. Many are raised on stilts, an adaptation to the tropical climate.

Intricate patterns of honeycomb weathering in cliffs near Sydney. Strong salt winds rapidy erode away the surface of the soft local sandstone.

their upper edge. A number of early colonial weatherboard buildings survive around the country, sturdy to this day.

The boards – of stringybark, box, ironbark or sheoak – were pit sawn. It was hard to achieve uniformity, so timber slabs were much more popular for houses at first. But the advent of mechanical saws and milling machines in the 1840s meant accurate planks could be produced in a fraction of the former time, and at a fraction of the cost.

In the gold rushes of the 1850s the population soared, and cheap, easily-built houses were desperately needed. A solution came from the west coast of America with its similar experience. The 'balloon frame' house (so called for its lightness) had a timber frame, was clad with weatherboards, and was roofed with the new corrugated iron. Its components were easily transported. Australia had plentiful timber for the cladding. Although joists and studs were of imported softwoods, the expense was balanced by the ease of handling the materials. New machine-made nails meant that the former complex and precise joints and wedges and pegs were unnecessary. For the cladding, only one nail was knocked

through each weatherboard into the studs, so that if the timber shrank it would not split. With an overlap of 375 mm, shrinking would not result in gaps between boards.

Within a short time weatherboard buildings abounded – from cottages and commercial buildings to churches. So cheap and simple was the weatherboard house that it had no prestige, except in parts of the country where the poorest houses had corrugated iron walls. By the early 1900s brick veneer houses were solidly established on city outskirts, but in the country weatherboard prevailed for another 30 years.

WEATHERING

Weathering is the destruction of rocks on earth's surface by the power of wind and water. These slow, inexorable forces have shaped the Australian landscape, eroding the Great Dividing Range, for example, reducing it from a massive mountain chain to stunted hills.

Rocks react with the atmosphere over long periods of time just as a cake goes stale when left exposed to the air. The constant action of wind can pluck grains from rock creating strange shapes. The famous Wave Rock in Western

WEB SPINNER

Web spinners are a small group of insects which are unique because as adults they can spin silk. Many insect larvae can do this, but the only adults which can are web spinners, *Embioptera*. They are 10 mm long on average, and are related to termites and earwigs. The silk is produced from glands in their very swollen front feet. Their feet, and their habit of living together in silken tunnels, identify them, although they are not often seen. The insects make their tunnel by paying out silk and rotating their bodies at the same time. In damp regions they may be seen on tree bark, but more often they live in crevices. Some live on fence palings in Perth. Females are always wingless and males often so. They are vegetarian and eat plant scraps, mosses and lichens, although some females also eat males after mating is complete.

WEED

Weeds are plants that grow where they are not wanted, causing economic loss, inconvenience, or displeasure to those who own the land on which they grow. The losses are due to the fact that they compete effectively with other plants, such as crops, and reduce their growth. In Australia the concept of weed is often restricted to INTRODUCED PLANTS, but there are also a few native species which have proved troublesome to farmers, graziers and even suburban gardeners.

The spread of weeds in Australia is limited by three main factors – lack of water, infertility of soils and the stability of existing vegetation. Most weeds are therefore concentrated in the higher rainfall settled areas on good soils. They are opportunistic plants, ready to move in quickly and multiply, siezing the available light, moisture and nutrients. This requires an initial disturbance, making bare soil available for colonising. Disturbances come from various human activities, particularly cultivation of crops, roadmaking and urban development. Weed control in crops calls for the greatest expenditure of money and effort, and is the most scientifically based. Weeds along road edges and on urban waste ground are not regarded so seriously, and they are consequently the best places to find rich collections of introduced species. Other forms of disturbances which benefit weeds are grazing and fire. Weeds will inevitably move in on overgrazed – or undergrazed – pasture, and heavy infestations of plants such as thistles are commonly seen on such land. If allowed to flower and seed they can build up vast 'seed banks' in surface layers of the soil, ready to germinate when conditions become favourable following ploughing or heavy rain.

Bitou Bush, growing here on the shores of Botany Bay, is one of Australia's most serious problem weeds. Introduced from South Africa and planted to stabilise coastal dunes, the plant is now out of control.

Specimens of the Botany Bay Diamond Beetle – a weevil – were gathered in May 1770 by botanists from Captain Cook's expedition.

WEEVILS

Weevils – a group of vegetarian beetles – form the largest family in the animal kingdom: there are about 60 000 in the world and about 4300 are known in Australia. They greatly outnumber all the animals with backbones put together. They range in size from minute (1 mm) to large (50 mm), and are easily recognised by their face, which is drawn out into an often ridiculously long snout, with the mouthparts at its tip. There are also clubbed, elbowed antennae set along the length of the snout. Weevil larvae are legless grubs, usually found in food. Many weevils, such as the 3-mm-long *Sitophilus* species, are borers in stored grain, although the weevils of weevily ship's biscuits were not weevils at all. The 12 mm long *Cosmopolites sordidus* is an important introduced borer in banana plants, often causing them to topple over. The many native species include the largest – the rare 50-mm-long *Eurhamphus fasciculatus* whose larvae bore into hoop pines – and the beautiful iridescent, 20-mm-long Diamond Beetle *Chrysolopus spectabilis*, of wattle, one of the first insects collected at Botany Bay by Sir Joseph Banks and his colleagues.

WETHER

Wethers – adult, male, castrated sheep – are perhaps the most truly commercial animals in the sheep industry. Unlike ewes and rams, which are important for breeding, wethers are good only for the butcher's window and the shearing shed. Wethers are meatier and provide more wools than ewes do. With an average fleece weighing around 5.5 kg, wethers generally produce 500 g more wool than ewes. Greater numbers can also be run on a given area of land, and they are easier to manage. In the last 20 years large numbers have been shipped live to Middle Eastern countries.

WHEAT

The waving stands of wheat which fill southern Australia's farming horizons for six months of the year constitute far more than a pretty, rustic landscape. These knee-high plants, sown in their millions on every wheat growing farm, represent the lifeblood of many Australian country towns. To the wider economy, they contribute up to $3 billion a year in export income. On a domestic scale, Australia's wheat harvest produces enough grain to make 23.4 billion loaves of bread.

Wheat has been grown in Australia since Europeans first settled the continent 200 years ago. The first crop was sown by convicts at a government farm on a site now in the heart of Sydney. But it was not until a century later that the colony was able to produce more wheat than it needed, and not until the start of the 1900s that the wheat industry became a rapidly growing part of the economy. Australia's first farmers had to battle infertile soil, plant diseases, low and unreliable rainfall, lack of farm implements, labour shortages, the need to clear land before crops could be planted and imported seed bred for a vastly different environment. There were even widespread doubts about whether the struggling colony would ever become self-sufficient in food.

The 20th century, however, brought with it new wheat varieties developed specially to suit Australian conditions. William Farrer (see box p 388) was one of the plant breeders responsible for this critical progress. In the same period, machinery like the STUMP JUMP PLOUGH and the McKay stripper-harvester reduced dependence on labour and allowed farm sizes to increase.

Throughout this century, wheatgrowing has become increasingly complex, with the introduction of chemicals and fertilisers, improvements in cultivation techniques and machines – including the replacement of horses with tractors.

The development of bulk grain-handling equipment, introduced in the 1930s and 1940s to replace bags, has taken much of the backbreaking work out of sowing, harvesting and transporting a harvest. Now the only seed or fertiliser still bagged is that which is used in small quantities. Farrer's successors, too, have given today's farmers higher yielding, more disease-resistant varieties of better quality wheat.

Australia how has about 44 000 wheat farms spread over a 4000-km band of land which stretches around the southern half of the continent. Although a vast country, Australia's capacity to produce wheat is limited by rainfall – either too much or too little – and soil fertility. The grain belt seldom extends more than 400 km inland from the coast. Beyond that, there is just not enough rain to satisfy a growing crop, or what there is, is too unreliable. Within the coastal band, most of the wheatbelt lies in the 'growing period' from May to October. In wetter regions,

Wheat varieties for every purpose

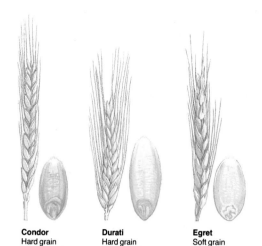

Condor
Hard grain
Bread wheat

Durati
Hard grain
Macaroni wheat

Egret
Soft grain
Biscuit wheat

Songlen
Hard grain
Bread wheat

Isis
Soft grain
Multi-purpose wheat

Tincurrin
Soft grain
Biscuit wheat

Gamenya
Soft grain
Bread wheat

Halberd
Hard grain
Multi-purpose wheat

Madden
Hard grain
Bread wheat

Olympic
Soft grain
Multi-purpose wheat

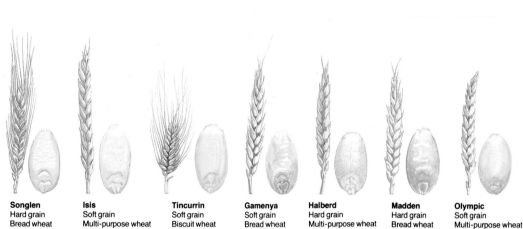

Just ten of dozens of wheat varieties that are available to farmers today. New ones appear every year. Each variety is recommended for particular areas and growing conditions, and yields grain that is suitable for one of a number of purposes.

other enterprises like dairying or horticulture have proved to be more profitable. In any case, it is the relatively dry conditions under which Australian wheat is grown that produces the type of grain – dry, white, with high protein – which makes it among the best in the world.

To many people who live in the city, wheat farmers seem a discontented bunch. They are reported to grumble frequently of too little rain, or too much – often the two within days of each other. Such complaints reflect the capricious nature of wheat farming. From the chilly winter days when the crop is sown to the windy, drying days of summer when the dead grain heads are harvested, each and every week starts a new, critical phase in the life of a wheat plant. At times the farmer wants a lot of rain, at others,

WHEATGROWING AREAS

Where wheat
is grown

The Australian wheatbelt – a crescent of land where soil type, rainfall and climate all combine to make grain growing possible and profitable.

moderate but regular falls, at still others – in the lead up to harvest – none at all.

The significance of the rainfall pattern changes across Australia. In Western Australia, growth of the crop depends heavily on winter rain, as falls during spring are usually unreliable. In South Australia, Victoria and southern NSW, spring rainfall is more reliable and very important in determining yields. In northern NSW and Queensland the success of the harvest depends on the conservation of subtropical summer rains by fallowing – that is, by killing, either with cultivation or chemicals, the plant life that would otherwise have grown after the summer rain. In these areas, where the soils are deep and retain moisture well, much of the 130 to 180 mm of rain that falls from February to April can be conserved before sowing. This moisture 'well' becomes available to the deep-rooting wheat plant at the time of peak moisture demand, in August and September, when there is not enough rain for crop growth.

Soil fertility also varies across the country. Queensland and northern NSW have highly fertile black soils. Red-brown loams predominate over much of the rest of the continent, while Western Australia grows much of its wheat in lower fertility sandy soils. Other than the richer earth, most wheatbelt soils are relatively poor and need regular applications of inorganic fertilisers like superphosphate.

Rotation of cropping paddocks and careful use of the pasture phase in between crops is the key to successful wheatgrowing in most of Australia, overcoming, cheaply, problems of low fertility. Pasture legumes – the most familiar of which are the three-leafed clovers – enrich the soil with nitrogen and organic matter through their ability to 'fix' nitrogen. This allows wheat to be grown continuously for several seasons.

Until a few years ago, pasture phases of three

to five years were usual, but more recently many farmers have shortened their rotations – the number of years any particular paddock is rested from cropping – to one or two years. Greater cropping intensity could mean that more farms will have to use nitrogen fertilisers in coming years. There is also concern about the long-term effects of intensive cropping on soil fertility and stability. Many of the dust storms which have reached as far as Australia's capital cities in recent years have been blamed on excessive cultivation in the wheatbelt.

In a bid to help solve this problem, as well as to cut farmers' costs, less working of the soil before a crop is sown is now widespread farming practice. It has been encouraged by the development of better herbicides, 'minimum tillage' cultivation, and sowing equipment which can work land on which crop or pasture residues have been left, without constantly becoming blocked with plant material.

Wheatgrowing in Australia is still a family operation, and production is highly mechanised. It is common for more than $250 000 of machinery to be brought out of storage for just the few weeks of the year when a wheat crop is being sown and harvested. In autumn, the lonely lights of high-powered tractors blaze long into the night as farmers work, often around the clock, to get their crops sown as quickly as possible after the 'break' of the season. Yields can fall dramatically for every week that sowing is delayed beyond the best date for a region. Often delays are unavoidable when the 'break' itself – the first substantial downpour of the season – is late, or does not really come at all. Then the earth is too dry either to cultivate or to sprout and nourish a young wheat seed. Alternatively, it may be too wet at planting time, leaving heavy machinery floundering in soggy earth, ruining the structure of the soil in the process.

Through the sowing and growing season, chemicals must be used frequently in a never-ending battle against unwanted weeds and pests. At harvest time – which starts in Queensland in September and works its way southwards with the onset of the hotter months – the largest item in the farmer's fleet, the grain harvester, emerges to devour the ripe crop.

Even then, uncertainty is far from over for farmers. The selling of Australian wheat may be a highly regulated activity, but returns are dictated by the vagaries of world wheat markets.

Production of wheat in Australia varies enormously. In 1982–83, a year rated by many farmers as one of the worst in living memory, only nine million tonnes of wheat were produced in Australia, much of that in Western Australia, which ironically enjoyed one of its best seasons. A year later, much to the joy of both farmers and their bankers, a record 22 million tonnes poured into the handling system after near perfect growing conditions over much of the wheatbelt.

The average yield of Australian wheat is 1.3 tonnes per hectare, compared with around eight tonnes per hectare in Britain.

The system for selling wheat is rigidly controlled in Australia, with the Australian Wheat Board (AWB) – a non-profit organisation set up by growers – controlling most of it. All wheat grown, apart from that kept on farms for livestock feed or seed for the next crop, or sold directly for domestic stockfeed use, is received by the AWB after harvest. It becomes the property of the Board once a grower delivers it to his local silo. The AWB is then responsible for selling the crop. In return it gives the grower a large initial payment – financed by a massive annual borrowing programme – and later pays out any further money it makes as sales of the crop progress. The AWB has been operating for 50 years, and was set up by growers in its present form in a bid to protect themselves against greedy grain merchants, and to reduce the possibility of a number of Australian wheat exporters undercutting each other to get sales. Although it has successfully marketed the Australian crop during its history, even during the slump of the 1980s, its monopoly control of the industry has often been questioned, and it seems likely that its tight grip on the wheat crop will eventually be loosened.

The Australian wheat industry is probably unique in the world in that almost all of the crop is delivered into a centralised storage and handling system within days of the harvest. Very little wheat is stored on farms. The most obvious physical evidence of this system are the towering concrete or steel grain silos which interrupt the otherwise flat horizons of most country towns in the wheatbelt. Trucks queue at these silos every

summer to deliver the harvest of the town's surrounding farms. In bumper seasons – when the permanent storage system is unable to cope with the quantity of grain delivered – low cost temporary stores called bunkers are built at convenient locations. Australia's total grain storage capacity, including these bunkers, is about 35 million tonnes.

At country receival points wheat is weighed, sampled and separated into six different categories, which are also the basis on which farmers are paid. The biggest category, into which about 70 per cent of the Australian crop falls, is called Australian Standard White. But a comprehensive range of wheat types is available as a result of the different environments in which wheat is grown around Australia, varying in hardness, protein content, dough properties and milling qualities. Consequently the crop can be used to make most wheat-based product, from biscuits to noodles.

Once delivered into storage, grain is transported to country sub-terminals and large seaboard terminal storages, almost exclusively by rail. Each year, the Australian Wheat Board, in conjunction with the state-run bulk-handling authorities in each state, coordinates the loading

The man on the two dollar note

William Farrer has received little recognition for his great contribution to Australia's prosperity.

One hundred years ago, Australia was producing wheat for the home market only, on merely 1.4 million hectares of high rainfall land. Losses from stem rust – a disease which makes the grain shrivel – were very high in the late-maturing varieties mostly grown then. By 1912 Australia had become a wheat exporter, and today, with eight times as much land under wheat, is one of the world's major wheat producers. One man fired this revolution – the pioneering and little-recognised wheat-breeder William James Farrer.

Born a farmer's son in England in 1845 he studied medicine before illness ended that career. In 1870 he came to Australia, and in 1875 worked as a surveyor around Cooma, Cobar and Dubbo. There he saw the effects of disease on wheat crops. In 1886 Farrer devoted his life to improving Australian wheat. On his property, Lambrigg, near Tharwa in the ACT, he built a small laboratory and established wheat-breeding plots on a hectare of land beside the Murrumbidgee River. Every year for the next 20 years, with infinite patience, he made between 200 and 400 crosses of varieties, concentrating on early-maturing strains, believing them to be stronger. Among the many disease- and drought-resistant varieties he produced, the most famous was Federation, the main wheat in Australia for many years. Farrer died in 1906. Australia's debt to him was acknowledged by his portrait being placed on the $2 note.

of about 700 ships at 18 ports with 15 classes of wheat for export to nearly 50 countries, as either flour or bagged or bulk grain.

Australia is one of the world's major wheat exporters, along with the United States, Canada, Europe and Argentina, providing about 15 per cent of the international wheat market each year. Although production – at around 15 million tonnes a year – is relatively small, accounting for only about three per cent of the total global wheat harvest, an average of 80 per cent of that is usually exported.

WHIPBIRD

The Eastern Whipbird *Psophodes olivaceus* is heard far more than it is seen. It lives in thick, wet forests where pairs establish permanent territories. The male calls with a whip-crack, and the female answers with two or three chirruping notes. They probably call in this way to maintain contact while foraging in the litter for insects, and to advertise their occupation of the territory. The Western Whipbird *P. nigrogularis* (220–250 mm), of Western Australia and the South Australian-Victorian border, leads a similar life, but its call is described as a repetitive rising tinkling. Whipbirds are related to two wedgebills – Chirruping *P. cristatus* (190–200 mm), and Chiming *P. occidentalis* (200–220 mm) – of the arid lands. The widespread and unrelated Rufous Whistler *Pachycephala rufiventris* (160–170 mm) is sometimes called the Mock Whipbird because of the explosive last syllable of the male's song.

WILD WHITE MEN

Of all the white men who lived among Aborigines, the most famous was William Buckley. Transported to Port Phillip in 1803, he escaped. After some months' desperate existence, he was befriended by Aborigines who believed him to be the ghost of a kinsman from whose grave Buckley had taken a piece of spear for a walking stick. For 31 years Buckley was honoured and respected, given the choicest portions of food, and made to stand aside during the frequent bloody fights. In 1835 John Batman's party, arriving at Indented Head south of Geelong, were astonished and fearful at meeting a huge figure clothed in skins with flowing beard and hair – Buckley stood two metres tall. As his English gradually returned, he constantly saved the whites from attack. He was pardoned, and employed as a go-between by the settlers. After two years, despairing of fair treatment for his old friends, he went to Hobart, married, and was given a small pension by the government. He died in 1856, aged 76. 'Buckley's chance' – very nearly none – probably has nothing to do with him. The phrase is more likely a pun on Buckley & Nunn, a Melbourne store.

The position of 'white blackfellows' was precarious. They might be 'recognised' as an enemy,

***William Buckley**, after his return to white society. For many years he worked as a gatekeeper at a women's prison in Tasmania. He died in 1856.*

and be murdered. They might easily commit some blunder or profanity before they learned language and customs. A score or so lived to tell their tales. Often their experience was put to good use. The convict John Baker lived as a 'white ghost' among Queensland tribes from 1836 to 1840 and was later employed as an interpreter. Convict John Graham, another recognised tribesman, lived with coastal Queensland people from 1827 to 1835 until he gave himself up. In 1836 he guided searchers looking for survivors of the shipwrecked *Stirling Castle*, and himself made the celebrated and brave rescue of Mrs Eliza Fraser. He was freed. Two more 'white ghosts' were rescued from Aborigines near Wide Bay in Queensland in 1842. The convicts James Bracefield – with a tribe for six years – and James Davis – with another tribe for 13 years – were both freed. Davis worked as a guide and interpreter until he died aged 81. Shipwrecked sailor James Morrill (or Murrell) lived near Cape Cleveland for 17 years from 1846. He later helped explorers and squatters. On his death, after two years in white society, he was mourned by many black friends.

There was at least one wild white woman, Barbara Thompson, shipwrecked at the age of 16 on Possession Island in 1844. Four years later she managed to reach a party from the surveying ship HMS *Rattlesnake*. With difficulty she found enough English to make herself known as a white woman, and she was eventually restored to her parents in Sydney.

***A field of ripening wheat**, soon to become part of the mountain of grain (below) produced in Australia each year. Twenty-two million tonnes were produced from 12.9 million hectares in 1983–84, a record year.*

Common wildflowers of the Australian countryside

There are over 25 000 species of plants to be found growing in Australia, and most of them have flowers. Despite the enormous variety, most are restricted to relatively small areas where the type of soil, climate and moisture suits them. One hundred and eighty flowers are illustrated on the following pages, all carefully chosen to represent those most commonly encountered in normal circumstances. The flowers are grouped by colour under the headings: red-pink, blue-purple, white-cream and yellow-green. Distribution, which can only be approximate, is given by state according to the following simple code: N = NSW; V = Victoria; T = Tasmania; S = South Australia; W = Western Australia; Nt = Northern Territory; Q = Queensland and C = Central Australia.

RED-PINK FLOWERS

Adenanthos barbigera
Hairy Gland Flower (W)

Amyema congener
Mistletoe (N)

Baeckea ramosissima
(NTVS)

Banksia coccinea
Scarlet Banksia (W)

Bauera rubioides
River Rose (NVTS)

Blandfordia grandiflora
Christmas Bell (NQ)

Boronia mollis
Soft Boronia (N)

Boronia serrulata
Native Rose (N)

Boronia heterophylla
Red Boronia (W)

Calandrinia balonensis
Broad-leafed Parakeela (C)

Callistemon citrinus
Crimson Bottlebrush (NVQ)

Calothamnus asper
(W)

Calytrix fraseri
(W)

Carpobrotus glaucescens
Angular Pig Face (NQ)

Chamelaucium uncinatum
Geraldton Wax (W)

Chorizema cordatum
(W)

Clianthus formosus
Sturt's Desert Pea (C)

Correa reflexa
Wild Fuschia (NVT)

Corybas undulatum
Helmet Orchid (NVTSW)

Crowea saligna
Bright Pink Waxflower (N)

Darwinia fascicularis
Clustered Scent Myrtle (N)

Dendrobium bigibbum
Cooktown Orchid (Q)

Dipodium punctatum
Hyacinth Orchid (NVTSQ)

Doryanthes excelsa
Gymea Lily (NQ)

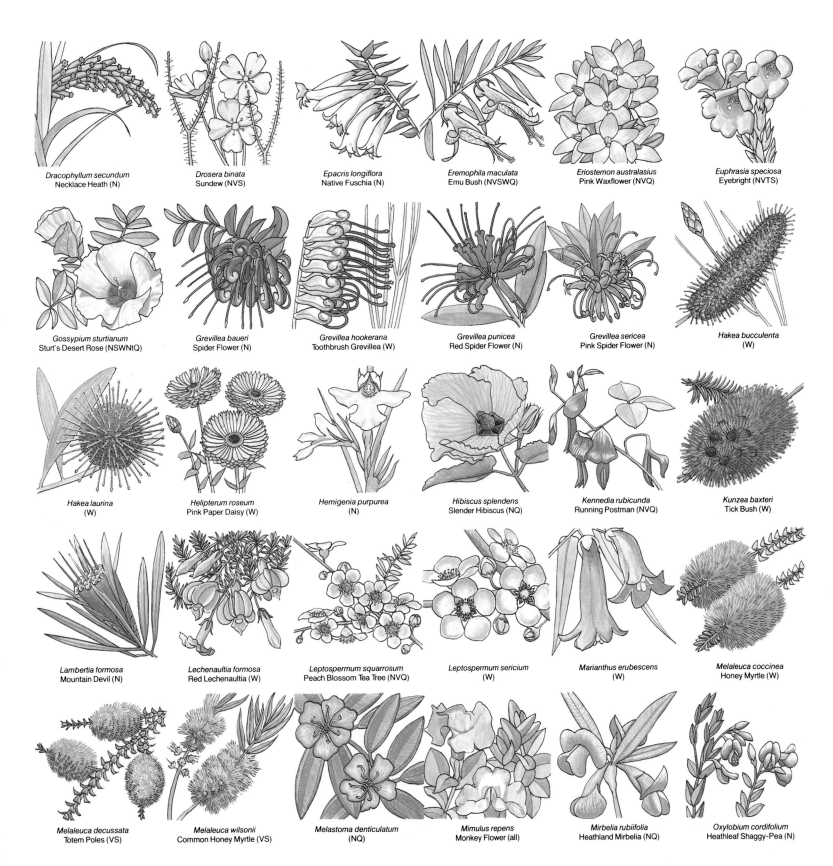

Dracophyllum secundum
Necklace Heath (N)

Drosera binata
Sundew (NVS)

Epacris longiflora
Native Fuschia (N)

Eremophila maculata
Emu Bush (NVSWQ)

Eriostemon australasius
Pink Waxflower (NVQ)

Euphrasia speciosa
Eyebright (NVTS)

Gossypium sturtianum
Sturt's Desert Rose (NSWNtQ)

Grevillea baueri
Spider Flower (N)

Grevillea hookerana
Toothbrush Grevillea (W)

Grevillea punicea
Red Spider Flower (N)

Grevillea sericea
Pink Spider Flower (N)

Hakea bucculenta
(W)

Hakea laurina
(W)

Helipterum roseum
Pink Paper Daisy (W)

Hemigenia purpurea
(N)

Hibiscus splendens
Slender Hibiscus (NQ)

Kennedia rubicunda
Running Postman (NVQ)

Kunzea baxteri
Tick Bush (W)

Lambertia formosa
Mountain Devil (N)

Lechenaultia formosa
Red Lechenaultia (W)

Leptospermum squarrosum
Peach Blossom Tea Tree (NVQ)

Leptospermum sericium
(W)

Marianthus erubescens
(W)

Melaleuca coccinea
Honey Myrtle (W)

Melaleuca decussata
Totem Poles (VS)

Melaleuca wilsonii
Common Honey Myrtle (VS)

Melastoma denticulatum
(NQ)

Mimulus repens
Monkey Flower (all)

Mirbelia rubiifolia
Heathland Mirbelia (NQ)

Oxylobium cordifolium
Heathleaf Shaggy-Pea (N)

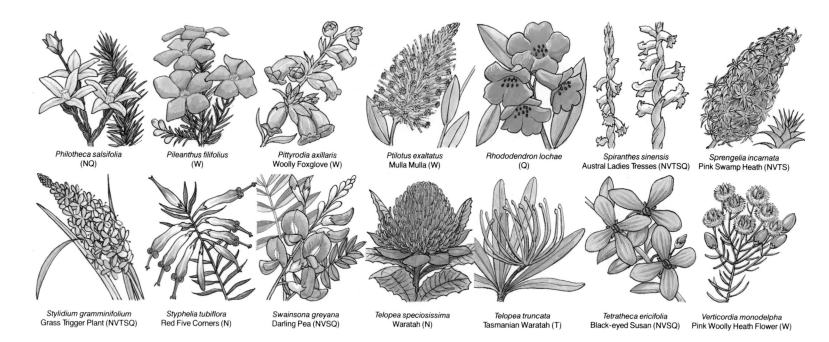

Philotheca salsifolia
(NQ)

Pileanthus filifolius
(W)

Pittyrodia axillaris
Woolly Foxglove (W)

Ptilotus exaltatus
Mulla Mulla (W)

Rhododendron lochae
(Q)

Spiranthes sinensis
Austral Ladies Tresses (NVTSQ)

Sprengelia incarnata
Pink Swamp Heath (NVTS)

Stylidium gramminifolium
Grass Trigger Plant (NVTSQ)

Styphelia tubiflora
Red Five Corners (N)

Swainsona greyana
Darling Pea (NVSQ)

Telopea speciosissima
Waratah (N)

Telopea truncata
Tasmanian Waratah (T)

Tetratheca ericifolia
Black-eyed Susan (NVSQ)

Verticordia monodelpha
Pink Woolly Heath Flower (W)

BLUE-PURPLE FLOWERS

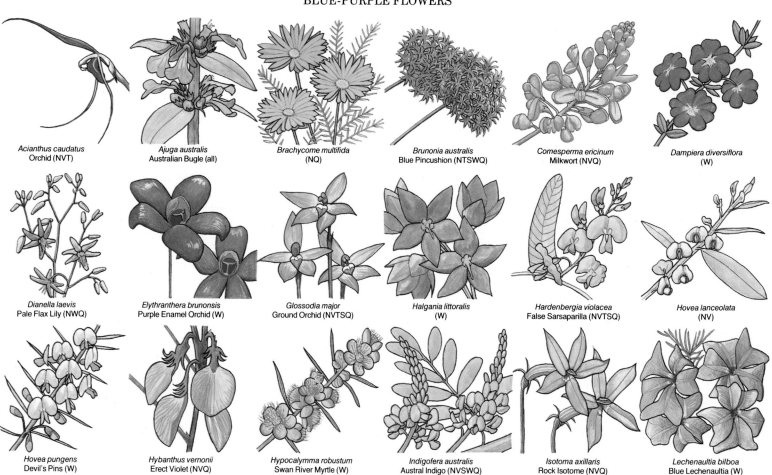

Acianthus caudatus
Orchid (NVT)

Ajuga australis
Australian Bugle (all)

Brachycome multifida
(NQ)

Brunonia australis
Blue Pincushion (NTSWQ)

Comesperma ericinum
Milkwort (NVQ)

Dampiera diversiflora
(W)

Dianella laevis
Pale Flax Lily (NWQ)

Elythranthera brunonsis
Purple Enamel Orchid (W)

Glossodia major
Ground Orchid (NVTSQ)

Halgania littoralis
(W)

Hardenbergia violacea
False Sarsaparilla (NVTSQ)

Hovea lanceolata
(NV)

Hovea pungens
Devil's Pins (W)

Hybanthus vernonii
Erect Violet (NVQ)

Hypocalymma robustum
Swan River Myrtle (W)

Indigofera australis
Austral Indigo (NVSWQ)

Isotoma axillaris
Rock Isotome (NVQ)

Lechenaultia bilboa
Blue Lechenaultia (W)

Linum marginale
Wild Flax (NVT)

Lobelia dentata
Wavy Lobelia (NQ)

Lobelia tenvior
(W)

Nymphaea gigantea
Water Lily (NTQNt)

Patersonia grabrata
Native Iris (NVQ)

Prostanthera caerulea
Blue Mintbush (N)

Scaevola ramosissima
Hairy Fan Flower (N)

Solanum aviculare
Kangaroo Apple (NVTSQ)

Sollya heterophylla
Bluebell (W)

Thelymitra ixioides
Spotted Sun Orchid (all)

Thysanotus tuberosus
Fringed Lily (all)

Utricularia dichotoma
Bladder Wort (NVT)

Viola hederacea
Wild Violet (NVTSQ)

Wahlenbergia stricta
Bluebell (NVTQ)

WHITE-CREAM FLOWERS

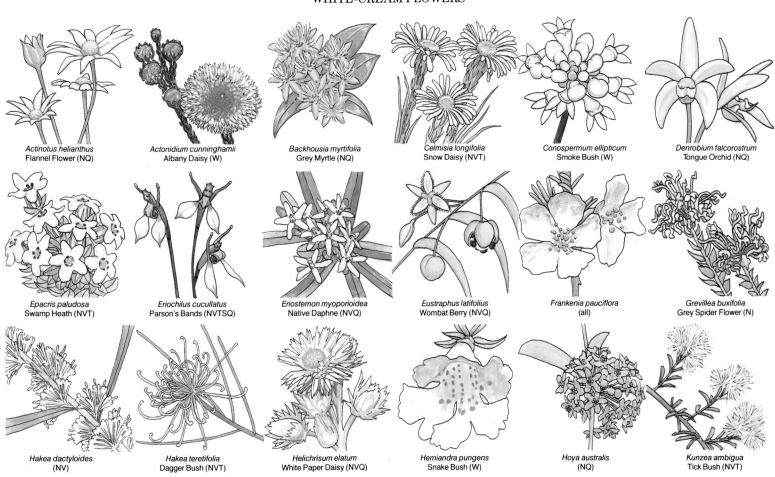

Actinotus helianthus
Flannel Flower (NQ)

Actonidium cunninghamii
Albany Daisy (W)

Backhousia myrtifolia
Grey Myrtle (NQ)

Celmisia longifolia
Snow Daisy (NVT)

Conospermum ellipticum
Smoke Bush (W)

Denrobium falcorostrum
Tongue Orchid (NQ)

Epacris paludosa
Swamp Heath (NVT)

Eriochilus cucullatus
Parson's Bands (NVTSQ)

Eriostemon myoporioidea
Native Daphne (NVQ)

Eustraphus latifolius
Wombat Berry (NVQ)

Frankenia pauciflora
(all)

Grevillea buxifolia
Grey Spider Flower (N)

Hakea dactyloides
(NV)

Hakea teretifolia
Dagger Bush (NVT)

Helichrisum elatum
White Paper Daisy (NVQ)

Hemiandra pungens
Snake Bush (W)

Hoya australis
(NQ)

Kunzea ambigua
Tick Bush (NVT)

WILDFLOWERS

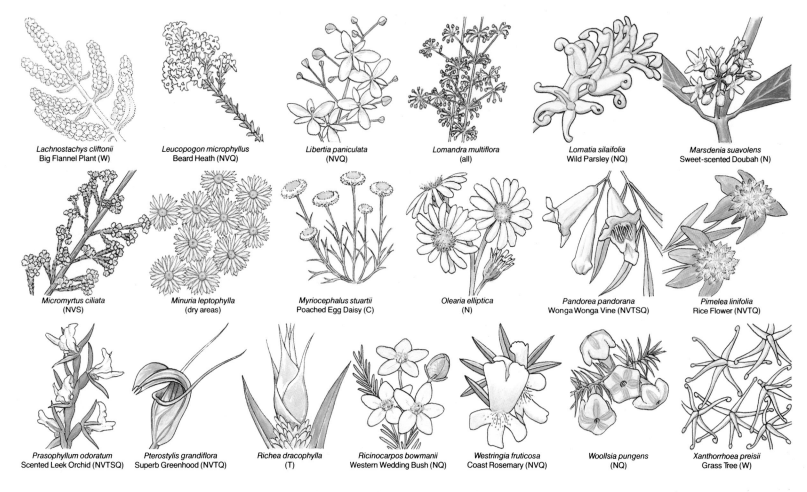

Lachnostachys cliftonii
Big Flannel Plant (W)

Leucopogon microphyllus
Beard Heath (NVQ)

Libertia paniculata
(NVQ)

Lomandra multiflora
(all)

Lomatia silaifolia
Wild Parsley (NQ)

Marsdenia suavolens
Sweet-scented Doubah (N)

Micromyrtus ciliata
(NVS)

Minuria leptophylla
(dry areas)

Myriocephalus stuartii
Poached Egg Daisy (C)

Olearia elliptica
(N)

Pandorea pandorana
Wonga Wonga Vine (NVTSQ)

Pimelea linifolia
Rice Flower (NVTQ)

Prasophyllum odoratum
Scented Leek Orchid (NVTSQ)

Pterostylis grandiflora
Superb Greenhood (NVTQ)

Richea dracophylla
(T)

Ricinocarpos bowmanii
Western Wedding Bush (NQ)

Westringia fruticosa
Coast Rosemary (NVQ)

Woollsia pungens
(NQ)

Xanthorrhoea preisii
Grass Tree (W)

YELLOW-GREEN FLOWERS

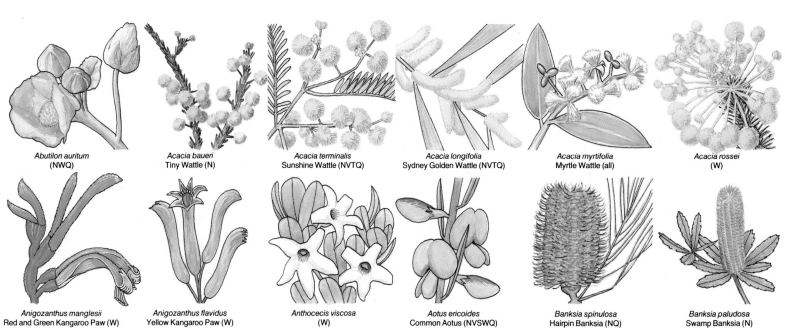

Abutilon auritum
(NWQ)

Acacia baueri
Tiny Wattle (N)

Acacia terminalis
Sunshine Wattle (NVTQ)

Acacia longifolia
Sydney Golden Wattle (NVTQ)

Acacia myrtifolia
Myrtle Wattle (all)

Acacia rossei
(W)

Anigozanthus manglesii
Red and Green Kangaroo Paw (W)

Anigozanthus flavidus
Yellow Kangaroo Paw (W)

Anthocecis viscosa
(W)

Aotus ericoides
Common Aotus (NVSWQ)

Banksia spinulosa
Hairpin Banksia (NQ)

Banksia paludosa
Swamp Banksia (N)

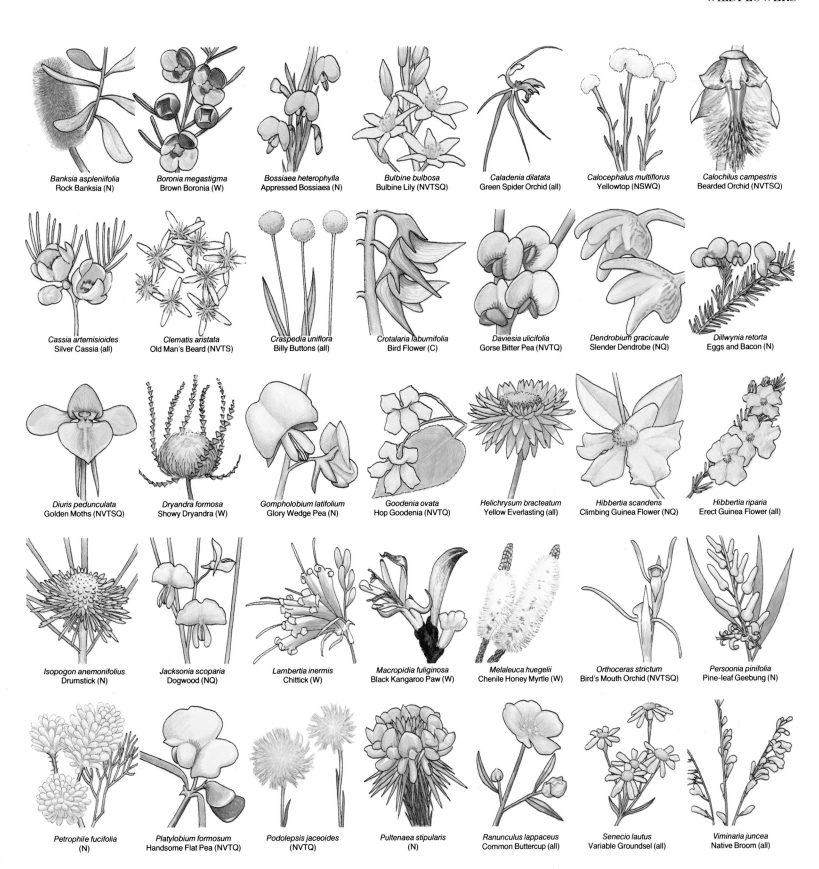

Banksia aspleniifolia
Rock Banksia (N)

Boronia megastigma
Brown Boronia (W)

Bossiaea heterophylla
Appressed Bossiaea (N)

Bulbine bulbosa
Bulbine Lily (NVTSQ)

Caladenia dilatata
Green Spider Orchid (all)

Calocephalus multiflorus
Yellowtop (NSWQ)

Calochilus campestris
Bearded Orchid (NVTSQ)

Cassia artemisioides
Silver Cassia (all)

Clematis aristata
Old Man's Beard (NVTS)

Craspedia uniflora
Billy Buttons (all)

Crotalaria laburnifolia
Bird Flower (C)

Daviesia ulicifolia
Gorse Bitter Pea (NVTQ)

Dendrobium gracicaule
Slender Dendrobe (NQ)

Dillwynia retorta
Eggs and Bacon (N)

Diuris pedunculata
Golden Moths (NVTSQ)

Dryandra formosa
Showy Dryandra (W)

Gompholobium latifolium
Glory Wedge Pea (N)

Goodenia ovata
Hop Goodenia (NVTQ)

Helichrysum bracteatum
Yellow Everlasting (all)

Hibbertia scandens
Climbing Guinea Flower (NQ)

Hibbertia riparia
Erect Guinea Flower (all)

Isopogon anemonifolius
Drumstick (N)

Jacksonia scoparia
Dogwood (NQ)

Lambertia inermis
Chittick (W)

Macropidia fuliginosa
Black Kangaroo Paw (W)

Melaleuca huegelii
Chenile Honey Myrtle (W)

Orthoceras strictum
Bird's Mouth Orchid (NVTSQ)

Persoonia pinifolia
Pine-leaf Geebung (N)

Petrophile fucifolia
(N)

Platylobium formosum
Handsome Flat Pea (NVTQ)

Podolepsis jaceoides
(NVTQ)

Pultenaea stipularis
(N)

Ranunculus lappaceus
Common Buttercup (all)

Senecio lautus
Variable Groundsel (all)

Viminaria juncea
Native Broom (all)

WILD FOOD

In most parts of Australia it is not easy for Europeans to live off uncultivated land. The Aborigines developed over thousands of years skills in obtaining food from a wide variety of plants and animals, as did hunter-gatherers in other parts of the world. But even the Aborigines found food difficult to obtain in many less fertile regions, such as the poor sandstone ridges of parts of the Great Dividing Range. In these areas they lived mainly along the more fertile river valley. The arid centre is obviously a difficult place in which to survive, but there the chief problem is usually finding water rather than food.

Early explorers crossing Australia thought of wild food almost entirely in terms of birds and mammals which could be shot, and fish which could be caught in the rivers. These were also central to the Aboriginal diet, but were joined by a wide range of other animals, including reptiles, insects, and shellfish, and many plants. FRUITS were obviously important to Aborigines, but so too were many roots, stems, leaves and seeds.

In the monsoonal north of the continent there are several species of plants which die down in the dry season, surviving as swollen roots, or tubers. Some were important Aboriginal food items. They include the well known YAMS, species of *Dioscorea*, although this term has been used loosely for other plants with tubers as well. Some plants in monsoonal areas have very large tubers,

Children gathering food in a Northern Territory swamp. Aborigines had little need to develop agriculture when all the food they needed could be gathered after just a few hours work each day.

Long Yams, a popular Aboriginal food, are common in rainforests and wetter eucalyptus forests. They can be baked in the ashes of a fire or lightly boiled.

an example being *Tacca* or Polynesian Arrowroot, but these are usually bitter and poisonous when raw, and need careful washing and cooking to convert their starch into an edible form. There are also a few plants with edible roots living in wet east-coastal areas among the tall eucalypt forests and rainforest margins. They include the Long Yam *Dioscorea transversa*, and Wombat Berry *Eustrephus latifolius*. Orchids, such as the Greenhoods, Doubletails, Sun Orchids and Spider Orchids, which live in temperate areas, also have small edible tubers.

Leafy shoots of a large range of plants can be used as green vegetables, either cooked or raw. One of the earliest plants discovered by white explorers was Native Spinach· *Tetragonia*, a creeping semi-succulent plant common on seashores as well as on inland plains. Captain Cook's crew found it palatable and nutritious. The tender leaf-buds of palms are also edible, but gathering them requires a whole tree to be killed. Young shoots of stinging nettles become edible after being boiled briefly, and the coiled young leaves of various ferns – including common BRACKEN – are edible and may be eaten raw or cooked. However, some ferns may be carcinogenic.

The seeds of many native plants are edible, and were mostly ground into a meal by Aborigines. They include a number of native grasses, which were especially important in the inland where they spring up in great abundance after flooding. Nardoo *Marsilea*, a semi-aquatic fern,

has edible, seed-like spore-cases which were ground into a flour, although their nutritional value has been questioned. The very large seeds of CYCADS are rich in starch, but poisonous. Aborigines washed them in running water for days to remove the poison before cooking and eating them. In the tropical north the seeds of waterlilies and sacred lotus were also an important source of food.

The swollen bodies of Honey Ants Melophorus spp. are still regarded as a great delicacy. They are widespread throught the arid inland.

WILLOW

In its English meaning, willow refers to European trees or shrubs belonging to the genus *Salix*. A variant name which is connected to both willow and salix is 'sallow' or 'sally'. There are about 300 *Salix* species in the world, native in all continents except Australia. Here they have been introduced as ornamental trees and sometimes for timber, going back to the earliest white settlement. Willows succeeded best in cooler, moderately wet areas, mainly south of a line between Sydney and Perth. River banks are one of their favoured habitats, and they have become thoroughly established along some rivers, in places displacing all native trees. The commonest species are Weeping Willow *S. babylonica*, a native of northern China, but taken to the west hundreds of years ago; White Willow *S. alba*, and Common Sallow *S. cinerea*, both native to Europe. Weeping Willow is one of the largest and most ornamental willows. It can be grown by sticking a thick branch in damp ground. Most Weeping Willows in Australia are alleged to have come from cuttings from a tree growing in Napoleon's grave on the island of Saint Helena. Although willows have flowers of different sexes on different trees, only female Weeping Willows are known in Australia, and no fertile seeds are produced. The bark and leaves of willows are the original source of salicylic acid, from which aspirin is derived, and their pain-deadening properties were known in Europe and American folk medicine.

The name Willow has also been given to a number of different native trees having narrow, drooping leaves, such as Native Willow *Pittosporum phylliraieoides* and Willow Cooba *Acacia salicina*.

WILLIE WAGTAIL

Willie Wagtails *Rhiphidura leucophrys* (190–210 mm) – FLYCATCHERS in the fantail group – are among the most familiar of Australian birds because they are common in cities and towns, as well as in lightly-timbered areas where there are suitable clearings for insect-hunting. They hop and zig-zag over the ground to catch prey, then fly to a convenient perch. Even there they are constantly moving, fanning their tails.

During breeding a pair maintains a territory around a small cup-shaped nest, made of grass and cobwebs, and placed in a tree fork. If human intruders stray near the nest the birds become excited and one or the other tries to lead them away by fluttering over the ground as if injured. The birds may rear several broods in a season.

Sometimes birds will sing from the nest during the night, a habit which has earned them the old name of Australian Nightingale. When birds which are normally active during the day sing at night it is often an alarm prompted by the approach of a predator.

WILLY-WILLY

Willy-willy is an Australian term – probably coined by an early settler – to describe a small but intense whirlwind capable of picking up dust and small objects and carrying them sometimes hundreds of metres into the air. Willy-willies are called dust devils elsewhere in the world. They occur when strong sun heats the ground during calm conditions. As air near the ground is heated and rises, it forms a column of buoyant air called a thermal. When surface air flows into the base of the thermal to replace rising air, a vortex may form, causing the column to rotate. Willy-willies are observed to rotate in either direction and may last for periods of between a few seconds and 20 minutes. The size of willy-willies varies, but their diameters range from 1 to 50 m, and they may reach a maximum height of about 700 m. They occur almost every day during summer in hot places like Marble Bar in Western Australia. Willy-willies may remain stationary, but they usually travel at a brisk pace, sometimes at speeds up to 30 km/h.

A column of dust, held aloft by a willy-willy, rises high into the air over arid country in South Australia. These miniature whirlwinds can travel at speeds of 30 km/h.

THE WIMMERA

In western Victoria about 24 000 sq. km of undulating wheatlands, scattered with salt lakes, stretches from the South Australian border to the Loddon River in the east. Taking its name from a river that rises in the Grampians and flows north to Lake Hindmarsh, the Wimmera encompasses the Little Desert, part of it a national park of 35 300 hectares which offers a haven for lowan or Mallee-fowl among its mallee eucalypts and sandhills. The 356-m sandstone monolith Mt Arapiles near Natimuk was climbed by Major Thomas Mitchell in 1836, after which much of the region was soon taken up for sheep runs. In the early 1900s thousands of hectares of Mallee scrub was cleared with primitive machinery, particularly by German settlers around Rainbow and Murtoa. In the 1930s a zinc deficiency in the soil was corrected with trace elements, enabling wheat to be sown. Stawell, in the south-east, saw a goldrush in 1857. The town is the home of the Stawell Easter Gift, a 120-m foot race run on Easter Mondays. Just south of Stawell is the township of Great Western where Seppelts produce champagne which is stored in 6 km of racks in vaulted cellars built by miners. Olives grow nearby and around Edenhope. Rainfall around Horsham – the city hub of the Wimmera – averages only about 450 mm a year, but the region's many lakes support large populations of waterbirds, which once sustained many Aborigines. Canoe trees can be seen in Dimboola and Edenhope. West of Dimboola is the salt Pink Lake, its tint caused by microscopic organisms.

Vast tracts of scrubland once covered the Wimmera, home for countless thousands of native animals. All of it was cleared away early this century by settlers.

WIND

Winds occur when air flows from places of higher air pressure to places where the air pressure is lower. The speed of the wind depends on the difference between air pressures. Thus, the highest wind speed ever recorded in Australia – 260 km/h – occurred when tropical cyclone Trixie struck the town of Mardie, in north-western Australia. Pressure differences, or pressure gradients, are very strong in tropical cyclones. Lower wind speeds are more common because of the relatively gentle pressure-gradients associated with anticyclones which move across Australia throughout the year. Travelling anticyclones bring mostly easterly winds to the northern half, and westerlies to the southern half of the continent, with variations provided by mid-latitude low-pressure systems in the south and tropical low-pressure systems in the north. Sea and land breezes are also common in coastal regions around Australia. Perth is the windiest capital city in Australia with an average wind speed of nearly 16 km/h, whereas Canberra is the least windy capital with an annual average wind speed of only 6 km/h.

WIND RECORDS (km/h)

Capital City	Average Speed January	Average Speed July	Highest Gust January	Highest Gust July	Windiest month
Adelaide	13	12	115	148	Nov–Jan
Brisbane	12	10	90	112	Dec
Canberra	7	5	104	101	Nov–Jan
Darwin	9	9	104	61	Feb
Hobart	13	11	130	130	Oct
Melbourne	13	13	104	108	Jan
Perth	17	14	83	137	Dec
Sydney	12	11	151	104	Dec–Jan

Vegetation can often give a good indication of the direction and strength of prevailing winds. This horizontal tree is at Greenough, on the coast of Western Australia, where powerful south-westerlies blow.

WINDBREAK

Farmers throughout Australia use windbreaks to protect crops and stock from damage caused by the chilling effect and strength of high-speed winds. On sheep properties, excessive winds, especially following rain, can cause several hundred deaths in a single night. The stock literally freeze to death.

Windbreaks are usually a band of trees planted close together. Depending on the type and spacing of the trees, the break can provide shelter up to ten times the height of the trees. For instance, a 20-m-high line of dense trees, such as firs or poplars, can provide an area of low-wind speeds for up to 200 m across a paddock. Such tree belts – which usually stretch for between 200 and 800 m – are generally planted along fencelines in such a way as to protect stock from the prevailing winds.

On more intensive properties, such as orchards, trees or tall tropical grasses are used to protect fruit and foliage from damage. Windbreaks are also used to protect homesteads and other major buildings.

WINDMILLS AND WINDPUMPS

There are great basins of artesian water under some of the best grazing country in Australia, and some of the world's most efficient windmills and pumps have been developed to bring that water to the surface.

There are two main types of windmills in Australia. One harnesses the wind's energy *via* a gear box and a pump mechanism. The other – an

Australian development – is the Comet Mill which uses an eccentric cam to pump on every stroke (see diagram above).

Mills are used either to pump water up from underground or, as a cheap energy source, to pump water from a dam to a trough.

If the source of water is underground, a bore is drilled down into the WATER TABLE. This shaft is lined with a bore casing, the lower end of which

Few sights can be more typically Australian than a lonely windmill in an empty paddock. This machine sits on the temporarily waterless bed of Lake George, NSW.

PUMP ACTION

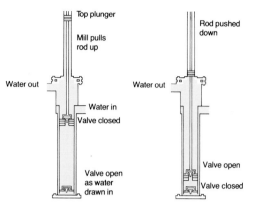

This windmill pump works on both the upstroke and the downstroke. Water is sucked in from the bore or other source on the upstroke, and forced out into a tank on both the up and downstroke.

is fitted with a screen to keep debris out, but which allows water to pass through.

Next a long delivery pipe and lift pump – with its foot valve – is lowered into the bore casing. Inside the delivery pipe, and connected to the pump plunger, is the pump-rod.

The pump itself is a simple brass cylinder. The piston plunger inside is fitted with a number of leather buckets which swell in contact with the water and make an air-tight seal.

The tail pipe, delivery pipe and pump-rod are in sections so that a two-man team, working from above, can connect the system six metres at a time and lower it down into the bore casing.

There are a number of safety features built into the system. The pump and the pump-rod are brass to prevent corrosion in bore water, which often contains a high percentage of dissolved minerals. The last connection of the pump-rod to the gear box at the top of the mill stand is a wooden shaft so that, should the pump jam for any reason, the wooden shaft will break, rather than the expensive brass pump-rod.

The mill wheel on the top of the stand is made up of a number of angled blades, a gear box and the mill tail. To set the mill in motion the wheel is turned into the wind so that the tail stands out straight behind. It will react to any shift in wind and keep the wheel facing into the breeze.

Another type of windmill which is much less popular these days is the wind generator. Used in isolated areas where no electricity was available, wind generators were used to keep a bank of storage batteries charged, and the homestead supplied with power.

WITCHETTY BUSH

This species of wattle, *Acacia kempeana*, is widely distributed in central Australia, extending from western Queensland to inland Western Australia, but is not found in NSW and Victoria. It is a many-stemmed shub, mostly two to four metres high, with short leaves which are broader and more spreading than those of its relative the MULGA (a more common plant in the same region), but with similar, short, yellow flower-spikes. Its bark is fibrous and peels off in strips. Witchetty bushes grow on flat sandy country, or sometimes on sand dunes or along dry water-courses. The name Witchetty is Aboriginal, and may have been used for several *Acacia* species. The connection between them and WITCHETTY GRUBS is uncertain, although the latter are often found in dead wattle trunks.

WITCHETTY GRUB

Strictly speaking the witchetty grub is the cater-pillar of the Goat MOTH *Xyleutes leucomochla*, but the name is also used for various other grubs. Goat Moth caterpillars live in the soil in silk-lined burrows and eat the roots of Witchetty Bushes *Acacia kempeana* in some dry inland areas. Goat Moths are fast-flying, grey, furry insects. Their name comes from the European species which is said to stink like a goat. The woodboring larvae of longhorn BEETLES are also esteemed. All can be eaten raw or singed, and a witchetty grub is said to have as much protein as a pork chop.

Witchetty grubs may be eaten raw or roasted. If eaten raw they should be held by the head which is bitten off and discarded. Grilled grubs are reputed to be delicious by those who have tried them and have a nutty flavour, due to the wood they eat.

WOMBAT

Wombats are the closest relatives of the Koalas. In both animals their pouch opens backwards, an odd arrangement for a tree-climbing Koala, but ideal for an animal that burrows. As a burrowing plant-eater, the Wombat's ecological equivalent in other countries would be marmots and similar rodents. Wombats spend their days in burrows, and emerge at night to graze.

Like many rodents they live on an abrasive diet rich in silica, so like them they have rootless teeth which can grow continuously, so that the molars are constantly wearing down to a ridged grinding surface. Wombats have stocky bodies, very short tails, short powerful limbs and strong claws and, despite their reputation, they have proportionately more grey matter in their brain than any other marsupial.

Wombat burrows often enrage farmers, but more serious is their habit of barging through rabbit-proof fences, often along stretches separating cultivated land from rough country where rabbit control is difficult. They make a highway for rabbits and other pests. One suggested solution is to fit small doors, on horizontal hinges, for the wombats to push through. They would close behind them and be too heavy for rabbits to open. The door should be erected on an existing hole in a wombat track, as too much reliance should not be put on their intelligence.

Common Wombats *Vombatus ursinus* (mean body length, 985 mm, tail 25 mm) live in forested areas on the south-east of the mainland and Tasmania, often in hilly areas. Although they have disappeared from much of their former range, they are still common and are often seen dead on roadsides. Their nose is large and naked, and their fur coarse and thick.

Southern Hairy-nosed Wombats *Lasiorhinus latifrons* are a little smaller and live in semi-arid regions of South Australia and the south-east of Western Australia. Rainfall there is only around 200 to 500 mm a year so the wombats often cannot drink for weeks, and conserve moisture by spending the day in damp burrows. They are still common over their limited range. Northern Hairy-nosed Wombats *L. krefftii* (about 1 m, 50 mm) have always had a limited distribution, at least since European colonisation. There was a small colony near Jerilderie in NSW, and one just north of the Queensland-NSW border, but as far as is known the animals are now only found in the Epping Forest National Park, Qld, where they live in semi-arid grassland and woodland. This species was known to scientists as a fossil skull before a living specimen was found.

Hairy-nosed Wombats have silkier fur and longer ears than Common Wombats.

WOODCHIPPING

It is hard for many people to sympathise with the felling of eucalypt trees to reduce just their trunks to chips about the size of an AA battery for pulping. But in south-eastern NSW, in Tasmania, in east Gippsland and the south-west of Western Australia, woodchipping means jobs and the spreading benefits of local industry. High quality paper can be made from hardwood fibre and Australia wants the Japanese money that nearly five million tonnes of woodchips earn yearly. The trouble is that felling of trees for woodchips occurs simultaneously with the taking of straighter trees for sawn timber, so clear-felling takes place over large tracts of forested country. The visual effects produce strong emotions among conservationists and even just casual observers. Small trees may be left, and trees considered likely to become suitable for sawn timber. Patches of forest of about 10 to 100 ha are logged in turn. Over about 40 or 50 years the whole region is logged, except for buffer strips left along major creeks, steep terrain, and stretches that are visually important, such as along skylines and beside roads.

Forests can regenerate vigorously, but wildlife ecologists are concerned because the new trees do not provide the diverse resources of mature forests. Not the least of those are the hollows found mostly in trees over 100 years old. Many species of birds, bats and possums need them for homes. Although a few small ground animals and several bird species preferring dense vegetation increase in numbers in regenerating forests, the losses are much greater than the gains.

Scientists feel that with much more attention to wildlife than has been evident so far, including setting aside large areas for national parks, animals or plants need not be endangered and erosion need not result from woodchipping.

WOODLOUSE

Woodlice, slaters or sowbugs are land-dwelling crustaceans, and are therefore related to crabs and lobsters. They need moist conditions because they breathe through gills on the underside of their abdomen, which are protected by projections from their legs. Their bodies are roughly oval and flattened, but are divided into head, thorax and abdomen. They have no shell – like that of a crab – overhanging their thorax. Woodlice have seven pairs of walking legs, and two pairs of antennae, although only one pair is obvious. Many Australian woodlice are introduced, including the common garden *Porcellio scaber*, a 12-mm-long, brown to blue-grey species found under stones and logs. It is a scavenger, but sometimes does minor damage to plants. Some native species are found in extremely salty lakes, such as Lake Corangamite in Victoria. Woodlice have many marine and freshwater relatives.

Common Wombats – this is a young female about eight months old – were called badgers by the early settlers. They dig many burrows, the largest of which can stretch for 20 m or more.

WOOL

Australia rides on the sheep's back, or to be more precise, on the wool produced by the nation's 164 million Merino sheep. The saying first became relevant in 1849 when the country's 16 million-strong sheep flock made Australia a solvent nation for the first time. Wool has consistently been one of the country's largest export earners since that time. In some 'wool boom' years, it has earned Australia more than $5 billion, surpassing coal's contribution to the national purse.

The Australian flock – soundly based on the foundation laid by the great sheep breeders of the past 200 years such as John Macarthur, Samuel Marsden and Alexander Riley – is the second largest in the world after that of the Soviet Union. It regularly produces more than 30 per cent of the world's wool clip. Because of this achievement, Australia is considered the wool industry's global leader. But like other primary producers, wool growers have experienced many 'booms and busts' since the first fat-tailed and hairy sheep arrived from South Africa in 1788 (and died within the next few months). In 1970, for example, a record woolclip of almost 930 000 tonnes outstripped world demand, sending prices crashing to low levels.

Continued high demand from major international buyers, namely Japan, Russia, China and European countries such as Italy and France, has played an important role in the industry's prosperity. The amount of wool produced is also an important factor contributing to the price received by growers. In times of war the demand for wool tends to increase because of the need to make uniforms. Thus, Australia reaped benefits from the Napoleonic War (1803–15), World War I (1914–18) and the Korean War (1950–53).

Demand is also strongly linked to the whims of the fashion industry. In the 1960s synthetic fibres such as nylon and rayon replaced wool in many garments, causing prices to fall.

The Australian wool industry extends to every state and territory, and spans an arc from just south of Hughenden in Queensland through all states across to Geraldton in Western Australia. NSW is the largest producing state, accounting for around 34 per cent of the national clip. Victoria and Western Australia produce around 20 per cent each, while South Australia accounts for 13 per cent. Queensland and Tasmania produce nine and three per cent respectively.

Raw wool has to go through a series of processes before it appears in either a carpet or garment. The first link in the chain is a decision made by the farmer about what type of sheep he is to produce. This is governed by many factors, including the suitability of the climate for coarse, fine or medium-strength wool. The farmer then embarks on a breeding program, usually based around one or more bloodlines of a particular breed of sheep. A bloodline – as the name implies

How wool is classified

Because of its range of climates, the Australian wool industry has the ability to produce all types of wool – superfine, fine, medium and strong. Wool is classified by the average fibre width of a fleece. The unit of measurement is the micron – one-millionth of a metre. In Australia, strong wool ranges from 22 to 25 microns; medium from 20 to 22; fine from 18 to 20; and superfine is anything under 18 microns. Around three-quarters of the clip is produced by pure Merinos, descendants of the Spanish stock brought to NSW in 1797. Most of the remainder of the clip comes from Merino-based crossbreeds. There is also a small, although growing, carpet-wool industry which produces extremely coarse wool. Carpet-wool sheep include the Tukidale and the Drysdale. Four grades of wool are shown below, with their thicknesses and typical uses to which they might be put.

A fleece of fine Merino wool with a thickness of about 19 microns. It will be used to make top-quality suiting.

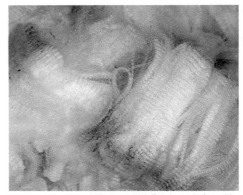

Medium (21-micron) Merino wool. Fabric made from this fibre is used in most medium-quality men's suits.

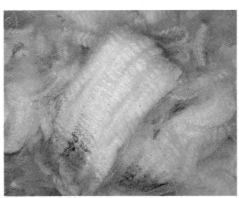

Strong Merino wool, measuring about 24 microns. The heavy cloth made from this is not worn much in Australia.

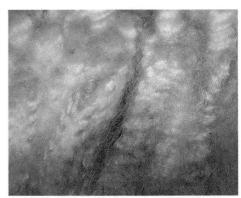

This coarse (32-micron) wool from Border Leicester sheep will be used in the manufacture of carpets.

– refers to sheep with a common parent, and relates usually to a particular stud. Such lines include the Peppin, Saxon and Booroola.

The moment of truth for a producer comes at shearing time when the newly-shorn fleeces are examined by a wool classer. He or she grades the wool into groups such as AAA, BB and AA. Woolclassers must sort the fleeces into lots which share the same fibre-width, strength, style, colour and yield. The wool is then sold, usually at public auction. From July to April in several selling centres – including Goulburn and Sydney in NSW, Fremantle in Western Australia and Geelong in Victoria – the auctions are held. Wool

buyers, who represent processors in Australia and overseas, bid for each lot of wool. After it is sold, the greasy wool is washed or scoured to remove grease and dirt. The wool then enters the textile chain, where fleeces are again cleaned and separated by fibre strength and type before spinning. Spinning is carried out in a mill, usually located in northern Europe. The Chinese and the Russians also have large spinning industries. After spinning, the wool is then dyed. This involves treating batches of wool in boiling dye liquids for one or two hours. The dyed fabrics are then made into garments.

The Australian wool industry has a history as

colourful and interesting as the nation it has so vigorously supported. One of the most significant events was the arrival of John Macarthur with the Second Fleet in 1790. As a young lieutenant in the NSW Corps, earning around 35 cents a day, Macarthur quickly realised the potential of wool in the harsh Australian climate. After receiving his first land grant of 100 acres (40 ha) at Parramatta, Macarthur set about finding the most suitable sheep for the climate. In 1797 he made his first breakthrough by buying some of the first South African Merinos shipped to Australia. By 1800, there were 6124 sheep in the colony, with Joseph Foveaux, William Cox and Samuel Marsden joining Macarthur as the main owners. Much credit should also go to John Macarthur's wife Elizabeth, who carried out much of the work involved with the early development of the Merino while her husband was in England facing a court martial for fighting a duel with his commanding officer.

In 1807 the English received the first bale of Australian wool, and its fine quality aroused great interest. The industry continued to expand as more people gained access to pure-bred Merino stock and were able to develop their flocks. By 1819 about 32 200 kg of wool were exported to Britain. Just two years later, that figure had increased to 78 400 kg. In 1827 Macarthur received the equivalent of $1.63 a pound ($3.59 a kg) for a bale of wool, setting a record which was not beaten until 1949. It is little

wonder that Macarthur's head now sits proudly on the Australian two dollar note. Between 1860 and 1930 annual wool production increased from 27 kilotonnes to 425 kilotonnes, as large tracts of 'good wool' country were opened up.

The industry also supported an ever-growing infrastructure. Workers included shearers, who received $2 per 100 sheep shorn, and shepherds. A haulage industry also developed to cart wool bales by bullock cart to the major ports. The bales were transported by barge on the Murray River and on Western Australia's Swan River. However, the history of the industry also contained some dark days. In the late 1880s, for example, the blowfly emerged as a serious pest. Despite the continuing work of scientists and farmers, it remains one of the most destructive pests that farmers have to contend with.

The industry has continued to take advantage of technological advances such as mechanical shearing, first demonstrated in 1900 by its inventor Jim Davidson.

By 1905 wool was Australia's largest export earner, a position it held until 1970. The survival of wool producers through 'lean' years is made easier by the industry's price stabilisation scheme – the Reserve Price Scheme. Under this scheme, the Australian Wool Corporation – the industry's statutory body, established in 1973 – buys lower-priced wool to maintain a 'floor' in the market, and thus support returns to growers, while providing stable prices.

SHEEP GROWING AREAS

Australia's sheep-growing areas take in a broad sweep from central Queensland to Western Australia. Largest numbers are in the south-east and south-west.

WOOL KING

Before 1836 many squatters occupied land without permission, and not having to pay, naturally took vast areas. Even after the introduction of a licence fee in 1836, and the passing of closer settlement laws in the 1860s, sheep stations tended to remain large. Some pastoralists, by acquiring a number of stations, came to own more sheep than any other individuals in history.

Among the first of the 'wool kings' was William

Bales of wool being loaded onto a wagon ready to be transported to the rail head. Temporary props hold the bales in place until loading is complete, and the entire cargo can be lashed down.

The welcome wool cheque

Wool growers receive a wool cheque once a year. It is payment for the amount of wool produced and sold off the property during the past selling season, which runs from August to June each year.

The cheque, which can often exceed $100 000, is the single most important source of income for wool producers, and many country towns and districts. It is paid by the wool merchant or broker responsible for selling the property's woolclip at the season's sales.

The cheque enables many farmers to settle up debts with local shops and hotels which have been incurred during the months spent waiting for payment. Its arrival also often prompts a spending spree in local towns as farmers buy new equipment and machinery. In 1974 – a boom year for wool – many country suppliers found it difficult to keep up with the demand for products such as fencing wire and tractors.

Under the provisions of the Wool Tax Act, all farmers pay a tax on the gross value of their wool to fund industry promotion, research and to operate the market reserve price scheme. What is left – after broking and handling fees – is the wool cheque.

Suttor (1805–77), who acquired properties on the Lachlan, Bogan, Darling and Macquarie Rivers, and on the Darling Downs. However his flocks were later dwarfed by men such as Sir Samuel Wilson, who paid for Melbourne University's Wilson Hall, and whose stations in Victoria, NSW and Queensland were said to hold over 600 000 sheep. More notable still was George Fairbairn (1816–95), who owned stations in the Western District of Victoria, the Riverina and elsewhere throughout eastern Australia; and Sir Samuel McCaughey (1835–1919), who finally owned 12 stations in NSW and three in Queensland, on which over a million sheep were shorn annually. His land stretched continuously along the Darling River for over 450 km.

WORMS

To the Saxons a 'wyrm' was a serpent, snake or dragon. Later a worm was any animal that creeps or crawls. Nowadays the word is used only for animals that are long, thin and usually legless. That is about all they have in common, for some of them – the blindworms – even have backbones.

A zoologist would describe an annelid – a member of group which contains EARTHWORMS, LEECHES and bristleworms – as true worms. All other kinds would be regarded as worm-like. The following are some of these groups which are found on land or in freshwater.

Eelworms and roundworms (Nemetoda) These simple animals can be found virtually everywhere where there is some water. One scientist has written that if all the world disappeared save nematodes, then these would remain forming the ghostly shape of the world and its living things. Others believe that there may be more species of nematodes than there are of insects. Yet – despite their abundance – many people have never seen one because most of the free-living species are microscopically small. Under one square metre of grass in good pasture, there can be four to twenty million, weighing 6 to 18 g. They live on bacteria, fungi, plant roots, decaying organic matter or each other. Many others are parasites, the largest being the roundworm *Ascaris* (to 350 mm) of humans and pigs. Other important nematode parasites of humans and their livestock are the Barber's Pole Worm *Haemonchus* of sheep, so-named from its red and white spiral colouring; the hookworms; the pinworms; and the mosquito-borne microfilarial worms which cause filariasis (elephantiasis), once a disease in Australia.

Hairworms (Nematomorpha) These long, thin worms resemble coarse thread, and people once believed that they developed from horse hairs which fell into water. They arrive, in fact, as parasites of insects or crustaceans, and burst out to mature into adults. Some live in damp soil.

Bootlace or Ribbon worms (Nemertea) Members of this small group of somewhat flattened

animals attack other animals with a proboscis that is normally stored in a pocket in their head. When it is shot out, the whole thing turns inside out in the process. This is a marine group, but some species are commonly found under stones and rotting logs, up to an altitude of 1500 m. One Western Australian species is now established in European glasshouses.

Flatworms (Platyhelminthes) This group contains the parasitic FLUKES and TAPEWORMS, but there are many marine and freshwater, free-living, fluke-like, predatory flatworms. One group – the planarians – has been used in maze experiments in animal behaviour studies and there was a scientific periodical called *The Wormrunner's Journal*. The shovel-headed garden worm *Bipalium kewense* (first described at Kew Gardens) and the blue *Geoplana caerulea* can often be found under stones in gardens.

WREN

The English Wren *Troglodytes troglodytes* is a small (95-mm-long) brownish bird with a short cocked tail which scurries through shrubberies, rather like a mouse, foraging in the litter. Over the centuries it has gathered a host of superstition and beliefs, mostly favourable. Not surprisingly British settlers in Australia called any small birds with cocked tails wrens. Had the process stopped there there would be no confusion, but they also used the name for many other small birds which forage on the ground, even when they had no cocked tail. One family, the Maluridae, deserves the name, for its 20 Australian members – fairy-wrens, emu-wrens and grasswrens – all have cocked tails.

Fairy-wrens are often called blue wrens, but some of the ten species have no blue colouring at all. They forage on open ground for insects, but never far from cover to which they can retreat. Most species are shy of humans, but the Superb Fairy-wren *Malurus cyaneus* (120–150 mm) from the south-east of the mainland and Tasmania has grown so used to human company that it will feed happily in gardens. They forage in groups consisting of the parents, the current young and, often, several extra males which may have brown, non-breeding plumage. Females are also brownish. Most of the year the group sticks fairly closely to its territory. When not feeding they perch close together, and sleep or indulge in mutual preening. Their nests are usually about one metre above the ground, near the edge of cover, and are shaped like small balls made of grass and cobwebs. Young may be raised by the parents alone, but often they are helped by other members of the group, which are apparently sometimes not closely related.

The three emu-wrens have six tail feathers which resemble emu plumes. They cock the tails when perching. The species most likely to be seen is the Southern Emu-wren *Stipiturus*

malachurus (150–190 mm) of heathlands in the south-east and south-west of the continent.

The eight grasswrens are among the rarest, or hardest to see, of Australia's birds. Between them they could only muster 343 reports in the recent extended national bird survey, compared with the Superb Fairy-wren's 26 146. The reason is partly the remoteness of their habitats. The Eyrean Grasswren *Amytornis goyderi* (140–165 mm), for example, lives only among sandhill canegrass in the Simpson and Strzelecki Deserts. It was discovered in the 19th century, and then not seen again till 1976, but nevertheless is thought to be reasonably abundant in its region. The Carpentarian Grasswren *A. dorotheae* (160–180 mm), is known from only two sites near the Gulf. They are like large fairy-wrens, but with streaked, camouflaged plumage.

Several other birds have been called, at one time or another, wrens. There is a move among ornithologists to restrict the word to the following, all in one family.

The Australian Fernwren *Crateroscelis gutturalis* (120–140 mm) is a small, mainly dark brown bird that is seen on rainforest floors in north-east Queensland.

Scrubwrens (five of twelve *Sericornis* species) are small brownish birds with strong songs, sometimes with contrasting underparts. They gather insects and small snails from foliage or the ground. One of the commonest is the Large-billed Scrubwren *S. magnirostris* (110–125 mm), a plain brown bird of eastern rainforests. In regions where other scrubwrens are found they almost always take away their nests.

Variegated Fairy-wrens Malurus lamberti *try to satisfy the hunger of a young Horsfield's Bronze-Cuckoo.*

Popular tales of country life

Two names spring immediately to mind when 'bush literature' in mentioned – 'Banjo' Paterson and Henry Lawson. Both managed to capture in their work all the characteristics and attitudes about which Australians – both city and country – are most proud. The power and popularity of their work is demonstrated by their enormous popularity today.

For many years, Australian literature tended to follow English models in both style and outlook. In poetry, for example, Adam Lindsay Gordon, Charles Harpur and Henry Kendall wrote in the prevailing English romantic tradition; and in prose, Henry Kingsley's *Geoffrey Hamlyn* tells a story of middle-class English ladies and gentlemen behaving in much the way they would have done in the home country, but with Australian scenery as a backdrop. In both prose and poetry, descriptions of the bush tended to be unconvincing, and there was little reflection of the growth of an Australian national character.

Stirrings of national pride

The 1880s brought some change. 'Rolf Boldrewood' (T.A. Browne), in *Robbery Under Arms*, was at least fairly successful in depicting characters who were distinctively Australian; and poems such as *Where the Pelican Builds Her Nest*, by Mary Hannay Foott, showed a genuine feeling for the Australian natural environment. However it was in the 1890s that a distinctively Australian literature became firmly established. Its themes were drawn from the bush rather than the cities, and reflected in particular the social values and attitudes of bush workers. It received particular encouragement from the *Bulletin*, which had been founded in 1880 and by the 1890s had become the most popular and influential magazine in Australian publishing history.

Genesis of the 'Typical Australian'

This literary movement was a natural consequence of the development of a sense of Australian nationalism. In very early colonial times the settlers naturally thought of England, or some other part of the British Isles, as home. By the late nineteenth century, however, the majority were Australian-born. They began to see themselves as different from British-born settlers, and built up in their minds a picture of the 'typical Australian', as being more resourceful, independent and hospitable, and less class-conscious than others. These characteristics were believed, rightly or wrongly,

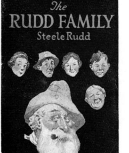

Stories of the Rudd family – Dad, Dave, Joe, Sarah, Fanny and Mother – were written by Arthur Hoey Davis. They first appeared in On Our Selection, *published in 1899, and later starred in plays, films, a radio serial and more novels.*

to be particularly strong among people living in the harsh environment of the bush.

Its two outstanding figures were, of course, Henry Lawson (1867–1922) and Andrew Barton ('Banjo') Paterson (1864–1941). Lawson was born on the Grenfell goldfield in NSW, but grew up on a selection in the Mudgee district. The sadness of his later life, which was marked by family separations, deafness, poverty, ill health and alcholism, seems to have sharpened his sympathy for others undergoing hardship; and his writing depicts the nobility and humour to be found in ordinary people. Most of all, he stressed the spirit of 'mateship' and hospitality among Outback workers:

'Tis hardship, drought and homelessness
That teach these Bushmen kindness:
The mateship, born in barren lands,
Of toil and thirst and danger,
The campfire for the wanderer set,
The first place to the stranger.

Among his many collections of short stories and poems are *In the Days When the World was Wide, While the Billy Boils, Verses Popular and Humorous, On the Track and Over the Sliprails* and *Joe Wilson and His Mates*. His most popular single piece of writing is probably the story *The Drover's Wife*.

Henry Lawson *began writing in 1907, at the age of 20. Six years later he began to write and publish the short stories that would eventually make him famous.*

Joseph Furphy *did not start to write until he was middle-aged. His rambling novel* Such is Life *brought together his experiences and thoughts about the country and country life.*

Henry Lawson *'The Sad Genius' drawn by David Low. The demon drink bedevilled Lawson's later years, and eventually killed him in 1922.*

Paterson wrote some works of fiction, but became famous only as a poet. He grew up on a station near Yass, and after working as a solicitor, a journalist, a war correspondent and an editor, he became a pastoralist in the Monaro district of NSW. The picture he gives of country people and events reflects this background, and is therefore very different from that of Lawson. He tends to avoid the grimmer aspects of bush life, concentrating on the exciting and humorous, but within these limits he gives a realistic picture, and reflects faithfully the feelings of Australians for the country. The immense and lasting popularity of his work can be judged from the fact that his first collection, *The Man from Snowy River and Other Verses*, went through several editions from 1895 to 1924, and his *Collected Verse* ran to nine editions between 1921 and 1938. The single poem *The Man from Snowy River*, in various collections, sold about 100 000 copies, and the still much read *Clancy of the Overflow* rivalled it in popularity.

Other writers of bush ballads included Will Ogilvie (1869–1963), Harry ('Breaker') Morant (1865–1902) and Barcroft Boake (1866–1892), who is remembered only for the powerful *Where the Dead Men Lie*. Other short story writers dealing with bush themes included

Edward Dyson (1865–1931), and Joseph Furphy ('Tom Collins', 1843–1912). Furphy, however, is best remembered for the rambling novel *Such is Life*. Set in northern Victoria and the Riverina, it is presented in the guise of a series of extracts from the pocket diary of the narrator. Although usually classed as a novel, it has no connecting plot, but consists of loosely-linked anecdotes and reminiscences, not only on country life, but on a wide range of human affairs. Furphy's own description of it was, 'temper: democratic; bias: offensively Australian'.

Rural myths live on in urban Australia
Although a great deal of later Australian literature is set in the country, the term 'bush literature' still brings to mind the writings of Lawson and Paterson. Moreover their popularity has lasted in spite of the fact that even in their time the proportion of the population living in the bush was falling, and that Australia is now one of the most urbanised nations in the world. Partly because of their writings, many people still like to think of the bushman as being typically Australian – even though the great majority of the population live in large cities on the sea coast – and still think of 'mateship' as an Australian virtue.

Y Z

YABBY

Lobsters and crayfish, more than any other group of animals, show why professional biologists stick to their cumbersome scientific names. The sea lobsters eaten in Australia are not closely related to the true lobsters of the northern hemisphere but are marine crayfish. There are also two families of freshwater crayfish, one in the northern, and one in the southern hemisphere. The last, the Parastacidae, which is most developed in Australia, includes the yabbies. Some people, however, call all of this group yabbies, others restrict the name to certain groups (as here), Tasmanians call their yabbies lobsters, Queenslanders call theirs lobbies, and give the name yabby to an estuarine burrowing shrimp, and Western Australians talk of their gilgies, koonaks and marrons.

All crayfish have ten walking legs, although most people would regard the first pair as nippers. They have a carapace covering their thorax, but unlike the crabs, not their abdomen, which is flexible and ends in a tail-fan which is used for swimming.

The true Yabby is *Cherax destructor*, one of the semi-aquatic species, which lives in inland streams, dams and irrigation ditches over much of eastern Australia. It reaches a length of 160 mm, and a weight of 150 g. Unlike the MURRAY CRAYFISH and its relatives, its body is relatively free from spines, and although its colour varies according to its surroundings, it is usually dull in appearance. Semi-aquatic crayfish – among which the genus *Cherax* is the main one – live in burrows which are connected to the water, and can survive the drying out of their dams. Their burrows often damage the banks.

Terrestrial crayfish live in many places, as long as the water table is within 2 m of the surface, and are too small to be useful for anything except fish bait. Their tail is greatly reduced, but they have large burrowing claws. Some are brightly coloured. They are gregarious, and several shafts will lead down into a large communal chamber. They can damage fruit tree roots, lawns and house foundations, and their extensive burrows can make land dangerous for farm machinery and horses.

This colourful Tasmanian freshwater crayfish, Astacopsis gouldi, *can reach a great size – up to 4 kg and 610 mm. It is Australia's largest freshwater crayfish, and may be the largest in the world.*

The common yabby of eastern Australia is Cherax destructor *(above). The tiny specimen below is* Parastacoides tasmanicus insignis, *from Tasmania.*

YAM

Yams from the twisting vine *Dioscorea* are an important starchy food in many warm countries. The edible part is usually the rootstock, but occasionally bulb-like growths on the stem are eaten. Of about 600 species world-wide, Australia has five. The Long Yam *D. transversa* grows as far south as Stanwell Park in NSW. Long Yams are unusual in that the small tubers can be eaten raw or simply boiled or baked. Nearly all other yams have to be carefully processed to get rid of a bitter poison. 'Top End' Aborigines call yams 'cheeky' because they can burn the mouth. The methods of preparation vary, but all entail leaching by water. The yams are cooked before or after the soaking and rinsing. In Arnhem Land, yams are baked then grated on a snail-shell tool or sliced fine with a kangaroo shoulder-blade knife. Some yams are very fibrous, and the Aborigines of north Queensland bake theirs first, mash them in a grass dilly-bag and discard the fibre. They then rinse the mealy mash in a bark trough using up to eight changes of water. The mash is left to drain in a hollow in sandy soil and has to be eaten the same day. Aborigines in the Greenough area of Western Australia were largely dependent on *D. hastifolia*.

Various other plants with water-storing tubers were used by Aborigines, such as Yam-daisy *Microseris scapigera*, an important food in Victoria; Blue Yam *Brunoniella australis* in eastern Australia; and the Kurrajong or Yam Tree *Brachychiton populneus*. In America, unrelated sweet potatoes are also called yams.

An Aboriginal woman gathering yams in northern Australia. The starch was an important source of food.

YEARLING

A yearling is a young horse between the age of 12 months and two years. By the time the horse becomes a yearling it has normally been separated from its mother. The environment in which a yearling grows up is significant. The lack of stress, disease and the contact with other horses of the same age is vitally important in developing a sensible horse that is easy to train for a successful career. Play and interaction with other young horses is essential in learning and reinforcing codes of behaviour and relationships. Learning in isolation can cause behavioural problems for the yearling which become apparent as the horse is trained.

Yearlings being sold at the Randwick (Sydney) sale ring of William Inglis and Sons, one of Australia's biggest bloodstock agents. The record price paid for a yearling in Australia was $825 000 in 1981.

YOWIE

There are reports from many countries of man-like creatures – sasquatches, yetis, Siberian snowmen, almas and the like – living in the wild and avoiding *Homo sapiens*. Before the scientific community will officially accept the existence of a new species of animal, a specimen must be described and deposited in a suitable institution. This has certainly not been achieved with any of these creatures, although evidence in the form of hairs, faeces, footprints and recordings of calls has been offered. Nevertheless, most biologists are reluctant to accept the reality of these animals, although a few reputable zoologists, anatomists and anthropologists believe there may be some substance behind the stories. It has been suggested that if they do exist they could be surviving specimens of a Neanderthal race, or even of the large ape-man, *Gigantopithecus*, which formerly existed in China where its teeth were first discovered in a drug store.

The Australian version is known as the Yowie, or, according to some versions, as the Yahoo. The latter is alleged to be an Aboriginal name, but it may be that this was a mis-hearing of a word that simply sounded like the name of the human-brutes described in Jonathan Swift's famous book *Gulliver's Travels*.

Most Yowie reports come from south-eastern Australia and mainly from hilly country. Graham Joyner has brought together and published privately dozens of newspaper and book reports of sightings from the region. Many of the earlier ones described the animal as gorilla-like. Size seemed to vary from the height of an average man to about 3.6 m. The creature's arms are usually long – to its knees, or to the ground – its body is extremely hairy, although the colour varies from dark to light. Remarks about the face are generally uncomplimentary, and sometimes refer to eyes which glow from within. Its neck is extremely short so that its head sinks into its shoulders. The Aborigines sometimes added a nice touch – the feet point backwards, making it difficult to track the animal. Oddly enough this is said of some other varieties in other countries. There is also a report of Aborigines having killed one. In 1903 a certain Mr Harry Williams claimed to have seen them killing a creature and dragging it away: 'It was like a black man covered all over with grey hair'.

The only proved primate in Australia is *Homo sapiens* and the first representatives of this species had to make several lengthy sea crossings to reach the continent. This makes it difficult to believe that any primate other than a very advanced one could have done so. It may be that recent Aboriginal stories are based on former encounters with a more robust form of human who may have reached Australia. Some researchers suggest that there is ample fossil evidence for their existence, and that they may have co-existed with modern Aborigines.

ZIRCON

Zircon crystals can change colour when exposed to light or heat. For this reason they are sometimes confused with diamonds. The deception does not last, however, as in time the original colour is partially restored.

Zircon is the heaviest of all precious stones. It has a simple chemical composition of oxygen, silica and zirconium. It is found in a variety of colours, but most commonly yellow, yellow-brown, brown, brownish-red, red, more rarely colourless, green and rose-red to bright-red. Most crystals are cloudy and flawed. Despite the fact that it is a hard substance, imperfect crystals will shatter easily.

Transparent stones are used as gems. In recent times zircons have also been used as a source of zirconium metal which is employed in the construction of nuclear reactors. In Australia zircon is produced from beach sands, notably along the east coast. Zircons are also found embedded in igneous and sedimentary rocks.

Index

Page numbers in bold type indicate main entries, while those in italic refer to illustrations. Illustrations have not been separately indicated where a main entry is marked. Latin names have only been indexed in cases where the plant or animal referred to does not have a common name.

410

Acknowledgments

Many people and organisations assisted in the preparation of this book. The publishers would like to thank them all, particularly:

Australian Dairy Corporation; The Australian Dried Fruits Association Inc.; Beverly Barnes; Des Beechey; Graham Brown, NSW Department of Agriculture; Bush Fire Council, NSW; Graeme Chapman, CSIRO Division of Wildlife and Rangelands Research; Charlie and Frank Cleary; Julian Cribb; Derek Dolstra, Mining Museum, Sydney; Hugh Edwards, Elders Pastoral, Yennora Woolstore; Electricity Commission of New South Wales; John Gasparotto, NSW Department of Agriculture; Dave Griffin, Nymboida Bush Fire Captain; Joseph Grossman, Office of the Minister for Finance and Co-operatives, NSW; Daniel Lunney, NSW National Parks and Wildlife Service; Henry Lyon; Kevin, Wilfred and Terry Mardling; Kirstie McRobert, LaTrobe Library; Paul Nixon; Nick Otway; Kevin 'Chif' Rhodes; Geoffrey Ritchie; Gordon Rogers, Ryde School of Horticulture; Royal Flying Doctor Service of Australia; Graham Smith; John Sutcliffe; Angela Webb; Mrs Wehner, Jindera Museum; Dr J. Peter White

The publishers acknowledge their indebtedness for information gained from the following books:

Ancient Australia Charles F. Laseron (A&R, Sydney, 1955); *Arid Australia* H.G. Cogger and E.E. Cameron (eds) (Australian Museum, Sydney, 1984); *Atlas of Australia* (Reader's Digest, Sydney, 1977); *Atlas of Australian Resources, Third Series* (Division of National Mapping, Canberra, 1986); *Australia: A History in Photographs* Michael Cannon (Currey O'Neil, Melbourne, 1983); *Australian Agriculture* Julian Cribb (ed) (Morescope, Melbourne, 1987); *Australian Butterflies* Charles McCubbin (Nelson, Melbourne, 1971); *Australian Encyclopedia* John Shaw (ed.) (Collins, Sydney, 1984); *The Australian Environment: Frogs* Rebecca Pinchin (Hodder, Sydney, 1986); *The Australian Fisherman's Companion* Harold Vaughan (Lansdowne, Sydney, 1986); *The Australian Gardener's Wildflower Catalogue* Denise Greig (A&R, Sydney, 1987); *Australian Geographic* (various editions); *Australian Grasses* Nancy T. Burbidge (A&R, Sydney, 1984); *Australian Insects* Keith C. McKeown; *Australian Medicinal Plants* E.V. Lassak & T. McCarthy (Methuen, Sydney, 1985); *Australian Rocks, Minerals and Gemstones* R.O. Chalmers (A&R, Sydney, 1967); *Australian Sea Shores* William J. Dakin (A&R, Sydney, 1953); *Australian Spiders in Colour* Ramon Mascord (Reed, Sydney, 1970); *Australian Traditional Bush Crafts* Ron Edwards (Lansdowne, Sydney, 1980); *Australian Wheat Varieties* R.W. Fitzsimmons et al. (CSIRO, Canberra, 1983); *Australians to 1788* D.J. Mulvaney and J. Peter White (eds) (Fairfax, Sydney, 1987); *Australia's Dangerous Creatures* David Underhill (Reader's Digest, Sydney, 1987); *Australia's Living Heritage* Jennifer Isaacs (Lansdowne, Sydney, 1984); *Beetles of Australia* Trevor Hawkeswood (A&R, Sydney, 1987); *Birds of Australia* J.D. Macdonald (Reed, Sydney, 1984); *Building and Ornamental Stones of Australia* R.T. Baker (NSW Government, Sydney, 1915); *The Bush* Ian G. Read (Reed, Sydney, 1987); *Butterflies of Australia* I.F.B. Common and D.F. Waterhouse (A&R, Sydney, 1981); *Common Australian Fungi* Tony Young (NSWU Press, Sydney, 1982); *Complete Book of Australian Birds* (Reader's Digest, Sydney, 1977); *Complete Book of Australian Dogs* Angela Sanderson (Currawong Press, Sydney, 1981); *Complete Book of Australian Mammals* Ronald Strahan (ed.) (A&R, Sydney, 1983); *The Countryman Farm Handbook* (St George Books, Perth, 1985); *The Exploration of Australia* Michael Cannon (Reader's Digest, Sydney, 1987); *The Farming of Australia* Robin Bromby (Doubleday, Sydney, 1986); *A Field Guide to Australian Native Shrubs* Ivan Holliday and Geoffrey Watton (Rigby, Sydney, 1978); *A Field Guide to Australian Shells* B.R. Wilson and K. Gillett (Reed, Sydney, 1971); *A Field Guide to Australian Trees* Ivan Holliday and Ron Hill (Rigby, Sydney, 1986); *Flora of Australia, Volume 1* (Commonwealth of Australia, Canberra, 1981); *Forest Trees of Australia* D.J. Boland (co-ordinator) (Nelson, Melbourne, 1984); *A Gardener's Guide to Eucalypts* Ivan Holliday and Geoffrey Watton (Rigby, Sydney, 1987); *The Great Australian Bird Finder* Michael Morcombe (Lansdowne, Sydney, 1986); *The Greats* Kramer et al. (A&R, Sydney, 1986); *The Greening of Gondwana* Mary E. White (Reed, Sydney, 1986); *Guide to the Australian Coast* (Reader's Digest, Sydney, 1983); *The Insects of Australia* CSIRO (MUP, Melbourne, 1979); *Insects of Australia* John Goode (A&R, Sydney, 1980); *An Introduction to Australian Insects* P.W. Hadlington and J.A. Johnston (NSWU Press, Sydney, 1982); *The Kangaroo* M. Archer et al. (Weldon, Sydney, 1985); *Kelpie and Cattle Dog* Monty Hamilton-Wilkes (A&R, Sydney, 1967); *Key Guide to Australian Wildflowers* Leonard Cronin (Reed, Sydney, 1987); *Kosciusko Alpine Flora* A.B. Costin et al. (CSIRO/Collins, Sydney, 1979); *Life in the Country* Michael Cannon (Currey O'Neil, Melbourne, 1983); *The Living Centre of Australia* Alec M. Blombery (Kangaroo, Sydney, 1985); *Lizards of Australia* Stephen Swanson (A&R, Sydney, 1980); *Mammal Tracks and Signs* Barbara Triggs (OUP, Melbourne, 1985); *A Manual of Australian Agriculture* R.L. Reid (Heinemann, Melbourne, 1981); *Native Trees and Shrubs of South-Eastern Australia* Leon Costermans (Rigby, Sydney, 1983); *Plants of Western New South Wales* G.M. Cunningham et al. (NSW Government Printing Office, Sydney, 1981); *Reptiles and Amphibians of Australia* Harold G. Cogger (Reed, Sydney, 1986); *Seaweeds of Australia* I.G. Christianson et al. (Reed, Sydney, 1981); *The Settler's Guide* compiled by Keith Smith (Nelson, Melbourne, 1981); *Snakes of Australia* Graeme F. Gow (A&R, Sydney, 1986); *Spiders* Barbara York Main (Collins, Sydney, 1976); *Toxic Plants and Animals* J. Covacevich, P. Davie, J. Pearn (eds) (Queensland Museum, Brisbane, 1987); *Trees and Shrubs for Eastern Australia* J.O Dark (NSWU Press, Sydney, 1986); *Urban Pest Control in Australia* P. Hadlington and J. Gerozisis (UNSW Press, Sydney, 1985); *Useful Wild Plants in Australia* A.B. and J.W. Cribb (Collins, Sydney, 1982); *Vertebrate Zoogeography and Evolution in Australia* M. Archer and G. Clayton (eds) (Hesperian, Perth, 1984); *What Bird is That?* Neville W. Cayley (A&R, Sydney, 1986); *What Wildflower is That?* Alec M. Blombery (Lansdowne, Sydney, 1985); *Wild Food in Australia* A.B. Cribb and J.W. Cribb (Collins, Sydney, 1975); *Wild Medicine in Australia* A.B. Cribb and J.W. Cribb (Collins, Sydney, 1981)

Typesetting by Best-set Typesetter Ltd, Hong Kong
Colour separations by Curman Lithographics, Sydney
Printed and bound in 1989 by Everbest Printing Company Ltd, Hong Kong
for Reader's Digest Services Pty Limited (Inc in NSW),
26–32 Waterloo Street, Surry Hills, NSW 2010